The Urban Experience

The Urban Experience
An Interdisciplinary Policy Perspective

SECOND EDITION

BARRY BLUESTONE
MARY HUFF STEVENSON
RUSSELL WILLIAMS

New York   Oxford
OXFORD UNIVERSITY PRESS

Oxford University Press is a department of the University of Oxford.
It furthers the University's objective of excellence in research, scholarship,
and education by publishing worldwide. Oxford is a registered trade mark of
Oxford University Press in the UK and certain other countries.

Published in the United States of America by Oxford University Press,
198 Madison Avenue, New York, NY 10016, United States of America.

For titles covered by Section 112 of the US Higher Education
Opportunity Act, please visit www.oup.com/us/he for the latest
information about pricing and alternate formats.

CIP data is on file at the Library of Congress

978-0-19-752731-3

Printing number: 9 8 7 6 5 4 3 2 1
Paperback printed by Marquis, Canada

Dedication

To our parents––Irving and Zelda, Samuel and Julia, Russell and Alma––to our sisters and brothers––Maura, Karen, Jaclyn, Estelle, Julian, Kenneth, and Percy––and to love that spans distance, time, and the barriers between this life and beyond.

And to Seth and Jenn, Elizabeth, Joshua, Alex, Michelle, Rachel, Nicole, Brian, Sammy and George, and Catalina and Teddy, and all others of the next generations who will inherit both the joys and the challenges of cities and suburbs our generation helped create.

Table of Contents

2 Cities of the World: How Metro Areas Rank   27

PART II   THE DYNAMICS OF METROPOLITAN DEVELOPMENT   63

3 Metropolitan Development: From the Seventeenth Century to the Early Twentieth Century   65

4   Cities and Suburbs Moving Into the Twenty-First Century   102

PART III   FOUNDATIONS OF METROPOLITAN AREA PROSPERITY   143

5   Urban Prosperity and the Role of Trade   145

6   Urban Labor Markets and Metro Prosperity   173

PART IV   CURRENT POLICY ISSUES IN METROPOLITAN AREAS   207

7   The Urban Public Sector   209

8   Urban Public Education and Metro Prosperity   253

9   Urban Physical Infrastructure: Water, Sewer, Waste, and Energy   291

10   Urban Area Transportation   315

15 Urban Resilience and Adaptation to Climate Change   466

16   Urban Economic Development Strategies   507

17   Urban Well-Being and Civic Engagement in the Twenty-First Century   547

Preface

In 2008 when the first edition of *The Urban Experience* was published, the nation and much of the world was in the midst of a great recession which had its roots in a subprime mortgage crisis that led to the collapse of the housing market in many cities throughout the country. The crisis led to the failure of a number of the largest US financial institutions. The nation's automobile industry was hit hard by the economy's downturn, which had a devastating impact on metro areas in the Midwest and the South. City leaders across the country had to address a decline in revenue while trying to assist millions who faced unemployment.

As we, the three authors, were completing this new and highly revised edition of *The Urban Experience*, the planet was hit by the COVID-19 pandemic, the worst outbreak of disease since the flu epidemic of 1918–1919 a century earlier. Urban areas were especially vulnerable because of their population density and their roles as hubs of international travel. Eventually, though, the virus would spread even to sparsely populated areas. World leaders, and perhaps even more importantly, state and local government officials, had to impose severe measures to keep the pandemic from affecting even more of their citizens. Life as we had known it came to a near standstill.

At the same time, there was a new call for racial equity in the form of the Black Lives Matter movement following the homicide by police officers of a number of Black men and women, most prominently Eric Garner, Breonna Taylor, and George Floyd. While such horrific crimes were hardly new in America, these were caught on cell phone cameras and police body-cameras whereby everyone could see exactly what had occurred. Massive protests followed in cities around the United States and to cities in Europe and elsewhere in solidarity with the movement in America.

It was in this new context that we were writing this second edition. But equally important, we decided at the outset that we wanted this new version to be even more interdisciplinary than the first edition. This meant adding new material from the fields of political science, sociology, and urban studies. We hope we have made it clear that to get involved with your community with real impact, you need to have an understanding not only of the economics of cities and metro areas but the social conditions, politics, and policy.

We also thought it necessary to go beyond stories and data that reference US urban areas. As such, you will find in this new edition a good deal of information about cities in Europe, Asia, South America, and Africa that highlight and compare the roles they are playing in everything from local economic development, education, housing, and transportation to their attempts to deal with climate change. Indeed, in this new edition one chapter is devoted solely to global warming, its impacts on cities and metro areas, and what cities are doing to remain sustainable.

All in all, we hope you will find this edition abundant with new information; extensions of theory from economics, sociology, and political science; and the beginning of what Germans would call a "Weltanshaung" or "worldview" that will permit you to better understand the workings, the challenges, and the promises of urban life.

As we said in the first edition, from the beginning our focus has been on the variety of urban experiences, perhaps reflecting the diversity of our own experiences. Among the three of us, one or another has lived in a big city, in a small town, in a suburb, and for a brief time, on a farm at the fringes of a metropolitan area. We have lived in a tenement slum, a public housing project, a tract house, a two-family home, and a single-family house on a large plot of land. We have lived in the Northeast, the Midwest, and the South. We are the children of college graduates and high school dropouts. We are Black and White, male and female.

We recognize that no three individuals could possibly span the full range of urban experience—for instance, none of us is disabled, none speaks English as a second language—but each of us does come with a distinctly different perspective on the question of what it means to live in a metropolitan area. Each of us cares passionately about making cities and suburbs work more effectively—putting scarce resources to better use, spreading the fruits of prosperity more equitably, holding decision-makers accountable for their choices, and helping the voiceless to make their viewpoints heard.

Our narrative describing and analyzing the ways that US cities have grown and changed makes a deliberate connection between events that occurred more than two centuries ago with events that may have occurred last week. We have made a special effort to understand some of the most recent changes, particularly the impact of globalization, that make life in twenty-first-century US metro areas so distinctly different from that of the late twentieth century.

We hope that readers will gain a deeper understanding of how and why metropolitan areas function as they do and that this knowledge will stimulate the investigation and review of current policies and practices. Much of this book focuses on the role of public policy in shaping metropolitan areas. We also hope that readers will see the role they can play, as individuals and in concert with others, in shaping public policies of the future.

This book has four major sections: Part I, "Introduction to Cities and Suburbs: A Global Perspective," provides the reader with a context for understanding contemporary metropolitan areas in the United States and elsewhere and introduces the key issues and concepts that are the tools of the trade. It also begins to provide data on a broad range of metro areas across the globe.

Part II, "The Dynamics of Metropolitan Development," provides a historical narrative of how American cities and suburbs, as well as other metro areas, developed from colonial times to the present. The chapters in this section incorporate basic theories and formal models from economics, sociology, and political science that are used throughout the text to provide insight and analysis into the dynamics of metro areas.

Part III, "Foundations of Metropolitan Area Prosperity," examines the conditions necessary for promoting and sustaining urban prosperity. It focuses on the role of trade and labor markets.

Finally, Part IV, "Current Policy Issues in Metropolitan Areas," contains a large number of chapters covering such critical issues as the role of the public sector in cities around the world; the growing importance of public education in assuring urban prosperity; the need for physical infrastructure to assure adequate water, waste removal, and energy resources for residents and businesses; the provision of adequate transportation in metro areas; the important role of public health and public welfare policy; law enforcement; land-use controls and smart growth; urban housing markets; the urban response to climate change; and urban economic development policies. The final chapter addresses urban well-being, civility, and civic engagement.

We have many colleagues and friends to thank for helping us complete this enormous work. We thank the Robert and Mary Priedeman Brown Fellowship, which through an endowed chair in Urban Planning and Environment supported Russell Williams's teaching and urban research at Wheaton from 2013 to 2019. We were especially fortunate to have a vast number of reviewers who helped us improve every section of this book based on their review of the first edition: Thomas Vicino, Northeastern University; Rob Wassmer, California State University, Sacramento; Rasha Ahmed, Trinity College; Junfu Zhang, Clark University; Nilopa Shah, University of California, Irvine; Nicholas Montgomery, University of Maryland; and Phillip Granberry, University of Massachusetts, Boston. We also had the benefit of an enormous amount of feedback from our graduate students, who were kind enough to provide comments on the substance and readability of each chapter. Thanks also to Diana Silvester, who sifted through the entire manuscript with a fine-tooth comb, finding all kinds of ways to improve on the text.

Our sincere thanks to Oxford University Press and especially our editor, Jennifer Carpenter, for the faith placed in us in developing the original edition of *The Urban Experience* and now this second edition. Jennifer and OUP understood truly the need for an up-to-date textbook that conveyed the excitement and mystery of the modern city and provided readers with a multidisciplinary way to investigate the places where we live.

PART I

Introduction to Cities and Suburbs: A Global Perspective

The Wonder and Paradox of Urban Life

1

LEARNING OBJECTIVES

- Explain the advantages and disadvantages of living within a central city or a suburb

- Differentiate between the approaches taken by economics, political science, and sociology to explain human behavior

- Specify the distinctive features of urban economics, urban political science, and urban sociology within their respective social science disciplines

- Explain positive and negative externalities and demonstrate why densely populated areas are likely to contain more of each

- Explain each of the factors that produce change in metropolitan areas and give an example of how they can be applied

- Explain and apply the concept of opportunity cost and the criteria of equity and efficiency

Place matters. Whether it's the exhilaration some of us feel when the hometown team wins the big game, or the desire to escape our surroundings and seek our fortune elsewhere (or, paradoxically, the ability to feel both sentiments simultaneously), we care passionately about the places where we live. Even when we choose to leave the places where we grew up, we are often nostalgic for "the old neighborhood" or "the old country." We carry our origins with us even as we reinvent ourselves, crafting lives that are different from those of our parents or grandparents. While the reach of technology—radio, television, and the internet—permits us to share more in common, the place we call home still affects us in profound ways.

Where we live says a lot about who we are and what our daily lives are like. Four-fifths of Americans today live in metropolitan areas—in central cities or suburbs. Worldwide, more than 55 percent of the nearly 8 billion people who live on this planet live in cities or suburbs, and by 2030 demographers estimate 60 percent will do so. And according to new research by the World Urban Forum, there are now around 10,000 cities worldwide, half of which did not exist as late as 1980. Each of these cities has a population of at least 50,000 inhabitants. Some of them, like Shenzhen, have even become megacities in almost no time at all. Shenzhen was a small fishing village in Guandong Province in China in the 1970s. By 2020, it had over 12 million residents as the city became a major industrial center (Scruggs 2020).

This means that urban living, with its challenges and promises, is essential to most of us, just as the exigencies of rural life were for 95 percent of the nation's families who lived in villages or on farms at the time of the American Revolution. Moreover, understanding urban issues, from the causes and consequences of local economic development and suburban sprawl to the problems associated with urban and suburban income inequality and disparity in the provision of public services, helps us to better understand—and possibly find remedies for—some of the most persistent problems facing American society and nations across the globe.

Urban Issues and the Social Science Lens

Social science looks for patterns in human behavior and tries to explain them. Each of the key social science disciplines—economics, political science, and sociology—approaches social phenomena in a different way. Economics focuses on the role of markets in understanding how people relate to each other; in a sense, dollars count. Political science examines the role of nonmarket institutions (such as political parties) that operate through an array of public institutions where votes and political influence count. Sociology analyzes human social relations beyond the bounds of the market or government institutions; social standing and the web of relationships within one's community matter.

Urban Economics

As a field of study, economics is divided into two broad areas. **Macroeconomics** looks at the big picture: the behavior of large aggregates of consumers or businesses, focusing on factors that determine the level of total production in a society. Essentially, macroeconomists try to understand why an economy experiences booms and busts and what can be done to smooth out the economic rollercoaster of inflation and recession. **Microeconomics** studies the behavior of individual consumers and firms, how prices are set in individual markets, and how output is divided among workers and families and among firms.

Putting economics in geographic space is the focus of urban economics. It is important because it takes macroeconomic and microeconomic concerns and places them in a context—a physical space where they can be studied with a microscopic eye. We can look at all the factors that determine the general level of output in a particular city or metropolitan area. Why was median household income in the city of Seattle in 2017 more than double (+106%) that of St. Louis? Why is per capita income growing rapidly in Phoenix while it is stagnant in Newark and Cleveland? Or for that matter, why is per capita income in Berlin 20 percent higher than in Chicago? Instead of looking at individual markets in the abstract, we can study specific conditions—the kind that determine the price of housing in cities and suburbs, or why the wages of janitors in San Francisco are so much higher than in Birmingham or Kansas City. The study of urban economics provides a special lens through which we can understand human behavior in the real world, in places where people live.

By itself, though, economics cannot do justice to an understanding of urban issues and urban public policy. We need to add the perspective of other social sciences, including political science and sociology, if we are to explain both behavior and outcomes in cities and suburbs. In a thousand different ways, political decisions involving public expenditure, taxation, and direct and indirect regulation influence and often trump the pure economic calculus of the market. Cities and towns that have instituted a minimum or "living" wage try to change the outcome of local labor markets. Zoning determines where housing and commercial properties will be developed. Building codes alter the way our homes are constructed.

Urban Sociology

As a field, sociology is the scientific study of human social relations and group life. This discipline is central to understanding how large numbers of people live in close proximity to each other in cities and suburbs. By studying social class, race and ethnicity, family and community, and the social uses of power, sociology adds to the study of metropolitan regions the subtle but powerful impact of neighborhood groups, community organizations, and similar nongovernmental units that affect daily life. A "Not In My Back Yard" mentality (NIMBYism) often better explains—more so than anything we know about land values and real estate law—why there is an insufficient supply of new housing to meet increased demand. Community organizations made up of active neighborhood residents can use their power to influence how mayors and city councils implement public regulations that affect the market decisions of commercial developers.

Urban Political Science

As a field, political science deals with systems of government and the analysis of political activity and behavior. How are individuals selected to represent the public, and how are laws and regulations designed and implemented? By studying election activity, interest groups, protest organizations, and even the role of street demonstrations in affecting public policy, political scientists try to understand how public policy is implemented.

In urban areas, political science has a lot to tell us about who becomes city mayor, how zoning laws are implemented, and how urban infrastructure comes to be funded and developed. Beyond the study of political parties, it tells us a good deal about what people want from their government leaders.

Urban Public Policy

Urban public policy draws on economic, political, and sociological theory and combines them to yield important insights about the well-being of various racial and ethnic groups living in central cities and suburbs; the reasons for rising or falling crime rates; the location of housing, commercial, and industrial properties within a city or suburb; and a myriad of other matters that affect where and how we live. The metro area becomes the laboratory for exploring economic, political, and social issues that affect how our communities and neighborhoods are organized across the entire globe.

Our Love–Hate Relationship with the City

As in the classic children's fable about the city mouse and the country mouse, some of us are energized by the bounteous offerings of the big city, while others prefer the peace and tranquility of smaller places. But our fascination with the big city is evident both in popular culture and in works of literature. New York City, often called the Big Apple or the City That Never Sleeps, is the setting for numerous TV sitcoms and dramas that shape—and distort—our image of the place. Likewise, Los Angeles, the City of Angels; Chicago, the City of Big Shoulders; Boston, the Hub of the Universe; and New Orleans, the Big Easy, have all been the settings for popular TV series and Hollywood films. The great cities of Europe—London, Paris, Rome, Madrid, and Lisbon—beckon visitors from around the world. In earlier times, the endless possibilities offered by the city were exuberantly celebrated in the poetry of Walt Whitman.

For many of those who live in them and others who visit, cities offer the thrill of a fast-paced life. Research by sociologist Robert Levine (1997) reveals that the pace of life varies according to where one lives. Within the United States, Levine finds important regional differences, with the cities of the Northeast having a faster pace (as measured by speed in walking, talking, banking transactions, and the proportion of people wearing wristwatches) than those of the laid-back Southwest.

Besides its quick pace, many observers of city life have celebrated its theatrical aspects. Lewis Mumford (1961), a leading urban historian of the mid-twentieth century, likens the city to a "stage," while the insightful urban commentator Jane Jacobs (1969) describes the "ballet" of daily life on a busy neighborhood street. The sociologist William H. Whyte (1989) harkens back to the "agora," or marketplace, of ancient cities, but he is less concerned with economic interchange than with the role of the city as a public meeting place. These urbanists prize the serendipity of life in the city, the unexpected delights, the chance encounters, the sheer pleasure of watching people in a place with so many people to watch.

Yet even as the metropolis captures our imagination with its infinite offerings, there is also ingrained deep within our traditions a distrust and fear of big cities. Thomas Jefferson envisioned a nation of yeoman farmers living in small towns, far removed from the industrial cities of England with their "dark Satanic mills," as the poet William Blake described them. In *Sister Carrie,* the early-twentieth-century American novelist Theodore Dreiser (1900) tells the story of a sweet and innocent young woman from a small town who loses her virtue when she goes to the big city of Chicago; from there she travels on to New York, an even bigger metropolis, and descends into greater shame and corruption. In Dreiser's narrative, Carrie is not just corrupted *in* the city, but she is also corrupted *by* the city. On TV, we have seen not only the mischievous urban humor of *Seinfeld* and *Friends* but also the depictions of mean streets and urban violence found in *NYPD Blue, CSI Miami,* and *The Sopranos.*

Our Love–Hate Relationship with the Suburbs

The desire to avoid the crime, disease, poverty, noise, and congestion that often typified city life fueled a centrifugal movement away from the centers of large cities even before the advent of automobiles at the beginning of the twentieth century. When people left big cities, they generally did not move to rural areas, but instead settled in the quieter places just outside the city limits. Although these suburbanites no longer lived inside the city, they usually continued to identify with it. Even today, if travelers far from home are asked where they are from, they are likely to say "Chicago" or "Detroit," when they actually live in suburban communities like Evanston or Southfield. There is a good chance that people outside the Midwest will recognize the names of the two big cities, and a much smaller likelihood that they will recognize the names of the suburbs. The same is true for those who live on the outskirts of Tokyo, Rio de Janeiro, or any large metro area.

In the United States, the quintessential symbol of the American Dream for many is the suburban single-family house complete with lawn (white picket fence optional). In his study of Levittown, a New York suburb built right after World War II on Long Island, sociologist Herbert Gans (1967) argues that "perhaps more than any other type of community, Levittown permits most of its residents to be what they want to be—to center their lives around the home and the family, to be among neighbors whom they can trust, to find friends to share leisure hours, and to participate in organizations that provide sociability and the opportunity to be of service to others." It is much easier and much less expensive to build such communities on the cheaper, often unoccupied land at the periphery of the metropolitan area than to do so in the central city.

As Levittown and the older suburbs of the East and the Midwest began to age, a newer generation of American suburbs was being created in the Southwest, on wide-open land that stretched to the horizon. The journalist David Brooks (2002) refers to these as "Sprinkler Cities," because so many of them are being carved out of the often-arid land of the southwestern desert. He notes that "people move to Sprinkler Cities for the same reasons people came to America or headed out West. They want to leave behind the dirt and toxins of their former existence—the crowding and inconvenience . . . Sprinkler City immigrants are not leaving cities to head out to suburbia. They are leaving older suburbs—which have come to seem as crowded, expensive, and stratified as cities—and heading for newer suburbs, for the suburbia of suburbia." In these newer communities, as in Levittown, people seek orderliness, cleanliness, easy friendships, leisure-time (often sports-related) activities, and rich, healthy childhood experiences for their kids.

Of course, there are many critics of the suburban lifestyle. They focus on its mass-consumption aspects: the "need" for every household to have its own lawn mower, snow blower, megasize gas grill, and, in many cases, more automobiles per household than there are drivers. Others emphasize the lack of aesthetic considerations in the design of suburban housing, and the unrelenting sameness of suburban subdivisions across the United States.

Along with the suburban housing developments themselves, there has been a growing worry about the "malling" of America, as one strip mall after another is built in suburban communities. While wonderfully convenient, these palaces of consumption look nearly identical no matter where they are located. Hence, the title of James Kunstler's (1993) critique of the suburbs, *The Geography of Nowhere,* which dwells on the undifferentiated sameness of suburbs with their nearly identical homes and identical shops as compared with the rich diversity of central city life. Even though a majority of the US population now lives and works in a suburb (Hobbs and Stoops 2002), Eric Bogosian's play *SubUrbia* paints a dark vision of the sterility and boredom of such places, with their supposed conformity, materialism, and lack of drama.

To some extent, our love–hate relationship with cities and suburbs is based on stereotypes. Suburbanites may exaggerate the dangers of the big city; city-dwellers may underestimate the range of people and activities that actually can be found in the suburbs. People often stereotype the racial, cultural, and social characteristics of city or suburban residents, but the complexity of both city and suburban life is such that any stereotype will always be more misleading than not. Life in many central cities is safe and clean, and there are suburbs that offer rich diversity in the racial and demographic composition of their residents, in their housing, and in their retail districts.

To be from New York, Los Angeles, Chicago, or any other major metropolitan area may mean one thing to the baby boomers who came of age there in the post–World War II era and quite another to young adults today. A program from the early days of television, *The Naked City,* proclaimed that there were "eight million stories" to tell (a reference to New York City's population at the time). Race, gender, ethnicity, income, and social class all have a profound influence on the way we experience our surroundings. To paraphrase Charles Dickens, "it was the best of places, it was the worst of places."

Annie Dillard (1987) wrote a well-regarded memoir, *An American Childhood,* about growing up in Pittsburgh in the 1950s. Dillard grew up in a relatively privileged, White, native-born household. However, growing up in Pittsburgh during that time would likely have been a substantially different experience for another young girl who was the child of Hungarian immigrants or for a young boy who was the great-grandchild of slaves.

Moreover, it is not just that the city will be experienced differently by *different* people but also that a large city offers the anonymity necessary for the *same* individual to explore different facets of his or her personality. Sociologists use the concept of **multiple identities** to describe a situation in which an individual may have one persona within a specific group at one time and a completely different persona with another group at another time. For example, a gay teen from a religious family background might find that the city affords sufficient anonymity to express both aspects of his personality while continuing to build a comprehensive sense of self. The anonymity of the city also allows for fresh starts; it facilitates that celebrated urban practice of "reinventing" oneself. In small towns and rural communities, this is often difficult to do. Everyone there knows everyone else and much that is private quickly becomes public.

Vibrant metropolitan areas theoretically provide a range of neighborhoods from which people can choose the physical and social environment that suits them best. But how much freedom they have in choosing where they live has always had a lot to do with income, and often with race and ethnicity. Residential segregation of Black Americans was nearly universal in both the South and the North just a generation ago—often enforced through racial covenants and bank lending policies. Even today, many of our cities remain largely segregated by both income and race. As such, metropolitan areas provide an economic, political, and social laboratory where we can seek to better understand the promises and challenges of society as a whole and help develop urban policies to enhance opportunities for all.

The Importance of Density   Large numbers of people living in close proximity to each other—what sociologists and demographers call **population density**—is the hallmark of urban areas. It provides cities and their environs with a range of activities that rural areas could never afford nor duplicate. If, for example, only one in a hundred people ever attends a professional hockey game or a ballet performance, the economic survival of a National Hockey League franchise or a dance company can only occur in a metro region where there are hundreds of thousands of people. Similarly, other businesses catering to rare or expensive tastes need to have a critical population mass and this, too, will be found only in the larger cities.

Even among some of the largest metro areas in the world, density varies enormously. London's metropolitan region covers 3,200 square miles with nearly 8.8 million residents. That equals more than 2,700 people per square mile. That is nothing, however, compared to Shanghai, where 24.2 million residents occupy just 2,450 square miles or nearly 10,000 people per square mile. By that standard, Los Angeles is hardly congested. Its 4.1 million residents live in an area of 4,850 square miles—836 people per square mile.

Because of density, metropolitan regions function in ways that are different in kind, not just in degree, from places where households are more sparsely settled. Residential neighborhoods are more likely to have the critical mass necessary to provide elementary schools within walking distance of their pupils, restaurants that can cater to varied tastes, and a range of recreational and cultural attractions that can please even those with unconventional preferences. Similarly, density is what allows the construction of a well-developed physical infrastructure—the road network, the mass-transit system, water and sewer systems, and power grids—at a relatively low cost per household. Density also permits a complex social infrastructure to develop based on a wide array of neighborhood and community-based organizations and formal and informal interpersonal networks for the exchange of ideas and information. If, as the saying goes, "variety is the spice of life," large cities are generally "spicier" than other places simply because they have the population density to permit it. This is also why cities are particularly good at fostering creativity, a major advantage in an era when economic success increasingly relies on the production of ideas, which flourish where there are many creative minds concentrated in one place (Florida 2002).

Urban Spillovers

With so much activity taking place, cities are littered with **spillover effects** or what economists call externalities. An externality is the cost or benefit that affects a third party who did not choose to incur that cost or benefit. One can enjoy window shopping along a street filled with specialized boutiques without spending a penny. However, the exhaust from cars, trucks, and buses along the route could make a person dread such a stroll downtown. The first represents a positive spillover; the latter a negative one. The closer people live to one another and the denser the level of economic activity, the greater the number of such externalities and the greater their impact. In the nineteenth century, before major reforms in public health and sanitation, the extraordinarily high densities in large cities made them centers for air- and waterborne illnesses. Today, central city residents often suffer a higher incidence of asthma and other diseases. In shifting to a less dense pattern of sub-urban development we have also changed the way we use land, however, leading to current concerns about urban sprawl and environmental degradation. Because these problems are usually more prevalent in metropolitan areas than rural com-munities, they have become urban policy issues worthy of careful study.

Economic Geographies and Political Geographies

As the economic activities of the dense central core of early American cities spilled over into surrounding areas, cities typically expanded their political boundaries through annexation of adjoining towns to keep pace with the geographic expan-sion of the area's economy. By the end of the nineteenth century, however, efforts to annex independent suburban jurisdictions met with resistance across the estab-lished metropolitan areas of the Northeast and mid-Atlantic states. From then on, as the economic boundaries of the metropolitan area expanded, the political boundaries remained unchanged, leading to a curious duality: a metropolitan area is a single economic unit—encompassing most of the residences of those who work there and most of the workplaces of those who live there—but with a set of frag-mented political units containing, in some instances, dozens if not hundreds of separate municipal jurisdictions. This tension between economic integration and political fragmentation often places severe constraints on the development of area-wide public policies. Initiatives that would benefit the entire metropolitan area but adversely affect any one jurisdiction (e.g., the expansion of a major research univer-sity that would bring economic growth to the region but remove property from the tax rolls of the municipality in which it is located) will require a lengthy and often contentious process of negotiation.

The Dynamics of Metropolitan Area Development

Places change constantly. The sturdy, working-class neighborhood of one genera-tion might become the dangerous slum of the next. The seedy warehouse district of a previous era might be transformed into today's trendy neighborhood of artists' lofts. The changing fortune of individual neighborhoods might also mirror the changing fortunes of entire cities, metropolitan areas, and even regions. The Sunbelt states of the South and West continue their rapid expansion, while many cities in the Snowbelt states of the Northeast and Midwest stagnate or decline. The fact that some places might be on the upswing while others fall on hard times has important implications for the well-being of families, businesses, and communities.

While many changes might appear to be random, a well-trained eye can often spot an underlying pattern. As any accomplished sleuth would testify, recognizing the pattern is the first step in finding the solution to the mystery. In Figure 1.1, we introduce a framework for understanding such patterns. This framework, which helps us to organize the pertinent information, will undergird the chapters that follow.

An Analytic Framework for Understanding Metropolitan Area Dynamics

The mystery of what we call metropolitan area dynamics—the rise and fall (and sometimes the rise again) of individual cities and suburbs—can best be understood by keeping our eye on the six elements noted in Figure 1.1. We want to follow **demographic shifts**, or changes in the racial and ethnic composition of cities and suburbs. We need to pay special attention to **industrial transformation,** as certain industries expand and prosper while others become technologically obsolete. And we want to trace the **spatial relocation** of households and businesses from one region to another (including immigration from abroad), from one city to another, or from city to suburb and back again. These three at the top of the figure interact and are affected by the three elements at the bottom of the figure: private market forces; federal, state, and local public policies; and social networks and community process. These six elements largely determine the ebb and flow of urban life across any nation.

Using this analytic framework will help us to understand a range of problems that face metropolitan areas. For example, many large cities of the world are in coastal areas and now face the challenge of rising sea levels. How will the interplay of market forces, public policy, and community considerations create demographic, industrial, and spatial change?

Let's start with the market forces that underlie rising sea levels. As we noted earlier, the use of fossil fuels creates negative spillovers—costs of production that are not taken into account as they damage the environment and lead to warmer temperatures, glacial melting, and thus rising sea levels. In the United States, existing public policies may have compounded the problem: lax zoning regulations allow new development in vulnerable areas and efforts to enact stricter regulations are often resisted by politically powerful real estate interests. A family's ties to its home, its neighbors, and to the community institutions that shape its life often lead to a reluctance to relocate until catastrophe hits. When it does hit, whether in the form of a destructive hurricane or a slowly eroding coastline, those areas become less desirable and spatial relocation will occur. Some businesses and some households with the resources to move to less vulnerable areas will do so. Those that remain often have fewer resources and fewer options and are likely to face difficult challenges in a declining and still-vulnerable area.

Metropolitan areas are affected by changes in the size and composition of their populations and their businesses, along with changes in the way these households and businesses are located across the area. All these changes are affected by the

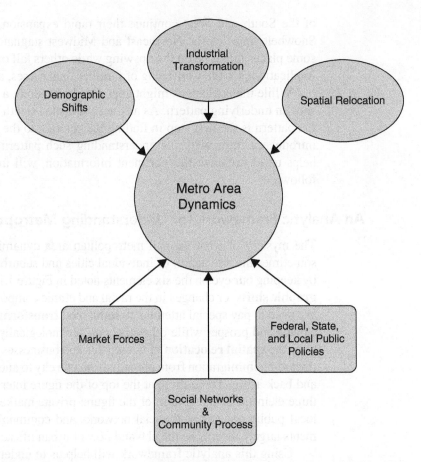

FIGURE 1.1. Metropolitan areas are affected by changes in the size and composition of their populations and their businesses, along with changes in the way these households and businesses are located across the area. All of these changes are affected by the complex interplay of private markets, government interventions, and informal community practices and traditions.

complex interplay of private markets, government interventions, and informal community practices and traditions.

Using this framework to understand metropolitan area dynamics in the face of rising sea levels helps us to identify promising policy options. It gives us the necessary information to discuss the range of policy options that could be adopted, from international agreements to reduce greenhouse gases, to federal changes in flood insurance regulations that would give greater incentives to relocate rather than rebuild, to state regulations protecting wetlands as a way to reduce flooding, to local ordinances that require stricter zoning in flood-prone areas. Each of the six elements interacts with the others, leading to constant change in the fortunes of cities, as some flourish and others decline.

Further Applications of the Analytic Framework

In part, the individual choices made by thousands upon thousands of households and businesses determine whether places will grow and prosper or whether they will wither and decay. People might be drawn to a place for any number of reasons:

a mild climate, proximity to natural beauty, or a population that shares the same ethnic or religious background, educational opportunities, or employment opportunities. But as they flock to a location, they also transform it. What was once a sleepy little town is now a bustling suburb. The places left behind are also transformed, as declining populations translate into fewer stores on Main Street and bleaker prospects for attracting new companies. Businesses, too, might be attracted to a particular location because of cheap land, superb transportation facilities, or a skilled workforce. Their relocation also transforms both the place where they came from and the place where they went.

Even as thousands of individual choices accumulate into good news or bad for specific neighborhoods, cities, and entire metropolitan areas, the well-being of these geographic entities exerts its own influence on the choices available to individuals. A prosperous community can provide safety, security, and high-quality education for its children; an area that has fallen on hard times will be far less able to do so. These feedback effects—success breeds success; failure breeds failure—make it ever more difficult for places that have fallen behind to catch up. But through the good luck of having industries that would later blossom, or exceptional political and civic leadership, some communities down on their luck do come back, and more could do so with good public policy. Take the older US cities of Pittsburgh and Boston as good examples: both cities thrived on early industry, then lost their competitive edge, and recently have returned to economic health.

Before the rise of the steel industry, which would become the backbone of America's manufacturing prowess, the population of Pittsburgh was just 21,115 in 1860—a mere small town. But by 1920, the City of Steel boasted a population of nearly 590,000—a 28-fold increase. And by 1950, when steel was king, the population soared to more than 675,000.

When the steel mills in Pittsburgh began to close down, younger and better-educated residents often left to build their futures elsewhere. For a time, this made Pittsburgh even less attractive to potential new businesses. The ever-declining prospects of the city led to further rounds of destructive selective migration. When people begin to abandon a city, the city's tax base erodes, making it more difficult to support good schools and public amenities. This leads to successive rounds of out-migration and diminished services in a downward spiral—at least until new industry springs up or existing industries undergo a renaissance. By 2010, Pittsburgh population had shrunk to just 305,000, less than half that of 1950.

Now Pittsburgh and its suburbs have been able to build a new employment base and stem the city's population loss by attracting new businesses and diversifying its industrial base, in part because of its relatively depressed land costs and its highly respected universities. Today, the Pittsburgh metro region boasts more than 60 regional universities, colleges, and other institutions of higher education, anchored by Carnegie Mellon University and the University of Pittsburgh. Its nationally ranked medical institutions have made it possible for the city to attract bioscience firms that have done a good deal to boost the economy. As such, the city's population has now stabilized.

The Boston story is similar. Boston's heyday based on shipping came to an end by the early nineteenth century, but it was replaced by a resurgent economy based on manufacturing. With such a strong economic base, the city attracted new residents from throughout the country and from abroad. Its population exploded from 250,000 in 1870 to a peak of 801,000 in 1950. Yet its fortunes declined sharply after World War II. By 1980 the city boasted just 563,000 residents, nearly 30 percent less than in 1950. Most of the city's loss went to Boston's suburbs, which expanded rapidly. With the construction of major highways running around the city and through it, families could move to the suburbs even when their breadwinners continued to work downtown.

Only after 1980 did Boston's fortunes turn up once again when its existing universities and medical centers became thriving businesses, with a majority of American high school students going onto college and with medical care increasing from just 4 percent of national income to more than 18 percent. Furthermore, as more families owned stocks and bonds, the city's mutual fund industry expanded, led by Fidelity Investments. And most recently Boston has become the hub of bioscience, based on its rich array of research universities and hospitals. Today the city's population exceeds 700,000—an increase of nearly 25 percent since 1980. Because of its great success, the cost of housing has exploded and the city ranks first in highway congestion—new challenges to its future viability.

But urban success or failure is not merely a matter of individual industries or individual choices made by households and businesses. The various branches of government—at the local, state, and federal level—make decisions that have an impact on which places will flourish and which will languish. Early massive public investment in public works played a crucial role in catapulting New York, Chicago, and Los Angeles to the top of the charts among US metropolitan regions. Intriguingly, the key public works projects in all three cities had to do with redirecting the flow of water. In the case of New York, the development of the Erie Canal in 1825 provided the impetus for growth by creating the best route from the Atlantic Ocean to the Great Lakes. This gave the Port of New York an edge over the East Coast port cities of Boston, Philadelphia, and Baltimore, and fueled the phenomenal growth of this world-class city of commerce. In Chicago, the stupendous engineering feat of reversing the flow of the highly polluted Chicago River so that it emptied into the Des Plaines River rather than into Lake Michigan allowed the city to protect the safety of its water supply. This gave Chicago its competitive edge over such midwestern contenders as Cincinnati and Indianapolis. In Los Angeles, redirecting the rivers of Northern California to flow into the parched region surrounding the city made the City of Angels what it is today. Without the water supply from these rivers passing through an elaborate system of aqueducts, the city could not have supported anywhere near its current population.

What has been true for American cities is true for most of the global cities of the world. Waterworks, street systems, public docks on riversides, canals, and a host of other public works have made London, Paris, Amsterdam, Berlin, and Tokyo major centers of commerce.

The interplay of private-sector decisions and public policy helps to explain the rise of that quintessential Sunbelt city, Houston. The development of air-conditioning made it livable and an economy based on oil and gas made it prosperous, but it was the enthusiasm and political clout of then Vice President Lyndon Johnson that helped to bring the headquarters of the National Aeronautics and Space Administration (NASA) to the city, thereby aiding Houston's growth.

The interplay of market forces and public policy propelled the growth of suburbs throughout the country and dramatically changed the shape of metropolitan areas in the mid-twentieth century. Federal housing programs and federal highway dollars made suburbs affordable and accessible. Successive rings of suburbs have grown and receded around many of America's major cities. Inner-ring suburbs have often seen their fortunes decline, while outer suburbs and the even farther out **exurban regions** grow rapidly. Cities and suburbs never stay the same for very long; they are always changing.

Well-Being and Public Policy

As realtors tell us, "The three things that are most important in valuing property are location, location, and location." Place is important for several reasons. A particular site might be appealing for its inherent beauty, or repugnant because of the toxic wastes it contains. Alternatively, we may be interested in a specific place because of its proximity to something else. When we choose where to live, for example, we might take into account how long it takes to commute to work, or whether friends and family are close by.

Place also may be important because each specific location ties us into a different network of opportunities and constraints. Just as communication systems and transportation networks link some places and leave others out of touch, there are neighborhood-based social networks that can provide access to important resources. Being in the right network makes a difference. A family living on one side of a district line sends its children to a school considered exceptional, while a family on the other side sends its children to a school with a poorer reputation. One town provides excellent connections to neighborhood associations and community resources while another does not. Every location offers a different mixture of advantages and disadvantages. How well individuals are connected to places, to things, and to other people will help to determine their well-being in various parts of the metropolitan area.

The economist George Galster has introduced the concept of **opportunity structures** to capture the fact that where people live has a major impact on their access to resources (Galster and Killen 1995). These opportunity structures are continuously shaped and reshaped by the interaction of individual choices, private business decisions, and government policy.

Opportunity structures vary across race, ethnicity, income, and wealth, contributing to tensions within a metropolitan area. Various groups attempt to use government to address their own needs and to expand their choices. This inevitably leads to conflict over public budget priorities, regulatory decisions, and tax policy. As a result, the intersections of public policy and private decision-making present some of the most complex aspects of urban life. How much should be spent on public works such as water and sewer lines, roads, and bridges? How much should be spent on public primary and secondary education, police and fire protection, and public health and sanitation?

These decisions are fraught with controversy as individuals and interest groups contest both for resources and over who should pay for them. When the commonwealth of Massachusetts spent more than $14 billion to depress Boston's Central

Artery as part of its famous "Big Dig" project, the overriding question was how much the taxpayers of Massachusetts would pay for the new road and how much would be paid by the federal government. When cities face severe fiscal crises as a result of a downturn in the national economy, mayors and city councilors have to decide where to make budget cuts: Should teachers' jobs be sacrificed to avoid laying off police and firefighters, or vice versa? In either case, some jobs will be lost and some constituents will lose valuable services.

The Role of Political Power and Interest Groups

Put more generally, politics and political power count. Metro areas constantly evolve, at least in part, as the result of external pressures. Detroit's decline from its status as one of America's wealthiest cities was due in large measure to the globalization of the auto industry. The rise of San Jose, Boston, and the Raleigh-Durham-Chapel Hill metro area in North Carolina owes much to the information revolution and the role that great research universities have played in spawning industries related to the computer, biotechnology, and nanotechnology in the late twentieth and early twenty-first centuries. Prodigious increases in agricultural productivity have sharply reduced the need for farm labor, compromising the growth of cities and towns that sprung up to serve them in the Farm Belt.

Yet the quality and pace of change in the urban setting is also intimately related to the array of interest groups and political alignments within each metro area. As Logan and Molotch (1987) argue, there are powerful local interest groups who have a stake in promoting growth because of its subsequent enhancement of land values. This **growth machine** includes real estate interests and the politicians who rely on them for campaign contributions, along with the local media (such as newspapers and radio and television stations), whose power and profits depend on population growth, as well as others (like utility companies), whose fortunes are tied to a specific locality. Even if these groups disagree on other matters (e.g., even if construction companies and unions in the building trades are adversaries in wage negotiations), they would nevertheless be aligned together as part of the area's pro-growth coalition.

Businesses, labor unions, nonprofit voluntary organizations, and community groups all interact to influence the political process and the fate of cities and suburbs. Through the chambers of commerce and other business groups that exist in virtually every municipality, business leaders use their economic clout to influence the mayor and city council or town selectmen to make decisions over taxes, regulations, and spending that support the interests of business. Public-sector unions strive to use their power to increase the wages and benefits of police officers, firefighters, teachers, and other city employees and to set work rules regarding what their members can and cannot do on the job. Voluntary organizations that range from advocates for public transit, neighborhood parks, and the homeless to Parent-Teacher Associations (PTAs) and community development corporations all vie to influence political leaders to address the issues that stir their passion. Neighborhood associations work to protect the value of the homes in their communities and to serve the interests of those who live there.

Inevitably, there are conflicts—often powerful ones—that erupt among these many interest groups as they all compete to support their own interests. Businesses often fight for lower taxes, arguing that high taxes discourage investment in the city and would cost the community jobs that are badly needed. But with lower taxes, how would the city or suburb pay for quality schools, police and fire services, and pleasant parks? Public-sector unions usually take every opportunity to push for better compensation for their members, but this often strains municipal budgets. Housing developers try to get zoning laws changed and building regulations modified in order to make it easier for them to build new homes. But neighborhood associations often fight back if they feel that the developments being planned will change the character of their communities or bring in new families that are "different" from them. Conflicts arise regarding where to place new highways and roads, since these inevitably affect property values in adjacent neighborhoods. This often pits one local neighborhood against another.

Every group attempts to gain political favor by contributing to local political candidates and lobbying the city council or the school board. Every group tries to mobilize its members to act in solidarity for the positions they take. In the end, given the unequal power of individual interest groups, what comes out of the political process is not always what benefits the entire community, but what serves the interests of those who are most adept at political maneuvering.

Since the 1960s, political scientists have debated whether the interest groups that exert influence on local governments are best described as a business elite united around issues like economic growth and redevelopment (as in Floyd Hunter's 1953 study of Atlanta) or a more disparate group of organizations with competing interests that require negotiation and compromise (as found in Robert Dahl's 1961 study of New Haven). More recently, this dichotomy between **elitism** and **pluralism** has been leavened by a concept introduced by Norman and Susan Fainstein (1983) and Clarence Stone (1989)—**regime theory**—broadly described as the informal channels and arrangements that influence formal government authority. According to Stone (1993), these regimes can take several different forms: development regimes that emphasize growth; middle-class progressive regimes that endorse neighborhood and environmental protections that slow growth; lower-class opportunity expansion regimes in which disadvantaged groups press for a greater share of resources; and maintenance regimes, which tend to be static caretaker governments less reliant on private-sector resources. It is less clear within these categories, but just as important, that the competition for power and influence in cities and suburbs is part of an ongoing and probably never-ending struggle.

Paradox and Urban Inquiry

Adding even more excitement to the study of metropolitan areas is an array of puzzles and paradoxes that require an understanding of how urban economics, sociology, political science, and public policy tie together. Why do poor people tend to live on the expensive land close to the center of the city, while wealthier people live on the cheaper land at the periphery? Why does rush-hour traffic seem to get even worse after a new highway is built to relieve congestion? When artists convert a marginal neighborhood into a more attractive and livable community, why do they wind up not being able to afford to live there themselves? Why are suburban subdivisions so often named for the orchards or forests they destroyed, so that the innumerable "Shady Groves" dotting the landscape offer no shade and contain no groves? Why is wine bottled in rural areas, close to where the grapes are grown, but beer is bottled close to major metropolitan areas, far away from where the barley, malt, or hops are grown? Why will a new restaurant want to locate on a street with many other restaurants, rather than finding a street where it wouldn't have to share potential customers with its competitors?

In each of these cases, the spatial aspect of the decisions made by households and businesses forms the core of our analysis. In looking at the dynamics that affect the quality of poor inner-city urban housing, for example, we need to understand the forces that led to its deterioration. Unlike some of the housing in rural areas, which might have been poorly constructed initially, or perhaps built without indoor plumbing, housing in urban areas is more likely to have been built originally to conform to prevailing middle-class standards. However, if middle-class households decide to move elsewhere, and landlords then rent to people with less ability to pay, these property owners might decide to skimp on maintenance and repairs, assuring that these buildings will begin their descent to lower quality. The process by which we get poor-quality housing in rural areas is entirely different from the process whereby urban housing deteriorates. And it is the location decisions of households and businesses that make all the difference between the two instances.

Key Issues in Urban Policy

Metropolitan areas are where many of the hottest domestic issues of the day are being played out—issues around disparities in income and wealth, inequalities by race and ethnicity, inequities in educational resources, and the integration of new immigrants into the mainstream, to name but a few. Cities are simultaneously places of boundless opportunity for some and deadly poverty traps for others. Some cities are faring well economically, but one in three central cities of metropolitan areas have poverty rates of 20 percent or more, even when poverty rates for the nation as a whole have been at or below 15 percent since the mid-1960s. Why are some cities wealthier than others? Why have cities provided upward mobility for some, but not others? What factors contribute to the distribution of income and wealth in a metropolitan area? Why do central cities often include the metropolitan area's wealthiest families and at the same time its poorest? These are all questions of urban policy.

Understanding urban dynamics is also necessary for insightful public policy in the crucial area of education and the labor market. Among the important services provided by local governments is schooling from kindergarten through twelfth grade. Individuals need access to *effective* education, and also need to have *opportunities* to transform the education they receive into income. Providing for good schools and making them available in the inner city as well as the suburbs raises many questions. How does education relate to the economic dynamics of a metropolitan area? What determines differences in access to high-quality education? Why can some people find jobs, while others with equal training levels cannot? What particular factors distinguish urban labor markets? Why do some metro areas have higher unemployment rates than others?

Besides good schools and good jobs, a thriving metro area needs to find a way to provide all its households with decent housing at affordable prices. Yet in numerous communities, the price of housing exceeds what many families can afford. What determines the cost of housing? Why does a house in one location cost a great deal more than an exact duplicate of that house located elsewhere in the same metro area? Why are housing prices in San Francisco and Boston so much higher than in Detroit, Albuquerque, and Boise? How, if at all, should city governments respond to problems of housing affordability? How can cities respond to problems of homeless-ness? How do some world-class cities like Stockholm find ways to provide housing for nearly all their citizens while others like Mexico City leave tens of thousands or more homeless? Why does a wealthy city like Los Angeles with its multimillion-dollar mansions still find more than 90,000 of its residents sleeping in tents on the streets on the cusp of the third decade of the twenty-first century?

For many economic and social reasons that are discussed later in this book, housing is different from most other goods. It is more costly, more durable, and less transportable. It requires land, and consequently places those who seek hous-ing in competition with other potential land users. Since the early 1900s, housing has been subject to zoning regulations implemented by local governments. While some zoning laws are designed to protect residential areas from noxious industrial activities, zoning has also been used to exclude households on the basis of race or income—or both.

Transportation is another vital area of public policy. The economic and social well-being of cities depends upon the ability of workers, consumers, and residents to move from one point to another within the metropolitan region. In addition to moving people, it is also necessary to have an efficient way to move goods. The repair of pot-holes, the design of new thoroughfares, the enforcement of parking regulations, and the creation and management of public transportation are all among the many impor-tant tasks undertaken by governments in metropolitan areas. Why do some cities have worse traffic jams than others? How have commuting patterns changed over time? Why do some metropolitan areas have a great deal of public transportation, while oth-ers have relatively little? What determines the availability of public transportation in different parts of a metropolitan area? Who should bear the cost for highways?

Other questions of public policy and quality of life surround many aspects of metropolitan growth. What conceptual tools do we need to understand the effect of metropolitan growth on environmental quality? How do activities in one part of the metropolitan area affect the well-being of other parts? How does urban sprawl affect the costs and quality of water supply and sewer lines? How does it alter our decisions about transportation planning and other components of metropolitan infrastructure?

In the chapters to come, we use the tools of economics, political science, and sociology to address the questions and issues we have just posed, as well as many others. We examine how and why particular industries grew up in specific met-ropolitan areas, and how that changed over time. Cities developed initially as a result of proximity to some natural resource or an advantageous feature, such as a deep harbor. With changes in transportation and communication costs and new technology, those advantages declined in importance, and other factors made cities desirable or undesirable places in which to locate. Cities that came of age during different transportation eras have different configurations. Nineteenth-century cities were highly centralized, but newer cities tend to be decentralized. Some metropoli-tan areas have been able to reinvent themselves, as the emerging industries of one era have become the sunset industries of another. Others have had a more difficult time adapting to change. The separate political jurisdictions within a metropolitan area have an incentive to cooperate for the good of the area as a whole, but they are also in competition with each other. The prospects for the well-being of house-holds, businesses, and communities within the metropolitan area depend on the successful resolution of these conflicting forces.

Globalization and the Changing Role of US Cities

Just as changes in transportation and communication technologies reshaped cit-ies around the world in the eighteenth, nineteenth, and twentieth centuries, they continue to play a role in determining which metropolitan areas will thrive and which will fall on hard times, as well as determining changing patterns of land use within metropolitan areas. While previous eras of technological change intensi-fied the competition between US metropolitan areas, current technological devel-opments have intensified the competition between metropolitan areas worldwide. With falling transportation costs and declining communication costs, it is feasible for an increasing amount of work to be done far afield of the initial supplier or the final customer. The most efficient location for production of any particular product or service—in economics jargon, the place that has an **absolute** or **comparative advantage** relative to all others—can now be selected from a vastly wider array of metro areas, both domestic and foreign.

To use Thomas Friedman's (2005) metaphor for the leveling of the playing field between potential competitors, the world is indeed becoming "flat," and in such a flat world, the key to metropolitan prosperity depends even more on developing a workforce with specialized skills, talents, and expertise that cannot easily be replicated elsewhere. This is what Michael Porter (1998) refers to as establishing a **competitive advantage.** If older metropolitan areas are able to reinvent them-selves, the sturdily built factories, lofts, and warehouses that provided industrial jobs to previous generations will be recycled to provide postindustrial jobs as well as attractive living spaces for its current generation of residents.

When a wide variety of goods and services can be produced almost anywhere, does place still matter? Surely, but it matters for different reasons. As we will dis-cuss more extensively later in the book, successful places do not necessarily offer proximity to raw materials, nor do they offer especially favorable transportation costs in an era in which transportation costs are so low that they don't matter very much. Instead, successful places offer the social interactions that help people create and transmit knowledge, and they provide the amenities—recreational, cultural, and environmental—that enhance the quality of life and therefore attract work-forces with needed skills.

The Tools of the Trade

To address the wide range of issues raised here, we need to rely on a battery of con-cepts and research tools that are the province of the economics profession, but that are important to political scientists and sociologists alike—even if they do not use the economist's jargon. We use these because they provide insight into the mysteries of how metropolitan areas operate. A few of these concepts—opportunity cost, the criteria of equity and efficiency, externalities, and unintended consequences—appear as themes throughout the book and, because of their importance, are briefly introduced here. Additional concepts are explained as needed in later chapters.

Opportunity Cost

Who was the better economist, poet Robert Frost or baseball catcher Yogi Berra? We believe the poet Frost. Here's why. Berra, known now as much for his hilariously fractured use of English as for his legendary skills as a catcher with the New York Yankees, once said, "When you come to a fork in the road, take it." It would be impossible, of course, to follow that advice, since you cannot travel down two roads simultaneously. You have to choose. Frost, on the other hand, understood this. In his poem "The Road Not Taken," he comes to a fork in the road and must make a choice, knowing full well that his choice has consequences—that it "made all the difference." In choosing the one, he necessarily forgoes the other.

This is the crux of **opportunity cost**, one of the most fundamental concepts in economics. We can't have everything, so we must make choices. And every time we make a choice, we give up the chance to follow an alternative path. The cost of choosing A is the forgone opportunity of being able to have B, if your income only permits the purchase of one. To economists, this sacrifice of the next best alternative is the "true" cost of making a choice, and it applies to time as well as money. Your out-of-pocket cost for a movie ticket might have been $8, for example, but an economist would want to know not only what else you could have done with that money but also what else you could have done with that time. The value of the next best alternative is the most important way to measure the cost of making a choice.

THE ROAD NOT TAKEN

Two roads diverged in a yellow wood,

And sorry I could not travel both

And be one traveler, long I stood

And looked down one as far as I could

To where it bent in the undergrowth;

Then took the other, as just as fair,

And having perhaps the better claim,

Because it was grassy and wanted wear;

Though as for that the passing there

Had worn them really about the same,

And both that morning equally lay

In leaves no step had trodden black.

Oh, I kept the first for another day!

Yet knowing how way leads on to way,

I doubted if I should ever come back.

I shall be telling this with a sigh

Somewhere ages and ages hence:

Two roads diverged in a wood, and I—

I took the one less traveled by,

And that has made all the difference.*

—Robert Frost

In the urban setting, there are all kinds of opportunity costs. A tax dollar spent on repaving a road is a dollar that cannot be used to pay for improving a subway system. A dollar spent on public health is a dollar that cannot be spent on improving public schools. The choices made by taxpayers and their municipal governments can sometimes make all the difference in whether a city or town grows or declines, whether it becomes a more attractive place to live or one that residents wish to leave.

The Criteria of Efficiency and Equity

Efficiency and equity are criteria used to evaluate economic and social outcomes, especially the outcomes produced as the result of public policy initiatives through laws, regulations, and judicial decisions.

Efficiency refers to being as productive as possible with limited resources. Technically speaking, a process is efficient if it results in producing the most output (of given quality) with a given amount of input. Alternatively, efficiency occurs whenever a given output of given quality is produced in a manner that uses the least input. Implicitly, efficiency requires being mindful of the opportunity cost of using scarce resources. Because almost all resources are scarce—from basic building materials and skilled labor to natural resources like clean water—efficiency requires not only using resources in the least wasteful manner but also using those resources for the best purpose.

Equity, on the other hand, refers to fairness with respect to the distribution of resources or income. This concept can be quite elusive, since each of us might have a different idea regarding what constitutes fairness. Many of us would argue that equity requires that all residents of a city have clean water, a decent and safe place to live, and a fair chance to get a good education and receive adequate healthcare. To the extent that there is great inequality in access to a clean environment and to housing and a great disparity in education and health resources, one could argue that the goal of equity has not been fulfilled.

Ideally, we would like our local, state, and federal governments to enact only those programs that are both efficient and equitable. Some of the most difficult choices occur when the criteria are in conflict and there are trade-offs that must be made: a program that is warranted on the grounds of efficiency might not be

---

Source: This poem, first published in 1916, is widely available on many websites, including www.bartleby.com.

equitable, or vice versa. Efforts to reduce traffic congestion, for example, might justify subsidizing high-speed commuter rail lines to attract a ridership among high-income suburban motorists, even if those rail lines do nothing to address the transit needs of lower-income communities. When the criteria of equity and efficiency conflict, economic analysis cannot determine which of the two should take precedence; that becomes a political and social question, rather than a purely economic one. How much to sacrifice efficiency for equity (or vice versa) is one of the toughest issues before any mayor or city council, before any governor or state legislature, or before the US president and the Congress or in many countries, a parliament.

Externalities

When a market functions smoothly, it automatically takes into account *all* of the costs of producing a good and *all* of the benefits of consuming it. In some instances, though, the market is incapable of doing this and some costs or benefits remain unaccounted for. A transaction between a buyer and a seller leaves some third parties better off or worse off, but compensation to or from the third party cannot be easily made.

Examples of such **externalities** (or spillovers) abound. Mrs. Frisoli, for example, has a lovely rose garden that she has planted next door to Mr. Jones. She paid a good deal of money to a nursery to plant these roses and she has worked hard to keep them well fertilized and healthy. From his porch, Mr. Jones gets enormous pleasure from seeing Mrs. Frisoli's roses and smelling their beautiful aroma. Yet he doesn't pay a cent for this benefit. It is a purely positive externality to him. Perhaps he should subsidize Mrs. Frisoli to help her pay for the roses, but he has never done so and no one is forcing him to do it.

Unfortunately, Mrs. Frisoli's roses pose a severely negative externality for Mr. Jones's wife, who is allergic to the pollen and coughs and sneezes every time they bloom. Perhaps Mrs. Frisoli should compensate Mrs. Jones for the discomfort she experiences and for the cost of prescription drugs she takes that allow her to breathe more easily. But no such compensation has ever been offered or required.

In other cases, we have resorted to government to "internalize" externalities. That is, the government has stepped in to subsidize a positive externality, tax a negative externality, or regulate the production of goods that would otherwise generate huge positive or negative externalities to society at large.

Pollution is a good example of a negative externality. If a new paper mill opens up and pollutes a stream that residents had been using for fishing and swimming, the residents have been made worse off, but have no recourse to receive compensation through the normal workings of the market. Government action of some sort is required—minimally, to define property rights, impose a tax on the polluter that is used to clean up the pollution, or more forcefully, to pass strict antipollution laws.

Elementary and secondary education provides positive spillovers for others in the community, who reap the benefits of a more productive workforce and a better-informed citizenry—including those who have no children in school or purchase private education for them. In the absence of government subsidies, families might not purchase enough years of education for their children, since they would not take the positive spillovers into account. As a society, we believe so strongly in the positive externalities of elementary and secondary education that we collect the necessary tax revenue to offer the service free of charge to the consumer. If that is not inducement enough, we also regulate education by making attendance mandatory for children up to age 16.

As we pointed out earlier in this chapter, although positive and negative externalities can occur anywhere, we are particularly cognizant of them in urban areas because they are more likely to occur when people live at higher densities. Playing your sound system at top volume will generate more negative externalities if you live on a street of apartment buildings than if you live 5 miles from your nearest neighbor; being inoculated against polio and thereby helping to avoid an epidemic will generate more positive externalities in a dense city than a rural town.

Unintended Consequences

Although much of this book addresses the role of public policy in trying to improve the workings of metropolitan areas and the lives of the people who reside there, it is best to approach the topic with a large dose of humility. As we shall see, many of the public policy initiatives launched with great fanfare in previous generations have ultimately failed because their full consequences were not foreseen.

Consider the case of kudzu, a plant native to China and Japan, where its growth is kept in check by natural enemies. It was used as a ground cover in the United States to protect against soil erosion, and planted across the nation by Civilian Conservation Corps workers during the Great Depression of the 1930s. With ideal growing conditions and the absence of any natural enemies in the southeastern United States, it has overrun many areas in that part of the country, engulfing cars, houses, and just about anything else in its path. In 1970 the US Department of Agriculture declared kudzu to be a weed, but efforts to eradicate it have been notably unsuccessful. A seemingly good idea to make abandoned open-pit coal mines more attractive ended up having serious unintended consequences.

Other Important Economic Concepts

Concepts like supply and demand, income and price elasticities, fixed and variable costs, absolute, comparative, and competitive advantage; path dependency; negative sum, zero sum, and positive sum games; economies and diseconomies of scale; and specialization and the division of labor are all incredibly useful in deciphering how cities and suburbs work and how people thrive or suffer within them. We introduce these terms as we need them, not because of their intrinsic value, but because of their power to help explain the mysteries, paradoxes, and secrets of urban life. For those already familiar with such concepts, insight will be gained as to how these ideas can be used in the specialized study of metropolitan areas. For those not already familiar with these terms and ideas, we have tried to explain all in nontechnical language.

This book is also data rich. We use a large number of charts and tables to present information that helps bring the more abstract concepts and ideas of urban economics, political science, and sociology to life. With the statistics presented here, you will be able to compare metropolitan areas across the country and contrast urban outcomes whether related to family incomes, housing values, or crime statistics.

The theories, concepts, and tools of social scientists are brought together with a rich array of city and suburban data, all calculated to provide a new, exciting, and in-depth understanding of the urban world around us. Read on, learn, and enjoy.

References

Brooks, David. 2002. "Patio Man and the Sprawl People: America's Newest Suburbs." *The Weekly Standard,* August 12, pp. 19–29.

Dahl, Robert A. 1961. *Who Governs?* New Haven, CT: Yale University Press.

Dillard, Annie. 1987. *An American Childhood.* New York: HarperCollins.

Dreiser, Theodore. 1900. *Sister Carrie.* New York: Doubleday.

Fainstein, Norman I., and Susan S. Fainstein. 1983. "Regime Strategies, Communal Resistance, and Economic Forces." In *Restructuring the City: The Political Economy of Urban Development*, edited by Normal Fainstein and Susan Fainstein. New York: Longman Publishing Group, pp. 245–282.

Florida, Richard. 2002. *The Rise of the Creative Class.* New York: Basic Books.

Friedman, Thomas L. 2005. *The World Is Flat: A Brief History of the Twenty-First Century.* New York: Farrar, Straus and Giroux.

Galster, George C., and Sean P. Killen. 1995. "The Geography of Metropolitan Opportunity: A Reconnaissance and Conceptual Framework." *Housing Policy Debate* 6, no. 1: 7–45.

Gans, Herbert. 1967. *The Levittowners: Ways of Life and Politics in a New Suburban Community.* New York: Random House.

Hobbs, Frank, and Nicole Stoops. 2002. *Demographic Trends in the Twentieth Century.* Census 2000 Special Reports, November. Washington, DC: US Bureau of the Census.

Hunter, Floyd. 1953. *Community Power Structure.* New York: Anchor Books.

Jacobs, Jane. 1969. *The Economy of Cities.* New York: Random House.

Kunstler, James. 1993. *The Geography of Nowhere: The Rise and Decline of America's Man-Made Landscape.* New York: Simon & Schuster.

Levine, Robert. 1997. *A Geography of Time.* New York: Basic Books.

Logan, John R., and Harvey L. Molotch. 1987. *Urban Fortunes: The Political Economy of Place.* Berkeley: University of California Press.

Mumford, Lewis. 1961. *The City in History: Its Origins, Its Transformations and Its Prospects.* New York: Harcourt, Brace, and World.

Porter, Michael. 1998. *Competitive Advantage: Creating and Sustaining Superior Performance.* New York: Free Press.

Scruggs, Gregory. 2020. "There Are 10,000 Cities on Planet Earth. Half Didn't Exist 40 Years Ago." Urban Planet, February 12. https://nextcity.org/daily/entry/there-are-10000-cities-on-planet-earth-half-didnt-exist-40-years-ago.

Stone, Clarence N. 1989. *Regime Politics*. Lawrence: University Press of Kansas.

Stone, Clarence N. 1993. "Urban Regimes and the Capacity to Govern." *Journal of Urban Affairs* 15, no. 1: 1–28.

Whyte, William H. 1989. *City: Rediscovering the Center*. New York: Doubleday.

Questions and Exercises

1. Using available "Quick Facts" from the US Census (https://www.census.gov/quickfacts), type in the name of a city or town that you would like to study and learn as much about it as you would like. You can compare statistics on this community against the United States as a whole or any other city, town, or county in the nation. Examine as much data as you can on the following:

   Size of Population
   Age/Sex Demographics
   Race & Hispanic (Latinx) Origin
   Population Characteristics
   Housing Characteristics
   Families & Living Arrangements
   Computer & Internet Usage
   Education
   Health
   Economy
   Transportation
   Income & Poverty
   Businesses
   Geography

2. List and describe three of the major externalities in your home city or town.

3. How do these externalities affect you and your household?

4. How does your city or town attempt to deal with these externalities?

5. In your city or town, which individuals and groups are powerful? What power do they have and how do they exercise it?

6. What types of changes do you think residents of your city or town would want to make regarding municipal agencies or programs?

7. Which organizations, city officials, and individuals in your city or town are important in making changes in education, housing, access to jobs, crime, public transportation, healthcare, and business growth?

Cities of the World: How Metro Areas Rank

2

LEARNING OBJECTIVES

- Identify the important roles of cities in the ancient world
- Distinguish between the political boundaries and the economic boundaries of a metropolitan area and how this distinction can affect challenges facing cities and suburbs
- Summarize the various geographical definitions used to delineate cities, metropolitan areas, and regions
- Summarize the taxonomy of twenty-first-century cities so as to distinguish between the several types of cities and their particular functions

More than 5,000 years ago, the earliest known cities on the planet arose in Mesopotamia and the Nile River valley (present-day Iraq and Egypt, respectively). These early urban settlements offered protection, security, and the ability to trade and control resources. Well over 2,000 years ago, they were followed by cities in the Indus Valley, in Mediterranean Europe, in the Yellow River valley of China, and in Mesoamerica (today, Central and South America). These cities of antiquity served one or more purposes: defense against invaders, places of trade, centers of religion or government, and places where such handicrafts as metalworking and jewelry-making could be practiced (Brunn et al. 2016). Many early cities were surrounded by walls that provided safety for inhabitants and for the activities carried on within (Bruegmann 2005).

Between the seventh and tenth centuries, Islam created an urban landscape in the Middle East that included mosques, religious schools, and universities. They were famous for their urban markets, palaces, and city walls. The original inhabitants were nomads who settled in these cities for protection and for religious study. Over the years, great cities like Cairo, Egypt, and Istanbul would become major centers for the arts and for commerce as well as trade in food and fabrics, gold and copper, and spices and perfume (Salim et al. 2016).

While lesser known, there were five major urban centers in Africa before the year 1500. The oldest was along the ancient Upper Nile, where the cities of Meroe, Axum, and Adulis were founded. The medieval Sahelian (or Western Sudan) cities of West Africa served as great trading empires with caravan routes that crisscrossed the Sahara Desert. Other early trading cities along the East African coast including Mogadishu and Mombasa, now urban centers within Somalia and Kenya, respectively. Coastal cities on the Red Sea and Indian Ocean arose in ancient times and provided for trade with the African interior. Some of these cities date back to the ninth century as trade with the Arabian Peninsula and the Gulf area increased (Myers et al. 2016).

The rise of many of these early cities was roughly contemporaneous with the development of agriculture in these regions. Many anthropologists speculate that improvements in agricultural practice allowed the creation of a food surplus, which, they argue, is what allowed cities to develop by freeing up labor to move from rural areas to central locations where they could work in activities other than food production. According to conventional wisdom, without the development of more efficient agricultural methods, there would be no cities (Palen 2002). The renowned urban expert Jane Jacobs argues just the opposite, however, in *The Economy of Cities* (1969). She points to early cities as places where goods and ideas were exchanged and where innovations occurred. She posits that the ideas underlying the productivity gains in food production originated in the cities and that without these early cities, more efficient agriculture would never have developed.

We may never have the evidence to resolve this chicken-and-egg question in the case of the earliest cities. But we do know that when the first colonists traveled from the cities of Europe to the New World, they initially established towns along the eastern seaboard as outposts of their civilization; they did not scatter over the countryside. From the first villages and towns, the agricultural hinterlands then developed, allowing the small population of the colonial towns to spawn a much larger rural population. Similarly, as demonstrated in Richard C. Wade's *The Urban Frontier* (1959), the establishment of urban outposts in places like Pittsburgh, St. Louis, Cincinnati, Louisville, and Lexington, Kentucky, allowed the expansion of agriculture into the Midwest.

But these early American colonists were not the first to have what we would consider to be urban communities. From 1050 to 1350 CE, in an area across the Mississippi River from where St. Louis, Missouri now is situated, lies Cahokia, a pre-Columbian Native American city. At its apex around 1100 CE, according to archeologists and anthropologists, the central core of Cahokia covered about 0.7 square miles and had a population of 14,000 to 18,000 (Munoz et al. 2014). Including outlying areas—what today we would call suburbs—the population was perhaps as high as 40,000. If this estimate is accurate, Cahokia was larger than any subsequent city in the United States until the 1780s, when Philadelphia's population of European immigrants and their descendants grew beyond 40,000. Scholars suggest that environmental factors including overhunting, deforestation, and flooding led to this early city's abandonment (Henderson 2000).

What we know today is that the entire world is urbanizing rapidly. In 1950 only 30 percent of the globe's population lived in cities. By 2018, more than 55 percent lived in urban settlements of one type or another. And by 2030, the United Nations projects that 60 percent of all people will live in urban areas and one-third will live in cities with at least half a million inhabitants. Moreover, the number of large cities—the "megacities" of the world—is on the rise. In 2000, the UN counted 371 cities across the globe with 1 million inhabitants or more. Less than twenty years later the count stood at 548, and by 2030 it is estimated that there will be 706 such large cities worldwide. The number of megacities—cities with more than 10 million residents—is expected to increase from 33 in 2018 to 43 by 2030.

The United States is even more urbanized than the world at large. By the time the American colonies declared their independence from England in 1776, there were only a handful of cities along the Atlantic Coast, with most of the population living in small villages or in rural outposts. The new nation's first census, taken in 1790, revealed that only 5 percent of the population lived in cities with 2,500 people or more. During the next two centuries, the urban population expanded dramatically while the share living in nonurban areas declined. As noted in Chapter 1, today more than four out of five US residents live in metropolitan areas with the majority in the very largest metropolises that have populations of more than a million.

In this chapter, we will delve more deeply into how cities rank in terms of population and how the population has shifted not only from rural areas to metropolitan regions, but how central cities and suburbs have evolved within these large urban conglomerations.

Defining Cities

For most of us, we rely on "cognitive" maps that we carry around in our heads to define a city. To sports fans, for example, Detroit, Michigan is the home of the Tigers, the Lions, the Pistons, and the Red Wings. For older folks, Detroit is still remembered as the automobile capital of the world. To the generation of postwar baby boomers, Detroit is Motown—the city that spawned a musical tradition including Diana Ross and the Supremes, Stevie Wonder, and Smokey Robinson and the Miracles. A later generation of music fans know it as the home of rapper Eminem. Current or past residents of other cities carry their own cognitive maps about the places they call home. If you are in Europe or the Far East, you have some idea of the urban area called Paris or Berlin or Beijing.

But for a more concrete definition or map of an urban area, we need to turn to official definitions to give meaning to what we describe as a city or metro area. As it turns out, there are several different ways to characterize cities depending on political jurisdictions, urban-suburban sprawl, and commuting patterns. Most people can agree that cities are places where large numbers of people live and work and they are usually the hubs of government, commerce, and transportation. But simple political boundaries no longer have much meaning in terms of where people live and work. Commuting across political jurisdictions is commonplace and therefore there is the need for urban definitions that encompass more than where the city line ends.

In 2018, the United Nations released its comprehensive report on world cities (United Nations 2018). In this report, they note there is no standardized international criteria for determining the boundaries of a city and noted that often there are multiple boundary definitions for any given city. The report suggests that one type of definition, sometimes referred to as the "city proper," describes a city according to its administrative boundary. A second approach, which the UN terms the "urban agglomeration," considers the extent of a contiguous urban area including built up suburbs beyond the city's political boundaries. A third concept is the "metropolitan area," which defines an urban area according to the degree to which its economic and social life is interconnected by commerce and commuting.

In the United States, a good deal of attention has been paid to defining metro boundaries since 1950. Before that time there was no uniform definition of urban areas. There were political boundaries, to be sure, in the form of **municipalities**—areas over which a local government exercises *political* authority and provides public services. But these seldom corresponded to the *economic* boundaries of a region. Each federal and state government agency used a map of its own to define the economic borders relevant to that agency. The US Department of the Interior looked at watershed regions. Local transportation agencies used maps that included all the bus and subway transit stops in their networks. But only beginning with the 1950 census did the federal government create the first set of uniform and consistent definitions of metro areas based on the economic concept of commuting patterns. With some modification and new terminology, these census definitions have continued to evolve. Let's look at some of the key terms used for defining urban and suburban areas:

- **Urban cluster**: A geographical region consisting of a central place (or places) and adjacent densely settled territory that together contain at least 2,500 people, generally with an overall population density of at least 1,000 people per square mile.

- **Urbanized area**: An area with a total population of at least 50,000, consisting of one large central city together with adjacent areas with a population density of 1,000 or more people per square mile.

The Bureau of the Census has also defined something called the **urban population** in order to measure what share of the nation's entire population can be considered living in an urban setting as opposed to a rural community. Officially, the urban population includes all people living in official urbanized areas plus people outside of these areas who live in urban clusters (i.e., towns with more than 2,500 inhabitants). The total urban population currently comprises 80 percent of all US residents.

The first official definitions issued in 1950 by the Bureau of the Budget, the predecessor to today's US Office of Management and Budget (OMB), designated large metro areas as "standard metropolitan areas." In 1959, the term was changed to **standard metropolitan statistical areas (SMSAs)**. In 1983, the OMB dropped the word "standard" and just referred to them as **metropolitan statistical areas (MSAs)**, the same term used today. Seven years later, the term **metropolitan**

area (MA) was adopted to refer collectively to metropolitan statistical areas, while **consolidated metropolitan statistical areas (CMSAs) was** reserved for areas around the very large cities that contain more than one MSA. Finally, **primary metropolitan statistical areas (PMSAs) was** the name given to the MSAs that were part of a large CMSA.

New Definitions

Confusing as all this may be, the OMB changed definitions again in 2003, and the terms CMSA and PMSA disappeared. Now, urban regions are divided into metropolitan and **micropolitan statistical areas** (US Bureau of the Census 2003). As you might guess, metropolitan statistical areas are larger entities.

- **Metropolitan statistical area:** A large urban area with at least one urban cluster that has a population of at least 50,000 inhabitants.

- **Micropolitan statistical area:** A smaller urban area with at least one urban cluster of between 10,000 and 50,000 inhabitants.

Together, metropolitan and micropolitan statistical areas are now referred to as **core-based statistical areas (CBSAs).** As of the 2015, there were 389 metropolitan statistical areas (including 7 in Puerto Rico) and 556 micropolitan statistical areas (including 5 in Puerto Rico), totaling 945 large and small CBSAs.

Determining what counts as a CBSA and what its boundaries are is a complicated process. But the government begins with a general concept that has remained central to the definition of an urban area for decades and still holds for the newfangled CBSA:

- A CBSA is a core area containing a substantial population nucleus, together with adjacent communities having a high degree of economic and social integration with that core.

Under this definition, the government begins with the political unit of the county—everywhere but in New England—to define a metropolitan statistical area. The county (or counties) containing the largest city in a region becomes the "central county" (counties). Then any adjacent counties—in that state or in an adjacent state—that have at least 50 percent of their population in the urbanized area surrounding the largest city are added to the MSA. Additional outlying counties are also added to the MSA if they meet specified commuting and population density requirements. The boundaries of a particular MSA are set when it is far enough away from one of its central counties to make commuting between the periphery and the central counties unlikely. The very largest MSAs may have one or more geographically concentrated metropolitan divisions within them, each covering several counties.

Atlanta (or more correctly, the Atlanta-Sandy Springs-Marietta metropolitan statistical area in Georgia) is a good example of an MSA. It contains more than 3.7 million residents living in twenty-eight different counties with the city of Atlanta at its core. Atlanta is the largest **principal city** in the Atlanta MSA; Sandy Springs and Marietta are considerably smaller but are still considered to be principal cities since both municipalities have more than 10,000 residents. Principal cities used to be known as **central cities** under the old OMB and census definitions, and we continue to use that familiar term in this book. Principal or central cities are political jurisdictions defined by municipal boundaries, not necessarily economic logic.

In the six New England states, where counties are less important units of government and where all land is part of one municipality or another, MSAs are collections of cities and towns rather than counties. The largest urban unit in the New England states is now known as a NECTA—a New England City and Town Area.

The US Bureau of the Census also has a new definition for the largest urbanized areas in the country. They used to be called consolidated metropolitan statistical areas (CMSAs), a term introduced earlier. Now they are called **combined statistical areas (CSAs)**, which link together MSAs where there is a substantial amount of commuting between individual metropolitan areas. Hence, within the largest CSAs there can be several MSAs, each with one or more counties and principal cities. These combined statistical areas can cover hundreds and even thousands of square miles.

Of the entire array of CSAs, the largest is New York, which covers New York City and other adjacent communities in New York State, parts of northern New Jersey and eastern Pennsylvania, and a few counties in southwestern Connecticut. It now spreads over nearly 8,300 square miles—nearly eight times the size of the entire state of Rhode Island and nearly as large as the state of New Hampshire—and includes the following metro areas:

- Bridgeport-Stamford-Norwalk (Connecticut Metropolitan Statistical Area)

- Kingston (New York Metropolitan Statistical Area)

- New Haven-Milford (Connecticut Metropolitan Statistical Area)

- New York-Northern New Jersey-Long Island (New York-New Jersey-Pennsylvania Metropolitan Statistical Area)

- Poughkeepsie-Newburgh-Middletown (New York Metropolitan Statistical Area)

- Torrington (Connecticut Micropolitan Statistical Area)

- Trenton-Ewing (New Jersey Metropolitan Statistical Area)

This single CSA contained more than nearly 22.7 million residents in 2018. One out of every 15 Americans live in this one mega region residing in one or another of six metropolitan statistical areas and one micropolitan area spread out over 30 counties.

Interstate 95, the Saw Mill River Parkway, the Long Island Expressway, the New York subway system, and commuter rail make it possible for all of these people to commute to work within the same geographically defined labor market, and therefore this region is designated as a single combined statistical area. All combined statistical areas across the country are defined in the same way, their boundaries dependent on the extent to which the local transportation system permits residents to commute to work. The better the transportation system, the larger the CSA. If CSAs existed in the nineteenth century, they would have been considerably smaller than they are today simply because it was infeasible for residents to commute very far to work given horse-drawn carts, a primitive highway system, and only limited street railways.

New York City itself, with its five boroughs, is the largest principal city in the CSA with more than 8 million inhabitants. There are also 20 other principal cities in this one CSA, including Poughkeepsie, Newburgh, and Middletown in New York State; Newark, Edison, and Union in New Jersey; and Bridgeport, Stamford, Norwalk, Danbury, New Haven, and Stratford in Connecticut.

Ranking the World's Metropolitan Areas

By far, Tokyo leads the pack in terms of being the world's *most populous metropolitan area* with more than 37,000,000 residents. To give some idea of how many this is, the number of residents in the metro area of Tokyo alone in 2018 nearly equals the number of residents in the entire state of California (39.9 million) and is considerably larger than the populations in each of the other 49 states within the United States.

Following Tokyo in second and third place are the metro areas of Delhi and Shanghai. Each has a population that exceeds 25 million. New York City ranks 11th in the world with a metro-wide population of nearly 19 million. Of all the metro areas in the United States, Los Angeles is the only other US metro area ranked in the top 25 of the world's largest metropolitan areas.

What is fascinating is how many countries are listed in Table 2.1. Sao Paolo in Brazil ranks 4th, followed by Mexico City in Mexico ranked 5th and Cairo, Egypt ranked 6th. Among the largest 25 metro areas in the world are Dhaka in Bangladesh (#9), Osaka, Japan (#10), Karachi, Pakistan (#12), Buenos Aires, Argentina (#13), and Istanbul, Turkey (#15). In Africa, both Kinshasa in the Democratic Republic of the Congo and Lagos, Nigeria are found on this list of the largest metro areas in the world.

Roles in the World Economy

There is a big difference, however, in the role each of these large cities play in the world. New York is known as one of the greatest financial capitals in the global economy. Tokyo is still the center of a global network of manufacturing. With its concentration of research universities, the Boston-Cambridge metro region of Massachusetts can now claim to be the world's #1 center for biotechnology research.

By contrast, most of the large African cities still have little economic impact in terms of global commerce and in this sense many demographers do not consider these large urban communities to be "world cities" (Brunn et al. 2016). They may be centers for their national economies, but they are not fully integrated into the global economy. Nonetheless, over time many of these cities will become world cities in the sense of increased trade with other of nations of the world. Nairobi is one sub-Saharan city on its way to world status. Brunn and his colleagues suggest this city in Kenya is a prime example of a "splintering urbanism" where one

TABLE 2.1.   WORLD'S LARGEST METROPOLITAN AREAS AND THEIR CENTRAL CITIES - 2018 ESTIMATES

RANK	CITY	COUNTRY	METRO POPULATION (IN MILLIONS)
1	Tokyo	Japan	37.40
2	Delhi	India	28.51
3	Shanghai	China	25.58
4	Sao Paulo	Brazil	21.65
5	Mexico City	Mexico	21.58
6	Cairo	Egypt	20.08
7	Mumbai	India	19.98
8	Beijing	China	19.62
9	Dhaka	Bangladesh	19.58
10	Osaka	Japan	19.28
11	New York City	United States	18.82
12	Karachi	Pakistan	15.40
13	Buenos Aires	Argentina	14.97
14	Changqing	China	14.84
15	Istanbul	Turkey	14.75
16	Calcutta	India	14.68
17	Manila	Philippines	13.48
18	Lagos	Nigeria	13.46
19	Rio de Janeiro	Brazil	13.30
20	Tianjin	China	13.22
21	Kinshasa	Congo	13.17
22	Guangzhou	China	12.64
23	Los Angeles	United States	12.46
24	Moscow	Russia	12.41
25	Shenzhen	China	11.91

Source: United Nations

portion of the city is highly integrated with the world economy while another larger portion is disintegrated both literally and figuratively with many of its residents newly arrived from rural areas and not yet integrated into the core functions of the city, with many living in informal squatter settlements just east of downtown. Yet the increase in the central city population of Nairobi to 4 million inhabitants has helped make the city a transport hub for much of East Africa and now is becoming a major industrial urban center in the region and prominent in commerce, retailing, tourism, banking, and education (Brunn et al. 2016).

Moreover, if we correlate the annual average growth rate in a country's gross domestic product for the period 2000–2010 with the average growth rate in its major metro area population for the period 2006–2020, we find a 52 percent positive correlation between the two series. This suggests that urbanization is a major contributor to economic growth.

Nonetheless, many sub-Saharan African countries have been trying to stem rural to urban migration because of the splintering urbanism where many of the new migrants remain poor and unemployed and pose serious health risks on the community. The country of Senegal in West Africa is now trying to put the brakes on in-migration into its capital city Dakar through the development of "ecovillages." The strategy focuses on equipping existing rural communities with the means to utilize solar energy, sustainable water storage, and waste management techniques (Brunn et al. 2016). If these are successful, these ecovillages may provide a boost to the nation's economic growth while limiting the adverse effects of too many migrants fleeing rural areas for large cities.

Ranking US Metropolitan Areas

As we saw in Table 2.1, the New York metropolitan region was the 11th largest in the world in 2018, but it clearly has the largest population in the United States. The 25 largest metropolitan regions in America are listed in Table 2.2, where data on population from 1990 through 2018 can be found.

By 2018, the New York-Newark-Bridgeport consolidated statistical area had an estimated population of nearly 22.7 million, nearly four million more than the second place Los Angeles-Long Beach-Riverside CSA. Rounding out the top five are the Chicago-Naperville-Michigan City, Washington-Baltimore-Arlington, and San Jose-San Francisco-Oakland CSAs.

All these large metro areas have been growing at vastly different rates and none have grown faster than the Phoenix-Mesa consolidated area in Arizona which more than doubled its population between 1990 and 2018. By contrast, midwestern metro areas like Detroit-Warren-Ann Arbor, Michigan and Cleveland-Akron-Canton, Ohio have hardly grown at all since 2000—the former by just 5.1 percent and the latter by less than 1 percent. The same is true for the Pittsburgh-New Castle-Weirton, Pennsylvania CSA which experienced less than a 2 percent increase in its population over a period of almost two decades.

These trends, as we shall see in other sections of this text, reflect major shifts in the underlying economies of these metro areas. In the case of Atlanta, it has become the "capital" of the South with its growth in industry. Delta Airline's corporate headquarters are in this city with its 34,500 employees. Emory University, the corporate headquarters of Home Depot, and the division headquarters of Publix Supermarkets all make their home in this consolidated metro area—along with the corporate headquarters of the United Parcel Service (UPS), the Coca-Cola Company, and the regional headquarters of Bank of America.

By contrast, Detroit which was once the fifth largest city in the nation has grown slowly as some of its key industries—most importantly the automobile industry—have shrunk in size. Two other midwestern metro areas—centered in Cleveland and Pittsburgh—have suffered something of the same fate. In both of those cities, the steel industry once ruled supreme, but with the rise in steel imports from other countries and the relocation of steel production to the American South, population growth has been very limited.

TABLE 2.2. LARGEST METROPOLITAN AREA POPULATIONS IN THE UNITED STATES 1990-2018

RANK	COMBINED STATISTICAL AREA	STATE(S)	2018	2010	2000	1990	PERCENT CHANGE 1990-2018
1	New York-Newark-Bridgeport	NY-NJ-CT-PA	22,679,940	22,255,491	21,361,797	19,710,239	15.07%
2	Los Angeles-Long Beach-Riverside	CA	18,764,814	17,877,006	16,373,645	14,531,529	29.13%
3	Chicago-Naperville-Michigan City	IL-IN-WI	9,866,910	9,840,929	9,312,255	8,385,397	17.67%
4	Washington, D.C. -Blatimore-Arlington	DC-MD-VA-WV-PA	9,778,360	9,032,651	7,572,647	6,665,228	46.71%
5	San Jose-San Francisco-Oakland	CA	9,666,055	8,923,942	7,092,596	6,290,008	53.67%
6	Boston-Worcester-Providence	MA-RI-NH-CT	8,285,407	7,893,376	7,298,695	5,348,894	15.90%
7	Dallas-Fort Worth	TX	7,957,493	6,816,237	5,487,956	4,138,010	92.30%
8	Philadelphia-Reading-Camden	PA-NJ-DE-MD	7,204,035	7,067,807	6,207,223	5,573,521	29.25%
9	Houston-The Woodlands	TX	7,197,863	6,114,562	4,815,122	3,855,180	86.71%
10	Miami-Port ST. Lucie-Fort Lauderdale	FL	6,913,263	6,199,860	5,519,891	4,475,531	54.47%
11	Atlanta-Athens-Clark County-Sandy Springs	GA-AL	6,775,511	6,054,858	4,548,344	3,317,380	104.24%
12	Detroit-Warren-Ann Arbor	MI	5,353,002	5,318,744	537,538	5,095,695	5.05%
13	Phoenix-Mesa	AZ	4,911,581	4,246,484	3,303,182	2,278,714	115.54%
14	Seattle-Tacoma	WA	4,853,364	4,274,767	3,604,165	3,008,669	61.31%
15	Orlando-Deltona-Daytona Beach	FL	4,096,575	3,447,950	27,901,791	2,080,740	96.88%
16	Minneapolis-St. Paul	MN	3,999,565	3,706,276	3,353,813	2,882,826	38.74%
17	Cleveland-Akron-Canton	OH	3,599,264	3,630,188	3,694,214	3,572,338	0.75%
18	Denver-Aurora	CO	3,572,798	3,091,010	2,630,026	2,007,649	77.96%
19	San Diego-Chula Vista-Carlsbad	CA	3,343,364	3,095,349	2,813,839	2,498,839	33.80%
20	Portland-Vancouver-Salem	OR-WA	3,239,412	2,921,412	2,549,327	2,045,922	58.34%
21	Tampa-St. Petersberg-Clearwater	FL	3,142,663	2,783,462	2,396,038	2,067,959	51.97%
22	St. Louis-St. Charles-Farmington	MO	2,909,777	2,892,556	2,772,883	2,650,805	9.77%
23	Charlotte-Concord	NC-SC	2,753,754	2,402,623	1,897,034	1,5010,663	83.38%
24	Sacramento-Roseville	CA-NV	2,619,754	2,414,783	1,930,149	1,587,249	65.05%
25	Pittsburgh-New Castle-Weirton	PA-OH	2,612,492	2,660,727	2,525,730	2,564,535	1.87%

Source: U.S. Census Bureau

What's growing rapidly are metro areas in the South and West led by Dallas-Fort Worth and the Houston-Woodlands CSAs in Texas, Phoenix-Mesa in Arizona, Denver-Aurora in Colorado, and Charlotte-Concord in North and South Carolina.

Cities and Their Reputations

Another way that we might rank cities is not by population size, but by the reputation they have for the quality of life for their residents. When *Travel + Leisure* magazine surveyed more than half a million travelers in 2020 about the cities they liked the most, the respondents named Charleston, Honolulu, and San Francisco as the three most romantic cities in the United States. Of the 25 major cities in this poll, travelers found the following US cities to be the most interesting of all because of their arts, entertainment, architecture, or physical beauty:

1. Charleston, South Carolina
2. New Orleans, Louisiana
3. Santa Fe, New Mexico
4. Savannah, Georgia
5. Chicago, Illinois
6. New York, New York
7. San Antonio, Texas
8. Honolulu, Hawaii
9. Ashville, North Carolina
10. Austin, Texas

In a similar survey of world travelers, the magazine's respondents named the following cities as the best global destinations in terms of similar traits:

1. Oaxca, Mexico
2. San Miguel de Allende, Mexico
3. Hoi An, Vietnam
4. Chiang Mai, Thailand
5. Florence, Italy
6. Kyota, Japan
7. Udaipur, India
8. Luang Prabang, Laos
9. Ubud, Indonesia
10. Istanbul, Turkey

Of course, how one ranks cities by reputation depends very much on who is doing the ranking. If one is not simply interested in travel, but in finding the best place to live, one might wish to consider the list of US cities named by *Curbed Magazine* (2020) as having the best "livability." Their criteria for best place to live was based on such factors as walkability, park access, diversity, housing costs, job opportunities, and entertainment venues. Their list put Arlington, Virginia— just outside of Washington, DC—as #1. Besides having all the advantages of the Capitol City next door, it was ranked high on walkability, biking, a park within a 10-minute walk of nearly anyplace you might live as well as cultural diversity and a wide-ranging restaurant scene.

Number 2 was Boise, Idaho, which boasts a beautiful natural setting and a booming economy. Charlotte, North Carolina comes in #3, so it is found on both the *Travel + Leisure* Ranking and this one as well. It boasts music, tech, cuisine, and a strong economy. Rounding out the top 10 most livable cities in the *Curbed Magazine* ranking are Dallas, Texas (#4); Denver, Colorado (#5); Madison, Wisconsin (#6); Minneapolis, Minnesota (#7); Provo, Utah (#8); Raleigh, North Carolina (#9); and St. Louis, Missouri (#10).

The Mercer Company, a human resources firm that helps its clients determine whether they should offer a "hardship allowance" to top company executives who are relocated to a new city, has a created a Quality of Living index (Mercer Consulting 2007). It is based on how safe and stable a city is and whether it has a "dynamic *je ne sais quoi*" (a quality or attribute that is difficult to describe or express) like that often attributed to Paris, Tokyo, London, or New York. As of 2007, the Mercer index puts Zurich and Geneva, Switzerland, at the very top of the list of desirable places to live, followed by Vancouver, Canada; Vienna, Austria; and Auckland, New Zealand. The first US cities do not show up until #27, with Honolulu and San Francisco in a tie, followed by Boston (#36), Washington, DC (#42), New York (#47), and finally Seattle (#49). In evaluating the credibility of this index, it may be useful to know that the author of the Mercer report resides in Geneva, Switzerland!

Closer to home, That Sister.com (2021) ranks the best US cities for Black families. According to their research, #1 is Raleigh, North Carolina. It gained this ranking for its low unemployment rate, its highly diverse population, its four distinct seasons, and loads of entertainment. Orlando, Florida ranked #2 for its great housing market and the strong economy around Disneyworld and other theme parks. Richmond, Virginia was ranked #3 as being particularly safe and prosperous. Lansing, Michigan was ranked #4 as it is apparently not only diverse, but also embraces the diversity. San Antonio, Texas is ranked #5. Rounding out the top 10 are Washington, DC; San Diego, California; Columbus, Ohio; Dallas, Texas; and Seattle, Washington. Key factors in each of these were either a strong economy or lower cost of living, high diversity, and quality of life.

If you are a major league baseball fanatic, you probably would rank Boston, New York, and Chicago as the greatest places to live. After all, the Red Sox–Yankees rivalry is legendary: the Sox consistently sell out home games, and Red Sox Nation has hundreds (if not thousands) of loyal Boston fans at virtually every away game, no matter where it is played. The Chicago Cubs have few rivals when it comes to committed followers. St. Louis and Cincinnati can also lay claim to being great baseball towns.

All these rankings, of course, are highly subjective. Social scientists continually look for more objective measures to assess cities and suburbs. We can begin to assess metro areas by considering a taxonomy of cities based on their economic and social function.

A Taxonomy of Twenty-First-Century Cities

The growth pattern of individual cities and metro areas around the globe is underpinned by the function they serve in the economy. While each urban area has aspects of most economic functions, each city or metro area has one or two that are most prominent. We can count six broad types of cities in terms of a taxonomy.

Manufacturing cities (centers) continue to constitute a significant part of the economic structure in many metro areas and are a key factor in economic growth for some. In the automobile industry, the Toyota plant in the Evansville, Indiana metro area (opened in 1995) and the BMW and Michelin plants (and national headquarters) in the Greenville-Spartanburg, South Carolina metro area (opened in the mid-1990s) have been important sources of growth in these two urban areas. However, in many metropolitan areas manufacturing is a less secure part of the economy, as businesses are more subject to failure in a world of global competition where firms either go out of business or search for locations with lower costs. In the United States, manufacturing employment peaked in July 1945 just as World War II was drawing to a close. In that month, 35.7 million workers toiled in American factories. By 1982, the number was down to 19.9 million and by 2020 less than 8.5 million were employed in this critical sector (Federal Reserve Bank of St. Louis 2019). Many US manufacturing cities, most centered in the Northeast and Midwest, faced decline as work shifted to Mexico, India, China, and other countries. Cities like Detroit, Cleveland, Akron, and Pittsburgh were particularly hard hit because so much of their industry was tied to manufacturing.

Transportation hubs of the early twenty-first century attract economic activity because of their proximity to regional, national, and international production sites and markets. Finished products, intermediate inputs (products or substances to be used for further manufacture), passengers, and communications are channeled through these transportation hubs. But as transportation has changed, the location of hubs and the tasks related to transportation shipments have also changed. Today, airline hubs near the middle of the country, such as the FedEx hub in Memphis, Tennessee, and the UPS hub (Worldport) in Louisville, Kentucky, are among the primary sites for swiftly delivering packages to cities across the United States (Friedman 2005).

The volume and speed of activity in the transportation hubs—Worldport can sort 304,000 packages per hour—has had several spin-off activities, evincing what Jane Jacobs referred to as "creating new work out of old" (Jacobs 1969). Memphis and Louisville are not only expediting the movement of material, but they are also becoming centers for repair of appliances—consolidating the location of parts and expertise in repair to handle high-volume work that otherwise would be spread among many diffuse locations. In addition to the airline hubs, other cities serve as hubs for surface transportation lines. For example, Dallas has developed its

International Inland Port District or IIPOD as a major connector to local, regional, national, and global markets. The district covers more than 7,500 acres (equivalent to nearly 12 square miles) and extends into five municipalities within the Dallas metro region. The Inland Port has trucking and rail facilities to capitalize upon Dallas' location between Atlanta and Los Angeles (along an east–west axis) and between Mexico and Chicago-Detroit (along a northeast–southwest axis) (City of Dallas 2007).

With such massive growth in international commerce, seaports have become critical for moving goods globally—now in super cargo ships. The top five seaports in the world today are in Asia, where the largest is in Shanghai and the second largest is the capital city of Singapore. Rotterdam in the Netherlands is ranked 6th in cargo transfer.

International airports are just as important both for passenger travel and cargo. Perhaps surprisingly, the busiest air hub in the world is the Hartsfield-Jackson Atlanta International Airport in Georgia. The next busiest airports are the Beijing Capital International Airport, Dubai International Airport, O'Hare International Airport, Tokyo Haneda Airport, London Heathrow Airport, Los Angeles International Airport, Hong Kong International Airport, Paris International Airport, and Dallas/Fort Worth International Airport (VanDigit 2021).

Financial centers of the twenty-first century remain among the metropolitan areas with the most lucrative economic activities, as the removal of barriers to international financial investing and the financial returns to companies that correctly interpret information about economies in other countries have led to high profitability. According to the Global Financial Center Index (GFCI), the New York metro area has retained its role as the foremost financial industry site in the United States and worldwide (Yeandle and Wardle 2019). It is one of the two most important financial centers in the world (along with London) and is particularly well known for its trading and financial expertise associated with buying firms—or building new firms—in other countries as part of global economic activities (Sassen 2006). According to the GFCI, the next most important financial centers are spread across the world from Hong Kong (#3), Singapore (#4), Shanghai (#5), and Tokyo (#6). On the European continent, the two metro areas with large financial sectors are Zurich (#14) and Frankfurt (#15).

Like other finance centers of the twenty-first century, New York's financial industry has experienced increasing consolidation of firms due to mergers reflecting economies of scale which take advantage of information technology and efforts to expand the variety of expertise available in expert teams within financial companies. As a result of these mergers, it has retained its #1 GFCI ranking in the world.

Recently, Chicago and Charlotte have grown as finance centers in the United States. In 2007, two previously rival financial companies in Chicago, the Chicago Mercantile Exchange and the Chicago Board of Trade, merged to create the largest single market location in the world for the trade of financial instruments related to grain, livestock, and other agricultural products. Within a matter of years, the newly merged company now called CME was executing as many as 9 million contracts per day. Based in the Chicago Loop, CME continued to expand. In 2008, the New York Mercantile Exchange (NYMEX) accepted an offer from CME to purchase NYMEX for $8.9 billion in cash and CME Group stock. And then the

Chicago-based corporation entered a joint venture with the Dubai Mercantile Exchange (DME) on the Arabian Peninsula.

In 2012, the CME Group continued its expansion from its Chicago base when it acquired the Kansas City Board of Trade for $126 Million in cash. In 2017 it began trading in Bitcoin futures and finally in 2018 CME bought the London-based NEX Group for $5.5 billion. As such, Chicago now is poised to move up in the GFCI index for leadership in the highly valuable financial sector. As of 2020 it was ranked just behind Frankfurt, in 16th place.

Meanwhile, Charlotte, North Carolina, has grown as a major financial center throughout the final years of the twentieth century and the early years of the twenty-first century. In 1998, Charlotte-based NationsBank purchased Bank of America, and moved the Bank of America headquarters from San Francisco to Charlotte to merge with NationsBank. Consequently, Charlotte became the home of both Bank of America (the largest consumer and small business bank in the United States) and Wachovia Bank (the fourth-largest bank in the United States). According to the US Chamber of Commerce, the financial industry in Charlotte now employs more than 55,000 people.

Innovation centers play an increasingly valued role in the economy of the twenty-first century because such cities attract and support creativity that will extend the ongoing technological revolution of recent decades into new products and new production technologies. Many of the recent technological advances in microprocessors, optical technology, biotechnology, and other areas are being developed in the metro areas that have taken the lead in these fields, as insight and creativity transform laboratory research into useful products and services. Cities including Austin, Boston, San Diego, Seattle, Raleigh, Washington, DC, and Denver are important not only for the innovation that occurs within the research and development departments of established firms like Microsoft (Seattle), Dell Computers (Austin), Qualcomm (San Diego), and Biogen (Boston), but also for the new products and services that emerge from the many start-up businesses that flourish in these areas.

In one ranking of innovation centers based on job opportunities for tech workers and those with digital skills, London is today considered the best place to look for employment in these fields (Phillpot 2019). In 2017, London-based firms received more equity investment than any other European nation. New York City, now nicknamed "Silicon Alley," was ranked second with 7,500 tech companies with 120,000 employees operating in the city and $40 billion invested in local startups over the period 2014–2019. In third place is Boston, which based on its fine array of universities including Harvard, MIT, Boston University, and Northeastern and more than $1 billion of state government investment in this sector, has become the biotech capital of the world. Rounding out the top 10 are Singapore (#4), with major offices housing both Facebook and Google; and the San Francisco Bay area (#5), affectionately known as "Silicon Valley" with its emphasis on computer and web-based technology. Just behind these top five are Tokyo, Berlin, Amsterdam, Toronto, and Austin.

In *Rise of the Creative Class,* Richard Florida suggests that within the increasingly important "creative class," there are two tiers of people who provide innovation—a "super-creative core" of individuals who provide path-breaking insights and produce "new forms or designs that are readily transferable and broadly useful," and "creative professionals," who are not path breakers in the same sense, but who are problem solvers "drawing on complex bodies of knowledge to solve specific problems" and who "apply or combine standard approaches in unique ways to fit the situation" (Florida 2002).

Successful innovation centers are characterized by an educated workforce, the presence of universities and hospitals, a high-quality telecommunications infrastructure, a number of employment opportunities that provide both lateral and upward mobility, and a quality of life that attracts and retains highly skilled creative people. Harkavy and Zuckerman (1999) have argued that the presence of institutions of higher learning and medical facilities—"Eds and Meds"—are particularly important as a part of the infrastructure that helps to anchor creativity in a specific metro area. These institutions generate large numbers of jobs, continuously engage in research, and disseminate knowledge to their students and workers. Moreover, because they are inherently immobile, they are not likely to be lured away to other places.

Cultural, tourism, and recreation centers have developed in many parts of the globe, reflecting the fact that the increased speed of transportation has not only made the world a smaller place for delivery of products and business services, but has also made sites of historical importance, recreation areas, and other culturally significant venues more accessible to vacationers. Cities such as Venice attract upwards of 20 million visitors a year. Beijing now has 140 million Chinese tourists visiting the capital city annually, along with 4.4 million international tourists. Nearly 30 percent of the workers in the Las Vegas, Nevada metro area, which markets itself as the Entertainment Capital of the World, are employed in leisure and hospitality industries. In 2016, visitors to Las Vegas spent a total of nearly $60 billion (Prince 2017). With the expansion of casinos and resorts fueling economic growth, the Las Vegas metro area attracts many new residents and is currently one of the fastest-growing urban regions in the United States, having nearly tripled in size between 1990 and 2018, from 797,142 to 2.23 million residents.

Similar dynamics have occurred in the Orlando metropolitan area, home of Walt Disney World, Sea World, the Epcot Theme Park and other attractions. The thriving Orlando area experienced more than a doubling of its population between 1990 and 2017, from 1.2 to 2.5 million residents. In 2018 metro Orlando received more than 68 million visitors, including 6.8 million who came from abroad. Indeed, tourism now accounts for fully one-third of the region's economy (Orlando/Orange County Convention and Visitors Bureau 2019).

Las Vegas and Orlando may be unique among US cities for the scale of their entertainment sites, but many other metro areas have smaller-scale attractions that contribute substantially to the area's economic activity. Philadelphia—the city in which both the Declaration of Independence and the Constitution were written, the capital of the United States from 1790 to 1800, and home of the Liberty Bell—has a unique historical legacy that brings many visitors to the city. Attracted by this rich history, visitors are also drawn to art museums on the Avenue of the Arts, recreational activities, restaurants, and retail stores. Since 2000, Philadelphia has enhanced its appeal to visitors by improving the Independence National Historic Park, opening a family entertainment complex on the waterfront, and building a 5,000-seat Regional Performing Arts Center.

Retirement centers have now emerged as a significant force in the US economy, as the 76 million members of the US baby boomer generation born between 1946 and 1964 begin to retire and seek new places to live. As such, the attraction of retirees has become part of the formal economic development plans of many areas. Retirees may be classified as one of three types: individuals who have lived in a particular area for much of their lives and choose to stay there, individuals whose health leads them to migrate to other locations near caregiving family members, and individuals who seek to migrate to a pleasant environment. Because travel and communication costs are much lower than they were in the past, retirees can live in a new location while still keeping in frequent touch with family.

Retirement centers target this last group, reasoning that amenity-seeking retirees often have sources of income that are not dependent upon local economic conditions and thus can contribute to the stabilization of a local economy. This relatively affluent group has good health and high education levels, add to the number of volunteers in an area, and pay more in local taxes than they use in locally supported services—largely because they do not have school-age children attending schools. Their relatively high levels of discretionary income can be spent in the local economy.

In addition to their immediate effects on the local economy, retirees are seen as potentially valuable to a local economy over the long haul because their relatively stable incomes generate public-sector tax revenue and private-sector spending that can "prime the pump" for future economic development activities in a community. As the numbers of migrant retirees increase, so does the overall spending from that cohort, stimulating the growth of service-based businesses and the in-migration of younger cohorts to fill the new jobs. This, in turn, can stimulate the growth of a wider range of businesses (Graff and Wiseman 1990; Fagan and Longino 1993; Skelley 2004).

Retirees often want locations with quality healthcare, warm climates, a low cost of living (including decent, affordable housing), safe neighborhoods, and convenient routine shopping. But they also often value being near cities that offer cultural events, recreation, and other attractions that would not be possible in a more distant small town.

In the United States, retirees have flocked to the Sunbelt and the Southwest to escape the cold winters of the north. Between 2000 and 2018, Texas experienced an increase of nearly 8 million new residents, an increase of 38 percent. Florida gained more than 5.3 million new inhabitants over this period, an increase of 33 percent. Other states with more than a 20 percent increase in their populations included Arizona (+40%), Utah (+42%), and South Carolina (+27%).

The states with little population growth over this time were in rougher climates. West Virginia actually lost population between 2000 and 2018, while Michigan and Rhode Island grew by just 1 percent and Illinois by a scant 3 percent. These are states where the economy has been weaker than most and the winters are tough.

Asset, Inc. lists what they consider to be the best places to retire worldwide. Within the United States, they consider Naples, Florida to be the best place to retire because of its climate and rich array of medical centers, recreations centers, and retirement communities (Kuffel 2019). In California they favor Beverly Hills, although it "isn't a cheap place to live." In Europe, they are partial to communities in Portugal because of their Mediterranean climate, history to explore, and favorable taxes. The cost of living in Portugal is about 30 percent lower than in the United States, making retirement dollars stretch further. Communities in Thailand also make the grade, given its relative affordability and ease with which to obtain a "retirement visa." Spain is favored for its beaches, especially in Barcelona. If you prefer South America, Asset, Inc. suggests Buenos Aires, Argentina.

Central Cities and Suburbs

Since at least World War II, there has been a near constant shift in population between the central city and the suburbs in the major metropolitan areas of the United States. Table 2.3 provides information on this shift over the period 1990 through 2018 for the nation's 25 largest metro areas.

Note that between 1990 and 2010, the proportion of a metro area's population residing in its Central City declined in almost every single instance. Atlanta saw its central city share of metro population decline from nearly 12 percent to less than 7 percent. Detroit experienced a decline from 20 percent to just 13 percent, while Houston's central city declined from 42 percent to 34 percent. Many of these central cities began to rebound after 2010. Indeed, in 18 of the 25 metro areas, the central city experienced an increase in the share of its metro area population. Central cities were once again a place where people were choosing to live.

The population dynamics of these metro areas were not necessarily similar. In many cases the central city continued to increase between 1990 and 2018, but since their suburbs were increasing so much faster, the central city's share of population declined. Table 2.4 reveals the change in the size of the central city and suburban population for our 25 largest metro areas.

In 19 of the largest 25 metro areas, the central city population increased over the past two decades. In New York, for example, the city itself, composed of its five boroughs of Manhattan, Brooklyn, the Bronx, Queens, and Staten Island, experienced a population explosion of nearly 1.1 million. The only reason the central city share fell was that the suburbs grew even faster, adding nearly 1.9 million residents between 1990 and 2018. The Detroit-Warren-Ann Arbor metro area experienced an enormous decline in its central city as many residents fled to its suburbs. The City of Detroit proper saw its population decline by more than one-third of a million residents while its suburbs experienced an increase of more than 600,000. Other midwestern metro areas experienced something of the same exodus from the central city, but not anywhere as severe. Cleveland lost more than 121,000 central city residents; St. Louis lost nearly 94,000; Chicago experienced a decline of nearly 78,000; Pittsburgh lost nearly 69,000: Philadelphia lost a comparatively modest number, under 1500. In each of these cases, their metro area suburbs saw large increases in population. This was particularly true of Chicago and Philadelphia..

Movement to the suburbs is not simply a US phenomenon. It has been happening in cities across the globe. The London metro area added nearly 1 million new residents between 2001 and 2021 (Trust for London 2021). Back in 1931, Inner London boasted a population of nearly 5 million while Outer London had just a little more than 3 million residents. By 1951 the suburban population already

TABLE 2.3. SHIFTS IN POPULATION BETWEEN CENTRAL CITY AND SUBURBS, 1990-2018

	CENTRAL CITY POPULATION AS PERCENT OF METRO AREA POPULATION					
	1990	2000	2010	2018	1990-2018	2010-2018
Atlanta	11.88%	9.16%	6.94%	7.35%	↓	↑
Boston	10.74%	8.07%	7.82%	8.38%	↓	↑
Charlotte	26.37%	28.51%	30.44%	31.68%	↑	↑
Chicago	33.20%	31.10%	27.39%	27.42%	↓	↑
Cleveland	14.15%	12.95%	10.93%	10.66%	↓	↓
Dallas	24.33%	21.66%	17.57%	16.90%	↓	↓
Denver	23.29%	21.09%	19.42%	20.05%	↓	↑
Detroit	20.17%	17.76%	13.42%	12.57%	↓	↓
Houston	42.30%	40.57%	34.35%	32.31%	↓	↓
Los Angeles	23.99%	22.57%	21.22%	21.27%	↓	↑
Miami	8.01%	6.57%	6.44%	6.81%	↓	↑
Minneapolis	12.78%	11.41%	10.32%	10.64%	↓	↑
New York	37.15%	37.49%	36.73%	37.03%	↓	↑
Orlando	7.92%	6.88%	6.91%	6.97%	↓	↑
Philadelphia	28.45%	24.45%	21.59%	21.99%	↓	↑
Phoenix	43.16%	39.99%	34.04%	33.80%	↓	↓
Pittsburgh	14.42%	13.25%	11.49%	11.52%	↓	↑
Portland	21.38%	20.76%	19.98%	20.16%	↓	↑
Sacramento	23.27%	21.09%	19.32%	19.41%	↓	↑
San Diego	44.44%	43.48%	42.24%	42.65%	↓	↑
San Jose	12.44%	12.62%	10.70%	10.66%	↓	↓
Seattle	17.16%	15.63%	14.24%	14.93%	↓	↑
St. Louis	14.96%	12.56%	11.04%	10.41%	↓	↓
Tampa	13.54%	12.66%	12.06%	12.50%	↓	↑
Washington, D.C.	9.11%	7.55%	6.66%	7.18%	↓	↑

Source: U.S. Census Bureau

outnumbered the central city population, and this differential has continued to increase through 2021. Indeed, London's central city continued to lose population through 1991, but since then its number of residents has almost continually increased. Between 2011 and 2021, Inner London's population count has increased by 300,000 to 3.5 million while Outer London has gained 350,000 to 5.3 million. Outer London's population is thus 60 percent of the total.

As is typical in major European core municipalities, most of the growth in London has come from net international immigration rather than internal migration. For London and other Western European cities, the largest number of immigrants have come from Eastern Europe.

TABLE 2.4.   CHANGES IN CENTRAL CITY AND SUBURBAN POPULATIONS, 1990-2018

METRO AREA	CHANGE IN CENTRAL CITY POPULATION	CHANGE IN SUBURBAN POPULATION
	1990-2018	1990-2018
Detroit-Warren-Ann Arbor	−355,312	612,619
Cleveland-Akron-Canton	−121,823	148,749
St. Louis-St. Charles-Farmington	−93,847	352,819
Chicago-Naperville- Michigan City	−77,917	1,559,430
Pittsburgh-New Castle-Weirton	−68,831	116,788
Philadelphia-Reading-Camden	-1,439	1,631,953
Minneapolis-St. Paul	57,020	1,059,719
Washington-Baltimore-Arlington	95,555	3,017,577
Atlanta-Athens-Clark County-Sandy Springs	104,027	3,354,104
Miami-Port St. Lucie-Fort Lauderdale	112,366	2,325,366
Tampa-St. Petersburg-Clearwater	112,875	961,829
Boston-Worcester-Providence	120,300	2,816,213
Orlando-Deltona-Daytona Beach	121,020	1,894,815
Sacramento-Roseville	139,164	893,341
Seattle-Tacoma	208,486	1,636,209
Portland-Vancouver-Salem	215,796	977,694
San Jose-San Francisco-Oakland	247,869	3,128,178
Denver-Aurora	248,882	1,316,267
San Diego-Chula Vista-Carlbad	315,427	529,098
Dallas-Fort Worth	338,070	3,481,413
Charlotte-Concord	476,564	775,527
Los Angeles-Long Beach-Riverside	505,058	3,728,227
Phoenix-Mesa	676,869	1,955,998
Houston-The Woodlands	694,949	2,647,734
New York-Newark- Bridgeport	1,076,184	1,893,517

Source: U.S. Census Bureau

Economic Ranking of Cities

Beyond ranking cities on the basis of their population growth, there are literally hundreds of ways to rank metro regions economically; using **median family income** is particularly effective, because it summarizes so much about the living standards in a particular area. If you array all the families in a city from the poorest to the richest and then take the middle one, you will have selected the family with the median income. Social scientists normally use this measure rather than mean (or average) income because a relatively few rich families in a city can make the "average" family in town seem better off than it is. The median, in most cases, represents a more "typical" family.

Urban areas with high median incomes tend to rank high on many other measures as well. More often than not, urban areas with high median incomes have lower poverty rates and crime rates and higher education and health levels. The housing stock is less dilapidated, and more money is normally spent on parks and recreation. Hence, simply knowing something about median family income in a city or suburb often tells a good deal about the quality of life in those communities along multiple dimensions.

Figure 2.1 provides a snapshot of median household income in 2016 for the central cities in the largest 25 metropolitan areas in the United States. Within this group, San Francisco boasts the highest median household income: $87,701. Half of the city's households live on more than this amount per year; the other half live on less. At the opposite extreme is Detroit, where median household income is only $26,249. Somewhere in the middle of these 25 cities is Los Angeles, with a median of $51,538. Miami, St. Louis, Philadelphia, Orlando, and Baltimore join Detroit at the bottom of the list. Seattle, Washington, DC, San Diego, Riverside (California), and Boston join the Golden Gate city at the top.

The disparity in household income across central cities is substantial. Median household income in Detroit is less than 30 percent of that in San Francisco and half that of Minneapolis. Not unexpectedly, median incomes are generally higher—often much higher—across the entire metropolitan areas where these central cities are located. Figure 2.2 provides the information for the largest 25 metro areas in the United States, while Figure 2.3 shows the ratio of the central city median to the metro area median for each of these metropolitan areas. Not surprisingly, perhaps, San Francisco's metro area ranks #1, as does its central city. Washington, DC's metro area ranks #2 and Boston is #3. While Detroit's central city had by far the

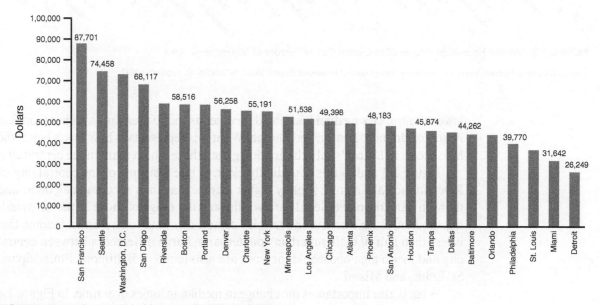

FIGURE 2.1. Median Household Income 2016 Central City

Source: US Census Bureau American Community Survey Briefs, "Household Income 2016", ACSBR/16-02, September 2017.,

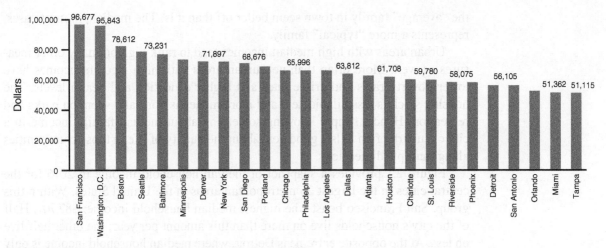

FIGURE 2.2. Median Household Income 2016 Metropolitan Areas

Source: US Census Bureau, American Community Survey Briefs, "Household Income 2016", ACSBR/16-02, September 2017.

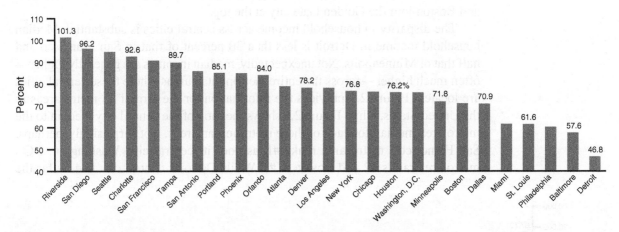

FIGURE 2.3. Median Household Income 2016 Central City as Percent of Metropolitan Area

Source: US Census Bureau, American Community Survey Briefs, "Household Income 2016", ACSBR/16-02, September 2017.

lowest central city median household income, its metro area ranks higher than San Antonio, Orlando, Miami, and Tampa. What this represents is how much better the households in Detroit's suburbs are doing than those who remain in the central city.

Figure 2.3 makes this abundantly clear. While residents of the central city of Riverside actually enjoy a slightly higher income than their suburban neighbors and those in San Diego and Seattle are within striking range of those in the surrounding suburbs, those who live in Detroit's central city have to live on an income that is less than half of their suburban counterparts. Large differences between central city and metro area household incomes are also found in Baltimore, Philadelphia, St. Louis, and Miami.

What is also important is the change in median incomes over time. In Figure 2.4 data are presented on the percentage change in nominal median family income between the years 2000 and 2017 for 20 large central cities. According to the US

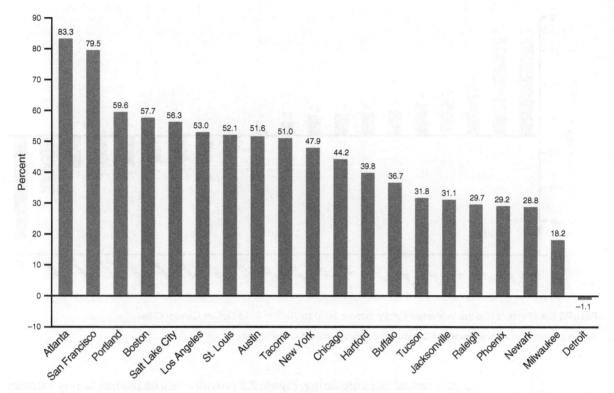

FIGURE 2.4. Percentage Change in Median Family Income 2000 to 2017 Central Cities

Source: https://www.statista.com/statistics/432876/us-metro-areas-by-median-household-income

Census Bureau, households include anyone living in a single housing unit related or not, including individuals living alone. Families, on the other hand, refer to the subset of households where there are two or more related individuals living in the same housing unit. Nominal income refers to income which has not been adjusted for increases in the cost of living.

Not accounting for inflation, residents of Atlanta have seen their family incomes increase by more than 83 percent between 2000 and 2017. San Francisco central city residents are not far behind with nearly an 80 percent increase in nominal median family income. But at the other end of the income scale, Detroit central city residents have experienced a slight drop in their family incomes even before accounting for the increased cost of living. Central city families in Raleigh, Phoenix, Newark, and Milwaukee have experienced increases in nominal median family income that are just a little more than one-third the increase in Atlanta and San Francisco.

The Cost of Living

Once we consider increases in the cost of living, using the **consumer price index** for urban families (CPI), which measures the change in the cost of purchasing a specified set of goods and services over time, the picture becomes much more striking and one begins to appreciate how well or poorly families in some of America's

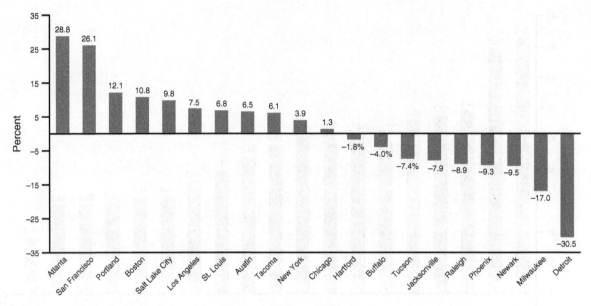

FIGURE 2.5. Percent Change in Median Family Income 2000 to 2017 in 2017 Dollars Central Cities

Source: https://www.statista.com/statistics/432876/us-metro-areas-by-median-household-income

largest central cities are faring. Figure 2.5 provides data on median family incomes for the same 20 cities we listed in Figure 2.2, but this time adjusts each median for changes in the national CPI.

The typical family living in the central city of Atlanta in 2017 enjoyed a median income adjusted for inflation that was nearly 29 percent higher than the typical family who lived there in 2000. Similarly, central city families in San Francisco, Portland (Oregon), and Boston enjoyed at least a 10.8 percent increase in their "real" inflation-adjusted incomes.

At the other end of the income spectrum were families in Detroit's central city. After adjusting for inflation, the typical family there had to live on nearly 31 percent less income in 2017 than the typical family in 2000. That is one powerful measure of how Detroit has suffered since the heyday of the automobile industry. Similarly, residents of Hartford, Buffalo, Tucson, Jacksonville, Raleigh, Phoenix, Newark, and Milwaukee now live on inflation-adjusted family incomes that are less than families who lived in these central cities in 2000.

While Figure 2.5 adjusted nominal family income for the *national* CPI, the Economic Policy Institute (EPI) in Washington, DC has developed a family budget calculator that takes into account the *actual* cost of housing, food, child care, transportation, healthcare, other necessities, and taxes for metro area in the United States. Since the average cost of these items differ across metro areas, the EPI calculations provide a better picture of the actual living standards in each city.

One can look at two cities to show the difference in the cost of living of a typical middle-class family with two adults and two children. This is shown in Table 2.5.

In 2017, median family income in the central city of Boston was $69,616, while in Buffalo it was just $41,837. This would seem to suggest that the typical family in Boston was enjoying a standard of living some 66 percent higher than such a family

TABLE 2.5. COST OF LIVING

ANNUAL COSTS 2 ADULTS AND 2 CHILDREN BUFFALO/CHEEKTOWAGA/NIAGARA FALLS METRO AREA	
HOUSING	$9.588
FOOD	$9.032
CHILD CARE	$23.354
TRANSPORTATION	$13.723
HEALTH CARE	$12.765
OTHER NECESSITIES	$7.512
TAXES	$12.896
Annual Total	**$88,071**
ANNUAL COSTS	
2 adults and 2 children	
Boston/Cambridge-Quincy metro area	
HOUSING	$20.880
FOOD	$10.519
CHILD CARE	$26.700
TRANSPORTATION	$13.234
HEALTH CARE	$10.041
OTHER NECESSITIES	$12.667
TAXES	$19.516
Annual Total	**$113,558**

Source: Economic Policy Institute's State of Working America Data Library, 2019

in Buffalo. But Boston is renowned for its very high cost of living while that in Buffalo is much lower, especially when it comes to the cost of housing, other necessities, and taxes. A typical middle-class family in Boston, according to the EPI budget calculator, needs more than $113,000 to cover living costs. In Buffalo, a family of four only needs about $88,000 to cover the same costs. So after controlling for differences in living costs, that median income family in Boston has a real adjusted income only 29 percent higher than a similar family in Buffalo—much lower than the 66 percent difference if we simply rely on using a national inflation factor.

Poverty

Closely related to how median household incomes are distributed across the United States is the distribution of poverty. In 2020, a family of four was considered officially poor if its money income—income excluding the value of food stamps or rent subsidies—fell below $26,200 for the year. That amounts to $2,183 per month or $504 per week to pay for rent, food, clothing, transportation, and everything else.

In 2020, the 10 central cities with the highest official poverty rates were:

1.	Detroit, Michigan	36.4%
2.	Cleveland, Ohio	34.6%
3.	Rochester, New York	32.6%
4.	Dayton, Ohio	32.1%
5.	Syracuse, New York	31.8%
6.	Hartford, Connecticut	30.1%
7.	Springfield, Massachusetts	28.6%
8.	Newark, New Jersey	28%
9.	Birmingham, Alabama	27.2%
10.	Jackson, Mississippi	26.9%

Source: Chris Kolmar, "The 10 Poorest Cities in American 2020," in Roadsnacks
http://www.roadsnacks.net/poorest-cities-in-America/.

What most of these cities have in common is that they were once among the premier manufacturing centers in the United States. Detroit was the center of the auto industry; Cleveland was a steel town; Rochester was famous for its clothing, shoe, and machine manufacturing; Dayton was the headquarters of National Cash Register and numerous automobile parts plants; Birmingham was, like Cleveland, a major steel producer. As these manufacturing cities faced deindustrialization, jobs dried up and poverty spiked. Most of these cities are still struggling to attract new industries to replace those that have left or downsized.

Migration to the suburbs played a role as well. With the post–World War II migration of middle-income households (particularly White families) from the inner city to the suburbs, there was a concern that particular neighborhoods in the central cities would become areas of concentrated poverty—where 40 percent or more of the households are living under the poverty line (Danziger and Gottschalk 1987; Kasarda 1993). The concern turned out to be fully justified. By 1990, there were more than 3,400 census tracts containing 10.4 million people living in concentrated poverty, most in inner cities. A **census tract** is a contiguous neighborhood of 2,500 to 8,000 persons who generally share similar population characteristics, economic conditions, and living standards. These 3,400 neighborhoods represented more than a doubling from 1970 in the number of high-poverty census tracts in the country. Across all the high-concentration poverty neighborhoods in the United States, 69 percent of the residents were Black or Latinx, while just 26 percent were White.

Only with the reemergence of the central city as a prime location for young professionals and older empty nesters has this trend been partly arrested. Still, most central cities today have neighborhoods that are dilapidated and often crime-ridden—a function in part of the growing income inequality throughout the nation.

Race and Ethnicity

Besides their population growth rates and income trends, metro areas also differ significantly in terms of racial and ethnic composition. For centuries in the United States, segregation by race was either enforced by law—particularly in the

South—or made a standard practice nearly everywhere else. Real estate agents and mortgage lenders often "red-lined" certain neighborhoods so that Black families could only rent or purchase homes in Black neighborhoods. This has been well-documented in Richard Rothstein's *The Color of Law* (2019).

What is also clear is how the racial and ethnic composition of *central cities* differs across the country, often the result of varying patterns of domestic migration and international immigration. To get some idea of the wide variance in this demographic feature, Figures 2.6a, 2.6b, and 2.6c present the racial and ethnic composition of the central cities of San Francisco, Houston, and Detroit.

San Francisco, now one of the wealthiest cities in the United States, has a fascinatingly diverse population. In 2017, just under 41 percent of its residents were White. The Asian population made up a little more than a third (33.9%) of the population, with many residents of Chinese and Japanese descent. About 15 percent of the residents are Latinx. Only about 5 percent of the population is Black.

In sharp contrast, the City of Houston has a small Asian population (less than 7 percent), but it has a large Latinx population (nearly 45 percent). Of these, about three-fourths are of Mexican ancestry. Whites account for just under a quarter

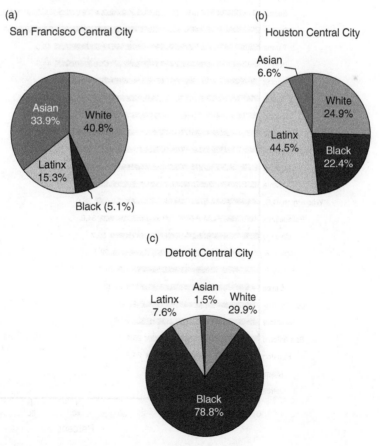

(a)
San Francisco Central City

Asian 33.9%
White 40.8%
Latinx 15.3%
Black (5.1%)

(b)
Houston Central City

Asian 6.6%
White 24.9%
Latinx 44.5%
Black 22.4%

(c)
Detroit Central City

Latinx 7.6%
Asian 1.5%
White 29.9%
Black 78.8%

FIGURE 2.6. Racial/Ethnic Composition 2017

Source: US Census Bureau, Quick Facts. https://www.census.gov/quickfacts/fact/table/US/PST045219

(24.9) percent of the city's population. The Black community is almost as large as the number of Whites, making up 22.4 percent of the city's residents.

Finally, we can look at the City of Detroit. By 2017, nearly 4 out of 5 Detroiters were Black—one the highest concentrations in the country. Many of these are descendants of southern Blacks who migrated up to Detroit during World War II to work in its defense plants and remained to work in the burgeoning auto industry. Today, less than 10 percent of the city's population is White, while Latinx residents make up just under 8 percent. Asian Americans account for less than 2 percent of Detroit's population.

Figure 2.7a through Figure 2.7d provide evidence of just how much variance there is across the largest central cities in the nation. The first of these reveals the share of each city's population who are non-Latinx White. Such Whites make up more than 70 percent of Portland, Oregon's population, followed by Minneapolis with 68.2 percent, Seattle with 65.3 percent, and Denver with 53.6 percent.

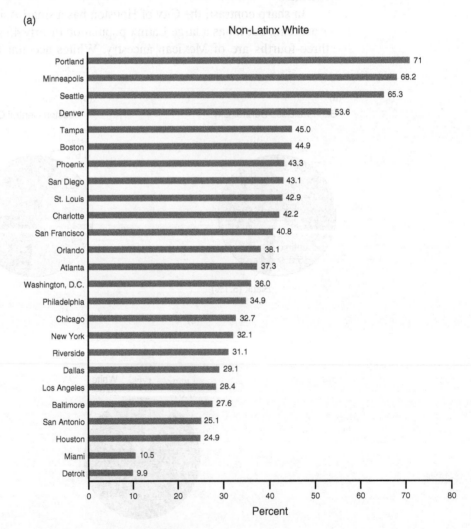

FIGURE 2.7. Racial/Ethnic Composition of Major Central Cities 2017

Source: US Census Bureau, Quick Facts. https://www.census.gov/quickfacts/fact/table/US/PST045219

(b)

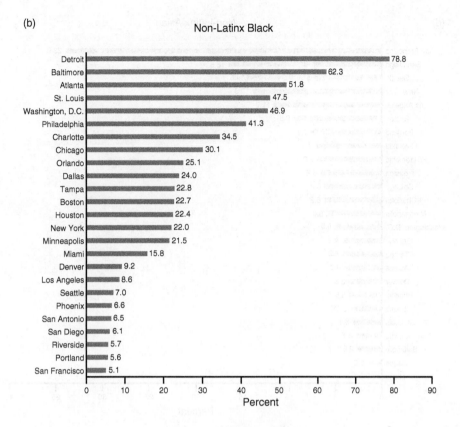

Non-Latinx Black

City	Percent
Detroit	78.8
Baltimore	62.3
Atlanta	51.8
St. Louis	47.5
Washington, D.C.	46.9
Philadelphia	41.3
Charlotte	34.5
Chicago	30.1
Orlando	25.1
Dallas	24.0
Tampa	22.8
Boston	22.7
Houston	22.4
New York	22.0
Minneapolis	21.5
Miami	15.8
Denver	9.2
Los Angeles	8.6
Seattle	7.0
Phoenix	6.6
San Antonio	6.5
San Diego	6.1
Riverside	5.7
Portland	5.6
San Francisco	5.1

Percent

(c)

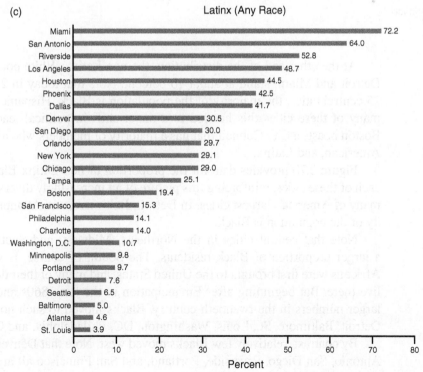

Latinx (Any Race)

City	Percent
Miami	72.2
San Antonio	64.0
Riverside	52.8
Los Angeles	48.7
Houston	44.5
Phoenix	42.5
Dallas	41.7
Denver	30.5
San Diego	30.0
Orlando	29.7
New York	29.1
Chicago	29.0
Tampa	25.1
Boston	19.4
San Francisco	15.3
Philadelphia	14.1
Charlotte	14.0
Washington, D.C.	10.7
Minneapolis	9.8
Portland	9.7
Detroit	7.6
Seattle	6.5
Baltimore	5.0
Atlanta	4.6
St. Louis	3.9

Percent

FIGURE 2.7. Continued

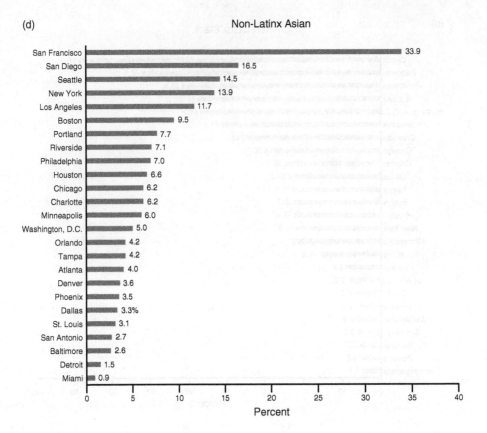

(d)   Non-Latinx Asian

FIGURE 2.7. Continued

At the other end of the distribution, the non-Latinx White population of both Detroit and Miami stand at about 10 percent. Note that today in 21 of the largest 25 central cities, the majority of the population is Black, Hispanic, and Asian. In many of these cities this has led to a major shift in political leadership. Today, Boston boasts a City Council that has a majority of members who are Black, Asian American, and Latinx.

Figure 2.7b provides data for the proportion of non-Latinx Black residents in each of these cities, reinforcing this picture of an increasingly diverse population in many of America's largest cities. In Detroit, Baltimore, and Atlanta, a clear majority of the population is Black.

Note that central cities in the Northeast, Midwest, and South tend to have a larger proportion of Black residents. The South, of course, is where enslaved Africans were first brought to the United States, and many of their descendants still live there. But beginning after Emancipation in the late 1860s and then in much larger numbers in the twentieth century, Blacks moved to such northern cities as Detroit, Baltimore, St., Louis, Washington, DC, Philadelphia, and Chicago.

By contrast, relatively few Blacks moved west. Note that Denver, Phoenix, San Antonio, San Diego, Riverside, Portland, and San Francisco all are at the bottom of the chart, and in each Blacks make up less than 10 percent of the central city population.

Figure 2.7c provides the city data for the Latinx community in each of these large central cities. Note that today Miami is essentially a Latinx city. More than 72 percent of the central city are identified as such. More than 35 percent of the population came from Cuba or are the descendants of Cubans. Many of them arrived soon after the Cuban revolution in 1959, and Miami welcomed them.

San Antonio is also heavily Latinx, with nearly two-thirds of the population (64%) having Latino/Latina roots. Of the total population, almost 58 percent— or nearly the entire Latinx population—has Mexican roots. This is perhaps not surprising, given that Mexico sits close to San Antonio's border. By contrast, central cities farther from Mexico and Cuba have much smaller Latinx populations. In St. Louis, less than 4 percent of the population identifies themselves as such. The same is true for Atlanta, Baltimore, and Seattle—all with fewer than 7 percent Latinx.

Asians are also becoming a significant part of America's new urban landscape, as shown in Figure 2.7d. In San Francisco, famous for its Chinatown, the proportion is now greater than one in three (33.9%). Not only is there a large population of Chinese descendants, but also a significant number from Southeast Asia, including Vietnam. Other West Coast cities also boast large Asian American communities, including San Diego (16.5%), Seattle (14.5%), and Los Angeles (11.7%).

Large Asian American populations also exist in the East. Nearly 14 percent of New York City's residents are of Asian descent, as are close 10 percent in Boston.

What these charts demonstrate is that now, in the twenty-first century, many of our cities can be considered "prismatic cities," to use a phrase coined by sociologist Larry Bobo and his colleagues (Bobo et al. 2002).

Racial and Ethnic Diversity in Global Cities

While the United States remains one of the most heterogenous countries in the world in terms of its racial and ethnic diversity because of its long history of immigration and its legacy of slavery, many global cities have become diverse as well.

London's population, for example, according to its 2011 census, was 59.8 percent White, 18.4 percent Asian, 13.3 percent Black, 5 percent mixed race, and 3.4 percent from other ethnic groups.

Paris' population, according to its 2015 census, was 61.9 percent White, 17 percent Black, 9.9 percent Latinx, 8.7 percent mixed race, and 0.8 percent Asian.

Melbourne is now 73 percent White, 10 percent Latinx, 10 percent Black, and 3 percent Asian.

Dublin is 82.7 percent Irish, but now 2.7 percent of its population is Polish, 2.9 percent Asian, and 1.6 percent African.

Oslo is 70 percent Norwegian, but its 30 percent population of immigrants come from Pakistan, Somalia, Sweden, Iraq, Iran, Vietnam, Turkey, and Morocco.

Of course, there are other major cities that have remained virtually homogeneous. Tokyo is 98.5 percent Japanese—although it is now allowing in a small number of guest workers from Bangladesh, Iran, Afghanistan, Chile, Mexico, and Peru. Moscow's population is 91.6 percent Russian. Hong Kong is 92 percent Chinese, with small numbers of Filipinos, Indonesians, and Pakistanis.

Income Disparities in Global Cities

While there has been some degree of racial diversity in many of the great cities of the world, wealth disparity remains a major challenge. In the United States wealth disparity is greatest in metro areas near New York and several in Florida and California. In 2018, the top 1 percent of the households in Los Angeles had an average income of more than $1.8 million while the average income for the bottom 99 percent was less than $54,000. The top-to-bottom ratio was 33.5 to 1. San Jose and San Francisco were not far behind with a ratios of 34.6 to 1 and 34.2 to 1. While this seems extreme, these ratios do not compare with Miami, where the average income of the top 1 percent was more than $2.3 million compared to an average of just over $42,000 for the bottom 99 percent. This translates into a 55.4 to 1 income ratio. Even higher is the Bridgeport-Stamford-Norwalk metro area in Connecticut, which borders New York City. Here the ratio was more than 62 to 1 (DePietro 2018).

Income inequality is even greater in other cities around the world. This is especially true in metro regions in Africa and in the Americas. In 2016, according to Euromonitor International (2020), Johannesburg, South Africa and Lagos, Nigeria were the two major cities of the world with the greatest income disparity. This was followed by Nairobi, Kenya; Santo Domingo in the Dominican Republic; Cape Town, South Africa; Kuala Lumpur in Malaysia; and Rio de Janeiro in Brazil. By contrast, there are a number of cities in which income inequality is much lower. These include Mumbai, India; Karachi, Pakistan; Wuhan, China; Berlin, Germany; and Leeds, England.

The disparities in all these metro areas and cities are tied to the nature of industry in each region and policies related to housing. Not surprisingly, with its global leadership in the financial industry, law, and advertising, where executives earn high salaries, income disparity in New York is quite high. In Los Angeles, Hollywood is famous for its highly paid movie stars. In cities such as Rio de Janeiro, where a quarter of its 13 million residents are housed in more than 600 depressingly poor low-income neighborhoods called "favelas," it is not surprising that this city is ranked #7 in the world in terms of income inequality. Racial segregation in Johannesburg, Lagos, Nairobi, and Cape Town helps explain the income inequality in these sub-Saharan African countries.

Using Data Wisely

This chapter is chock full of data. Data help to answer questions, but they are also useful for posing them. If you have been following the statistics closely, numerous questions might already have occurred to you, such as: Why is the population of some metro areas rising rapidly while it seems to be collapsing in others? How can median household incomes diverge so much between cities and between metro areas? Why are some communities highly diverse while others remain relatively homogenous? These but scratch the surface of a whole array of interesting questions that are raised whenever you use an urban lens to delve into a wide range of economic, social, and political issues.

Essentially, statistics provide the first step in a much longer process of inquiry. The first task is to try to decipher clear patterns in the data. Are there real differences between central cities in the old industrial Midwest and the newer central cities in the Southwest? If so, what do these differences represent and with what are they correlated? Can we trace the economic and institutional mechanisms that are responsible for the dynamic trends we see in the data? The answers to one set of questions will almost inevitably force us to dig deeper into the data to find root causes. In the chapters that follow, we will use economics, sociology, and political science to try to answer these questions and others. Hang on and enjoy the ride!

References

Bobo, Larry, Melvin Oliver, James H. Johnson Jr., and Abel Valenzuela Jr. 2002. *Prismatic Metropolis: Inequality in Los Angeles*. New York: Russell Sage Foundation.

Brinkhoff, Thomas. 2020. *City Population*. http:www.citypopulation.de.

Bruegmann, Robert. 2005. *Sprawl: A Compact History*. Chicago: University of Chicago Press.

Brunn, Stanley D., Jessica K. Graybill, Maureen Hays-Mitchell, and Donald J. Zeigler, eds. 2016. *Cities of the World: Regional Patterns and Urban Environments*, 6th ed. Lanham, MD: Rowman & Littlefield.

City of Dallas. 2007. "International Inland Port of Dallas," *Office of Economic Development*. http://66.97.146.43/inland_port.html.

City Mayors Statistics. 2020. http://citymayors.com/statistics/urban_2020_1.html.

City Population Data Set. https://www.citypopulation.de/ (accessed August 1, 2021).

Curbed Magazine. 2020. "The 10 Best Cities in the U.S. to Move to Right Now." https://www.curbed.com/2020/2/11/21126341/best-cities-to-live-united-states.

Danziger, Sheldon, and Peter Gottschalk. 1987. "Earnings Inequality, the Spatial Concentration of Poverty, and the Underclass." *American Economic Review* 77, no. 2: 211–215.

DePietro, Andrew. 2018. "Divided By Wealth: 13 Places in American with the Worst Income Inequality." *Forbes*, August 29.

Economic Policy Institute. 2005. "Family Budget Calculator." https://www.epi.org/resources/budget/

Economic Policy Institute. 2019. *The State of Working America*. http://www.stateofworkingamerica.org/

Euromonitor International. 2020. "Income Inequality Ranking of the World's Major Cities." https://blog.euromonitor.com/income-inequality-ranking-worlds-major-cities/

Fagan, Mark, and Charles F. Longino Jr. 1993. "Migrating Retirees: A Source for Economic Development." *Economic Development Quarterly* 7, no. 1: 98-106.

Federal Reserve Bank of St. Louis. 2019. "Is the Decline in Manufacturing Economically 'Normal'?" December 30. St. Louis: Federal Reserve Bank.

Florida, Richard. 2002. *The Rise of the Creative Class*. New York: Basic Books.

Friedman, Thomas L. 2005. *The World Is Flat: A Brief History of the Twenty-First Century*. New York. Farrar, Strauss, and Giroux.

Graff, Thomas O., and Robert F. Wiseman. 1990. "Changing Pattern of Retirement Counties since 1965." *Geographical Review*, 80, no.3: 239-251.

Harkavy, Ira, and Harmon Zuckerman. 1999. "Eds and Meds: Cities Hidden Assets." Washington, DC: Brookings Institution, Center on Urban and Metropolitan Policy.

Henderson, Harold. 2000. "The Rise and Fall of the Mound People." *Chicago Reader*, June 29. http://www.chiagoreader.com/chicago/the-rise-and-fall-of-the-mound-people/.

Jacobs, Jane. 1969. *The Economy of Cities*. New York: Random House.

Kasarda, John. 1993. "Inner City Poverty and Economic Access." In *Rediscovering Urban America: Perspectives on the 1980s*, edited by J. Sommer and D. A. Hicks. Washington, DC: US Department of Housing and Economic Development, 4-1–4-60.

Kolmar, Chris. 2020. "The 10 Poorest Cities in American 2020." *Roadshacks*. http://www.roadshacks.net/poorest-cities-in-America.

Kuffel, Hunter. 2019. "The Best Places in the World to Retire." https://smartasset.com/retirement/where-to-retire.

Logan, John, ed. 2014. *Diversity and Disparities: America Enters a New Century*. Russell Sage Foundation.

Mercer Consulting. 2007. "Highlights from the 2007 Quality of Living Survey." http://www.allianceau.com/pics/advant/2007_Mercer_Quality.pdf

Munoz, Samuel E., Sissel Schroeder, David A. Fink, and John W. Williams. 2014. "A Record of Sustained Prehistoric and Historic Land Use from the Cahokia Region, Illinois, USA." *Geology* 42, no. 6: 499-502.

Myers, Garth, Francis Owusu, and Angela Gray Subulwa. 2016. "Cities in Sub-Sahara Africa." In *Cities of the World: Regional Patterns and Urban Environments*, 6th ed., edited by Stanley Brunn, Maureen Hays-Mitchell, Donald J. Ziegler, and Jessica K. Graybill. Rowman & Littlefield, 323-368.

Orlando/Orange County Convention and Visitors Bureau. 2019. "State of the Market, November 2019." https://www.occc.net/Toolbox

Palen, J. John. 2002. *The Urban World*, 6th ed. Boston: McGraw-Hill.

Partners for Livable Communities. 2006. "America's Most Livable Communities." https://scrc.gmu.edu/finding_aids/plcrecords.html

Phillpot, Sion. 2019. "The 10 Best Tech Cities in the World." *Job Search*. https://www.careeraddict.com/best-tech-cities.

Prince, Todd. 2017. "Las Vegas Tourism Spending Near $60 billion." *Las Vegas Review Journal*, March 17.

Rothstein, Richard. 2019. *The Color of Law: A Forgotten History of How Our Government Segregated America*. New York: Liveright.

Salim, Zia, Donald J. Ziegler, and Amal K. Ali. 2016. "Cities of the Greater Middle East." In *Cities of the World: Regional Patterns and Urban Environments*, 6th ed., edited by Stanley Brunn, Maureen Hays-Mitchell, Donald Ziegler, and Jessica K. Graybill. Rowman & Littlefield, 277-322.

Sassen, Saskia. 2006. *Cities in a World Economy*, 3rd ed. Thousand Oaks, CA: Pine Forge Press.

Skelley, B. Douglas. 2004. "Retiree-Attraction Policies: Challenges for Local Governance in Rural Regions." *Public Administration and Management* 9, no. 3: 212-223.

That Sister.com. 2021. "10 Best Cities in America for Black Families to Live 2021." https://www.thatsister.com/best-cities-in-america-for-black-families-to-live/.

Trust for London. 2021. https://www.trustforlondon.org.uk/data/population-over-time/.

United Nations, Department of Economic and Social Affairs, Population Division (2018). *The World's Cities in 2018—Data Booklet (ST/ESA/ SER.A/417)*.

US Bureau of the Census. 2002. *Statistical Abstract of the United States*. Washington, DC: Government Printing Office.

US Bureau of the Census. 2003. *Metropolitan and Micropolitan Statistical Areas*. Washington, DC: Government Printing Office.

US Bureau of the Census. 2004. *State-Based Metropolitan and Micropolitan Statistical Area Maps*. Washington, DC: Government Printing Office.

US Department of Housing and Urban Development. 2007. "HUD User Policy Development and Research Information Service." *State of the Cities Data Systems (SOCDS) data set*. http://socds.huduser.org.

VanDigit. 2021. "Top Ten World's Busiest Airports in 2021." https://www.vanndigit.com/top-10-worlds-busiest-airports/.

Wade, Richard C. 1959. *The Urban Frontier: The Rise of Western Cities 1790–1830*. Cambridge, MA: Harvard University Press.

Yeandle, Mark, and Mike Wardle. 2019. "The Global Financial Centres Index 26." https://www.longfinance.net/media/documents/GFCI_26_Report_2019.09.19_v1.4.pdf

Questions and Exercises

Metropolitan and Micropolitan Areas

1. Go to https://www.census.gov/geographies/reference-maps/2020/demo/state-maps.html and take a look at the map of metropolitan and micropolitan statistical areas in your state. Which three MSAs within your state are closest to where you live?

   You also might want to look at MSAs in adjoining states. Do you live in a metropolitan or a micropolitan statistical area, or in neither?

2. As mentioned in this chapter, there are 370 metropolitan statistical areas and 565 micropolitan statistical areas in the United States. For the state you have chosen,

   • how many metropolitan areas are in your state?
   • how many micropolitan areas are in your state?
   • how many of the metropolitan areas in your state are part of larger CSAs?

Exploring and Comparing Important Characteristics of Metropolitan Areas

3. Using US census data at https://www.census.gov/data, select the MSA closest to your home or another MSA of your choice (other than the 20 presented in the book), and prepare charts for the racial and ethnic composition (percentages) of this MSA and its principal city. Of the 25 metro areas for which we have described the racial and ethnic composition in the book, which comes closest to describing the racial and ethnic composition in the MSA you have selected?

4. Using US census data at https://www.census.gov/data prepare tables for the median family income in the MSA and its principal cities that you used in question 3, which central (principal) cities in the chapter are most similar to your principal city?

PART II

The Dynamics of Metropolitan Development

Metropolitan Development: From the Seventeenth Century to the Early Twentieth Century

LEARNING OBJECTIVES

- ▪ Explain the concepts of centripetal and centrifugal force and apply them to the ways in which cities have developed

- ▪ Enumerate the five key economic factors underlying the dynamics of urban growth and illustrate each of them

- ▪ Define external economies and diseconomies in production and show how they affect a firm's location decisions

- ▪ Explain why the two subcategories of transportation-cost-oriented firms will make different location decisions from each other and from firms that are not transportation-cost-oriented

- ▪ Explain the two subcategories of agglomeration economies and give an example of each

- ▪ Identify the push and pull factors that affected internal migration and immigration from abroad and explain their impact on urbanization

By the time the American colonies declared their independence from England in 1776, there were only a handful of cities along the Atlantic Coast, with the vast majority of the population living in small villages or in rural outposts. The new nation's first census, taken in 1790, revealed that only 5 percent of the population lived in cities with 2,500 people or more. During the next two centuries, the urban population expanded dramatically while the share living in nonurban areas

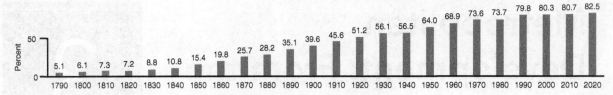

FIGURE 3.1. US Urban Population, 1790–2020 (Percentage of Total US Population).

Note: 1950–2000 reflect new MSA Urban Definition. *Sources:* US Bureau of the Census, "Selected Historical Decennial Census, Population and ј Housing Counts"; Marc J. Perry and Paul J. Mackun, "Population Change and Distribution: 1990–2000," US Bureau ofІthe Census, April 2001 (Washington, DC: Government Printing Office, 2001). The urban population percentage for 2020 is based on 2018 data extrapolated based on 2000–2010 growth rate.

declined. As noted in Chapter 1, today more than four out of five US residents live in metropolitan areas (see Figure 3.1), with the majority in the very largest metropolises that have populations of more than a million.

Closer inspection of Figure 3.1 reveals that there were particular periods when urbanization grew most rapidly in the United States. Between 1880 and 1930, during the period of massive immigration to America from both Western and Eastern Europe, the urban population increased from less than 30 percent to more than 56 percent. After World War II, there was another period of rapid urbanization as the percentage of those living in urban areas increased from under two-thirds (64%) to nearly three-quarters (74%) between 1950 and 1970. By 1990, nearly 80 percent of the US population lived in metro areas, a percentage that has been relatively stable since then.

Similarly, rapid urbanization has occurred across the globe as Table 3.1 indicates and the historical record indicates periods of particular expansion. As of 2018, Belgium was the most urbanized country of the world with 98 percent of its population living in metro areas. Uruguay, Israel, Japan, and the Netherlands all follow, each with better than 90 percent of their populations living in metropolitan areas. Note even Australia which we often think of as a vast country has 86 percent of its residents living in urbanized settings.

Several of these countries have seen enormous increases in urbanization since 1960. Back in 1960 only one Chinese resident out of six (16.2%) lived in urban areas. In less than 50 years, its urban population grew to nearly 6 out of 10 (59.2%). In Nigeria, with its enormous city of Lagos, the urban population percentage has increased over this period from 15.4 percent to fully half of the population. And in Iran, the urban population has increased from a third (33.7%) to three-fourths (74.9%) in this relatively brief period.

In this chapter, we will delve more deeply into the question of how cities originated, grew, and became the dominant places for economic activity and residential location in America. In the following chapter, we shall look at how cities themselves expanded into the suburbs and beyond.

The Geography of Growth: Centripetal and Centrifugal Forces

One important way to conceptualize growth in cities focuses on geography, using the concepts of centripetal and centrifugal force. **Centripetal force** drives businesses and households to seek locations at or near the center of a region. **Centrifugal**

TABLE 3.1. URBANIZED POPULATION OF MAJOR COUNTRIES 1960-2018

	1960	2018
Belgium	92.5%	98.0%
Uruguay	80.2%	95.3%
Israel	76.9%	92.4%
Japan	63.3%	91.6%
Netherlands	59.8%	91.5%
Brazil	46.1%	86.6%
Australia	81.5%	86.0%
United Kingdom	78.4%	83.4%
United States	69.9%	82.3%
France	61.9%	80.4%
Spain	56.6%	80.3%
Mexico	50.8%	80.2%
Iran	33.7%	74.9%
Russia	53.7%	74.4%
Italy	69.4%	70.4%
South Africa	46.6%	66.4%
China	16.2%	59.2%
Nigeria	15.4%	50.3%
India	17.9%	34.0%

Source: Macrotrends 1960-2018 www.macrotrends.net/countries

force encourages the dispersal of businesses and households to the outskirts. To illustrate, let's take a look at early American cities and their development through the nineteenth century.

Cities such as Boston, New York, Philadelphia, Charleston, and Norfolk were established by explicit decisions on the part of European colonial powers to create outposts in the New World. In an era when the most efficient form of long-distance transportation was by water, these cities were established in places with good, safe harbors. In the seventeenth and eighteenth centuries their role was to provide raw materials to the mother country, and therefore their primary purpose was commercial. The major economic focus of urban life was the transfer of agricultural products—cotton for European manufacturing inputs, and wheat, corn, rice, tobacco, and other staples for consumption in Europe, the West Indies, and other places. The activities related to this economic focus were centered around the docks, where the transfer of raw materials to ships took place. Access to the waterfront was crucial and the competition for space there was keen.

Cities of this era were compact and dense with a radius of only 2 to 3 miles at most. They were pedestrian cities, where people walked to get from place to place and parcels were transported by horse and wagon. Residences were jumbled together with workplaces. Wealthy families had grand homes along the street and poor families lived in humble shelters in the back alleys. In addition to trade with the mother country, these early American cities served as centers of government and housed craftsmen who produced items needed for commerce (e.g., shipbuilders to produce seagoing vessels and coopers who made barrels and crates) or artisans who produced luxury goods for the wealthy (e.g., silversmiths like Paul Revere, whose house can still be seen in the oldest part of Boston).

Indeed, most of the major cities of the world have been located along rivers for centuries, if not millennia. Rivers served not only as a source of fresh water for humans and animals, but as the main transportation mode before there were many roads and wheeled vehicles. Barges were used to transport goods and people. London on the Thames; Paris on the Seine; Rome on the Tiber; Amsterdam on the Amstel; Berlin on the Spree and Havel; Budapest on the Danube; and Hong Kong on the Pearl are examples of these river-based cities. Table 3.2 lists major world cities and the rivers that run through them.

TABLE 3.2. MAJOR CITIES AND THEIR RIVERS

CITY	COUNTRY	RIVER
Alexandria	Egypt	Nile
Amsterdam	Netherlands	Amstel
Baghdad	Iraq	Tigris
Bangkok	Thailand	Chao Phraya
Belgrade	Yugoslavia	Danube, Sava
Berlin	Germany	Spree, Havel
Bogotá	Colombia	Bogotá
Brussels	Belgium	Senne
Budapest	Hungary	Danube
Buenos Aires	Argentina	Rio de la Plata
Cairo	Egypt	Nile
Calcutta	India	Hugli
Damascus	Syria	Barada
Delhi	India	Yamuna
Dublin	Ireland	Liffey
Ho Chi Minh City	Vietnam	Saigon
Hong Kong	China	Pearl
Jakarta	Indonesia	Liwung
Kiev	Ukraine	Dnieper
Lisbon	Portugal	Tagus
Lima	Peru	Rimac
London	England	Thames
Madrid	Spain	Manzanares

CITY	COUNTRY	RIVER
Melbourne	Australia	Yarra
Montreal	Canada	St. Lawrence
Moscow	Russia	Moskva
Paris	France	Seine
Prague	Czech Republic	Moldau
Rome	Italy	Tiber
Saint Petersburg	Russia	Neva
Santiago	Chile	Mapocho
São Paulo	Brazil	Tietê
Seoul	South Korea	Han
Shanghai	China	Huangpu
Tokyo	Japan	Sumida
Vienna	Austria	Danube
Warsaw	Poland	Vistula
Zagreb	Croatia	Sava
Zürich	Switzerland	Limmat, Sihl

Source: www.MIStupid.com "Major Rivers of the World"

The Era of Water and Steam Power

In more recent eras, rivers would serve a new purpose. The first factories for milling grains and weaving textiles in the eighteenth and nineteenth centuries required new sources of power. Initially, the waterwheel replaced human power and horsepower. To take advantage of the waterwheel, mills had to be located at appropriate places along rivers where canals could be constructed to produce a steady flow of water. This resulted in the shift of many business locations from harbor-based cities to towns situated on rivers.

These new river-based factories soon developed their own centripetal forces. As the factories were built and began hiring, first hundreds and then thousands of individual workers and households moved to rooming houses or cottages built within walking distance of the factories themselves. In similar fashion, crafts persons moved to close-in locations where they could ply their products to new businesses and households.

The introduction of steam-powered manufacturing after 1800 made it possible to relocate business once again, this time away from the riverbank and canal. Freed from the constraints of rivers and streams, and eager to reduce the costs of obtaining labor, procuring raw materials, and distributing their products to markets, owners tended to establish new factories in the middle of cities. The owners of the new factories sought existing cities because there existed already a potential labor force in urban centers. There was no need to move families to new locations, and in an age dominated by dense housing and foot traffic, there was less need to worry about getting workers from their existing homes to factories. Centripetal forces dominated, leading to ever-increasing density in central cities.

Manufacturing was not the only type of business vying for central locations. Expanding business in shipping and in retail trade increased the competition for centralized land. Eventually, instead of buying land in the middle of the city where it was becoming more expensive, many manufacturers found it more profitable to buy land on the outskirts of the commercial district where they now had access to railroad lines via short stretches of track. Often the new manufacturing plants needed to buy residential land and convert it for manufacturing purposes. This forced residential developments to expand even farther outward.

The location dynamics for retail business during the nineteenth century were different. By 1850, urban retail shopping was changed by the emergence of the large department store. These new stores centralized the purchase of goods by marketing and selling many different types of products under the same roof (Bluestone et al. 1981). The first of these stores appeared in New York in 1846 and the concept spread quickly to other cities. Three years later, in 1849, the great British department store Harrod's was established in London and in 1852 Bon Marché opened its doors in Paris. By providing an abundance of many types of goods in one place, department stores reduced shopping time for customers and became retail centers for the entire urban area, despite the geographic expansion that was occurring. In the years to come, city downtowns became synonymous with the presence of large stores that offered a wide array of goods. In order to have sufficient customers and be profitable, these high-volume stores needed to be at the epicenter of surrounding residential neighborhoods.

The Era of Railroads, Electricity, and the Telephone

Railroads and harbors were important to these stores because they provided the means of transportation for the products that were sold. Also important were the streetcar lines that brought customers from all parts of the city to the stores. Transportation lines that converged on downtown were a powerful centripetal force for retail trade through their ability to create the high volume upon which such stores thrived. Retail stores were able to expand vertically (i.e., construct taller buildings), unlike manufacturing plants, where heavy equipment made vertical expansion problematic. Creating taller buildings allowed them to stock more goods, offer wider variety, and maintain their high-customer-volume locations. The development of new building technology, in the form of iron-girdered construction in 1889, followed on the heels of the invention of the elevator in the mid-1800s. This created new possibilities for vertical expansion in retail buildings.

In the last half of the nineteenth century the introduction of the telegraph, followed by the telephone, created new communication possibilities for offices that were not directly involved in production. Before these new technologies arrived, communication in person was necessary, either directly or indirectly through messengers. The new forms of communication allowed the transfer of information and instructions from spatially separated sites. Thus, an owner could be in the central city, where there were advantages of information transfer and proximity to a wide array of business services, and still be in communication with production supervisors at a plant in another part of the metro area. As in the case of the large department store, the creation of high-rise buildings with steel girder structures made it possible for these commercial offices to remain centralized, even while the staff devoted to such operations and the space they required increased dramatically.

The allure of downtown areas for entertainment was advanced with the introduction of electric power stations that provided a new source of lighting for evening activities. Indeed, the story of electric power is a story of urbanization (Citi I/O 2017). In 1878, Thomas Edison attended the Exposition Universelle in Paris, where arc lights powered by electric generators lined the Avenue de l'Opera and the Place de l'Opera. A year later, Edison unveiled his improvements on the incandescent light bulb and by 1882 he started the Edison Electric Light Company to distribute low voltage direct current (DC) power to homes and to city streets as well. William Stanley Jr. and George Westinghouse would introduce alternating current (AC), a safer form of electricity, in 1886. By 1888, Westinghouse had sold central generating equipment to New York City which was used to power 45,000 lights. Ultimately, AC would quickly displace DC as a power source, not only because of its safety but because it could be used more easily to power machines. By the late 1890s, electric power stations existed in many US cities and, in addition to lighting, were used to power electric motors for streetcars and factories.

The introduction of electricity made it possible for cities to become much livelier. Cities became much more nocturnal places than the countryside. For the majority of people who worked during the day, the fact that things could be lit up at night meant they had this entire additional period of leisure in their lives. Electricity also made elevators and thus taller buildings possible which would increase the density of cities and lead to the vertical appearance of major downtown areas. With electricity, subways and trolley cars could make commuting much easier and faster so that workers could more easily move from their homes to downtown offices and retail establishments.

By 1900, transportation, energy, and communication technologies had shifted the set of costs associated with location in ways that affected manufacturing, retail, and office functions quite differently. The interaction of railroad and related streetcar technology with the spatial needs of mass production had produced both centripetal and centrifugal forces. Retail and office functions had strong centripetal dynamics, while manufacturing increasingly located along the railroad lines that radiated from the city core, encouraged centrifugal activity. By the beginning of the twentieth century, the layout of the modern metro region was beginning to form: a dense downtown devoted to retail and office activity, residential neighborhoods surrounding the **central business district (CBD)**, and more and more factories on the outskirts of town.

Some Economic Concepts Underlying Urban Growth

To understand the dynamics of urban growth, it is helpful to keep in mind five key economic factors: (1) **trade** and **transportation costs**, (2) **agglomeration economies**, (3) **internal economies of scale**, (4) the size of **consumer markets**, and (5) **technological progress**. We will return to these over and over again to deepen our understanding of urban growth and the centripetal and centrifugal patterns that have accompanied the urban growth. In this chapter, we use these concepts to gain insight into why economic activity became concentrated in dense central cities in the nineteenth and early twentieth centuries. In the next chapter, we see how these factors were responsible for the great migration of businesses and households to the suburbs in the post–World War II era. The relative importance of each of these five factors varies for individual cities at any given point in time. The influence of each of these factors may change for any particular city as it evolves over time.

The implications of these five basic economic concepts are explained more fully as they are needed in this chapter. For now, a few thumbnail explanations will serve our purpose.

Trade and Transportation Costs

Why do some forms of economic activity concentrate at specific points on the map, and why do some places grow faster than others? On average, there are about 85 people per square mile across America's land mass of 3.5 million square miles, but the population density is many times higher than that in the largest metro areas and a fraction of it elsewhere. More than 26,400 people live in New York City per square mile. San Francisco and Boston have per mile densities of more than 18,750 and more than 13,840, respectively. In Wyoming, on the other hand, there are only five residents per square mile (US Bureau of the Census QuickFacts).

Even the population density of New York, San Francisco, and Boston pale by comparison with a number of cities around the world. Manila, the capital of the Philippines, is the densest city in the world. With more than 107,500 residents per square mile, the city is more than four times as dense as New York. Mumbai, India and Dhaka, Bangladesh each have a density of more than 73,900 residents per square mile. Paris has a density more than twice that of New York City (Migiro 2018).

What causes households and firms to gather at specific places rather than spreading themselves out smoothly? Sociologists note the importance of community. They suggest that belonging to a community helps satisfy a number of human needs (Moodpanda 2020).

> *Community gives hope*: In a painful, uncertain world the understanding and supportive nature of good, honest community can provide the hope necessary to press on and take chances—even in the midst of pain.

> *Community gives options*: Life without community is lonely; it is lacking in social events, intimate conversation, and deep relationships. A strong network of people grants options for a night out, a friend to call in a crisis, and someone with whom to share a funny story.

> *Community gives joy*: The long and short of it is that community is fun. The shared memories, laughter, and times spent with your closest circle of friends provide memories that truly last for a lifetime.

Economists, drawing on their own tools, view community as a context for meeting the basic needs of individual households. A relatively self-sufficient household may, with great effort, provide for all its needs: building its own shelter, growing its own food, weaving its own cloth, birthing its own babies, and burying its own dead. Such a household living in an isolated area is likely to have a low standard of living, at least in terms of material goods and services. By focusing on the production of one good and exchanging it for goods and services produced by others, this household and its trading partners can enjoy the benefits of **specialization** and **division of labor**. This is the economic and social basis for trade and explains the role of the city as a marketplace—a central location where people come together to exchange goods and services.

Bringing goods to market requires transporting them from one place to another. In a time when travel was difficult, dangerous, and expensive, transportation costs played an important role in determining which goods would be traded and where trading cities would be located. High transportation costs help explain why people live closer to each other than they might if travel were instantaneous and essentially free. Even if goods can be transported quickly and inexpensively between regions of the country and even globally, many services need to be close to the consumer because otherwise the transportation costs add up rapidly. Consider the cost of getting a professional haircut, in terms of travel time alone, if you live on a million-acre sheep station in the middle of Australia, 300 miles from the nearest town.

Agglomeration Economies and Density

As the original trading cities grew, they became large enough to support a variety of commercial specialists. A greater division of labor and increased specialization made it possible for individual firms to operate at lower cost in these locations. For example, a producer of salted cod in colonial New England who wanted to ship his product to Europe would find that he could operate more efficiently if he located near the barrel makers and trading companies he needed, virtually all of whom had set up shop in port cities. The existence of these city-based specialists meant that new firms could operate more efficiently in these places than at other points on the map, and port cities therefore increased in size. Greater density brought greater efficiency, which encouraged urban development, and greater efficiency spawned even greater density. There is an interaction between density and urban diversity, the two characteristics emphasized by Jane Jacobs (1961; 1969). As cities grew, they attracted newcomers with diverse sets of skills and different uses of land.

Cost-saving factors that emanate from *outside* the individual firm such as the barrel makers' contribution to the success of the salted cod producer and vice versa are known generally as **external economies** of production. In urban settings, they are often called agglomeration economies. Simply put, having your lawyer and your accountant nearby helps lower your operating costs and therefore boosts profits, or at least permits you to compete successfully against other firms that are trying to lower their costs. Technically speaking, agglomeration economies permit a firm to lower its **short-run average cost curve**—the cost per unit of output, as shown in Figure 3.2. The short run is defined in economics as a period brief enough that the firm does not have the opportunity to make new investments in its stock of **capital**, the buildings and equipment it uses to produce its output.

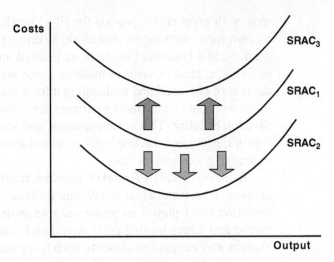

FIGURE 3.2. Effect of External Economies and External Diseconomies on Short-Run Average Costs

Conversely, **external diseconomies** are factors outside the firm that *raise* a firm's short-run average cost curve. Imagine what would happen to a firm's average costs if it relied on ferry service to transport its goods to market and the ferry company went out of business. Urban density can reach a point where congestion is so great that the cost of commuting and transporting goods becomes a real disadvantage for firms in the middle of the city. In this case, the benefits from agglomeration might be more than offset by the external diseconomies. Agglomeration economies tend to favor production in urban centers; external diseconomies tend to favor more dispersed production away from central cities.

In this figure, each short-run-average-cost curve is U-shaped, indicating that (1) at low levels of output average costs are high (due to fixed costs), but fall as the amount of output increases, and (2) as a firm continues to increase output, it becomes harder to find some inputs (perhaps labor). Therefore, average costs rise as less productive or more expensive inputs have to be used. **External economies** lower the firm's short-run average cost curve from $SRAC_1$ to $SRAC_2$. **External diseconomies** raise the firm's short-run average cost curve from $SRAC_1$ to $SRAC_3$.

Internal Economies of Scale

Just as external economies reduce a firm's short-run average cost curve, the existence of **scale economies** internal to a firm allow it to produce more efficiently—at lower unit cost—as it moves to larger facilities. Economists refer to this as occurring in the long run, when the firm can increase its plants and equipment. Suppose an industry has 100 plants, each producing 1,000 units of a good at a cost of $50 per unit. If **economies of scale** exist, then it would be cheaper (perhaps $40 per unit) to produce these 1 million units in two large plants, and cheapest of all (perhaps $30 per unit) if one single large factory produces all 1 million units.

Now suppose that 1 million units per factory is the most efficient scale of production possible. If the market demand for this good is 3 million units per year, there would then be room in this industry for only three very large firms. Smaller firms would disappear from the industry because their scale of operations would not permit them the luxury of the lower costs of the big firms. The big firms could easily price the smaller ones out of the market by charging a price higher than their own lowest cost per unit, but below that of the smaller firm and thereby continue to make a profit. The combination of agglomeration economies plus internal economies of scale are part of the reason why a few cities in Massachusetts, including Lawrence, Lowell, and New Bedford, grew to be the home of the US textile industry in the nineteenth century. Instead of being scattered over the entire national landscape, these industries with their very large producers were concentrated in a small number of cities, keeping their average unit costs near the bottom of their long-run average cost curve.

In the twentieth century, the same benefits of *agglomeration*, *external economies*, and *economies of scale* would help explain why Detroit became the center for the early auto industry, Pittsburgh for steel, and Akron, Ohio for tires.

As illustrated in Figure 3.3, the **long run average cost curve** (LRAC) curve indicates (1) the range of output over which moving to larger plant capacity would reduce average costs (economies of scale), (2) the range over which there are no advantages or disadvantages associated with size (constant returns to scale), and (3) the range over which larger plants are less efficient (diseconomies of scale). Each Short Run Average Cost (SRAC) curve provides information about the cost of production at a given level of plant capacity. The LRAC is derived from the most efficient points on the short run average cost curves, thereby showing the most efficient production with different amounts of plant and equipment. The LRAC curve declines initially, flattens out for a time, and often begins to rise only at very high levels of output. In the declining region of the curve, there are increasing returns to scale (scale economies), which means that moving to a larger plant size allows output to be produced at lower average cost. The flat section of the curve indicates the range of output where plants of different sizes can produce equally efficiently—in

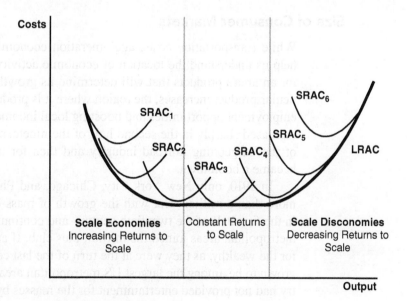

FIGURE 3.3. A Typical Long-Run Average Cost Curve

other words, a range of constant returns to scale where there are no advantages or disadvantages associated with size. The rising section indicates the range of output in which there are decreasing returns to scale (**diseconomies of scale**), where problems of coordination and control might make very large plants *less* efficient.

We can apply the same idea of economies of scale to the size and structure of metropolitan areas. Small places do not have a large enough population to support a wide variety of goods and services in the same way that a small factory can produce only a limited number of products. According to **central place theory**, there is a hierarchy of places within any given region.

The *central city* of a metropolitan area with its dense population is where large office buildings, department stores, libraries, museums, and professional sports stadiums will usually be located because all of these depend on large numbers of employees or consumers who can reach the central business district from many surrounding neighborhoods.

In the *suburbs*, one will find lower population density and, beginning in the early twentieth century, manufacturing plants. Farther out, one will find smaller towns and villages with a general store serving farm communities and mining companies.

For a time, there were efforts to define the optimum size for a city. Presumably, such an optimal-sized city would have a population large enough to benefit from scale economies in the provision of goods and services without encountering the diseconomies of scale—the congestion, pollution, and higher per capita costs for many big city public services such as education and public safety. The efforts came to naught because by the time a city reached the critical mass necessary to achieve economies of scale for some services, it was already encountering diseconomies of scale for others. The ultimate conclusion was that if a nation offered a wide variety of places, each of a different scale, every household could decide for itself the trade-offs of living in larger areas versus smaller ones—each optimal for the residents who choose it.

Size of Consumer Markets

While transportation costs, agglomeration economies, and scale economies can help us understand the location of economic activity, it is the strength of demand for an area's products that will determine its growth. When the market for a particular product increases, the region where it is produced usually benefits, creating employment opportunities and boosting local incomes. When the demand for steel increased sharply in the second half of the nineteenth century to fulfill the needs of the burgeoning railroad industry and then for use in skyscrapers, Pittsburgh became a boomtown.

In 1910, only New York City, Chicago, and Philadelphia had populations of more than a million. But with the growth of mass-consumer markets, beginning in the first half of the twentieth century and continuing to the present, many more metropolitan areas joined the million-plus club. If automobiles had remained toys for the wealthy, as they were at the turn of the last century, Detroit would not have grown to be among the largest US metropolitan areas. If the motion picture industry had not provided entertainment for the masses by the 1930s, Hollywood might still be just a sleepy little town with lots of sun.

Technological Progress

Finally, we cannot ignore the role that technology plays in urban development. Before the introduction of the waterwheel as a means to power such equipment as textile looms, bringing together a huge number of machines in one location was neither needed nor beneficial. Weavers and craftsmen could produce goods in their own homes and only the cost of transportation suggested the need for some amount of density. But once power looms were invented, with flowing water as their source of energy, it made economic sense to bring hundreds if not thousands of looms together in one "manufactory," where the power could be distributed to each machine from a central source through an elaborate network of belts and shafts. Needed now were hundreds and sometimes thousands of workers who lived close enough to the mills to walk to work. The result was the rapid expansion of cities that had rivers running through them. As we have noted earlier, the introduction of the steam engine as the dominant source of power in late-nineteenth-century factories encouraged density, but manufacturing cities no longer needed to be located near flowing water. Bringing workers together in a factory where they could be disciplined by managers if they slowed their pace was no doubt a benefit to the profitability of firms that came along with the establishment of large factories (Edwards 1980).

Thus, the fate of individual cities and towns, central cities, and suburbs rests on the ever-changing sands of transportation costs, agglomeration economies and diseconomies, changes in scale economies, the fickleness of consumer response to old and new products, and the evolution of always newer and more productive technologies.

In order to draw out some of the more complex implications for the creation and growth of urban areas, a closer look at these location factors is needed.

Transportation Costs Between Nineteenth-Century Cities

When steam power replaced waterpower in factories, and railroads replaced ships as the principal way to transport goods, firms were no longer tethered to port cities and mill towns, yet they still faced constraints. In the industrial age, an economy based on manufacturing takes raw materials and turns them into finished goods to be sold to consumers. The transportation of raw materials to the factory or finished goods to their final consumer markets often involves significant cost. The desire to minimize these costs places its own set of limitations on a firm's location decision.

Consider the following development in the economic history of the United States. For the first half of the 1900s, the tire manufacturing center in the United States was Akron, Ohio, as we noted earlier. Why Akron, instead of somewhere else? Almost all the crude rubber used in the manufacture of tires came from East Asia (the regions that have now become Malaysia, Indonesia, and Sri Lanka). Why not San Francisco, or one of the other West Coast port cities geographically closest to East Asia? Until the 1870s, practically all the US experience with working with rubber was in New England. Why not in Massachusetts or Connecticut, which together accounted for half of the rubber-using firms in 1870? Why not in Philadelphia, where Charles Goodyear discovered the important process of vulcanization of rubber in 1839, or in New York State, where B. F. Goodrich opened his first business? Part of the answer lies in the roles of transportation procurement and distribution costs. Keep Akron's tire industry in mind as we examine the impact of transportation costs on industry location.

In the nineteenth century and much of the twentieth, before the introduction of super-cargo container ships and large jet cargo aircraft, transportation costs were a much larger share of the total costs of delivering raw materials to manufacturers and final goods to customers. Moreover, before the introduction of high-speed computerized communication, it was often useful for firms to be in a central location to limit the cost of coordinating activities. As such, the location of manufacturing was heavily influenced by large businesses trying to reduce their transportation costs and maintain rapid and direct communication. Hence, which cities would expand rapidly, and which would remain as smaller towns, had much to do with the role of transportation costs and limits to communication in determining where manufacturing would take place.

Think of the wide variety of economic activities as arrayed along a spectrum, from those whose location choices are most constrained to those whose choices are least constrained. At one extreme are the extractive industries, along with others that are based on some natural feature. If you want to operate a coal mine, you have to go where there are deposits of coal; if you want to operate a lumber mill, it is useful to locate near forests. At the other extreme, there is the occasional poet or philosopher, who can work equally well on the highest mountain, in the deepest valley, or along the most densely populated city street. For all firms except those that mimic our poet-philosopher, location matters, either as an absolute constraint or, more commonly, as a major cost consideration.

In general, the profits of an enterprise represent the difference between revenue generated from sales and the costs incurred in production. Consider a simple categorization of types of costs:

1. **Site costs:** the costs of the land and physical plant

2. **Operating costs:** the costs of materials, labor, energy, and other inputs used in the operation of the firm

3. **Transportation costs:** the costs of moving raw materials to the firm and finished products to the market

Firms for which transportation costs are the primary determinant of location are called **transportation-cost-oriented firms**. The cost of moving inputs from their source or sources to the place where they will be used to manufacture goods is called **procurement cost**. The cost of moving the final product to the places where it will be sold is called **distribution cost**. For a manufacturing firm, total transportation costs equal the sum of procurement costs plus distribution costs. The goal of the firm is to minimize total transportation cost by locating where the sum of procurement costs and distribution costs is lower than anywhere else.

Firms that produce goods or services entailing high transportation costs must locate at a site that minimizes the sum of these costs. Otherwise, they will be at a competitive disadvantage relative to firms that make cost-effective location decisions. In some cases, the location that minimizes transportation costs will be close to the source of its raw materials and in other cases, closer to its consumers.

Transportation costs are determined for the most part by the nature of the material being transported and the type of transportation being used. Suppose for the moment that the same means of transportation—say, railroads—is used for both procurement and distribution. Then the cost of transportation depends upon the weight of the material (heavier items require more fuel for the engine), the bulk of the material (more railroad cars are needed if the shipment takes up more space), and the fragility of the items (more packing material is needed for items that carry a risk of breaking). The location that minimizes transportation costs would then depend upon whether the raw materials are heavier, bulkier, or more fragile than the finished product.

If the production process that transforms the raw material into a finished product involves the loss of weight, a loss of bulk, or a reduction in fragility, the finished product will be cheaper to transport. For example, sawmills are located close to forests because it is less expensive to transport finished two-by-fours or plywood sheets than to transport the logs and cut them up at their final destination near the local Home Depot or Lowe's. Similarly, fruit and vegetable canneries (and wineries) are located near the fields where the crops are grown, because fresh fruit and vegetables are more likely to be damaged or spoil en route than canned vegetables or bottles of wine. These are examples of **materials-oriented firms** in which transportation costs are minimized by locating the processing plant close to the source of raw materials.

If, on the other hand, the finished product is heavier, bulkier, or more fragile than the raw materials, transportation costs will be minimized by shipping the raw materials close to the final consumer markets before processing them. These are called **market-oriented** firms. For example, large national firms in the baking, brewing, or bottling industries use regional processing plants because it is cheaper to ship the ingredients than the final product. The bread is bulkier and more perishable than the flour and yeast. If a decent water supply is available locally, it is cheaper to ship the hops or syrup than the beer or soda. These market-oriented industries minimize their transportation costs by operating regional processing facilities. Those who prefer Heineken to Budweiser or Perrier to Poland Spring are paying a premium partly because they are paying to transport from Europe a product that is mostly water.

Similarly, the geographic expansion of consumer markets has implications for firm location because of the distribution costs to potential buyers who are relatively far away. Instead of incurring high distribution costs, it is sometimes more cost efficient for firms to establish branch plants—production centers in various cities—to lower distribution costs. Branch plants and their retail counterpart—chain stores—proliferated beyond the cities where firms were founded, both responding and contributing to the growth of more cities. Still, such businesses capitalized on economies of scale in certain enterprise functions—accounting, design, and so forth—by locating their corporate headquarters in a single city.

To account for differences in the type of transportation used, economists refer to the **monetary weight** of transportation, which is calculated by multiplying the monetary cost of transporting a given number of units of a particular product and the weight of the product. The term "monetary weight" may sound strange at first, but it actually follows a long tradition of mathematical nomenclature. For example, in physics, one of the measurement units of energy is the foot-pound, obtained by multiplying the distance that a force moves an object by the pounds of force applied. In economics, we use the concept of person-hours, obtained by multiplying the number of workers by the hours that they worked.

The difference in the monetary weights of procurement and distribution provides an important insight for the answer to our question about Akron. Rubber was transported to manufacturing sites in bales, packed as tightly as possible. By contrast, the tires that were produced were bulkier, since the shape of tires includes space where there is just air. Because the number of conveyances (boxcars, trucks) needed to transport bulky items is greater than the number needed to transport more closely packed items, the costs of transportation for the bulkier tires was greater than the cost of the inputs. The monetary weight of the tires was greater than the monetary weight of the inputs. Therefore, it made more sense for tire manufacturers to locate near the final market for the tires: the automobile industry based in Michigan.

In some instances, as goods are transformed from raw material to finished product, their journey is partly by water and partly by land. Processing plants often arise at these junctures. Historically, that is how the Chicago stockyards originated. Live animals were transported across the land (first on hoof, later via cattle car), slaughtered and partially disassembled in Chicago, and then sent to other cities and towns—originally by ship across the Great Lakes and down rivers, and after the mid-1800s by specially made railroad cars refrigerated with ice—where the final cutting and trimming was done in local butcher shops (Cronon 1991; Miller 1996). Similarly, wheat is refined into flour in Minneapolis (nicknamed the Flour City) and shipped all over the country by rail and truck.

Weber's Graphical Model of Transportation Costs

The standard figures used in urban economic theory to visualize the impact of transportation costs on the location decisions of firms were first developed by Wilhelm Launhardt (1885) and later refined by Alfred Weber (1909). These figures, in the form of graphs, are central to the so-called Weber model.

Weber's approach assumes that transportation costs play the fundamental role in location decisions, and that other cost factors (including the cost of labor) play a secondary role. This made sense a century ago, when transportation costs were huge and most of the modern transportation network we now take for granted did not exist at all. Weber imagined a featureless geography, with a single source of raw materials, a geographically separate single market, and a road connecting the two. Suppose that, except for the raw materials, all other inputs—such as labor and capital—were available at identical costs at every point between the resource site and the market. Where would a profit-seeking firm locate—at the site where all the raw materials needed to make its products come from, at the market where its products will be sold, or somewhere in between? This is obviously important for understanding where cities will be located and how big they will become.

In the basic Weber graph there is one resource site and one market, as shown in Figure 3.4. The horizontal axis represents the distance between these two sites, and thus each point along the axis is a potential location for the firm. Procurement

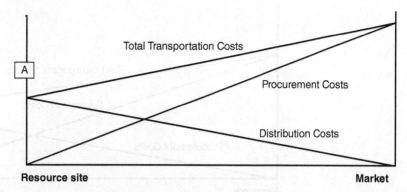

FIGURE 3.4. Transportation Costs for a Resource-Oriented Firm (also called a materials-oriented firm)

costs are represented by the upward sloping line extending from the origin at the resource site. Since it costs more to move materials longer distances, procurement costs increase as we consider potential sites moving from left to right, from the resource site toward the market. Similarly, distribution costs are represented by a line extending from the origin at the market leftward toward the resource site, indicating that the costs of moving final goods from the firm to the market increases as we move away from the market toward the resource site. The rate of increase in costs (and thus the actual costs at any point along the horizontal axis where the firm might choose to locate) depends upon (1) the characteristics of the raw materials (for procurement costs) or final goods (for distribution costs), and (2) the type of transportation used.

A firm considering where to ideally locate will take into account total transportation costs (procurement plus distribution) at each potential firm location, and, if transportation costs are the deciding factor for location, will locate at a point that minimizes total transportation costs. As shown in this graph, if the increase in procurement costs from the resource site origin is greater than the increase in distribution costs from the market origin, the lowest total transportation cost (indicated by A) will be at the resource site, and consequently the firm will try to locate near its source of raw materials.

In Figure 3.4, the procurement costs for raw materials per mile are greater than the distribution costs to consumers per mile. Accordingly, as is indicated by the "Total Transportation Costs" line—representing the vertical sum of transportation procurement and transportation distribution costs—the firm will minimize its transportation costs if it locates at the resource site, point A. Point A will be a location where economic activity takes place and at least a small urban area will begin to develop.

In Figure 3.5, the procurement costs per mile are less than the distribution costs per mile. This firm will minimize its total transportation costs if it locates at the market site, point B. Point B, like point A, is where urban activity will take place and density will presumably increase.

Figures 3.4 and 3.5 are predicated on the idea that there is one site where raw materials are obtained. But what if two or more raw materials are needed, and each comes from a different location? The problem once again, according to the Weber

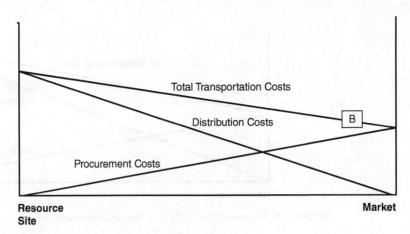

FIGURE 3.5. Transportation Costs for a Market-Oriented Firm

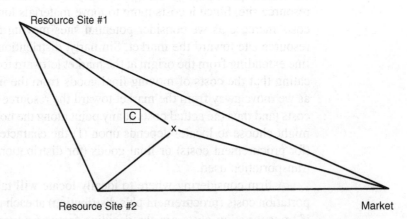

FIGURE 3.6. The Weber Location Polygon for Two Resource Sites and a Single Market

formulation, focuses on the minimization of total transportation costs under the assumption that other costs are the same, regardless of location.

In the case of *two* resource sites and *one* market site, the optimal location for the firm—which minimizes transportation costs and maximizes profits—may be at one of the sources of raw materials; at the location of the distribution market (as in the simple models depicted in the previous two figures), or somewhere within the area bordered by the triangle connecting each of these points. This is shown in Figure 3.6. Exactly where transportation costs are minimized depends upon the same considerations—the weight of the shipment, the cost of transporting that weight given the objects being transported, and the distance transported. Cost minimization occurs at point C somewhere between raw material locations and the final market. Point C minimizes the sum of the costs of transporting the two resources to a central manufacturing plant and transporting the final product to the consumer market. It is precisely at such points that new production centers can arise with all of the related services that firms and workers need. Housing will be constructed along with retail outlets, and thus a small urban area comes into existence. If the site proves a cost-minimizing location for an important industry such as autos or steel, the emerging urban area can become a burgeoning, wealthy city and ultimately a large metro area.

While transportation costs today are a fraction of what they were in the nineteenth and early twentieth century, the Weber model certainly provides some guidance as to where the urban centers of this bygone era were located in the United States and much of the world. Hence ocean ports, sites on rivers, and other locations that reduced transportation costs became the centers for burgeoning cities.

Other Important Ideas from Weber and Isard

Let us turn back to the example of Akron and the tire industry. We have explained why the tire industry emerged in the Midwest, near Detroit, rather than in other regions of the country. But why was it not located *in* Detroit? Part of the answer is historical. In 1870, when B. F. Goodrich opened his rubber company in Akron, his chief vision for the company was to produce fire hoses and industrial belts for the expanding cities and manufacturing companies in the Midwest, not bicycle or automobile tires (bicycles did not become popular until the 1880s, and the auto industry had not yet been born). But Goodrich and his firm were interested in taking advantage of new opportunities involving rubber, so in 1888, in response to the sudden popularity of bicycles, the Goodrich firm began to produce bicycle tires. From there it was an easy step in 1896 to becoming a pioneer in the manufacture of automobile tires (Blackford and Kerr 1996). The location of the BFGoodrich Company as a tire manufacturer was therefore tied to the original location chosen for producing hoses and belts.

This illustrates a more general point. As Jane Jacobs emphasizes in her classic book *The Economy of Cities* (1969), many new products emerge from businesses that were originally making something else, either because of insights gained during manufacture or—as was the case for BFGoodrich—because the manufacturing process of new products is similar to that of the old.

This can be partially explained by what social scientists call **path dependency**—when, in any period of time, events and characteristics are dependent upon the historical path of the past. But another part of the answer takes us to one more important insight of Weber's. While transportation-cost-oriented firms pay primary attention to the patterns of transportation costs, they cannot be totally oblivious to other costs. Weber realized that if costs other than transportation dropped sharply in areas around the market or resource site, these differences could change the cost-minimizing location for the firm. Discussing a site that might be different from the transportation-cost-minimizing site, Weber stated that even for a transportation-cost-oriented firm, it makes sense to locate at a site of lower labor costs, "if the savings in the cost of labor which this new place makes possible are larger than the additional costs of transportation which it involves" (Weber 1909, p. 103).

Weber's insight was expanded upon by Walter Isard, who considered the theoretical case of a site where labor costs are $5 per unit of output cheaper than at the transportation-cost-minimizing site, while the increase in transportation costs is only $4 per unit of output. Noting the offsetting costs of labor and transportation, Isard demonstrates that the site of cheaper labor "offers a net gain of $1 per ton relative to the optimal transport point . . . In similar manner we can examine

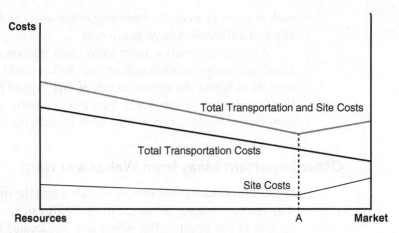

FIGURE 3.7. The Weber/Isard Graph with Offsetting Costs

the pull of cheap power locations, cheap tax locations and other locations having specific advantages" (Isard 1975, p. 98). The general idea of this concept can be illustrated through the graph in Figure 3.7.

If only transportation costs were important, production would take place near the center of the market—the far right of the figure. However, because of other site costs, the location that minimizes transportation costs + site costs is at point A.

In fact, this insight is part of the story of Akron. When Goodrich was exploring where to build his firm in 1870, some businesspeople in Akron wanted Goodrich to open the firm there and offered to provide some of his financing, but only if he built his rubber company in Akron. Similarly, in 1898, when Frank Sieberling started Goodyear Tire and Rubber, specifically to target the growing bicycle and auto tire business, his location of the firm in his hometown of Akron was related to the fact that he had been able to obtain an abandoned factory at a very cheap price, say at point A, and that he was able to draw upon local investors for the financing to start the firm (Allen 1949; O'Reilly 1983).

One other factor is relevant to the question of how Akron became the location for the tire industry. In the late 1890s, it was not at all clear that Detroit would be the center of the automobile industry. There was still uncertainty about where automobile manufacturing would become successful, and several other cities in the Midwest, including Cleveland, were producing cars with hopes of participating in the new automobile industry (Blackford and Kerr 1996). So uncertainty at a key point in the development of the auto industry sheds a bit more light on the decisions that eventually led to Akron's ultimate role.

Whether automobile manufacturing occurred in Detroit, Indianapolis, or Cleveland, the amount saved in site costs originally compensated for whatever difference in costs were incurred by moving the finished tires to those other cities. Over time, differences in costs that emerged from agglomeration economies (as firms related to tire production moved to Akron), and perhaps the importance of carving out its own local labor market rather than competing in the same local labor market as the Detroit auto manufacturers, gave reason for the tire industry to stay in Akron.

Weber's insight into the effect of the relationships between transportation cost, site costs, and operating costs for the location of firms provides a key to understanding the location of firms in the nineteenth and early twentieth centuries and, therefore, the development of cities. As we shall see in Chapter 4, despite the technological marvels of the late twentieth and early twenty-first centuries, Weber's insights are still of some relevance.

Transportation Costs Within Nineteenth-Century Cities

At the dawn of the twentieth century, cities still relied on the railroad to transport people and goods from one place to another and manufacturing was still the core of economic activity. Although streetcars allowed some wealthier households to move away from the hustle and bustle of the downtown, most business activity was still confined to the core, as were the majority of households. Nationwide, the proportion of the metropolitan population living in central cities reached its peak of 66 percent in 1920. This high degree of centralization meant that as urban populations grew, the bulk of that growth was still contained inside city limits. Although city populations would continue to grow, suburbs would grow more quickly after 1920.

In the late nineteenth century, a factory owner in New York who wanted to ship merchandise to Chicago would find that the most cumbersome part of the task was getting the merchandise from the factory to the railroad depot in New York and, at the other end, getting it from the railroad depot in Chicago to its final destination. As Moses and Williamson (1967) point out in their explanation for why late-nineteenth-century cities were so highly centralized, it was cheaper per mile to move goods *between* cities via the railroad than *within* cities via horse and wagon. For this reason, factories and warehouses were near the centrally located railroad depots. Although the streetcar lines radiating away from the downtowns did allow some wealthier households to escape from the center, they reinforced the center as the only place where a large labor force could be collected, since that was the only spot where the lines converged. This helps account for the growing density of the central business district in American cities in the nineteenth and early twentieth centuries.

Other technological developments of the era contributed to the highly centralized development of the city. Because access to the downtown was so valuable, the price of centrally located land was very high. One way of counteracting the high price of land is to use it more intensively. As noted earlier, the advent of the elevator, in the middle of the nineteenth century, and steel beam construction in the 1880s, meant that buildings could rise more than four or five stories, the limit for non–steel reinforced masonry construction. Though these early skyscrapers are dwarfed by the heights of today's megastructures, they nevertheless multiplied the square footage of floor space that could be obtained from a plot of land by fourfold or more, making downtown commercial and production locations more affordable than they otherwise would have been. Thus, technology in the form of new energy sources, new transportation modes, and new construction materials contributed mightily to the location, size, and density of the nineteenth- and early-twentieth-century city.

Agglomeration Economies and the Growth of Cities

A business looking for the very lowest wage labor or the very cheapest land will not find either of them in large cities. Yet cities continued to grow throughout the nineteenth century, along with the growth of the railroads and factories. In the period from 1830 to 1860, the total US population more than doubled, from 13 million to 31 million, but New York's population quadrupled from just over 200,000 to more than 800,000. By 1910, 50 US cities had populations of 100,000 or more. Large as this must seem for a city before the US Civil War, New York was still substantially smaller than European cities at the time. By 1861, Paris had a population of nearly 1.7 million with a density of nearly 42,000 per square mile (Demographia 2003). Even much larger was London, which had nearly 3.2 million residents in 1860 (Emsley et al. 2020).

If these and other cities did not offer the cheapest land or the cheapest labor, they did offer to businesses the cost advantages that come from locating near other firms. As we learned earlier in this chapter, these advantages are called external economies or agglomeration economies because they exist outside any one individual firm, but allow all of the firms to operate more efficiently (i.e., at lower cost). Urban economists call these **localization economies**, if the firms benefiting from locating near each other are all in the same industry and produce the same product or service.

Locating near your competitor may not sound all that appealing, but being able to draw from a common pool of specialized suppliers, skilled workers, or eager consumers reduces costs, leading in a competitive market to lower prices for consumers. For firms on the cutting edge of new technologies, **knowledge spillovers** play an important role in disseminating new advances. In a city dense with skilled workers and many firms, these can be quickly communicated through formal channels of industry symposia, but perhaps even more importantly, through informal channels as engineers and other workers from various firms get to know each other. These turn out to be especially significant localization economies. Sociologists often refer to such relationships in terms of social network theory. A **social network** is a social structure made of "nodes" (generally, individuals or organizations) that are linked together by one or more specific types of relations, including shared expertise and skill. Social networks play a critical role in determining the way problems are solved and organizations are run. In an age well before the internet, social networks required physical proximity.

As places where external economies and social networks are plentiful, big cities provide the advantage of a location where you can find whatever you need to run your business effectively and at lowest cost. Imagine a new firm, just starting out, with a newly invented product to sell. Often such a firm will not be able to afford to construct its own building at the outset. It will not be able to buy machinery designed specifically for its purpose. It will not have its own in-house fleet of delivery trucks, nor will it have its own patent lawyer to protect it if its nearest competitor sues. It might need to hire a printing company to print its business stationery and an accounting company to help keep the books. All these business services exist outside of the firm, but it usually will be cheaper for the firm to do business if they are available within the local environment. Our new firm might need to rent loft space. It might need skilled machinists to adapt existing machinery to suit its purpose. A ready supply of such workers who are available in the local community will normally benefit the firm in the form of lower production costs. In this case of locally available resources, the agglomeration economies are called **urbanization economies**.

Firms that need face-to-face communications will be attracted to large cities to take advantage of such economies of scale. These are the head offices of large corporations and portions of the publishing, advertising, and fashion industries, as well as specialized legal and banking services. Raymond Vernon (1972) found that it was just such factors that allowed the New York City metropolitan area to sustain a healthy rate of economic growth, even though the city had among the highest rents and highest costs of living in the nation. If it were not for agglomeration economies, there would be fewer large cities, urban areas in general would be much smaller, and more of the population would live outside of metropolitan areas altogether.

Technological Progress and Innovation

We discuss technological progress last—but it certainly is not least—because over time, it has been one of the most powerful dynamics in urban growth, affecting the geography of growth and the dynamics of trade and transportation, agglomeration economies, internal economies of scale, and the size of consumer markets. To take a deeper look at technological progress, first think back to the centripetal and centrifugal forces discussed near the beginning of this chapter. As our history of centripetal and centrifugal forces illustrates, a firm may be located in a particular part of a city or region because its energy requirements require that it be near necessary resources—such as a port facility, which may be available only at certain sites such as the fall line of a river—or because the firm's production process may require buildings of certain dimensions that cannot be found elsewhere.

What is so important about technological change is that it can remove or relax constraints—creating new location possibilities for businesses and for households, Technological change can create new incentives that allow firms to find new ways to maximize profits and new ways for households to pursue their own goals. Since the seventeenth and eighteenth centuries, US cities have undergone several waves of technological innovation which have changed (1) the constraints and incentives that affect business and residential location; (2) the subsequent centripetal or centrifugal forces of urban areas; and (3) the cost of transportation, the value of agglomeration economies and economies of scale, and the dynamics of consumer markets.

Douglas Rae (2003), an urban political scientist, examines both the general process of technological change and the impact of such innovation on American cities. Building upon the idea of "creative destruction"—the replacement of older industries with newer ones—originally advanced by the economist Joseph Schumpeter, Rae states that within all cities, competition and the desire to increase profit create pressure on firms to discover new ways to do things, and thus to constantly seek out new techniques that lower costs or improve the quality and consequently the demand for their goods or services.

As Rae describes it, in different historical periods, this unrelenting "creative edge of capitalism" has forced company managers to fasten upon particular aspects of their production processes in a constant search for ways to take advantage of new production techniques, transportation modes, or communication media. When this process is successful a series of innovations ensue, removing old constraints and creating new possibilities. In response to these technological innovations, firms and households make adjustments about the location and content of their economic activities, and new location patterns of economic activity are formed. As in the case of the steam engine that allowed production to move away from riverbanks, new technologies make some areas hotbeds of economic activity while making others obsolete. According to Rae, the timing and characteristics of such changes vary from one urban area to another, since innovation and the subsequent adoption of new technology depend upon each city's natural resources, the financial capital available, and the acumen of the city's economic and political decision-makers.

Technological progress therefore changes the cost, speed, reach, and methods of transportation and consequently the fortunes of individual cities. By changing the raw materials that firms use in production, technological change affects the types of firms that benefit from particular localization economies. Advances in technology such as transportation that allowed producers to move goods to a greater numbers of buyers, and communications technology that allowed producers to communicate with more potential buyers, have contributed to the increased size of consumer markets.

As the Nobel prize-winning economist Robert Solow demonstrated in his work on economic growth, increases in capital and labor both contribute to increases in output. But over time, only with the introduction of new technologies that boost productivity can an economy continue to grow rapidly (Solow 1956). In the nineteenth century and even more so in the decades to follow, new inventions that would increase the efficiency of production would be the driving force for increased living standards throughout the world.

Demographic Growth and Change in Urban Areas

A huge labor force was needed to work in the nineteenth- and early-twentieth-century factories, to drive the streetcars and lorries, and to service the new industries spawned by American technological prowess. After all, to staff an ever-greater number of larger and larger firms located within the central city, it goes without saying that you need a lot of people. Where did they come from?

In order to understand the emergence of the rapidly increasing urban labor force, we require not only an insight into market forces but into a set of institutional factors that led to huge demographic shifts. Although some of the growth in the urban population was due to natural increase among city-dwellers, there were two major flows that brought newcomers to the city: (1) the shift of US households from rural to urban areas, and (2) the arrival of waves of immigrants from abroad.

London's emergence as the largest city in the world in 1860 was due in part to immigration from Ireland in the wake of the Great Potato Famine (1846–1849) and the arrival of refugees from France, Italy, Germany, and Spain who were forced to flee from political revolutions in those countries in 1830 and 1848. There were even small numbers of Chinese, Indian, and African sailors who made port in London and decided to remain there.

A combination of both **push factors** and **pull factors** has been responsible for bringing millions upon millions of immigrants to America's shores as well as to her cities. Like centrifugal and centripetal forces—the one pushing outward as a mass spins and the other pulling inward—these two great immigration factors explain much of the growth of urban America. Push factors refer to all the reasons people feel they must leave one place to go to another. Pull factors are all those that attract people to a particular region or city. The same factors underlie migration within the country from rural areas to central cities and, later, from central cities to the suburbs.

Internal Migration: From Rural to Urban America

The growth of US cities in the late nineteenth and early twentieth centuries involved not only changes in the economic alternatives available to firms, but consideration of lifestyles and economic possibilities for individual workers and their families. Rural life had many positive aspects. Thomas Jefferson lauded the political independence of farmers who owned their own land. The quality of agricultural life was often compared favorably against conditions in cities, but rural life presented numerous challenges. Crops and animals need daily attention, and the demands of agricultural work could be unforgiving when the farmworker suffered illness or injury. The financial rewards to farming were highly uncertain as a result of weather, crop disease, and insect infestation.

Consequently, for families contemplating a move to a city, there was an interplay between the perceived quality of city life and the experience of life in rural areas. Push and pull factors led individuals to reexamine their physical surroundings and economic situations. Did cities offer a better alternative to the structures of opportunity in rural settings? Was it time to seek a different type of life in the city? In the late 1800s and early 1900s there were a number of push factors, including a series of weather-related disasters, insect plagues, and economic recessions that struck agriculture. These factors brought on hunger, foreclosure, and displacement for many of those affected (see Table 3.3). Moving to the city seemed to be the only good opportunity for many who tried unsuccessfully to keep their farms profitable.

Among those who worked on farms but did not own them, the weather, insect plagues, and recessions were significant factors that led to migration to cities, but there were other developments that contributed significantly to the push toward urban areas. Since the mid-1800s, various inventors had tried to develop and market steam-powered machines to aid agricultural production—with limited success. By the 1890s these initiatives had turned to gas-powered farm vehicles, which ultimately had greater commercial success. For many farmworkers, regardless of race or geographic region, the increasing mechanization of agriculture through the development of tractors and increasingly sophisticated weeding and harvesting machines meant wholesale displacement from farm jobs (Rasmussen 1982). The city became the only viable option for those who no longer could make a living in agriculture. In 1810, 81 percent of the American labor force was employed on farms and ranches. By 1870, the proportion was less than 52 percent. And by 1910, only 31 percent of the labor force was still employed in agriculture (Lebergott 1966).

TABLE 3.3.	ECONOMIC AND BIOLOGICAL *PUSH FACTORS* AFFECTING MIGRATION FROM FARMS TO CITIES
1874–1876	Grasshopper plagues destroy crops in Western United States.
Late 1870s and 1880s	Wheat, corn, and cotton prices fall; many small farmers lose their farms.
1886–1887	Blizzards in Great Plains harm cattle ranches.
1887–1897	Drought in Great Plains states devastates farms.
1890s	Depression in the United States; cotton prices fall from 8.6 cents per pound in 1890 to 6.98 cents in 1899.
1894–1895	Double-freeze winters destroy Florida citrus crops.
1900–1910	Cotton prices rebound, rising from 9.1 cents in 1900 to 13.5 cents in 1910. But boll weevil infestation spreads east from Texas to Louisiana and Mississippi.
1904	Stem rust epidemic destroys wheat in wheat-growing states.
1910–1920	Cotton prices fall in first half of decade, reaching a low of 7.4 cents in 1914, but then rise from 11.2 cents in 1915 to 35.3 cents in 1919. But boll weevil plague spreads across Alabama, Georgia, South Carolina, and Florida.
1920–1930	Overproduction of cotton leads to an agricultural depression, creating more poverty in the South. Boll weevil problem persists through 1925. Cotton prices vary from year to year, from a low of 15.9 cents in 1920 to a high of 28.7 cents in 1923 and end the decade at 16.8 cents. Blacks migrate away from areas of heaviest depression to cities in North and South. Many White farm owners lose land and are forced into farm tenantry or migration.
1920–1930	Number of tractors in use in nine southern states increases from 25,203 to 89,016, reducing owners' need for farm laborers.
1930–1940	Cotton prices fall drastically; beginning at 9.5 cents in 1930, falling to 5.7 cents in 1931, rising only as high as 12.4 cents, and ending the decade at 9.1 cents. Use of tractors spread east from Texas and Oklahoma, doubling in number from 89,016 to 171,431. Increased tractor use continues to reduce owners' need for farm laborers.
1932–1936	Dust bowl conditions devastate farms in Great Plains states.
1933–1939	U.S. government intervenes in cotton markets by introducing subsidies to farm owners if they restrict acreage. Resulting decrease in acreage lessens demand for labor, displacing some farmworkers. Acreage harvested falls from 42,444 in 1930 to 23,805 in 1939.

Sources: US Department of Agriculture, "A History of American Agriculture: 1776–1990," http://www.usda.gov/history2; Work 1925, 1930, 1940; Agricultural Extension Service at University of Georgia, "Cotton Production and the Boll Weevil in Georgia," www.ces.uga.edu/pubs/PDF/RR428.pdf.

For some groups, there were additional push factors. The tenant farming system, common in the South, institutionalized some forms of economic hardship for sharecroppers and other tenant farmers, as they rented their land and tools from owners and persistently found themselves in debt to them. For Black farmworkers economic exploitation was particularly oppressive, as they had no legal recourse if they were cheated by their bosses, and raising complaints about such situations could be life-threatening. This oppression of former slaves was buttressed by the systematic political disenfranchisement institutionalized during the 1890s and the physical violence perpetrated upon Blacks with the tacit, if not explicit, support of many White business and political leaders in the South. Between 1900 and 1914, more than a thousand Blacks were murdered, the victims of brutal lynchings, most in the South (Work 1938). For Blacks, "Going to Chicago" became a euphemism not only for the search for new job opportunities, but for an escape to places with less political and social brutality (Work 1924; Fligstein 1981).

Between 1910 and 1930, in the first wave of what has come to be known as the Great Migration, more than a million Blacks, mostly from rural communities, moved from the South to the North, with most going to northern cities, among them New York, Philadelphia, Chicago, Indianapolis, St. Louis, and Kansas City (US Bureau of the Census 1979; Work 1938). Hundreds of thousands more moved from farms and former plantations to southern cities, such as Atlanta, Birmingham, Jackson, and Memphis.

The migration slowed during the 1930s, but during this decade, federal policies that were introduced to help farm owners (in particular, the Agricultural Adjustment Act of 1933) ultimately had the unintended consequence of intensifying the economic push factors affecting farmworkers, which led to increased migration in the decades that followed. By stabilizing the market price for cotton and other agricultural products that had suffered from low prices due to overproduction relative to demand, and by giving subsidies to farm owners if they reduced the amount of land under cultivation, hundreds of thousands of farmworkers became redundant.

The reduction in farm owners' demand for labor was augmented by still another impact of the federal subsidies. Subsidies provided farm owners with an infusion of cash, making it more feasible for them to buy tractors and, after 1945, new chemical weed killers and mechanized cotton pickers. These developments reduced the need for farm labor in the South, displacing tens of thousands of sharecroppers, intensifying the economic reasons for leaving southern farm areas, and greatly accelerating outmigration. Coupled with the continuing social and political barriers in the South after World War II that kept Blacks from access to voting, schools, and other activities, these new push factors created powerful incentives for Blacks to leave the South, in the second wave of the Great Migration, for what they hoped would be better conditions in the North (Lemann 1991).

While awareness of these push factors is very important for understanding this internal migration, the massive relocation of Blacks and native-born Whites to cities cannot be understood without contemplating the pull factors exerted by cities. In the late 1800s and early 1900s, the growth of employment opportunities in the nation's manufacturing centers, such as those presented in Table 3.4, was a major factor as families considered where to move. With the exception of the Depression years in the 1930s, pull factors continued to be strong in the decades from 1910 to

TABLE 3.4. ECONOMIC *PULL FACTORS* AFFECTING MIGRATION TO CITIES

1890–1910	Textile manufacturing, introduced into the South in the 1880s expands, drawing workers to southern cities. By 1910, half of all U.S. textile manufacturing is being done in the South.
1900–1910	Cities in the North and South grow rapidly.
1914–1918	Expansion of manufacturing during World War I attracts Whites and Blacks to cities in the North and South.
1920s	Displacement due to introduction of machinery is negligible.
1930–1940	Number of Black farmers decreases by 23 percent, from 749,000 to 574,000 (a decrease of 175,000). Number of White farmers decreases by 50,000 (less than 4 percent). Reverse migration by whites from cities is substantial, as some Whites leave cities and take on subsistence farming to weather the Great Depression (the number of White farm owners increased by 74,000, or 12 percent).
1940s	War industries (steel, refineries, textiles) spur city development.

Source: Fligstein 1981.

1970, as automobile and steel industry jobs opened up in Michigan, Ohio, Illinois, and Pennsylvania, attracting Blacks from the South and Whites from rural areas to cities in the country's booming manufacturing belt. The allure of cities was particularly strong during World War I and World War II, as wartime industries offered wages much beyond the average paid to farmworkers. At mid-century, with the economic boom of the late 1940s and the 1950s, the employment opportunities in cities of the North and West continued to stoke internal migration, pulling large numbers of people from rural areas and small towns to city life.

Thus, the combination of push factors in rural areas and pull factors in US cities created a massive flow of internal migration to the growing cities. As early as 1920, half of all native Whites and a third of Blacks lived in urban areas. Between 1900 and 1940, the number of native-born Whites living in urban areas increased by 30 million, doubling the total number to 59 million. The number of Blacks living in urban areas tripled, from 2 million to 6 million. Rural White families moved in all directions to cities across the nation, while Black migration tended to go from the rural South to cities in the South, North, and West. In turn, the internal migration contributed to changes in the geographic size of urban areas, their demographics, and their socioeconomic dynamics.

This migration from lower-wage to higher-wage areas led to regional income convergence—some decline in income inequality—as labor supply increased in the latter and decreased in the former. Ganong and Shoag (2017) describe the century from 1880 to 1980 as such a period of regional convergence in which higher wages offset the higher cost of living in cities, especially higher housing costs, for workers at all skill levels (in their example, janitors and lawyers alike).

Yet at least since 1980, land-use restrictions that limit housing supply have caused higher housing costs to outstrip higher wages for less-skilled workers: the move is still attractive to lawyers, but not to janitors. As high-wage areas exert less of a pull factor for lower-skilled workers, regional convergence ends and regional patterns of income inequality increase dramatically.

Immigration and the Growth of American Cities

The new American city of the nineteenth century and later in the early twentieth century was populated not only by those who came from small villages and farms, but by millions who came from abroad. In 1830, a year after Andrew Jackson's inauguration as the nation's seventh president, 12.5 million people lived in the United States. Just 20 years later the number had nearly doubled to 23 million, and a decade later it had grown to 31 million. Of these, more than 5 million—one in six—were immigrants. Many of those who disembarked in port cities along the East Coast quickly moved to the interior of the country to renew or take up a life of farming, mining, or working in America's vast timberlands. But many made their new home in urban America, practicing trades they had learned in the old country or learning new ones. In New York in 1850, 45 percent of the population was foreign born, with Ireland and Germany responsible for most of the new immigrants. In Philadelphia, about one in four residents had been born in Europe (Kraus 1959).

More than a million Irish men, women, and children, mostly from rural areas, came to the United States between 1815 and 1845. In the early days of this great wave of emigration, they were escaping—pushed out—of their emerald homeland, forced off their farms to make way for pasturage. Later, the trickle turned into a torrent of Irish emigration as the great potato famine struck with a vengeance in the 1840s. Trying to escape starvation, the Irish not only moved to such cities as London, as we noted earlier, but filled boats bound for the United States and Canada, their passage often paid for by the Irish government or private philanthropy. Meanwhile, the emerging factory system in Britain and Germany undermined the skills of highly trained craftsmen who saw their wages fall and their working day lengthen. Religious and social persecution added to the push away from Europe and would have done so even if the United States had little to offer.

But indeed, the United States had much to offer. In the nineteenth and early twentieth centuries America's abundant land and the growth of jobs in its expanding cities beckoned, pulling millions of these immigrants to our shores. Guidebooks, travel accounts, and newspapers afforded prospective emigrants a vision of the better life awaiting them in the New World. Innkeepers and labor contractors helped round up emigrants for America with promises of good jobs at good pay. For as little as $5, an immigrant could make it to North America on a Canadian lumber vessel or a fishing boat. But those arriving with nothing could rarely leave the cities where they disembarked. Only about 10 percent of the Irish moved to rural areas, the vast majority staying in the cities to work in the emerging textile industry, in construction, and on the docks (Bluestone and Stevenson 2000). Those who came with some wealth began their own businesses, contributing capital and entrepreneurship to American industry.

The immortal words of Emma Lazarus inscribed on the Statue of Liberty in New York Harbor represent both of these forces—the push away from poverty and political repression, the pull toward what many saw as the golden opportunities beckoning in the United States:

> Give me your tired, your poor,
>
> Your huddled masses yearning to breathe free,
>
> The wretched refuse of your teeming shore,
>
> Send these, the homeless, tempest-tossed to me,
>
> I lift my lamp beside the golden door!

During the second half of the nineteenth century, new immigrants poured into the United States from both Western and Eastern Europe. By 1900, the countries sending the largest number of emigrants to America were Germany, Ireland, Canada, Great Britain, Sweden, Italy, Russia, and Poland. Between 1900 and 1920, more than 14.5 million new immigrants arrived in the United States—a number not surpassed until the last two decades of the twentieth century, 1980–2000.

In the West, immigration became a major factor as well. Between 1850 and 1880, 300,000 Chinese entered the country, most coming from Kwantang Province in southeastern China, and settling in California. Nine in 10 of these new arrivals were men, many recruited as contract laborers by the "49ers" who had come West to pan for riches in California's gold rush. Others were taken against their will and forced to join railway gangs to help build the transcontinental railroad. By 1860, 9 percent of

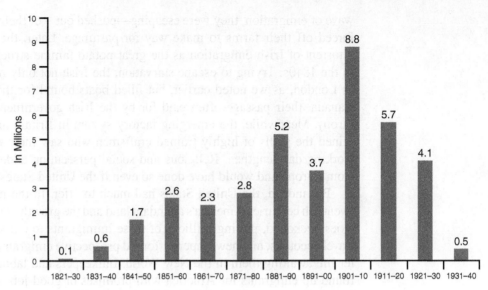

FIGURE 3.8. US Immigration 1821–1940

Source: US Department of Justice, Immigration and Naturalization Service. 2002. "1999 Statistical Yearbook of the Immigration and Naturalization Service," p.19 https://www.dhs.gov/sites/default/files/publications/Yearbook_Immigration_Statistics_1999.pdf

California's population was Chinese. By the early 1880s, 25,000 to 30,000 people of Chinese descent lived in San Francisco, most in a single neighborhood known even today as Chinatown. By the end of the nineteenth century you would have heard a great number of languages spoken in America's cities, whether you stood under a gas lamp on the Bowery in lower Manhattan, in the crowded precincts around the slaughterhouses in Chicago, or near San Francisco's bustling waterfront.

Yet the boom in immigration had just begun. Between 1880 and 1890, according to historical statistics compiled by the US Immigration and Naturalization Service (INS), nearly 9 million new immigrants reached American shores and nearly the same number in the following decade (see Figure 3.8). To be sure, many of those who came to America returned to their homelands or moved elsewhere. Many left because they were homesick, others because they could not find good jobs. A few who were born in the United States chose to move to other countries because of marriage or wanderlust. Times were so difficult during the Great Depression of the 1930s that more people left the United States than entered. Still, the net inflows—arrivals minus departures—were so great earlier in the century that by 1910 there were 13.5 million foreign-born residents in the United States—nearly 15 percent of the nation's total population. Only in the last decade of the twentieth century did official immigration come close to matching the level reached at the beginning of the century. The 2000 census found that more than 1 in 10 (10.4%) of those in the United States were foreign born, a total exceeding 28 million (US Bureau of the Census 2001).

Immigration is not simply a matter of push and pull factors. Politics and legislation play a key role. In 1882, the US Congress passed the Chinese Exclusion Act, which restricted the migration of immigrants from China and declared Chinese immigrants to be ineligible for citizenship. After the massive wave of foreigners came to the United States between 1880 and 1910, the rate of immigration slowed because of World War I, as well as Congressional passage of laws in 1921 and in 1924 that severely restricted immigration. The new legislation reduced the overall amount of immigration allowed, while establishing immigration quota systems that strongly favored countries in the Western Hemisphere and northern and Western Europe. During the Great Depression of the 1930s and then during World War II, immigration was also quite low. By 1950, the number of foreign born was down to just 6.9 percent of the total population.

The standard narrative of late-nineteenth- and early-twentieth-century immigration is one of assimilation of these immigrants and their children into the broader American culture. Still, Douglas Massey questions whether that narrative can be generalized to other periods. He argues that assimilation depends on the attitudes of the native-born population as well as those of the immigrants, as tempered by economic conditions (Massey and Magaly 2010). Those late-nineteenth- and early-twentieth-century immigrants were European, viewed as White; later immigrants were non-European, viewed as non-White. Moreover, the period from 1945 to the 1970s, when many of the barriers against the children of immigrants became blurred, was a time of prosperity and rising incomes. Later immigrants, especially those with lower skills and education, arrived during a time of growing income inequality and stagnation of middle-class incomes, along with greater hostility on the part of the native born. These factors present barriers to assimilation.

In the final analysis, American cities in the nineteenth and early twentieth centuries grew rapidly as a result of rising demand for workers, given the expanding factory system and the increase in the supply of workers who were migrating from rural areas or emigrating from abroad. The coming together of central city economic demand as a result of transportation economies, agglomeration economies, economies of scale, and mass markets with a ready supply of labor and capital produced America's great and small cities.

US cities grew both in population and in geographic size. As economic activity in cities developed, both the demand for labor and the opportunities for additional businesses expanded. As people moved to cities in response to increased labor demand and expanding business opportunities, the demand for housing and for commercial and industrial space increased. With the urban population increasing, new service businesses were founded and cities became even more alluring. The explosion in the size of cities was the result of this interaction between business expansion and population growth.

Ultimately, this created new possibilities for the owners of farmlands adjacent to the growing cities. If the profits from the sale of land for residential or business purposes exceeded the profits that could be expected from agricultural use, why continue farming? Hence, the expansion of population and of commercial activity pushed the borders of cities outward, swallowing up the surrounding farms. Cities became denser at their core while expanding outward to their fringe.

Annexation and the Growing Size of Cities

Until the late nineteenth century, as economic activity expanded, the political boundaries of most cities expanded to accommodate it. For outlying areas, the need to access water and sewage systems and a variety of other public services provided a strong incentive to become part of the city. Through the process of **annexation**, central cities encompassed larger and larger areas. Philadelphia, for example, expanded from just 2 square miles in 1850 to 130 square miles two decades later. The city of New York increased its geographic size sevenfold between 1890 and 1910 (from 44 to 299 square miles) by annexing Brooklyn, Queens, Staten Island, and the Bronx. Chicago expanded from 10 square miles in 1850 to 169 square miles in 1890.

However, as political discord intensified in the late-nineteenth-century city, and as states chose to provide public services to their municipalities through the creation of special water and sewer districts, many suburban communities had little need to join the central city and fought further annexation attempts. Fischel (2001) has argued that the communities' desire to maintain control over land-use decisions within their boundaries was a major motivation in their resistance to annexation attempts by the central city.

Suburban communities sought to maintain their independence from city political power, to control their own environments, and in many cases to maintain their economic, ethnic, or racial exclusivity. This was the case in metropolitan Boston, for example, where annexation has been successfully resisted since the late nineteenth century. Nonetheless, annexation continued well into the twentieth century in the newer cities of the South and West. Los Angeles grew from 85 square miles in 1910 to 440 square miles in 1930. In the period after 1950, Jacksonville expanded from 30 square miles to 827 square miles, while Indianapolis expanded from 55 square miles to 379 square miles.

As a result, today the proportion of the geographic area occupied by the central cities of metropolitan areas varies considerably. According to the 2018 census figures, only 2.8 percent of the land in the Greater Boston metropolitan area is actually in the city of Boston, and the city proper contains just 14.2 percent of the area's total population. By contrast, the city of Phoenix occupies nearly three-fifths of its surrounding metro area and accounts for nearly half of the MSA's population.

The Changing Pattern of Urban Population Growth

While economics and politics were transforming the boundaries of cities, technological marvels were also transforming the urban home. As noted earlier, Thomas Edison's incandescent bulb made electric lighting common beginning in the early twentieth century. Electric lights replaced gas lamps on city streets. In the 1880s and 1890s, hot air furnaces were first introduced, gas stoves replaced coal-burning cast iron ranges, and iceboxes were becoming standard, even before the electric refrigerator made its debut. Factory-made products replaced homemade, from breads and canned goods to clothing. As historian Foster Rhea Dulles notes, most of these new innovations were still largely confined to the city, and "the traditional divergence between urban and rural ways of living was sharply accentuated. The future, indeed, belonged to the city and ultimately its culture would invade even the most isolated country areas" (Dulles 1959, p. 91).

Cities were becoming the intellectual, artistic, and literary centers of the nation. With the exception of the land-grant universities, most of the great institutions of higher education were located in cities along with the nation's most prestigious museums and libraries. America's wealthiest moved into the cities to take advantage of their great and growing amenities.

Meanwhile, members of a growing middle class were moving into their first owner-occupied homes in the city, often on quiet streets farther from the central business district. Chicago, Detroit, and Philadelphia boasted of thousands of single-family homes built for professionals, small business owners, and increasingly even for some of the better off among the blue-collar working class.

Yet even a century ago, the urban paradox of poverty among plenty ruled. The urban experience was truly diverse for those who populated the cities. At the beginning of the twentieth century, approximately one-tenth of the population in the largest cities lived in slums. In New York City alone, it was estimated that more than 1.5 million people were crowded into 43,000 tenements where they were closely packed together in five- and six-story buildings, hurriedly built with plumbing, heating, and lighting that was primitive at best. Deadly fires, disease, crime, and juvenile delinquency were common. Although some immigrants to the United States had been told that in this land of opportunity the streets were paved with gold, most streets still did not even have asphalt. City populations were often divided along ethnic, racial, religious, and income lines (Chudacoff and Smith 2000). Reflecting such divisions, various interest groups exerted important influences in both market (e.g., housing, employment) and nonmarket (e.g., political and social) activities. Later, in the mid-1900s, when many in the middle class left for the suburbs, the largest cities became more polarized along the dimensions of income and race. Some of the richest and many of the poorest families in America ended up as the residents of central cities, as working-class and middle-class families sought their dream homes in the suburbs.

In the industrial age, the high concentrations of population and economic activity within the city limits allowed for the creation of many of the institutions that define our cities today. The physical infrastructure of the city—from paved roads to lighted streets to reliable water supplies—depended on a large critical mass of people to be served. To be sure, it was the dense population of cities that contributed to the diseases associated with filth. But it was in response to these diseases that the public health movement was born, resulting in sanitation departments, health departments, and the movement for the construction of public parks in the middle of cities.

It was both the concentration of people in large cities and the great fortunes that sprang from the urban industrial age that allowed new cultural, religious, medical, and educational institutions to flourish there. Many of our finest urban facades—public libraries, museums, concert halls, railroad stations, and courthouses—date from this period.

Certainly, the positive economies of scale in the central city represent only one side of the urban coin. The flip side contains the story of vice and corruption, congestion, violence, and danger in ever more densely packed central cities. While technology was reinforcing the primacy of central locations, its need for large manufacturing workforces and the consequent gathering of huge populations that were new to industrialization and urbanization led to turmoil.

Metropolitan growth has spread from the Northeast and Midwest to the South and West, and this also can be seen as an interaction between market forces and public policy. In addition to the economic and technological changes that expanded the location choices of firms and households, politics contributed to the growth of cities in places where vacant land was cheaper and more available and where labor costs were lower. The seniority of a number of southern congressmen and senators allowed them key committee chairmanships. They used their influence to bring a disproportionate number of military facilities to southern states and to relocate large military contractors to the Sunbelt, raising the South's share of all Department of Defense prime contract awards from 7.6 percent in 1951 to 23.5 percent in 1967 (Schulman 1991). Moreover, Congress passed the Taft-Hartley Act in 1947, which made it more difficult for northern unions to follow their workers to the South and made it almost impossible for them to organize in states with right-to-work laws—most of which were in the South. These laws limited the ability of unions to collect dues from workers who were covered by union contracts but were not willing to help underwrite the cost of union representation. By moving to the South, firms found locations where they could lower the cost of labor and often their local and state taxes. Such political factors helped redirect where growth would take place and where small towns would turn into burgeoning cities—mostly in the South and West.

In the newer metropolitan areas, where lower-density development was the rule, both the cities and the suburbs were more likely to be oriented around the needs of the motorist rather than those of pedestrians or public transit users. The lower density itself made these areas costly locations for public transportation, especially with the auto industry lobbying for more highways and roads. The role served by the waterfront in colonial cities and the railroad depot in industrial cities was now served by the highway interchange in the postindustrial twentieth-century metropolis, as we see in the next chapter.

References

Allen, Hugh. 1949. *The House of Goodyear*. Cleveland, Ohio: Corday and Gross.

Blackford, Mansel G., and K. Austin Kerr. 1996. *BF Goodrich: Tradition and Transformation, 1870–1995*. Columbus: Ohio State University Press.

Bluestone, Barry, and Mary Huff Stevenson. 2000. *The Boston Renaissance: Race, Space, and Economic Change in an American Metropolis*. New York: Russell Sage.

Bluestone, Barry, Patricia Hanna, Sarah Kuhn, and Laura Moore. 1981. *The Retail Revolution: Market Transformation, Investment and Labor in the Modern Department Store Industry*. Boston: Auburn House.

Chudacoff, Howard, and Judith E. Smith. 2000. *The Evolution of American Urban Society*. 5th ed. Upper Saddle River, NJ: Prentice Hall.

Citi I/O. "How Did Electricity Change the Way People Lived in Cities?" March 16, 2017. https://citi.io/2017/03/16/how-did-electricity-change-the-way-people-lived-in-cities/.

Cronon, William. 1991. *Nature's Metropolis: Chicago and the Great West*. New York: Norton.

Demographia. 2003. "Ville de Paris: Population & Density from 1600." http://demographia.com/dm-par90.htm.

Dulles, Foster Rhea. 1959. *The United States since 1865*. Ann Arbor: University of Michigan Press.

Edwards, Richard C. 1980. *Contested Terrain: The Transformation of the Workplace in the 20th Century*. New York: Basic Books.

Emsley, Clive, Tim Hitchcock, and Robert Shoemaker. 2020. "London History—A Population History of London." *Old Bailey Proceedings Online, version 7.0,* March 24. https://www.oldbaileyonline.org/static/Population-history-of-london.jsp.

Fischel, William A. 2001. *The Homevoter Hypothesis: How Home Values Influence Local Government Taxation, School Finance, and Land-Use Policies*. Cambridge, MA: Harvard University Press.

Fligstein, Neil. 1981. *Going North: Migration of Blacks and Whites from the South, 1900–1950*. New York: Academic Press.

Ganong, Peter, and Daniel W. Shoag. 2017. "Why Has Regional Income Convergence in the U.S. Declined?" *National Bureau of Economic Research Working Paper 23609*. Cambridge, MA: National Bureau of Economic Research.

Isard, Walter. 1975. *Introduction to Regional Science*. Englewood Cliffs, NJ: Prentice Hall.

Jacobs, Jane. 1961. *The Death and Life of Great American Cities*. New York: Random House.

Jacobs, Jane. 1969. *The Economy of Cities*. New York: Random House.

Kraus, Michael. 1959. *The United States to 1865*. Ann Arbor: University of Michigan Press.

Launhardt, Wilhelm. 1885. *Mathematische Begrundung der Volkswirtschafslehre*. Leipzig: W. Engleman. Trans. John Creedy (1993) as *Mathematical Principles of Economics*. Aldershot, UK.: Edward Elgar.

Lebergott, Stanley.1966. *Labor Force and Employment 1800–1960*. Cambridge, MA.: National Bureau of Economic Research.

Lemann, Nicholas. 1991. *The Promised Land: The Great Black Migration and How It Changed America*. New York: Knopf.

Massey, Douglas S., and Sanchez R. Magaly. 2010. *Brokered Boundaries: Creating Immigrant Identity in Anti-Immigrant Times*. New York: Russell Sage Foundation.

Migiro, Geoffrey. 2018. "The World's Most Densely Populated Cities." *World Atlas*, November 15.

Miller, Donald L. 1996. *City of the Century: The Epic of Chicago and the Making of America*. New York: Simon & Schuster.

Moodpanda Blog. 2020. "Five Reasons Why Community is Important." https://moodpanda.tumblr.com/post/49460339385/five-reasons-why-community-is-important.

Moses, Leon, and Harold F. Williamson Jr. 1967. "The Location of Economic Activity in Cities." *American Economic Review* 57 (May): 211–222.

O'Reilly, Maurice. 1983. *The Goodyear Story*. New York: Benjamin Company.

Rae, Douglas. 2003. *City: Urbanism and Its End*. New Haven, CT: Yale University Press.

Rasmussen, Wayne D. 1982. "The Mechanization of Agriculture." *Scientific American* 247, no. 3 (September): 76–89.

Schulman, Bruce J. 1991. *From Cotton Belt to Sunbelt: Federal Policy, Economic Development, and the Transformation of the South, 1938–1980*. New York: Oxford University Press.

Solow, R. 1956. "A Contribution to the Theory of Economic Growth." *Quarterly Journal of Economics* 70, no. 1 (February): 65–94. .

US Bureau of the Census. 1979. "The Social and Economic Status of the Black Population in the United States: An Historical View, 1790–1978." *US Department of Commerce Special Studies Series P-23*, No. 80. Washington, DC: Government Printing Office.

US Bureau of the Census. 2001. *Selected Historical Decennial Census, Population and Housing Counts*. April. Washington, DC: Government Printing Office.

Vernon, Raymond. 1972. "External Economies." In *Readings in Urban Economics*, edited by Matthew Edel and Jerome Rothenberg. New York: Macmillan, pp. 37–49.

Weber, Alfred. 1909. *Uber den Standort der Industrien*. Tübingen: J. C. B. Mohr Publisher.

Work, Monroe N. 1924. "The Negro Migration." *Southern Workman* (May): 202–212.

Work, Monroe N. 1938. *The Negro Year Book 1937–1938*. Tuskegee, AL: The Negro Year Book Publishing Company.

Questions and Exercises

The Economic Roles of Early US Cities and Towns

1. Consider the city or town in which you live (or where you grew up). Using the official website of the municipality or the community's historical society, identify the products (goods or services) that seem to have contributed most to the early growth of this area. What connection, if any, can you make between these early economic activities and Weber's theory linking business location and transportation costs?

2. Was the city or town you studied in question 1 famous nationwide for a particular product (good or service) produced there? Were there many companies producing this product in your city or town? Does this represent agglomeration economies?

Immigration and Internal Migration

3. Using http://data.census.gov, explore the size of the foreign-born population in the city closest to your home and two other cities. For each of your selected cities, in which decade was the fastest growth in population experienced? Does the population boom for each of those cities seem to have been most strongly caused by an increase in immigration or an increase in internal migration?

4. For the three cities you chose in question 3, take a look at the city's website, the local historical society's website, or some other source giving the history of the city. Which economic pull factors stimulated migration to those cities during the periods of peak population growth?

4

Cities and Suburbs Moving Into the Twenty-First Century

LEARNING OBJECTIVES

- Describe the three formal models of land-use patterns and compare the implications of each on the shape of the metropolitan area

- Explain the Alonso model and use it to resolve his residential paradox

- Show how considering costs other than transportation affect location decisions

- Explain how late-twentieth and early-twenty-first-century immigration patterns have shaped urban areas

- Explain the concepts of edge city and gentrification and show how they can be incorporated into the Alonso model

The Dynamics of Metropolitan Expansion

If you stand at the center of most large cities and look skyward, you will see high-rise office towers, some of which soar 50 stories or more—unless, of course, it is a city with explicit government-imposed height restrictions such as Washington, DC or Paris. Now, if you travel to a point 1 mile from the geographic center of the city, what do your surroundings look like? How about at 5 miles or 15 miles? The answer depends upon the particular city you are in and often on whether you travel north, south, east, or west from the city center. You may find yourself in an area of small single-family homes or large apartment buildings, in a new high-tech industrial park, or in a small business area that has existed for decades. It could be a neighborhood characterized by large expensive mansions, a community of small bungalows, or, alternatively, a rural area of farms or forests. Depending more on politics than economics, you may still be within the city's jurisdiction, in a suburb, or in an unincorporated area. Most likely as you move away from downtown, the average scale of the buildings will decline, although today there are places other than the geographic center where there is the equivalent of a high-rise village.

How each metro area is laid out depends upon millions of choices made by individual families and firms over time. Some of these choices are made in the marketplace, others through the ballot box. But they are almost invariably influenced by *land prices*, which are in turn influenced by advances in transportation and communications technology, changing social mores, and the evolution of political institutions.

It is clear, however, that the pattern is not random. To understand where businesses and families locate within metro areas, where greater density in population and economic activity occurs, how the landscape will be spiked with high-rises and office towers, and how each of these changes over time, it is useful to turn first to a set of formal models developed by economists, sociologists, and urban geographers. All these models have a common goal: to understand the patterns of land use and the physical structure of the landscape in terms of land prices, or what economists refer to as **rent**.

Once we have explored these formal models, we will use them to explain the evolution of metro areas in the late twentieth century and the early twenty-first. In doing so, we need to also bring in a number of important insights from political science and sociology.

Formal Models of Urban Growth and Development

There are three principal descriptive models of land-use patterns in urban areas. The first, set forth by Ernest Burgess in 1925 (and slightly revised in 1929) as part of the so-called Chicago School of urban sociology, described cities in terms of concentric rings:

Zone 1:   Inner ring containing the city's central business district (CBD).

Zone 2:   Subsequent ring just outside the CBD or the "zone of transition," which Burgess's 1929 article described as containing factories on the innermost side and "areas of residential deterioration caused by the encroaching of business and industry from Zone 1" and populated by newly arrived immigrants in rooming houses and homeless men.

Zone 3:   Neighborhoods where "skilled and thrifty" factory and shop workers live.

Zone 4:   Residential zone of somewhat higher incomes that included single-family homes, apartment houses, residential hotels, and "bright light areas."

Zone 5:   Commuters' zone where workers may live, but must commute into inner rings where they work.

In Burgess's view, changes in land use proceeded from the inner ring outward, with each ring "invading" the next in a competition for use of the land as city expansion occurred (Burgess 1925; 1929).

The second major descriptive model, advanced by Homer Hoyt in 1939, is known as the sector model. Instead of concentric rings, this model envisioned cities developing in sectors or wedges. The sector model proposes that as cities expand and wealthy families move to well-to-do suburbs, retail businesses follow, locating along the transportation routes leading to these suburbs. Subsidiary development then follows along the outskirts of transportation routes, creating wedge shapes. Topography (the characteristics of the land) can also be a factor in the development of sectors. Individual sectors associated with a specific industry may arise, since (as noted in Chapter 3) some industries seek locations near bodies of water. Sectors of distinct income levels may arise because high-income families seek land with the best qualities, while poor families may not be able to afford the most desired land.

The third major descriptive model of land use, known as the multinucleic or polycentric model, was developed by Chauncy Harris and Edward Ullman in 1945. Harris and Ullman rejected the concept that cities have just one center. "In many cities," they wrote, "the land-use pattern is built not around a single center but around several discrete nuclei. In some cities these nuclei have existed from the very origins of the city; in others they have developed as the growth of the city stimulated migration and activities and the concentration of like functions" (Harris and Ullman 1945, p. 14). They attributed the existence of distinct nuclei to four factors:

1. Some industrial or cultural activities require specific types of facilities

2. Some production activities benefit from the existence of "localization economies" where increased size leads to increased productivity

3. Some activities are environmentally incompatible with others and therefore should or must be separated from other activities

4. Some areas are not affordable for some uses

Each of these models foretold the changes that metro areas would undergo, particularly after World War II. Figure 4.1 provides a pictorial representation of the concentric zone, sector, and multiple nuclei models of metro area location.

The top figure depicts the concentric model of cities as envisioned by Ernest Burgess, one of the prominent early members of the Chicago School of Sociology. As mentioned earlier, Burgess envisioned cities as composed of five concentric zones:

1. central business district (CBD)

2. zone of transition

3. zone of independent workingmen's homes

4. zone of better residences

5. commuter zone

The middle figure is a depiction of the sector model. In the sector model, there is a central business district with wedges of various sizes emanating from the CBD. The multinucleic model, an example of which is shown in the bottom figure,

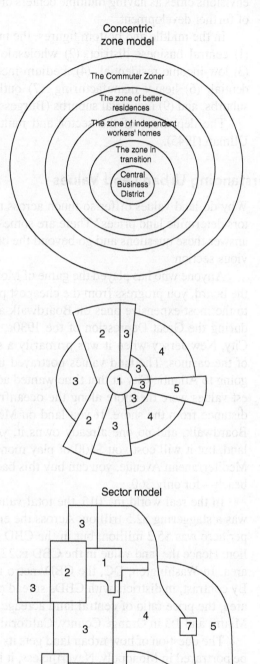

Concentric zone model

The Commuter Zoner

The zone of better residences

The zone of independent workers' homes

The zone in transition

Central Business District

Sector model

Multiple nuclei

FIGURE 4.1. An Illustration of Concentric Zone, Sector, and Multiple Nuclei Urban Structures

envisions cities as having multiple centers of activity, each of which can be a source of further development.

In the middle and bottom figures, the numbers indicate different uses of land: (1) central business district, (2) wholesale businesses and light manufacturing, (3) low-income residential, (4) medium-income residential, (5) high-income residential, (6) heavy manufacturing, (7) outlying business district, (8) residential suburbs, and (9) industrial suburbs (Burgess 1925).

The depictions of the sector and multinucleic models are from Harris and Ullman (1945).

Understanding Urban Land Values

Why do land values differ so much across the metropolitan landscape? What factors determine land prices? There are some fascinating economic models that help answer these questions and go beyond the descriptive models described in the previous section.

Anyone who has played the game of Monopoly knows that as you travel around the board, you progress from the cheapest properties on Baltic and Mediterranean to the most expensive ones on Boardwalk and Park Place. The game was created during the Great Depression of the 1930s, and the street names refer to Atlantic City, New Jersey when it was primarily a summer resort, long before the advent of the casinos. The land values portrayed in the game reflect the fact that people going to Atlantic City at that time wanted access to its beach and ocean. The highest values were therefore along the oceanfront; land values declined with greater distance from the shore. If you land on Monopoly's premier waterfront property, Boardwalk, and no one already owns it, you can buy this piece of undeveloped land, but it will cost you $400 of play money. If the roll of the dice lands you on Mediterranean Avenue, you can buy this back-alley property—a distance from the beach—for only $60.

In the real world in 2015, the total value of land in the New York metro area was a staggering $2.5 trillion. Across the entire metro area the average land value per acre was $5.2 million, but in the CBD the per acre land value was $123 million. Hence the land value in the CBD is 22.3 times the average value in the metro area. In Washington, DC, the CBD/metro region land value is even higher: 32.6. By contrast, in districts with CBDs spread out across a broader swath of the metro area, the price ratio of central land acreage to metro area price is as low as 3:2 in Miami and 1:3 in Orange County, California (Albouy et al. 2018).

The question of how urban land gets its value is far more complicated than can be portrayed in Monopoly. Nevertheless, it is useful to begin with a stripped-down model to help us understand the underlying forces that affect the price of land. Such a model will not fully explain land use and land values in any one specific city, but it will provide a template that can be adapted to accommodate the geographical, historical, legal, and cultural differences that have made each place unique and help us to understand how places change over time. In the course of this chapter, we begin with a simple model and add complexity as we go along. To start, we hearken back to the early twentieth century, when transportation costs were still a significant factor in business location.

The Basic Alonso Model: Learning About Cities from Rural Farms

The economist William Alonso (1964), building on the earlier work of German economists on the value of agricultural land, created a simple model of urban land markets in the mid-1960s (von Thunen 1826; Launhardt 1885; Dunn 1954; Isard 1956). He was interested not only in explaining how land obtained its value but also how it was distributed across different categories of users, including businesses and households. Just as everyone in Monopoly wants access to the beachfront, everyone in the basic Alonso model desires access to the central marketplace. As such, in the Alonso model, land values decrease the farther away you move from the center city.

Here is his reasoning. While Alonso's ultimate goal was to understand complex *urban* land markets, he started with the simplest case of an agricultural land market in which identical farmers produce the same crop in the same way on the same amount of acreage (von Thunen 1826; Alonso 1964). The only difference between the farmers is that some have land very close to the central marketplace to which they transport their crops for sale, while others live and farm farther away. Assuming that these individual farmers actually own the land they farm and therefore need not pay rent, and that the cost of transporting goods is substantial and increases the farther one has to carry those goods, the farmers who are located nearer the market will be more profitable. Economic profit will decline as the distance to the market increases.

This is true because profitability is the result of the difference between total revenue and total cost, where total cost is comprised of production costs *plus* transportation costs. For example, if each farmer's acreage produces 1,000 pounds of wheat for bread production and the market price for wheat is $2 per pound, each farmer will receive $2,000 in revenue from the sale of his output. Under the assumptions mentioned in the preceding paragraph, production costs would be the same for each farmer but transportation costs would vary with the number of miles traveled. If production costs amounted to $1,500 and transportation costs were $10 per mile, the farmer right next to the marketplace would wind up with an economic profit of $500 ($2,000 - $1,500 - $0 transportation costs), while the farmer 20 miles down the road would have an economic profit of only $300 ($2,000 - $1,500 - $200 transportation costs). Given fixed costs of transportation per mile, the farmer who tries to make a living on a farm 50 miles from the marketplace will earn no profit at all, since his or her transportation costs will equal the value of wheat he can sell there. Any farmer trying to compete in this market farther from the central marketplace would suffer an economic loss. In this case, all of the crop would be grown within a 50-mile radius of the marketplace. It would not be financially feasible to grow it any farther away. As this example illustrates, there is an essential link between market forces and patterns of land use.

So how does this affect the price of land? The answer lies in understanding how a bid rent curve is established. So far, we have assumed that all the farmers own their land, but what if they have to rent the farmland from others, as tenant farmers and sharecroppers do? The farmer on the land closest to the marketplace still has the lowest transportation cost and the farmer on the land 50 miles away has the highest. Therefore, farmers working the land 50 miles away would be willing to pay no more than $500 to rent the land at the center, since that is what they would save in transportation costs, but they would be willing to pay no more than $300 to rent the land 20 miles out. These values are called the **bid rents** and refer to what a renter or buyer would be willing to bid in order to gain access to and use of a specific parcel of land. Ultimately, as shown in Table 4.1, the landlord closest to the center can charge the farmers on his or her land $500 in rent; the one 20 miles out can charge only $300. Beyond the 50-mile radius, the land would have no economic value, at least with regard to this one crop.

When every tenant farmer is paying the market-determined rent, none is better off than any other. Those closer to the center pay more for rent and less for transportation. Those farther away pay more for transportation and less for rent. The sum of rent plus transportation costs is the same for every tenant farmer, and leaves each with an income but an economic profit of zero. For every farm, the difference between the revenue received and the cost of production ends up with the landlord. Those landlords who are lucky enough to own land near the central marketplace profit the most; those farther away earn less and less rent, the farther their land from the center. The outcome of this process is illustrated in Panel A of Figure 4.2, which shows how the rent the farmers are willing to pay varies inversely with distance from the marketplace.

TABLE 4.1. UNDERSTANDING BID RENTS

			PRODUCTION COSTS				
Distance between farm and marketplace (miles)	Revenue from sale of 1,000 pounds of wheat	Amount farmer pays to others (for seed, fertilizer, etc.)	Minimum amount farmer pays to himself (the amount the farmer would receive from his next-best alternative to farming)	Transportation costs to take wheat from farm to marketplace	Economic profit before paying rent for farmland	Maximum amount farmer is willing to pay to rent the farmland	Economic profit after paying rent for farmland
0	$2,000	$1,300	$200	-0-	$500	$500	-0-
10	2,000	1,300	200	$100	400	400	-0-
20	2,000	1,300	200	200	300	300	-0-
30	2,000	1,300	200	300	200	200	-0-
40	2,000	1,300	200	400	100	100	-0-
50	2,000	1,300	200	500	-0-	-0-	-0-
60	2,000	1,300	200	600	−100	Farmer chooses another occupation	

Note: In a situation in which farmers rent land, they will be willing to pay any amount of rent that leaves them with a profit greater than their next-best alternative occupation. Accordingly, landowners can charge rent up to those levels. The amount of profit, however, depends upon the costs of transporting the crops to the market. Higher transportation costs leave less profit. This leads to the array of rents in the column second from the right. For example, a farmer renting land at the marketplace would pay up to $500, while a farmer at 30 miles out would be willing to pay a maximum of only $200. A farmer at 60 miles out would be operating at a loss, compared with his next-best alternative occupation, and so would choose to stop farming.

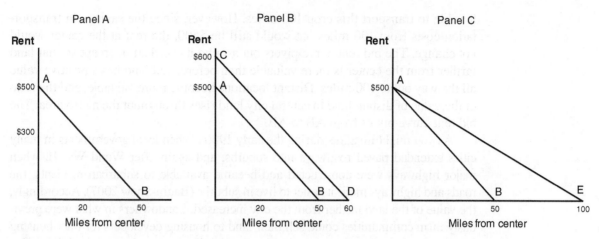

FIGURE 4.2. The Bid Rent Curve and Effect of a Change in Product Price or a Change in Transportation Costs

What if the market price of the crop increases? Each producer is a small part of the whole market, so no individual producer has any influence over price. But if the demand for the crop rises, its price will rise as well. Panel B of Figure 4.2 shows the effect of a rise in the market price of the crop, **ceteris paribus**—a Latin phrase used in economics to mean "holding everything else constant." If the market price of the crop rises from $2 to $2.10, total revenue would rise to $2,100 ($2.10 × 1,000 lbs. of wheat). With production costs of $1,500 and transportation costs of $10/mile, it would be feasible to incur up to $600 in transportation costs and to grow this crop up to 60 miles from the marketplace. Given the new higher price for his wheat, the farmer at the outer limit would be willing to pay up to $600 to rent the land at the center. The effect of an increase in the price of the product is to shift the **bid rent curve** out *parallel* to its original position, making land everywhere within the 60-mile radius more valuable. Landowners would benefit from the increase in the price of the farmers' crop. Now wheat production can take place further away from the central marketplace.

In Figure 4.2, Panel A, farmers face a trade-off between rent and transportation costs. If total revenue is $2,000 and production costs are $1,500, and if transportation costs are $10 per mile, it is feasible to operate only within a 50-mile radius of the center. Compared with a location 50 miles away, a central location will save the farmer $500 in transportation costs, and that is what farmers would be willing to pay in rent. The sum of rent and transportation costs are $500 anywhere along the bid rent curve, line AB. At a distance 20 miles out, for example, transportation costs are $200 and rent would be $300.

In Panel B, if the market price of the product increases, everything else being constant, so that total revenue rises to $2,100, it is now feasible to operate within a 60-mile radius of the center. Since a central location now represents a savings of $600 in transportation costs for the farmer who is farthest away, rent at the center rises to $600. The bid rent curve has shifted out from AB to CD.

What if transportation costs fell, instead of an increase in the price of the product? Panel C illustrates this case. If transportation costs fell to $5/mile, it would be feasible to transport this crop 100 miles. However, since the savings in transportation costs from 100 miles out would still be $500, the rent at the center would not change. The bid rent curve pivots out around its vertical intercept so that land farther from the center is more valuable than before, and land has a positive value all the way out to 100 miles. Distant locations become more valuable, and the ratio of the value of distant land to central city land rises throughout the metro area. The bid rent curve pivots from AB to AE.

As you might imagine, during the early 1900s, when local governments in many cities extended paved roadways into suburbs, and again after World War II, when major highways were constructed and became available to suburban residents, the roads and highways made it easier to live in suburbs (Baum-Snow 2007). Accordingly, the value of the land farther from the city increased. Landowners in what were previously farm communities could sell their land to housing developers for tract housing in new suburbs and to commercial and industrial developers who were building office parks and industrial parks far from the central city. What had been low-value farmland became more valuable suburban land for tract housing and industry.

Now consider a variant of this model. What if the land can be used to grow more than one kind of crop? What if a second group of tenant farmers comes along, growing a crop that brings in more revenue but is more difficult to transport (see Figure 4.3)?

If our first group of farmers is growing wheat, this second group might be growing tomatoes, which are more valuable but also more perishable and require special handling when they are transported. Assume that these tomato farmers are also identical to each other except for their location. They will also be arrayed along a bid rent curve, but their bid rent curve will be steeper. They have a greater desire to avoid transportation costs, so they place a higher value on accessibility and can pay more for it.

Compared with our original example, these tomato farmers might receive $3,000 in total revenue, have $2,200 in production costs, and incur higher transportation costs of $20/mile because of the perishable nature of their crop. Thus, the tomato crop can be grown no farther than 40 miles away from the center, because at this point the production costs ($2,200) plus transportation costs ($800) equal total revenue of $3,000. A tomato farmer, in this case, would be willing to pay $800 in rent for a site right next to the marketplace.

First consider Figure 4.3, Panel A. Here grain farmers compete against each other along bid rent curve AB. Tomato farmers, who grow a more profitable crop but incur higher transportation costs, compete against each other along bid rent curve CD. As a group, they outbid wheat farmers for the land within a 30-mile radius of the center while the grain farmers can outbid for the land in a concentric ring 30 to 50 miles away from the center. Now consider Panel B, where the resulting distribution of land is illustrated. Tomato farmers operate within a 30-mile radius of the center, while wheat farmers operate in the concentric ring 30 to 50 miles away.

Now there are two bid rent curves and there are three ways in which bidding to rent land occurs:

1. As individuals, the wheat farmers compete against each other along their bid rent curve (Line AB in Panel A of Figure 4.3).

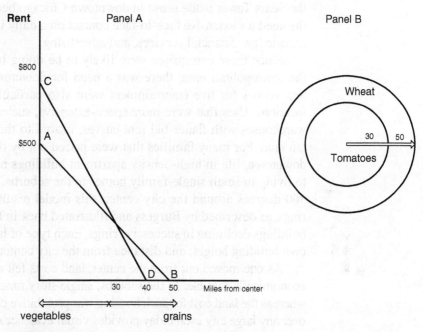

FIGURE 4.3. Bid Rent Curves for Two Different Uses of Land and the Resulting Land Distribution

2. As individuals, the tomato farmers compete against each other along their bid rent curve (Line CD in Panel A of Figure 4.3).

3. The wheat farmers as a group compete against the tomato farmers as a group.

The landlord will rent to the highest bidder, so the group with the highest curve at any location will have the winning bid. Since the tomato farmers have the steeper curve, they will win the competition for the land that is closer in. The wheat farmers will outbid the tomato farmers for the land that is farther out. The land within a 30-mile radius will be planted in tomatoes; the concentric ring with a radius from 30 to 50 miles out will be planted in wheat, as illustrated in Panel B of Figure 4.3. Other uses of land can be added with additional bid rent curves.

Applying the Bid Rent Model to Metro Area Development

As Alonso realized, these insights of earlier economists about farmers and the rent they pay had direct applicability to the pattern of land use and land values in metropolitan regions.

Essentially, the steeper the bid rent curve, the higher the value placed on accessibility to the center. And the higher the value per square foot of land, the more it made economic sense to use that land intensively by building multistory buildings that housed high-value operations—even if the construction cost per square foot of floor space in a skyscraper was significantly higher than the cost for a one- or two-story structure. The Empire State Building made sense in midtown Manhattan and the Sears Tower made sense in downtown Chicago because of the cost of land and the need for extensive face-to-face contact on a daily basis for core businesses that include law, financial services, and advertising.

Since these enterprises were likely to be doing business with people outside the metropolitan area, there was a need for downtown hotels. Some restaurants and venues for live entertainment were also particularly attracted to downtown locations. Uses that were more space-extensive, such as single-story factories and warehouses with flatter bid rent curves, moved to the outskirts of the metropolitan area. For many families that were priced out by the competition for land near downtown, life in high-density apartment buildings near the city center gave way to living in small single-family homes in the suburbs. If you rotate bid rent curves 360 degrees around the city center, this model results in a pattern of concentric rings, as described by Burgess and illustrated back in Figure 4.1, with the height of buildings declining in successive rings. Each type of land use had its own place, its own building height, and distance from the city center.

As one moved out from the center, land costs fell and lower-rise buildings were economically feasible. In the suburbs, single-story ranch-type homes were practical, whereas the land cost for such housing was prohibitive closer to the city center. Flying over any large city even today provides visual evidence of this land-use pattern.

There are some exceptions to this metropolitan skyline, but only because of political considerations. In some cities like Washington, DC and Paris, the government imposes height restrictions. In Paris, city law did not permit a building to be higher than 121 feet, so that at 1,063 feet the Eiffel Tower towered over everything in the city. Only in 2010 did the Paris City Council vote to raise the height limit to a revolutionary 590 feet—still little more than a third of the height of New York City's Empire State Building (Davies 2010). As of 2020, 18 buildings in Paris were at least 500 feet tall, changing the skyline considerably.

The Residential Paradox

The parable of the wheat and tomato farmers also provides the basic framework for Alonso's resolution of the **residential paradox**: his observation that the poor often live on expensive land in the central city, while the wealthy tend to live on cheaper land in the suburbs. Metaphorically, then, the poor play the role of the tomato farmers. Unlike the tomato farmers, though, the poor do not have greater revenue with which to outbid the wealthy, so how can they afford to live there? The resolution of this paradox can be represented by the bid rent curve in Figure 4.4, but the explanation is more complicated.

In this figure, all households prefer to live at low density. High-income households are able to absorb higher transportation costs in exchange for cheaper land and are represented by bid rent curve AB. Low-income households are unable to achieve this goal. They need to avoid high transportation costs and place a greater value on accessibility (bid rent curve CD). They pay for the more expensive land, but can do so only by living at higher density on smaller lots than they would otherwise prefer.

Alonso starts with the assumption that in the second half of the twentieth century most US families preferred to live at lower population density in the suburbs, and then shows why higher-income families were more likely to achieve that goal.

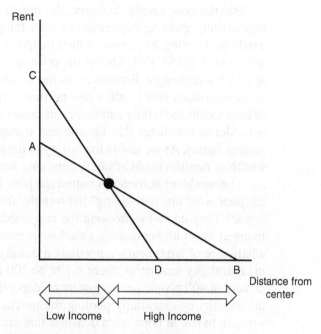

FIGURE 4.4. The Residential Paradox

Let us assume that a low-income family and a high-income family both prefer to follow the American Dream of owning a single-family house on its own plot of land somewhere outside the city center. Assume further, for simplicity, that the low-income family has a budget for shelter and transportation of $1,000 per month, while the high-income family has a budget of $5,000 per month. Land values fall and transportation costs rise as we go farther from the center. The transportation costs are $100 per month close to the center, $200 per month 10 miles out, and $300 per month 20 miles out. Thus, as shown in Table 4.2, after paying for transportation costs, the rich and poor families would have left over for shelter $4,900 and $900 near the center (respectively), $4,800 and $800 out 10 miles, and $4,700 and $700 out 20 miles. For each family, there is a trade-off between the falling price of land and the rising cost of transportation.

TABLE 4.2. IMPACT OF TRANSPORTATION COSTS ON LOW-INCOME AND HIGH-INCOME FAMILIES

TRANSPORTATION COSTS FOR FAMILY	LOW-INCOME FAMILY: BUDGET $1,000		HIGH-INCOME FAMILY: BUDGET $5,000	
	Transportation as Percent of Budget	Amount Remaining for Shelter	Transportation as Percent of Budget	Amount Remaining for Shelter
Close to Center: $100	10%	$900	2%	$4,900
10 Miles Out: $200	20%	$800	4%	$4,800
20 Miles Out: $300	30%	$700	6%	$4,700

Note: Although a low-income family and a high-income family may have the same transportation costs, those costs represent a higher proportion of the budget for low-income families, leaving them with much less for other needs. Because high-income families are more able to absorb higher transportation costs, they are more likely than low-income families to move to suburbs with greater transportation costs.

For the poor family, however, the transportation costs represent a large and dramatically growing percentage of their budget as they move farther out. They would be devoting 30 percent of their budget to transportation costs if they lived 20 miles out ($300/$1,000). The falling price of land does not compensate for the rate at which their budget diminishes. In the wealthy household, however, the increase in transportation cost is still a tiny portion of the family's budget. The lower price of land means the family can realize its desire to live at much lower density farther out. Alonso concludes that income and transportation costs constrain the lower-income family. As we saw in the history of the nineteenth-century suburbs, only the wealthier families could afford to commute downtown from their suburban homes.

The wealthier households outbid the poor for the land farther out. But how do the poor wind up "outbidding" the wealthy for the higher-priced land close to the center? They do so by choosing the best residential alternative available to them: living at much higher density. One four-person family in a single-family home on a half-acre of land means a population density of only eight people per acre. But in central city tenements, there might be 100 families per acre with a population density of 400 people per acre or more, depending on family size. The poor outbid the wealthy by essentially pooling the purchasing power of many more families per acre to live at population densities that are unacceptably high to suburbanites. In fact, they are not so much outbidding as they are forced to accept a living situation that is often much denser than they would choose if they could afford to live elsewhere.

Constrained Choice and Political Factors in Land Values and Location

The Alonso model, extended to take into consideration travel distances and highways, focuses on just a few key elements—as is true of nearly all models—and thus simplifies the underlying reality. The hypothetical farmers described by Alonso looked only at the trade-off between rent and distance in their quest to maximize profits. They did not consider, for example, the quality of the soil or irrigation. Alonso's urban households had preferences only with regard to the population density where they desired to live and their willingness and ability to trade commuting costs for additional space.

In order to fully understand land use in the real world and the location dynamics underlying twenty-first-century metropolitan areas, it is necessary to take into account a long list of physical constraints, individual preferences, social mores, and political considerations. For this reason, bid rent curves by themselves cannot tell the whole story about land values, where people live, or where businesses set up their operations. Understanding choice and constraints is important for understanding how individuals make decisions about where to live. As we will discuss more extensively in later chapters, the choices that individuals and firms can effectively make depend not just upon their individual proclivities but also upon their ability to wield various forms of power including income and wealth, and by the benefits they gain through actual or perceived membership in groups. The available set of choices changes over time, so these concepts are also important for understanding the consequences of changes in patterns of residential location and the development of cities.

Poor households are priced out of the market to the extent that municipalities enact laws and zoning regulations that prohibit no more than one or two houses per acre, thus driving up the price of housing. The problem for a low-income family willing to accept the higher transportation costs of living in a suburb is that the multifamily housing such a household could afford is simply not available as a result of large-lot **exclusionary zoning**. Thus, political decisions over land use changes the final disposition of land and its price from what the market would otherwise establish.

Taking factors other than simple bid rent curves into account is also necessary because there are many things that individuals want when deciding where to live. The ideal home might be a place with an incredible view, with just the right proximity to work, friends, and shopping. To be optimal, it would be exactly the right size and would have precisely the features desired by the owner. It would be far from the things that people try to avoid such as pollution and crime, but would have access to outdoor activities, entertainment, or other sources of enjoyment.

Typically, however, the ideal home in the ideal location is not attainable for any but the wealthiest families. Just about everyone else is faced with a range of constraints when making choices. One constraint is simply that the ideal home in the ideal place may not exist; it is a figment of imagination. More likely, there are budget constraints; most of us cannot afford the perfect place with all the features we desire. There are constraints imposed by social institutions. For example, a city may not allow the construction of housing in the most desirable location because of environmental laws. Social convention or outright discrimination may limit housing choices for particular racial or ethnic groups. Instead of being able to get everything we want, we have to consider what is feasible, examine the trade-offs contained in this more limited set of possibilities, and then select from among the available and affordable alternatives.

The Evolution of Twentieth-First-Century US Metropolitan Areas

With the Alonso theory and some understanding of the social and political constraints placed on location as preface, we can examine the way land use in American cities changed over the course of the twentieth century leading into the twenty-first. We first examine the factors that affected business location and then turn our attention to changes in residential location.

As technology opened up the possibility of new, cheaper forms of transportation, other costs of production became relatively more important. To remain competitive, company managers had to solve a more complex cost equation in which transport costs were only one item in a growing list.

Essentially, managers had to reconsider the fundamental equation for business profits:

$$profits = total\ revenue\ (TR) - total\ costs\ (TC)$$

where total revenue refers to the total value of the goods and services sold by the firm and total costs refers to all the costs a firm incurs in producing its product or service.

In our simple bid rent model, we assumed that all the wheat farmers faced identical production costs, as did all the tomato farmers. None of the farmers needed to take tax rates into account because our simple model did not include any role for government. Although the bid rent curve illustrates the trade-off between rent and transportation costs, we must acknowledge that production costs, site costs, taxes, and government regulatory burden can also vary at different locations throughout the metropolitan area and from one metro region to another. These factors can influence the choice of a site, once transportation is assured.

Looking more closely at the concept of costs, we can identify five broad categories:

- **Production costs** are incurred in the actual manufacture of a good or service, including the cost of labor and raw material

- **Transportation costs** are incurred in moving inputs to business and shipping the output to points of sale

- **Site costs** are incurred in procuring the land and buildings that the business occupies

- **Taxes** and **fees** comprise levies imposed on business by local, state, and federal government

- **Regulatory costs** are incurred by business in the course of complying with local, state, and federal law, including environmental protection requirements

As this list makes evident, to maximize profits, business owners must ultimately consider a large number of location-dependent costs and array these against the economies of scale and agglomeration economies offered by any particular location.

The location decisions of firms changed in the twentieth century, as transportation constraints weakened, the composition of industry shifted from resource extraction to manufacturing to services, and new products and new techniques of production emerged. The resulting shift in the geography of work sites contributed significantly to changes in the overall patterns of land use in urban areas. We can see this historically in the ever-changing location of business activity in the metro region with the rise of biotech in some regions and the contraction of autos and steel in others.

Post–World War II Business Location

As we noted in Chapter 3, early cities in the United States were built on the sea, along canals, or next to rivers because transportation costs dominated all others and water transport was the most efficient method available. In the nineteenth century, the railroad opened up the possibility of building cities away from the water and made it possible for cities to trade goods even when they did not share a common waterway. The early street railway and road systems made it possible for some people and some firms to move to the periphery beyond the central city, and thus the first inner-ring suburbs were born.

Constraints due to transportation costs continued to dissipate in the twentieth century. By 1950 fewer firms were limited by transportation, thanks to the dense web of paved highways and roads that had been constructed by local municipalities, states, and the federal government. Therefore, many locations could flourish in the production of each good and service. As we saw earlier, Detroit, still known as the Motor City because it was the center of production for the nation's three largest domestic producers—General Motors, Ford, and Chrysler—would lose its stature as the primary location for auto production throughout the last decades of the twentieth century. The corporate headquarters remained there, but production increasingly moved to other parts of the Midwest and the South, as well as to Canada and Mexico. With the ability to move parts and assemblies around the country by rail and by truck, Ford could assemble cars as cheaply in Atlanta and Chicago as in Dearborn, Michigan (a nearby suburb of Detroit). As transportation costs declined as a share of total costs, and as air-conditioning permitted comfortable living in the heat of Arizona or the heat and humidity of Florida, cities could expand almost anywhere, as long as there was a good reason for people to congregate at a particular place or region. Before the advent of air conditioning, Phoenix was hardly a town. With temperatures averaging greater than 100 degrees Fahrenheit in the summer, fewer than 5,600 called Phoenix home in 1900. By 1950, after air conditioning was becoming more common, the population had swollen to 107,000. Now, with air conditioning virtually available everywhere in the Southwest, Phoenix is home to nearly 1.7 million residents.

The post–World War II transportation revolution took many forms. The passage of the Federal-Aid Highway Act of 1956 (also known as the National Interstate and Defense Highways Act), which led to the construction of 42,500 miles of superhighways crisscrossing America, provided more direct, reliable, speedy truck transportation that reduced the costs of both short- and long-distance hauling. Wider, double-barreled highways with median strips permitted longer trucks and, in many locations, tandem trailers.

As for rail transportation, the full adoption of powerful diesel locomotives back in the 1940s and 1950s, replacing the slower and costlier steam-powered engines, made it possible to haul more container cars in a single train with fewer time-consuming stops to replenish fuel supplies. Double-stack container cars known as trailer on flat car (TOFC) provided more volume for cargo, further reducing transportation costs.

Perhaps most critically, new technology has also revolutionized ocean transport, making it ever easier and cheaper to ship goods from continent to continent. Containerization became the way to move goods across land to sea and back to land. The efficiency with which containers could be transferred and the economies of scale associated with larger ships led companies to greatly increase the size of cargo ships. While the first ships to carry containers (introduced in the 1950s and 1960s) were converted bulk cargo ships or tankers and carried fewer than 1,000 containers, ships specifically built for container shipping emerged in 1968. Built with space for between 1,000 and 2,500 containers, they were widely adopted in the 1970s. As container shipping became widespread, container size was standardized as 20-foot-equivalent units (TEUs). As international shipping continued to increase in the 1980s, ships as large as the Panamax standard (with capacity up to 4,800 TEUs, the limit for the Panama Canal) were created and by the mid-1990s ships larger than the Panamax limit (known as post-Panamax ships) were crossing the Pacific, Atlantic, and Indian Oceans carrying trade between Asia and West Coast ports such as Seattle and Los Angeles/Long Beach, within Asia, between Asia and Europe (through the Suez Canal) and between other continents around the world (CanagaRetna 2013; Rodrigue 2020). Ship size continued to grow from 6,000 to 8,000 TEUs during the 1990s.

To compete for more of the international shipping trade, to reduce the cost of shipping from Asia to the US East Coast, and to alleviate the long delays that often existed for passage through the Panama Canal, a major project was begun in 2011 to widen and deepen the Panama Canal to allow the passage of larger vessels. Completed in 2016, the new Panama Canal is able to handle ships of up to 14,500 TEUs (the new-Panamax limit). But the increasing demand for international goods and economies of scale associated with further improvements in ship technology and in dockside crane technology (to load and offload containers) have led to even larger container ships travelling through other routes—and to ports—that can handle their size. In 2017, Samsung introduced the first vessel capable of carrying more than 20,000 TEUs (the 20,170 TEU MOL Triumph). By the end of 2020, more than 70 ships of more than 20,000 TEUs were in operation. The seven largest of these, in a fleet operated by HMM in South Korea, each carry 23,964 TEUs.

The transportation revolution has made it possible for global corporations to build their products pretty much anywhere. By the end of the twentieth century, General Motors Corporation (GM) was producing its sporty Pontiac GTO for the American market in Australia, shipping key components from the United States for assembly Down Under and then shipping the completed vehicles back to the United States for distribution and sale. Excess assembly capacity in GM's Holden car division in Australia encouraged the company to use this production strategy for their specialized, limited-production, high-performance vehicle. Without the revolution in shipping technology and in communications that made such production coordination possible, long-distance manufacturing would not have become anywhere near as cost effective.

Satellite-linked telephone communication followed the successful launch of America's first human-made satellites in 1958, and now cell phone coverage is worldwide. By 2020, more than 5.1 billion people owned a cell phone, a full two-thirds of the global population. Jumbo jet aircraft—such as the Boeing 747 first introduced in 1969—provided nonstop service to most places on earth. By 2007, the European Airbus A380-800 had become the largest passenger jet airlines in the skies, capable of carrying more than 850 passengers on its double-deck configuration. Together, these technologies made it possible to ship higher-valued cargo across the globe at nearly the speed of sound, and gave corporate managers the ability to travel halfway across the earth in a single day and to coordinate worldwide production of goods and services at nearly the speed of light.

With all the new transportation and communications technology available to business, transportation costs plummeted in the second half of the twentieth century. Glaeser and Kohlhase report that by 2001, the average cost adjusted for inflation of moving a ton of goods one mile by rail was only one-eighth of what it had been in 1890. When all forms of transportation were taken into account (including trucking, which is more expensive than rail), the transportation costs for goods fell by more than 1 percent each year between 1960 and 1992 (Glaeser and Kohlhase 2004). The lowered transportation costs and the consequent freedom for businesses to consider locations farther away allowed firms to search widely in a bid to lower other input costs—most importantly, the cost of labor. In competitive industries, the ability to use lower-cost labor in the American South encouraged firms to take advantage of this option or to seek out highly specialized labor that added to the value of the end product. Atlanta, Miami, Houston, and other southern cities became powerful business centers that rivaled many in the Northeast and Midwest. The population center of the United States moved south and west.

The effect of these changes on manufacturing costs, and the subsequent decision by many manufacturing companies to move production to other geographic areas, has been called **deindustrialization**. In *The Deindustrialization of America,* Bluestone and Harrison (1982) identify four dynamics that affected cities: (1) the redirection of profits from successful plants in existing locations to build new facilities elsewhere, (2) decisions not to replace machinery that was wearing out or becoming obsolete so that the money saved could be used to build facilities elsewhere, (3) relocating some of the equipment from one facility to a new facility in a distant location, and (4) shutting down plants and moving or selling the building and equipment. As we shall see in Chapter 5, where we discuss the dynamics underlying the prosperity of cities, the relocation of key businesses and industries without their replacement by new businesses has both direct and indirect effects on the economy of metropolitan areas.

The key point is that in the decades following World War II, the viability of many older cities was placed in jeopardy as new locations vied to be production centers for their once-vaunted goods. With the revolution in transportation technology, older urban areas were threatened (e.g., Detroit, Akron, and Toledo), while newer urban areas in the South and West—and increasingly in Mexico, in Europe, and in Japan—became production centers for consumer products used everywhere in the country.

As they recovered from the devastation of the second World War, European countries including Germany, Denmark, Sweden, and England once again became major manufacturing centers offering products, including the BMW and Mercedes automobiles, to a worldwide audience. By 2015 China led the world in manufacturing output, generating more than $2 trillion in products that were being sold worldwide. China had 6 of the top 10 export ports in the world and six of the most important manufacturing cities including Shanghai, Beijing, Ningbo, Hangzho, Guanzhou, and Shenzhen. The top 10 products China now sells to its own citizens and to consumers across the world are, in order of value: (1) personal computers, (2) mobile phones, (3) solar cells, (4) air conditioners, (5) shoes, (6) cement, (7) energy-saving lamps, (8) ships, (9) clothing, and (10) coal.

Table 4.3 provides a list of the top industrial countries of the world with the dollar values of their industrial production. China alone was responsible for 20 percent of the total world output of manufactured goods, with the United States

TABLE 4.3. TOP 20 MANUFACTURING COUNTRIES WORLD-WIDE - 2015

COUNTRY	ANNUAL MANUFACTURING OUTPUT (USD IN $BILLIONS)	PERCENT OF NATIONAL OUTPUT	PERCENT OF TOTAL GLOBAL MANUFACTURING
China	$2,010	27%	20%
United States	1,867	12%	18%
Japan	1,063	23%	10%
Germany	700	23%	7%
South Korea	372	29%	4%
India	298	16%	3%
France	274	11%	3%
Italy	264	16%	3%
United Kingdom	244	10%	2%
Taiwan	185	31%	2%
Mexico	175	19%	2%
Spain	153	14%	2%
Canada	148	11%	1%
Brazil	146	11%	1%
Russia	139	11%	1%
Turkey	125	18%	1%
Indonesia	115	22%	1%
Poland	100	20%	1%
Switzerland	93	0.18	0.01
Netherlands	88	12%	1%

Source: United Nations Conference on Trade and Development 2015

in second place with 18 percent and Japan at 10 percent. In terms of percentage of national output, the two countries that lead in manufacturing are Taiwan (31%) and South Korea (29%).

The Rise of the Post–World War II American Suburb

Nothing transformed the relationship between city and suburb more than the automobile. It was the dramatic increase in automobile ownership after World War II that led to explosive growth in suburban residential development not only in the United States, but in countries across the globe. Instead of locating within walking distance of stops along the rail lines, individuals could locate any where there were roads. Residential development, which had been concentrated along the rail line spokes, spread out to cover a broader area. In 1948, there were 33 million automobiles registered in the United States. By 1960, there were 61 million cars on the road and the number doubled again to 124 million by 1980. By 2020, the number of registered automobiles reached 144 million. Counting trucks, the total number of vehicles in the United States exceeded 230 million.

The percentage of families owning at least one automobile surged from 54 percent in 1948 to 77 percent in 1960 (US Bureau of the Census 1950; 2006). By 2016, it is reported that more than 91 percent of US households either owned their own vehicle or had ready access to one. For those who live in suburbs, the percentage owning automobiles approaches 100 percent. Nationwide, there are about 1.8 vehicles per household.

Yet vehicle ownership in central cities is much lower and varies greatly from city to city based on the density of each city and the availability of public transit. Across all major cities in the United States, the percentage with a motor vehicle ranges from just 45.6 percent in New York City to more than 95 percent in Fort Worth, Texas (Naciag 2017).

While individual states built new highways that connected city to suburb and city to city, it was the passage of the 1956 Federal-Aid Highway Act that ultimately put the national economy on wheels. The interstate highway system not only facilitated interstate commerce but also allowed workers to commute longer distances and consumers to drive to the suburban mall for convenient retail shopping within the same metro area. Living in the suburbs became feasible for tens of millions of families whose breadwinners worked in the central city or in rapidly growing office parks and shopping centers constructed adjacent to suburban highways and circumferential roads.

Suburbanization was also spurred by changes in technology associated with the construction of housing. In the early twentieth century houses were typically built one at a time, with most contractors building no more than five houses per year. However, after World War II, new mass-production techniques—including the standardization of building components and the implementation of a division of construction labor into simple, repetitive steps—were increasingly used to build suburban housing. These changes led to house building on an unprecedented scale and the development of massive suburban subdivisions. The largest of these, in Levittown, New York, comprised 17,400 houses (Jackson 1985). With such techniques, houses were built faster and were available at lower costs than before, adding to the economic incentives for families to move to suburbs.

Along with changes in residential location came a further decentralization of business locations. Corporate headquarters generally remained downtown in what became taller and taller office towers, where managers could meet face-to-face with their accountants, lawyers, and other business service providers. With prime real estate downtown escalating in price per square foot, it no longer made economic sense for manufacturers and those who operated warehouses to stay there or in the inner ring of suburbs. Cheaper and faster transportation made it cost effective to move to suburban locations farther and farther from the central business district. The rapidly increasing highway and road system that surrounded the city made it possible for employees to travel to work and for their products to get to market.

The Impact of Federal Policies on Suburbanization

Not surprisingly, there was an emptying out of the residential areas in most older central cities after World War II, as the highway network expanded and autos and trucks became the primary mode of transportation. Downtown department stores and other retail outlets followed suit, moving to the suburbs to be near their customers. The federal government also reinforced this trend toward suburbanization through Internal Revenue Service (IRS) personal income tax provisions that favored homeownership and through the operations of two of its agencies, the Federal Housing Authority (FHA) and the Veterans Administration (VA). When federal income taxes were established in 1913, the provisions included a deduction for interest paid on home mortgages, which made homeownership more economically advantageous than renting. This did not help renters who lived in central city apartment buildings—at least until late in the twentieth century, when many apartments were converted to owner-occupied condominiums. For most of the post–World War II period up until then, this tax provision spurred the production of single-family homes in suburbia. The deductibility of local residential property taxes against the federal income tax made the bias in favor of homeownership even greater.

Changes in the structure of home mortgages added to the demand for homeownership, and therefore the choice of suburbia for many families. Before the early 1930s a five- to seven-year mortgage was typical, with a high down payment, interest rates of up to 12 percent, and a substantial final payment. The sudden economic downturn that began in 1929 created high unemployment and numerous defaults on mortgages. To stabilize the situation of both home buyers and lenders, the federal government created the Home Owners Loan Corporation (HOLC) in 1933 to provide a means for homeowners in cities and suburbs to refinance their loans at low interest rates over 15 years. A year later, the federal government created the Federal Housing Authority (FHA) to insure private bank loans used for buying or repairing homes. This made it possible for banks and other mortgage lenders to offer even lower mortgage interest rates and the extension of mortgages to as long as 30 years.

In practice, the FHA guidelines supported newly constructed single-family homes to the exclusion of other forms of new housing and to the detriment of the existing housing stock. Families who might have preferred homes in more densely populated parts of urban areas found that they often were not eligible for the new low-interest, long-term mortgages. For such families, there was a great incentive to build their new home in the suburbs. In sum, the HOLC and FHA provided another major shift in trade-offs for families' residential decisions not only by reducing the cost of moving, but also by reducing the forgone benefits of staying.

Meanwhile, in efforts to reduce housing shortages for veterans returning from World War II, the Veterans Administration created a mortgage program under the Servicemen's Readjustment Act of 1944, which allowed veterans to buy houses with no down payment. The mortgage loans were guaranteed by the federal government—if the person who took out the loan defaulted, the government would pay the lender the amount remaining on the loan—so that lenders incurred no risks (Jackson 1985; Palen 1995). The FHA and VA programs, together with the highway transport revolution, led to a mushrooming of suburbs at the end of World War II, when wartime restrictions on residential construction were removed.

By 1950, the population of suburbs was growing 10 times faster than the population in central cities. After 1950 central city populations began to decrease sharply in many metro areas, as the number of people leaving cities for suburbs surpassed the number of people moving to the central cities. We can see this general trend by looking at just two cases—San Francisco and Detroit—illustrated in Figures 4.5a and 4.5b. This figure presents the decennial central city population living in San Francisco from 1900 through 2000. Note that the population more than doubled through mid-century, but from 1950 through 1980, it declined. Only after 1980 was there a movement back into the central city, and it took until 2000 for the Golden City to regain the population peak it had a half-century earlier. Detroit's population had both a more meteoric rise and more meteoric fall than San Francisco. As Figure 4.5 reveals, Detroit's population grew six times over in the first half of the twentieth century only to see its population fall by 50 percent in the next half-century. Indeed, Detroit's central city population at the turn of the twenty-first century was smaller than it was in 1920, just after the end of World War I.

Among all metro areas in the United States, the percentage of the metropolitan population living in central cities remained roughly constant at 63 to 66 percent between 1910 and 1940. But just 20 years later in 1960, it was down to half (51.4%) of the total metro population. The suburbs were burgeoning. In the next 40 years, the central city population continued to decline so that by 2000 only 38 percent of the US metro population was living there. By 2018, central city residents comprised less than 31 percent of the nation's metropolitan population. More than three-fifths of metro area residents lived in the suburbs, which were spreading farther and farther over the landscape.

With residential funding focused on suburban areas and in the new cities of the South and the West, the housing stock in central cities deteriorated, particularly in the older industrial cities of the Northeast and the Midwest. Older housing in need of repair suffered from a lack of viable financing alternatives. Abandoned buildings became common in many cities. This generated another incentive to move

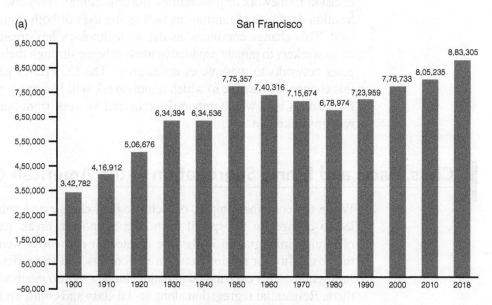

FIGURE 4.5A. City of San Francisco Population 1900–2018

https://www.biggestuscities.com/city/san-francisco-california

(b)

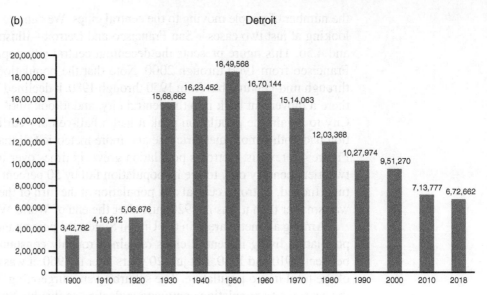

FIGURE 4.5B. City of Detroit Population 1900-2018

Source: https://www.biggestuscities.com/city/detroit-michigan

to suburbs for those who had the choice. In many metro areas this resulted in the juxtaposition of increasingly wealthy suburbs surrounding increasingly dilapidated central cities, a phenomenon we still see in many metro regions today.

In summary, during the past 200 years innovations in transportation and housing construction, and a changing set of economic and political constraints, have shifted the balance of centripetal and centrifugal forces. This has changed the decision framework of possibilities and opportunity costs and has transformed the location decisions of families as well as the uses of both central and more distant land. This change continues, as digital technology has created opportunities for some workers to pursue productive work at home through their connection to computer networks to workplaces miles away. The COVID-19 pandemic accelerated this change. The extent to which remote work will become a permanent condition for workers who were temporarily required to work from home during the crisis remains unknown.

Class, Race, and Ethnic Segregation in the American City

While the combined impact of technological change and public policy decisions led to changes in the spatial form of metropolitan areas, each successive wave of foreign immigration in the late nineteenth and early twentieth centuries held the possibility for tension between newcomers and those descended from earlier immigrants. This contributed to major changes, not so much across cities as within them. Residential segregation along social class and ethnic and racial lines ensued; many cities had their "Chinatowns," "Greektowns," and "Poletowns," where families of one or another ethnic group congregated.

In those cases where proximity to work was an important factor in residential location, recruitment and hiring dynamics also contributed to the creation of segregated neighborhoods with relatively homogeneous populations. Some employers chose to recruit among certain ethnic groups; other employers found that hiring individuals referred by existing workers was worthwhile, thereby reinforcing ethnic segregation. For other firms, word of vacancies quickly spread within ethnic neighborhoods, even if the employer was not consciously seeking to recruit certain groups. To some extent, segregation was also a matter of personal choice, as many families chose to live near their coethnics for various forms of networking support. Thus, within the overall contours of centrifugal and centripetal forces, social and market forces existed for the clustering of individual groups.

Until World War II, the greatest urban disparities in job opportunities and living standards were found among White ethnic groups, especially in northern cities. But after World War II, with the full mechanization of the cotton harvest, newly unemployed Black farmworkers and sharecroppers from the Mississippi Delta and other parts of the Cotton Belt came north in search of blue-collar jobs. Whites from depressed communities in West Virginia, Kentucky, and Tennessee also followed the trail to manufacturing jobs in Midwestern cities. These workers sought jobs in the burgeoning auto, steel, and other manufacturing industries in cities like Detroit; Chicago; Gary, Indiana; Newark, New Jersey; and Cleveland, Ohio. More than 1.5 million Black Americans migrated out of the South between 1940 and 1950, followed by similar numbers in the 1950s and 1960s. The overwhelming majority came to the northeastern and north central states (US Bureau of the Census 1979, Table 8). Leah Platt Boustan (2016), an economic historian, used census data to examine outcomes for those who left and those who stayed. She found that while Black migrants earned substantially more than those who stayed behind, they competed against Black workers already residing in the north, making it more difficult to close the racial earnings gap in a segregated labor market. She also found that an increase in an area's minority population contributed to White suburbanization.

The period from 1910 into the 1930s was characterized by what historians call the first wave of the migration. The peak of the first wave that lasted from about 1914 into the 1930s occurred during the 1920s, when 749,000 Black Americans from the South moved to other regions. The second wave of the migration, between 1940 and 1970, was much larger. During this period, nearly 4.5 million Black Americans moved from the South to other parts of the United States. In the 1940s alone, migration reached almost 1.6 million. The most common destinations before 1940 were the northeastern and north central states, but the western states were a very significant migration destination after 1940.

The demographic patterns within metropolitan areas during this period reflect a history of discrimination. Racism manifested itself in labor and housing markets. Many employers refused to hire Blacks or relegated them to the lowest-paying menial positions. This helped to create what became in the following decades an increasing gulf between a rapidly rising standard of living for a predominantly White middle class in the suburbs and an overwhelmingly Black "underclass," increasingly concentrated in the central city (Wilson 1987; 1996).

Before 1920, racially motivated violence in a number of cities had led to the destruction of Black-owned homes, the forcible removal of families from White neighborhoods, and, in some instances, even loss of life. Black-owned businesses were destroyed in Chicago, Philadelphia, Tulsa, and Wilmington, North Carolina. Anti-Chinese riots occurred in Los Angeles, Denver, and Seattle. Just as proximity to work was a major historical constraint in residential decision-making for many families, discrimination and violence operated as a major constraint for some groups, affecting the possibilities and opportunity costs involved in their location decisions.

From 1930 on, however, the most influential discriminatory influences were actually federal government programs that helped many White families move to the suburbs—the Home Owners Loan Corporation (1933) and the Federal Housing Authority (1934). The HOLC and the FHA advocated both residential segregation and "redlining"—the explicit classification of Black neighborhoods as the least desirable areas for financial institutions to make mortgages and other loans. From 1930 to 1950, the official code of ethics of the National Association of Real Estate Boards, the professional group representing real estate brokers, stated that selling homes in White neighborhoods to Blacks would be a violation of professional standards. Racially restrictive covenants that barred both current and future sale of housing and land to non-Whites became common. Even in the absence of such documents, refusal to sell to non-Whites was typical in new post–World War II suburban communities, including the affordable communities filled with mass-produced housing, such as Levittown. The resulting demographic geography of metropolitan areas came to reflect distinct racial patterns in the period between 1920 and 1970. The discrimination visited on Black families would have repercussions on their children and grandchildren.

These discriminatory federal housing policies contributed to racial inequalities in wealth and income. By denying homeownership opportunities to Black families and by restricting the geographic areas in which they could reside, the groundwork was laid for the special vulnerability of such families decades later during the coronavirus pandemic. Poor housing and neighborhood conditions contributed to the high toll the virus took in Black communities. In the spring and summer of 2020 demonstrations for social justice focused on police brutality toward Blacks, but also recognized the vulnerabilities caused by the government-supported housing discrimination of the previous century.

With jobs moving to the suburbs and most Black workers trapped by residential segregation in central cities, the employment opportunities for inner-city residents deteriorated. With a growing gap between the wealth of the suburbs and the poverty of the central cities, anger spilled over into the streets of many cities. Major urban riots scarred Detroit, Newark, Washington, DC, Los Angeles, and a host of smaller cities in the mid-1960s.

Segregation, especially with regard to race, still dominates virtually all cities in the United States. Nevertheless, from 1970 to the present, as a result of the passage and enforcement of antidiscrimination laws in employment, housing, and lending, as well as changing racial attitudes, there has been a movement of Blacks, Asian Americans, and Latinx to suburban areas—or at least to a few specific suburban towns and cities. Today's metropolitan areas are demographically different from those of 50 years ago, just as those of 1950 were different from those of 1900.

In 2000, there was no single pattern that described every metro area. According to studies of the 2000 census, in 24 of the 102 largest metro areas, Blacks constituted 10 percent or more of suburban residents. Latinx and Asian suburban residents were found in large numbers in 35 of these largest metro areas—specifically, in those metro areas that were major centers of immigration during the 1990s.

As it turns out, however, Black migration to the suburbs is limited to a few suburbs in cities where barriers to outright discrimination came down. Because informal segregation still exists in most suburban communities, suburbs that permitted Black families to move into them often became segregated themselves.

A good example of this can be found in the suburbs just north of the City of Detroit's boundary at 8-Mile Road (Wilkinson 2016). In 1970 in Oak Park, on the northern boundary of Detroit, only 0.2 percent of the population was Black. A decade later the Black population had increased to 12 percent. But as the number of Black families increased in this near-in suburb, White families moved out. By 2000, Black families comprised 45.7 percent of the community's population and by 2017, 58.1 percent. Southfield, another of Detroit's inner suburbs, had an even more striking reversal in its demographic makeup. In 1970, Blacks made up only 0.1 percent of the population. By 2000, the proportion was 28.9 percent. By 2017, more than 7 out of 10 residents in this suburb were Black. By contrast, suburbs near Oak Park and Southfield still had Black populations of less than 5 percent. As discussed further in Chapter 14, considerable segregation remains in many metropolitan areas (Frey 2001; Glaeser and Vigdor 2001; Logan et al. 2001; Frey and Myers 2005). The history of migration flows and differences in economic opportunity still play a crucial role in the demographic patterns of US metropolitan areas.

New Immigration and the Cities

Until the mid-1960s the labor force in cities grew mainly through internal migration, since immigration had been restricted for the previous four decades. After 1965, however, the United States experienced a new wave of immigration from abroad. Congress passed the Hart-Cellar Act in 1965, with the intent of removing discrimination against Southern and Eastern Europeans by eliminating the national origins quotas that had favored Great Britain, Germany, and Ireland. The act placed new emphasis on family unification, which should have favored European nations, but when it passed it also removed quotas on residents in former British colonies, including Jamaica and Trinidad and Tobago. With Great Britain limiting immigration itself, far more immigrants came to the United States from these Caribbean countries than expected.

The new law also permitted political refugees from other countries to enter without quota and allowed immediate family members of US citizens (spouses, parents, and minor children) to be admitted outside of quotas. As a result, during the 1970s and 1980s a new wave of immigrants came to the United States, many coming to cities in the West and Southwest. War refugees from Vietnam and Cambodia came to California and Texas. Political refugees from El Salvador, Guatemala, and Nicaragua came north to escape civil war and civil strife. On the

East Coast, a flood of Cubans settled in Miami. Haitians and Jamaicans, fleeing political and economic strife, immigrated to cities such as New York and Boston. Ethiopians, fleeing civil war, came to Washington, DC. In the course of all this immigration, the combination of powerful push factors that emanated from political and economic repression and the pull factors of American jobs and a better standard of living helped repopulate many US cities.

Like those who came before them, today's immigrants tend to settle in the largest metropolitan areas in the country and in cities throughout the world. Indeed, more than half (54.5%) of all the foreign-born people now living in the United States live in the largest nine metropolitan areas of the country, those with populations of 5 million or more. By contrast, only 27.3 percent of the native-born population lives in these large urban centers. Immigrants make up nearly 38 percent of the population in the Los Angeles metro area and the New York metro area, nearly 35 percent in San Francisco, and more than 30 percent in Houston. The concentration of immigrants is particularly high within the central cities of large metropolitan regions, where more than one in four residents (26%) is now foreign born.

Combined with the native born, who come to these same central cities, often as college students and young professionals, the composition of many of these cities has undergone a dramatic transformation. To take one extraordinary example, as late as 1950 the city of Boston's population was 95 percent White, with large numbers of first-, second-, and third-generation Irish and Italian families. A decade later, the "minority" population, mostly Blacks, made up nearly 10 percent of the central city's residents. Just two decades later, in 1980, nearly one in three residents was Black, Latinx, or Asian. In just another two decades, in 2000, Boston's booming economy was anchored in a central city which was "majority minority," with just over half of the residents reporting they were Black, Asian, Latinx, Native American, or multiracial. By 2017, non-Latinx Whites comprised just 44.9 percent of the city's population.

Indeed, without the increased flow of immigration into America's 25 largest cities during the 1990s, these cities would have seen their combined population decline in size. In seven of these cities—San Diego, San Jose, New York, San Francisco, Chicago, Los Angeles, and Boston—the central cities grew only because of the presence of new immigrants (Sum and Pond 2002).

Immigration is by no means limited to US cities. In London, more than 36 percent of the city's population is foreign born. In Sydney, foreign-born residents now make up more than 45 percent of the population. In Toronto, the percentage is even higher: 47 percent. Even in the most French of all places on earth, Paris, the foreign born now comprise nearly 15 percent of all Parisians. And in Milan, more than 1 in 10 residents is foreign born.

Cross-Currents of the Late Twentieth Century: Sunbelt Cities, Edge Cities, and Gentrification

Toward the end of the twentieth century, further changes in transportation and communications as well as a new source of demographic change—the aging of the US population—contributed to the rapid growth of new cities in the South and West that were organized around recreation and retirement. In addition to the growth of these new metropolitan areas, existing metropolitan areas found that more and more of the traditional functions of the central city were now being replicated in the suburbs. Yet even as these phenomena seemed to reduce the importance of established central cities, other changes led to the resurgence in the desirability of central city living among a self-selected group of higher-income households. We examine each of these phenomena in turn.

The Rise of Sunbelt Cities

As the core of the US economy shifted away from **primary sector industries** (agriculture and mining) to **secondary sector industries** (manufacturing and construction) and then to the **tertiary sector industries** that are composed of wholesale and retail trade and business and personal service industries, the size and location of metropolitan areas came to depend less heavily on satisfying the need for transportation and more on the growth of mass consumer markets for an array of goods and services that were once only affordable by the affluent.

Tourism and retirement communities provide good examples. While tourism *contributes* to the economies of such cities as New York, Boston, and San Francisco (which have long economic histories based on trading and manufacturing), it became an important *foundation* of economic growth for places like Orlando and Las Vegas. In 1960, before Walt Disney World was built in Orlando, the Orlando metropolitan area had a total population of 395,000. By the end of the century the Orlando metro area held almost 1.65 million residents, its growth fueled largely by its emergence in the last decades of the century as one of the foremost vacation and convention destinations in the world. By 2017, Orlando's population exceeded 2.57 million. Similarly, the Las Vegas metro area had fewer than 275,000 residents in 1970; three decades later, due to economic growth based mainly on tourism, it too had ballooned to 1.6 million residents and by 2017 it had 2.2 million.

Important changes in consumer spending made these developments possible. Through the course of the twentieth century, airplane travel ceased to be the province of the wealthy, as it had been before mid-century. Similarly, the paid vacation became a common job benefit during World War II, when unions could not easily negotiate wage increases because of wartime wage and price controls. Cheaper, quicker travel and more leisure time made tourism a skyrocketing industry. The growth in the number of relatively affluent retirees contributed not only to the demand for tourism but also for year-round retirement communities. These trends, augmented by the introduction and spread of air-conditioning, were responsible for propelling the boomtown cities of the South and Southwest as tourist destinations, convention locales, and places for northern retirees to leave their winter homes behind.

The Rise of Edge Cities

The term **edge city** was coined by the journalist Joel Garreau (1991) to describe a pattern of urban growth where there are multiple urban cores in the outer rings of metropolitan areas. Edge cities are often built around large retail malls or the intersection of two or more major highways located well beyond the central city. They are sometimes called suburban business districts, suburban cores, mini-cities, urban subcenters, or even superburbia, technoburbs, peripheral centers, urban villages, or suburban downtowns. An edge city, according to Garreau's criteria, must have a minimum of 5 million square feet of leasable office space and at least 600,000 square feet of retail space. Using these criteria, there were approximately 250 edge cities in North America by the end of the twentieth century, with Southern California, the metro area of Washington, DC, and metro New York having the largest concentrations. These edge cities contained two-thirds of all the office space in the United States, up from just 25 percent in 1970 (Soja 2001). With the rise of edge cities where both jobs and housing are located, cross-commuting between suburbs increased dramatically (Judd and Swanstrom 2004).

The archetypal edge city is Tysons Corner, Virginia, outside Washington, DC. It is located near the junctions of Interstate 495, Interstate 66, and Virginia 267 (the route from Washington, DC, to Dulles International Airport). Until a few decades ago Tysons Corner was little more than a small village, but by the end of the 1990s it was home to the largest retail area on the East Coast south of New York City, with 6 anchor department stores and more than 230 stores in all, more than 3,400 hotel rooms, more than 100,000 jobs, and more than 25 million square feet of office space. Using census tract data on commuting patterns from the 1960 and 2000 censuses, Baum-Snow (2010) was able to demonstrate the role of new highway construction in decentralizing the location of businesses as well as households.

Going back to the Alonso model, we can see how the rise of edge cities changes the shape of bid rent curves. The bid rent curves we presented earlier in this chapter were drawn on the basis of **monocentrism** or **mononuclearity**—one central city with land values that decline the farther away one moves from the center. Until the massive relocation of firms and households after World War II, this was an eminently reasonable model that described well the evolving pattern of metro areas. With the development of new centers of commerce and with residential communities located farther and farther away from the central city, monocentrism no longer prevailed. Nonetheless, the general implication of the bid rent curve analysis still applies: the places to which people want access will increase in value. In the final chapter of *Location and Land Use,* Alonso (1964) considered several types of polycentric metropolitan forms, one of which has two independent centers of unequal size. This model is similar to the notion of edge cities.

If the bid rent curves used to decline monotonically, we can now replace those bid rent curves with ones that decline with distance away from the center, but have upticks as the distance to an edge city or a circumferential highway interchange declines (see Figure 4.6).

In some metropolitan areas, such upticks occur in a radius around an inner-ring circumferential highway and again around an outer-ring circumferential highway. It is no coincidence that many of the newer edge cities are in just such places. Thus, although we need to recognize the limitations of the bid rent curve analysis, we can also acknowledge that the fundamental ideas contained in this formulation provide

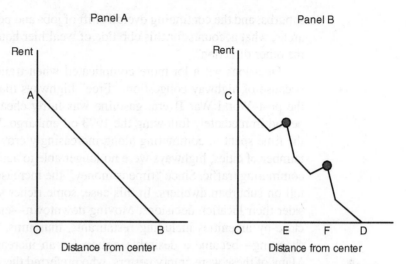

FIGURE 4.6. A Monocentric Bid Rent Curve versus a Bid Rent Curve for a Region with Edge Cities

Panel A: In a monocentric city, the bid rent curve declines steadily the farther away from the center one travels because the center is the only point to which people desire access.

Panel B: With the advent of edge cities, there is more than one place to which people want access. If there is significant economic activity in edge cities along an inner-ring circumferential highway OE miles from the center and an outer-ring circumferential highway OF miles from the center, access to these sites will raise their land value, as reflected in upticks on the bid rent curve.

a helpful tool in understanding the dynamics of urban land markets, even in this new era of edge cities and the dense suburb.

> Panel A: In a monocentric city, the bid rent curve declines steadily the farther away from the center one travels because the center is the only point to which people desire access.
>
> Panel B: With the advent of edge cities, there is more than one place to which people want access. If there is significant economic activity in edge cities along an inner-ring circumferential highway OE miles from the center and an outer-ring circumferential highway OF miles from the center, access to these sites will raise their land value, as reflected in upticks on the bid rent curve.

Since 1980, there have been new centrifugal forces emerging from developing technology. Information retrieval through the internet, videoconferencing, and other advances have made possible virtually instantaneous communication from remote locations. With this has come an even greater expansion in edge cities, which rely upon continuing advances in transportation technology to allow firms and customers to locate even farther out from central city locations.

Central Cities and Gentrification

Even as edge cities continued to grow, many central cities experienced a renaissance as they became more attractive to some higher-income households. Given all the reasons discussed earlier for why higher-income households moved to the suburbs, and the continuing overall shift of jobs and population growth to suburban areas, what accounts for this ebb tide of wealthier households choosing to move in the other direction?

Decisions get a lot more complicated when transportation costs rise sharply because of highway congestion. "Free" highways may exist, and during much of the post–World War II era, gasoline was fairly cheap, with the exception of the period immediately following the 1973 oil embargo. What became expensive was the time spent in commuting along increasingly crowded roadways. In a growing number of cities, highways were no longer able to accommodate the heavy load of commuting traffic. Since "time is money," the increase in commuting time took its toll on suburban dwellers. In this case, some richer suburbanites began to reconsider their location decisions. Moving downtown—especially given the variety of close-by amenities including restaurants, museums, music venues, and boutique shopping—became a desirable option for an increasing number of households. Many of these were empty nesters, who preferred the suburbs while raising school-age children, but for whom the central city now provided the preferred place to live. Young professionals—usually without children—were also attracted to the central city for the same amenities.

In some cities, this form of relocation gave way to a new model of residential land use: high-rent apartments and townhouses at the center for the well-to-do, a ring of low-income tenants in the city around the central core, and middle-income families in the suburbs. This process, called **gentrification**, can also be illustrated using Alonso's bid rent curves. Our earlier discussion of the residential paradox was based on the assumption that everyone wanted to live at low density. However, if we acknowledge that there are some groups who prefer high density and that these groups, albeit small in number, are growing, we can introduce a third bid rent curve into the analysis. Figure 4.7 illustrates this case by adding another bid rent curve to the previous figure that reflects the preferences of those who choose high density.

There is a small group of high-income households, represented by bid rent curve EF, who prefer high density and can outbid lower-income households for the land near the center. In places where this has happened, it is more difficult for low-income households to find affordable housing.

This group behaves analogously to the tomato farmers in our earlier agricultural example. The households in this group place a high value on access to the center, and they have the ability to outbid other groups. Many lower-income households find themselves squeezed out of some central areas but still not able to compete for places in more expensive suburbs. Instead, in many metro areas there has been a movement of lower-income households to some less sought after older industrial suburbs, just beyond the central city boundary. In some metro areas where this possibility does not exist, or where the supply of housing in such suburbs is insufficient for those being displaced, the problems of homelessness and the lack of affordable housing have reached crisis proportions. The poor are forced to accept even greater overcrowding in the central city or leave the metro area altogether.

Along with the growth of Sunbelt cities and edge cities, gentrification helps us to understand some of the changing patterns of location that affected US metropolitan areas toward the end of the twentieth century.

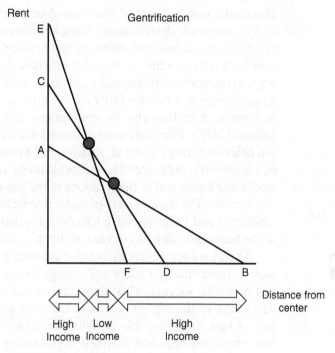

FIGURE 4.7. Bid Rents with Gentrification

The Changing Fortunes of Individual Cities

As the importance and location of particular industries have changed, so have the fortunes of their cities. The extraction of minerals and the production of other natural resources, including agricultural products and timber, continued to fuel the growth of a number of cities in the late nineteenth and early twentieth centuries. For example, Butte, Montana, the site for one of the largest copper mines in the world, expanded rapidly as copper was needed for wire, electric generators, and electric motors, given the inventions of Thomas Edison and Tesla. From less than 3,400 residents in 1880, Butte's population mushroomed to nearly 42,000 by 2020. By contrast, Charleston, West Virginia decreased in importance relative to places like Tulsa, Oklahoma and New Orleans once oil and gas replaced coal as a major energy source. In 1960 Charleston's population peaked at nearly 86,000; by 2019, its had shrunk to less than 47,000 as dependence on "King Coal" gave way to reliance on oil.

Similarly, the location of key manufacturing industries—including autos, tires, glass, and machine tools—dispersed from Detroit and other midwestern cities to rural towns in Tennessee and Kentucky, as well as to other countries including Japan, Sweden, Germany, and Korea. The interstate highway system and national rail networks made it possible to move assemblies, parts, and finished products over longer distances at cheaper prices, contributing to the decentralization of manufacturing.

As transportation modes switched from canal and railroad to truck and airplane, individual cities saw their fortunes rise or fall. Access to interstate highways and airports could help stimulate local business trade with other regions and could also attract new businesses, while the absence of such infrastructure could lead to a city's economic deterioration. Some cities were better able than others (because of differences in financial resources and political power) to finance, build, and support such infrastructure. Other cities exercised greater creativity and sought new ways to integrate air traffic and economic growth. Atlanta, for example, integrated its emergence as a hub for Delta Airlines into a larger economic development plan to become a leading city for conventions and corporate offices (Altshuler and Luberoff 2003). Even the center of financial activity changed with the times; southern cities including Charlotte, Atlanta, and Miami became banking hubs for much of the country. Advances in communications led to changes in the markets for stocks and bonds and in the locations of the businesses that handled such financial instruments. The development of major research universities, including Stanford in California and Duke in North Carolina, challenged the great Ivy League schools of the Northeast, such as Harvard, Columbia, and Princeton, as innovation centers.

As technology advances, no city is assured of continued prosperity or dominance. Those that can adapt and change have a much greater chance of survival and economic success, while those that cannot see their economic vitality sapped. The ranks of the top 100 cities in terms of population provide just one indication of how important this is. With the value of steel for skyscraper production, auto manufacturing, and railroads skyrocketing at the beginning of the twentieth century, Birmingham, Alabama rose from the 99th-largest city in 1900 to 34th in 1930—only to fall back to 76th by 2000, as the US steel industry lost out to other building materials and to steel produced in Japan and Korea. Duluth, Minnesota, the home of the iron range where taconite for steel production is mined, went from the 92nd-largest city in 1890 to the 69th by 1920. But already by 1940, it had fallen back to 90th (US Bureau of the Census 1998).

In manufacturing, Detroit went from the 13th-largest city in 1900 to the 4th-largest in the country in 1930; by 2018 it had fallen to #23. Cleveland, home to the steel industry as well as auto manufacturing, declined from the 5th-largest city in 1920 to #54 in 2018. Meanwhile, Long Beach, California—home to the aircraft industry and tourism—had moved up from #57 in 1930 to #34 in 2004, before falling back to #43 by 2018. San Jose—home to Silicon Valley and high technology—skyrocketed from the 57th-largest city in 1960 to the 10th largest in America today. Back in 1900, the 10th-largest city was Cincinnati, Ohio, famous as the headquarters for Proctor and Gamble, one of the nation's premier producers of personal care products. Just as Cincinnati was eclipsed by San Jose, some of today's largest cities are likely to be eclipsed by the cities now at the cutting edge of twenty-first-century technologies.

Globalization and the Competition for Industry in the Twenty-First Century

For more than three decades, social scientists and journalists have been chronicling the **globalization** of business and world commerce and the impact on employment and income. Of course, trade and production processes involving interaction across continents are not new. Trade between continents was an important part of economic dynamics in many parts of the world. However, it is generally recognized that during the last half-century there has been an acceleration of many developments that have changed both the volume and the characteristics of today's global transactions.

Social scientists have been studying the repercussions of this trend, including the rising influence of multinational corporations and the enhanced role of particular cities in the world economy (Friedmann 1995; Sassen 2006; Schaeffer 2003; Storper 1997; Taylor et al. 2002). As the twenty-first century began, the context for trade, production, and investment was considerably different from the context that had existed just a few decades earlier and the implications of this change were being felt by cities across the Unites States.

The revolution in transportation technologies ushered in with the introduction of the jumbo jet, the supertanker, and the container ship made it possible for manufacturing firms to move their operations farther and farther away from where their products are actually consumed. With such revolutionary telecommunications technology as high-speed internet, mobile phones, and satellite links, all kinds of business services—from banking services, teleconferencing, and online technical assistance—can be coordinated and delivered from nearly anywhere on earth. By 2008 imports of goods and services in the United States equaled 17.5 percent of gross domestic product (GDP), up from 10 percent in 1990 and just 4 percent in 1967. Indeed, the import share in 1967 was no different than the share back in 1929 just before the Great Depression began, suggesting how recent and how rapidly the world has changed in terms of trade and globalization. Recessions have generally reduced imports as a share of GDP. The deep recession beginning in 2008 saw a sharp cut in imports and since that time the foreign share of total US output has averaged around 15 percent per year.

As Friedman noted, "It is now possible for more people than ever to collaborate and compete in real time with more other people on more different kinds of work from more different corners of the planet and on a more equal footing than at any previous time in the history of the world—using computers, e-mail, fiber-optic networks, teleconferencing, and dynamic new software" (2005, p. 8). All the knowledge centers around the globe can now be connected into a single network of producers and consumers. Individuals as well as firms can connect to each other in ways not imaginable a decade ago. Cities are leading the latest advances in communications infrastructure because they house the largest information producers: banks, law offices, insurance companies, financial service providers, corporate headquarters of national and international manufacturing enterprises, and retailers (Moss 1998). All this new technology is radically changing the role and function of cities and suburbs.

The twenty-first-century technology revolution permits the unprecedented expansion of two forms of global enterprise. **Outsourcing** involves the moving of specific limited functions originally performed within a company—a call center or a research lab—to another firm that performs the function and then sells parts or services to the original company. General Electric, the publisher Simon & Schuster, and Texas Instruments were early adopters of foreign outsourcing, finding companies that could produce parts or services for them in China, India, and other countries offering some combination of lower wages, appropriate skills, English-speaking workers, and fewer regulations. Circuit design is being accomplished in India for Texas Instruments while Simon & Schuster uses Indian computer operators to convert manuscript drafts into electronic formats for publishing. A company in Bangalore does medical transcriptions for US doctors and hospitals, reducing the transcription time from weeks to two hours and the cost by 80 percent (Friedman 2005).

The more dramatic new form of global business is **offshoring**. Here companies move an entire factory or production center to another country, using a central office back in the United States simply to coordinate production and distribution. With its enormous supply of unskilled and semiskilled labor, and now increasingly a pool of highly skilled labor, China has become the prime location for offshoring activity. If you want proof of this, check out where your cell phone was manufactured, your home television, your computer, or nearly any electronic device you own. With China so successful at attracting US companies to its shores for production purposes, other countries including Thailand, Malaysia, Ireland, Mexico, Brazil, and Vietnam have offered low wages for increasingly high-skilled labor hoping to attract the offshore activity of American firms. The result: while in 1995, 90 percent of manufactured goods consumed by Americans were produced in the United States, less than a decade later the proportion had declined to 75 percent and continues to fall. By 2019, only about 51 percent of the manufactured goods that Americans purchased was produced domestically.

As outsourcing and offshoring have increased, American firms—as well as those of Europe and increasingly elsewhere in the world—have become truly multinational, buying companies in other countries. Ford bought Jaguar and Land Rover of the United Kingdom (in 1989 and 2000, respectively), half of Volvo of Sweden (acquired in 1998), and one-third of Mazda of Japan (acquired in 1999). General Motors is the parent company to Sweden's Saab (half of which it acquired in 1990 and the other half in 2000) and Germany's Opel (which it has owned since 1931). From 1998 to 2007, Chrysler was actually owned by the German company Daimler Benz. Sony Corporation of Japan bought Columbia Pictures of the United States in 1989 and 20 percent of the US media company MGM (Metro-Goldwyn-Mayer) in 2005. The Tata Group, one of the largest firms in India, bought the US firm Tyco's international network of underwater cables in 2005, and acquired Corus, a large English and Dutch steel firm, in 2007.

With so much multinational activity, managing the **supply chains** across far-flung operations has become a major activity of business executives. When done efficiently, these supply chains—linking together innovative research and development (R&D) activities, the actual production of parts and final assemblies, and the distribution of final products to customers across many suppliers—result in companies such as Wal-Mart, Home Depot, and IKEA being able to offer a wide array of consumer goods at very low prices to their customers. In the process, however, the ability to source parts and labor from all over the world eliminates large numbers of traditional jobs in the United States and exerts downward pressure on American workers' wages and benefits. The result for many cities in the late post–World War II period was a continuation of the **deindustrialization** we discussed in Chapter 4, the wholesale loss of factories and jobs to other parts of the country or to other nations. In the twenty-first century, these same pressures are bubbling up in more highly skilled fields and have invaded all kinds of services as well as manufacturing.

At the same time that the transportation and communications revolutions have allowed outsourcing and offshoring, computers have permitted more and more skilled people to do their work by **telecommuting** and **teleconferencing**. Instead of coming to a central workplace such as an office or retail shop, individuals can perform their work from home by reading and writing reports, meeting electronically with coworkers to coordinate production, or selling goods and services over the internet or by telephone. The exact extent and growth of telecommuting is not known, but a recent study of commuting data between 1990 and 2004 indicates that the category that encompasses such work, "working at home," is one of the fastest growing categories in commuting patterns (Pisarski 2006). The advent of COVID-19 in early 2020 led to an explosion in telecommuting and teleconferencing using Zoom. Many expect that when the pandemic ends some will return to work on-site but others will continue to work remotely, given all the new technology that permits such work activity. This is providing new—or at least different—forms of employment for an increasing number of workers and new and different opportunities and challenges for cities and suburbs.

Weber and the Twenty-First-Century City

In the location models of the twentieth century, transportation costs and communication costs were so important that they were seen as the prime determinants of where firms located. In the Weber models, transportation costs are the key determinant of firm location over *long* distances. A resource-oriented firm will locate near the source of its raw materials, while a consumer-oriented firm will locate near where its consumers live. Copper for electronic devices will not only be mined from deep deposits and open pits in Arizona, but also smelted and refined near the mines to reduce the weight of the product to be shipped to electronics producers. Haircuts, on the other hand, will be provided in barbershops close to where the consumers live or work, in order to cut down on the transportation costs of getting the barber to the customer or vice versa. If transportation costs are high in terms of the dollar cost of getting from point A to point B or high in terms of the opportunity cost of the time needed to traverse this distance, it makes sense for the producers of services to be near their customers.

The basic Weber graphs were reasonably appropriate as descriptive approximations of firm location decisions for most of the twentieth century, but as the turn of the current century approached and transportation and communication costs decreased dramatically, their direct applicability to location decisions in the real world became more tenuous. The internet and related technological developments particularly revolutionized the relationship between communication and physical proximity. By the end of the century it was possible to communicate with coworkers instantaneously via e-mail at virtually no cost, whether they were located next door, across the city, across the state, across the nation, or across the globe. Videoconferencing makes it possible to have real-time meetings even though the participants are separated by thousands of miles. A person in downtown Denver, another in suburban Denver, a third in Miami, and a fourth in Singapore can videoconference—all without leaving their buildings. The cost of transportation also continued to decline with the proliferation of business jets for corporate executives and overnight delivery services such as FedEx. As the twenty-first century began, factors other than transportation and communication costs were beginning to dominate the location decisions of firms. If labor costs decline with distance from the customer, then as transportation costs become less important, labor costs will become more important in determining location. As a result, producers will move to wherever labor costs are lowest. This could be anywhere in the world, but developing countries are especially attractive.

While reduction of transportation and communication costs to zero may seem an extreme assumption, something close to this is happening in some industries. Due to advances in communication technology, much information that in earlier times was carried from place to place and delivered as documents or as face-to-face conversation, can now be transferred virtually without cost around the globe. This has fueled the relocation not only of manufacturing plants but also call centers, accounting services, and other information-based services to countries where labor costs and site costs are lower than in the United States.

Some services, of course, must be located near the customer almost regardless of site costs or labor cost. McDonald's may be able to find cheaper labor to fry hamburgers and french fries in Bangladesh than in Boston, but even if jumbo jet service were nearly free, the increased cost of flying in Big Macs to Boston-area customers exceeds the labor cost savings of putting their franchises in Boston neighborhoods. On the other hand, the ordering functions can be spun off to distant locations using electronic transmission. When you pull up to the drive-up window at your local McDonald's, your order may be received by someone hundreds of miles away, who then transmits it electronically to the person who is actually preparing your food (Friedman 2005).

The only thing certain about metro areas is that they will constantly and inevitably change, which, of course, is true of most things. Some of this change will be advantageous, as when new products and services evolve and their production is concentrated in certain regions. Some of this change causes great disadvantage, as when old products and services lose their luster and their markets; the cities where these goods and services were produced find themselves challenged to remain prosperous.

Now, in the twenty-first century, new technologies and global relations seem to be evolving faster than ever. How these new technologies and new relationships will interact with the chronic threats posed by climate change and the acute threats posed by pandemics such as COVID-19 to influence the fortunes of metropolitan areas and the cities and suburbs of which they are comprised remains an open question.

References

Albouy, David, Gabriel Ehrlich, and Minchul Shin. 2018. "Metropolitan Land Values." *Review of Economics and Statistics* 100 no. 3, p. 454-466.

Alonso, William. 1964. *Location and Land Use: Toward a General Theory of Land Rent*. Cambridge, MA: Harvard University Press.

Altshuler, Alan, and David Luberoff. 2003. *Mega-Projects: The Changing Politics of Urban Public Investment*. Washington, DC: Brookings Institution Press.

Baum-Snow, Nathaniel. 2007. "Did Highways Cause Suburbanization?" *Quarterly Journal of Economics* 122, no. 2: 775–805.

Baum-Snow, Nathaniel. 2010. "Changes in Transportation Infrastructure and Commuting Patterns in U.S. Metropolitan Areas, 1960–2000." *American Economic Review Papers & Proceedings* 100, no. 2: 378–382.

Bluestone, Barry, and Bennett Harrison. 1982. *The Deindustrialization of America*. New York: Basic Books.

Boustan, Leah Platt. 2016. *Competition in the Promised Land: Black Migrants in Northern Cities and Labor Markets*. Princeton, NJ: Princeton University Press.

Burgess, Ernest. 1925. "The Growth of the City." In *The City*, edited by Robert Park, Ernest Burgess, and Roderick McKenzie. Chicago: University of Chicago Press, pp. 47–62.

Burgess, Ernest. 1929. "Urban Areas." In T. V. Smith and L. D. White, eds., *Chicago: An Experiment in Social Science Research*. Chicago: University of Chicago Press, pp. 113–138.

CanagaRetna, Sujit. 2013. "The Panama Canal Expansion and Ports in the Atlantic and Gulf Coast States." *The Book of the States, 2013*. Lexington, KY: Council of State Governments.

Davies, Alex. 2010. "Newly Freed from Height Limits, Paris Skyline Ready to Rise." *Greenhugger Magazine*, November 21.

Dunn, Edgar. 1954. *The Location of Agricultural Production*. Gainesville: University of Florida Press.

Frey, William H. 2001. "Melting Pot Suburbs: A Census 2000 Study of Suburban Diversity." Washington, DC: Brookings Institution, Center on Urban and Metropolitan Policy.

Frey, William, and Dowell Myers. 2005. "Racial Segregation in U.S. Metropolitan Areas and Cities, 1990–2000: Patterns, Trends, and Explanations." *Research Report 05-573*. Ann Arbor: University of Michigan, Population Studies Center, Institute for Social Research.

Friedman, Thomas. 2005. *The World Is Flat: A Brief History of the Twenty-First Century*. New York: Farrar, Straus and Giroux.

Friedmann, John. 1995. "Where We Stand: A Decade of World City Research." In *World Cities in a World System*, edited by Paul Knox and Peter Taylor. Cambridge: Cambridge University Press, pp. 21-47.

Garreau, Joel. 1991. *Edge City: Life on the New Frontier*. New York: Doubleday.

Glaeser, Edward, and Janet Kohlhase. 2004. "Cities, Regions and the Decline of Transport Costs." *Papers in Regional Science* 83, no. 1 (January): 197–228.

Glaeser, Edward, and J. Vigdor. 2001. "Racial Segregation in the 2000 Census: Promising News." Washington, DC: Brookings Institution, Center on Urban and Metropolitan Policy.

Harris, Chauncy, and Edward Ullman. 1945. "The Nature of Cities." *Annals of the American Academy of Political and Social Science* 242, no. 1: 7–17.

Hoyt, Homer. 1939. *The Structure and Growth of Residential Neighborhoods.* Washington, DC: Federal Housing Administration.

Isard, Walter. 1956. *Location and Space-Economy: A General Theory Relating to Industrial Location, Market Areas, Land Use, Trade, and Urban Structure.* Cambridge, MA: MIT Press.

Jackson, Kenneth. 1985. *Crabgrass Frontier.* New York: Oxford University Press.

Judd, Dennis R., and Todd Swanstrom. 2004. *City Politics: Private Power and Public Policy.* New York: Longman.

Launhardt, Wilhelm. 1885. *Mathematische Begrundung der Volkswirtschafslehre.* Leipzig: W. Engleman. Trans. John Creedy (1993) as *Mathematical Principles of Economics.* Aldershot, UK: Edward Elgar.

Logan, John, Deirdre Oakley, Polly Smith, Jacob Stovell, and Brian Stults. 2001. "Separating the Children." Albany, NY: The Lewis Mumford Center.

Moss, Mitchell L. 1998. "Technology and Cities," *Cityscape,* 3 no. 3: 107-127.

Naciag, Mike. 2017. "Vehicle Ownership in U.S. Cities Data and Map." *Governing Magazine*, November 18.

Palen, J. John. 1995. *The Suburbs.* New York: McGraw-Hill.

Pisarski, Alan E. 2006. *Commuting in America III.* Washington, DC: Transportation Research Board.

Rodrigue, Jean-Paul. 2020. *The Geography of Transport Systems*, 5th ed. London: Routledge.

Sassen, Saskia. 2006. *Cities in a World Economy*, 3rd ed. Thousand Oaks, CA: Pine Forge Press.

Schaeffer, Robert. 2003. *Understanding Globalization: The Social Consequences of Political, Economic, and Environmental Change.* 2nd ed. Lanham, MD: Rowman & Littlefield.

Soja, Edward W. 2001. *Postmetropolis: Critical Studies of Cities and Regions.* Oxford: Blackwell.

Storper, Michael. 1997. *The Regional World.* New York: Guilford.

Sum, Andrew, and Nathan Pond. 2002. "The Contributions of Foreign Immigration to the Demographic Revival of America's and the Northeast Region's Big Cities in the 1990s." Boston: Northeastern University, Center for Labor Market Studies.

Taylor, Peter, David Walker, and Jon V. Beaverstock. 2002. "Firms and Their Global Service Networks." In *Global Networks, Linked Cities*, edited by Saskia Sassen. New York: Routledge, pp. xx–xx.

US Bureau of the Census. 1950. *Statistical Abstract of the United States.* Washington, DC: Government Printing Office.

US Bureau of the Census. 1979. "The Social and Economic Status of the Black Population in the United States: An Historical View, 1790–1978." *Department of Commerce, Current Population Reports Special Studies Series P-23*, no. 80. Washington, DC: Government Printing Office.

US Bureau of the Census. 1998. "Population of the 100 Largest Cities and other Urban Areas in the United States: 1770–1990." *Population Division Working Paper #27.* https://www.census.gov/library/working-papers/1998/demo/POP-twps0027.html

US Bureau of the Census. 2001. *Statistical Abstract of the United States, 2001.* Washington, DC: Government Printing Office.

US Bureau of the Census. 2005. *Statistical Abstract of the United States, 2005.* Washington, DC: Government Printing Office.

US Bureau of the Census. 2006. *Statistical Abstract of the United States, 2006.* Washington, DC: Government Printing Office.

von Thunen, Johann Heinrich. 1826. *Der Isolierte Staat in Beziehung auf Landwirtschaft und Nationalokonomie.* Dusseldorf: Verlag Wirtschaft und Finanzen. Trans. Peter Geoffrey Hall (1966) as *Isolated State: An English Edition of Der Isolierte Staat.* Oxford: Pergamon Press.

Wilkinson, Mike. 2016. "Black Flight to Suburbs Masks Lingering Segregation in Metro Detroit." *Bridge*, December 6.

Wilson, William Julius. 1987. *The Truly Disadvantaged: The Inner City, the Underclass and Public Policy.* Chicago: University of Chicago Press.

Wilson, William Julius. 1996. *When Work Disappears: The World of the New Urban Poor.* New York: Vintage.

Questions and Exercises

Land Values and Land Use in Metropolitan Areas

1. In the metropolitan area closest to you, or another one of your choice, where are largest manufacturing firms located? How about the largest financial industry firms and the largest retail businesses (for food, clothes, and for other goods bought by families)? How, if at all, can you relate the patterns you find to the Alonso model of land costs and land use? How, if at all, do the patterns you find reflect the location of the markets for the industries? How, if at all, do they reflect access to railroads, highways, airports, or harbors? How, if at all, do they reflect agglomeration economies?

The Rise of the Suburbs

2. This chapter discusses the construction of highways that connected cities to suburbs and suburbs to other suburbs. Go to the following website: www.mapquest.com.

Type in the name of a city of your choice and look at the road map MapQuest provides. Identify the major routes used by commuters traveling by automobile. How many of these routes are interstates (identifiable by a red, white, and blue shield)?

How do you think access to interstate roadways has affected the growth of communities in your area?

The Relocation of Industry and Workforces to Other Metro Areas

3. The Bureau of the Census has data on the mean and median center of population of the United States. Go to the following Web address: https://www.census.gov/dataviz/visualizations/050. How has this center of population changed since 1900? Which factors caused this movement?

Metro Areas and Immigration After World War II

4. Using US census data, select any five cities in the United States and develop a chart indicating the percentage of foreign-born individuals from 1970 through 2010. Taking the city with the largest foreign-born population, consider what factors might have attracted these immigrants to this city.

PART III

Foundations of Metropolitan Area Prosperity

Urban Prosperity and the Role of Trade

5

LEARNING OBJECTIVES

■ Explain the difference between absolute advantage and comparative advantage and show why trade would be beneficial in either circumstance

■ Compare and contrast the implications of new trade theory, product life cycle theory, and competitive advantage for the prosperity of a region

■ Explain how export base theory distinguishes between goods produced for trade outside the area versus goods that are produced for local consumption

■ Explain the multiplier effect and identify the circumstances under which it applies

■ Explain how the competitive advantage approach can be applied to disadvantaged neighborhoods within cities

When a nation's economy is doing well, new college graduates have their choice of good jobs, households have more income to spend, and the future looks rosy. When a nation's economy turns sour, newly minted BAs take jobs behind the counter at a Starbucks or a Parisian patisserie, households rein in their spending, and prospects look bleak. As in the case of the well-being of individuals and households, metropolitan area prosperity is linked to the vicissitudes of its national economy, if not the global economy. The COVID-19 pandemic proved this most convincingly as the economies of one nation after another and one metro area after another suffered business closures and soaring unemployment.

Yet just as some individuals and households fare better than others, some cities and suburbs outperform other metro regions. When a nation's unemployment rate is 6 percent, more than 12 percent of the workforce might be jobless in some of its metro areas while only 3 percent are unemployed in others. Some cities experience buoyant growth and rising incomes for decades, while others have their day in the sun and then decline as other cities and regions surpass them. Some undergo an economic renaissance, while others fall from economic grace.

Chapter 2 called attention to the great differences in household income among the 25 largest metropolitan areas in the United States. As Figure 2.2-6 showed, the San Francisco metro area had a median household income of $96,677 in 2016 while Tampa's was $51,115. When we exclude suburbs and consider only central cities, San Francisco had a median household income of $87,701 in 2016, in contrast to Detroit's $26,249. As shown in Figure 2.5, from 2000 to 2017, central city real income increased nearly 30 percent in Atlanta but fell over 30 percent in Detroit.

What accounts for these extreme differences in household income and these stunning changes over time? Why are the residents of some metropolitan areas able to prosper, while others experience steep declines in income? Of the five major colonial cities from the eighteenth century, why are New York, Philadelphia, and Boston still the nuclei of top-ten metropolitan areas, while Newport (Rhode Island) and Charleston (South Carolina) have been eclipsed by the growth of other areas? What has made it possible for disposable personal income to more than double in China in the brief period between 2010 and 2019 (Trading Economics 2020)?

To answer these questions, we need to understand the role of trade in the metropolitan economy and how it affects the economic base of metropolitan areas—those activities that bring income and employment to an area and provide the foundation for further expansion and growth.

A Short Primer on the Economics of Trade

As we saw in Chapter 3, specialization and the division of labor are the basis for trade. In the same way that households can enjoy a higher standard of living if they focus on helping to produce only one or a few goods or services and purchase the rest from their earnings, entire metropolitan areas gain from specialization and trade. Although this may sound like a simple enough proposition, in execution it is complex.

To understand how trade actually works, we will start with the easiest case that appeals to common sense, and then move on to instances that may seem counterintuitive. Economic theory can help explain why trade is advantageous under a much broader range of circumstances than first comes to mind, and why cities and suburbs can thrive—at least for a while—when they specialize in the production of a few goods and services.

Absolute Advantage

People have different skills and abilities, partly because of natural talents and partly because of training. For example, consider two teenage cousins, Thelma and Louise, who live on opposite sides of town. Each has a paper route. Louise, the elder of the two, already has her driver's license while Thelma covers her route on bicycle. Louise has a weak throwing arm, while Thelma is an ace at throwing. Separately, each takes two hours to cover her route, a total of four hours of work. But if they team up to cover both routes with Louise driving and Thelma throwing, they find they can cover *both* routes in two hours—in effect doubling their productivity and, potentially, their income.

In this case, the benefits of specialization and trade are clear. When one party can do something better than another, that party is said to have an **absolute advantage**. One person is better at driving, the other is better at throwing. Their strengths and weaknesses are complementary, so by joining forces they can accomplish things together that neither could accomplish alone. A similar argument could be made for why Norway might want to trade its sardines for pineapples grown in Honduras, why Washington State should specialize in growing apples and trade with California for oranges, and why Houston should specialize in oil refining and trade for coal from Wheeling, West Virginia.

Comparative Advantage

Beginning with David Ricardo in the early nineteenth century, economists have long argued that the case for specialization and trade can often be made even in those instances where one party does *not* hold an absolute advantage in *any* of the endeavors. If that party is *less disadvantaged* in one task than in another, that is enough to justify specialization and trade, and the result will be beneficial to *both* parties. We can use a simple example to illustrate this more elusive concept of **comparative advantage**.

Consider Ellwood and Jake, the former a lawyer with a specialty in immigration law. He worked his way through college and law school doing yard work, at which he became extraordinarily adept. Jake is a recent immigrant who is earning his living doing yard work and taking courses as a paralegal at a local community college. He is very good at yard work, but not quite as good as Ellwood. Moreover, with his limited paralegal training, it takes him much longer than Ellwood to complete a standard legal document. Therefore, Ellwood has the absolute advantage in both occupations.

But Jake is at *less* of a disadvantage in yard work than in the preparation of legal documents, and this is the basis for mutually beneficial specialization and trade. Holding the quality of the work constant, it might take Ellwood 20 hours to do the yard work while it would take Jake 25. It would take Ellwood two hours to prepare a legal document, while it takes Jake five. Ellwood is quicker at both tasks, but while it would take Jake two and a half times as long as Ellwood to prepare the document (five hours versus two), it would take him only one and a quarter times as long to do the yard work (25 hours versus 20). Therefore, Jake has a comparative advantage (he is less disadvantaged) in doing yard work and Ellwood in preparing the legal documents. In this case, it is to the advantage of Jake to do yard work for himself *and* Ellwood and trade his yard work labor to Ellwood for the preparation of any legal document he might need. Both Jake and Ellwood benefit from this division of labor. The economic principle that underlies comparative advantage is none other than opportunity cost.

Look at it this way and follow the logic: Jake's opportunity cost for the five hours of work he would need to complete one legal document is equal to the time needed to complete one-fifth of the yard work (five hours of effort out of the 25 hours to complete the work on the yard.) Ellwood's opportunity cost for completing the same legal document is that in the two hours it took him, he could have completed one-tenth of the yard work. So Ellwood can complete the document at lower opportunity cost: sacrificing one-tenth of the yard work, rather than one-fifth. On the other hand, if Ellwood had decided to complete the yard work, the 20 hours devoted to this task would have cost him the equivalent of finishing 10 legal documents, while Jake's opportunity cost for completing the yard work in 25 hours is the foregone time he would have needed to finish five legal documents. So Jake can complete the yard work at lower opportunity cost: 5 documents rather than 10. If one party can produce something at a lower opportunity cost than another, that party is said to have a comparative advantage. Ellwood has the comparative advantage (as well as the absolute advantage) in producing legal documents. Jake has the comparative advantage in yard work even though he does not have the absolute advantage.

We can show the benefits of this trade based on comparative advantage in dollar terms. Even if Ellwood's hourly wage is twice as high as Jake's, they will *both* benefit from specializing and trading. Say, for example, that Ellwood earns $50 an hour and Jake earns $25. If Ellwood did the yard work himself, his opportunity cost is $1000 ($50 x 20 hours); if he hires Jake, it costs him $625 ($25 x 25 hours). If Jake prepared his own documents, his opportunity cost would be $125 ($25 x 5 hours); if he hires Ellwood, it costs him $100 ($50 x 2 hours). Each is better off hiring the other. If a comparative advantage can be identified, both parties benefit from specialization and trade.

In the same way that individuals benefit from comparative advantage, so can metropolitan areas and nations. For example, call centers have become an important source of employment for cities such as Albuquerque, New Mexico (Uchitelle 2002). Spouses of people working at a nearby military base form a readily available workforce who can respond to free "800" calls on behalf of companies located far away. A hotel in Manhattan that is part of a chain might use a call center to handle reservations. Formerly, the on-site clerk might have booked the reservation and fielded prospective guests' questions. The clerk might have known whether room windows could be opened for fresh air, whether rooms facing the street were noisy, and whether the express train to the Bronx ran on weekends. The operator in Albuquerque can book the room, but is unlikely to be able to answer these questions. Nevertheless, if work space in Manhattan hotels is scarce and expensive, booking reservations will be spun off to other places, even if it is more productive when done on-site. The same is true for similar jobs, while others—such as cleaning rooms and making beds—must be done on-site.

The distant call center workers have a comparative advantage, even if they are not as productive, in that their work *can* be moved, while the work of the cleaning staff cannot. The movement of back-office functions from a company's midtown skyscraper to the metropolitan area's suburban office park or to a claims processing site in a different state or a different country is another illustration of comparative advantage, because it shows the opportunity cost of using expensive real estate for functions that could be spun off to cheaper land. Today, the Philippines—in particular its capital city of Manila—has the largest share of the call center market, handling over 20 percent of all call center volume worldwide and employing more than one million of its citizens in this growing industry (Finances Online

2020). In this Pacific archipelago nation, the cost of labor and building space is much cheaper than in North American and European cities and therefore more and more businesses have contracted with Philippine-based call centers. Improvement in communications technology has facilitated this development.

Limitations to the Theory of Comparative Advantage

If we want to know how two individuals (or metropolitan areas or nations) can maximize their well-being given a fixed amount of resources each has available, comparative advantage tells us the answer. If one has the lower opportunity cost for producing X and the other has the lower opportunity cost for producing Y, they will maximize total output and both parties will benefit if they each specialize in just one product or service and trade for the other. This way of looking at the situation—**constrained maximization** or "maximization subject to constraint"— takes the starting situation as a given that cannot be changed. Once we accept this assumption, the merits of comparative advantage and free trade inevitably follow. Given their natural resource endowments and the quality of labor their residents possess, cities and regions will begin to specialize according to their comparative advantage. Towns in the Napa Valley in California and Tuscan villages in Italy will produce wine; cities such as Houston will produce natural gas and oil; metro regions such as Greater Boston with its powerful universities will produce biotech products.

As compelling as this may seem, the value of this approach has come under serious reconsideration (Vernon 1966; Ohlin 1967; Krugman 1990; Porter 1990; Fallows 1994). One major problem with comparative advantage is that it is essentially static. It tells you the best that can be done under the circumstances *at a given point in time*. It does not address the question of where the constraints—the fixed resources and the fixed opportunity costs—came from or what might be done to change them. It does not address the question of how an individual, a metropolitan area, or a nation could work to improve the quantity or quality of its productive resources.

These are questions about the dynamics of the situation: What causes things to change over time? What do those changes imply for human ability to foster prosperity by augmenting resources and therefore changing the terms of trade? How would the changes affect the type of production in which an individual, metro area, or nation has comparative advantage?

Let's go back to Jake and Ellwood. If Ellwood remains a lawyer and Jake remains in yard work, comparative advantage tells us how they can prosper under the circumstances. What happens if we do not take this static analysis as a given? Jake might complete his paralegal training and become adept at preparing legal documents. Ellwood might decide to leave his law practice and start a landscaping business because of his love of the outdoors. Over the years, Jake's and Ellwood's initial occupations might take each of them down unexpected paths, perhaps unrelated to their original specialized line of work. Comparative advantage switches in this case, so that Jake is now spending most of his time on legal work, while Ellwood uses his working time for yard work. In a dynamic context, the question is not the one raised by comparative advantage: How do you make the best of a given amount of resources? Instead it is: *What can you do to improve the quality and quantity of the resources at your disposal?* The Philippines could become dominant in the call center industry by providing extensive training and language instruction for its workforce.

Changing comparative advantage is not easy for cities and regions to do, but it often becomes necessary when technological change or new competitors reduce a metro area's ability to successfully continue to specialize in one product or service. Chicago had to switch from meatpacking, Detroit has had to try to switch from auto production, and Cleveland and Pittsburgh have had to switch from steel. Instead of blindly accepting the dictates of comparative advantage, nations, regions, and cities try to find ways to specialize in new goods and services rather than accept the fate comparative advantage would ascribe to them. Seoul, South Korea became adept at manufacturing technology and now produces a line of Hyundai and Kia automobiles and LG appliances that compete against US, European, and Japanese brands that have been the standard of excellence for decades.

Those cities that prove adept at marshaling the resources to gain comparative advantage in the production of new goods and services are the ones in which median household income generally rises. Those less adept see their positions erode, and the common consequence is slowly rising or actually declining household incomes.

New Trade Theory

Several new ideas have emerged that provide an expanded framework for understanding trade, each of which provides a more dynamic framework for the explanation and new insights into the relationship between trade and the prosperity of geographic areas.

New trade theory emphasizes the effect of economies of scale in production and the barriers that existing large-scale production pose for the entry of new firms to an industry (Krugman 1990). According to this theory, if market demand is not sufficient to support many sites of large-scale production, the product will be produced in only a few locations. In such cases, a country, a region, a metropolitan area or a city may benefit from **first-mover advantage**, where firms and the areas in which they are located are able to establish economies of scale or other benefits by being early entrants into the market for a new good or service. In this case, the early bird gets the worm. For example, when the auto industry got its start in Detroit, there were no areas that could effectively challenge the city's dominance— at least until after World War II.

By contrast, **product life cycle theory** postulates that the location of production for a particular good may change over time as differing production and marketing needs arise in the course of moving from initial product introduction to widespread use (Vernon 1966). When Jane Jacobs described how the economy of a metropolitan area develops over time, she used the metaphor of "adding new work to old" to capture such a process (Jacobs 1969). In the initial stage of the product's life, the site of production may be solely determined by the location of the creative insight. In Stage 2, as the product catches on and demand from other areas increases, the initiating firm exports more of its output. As this occurs, firms in other locations begin to attempt to copy its success by producing the same or similar products. In Stage 3, competition from other firms increases, buyers have more alternatives from where to procure the product, and the initial firm's exports decrease. Eventually, the initial region may become an importer of that good.

Today, Detroiters *import* most of their cars from other regions of the country and from foreign producers. The product life cycle theory illustrates that geographic patterns of trade may reflect dynamic processes of innovation, the growth of interest in the product by consumers, export decisions, and competition from other firms. Laptop computers are a good example. When first introduced, they were manufactured by Toshiba in Japan and by companies such as Dell in the United States. But as production ramped up, both companies built laptops or components in Taiwan, Malaysia, and China.

What this tells us is that individual metro areas need to be constantly adopting new technologies and constantly adapting to changes in tastes and demand to maintain their prosperity. In general, success depends on being able to produce new products and services and export them to other markets to maintain or increase the incomes of their residents. Successful trade is the foundation for urban prosperity.

The Theory of Competitive Advantage

The most recently introduced conceptual framework for the explanation of trade and prosperity, **competitive advantage**, has emerged from business economics. In contrast to the concept of comparative advantage, which focuses on a region's gains from trade that involves different goods, the concept of competitive advantage focuses on the success of a firm in a particular industry in comparison with its rivals that produce the *same* good or service. Competitive advantage takes on locational significance, becoming relevant to nations, regions, and metropolitan areas because of the connections between place and the ability of specific firms in particular locales to initiate and maintain successful strategies against rivals.

According to Michael Porter, competitive advantage can be gained either through low-cost production or through product differentiation. Low-cost production allows a firm to underprice its competitors to obtain and keep a greater share of the market, or to gain higher profits from goods sold at the same price as a competitor. Product differentiation gives competitive advantage if it leads potential buyers to choose the firm's products over its competitors' at the same price, or if it leads the buyer to pay extra for the good because of the perceived "unique and superior value to the buyer in terms of product quality, special features, or after-sale service" (Porter 1990, p. 37).

Like the product life cycle theory, the competitive advantage approach emphasizes that industry and firm characteristics change over time. Extended periods of economic prosperity for a geographic area rest on the ability of its firms to continuously innovate to sustain competitive advantage against their rivals. This is called **sustained competitive advantage**. Advantages gained through low-cost production are relatively difficult to sustain, because lower-cost sources for labor or materials are often found. Textile production, once a New England industry, moved to the South early in the twentieth century in search of ever-cheaper labor. By the 1960s and 1970s, many textile firms had relocated to a number of urban centers in Mexico to reduce their costs. In the early twenty-first century, the location choice shifted to cities in China where labor costs are lower still.

Product differentiation strategies may be easier to sustain because they are built upon things that are harder to duplicate, such as unique technology, brand-name recognition, expertise in repair or service, durability, access to unique inputs, or other features valued by customers. Yet since rivals can be expected to seek competitive advantage from product differentiation, sustained advantage from such sources requires constant research and development, innovation, and creation of new resources.

Porter emphasizes the role of **industry clusters**, by which he means the external economies that occur from the agglomeration of firms operating in the same industry or in closely related industries. Regional clusters provide several important advantages to firms and therefore to the metropolitan areas in which they are located. The firms in a regional cluster can benefit from sharing skilled labor pools, exchanging knowledge, and utilizing common infrastructure and other agglomeration economies. In the process, they give a city or region an advantage over other locations trying to produce similar goods.

The geographic concentration of specialized expertise is particularly helpful in making these industry clusters successful. Knowledge spillovers allow scientists and engineers to quickly and easily share information, often in informal settings. While the internet makes it possible for professionals to share information even if they live on opposite sides of the globe, face-to-face contact is judged even more valuable. If a metro area can build a monopoly or near monopoly in a particular type of expertise, it can specialize in an industry or industry cluster that utilizes those skills and thus become prosperous.

Detroit gained competitive advantage in auto production and all the related design, manufacturing, and service industries that belong to this industrial cluster by attracting more auto engineers than anywhere on earth. Hollywood, which had an early comparative advantage in movie production—in relation to many other parts of the United States—thanks to its year-round mild climate and large number of sunny days, attracted more producers, directors, set designers, and actors, creating an industry cluster around the silver screen. Boston, based on its huge array of universities and colleges, attracted more hardware and software engineers than almost anywhere else, giving it a competitive advantage in the information and biotech sectors. Each of these cities became a boomtown specializing in successful industry clusters.

Today, Cambridge, Massachusetts has become a center for cutting-edge biotechnology firms anchored by the city's two premier universities, Harvard and the Massachusetts Institute of Technology. Similarly, the northwest region of Italy is home to the "industrial triangle," which links the cities of Milan, Turin, and Genoa and is characterized by a modern group of industries focused on naval production, machinery, aerospace, and automobiles.

Attaining and sustaining a competitive advantage for a differentiated high-valued product, thereby contributing greatly to an area's prosperity, requires the full deployment of high-quality resources. Porter groups these resources into the following categories:

- **Human resources**: the size and quality of the labor force
- **Physical resources:** the amount and quality of natural resources, including location and proximity to other markets
- **Knowledge resources:** scientific and technical know-how produced by universities, government agencies, and private research and development firms
- **Capital resources:** the amount and cost of finance capital, including the availability of venture capital to fund new enterprises
- **Infrastructure:** the quality and cost of the transportation, communication, delivery, and banking systems, as well as institutions that affect the quality of life

As these five categories indicate, the resources for sustained competitive advantage typically involve the work of businesses, government, and educational institutions. Those regions that can put all or many of these resources together are destined for real prosperity that can endure over time.

Trade and Prosperity

The approaches to trade and prosperity represented by comparative advantage, new trade theory, product life cycle theory, and competitive advantage are perhaps best seen as complementary tools for understanding the economies of metropolitan areas.

- The essential idea of *comparative advantage*—that areas trade to take advantage of their different opportunity costs—is still a very important prescriptive notion for increasing production and describes much of the trade that actually occurs between cities, metro areas, and regions.
- New trade theory gives us the insight that economies of scale and industry structure are important aspects of trade for firms, cities, and regions.
- The product life cycle theory calls attention to the dynamic quality of product creation and the implications for firms and regions of the product's acceptance into widespread use.
- Finally, the theory of competitive advantage highlights the rivalry that occurs within market economies, and the significance of rivalry between firms and regions for investment and jobs.

No metropolitan area is entirely self-sufficient in the sense of being able to produce within its boundaries all the goods and services its residents want to consume. Currently, there are no automobile assembly plants in metropolitan Boston (or, for that matter anywhere in New England). The area's drivers must buy cars produced somewhere else—Jeep Grand Cherokees from Detroit, Hondas from

Ohio, Mercedes from Alabama, and a variety of imports from Japan, South Korea, Sweden, and Germany. Similarly, Chicagoans who want orange juice or Seattle residents who want grapefruits need to bring them in from places with warmer climates. If the residents of a metropolitan area want to *buy* products from the outside, they will need to have something to *sell* to the outside in order to afford them. They must have a comparative advantage in the production of *something* if they are to remain economically viable.

Metaphorically, when areas import automobiles, orange juice, or grapefruits from beyond their boundaries, they need to pay for those purchases with income that has been earned by exporting products to the outside. In this sense, metropolitan Los Angeles exports motion pictures not only to moviegoers on other continents but to those in Northern California; metropolitan Seattle exports software not only to countries around the world but to other places in the Pacific Northwest.

What makes a product an export is that it brings income into an area that was earned elsewhere. That is easy to see when a worker in Atlanta uses some of her income to buy a new Honda manufactured in Ohio. The funds leave the place where they were earned and provide income to another place hundreds or thousands of miles away. What if that worker decided to spend her vacation in Orlando or in Rio de Janiero? If she leaves home with a fat wallet and returns with a thinner one—or a larger balance on her credit card—it is the same underlying principle: the funds leave the city where they were earned and provide income to businesses or households in Florida or Brazil. Indeed, tourism is an important part of the economic base of many metropolitan areas including Orlando, Las Vegas, New York, San Francisco, Rome, Venice, Paris, and London.

The idea behind **export base theory** is that the demand for an area's exports is the key to understanding its prosperity. If outsiders are eager to buy what the metro area produces, income will flow to that area and it will provide the funds not only to pay for the area's imports, but to support the metro area's local service sector—those items that are produced and consumed within the region.

Think of Pittsburgh in the mid-twentieth century, the heyday of the domestic steel industry. As the demand for steel increased, more steelworkers were hired. They spent part of their new earnings on products imported from elsewhere—either other cities, states, or countries—but some of those new earnings stayed within the local economy to be spent in luncheonettes, barbershops, or bowling alleys. Hence, the increased demand for steel meant more income initially for the new workers hired in the steel industry, but it also meant more demand for local goods and new employment in those luncheonettes, barbershops, and bowling alleys. These service workers spent some of their new income on imports and some on local services, fueling another round of spending in the local economy. Each new round is smaller either because some of that new income is saved and not spent or because the portion spent on imports departs the area, leaving only the portion spent on local services to generate more income in the next round.

Thus, for every new job created in an export industry, there is additional employment created in the local service sector. These local jobs are not only in the private sector, such as barber or movie usher, but also in the public sector, including teachers and firefighters. An increase in the demand for a city's exports will initially fuel employment growth in the city's export industries, and subsequently job growth in the area's local public and private sectors.

This phenomenon works in forward gear as the demand for exports grows, but it works in reverse gear. If the demand for steel produced in Pittsburgh declines, steelworkers get laid off, followed by layoffs in the area's luncheonettes, barbershops, and bowling alleys. As local tax revenue declines, some teachers and firefighters might lose their jobs as well. Here again, for every hundred jobs lost in the export sector, there will be many jobs lost in the local service sector, including public and private services.

The 1989 documentary film *Roger and Me* provided vivid examples of the consequences of a decline in an area's export base. It depicted the vacant downtown storefronts that resulted from the decision by General Motors to shut down many of the automobile assembly plants in the company's birthplace in Flint, Michigan. It included a portion of a grim local TV news report documenting that the rat population of the county outnumbered the human population, both because households were moving away to places with better employment opportunities and because the county could no longer afford to collect the trash as often.

When people move away from a depressed area in search of better opportunities elsewhere, the movers do not usually represent a general cross-section of the population. They tend to be those who are younger, more educated, and more energetic. Demographers call this **selective migration**. When this occurs, it becomes more difficult for an area to recover because the most economically attractive portion of its workforce has left for greener pastures.

We can summarize the key elements of export base theory in the following way:

- An export is a product or service that brings income earned elsewhere into a metro area

- The demand for a metro area's exports is the driving force in determining an area's prosperity

- Income from exports is crucial: it pays for a metro area's imports and supports the area's local service sector, including both private and public services

- An increase in a metro area's export industries will cause a multiplied increase in the area's local service sector

- A decrease in a metro area's export industries will cause a multiplied decrease in the area's local service sector

- A sustained contraction will cause selective migration and will make it even more difficult for the metro area to recover

The Basic/Nonbasic Approach: A Simple Measurement Technique

To better understand the power of export base theory, it is useful to see how economists measure the impact of exports on the prosperity of a region. The most widely used technique is known as the **basic/nonbasic approach** which measures the impact on a metro area's economy as a result of a change in export demand by estimating the size of a **job multiplier**.

The technique begins by categorizing all jobs in the area as either part of the export base (basic) or part of the local service sector (nonbasic). Even if the jobs look similar, the basic/nonbasic approach treats them differently depending on whether they are part of the export sector or part of the local sector. For example, a janitor answering help-wanted advertisements might be indifferent between a job with a publishing company and a similar job at the public library. Both might offer the same wages and fringe benefits and both places have lots of books. But even though the jobs might be interchangeable from the viewpoint of the worker, they play very different roles in the basic/nonbasic approach. The *basic* job at the publisher has a **multiplier effect** associated with it since much of the income of the janitor is generated by sales of books from outside the area; the *nonbasic* job at the public library does not since little or none of the income of the library comes from outside the community. Part of the income earned by employees of the city's export sector is spent on other export goods such as automobiles, but part is spent on local products and services including restaurant meals, haircuts, and rent, thus generating local jobs in the local economy.

Job Multipliers

When every job in the area has been categorized as either basic or nonbasic, the job multiplier can be calculated. For example, a small metropolitan area might contain 50,000 jobs, 25,000 of which might be basic (export) and the other 25,000 nonbasic (local services). The ratio of export jobs to total jobs is 25,000:50,000, or 1:2; the ratio of export jobs to local service jobs is 25,000:25,000, or 1:1. Assuming that new jobs are similar to existing jobs, we conclude that when the demand for the area's exports rises, each new export job will support, on average, one new local service job. Ultimately, the increased demand for exports has created two new jobs in the area—one in the export sector, and another in the local service sector, hence a job multiplier of two.

The simple basic/nonbasic approach implicitly assumes that the ratio of basic employment to total employment remains constant as the area grows. Yet we know that larger areas are more self-sufficient than are smaller ones. As an area grows, it will be able to substitute local production for some of the items it imports. This is referred to as **import substitution**. Therefore, in larger metropolitan areas, every additional 100 export jobs will generate even more local service jobs because there will be fewer leakages from the spending stream in the form of imports.

If, as we have seen, the ratio of export jobs to total jobs changes as an area grows, it would make more sense to calculate a multiplier based on *changes* in export employment and *changes* in total employment, rather than *levels* of export and total employment. In either case, though, calculating the jobs multiplier requires that the area's jobs be categorized as either export or local service—and this is easier said than done. In our earlier example of Pittsburgh, it was easy to assume that most of the steel was exported and that all the barbers served local clientele. When we consider more complicated situations where some of the steel is used locally and some of the "local" services are exported we need to consider another concept.

Location Quotients

How would we categorize restaurant workers in New York City? Some of the Big Apple's restaurants cater primarily to tourists, others serve a local clientele, and some have a mixture of locals and visitors. We need some way to apportion the jobs in this industry into those that are part of the export base versus those that are not. Presumably, we could place interviewers with clipboards at the door of each New York restaurant and ask the exiting patrons for their zip codes, but that would be prohibitively expensive. So instead, we use a more indirect strategy—calculating a **location quotient**.

The location quotient is the proportion of the *area's workers* employed in a given industry divided by the proportion of the *US workforce* employed in that industry. The location quotient measures the degree to which an industry is over-represented (or underrepresented) in the local economy. We infer from this the degree to which each industry is part of the area's export base. For example, if 2 percent of the nation's workforce is employed in an industry but 6 percent of a given metropolitan area's workforce is employed in that industry, the location quotient for that metro area would be three (6% divided by 2%), and we would infer that one-third of the workers are producing for local needs, while the other two-thirds are producing for export. If the industry had 60,000 jobs within the metropolitan area, 40,000 of these jobs would be counted as basic (export) while the other 20,000 would be counted as nonbasic (local).

A location quotient greater than one implies an industry is producing more than enough to meet local need and is *exporting* the excess. A location quotient less than one suggests that a community must *import* some of this industry's product to satisfy local demand. A location quotient equal to one would imply that the area is producing enough to satisfy local needs, without having to import anything from this industry. We would expect the location quotient for the dry cleaning industry to be just about one in every metropolitan area, since people rely on local providers for this service. Hotels in Las Vegas or any large convention city would have location quotients well above one, indicating they are largely part of the export base.

Limitations of the Basic/Nonbasic Approach

While data on employment by industry is easily available, the **basic/nonbasic approach,** with its use of job multipliers and location quotients, is far from precise. In fact, it often tends to overstate the size of the job multiplier, because of an inherent tendency to understate the size of the export sector due to some questionable assumptions. Implicit to its construction, the location quotient assumes that an industry's product is homogeneous, meaning that the output of one producer is no different from the output of another. The underlying model assumes that households will always consume the output of local producers to save on transportation costs since this product is indistinguishable from the output of producers outside the area.

That may not be such a bad assumption in the case of dry cleaners where a location quotient equal to one would be an accurate indicator of self-sufficiency. Yet in other instances a location quotient equal to one would lead to the *mistaken* conclusion that the product was neither imported nor exported. For example, let's say that a metropolitan area had a location quotient of one for the recording industry.

The assumption of product homogeneity would imply that there was no difference between one compact disc and another, and therefore that all the compact discs produced in that area were consumed there.

Such an outcome was highly unlikely. The underlying reality is that compact discs produced in Nashville were sold in New York, and vice-versa. By not recognizing this "cross-hauling," our location quotient would have failed to identify the recording industry in Nashville and New York as export industries, and mistakenly labeled it part of the local service sector. In this case, the location quotient would have failed to identify some export jobs, thereby underestimating the export sector and consequently overestimating the jobs multiplier—the number of local jobs generated as the result of the export sector.

Another limitation of the basic/nonbasic approach is that it cannot distinguish the impact of a change in demand in one part of an area's export base from a change in demand in another. The Los Angeles export base includes the aerospace industry, the motion picture industry, and several other industries. An expansion in aerospace might play out very differently from an expansion in motion pictures in terms of its specific impact on local area jobs. The basic/nonbasic approach cannot distinguish between these two scenarios because although it divides jobs into export versus local service, it does not make any distinction among different industries within the export sector. Hence, the basic/nonbasic approach to understanding a metro area's economy must be used with great caution.

Input-Output Analysis: A More Complex Set of Tools

Just as scientists and physicians use tracer dyes to follow the path of fluids through a system—to identify leakages from a sewage treatment plant or diseased tissue in the human body—social scientists can use **input-output analysis** to follow the impact of a change in demand for exports as it wends its way through the economy of the metropolitan area. Unlike the basic/nonbasic approach, input-output analysis allows us to disaggregate the export sector into its component parts and to distinguish the impact of a change in demand for one export from a change in demand for another. It allows us to see the specific ways in which each industry interacts with the rest of the metropolitan economy—for example, how an increase in demand for the output of the biotechnology industry would raise the demand for its inputs, some of which would be imported from outside while some is provided by local suppliers. As more income is earned by households employed in that industry, it would be spent on additional goods and services.

Here again, some will be imported and some will be provided by local suppliers. By specifying the complete set of relationships between all industries on the input side (what each industry requires as inputs from every other industry to produce its output) as well as the output side (where the output of each industry goes), we have the equivalent of a tracer dye for the area's economy. While the overall interdependence of production in an economy was recognized by economists in the eighteenth and nineteenth centuries, this particular mathematical articulation was introduced by Wassily Leontief (1936; 1966), who is considered the founder of input-output analysis.

According to input-output analysis, one can model the economy of a geographic area as a set of "recipes" for producing the output of each industry in the area and as a set of destinations for that output. For example, production by a particular industry could be expressed as requiring 20 percent of inputs from source A, none from input B, 30 percent from source C, and so on. Similarly, the goods and services that are produced as output can be expressed as going to households, industries, and government. For example, an industry may have 10 percent of its value purchased by households, 15 percent as an intermediate good for industry B, 20 percent for industry C, and so on.

While the cookbook recipe for a cake specifies the ingredients in physical units—number of eggs, cups of flour, pounds of butter, ounces of water, teaspoons of vanilla—the input-output matrix specifies the ingredients in dollar terms. A recipe for cake would be translated as follows: to get a dollar's worth of cake, we need x pennies' worth of eggs, y pennies' worth of flour, z pennies' worth of butter, and so on, adding up to a dollar's worth of input. One of the basic tenets of input-output analysis is that all transactions have been taken into account and therefore a dollar's worth of input is always equal to a dollar's worth of output—including the profit each firm makes in supplying its inputs.

The use of monetary values rather than physical units is dictated by the need to find a common denominator by which to measure the output of industries as disparate as steel, publishing, biotechnology, and tourism. Each of these industries will have its unique recipe for a dollar's worth of output.

Taking these input equations and output equations and presenting them together, with the input recipes for production expressed vertically, and the destination of output expressed horizontally, the entire economy of a nation, a region, or a city can be expressed as a matrix of interdependent equations.

As computing power was enhanced during the information technology revolution, the acquisition, analysis, and use of input-output information became more efficient and more widespread. Today, input-output data is used frequently by cities, metro areas, states, regions, and nations for economic impact analysis (EIA)—studies of the effect or potential effect of businesses, transportation projects, or other initiatives that have an economic impact. In the United States, much of the data for the analysis is gathered by the US Bureau of Economic Analysis (BEA). Publicly available programs include the BEA's Regional Input-Output Modeling System (RIMS-II), and the US Department of Energy's JEDI (Jobs and Economic Development Impact) models. Commercial EIA software programs may supplement the BEA data with information from other sources. Among the widely used commercial EIA software programs are REMI (Regional Economic Models, Inc), IMPLAN (Impact Analysis for Planning), and REDYN (Regional Dynamics).

Typically, economic impact analysis provides estimates of three types of effects: direct, indirect, and induced.

- *Direct* effects concentrate on the impact at the specific initiative that is the center of the study. For example, what is the expected change in revenue and employment at a particular business if it builds a new distribution center?

- *Indirect* effects recognize that businesses have suppliers of raw materials, intermediate goods, and services and thus are a measure of the impact that a change in the business at the center of the study has on suppliers. These suppliers may be within the area being studied or elsewhere. Therefore, the overall economic impact for a given area depends upon the location of suppliers and the amount of purchases expected from those suppliers.

• Induced effects estimate changes in the area's economy from changes in total household income, due to either changes in the number of employees at the business and its suppliers, or changes in the wages and salaries of employees. They are the ripple effects created as new household income is spent and respent within the local economy. Induced effects measure the changes in employment and revenue from spending multiplier effects from changes in household incomes.

Limitations of the Input-Output Measurement Technique

Although input-output models provide a far more sophisticated method than the basic/nonbasic approach for understanding the impact of a change in an area's export demand, this technique has some important limitations. The model is only as accurate as the input matrix allows it to be, but this input matrix itself may be subject to change. If we start with an accurate recipe at a given point in time, it is possible that it will become inaccurate fairly rapidly or over time. One reason is that our recipe for producing small batches of output might not be the same as the recipe for producing larger batches, if there are some scale economies in production. Another is that over time, technological change brings us not only new products, but new processes to produce existing products more efficiently. In this case, the inputs needed for producing a given output could change dramatically.

Yet another reason is that relative prices might change. Although our recipes would still be valid if, say, all prices doubled (in that case, a dollar's worth of output would represent half as many physical units), our recipes would be worthless if the price of one input rose by 15 percent while the price of another fell 5 percent. Therefore, the input matrix would need to be recalculated to account for technological change or a change in relative prices, meaning that it is valid only for relatively short periods of time. The recipe can change, often dramatically, when a previously supplied input is imported from another region or foreign country—or when a previously imported input is produced locally. As such, input-output analysis must be used with caution when analyzing an urban or metro economy.

Limitations of the Demand-Side Focus

Quite apart from the limitations of the measurement techniques, there are limitations to focusing so intensely on the demand side of the area's economy. Knowing the comparative or competitive advantage of a particular city or suburb does not, by itself, provide the necessary information to accurately gauge the metro area's level of prosperity. Dalton, Georgia, for example, might be the carpet production center of the United States, but the demand for carpets depends on household incomes, tastes, alternative floor covering options, and a host of other factors about which Dalton has little influence in the short run.

Moreover, even though it is indisputable that at any given moment, the well-being of the area depends on the health of its export industries, cities that rely on a single export industry are often more vulnerable than cities with a diversified set of export industries. The old proverb "don't put all your eggs in one basket" turns out to be good advice. Also, smaller cities are much more dependent on exports than are larger ones, since larger areas can provide for more of their needs internally through import substitution, producing some items locally rather than importing them from outside. Detroiters can buy a Ford Mustang built in the nearby Ford Rouge plant in Dearborn; whereas residents of Wyoming need to import their cars no matter what brand they buy.

Shifting the Focus from the Demand Side to the Supply Side

Earlier in this chapter we described comparative advantage as a static analysis with greatest relevance for the short run. At any given moment, an area's exports will be comprised of industries in which the area currently has a comparative advantage. Its existing plant and equipment and other human and physical resources will be well suited to produce its current mix of output. Yet over time, the demand for an area's exports will likely change and the area will need to adapt. Resources well suited to today's export industries may not be equally suited to the economy of tomorrow. Before it became the motor city, Detroit was known as the nation's premier manufacturer of cast iron stoves, a consumer product that became obsolete with the introduction of the modern gas range. Fortunately for Detroit, just as the demand for cast iron stoves was drying up, the demand for cars was taking off.

Because demand is so fickle and technological change so pervasive, we need to take a closer look at how a city, suburb, or metro area deploys its resources. Using the framework of input-output analysis, we need to know more about how the area creates value-added and whether it has the resources to sustain a competitive advantage in high value-added production. For example, the input-output table for one area might reflect the fact that its export industries are low-value-added assembly plants: components are imported from other places and are turned into finished products in a few simple steps. Most of the value of the final product is contained in the imported inputs, not its final assembly. High-quality physical and human resources are not required for this operation, so they are unlikely to be nurtured and developed in the area. Although the area might temporarily possess a competitive advantage based on low cost—at least until a lower cost location can be found—it will be stymied in its attempt to create sustainable competitive advantage in the absence of its ability to nurture high-value-added product differentiation. Boston and its nearby city Cambridge were well placed to take advantage of the digital age and the coming to fruition of the biotechnology revolution. While its earlier industries including fishing, small scale manufacturing, and leather products were becoming less important, its array of top universities would produce the engineers and scientists needed for the new twenty-first-century economy of high-value products.

An area with a rich variety of resources described by Porter will have an input-output table in which the difference in value between imported inputs and final output is large yielding high profits and the wherewithal to provide high-wage jobs. These high-value-added export industries are more likely to be the basis of sustainable comparative advantage through product differentiation and the beneficial effects of industry clusters, rather than through low-cost production. For this reason, it is time to take a closer look at the supply side of the metropolitan area's economy.

The Supply Side: A Long-Term Perspective

In the late nineteenth century, the price of silver was high and there was great prosperity in the silver mining towns of Colorado. Grand avenues, fancy stores, and fine opera houses were built, befitting the families of the wealthy mine owners. When the price of silver fell, those once-prosperous places became ghost towns as their export base crumbled. By contrast, the Boston area has remained economically viable for over 300 years, although it has gone through long periods of economic drought. Its original export base of fishing, whaling, and shipping is long gone, but it has found new export industries to replace the old.

Why are some areas more resilient than others? Why is the loss of an export base a death sentence for some communities, but only a temporary setback for others? Aside from the fact that the Colorado mining towns had only one export and were therefore more vulnerable to changes in their demand than places with a more diversified set of exports, what determines an area's economic staying power?

As we have seen, at any given moment an area's well-being depends on the health of its export industries. Yet over the long term, export industries come and go. Products might become obsolete, consumers might change their tastes, or producers might relocate in response to lower costs elsewhere. Over the long term, the key to an area's viability is its ability to attract, invent, or otherwise create new export bases to replace the old by being a place that is inherently attractive to firms. It is the quality and quantity of an area's productive resources—the supply side of the area's economy—that ultimately determines the viability of the area. The quality of its supply of physical capital and human capital matters most.

In shifting our emphasis from the demand side to the supply side, we have shifted the focus away from an area where local policymakers have very little control to one where they have much more. Indeed, local policymakers can choose to improve the area's human and physical resources by investing in social infrastructure such as education and training programs, and physical infrastructure that includes transportation and communication networks.

Our shift in focus from the demand side to the supply side holds very different policy prescriptions for an area wanting to improve its well-being. It turns the key assumption of export base theory on its head: no longer does only the export sector matter with events in the local service sector being merely a passive consequence of changes in exports (Blumenfeld 1960). Now, what happens inside the local service sector matters most in maintaining the area's attractiveness as a place to do business.

Today, metropolitan areas with the most dynamic economies are those whose industries depend most heavily on the creativity of their workforce. Therefore, the metropolitan areas with a competitive advantage in this realm are the areas that are the best at providing the environments that "creative workers" seek. Florida's (2002) research shows that these places tend to score high on tolerance and acceptance of diversity, including not only ethnic and racial diversity but an acceptance of differing sexual preferences and gender identifications, venues where live music is performed, and access to active recreation in places of natural scenic beauty.

Interactions Between the Demand Side and the Supply Side

If the quantity and quality of the area's resources—its social and physical infrastructure—matter most over the long term, why do some areas have better resource endowments than others? Does the nature of an area's existing export industries affect the way its supply side evolves? In a classic 1961 article, the economist Benjamin Chinitz described the *contrasts in agglomeration* that distinguish Pittsburgh from New York City. Chinitz argues that Pittsburgh's export base was characterized by oligopoly—an industry structure such as the steel industry, in which the bulk of the output is produced by a few large firms, often called a shared monopoly—while New York City's export base was comprised of more competitive firms. He argues that places in which the export base is oligopolistic are areas where the social and physical infrastructure is stunted. There is less entrepreneurship and therefore less innovation; there are fewer business services since large corporations provide for more of their needs internally—with in-house legal, printing, and shipping departments, for example. We can infer from Chinitz's arguments that such places as Pittsburgh, Detroit, and Flint are less resilient, and have a more difficult time overcoming the loss of their oligopolistic export bases than New York City, Boston, or San Francisco, where entrepreneurship and innovation find more fertile soil. The same can be said of such global cities as Tokyo, Seoul, and Stockholm.

In work that focuses on the nature of knowledge spillovers in metropolitan areas, Glaeser et al. (1992) distinguish between three hypotheses:

- The first emphasizes the role of knowledge spillovers *within* industries, and argues that they are most effective when the industry is able to use its market power—its oligopoly status—to capture the gains.

- The second, represented in the work of Michael Porter, emphasizes the value of knowledge spillovers *within* industries, but argues that local competition is more effective for its dissemination.

- The third, represented by the work of Jane Jacobs, shares with Porter the emphasis on local competition, but argues that the most important knowledge spillovers occur *across* industries, rather than *within* them.

In testing these hypotheses with data from the 170 largest US metropolitan areas spanning the period 1956 to 1987, Glaeser and his colleagues find support for Jacobs's view—that knowledge spillovers across industries in a competitive environment are the most effective in generating innovation and employment growth.

Thus, while a high level of human capital is critical to the prosperity of any metro region, those areas with interlocking industries—what Porter calls **industry clusters**—apparently do best in taking advantage of knowledge spillovers to generate high levels of income for their regions. In the twenty-first century, Austin, Texas; Raleigh-Durham-Chapel Hill, North Carolina; San Jose, California; Seattle, Washington; and Boston, Massachusetts are typical of metro areas well suited to compete in the new industry clusters in biotechnology, nanotechnology, pharmaceuticals, and state-of-the-art information technology hardware and software.

Strategies for Less Resilient Metropolitan Areas

While the future looks rosy for such places as Austin and San Jose, it looks relatively bleak for Detroit, Pittsburgh, and Flint. As Glaeser and Saiz (2004) point out, the US population has been shifting to the Sunbelt states ever since the advent of air-conditioning in the mid-twentieth century. Cities with average January temperatures above 50 degrees Fahrenheit have grown far more quickly than cities with average January temperatures below 30 degrees Fahrenheit.

Among the cold-weather cities with their relatively less attractive climates, the key distinction between those that have prospered and those that have not is the education level of the population. Glaeser and Saiz argue that investing in education is therefore especially important for the older industrial cities of the Northeast and Midwest.

How to do this is no simple matter. While investing in human capital will make the area more attractive to potential businesses and new residents, it requires large expenditures. Paying for quality education requires high tax rates which can deter new businesses and residents from locating in the area. One way for metropolitan areas to resolve this dilemma would be for the states and the federal government to play a larger role in funding education. In addition, Glaeser and Saiz emphasize the need to reduce crime rates and to offer an attractive and affordable housing stock.

In a similar vein, a study from the Brookings Institution (Vey 2007) argues that many older industrial cities have assets that are worth preserving such as distinctive architecture, scenic waterfronts, and a host of educational, medical, and cultural institutions. With changing demographic and economic trends, including the growth of immigration and the aging of the US population, as well as the increased economic importance of urban-based institutions including universities, medical centers, and museums, these cities might be able to reverse their misfortunes. Detroit might be a good example as it hosts a major state university within its borders, four professional sports teams, and a number of business and civic leaders investing in the city to help bring a renaissance to this once proud Motor City. As such it has the potential for recovery, if not to its former glory but as a good place to live and make a living. Along with Glaser and Saiz, the Brookings study emphasizes the need for state governments to assist cities in their efforts to improve education, reduce crime, provide affordable housing, and promote an economic climate attractive to new business and residents.

Competitive Advantage in Inner-City Neighborhoods

While strengthening export base industries is a valid short-term focus for local policymakers, many economists believe that a longer-term strategy of investing in social and physical infrastructure should guide policy. Both Michael Porter and

Richard Florida look at the elements of an area's economic environment that give it particular strength—an area's competitive advantage, the basis on which it can build attractiveness that is unique and therefore more difficult for other areas to imitate.

Although Porter has written about the competitive advantage of nations, he has applied his insights to an understanding of how the concept would work for disadvantaged inner-city neighborhoods. Porter (1995) notes that as a result of prior demographic and industrial change, many low-income ghettos depend heavily on such transfer payments as welfare benefits and food stamps. But these areas often are near the prosperous downtowns of successful cities, and this proximity offers a hard-to-duplicate competitive advantage for firms that provide services to downtown clients.

Training inner-city residents to work in a range of services could make residents less dependent on transfer payments and better able to raise their living standards through employment. Porter uses the growing number of laundry and catering firms in the Roxbury section of Boston as an example of this competitive advantage—enterprises that are well positioned to provide for the needs of downtown hotels and restaurants, while providing decent job opportunities for Roxbury's residents.

Porter makes a persuasive case for retail investment in the inner city. He notes that while residents there often earn much less per household than in the richer suburbs, higher housing density in the inner city means more consumer dollars *per acre*. His theory has been borne out by numerous instances in which the inner-city locations of retail chain stores outperform those in the suburbs (Boston Consulting Group and Initiative for a Competitive Inner City 1998).

Understanding Metro Area Prosperity in Light of Economic Theory

Using all the trade theory we have reviewed, we can take a look at some of the metro regions that have become hubs for key industries across the globe. We begin with an older industry but one still critical for our way of life: automobile manufacturing.

Today, the largest car-making manufacturing plant in the world is not in the United States, but in Wolfsburg, Germany, where Volkswagen has a factory of over 70 million square feet where it produces 3,800 vehicles *per day* or more than 815,000 per year. The factory halls alone take up a surface area of nearly a square mile, enough to produce four Golf lines, the Touran, and Tiguan SUVs. By concentrating under one roof everything needed to produce motor vehicles from toolmaking to plastic production and boasting one of the world's largest paint shops, the Wolfsburg plan is one of the most efficient in the world gaining it absolute advantage in some aspects of auto production and comparative advantage in others.

The second largest auto plant worldwide is in Ulsan, South Korea, where Hyundai manufactures 14 different model vehicles in a five-building complex which can churn out a vehicle *every 12 seconds*. The plant employees 34,000 employees on-site and since most of its product is sold overseas, it benefits from its location in a seaside city where the company has its own cargo pier for shipping its vehicles around the world. The efficiency of the plant, its relatively lower wages, and its specific location provide this city with a comparative advantage in modern auto manufacturing.

The third largest auto facility in the world is in the United States. But instead of Detroit or another long-established Michigan-based auto city such as Flint or Lansing, this plant is in Belvidere, Illinois. Mitsubishi Motors, the Japanese auto producer, built this plant in 1965 to produce its own brand vehicle for the North American market. In 2015 it shuttered the plant because of lagging sales and sold the facility to the Chrysler Corporation based outside of Detroit. Today, this 3.5 million square foot facility handles assembly of the Jeep Compass, Jeep Patriot, and Dodge Dart with about 780 robots and over 280 acres of property. The purchase of a plant that already was equipped for the efficient manufacturing of vehicles with the latest in technology makes this factory an ideal place for the final assembly (Newcomb 2017).

Not surprisingly, another industry that requires a massive facility for production is jet aircraft. The world's largest building by volume, the 4.2 million square foot Boeing manufacturing facility north of Seattle in Everett, Washington, covers nearly 100 acres and rolls out the 747, 767, 777 and 787 passenger jet planes. Along with a museum, theater, 19 restaurants, and a store, the 1966-built facility includes 2.33 miles of pedestrian tunnels underneath the factory floor, its own railway spur, over 1,000 bicycles for moving around the plant, and even the world's largest mural. Everett had the undeveloped space for this facility which made it ideal for Boeing. The second largest aircraft plant in the world is located in Toulouse-Blagnac, France, where the Jean-Luc Legardére Plant assembles the parts for the Airbus A380. With the plane's parts crafted across Europe, the French facility handles assembly and testing of the final build in the 1.3 million square foot facility that includes 49 acres of runway outside the plant.

Perhaps the newest and most exciting industry is biopharma which produces the drugs that cure illnesses and save lives. During the COVID-19 pandemic, such pharmaceutical firms around the world were working 24/7 to develop a vaccine that would rid the world of this physically devastating and economically destructive virus. The top biotech-pharma hubs in the United States are located in the San Francisco Bay area and Cambridge, because that is where top universities and research hospitals are located.

The San Francisco Bay Area has been a key hub for the biotechnology and life sciences industry for a long time. In general, the whole Northern California region hosts many biotechnology and life science companies and start-ups, but San Francisco deserves special mention as it is considered the birthplace of the modern biotech industry. The San Francisco Bay Area hosts top tier universities that include Stanford, UC Berkeley, UC San Francisco, and the University of San Francisco, all of which have powerful chemistry and biology departments. These universities have spun off many new firms among the 1,400 life science and biotech companies in the area. BioMarin Pharmaceutical, Genentech, Novartis, Bayer, and Gilead Sciences are a few. What has been most useful to the booming biotech sector in San Francisco has been the location of venture capital firms that have provided the funding for many start-ups. The Bay Area has the highest density of venture capital firms in the world, boasting by investment volume 35 percent of all venture funds in the nation.

Beyond this, San Francisco has natural benefits that few cities can boast: its magnificent beauty, its diverse population, and its rich array of amenities, Chinatown, the waterfront, lush valleys, and nearby outdoor activities for sports enthusiasts of all types. In addition, AnnaLee Saxenian (1994) has argued that the culture of Silicon Valley, in which there is a high degree of collaboration between firms as well as a high degree of worker mobility between them, is particularly valuable in generating knowledge spillovers, their subsequent innovations, and the ability to adapt quickly to changing economic and technological conditions. The close proximity of firms in the area means that workers can change jobs without disrupting their informal social and professional networks. Research by Marx, Strumsky, and Fleming (2007) suggest that strong enforcement of postemployment noncompete covenants which place restrictions on a worker's ability to join a competing firm reduces worker mobility. The absence of these covenants in California may have facilitated the high degree of hopping between firms. Fleming and Marx (2006) argue that interfirm knowledge spillovers are becoming a more important ingredient for innovation across a wide span of industries.

The San Francisco area has been a magnet for innovative young entrepreneurs and brilliant engineers and scientists. Few places have been as successful in parlaying natural beauty and lifestyle into economic success. As a result of all these factors, the Golden City MSA has moved up since 1969, from 10th place to first place in household income.

For much the same reasons, the Boston-Cambridge region, known as the Life Sciences Corridor, hosts around 450 life sciences and biotech companies. The region is the home to some of the most prestigious institutes such as Harvard and MIT, and hosts top biopharma companies including Merck, Sanofi, Pfizer, Biogen-Idec, Johnson & Johnson, Vertex Pharmaceuticals, Glaxo Smith Klein, Boston Scientific, Haemonetics, and Novartis. The Boston-Cambridge corridor concentrates on core biotechnology and pharmaceutical drug research and development.

Other cities around the world have now become biotech-pharma hubs as well. The Canadian biotechnology industry is heavily concentrated in three provinces: Quebec, Ontario, and British Columbia. These provinces account for 75 percent of all biotech companies in Canada. Montreal boasts 70 percent of Quebec's nearly 1,000 biotech companies. Toronto boasts 170 such companies working in proteomics, genomics, stem cell research, biomaterials, and biomedical engineering. The University of Toronto, York University, and Ryerson University all provide the comparative advantage for this Canadian city's dominance in biotech, which employs nearly 30,000 professionals and adds more than $2 billion to its local economy. Top biotech players include Aventis Pasteur Limited, Biovail, Inventis, Lorus Therapeutics, and MDS Pharma Services. Ottawa and Vancouver are two additional Canadian cities leading in bioengineering based on their well-established research universities.

Other emerging biotech-pharma hubs around the world are located in the Golden Triangle in the United Kingdom consisting of London, Oxford, and Cambridge. Oxford is host to the Oxford biotech cluster, one of the most mature life science clusters in Europe, as well as business, science, and technology facility Milton Park, home to around 250 businesses. Just 70 miles from Oxford, Cambridge is another exciting place to be for biotechnology and biomedical students and graduates.

The two British cities are host to five globally renowned research institutes and the United Kingdom's two largest pharma firms.

In addition, biotech hubs in Europe can be found in Switzerland, Germany, and France. In Switzerland, the leading biotech hubs are in Zurich and Basel and the area between the two is often referred to as BioValley, one of the leading European life science clusters in the world. Companies in these Swiss cities focus on pharmacology, pharmaceutical biotechnology, nanotechnology, medical technology, chemistry, and agricultural biotechnology. As of 2019 the region includes more than 600 companies (up from only 69 in 2006), 14 technology parks, and 10 universities and academic research institutes. Three main international "big pharma" companies are present on BioValley's territory, with their headquarters: Novartis, Roche, and Aventis. Other global pharma and life science players in BioValley are Eli Lilly, Sanofi-Synthelabo, Amersham, Johnson & Johnson, Dow, DuPont, and Syngenta. About 40 percent of the world's pharma industry is established in this small country's BioValley as spinoffs from the University of Basel.

Today, because of its critical nature, biotech is expanding rapidly in Sweden and Denmark and in Spain, particularly around Barcelona. The Catalan biotech sector is currently in rapid growth, due to a solid scientific base together with the recent creation of industry-driven government instruments and policies. The current trend of the young Catalan biotech sector is to increase from the base, at a rate of more than 10 companies per year. Most of the strictly biotech firms focus on drug development and to a lesser extent, diagnostics. Already by 2020, this Barcelona-based cluster had 71 products in preclinical development, 71 products in phase I development, 33 in phase II development, and 19 in phase III developments. The cluster can boast 20 registered products and 23 marketed products currently in phase IV clinical studies. Other emerging biotech centers can be found in Amsterdam, Oslo, Vienna, Lyon, Paris, Milan, and Dublin (Ray 2019).

Newly Prosperous Metro Regions in the United States

As we just saw, biotech is creating new winners in the global race for economic success. In the United States, the real winners today are metro regions such as Austin and Raleigh. If Buffalo and Detroit are the poster children for deindustrialization, Austin is the poster child for the new economy. High tech slowly began to form a presence in the area during the 1960s, partly as a result of the University of Texas being located there and partly as a result of IBM opening a facility nearby in 1963. In 1966 Texas Instruments moved to town, and Motorola opened operations in 1974. The real watershed for Austin came in 1982, when a young Michael Dell began Dell Computers. From that point, Austin became a magnet for high tech industry. During the 1990s the region added 1,000 new businesses and 280,000 jobs. Today it boasts 85 bioscience companies, and the University of Texas has become one of the largest research universities in the nation, behind only the University of California and MIT in new patents issued annually.

Austin is home to 98 large semiconductor and electronics-related businesses that contribute 17,000 jobs. Along with hardware, the area claims a booming software industry that averaged 22 percent annual growth in revenues from 1990 to 1996. Today there are more than 500 software companies located in the metro area. Developing high tech early and being the birthplace of companies akin to Dell has been the key to Austin's economic success. Not surprisingly, its real median household income has increased faster than any of the other 20 metro regions we have followed.

Raleigh is not far behind. The area was predominately farm country until the 1970s. During the 1980s, income from farming was declining at a 30 percent annual rate. But based on its strong university base with Duke and the nearby University of North Carolina at Chapel Hill and North Carolina State, Raleigh has become one the top five biotech and life sciences regions in the world. Fearful of losing their well-trained college graduates, a consortium of state and local government, business, and academic institutions created Research Triangle Park in 1959 to provide employment opportunities for these highly skilled professionals. Today, the Research Triangle metro area of Raleigh, Durham, and Chapel Hill has more than 140 biotech firms and 65 contract research companies within its bustling pharmaceutical and biotech, computer software and hardware, and telecommunications industries. More than 250 companies have their headquarters in the region. Lower wages than those in the North have contributed to Raleigh's ability to attract firms, but incomes are rising quickly, at a rate only second to Austin's. A lower cost of living and pleasant weather year-round has contributed to Raleigh's ability to attract workers.

Newark, New Jersey is often maligned for its desperately poor inner city. But its metro region as a whole was tied for fifth place with New York among our 20 metropolitan statistical areas (MSAs) in 1969 and moved up to a tie for fourth place in 1999. What accounts for its success? Many of Newark's MSA households work in New York City, but their incomes are counted for census purposes on the basis of where they live. Despite the fact that it is considered a separate MSA from New York, it is part of the official combined New York-New Jersey- Pennsylvania metropolitan area based on the commuting patterns of area workers. Thus, the Newark MSA actually contains many of the affluent New Jersey suburbs of New York City. Newark boasts that it was the early pharmaceutical capital of North America. No other metro area had a larger share of the total pharmaceutical industry than this northeastern region. Chief among the employers in the area are Johnson & Johnson, Hoffman-LaRoche, Merck & Co., Novartis, Wyeth, and a number of US affiliates of international drug companies that include Daiichi Pharmaceutical and Eisai, both of Japan. Newark's long-term competitive advantage in this growing industry helps keep it near the top of the list of metro areas in the country.

How to Encourage Economic Growth

While prosperity is often fleeting, economists have developed important theories about what contributes to success—and what leads to failure of a metro region. Here we have focused on the theories of absolute advantage, comparative advantage, and competitive advantage. But as we shall see in further chapters, political and social factors are important as well to a city's success. Having forward-looking and talented political leaders can help encourage business to expand in their communities. Having regulations that protect the community, but do not disadvantage firms to the point where they are anxious about locating in that region is critical. Having adequate transportation and other infrastructure is important. And obviously a well-trained labor force is a critical ingredient in economic success.

The key question for public policy is how to encourage economic growth and to then find ways to assure that everyone in the community has an opportunity to prosper. The areas that have been the most successful—the ones that make it to the top of the charts and stay there for decades and even for centuries—have a desirable natural feature such as a deep harbor or a good climate. In addition, they have had the wisdom to use their good fortune to develop the social and physical infrastructure to keep the area attractive not only to new firms and new industries but to young and well-educated workers. These are the metropolitan areas where new enterprises continue to be born. The newer metro regions joining them at the top are ones that have learned how to encourage innovative new industries, attract highly skilled workers, and trade their goods and services to the rest of the world.

References

Blumenfeld, Hans. 1960. "The Economic Base of the Metropolis." In *The Techniques of Urban Economic Analysis*, edited by R. W. Pfouts. West Trenton, NJ: Chandler-Davis Publishing.

Boston Consulting Group & Initiative for a Competitive Inner City. 1998. "The Business Case for Pursuing Retail Opportunities in the Inner City: The Boston Consulting Group in Partnership with the Initiative for a Competitive Inner City." *Banking and Community Perspectives* Issue No. 3. Dallas: Federal Reserve Bank of Dallas.

Chinitz, Benjamin. 1961. "Contrasts in Agglomeration: New York and Pittsburgh." *Papers and Proceedings of the American Economic Association* 51 no. 2: 279–289.

Fallows, James. 1994. *Looking at the Sun: The Rise of the New East Asian Economic and Political System*. New York: Pantheon Books.

Finances Online. 2020. "88 Call Center Statistics You Must Read." https://financesonline.com/call-center-statistics.

Fleming, Lee, and Matt Marx. 2006. "Managing Creativity in Small Worlds." *California Management Review* 48, no. 4 (Summer): 6-27.

Florida, Richard. 2002. *The Rise of the Creative Class*. New York: Basic Books.

Glaeser, Edward L., Heidi D. Kallal, Jose A. Scheinkman, and Andrei Schleifer. 1992. "Growth in Cities." *Journal of Political Economy* 100, no. 6 (December): 1126–1152.

Glaeser, Edward L, and Albert Saiz. 2004. "The Rise of the Skilled City," *Brookings-Wharton Papers on Urban Affairs*. 5: 47–94.

Jacobs, Jane. 1969. *The Economy of Cities*. New York: Vintage Books.

Krugman, Paul. 1990. *Rethinking International Trade*. Cambridge, MA: MIT Press.

Krugman, Paul. 1992. *Geography and Trade*. Cambridge, MA: MIT Press.

Leontief, Wassily. 1936. *Input-Output Economics*. Oxford: Oxford University Press.

Leontief, Wassily. 1966. "Quantitative Input and Output Relations on the Economic Systems of the United States." *Review of Economics and Statistics* 18, no. 3: 105–125.

Marx, Matt, Deborah Strumsky, and Lee Fleming. 2007. "Noncompetes and Inventor Mobility: Specialists, Stars, and the Michigan Experiment." *Harvard Business School Working Paper No. 07-042*. Boston: Harvard Business School.

Newcomb, Tim. 2017. "7 of the World's Largest Manufacturing Plants." *Popular Mechanics*, January 6.

Ohlin, Bertil. 1967. "Reflections on Contemporary International Trade Theories." *Appendix II in Interregional and International Trade*, rev. ed. Cambridge, MA: Harvard University Press.

Porter, Michael. 1990. *The Competitive Advantage of Nations*. New York: Free Press.

Porter, Michael. 1995. "The Competitive Advantage of the Inner City." *Harvard Business Review* (May/June): 55–71

Ray, Tanmay. 2019. "Top Biotech-Pharma Hubs in the World." *Stoodnt*, November 16.

Saxenian, AnnaLee. 1994. *Regional Advantage: Culture and Competition in Silicon Valley and Route 128*. Cambridge, MA: Harvard University Press.

Trading Economics. 2020. "China Urban Households Disposable Income per Capita," https://tradingeconomics.com/china/disposable-personal-income.

Uchitelle, Louis. 2002. "Answering '800' Calls Offers Extra Income but No Security." *New York Times*. March 27.

Vernon, Raymond. 1966. "International Investment and International Trade in the Product Cycle." *Quarterly Journal of Economics* 80, no. 2 (May): 190–207.

Vey, Jennifer. 2007. "Restoring Prosperity: The State Role in Revitalizing America's Older Industrial Cities." May 1. Washington, DC: Brookings Institution.

Questions and Exercises

The Importance of Trade in Cities and Regions Today

1. As you did in Chapter 3, once again consider the city or town in which you live (or where you grew up). Using the official website of the municipality or the community's Chamber of Commerce website, identify the products (goods or services) that are most important *today* in providing your region with absolute or comparative advantage in the national or international marketplace.

2. What natural or human resources in your community are responsible for the growth in local companies that produce products or services that are successful in regional, national, or international trade?

3. Try to identify two or three national or international cities that are in competition for the production of the key products and services produced in your municipality. What are the some of the things that your city or region can do to improve its chances of remaining competitive in these products and services?

4. Given the natural and human resources in your municipality or region, what industries might be developed to provide your area with another source of comparative or competitive advantage?

Urban Labor Markets and Metro Prosperity

6

LEARNING OBJECTIVES

- Explain the difference between nominal and real wages and show how it might affect the affordability of metropolitan areas

- Define the marginal product of labor and discuss the strengths and limitations of the concept as applied to wages differences between workers

- Explain how human capital theory builds on the concept of marginal productivity and discuss the strengths and limitations of the theory as it applies to wage differences between workers

- Explain how factors such as a firm's market power or the existence of unions in an industry can produce wage differences between workplaces and across metropolitan areas

- Identify different forms of labor market discrimination and show how they affect wage differences between workers

- Explain the concepts of skills mismatch and spatial mismatch and show how they have affected wage differences between workers

In Chapter 2, we used median *family* income as a measure of a metro area's prosperity. The broader category is median *household* income which includes the total income of all members in a household regardless of family status. According to the US Census, a family is comprised of two or more related individuals living in the same domicile. A household can consist of a family, a single individual living alone, or a group of unrelated individuals who share the same residence.

In 2019, income from wages and salaries accounted for about half (46.5%) of total household income. But this represented only one part of total income related to the labor market. Including the value of such job benefits as employer-paid health insurance and contributions to employee pensions along with proprietors' income—the income of small business owners—brings the total labor market-related income to better than 65 percent (see Figure 6.1). Social Security and other transfer payments such as unemployment insurance tied to past labor market earnings accounts for another 15.8 percent of household income. As such, the labor market accounts for more than 80 percent of total household income. The remainder is the share of household income coming from the return on financial assets and rent.

With such a high proportion of household income coming from work-related activities, how most individuals and their families fare is heavily dependent on how successful they are in the labor market. Hence trends in urban labor markets remain critically important not only for individual households and families but for the well-being of entire cities and metro areas.

As we will learn, the specific labor market opportunities available to individuals depend on a wide array of factors, some of which have to do with where those individuals live. Residing in one metropolitan area rather than another can make a big difference in how much one works and how much one earns. Working in a metro area's suburbs can provide different job opportunities—often better, sometimes worse—than working in the central city. The industry composition of a metro area—the range of mining, manufacturing, construction, trade, and service sectors, along with government enterprise in a region—can affect employment and earnings as well, and the composition varies dramatically across metropolitan areas. Two generations ago, living in a city where the auto industry was king meant you had a chance at a better paying job than if you lived in a city where textiles or apparel were the leading industries. Today, living in a metro area once dominated by the US auto industry yields a greater likelihood of unemployment.

To understand the earnings prospects that face workers in different places, we need to delve into the dynamics of the US labor market. We shall do this by considering a number of theories about what determines earnings and by applying

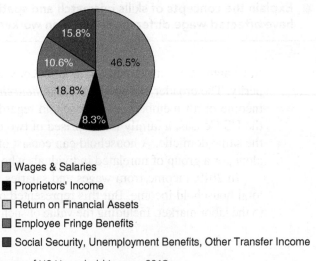

■ Wages & Salaries
■ Proprietors' Income
☐ Return on Financial Assets
■ Employee Fringe Benefits
■ Social Security, Unemployment Benefits, Other Transfer Income

FIGURE 6.1. Sources of US Household Income 2019

Source: Council of Economic Advisors, *Economic Report of the President, 2020.*

these theories to urban labor markets. But first we will take a look at how overall job opportunity is related to unemployment, first at the national level and then at the metro and city level and how your chances of getting and keeping a job—and what jobs pay once you secure employment—vary across metro regions.

The National Economic Business Cycle

Whether you can expect to work full-time all year long, year after year, depends on many phenomena. One is the state of the national economy. When the economy is expanding rapidly, firms are hiring and unemployment falls. When the economy falls into recession, officially defined as a time when total economic output declines for at least two quarters in a row (6 months), firms are doing little hiring and many are laying off their workers. As a result, job opportunity is generally dependent on the state of the economy and specifically the level of unemployment.

Figure 6.2 reveals the **business cycle**—the expansions and contractions of the US national economy in terms of unemployment rates from 1960 through 2017. The vertical bars represent periods of economic recession. Between 1960 and 2017, there were eight recessions—before the worst of all, caused by the onset of the COVID-19 pandemic which struck worldwide in early 2020.

There are many factors that can affect the business cycle and unemployment rates from domestic economic policy to international politics. The first recession in Figure 6.2 occurred between April 1960 and February 1961, with the national unemployment rate peaking at 7.1 percent. This recession was primarily due to an increase in interest rates by the US Federal Reserve Bank in an attempt to reduce

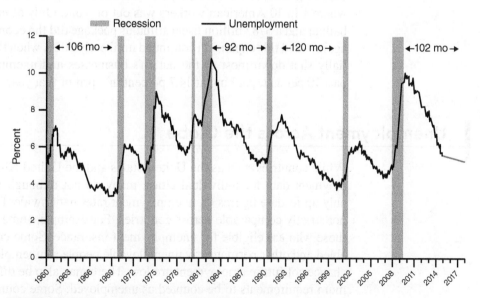

FIGURE 6.2. US Unemployment Rates 1960–2018

Source: US Bureau of Labor Statistics. 2021. "Labor Force Statistics from the Current Population Survey," https://data.bls.gov/timeseries/LNU04023554&series_id=LNU04000000&series_id=LNU03023554&series_id=LNU03000000&years_option=all_years&periods_option=specific_periods&periods=Annual+Data

inflation. This recession was followed by nearly a decade of increased output and falling unemployment, sparked by a tax cut ordered by President John F. Kennedy that provided households with extra disposable income allowing them to increase their spending. This, in turn, led to businesses rehiring laid-off employees.

The next recession began in December 1969 and was relatively mild, with the unemployment rate peaking at 6.1 percent. Then, with the quadrupling of oil prices in 1973 and long gasoline lines as a result of oil-rich Middle Eastern countries cutting petroleum production in order to punish Western nations for supporting Israel in its conflict with Egypt and Syria, the nation went into a more severe recession pushing unemployment to a new post–World War II high of 9 percent. After a brief recovery, the nation's economy regressed into recession beginning in January 1980 for a further six months.

And then the bottom fell out. The Iranian Revolution in 1979 led to another steep increase in the price of oil and the 1979 energy crisis. To counter a sharp rise in inflation, once again the US Federal Reserve Bank hit the monetary brakes by raising interest rates, slowing the economy and forcing up unemployment to levels not seen any time since the Great Depression of the 1930s. By November 1982, the jobless rate hit 10.8 percent. What followed was a period of 92 straight months—nearly 8 years—of economic growth and improved job opportunity. By 1990, the unemployment rate had been cut almost by half—to 5.6 percent—increasing job opportunity throughout much of the country.

A brief recession in 1990–1991 was followed by a long period of growing prosperity which lasted a total of 120 months—a full 10 years. Unemployment would fall to 4 percent in 2001. A short recession in 2001 was followed by improvement in the economy until December 2007 when the subprime mortgage crisis and the collapse of a housing bubble (which we shall discuss in more detail in Chapter 14) led to a recession that lasted 18 months leading to a peak unemployment rate where 1 in 10 American workers was out of work. Only after a $700 billion bank bailout and a $787 billion fiscal stimulus package did the economy begin to expand again—and this expansion continued until early 2020, when the coronavirus essentially shut down most of the nation's businesses and unemployment soared well past 10 percent, peaking at 14.7 percent in April of that year.

Unemployment Across the Globe

While countries such as the United States and the United Kingdom publish unemployment data for individual cities, many do not although most publish reasonably up-to-date figures on unemployment rates nationwide. Even these figures are not strictly comparable across countries. For example, some countries count only those who are eligible for unemployment insurance. Some count the severely disabled and other permanently unemployable people as unemployed even though the chances of future employment are low. There may also be differences in the minimum requirements to be counted as unemployed. Some countries consider people employed even if only marginally associated with the employment market. In the United States, for example, you are counted as employed as long as you work at least one hour a week. In addition, there can be differences in the age limit. For example, Eurostat uses 15 to 74 years old when calculating unemployment rates in European countries. For the same purpose in the United States, the Bureau of Labor Statistics uses anyone 16 years of age or older.

For purposes of comparison, harmonized values are published by the International Labour Organization (ILO). The ILO harmonized unemployment rate refers to those who are currently not working but are willing and able to work for pay, currently available to work, and have actively searched for work. These are the most comparable international unemployment statistics available. Figure 6.3 displays the unemployment rate for a selected set of countries in 2018 before the COVID-19 pandemic—using the ILO methodology.

Of the 24 countries exhibited in this table, Japan had the lowest unemployment rate at only 2.4 percent. Because of little immigration and the aging of its population, Japan actually faces a labor shortage. Germany, Poland, and Singapore all had jobless rates below 4 percent in 2018, levels which place these countries among those with what economists suggest is close to "full employment." Since some workers are "unemployed" between the time they leave one job for another or move to take a job in another part of the country, there is always some "frictional" unemployment. Indeed, in countries with very strong economies frictional unemployment may be a bit higher if workers feel secure in finding a better job if they quit their present one.

For much of the world in 2018 economies were flourishing, and therefore their unemployment rates were reasonably low. In the United Kingdom, in the United States, and in Israel the jobless rate was just 4 percent—among the lowest rates in these countries in the post–World War II era. In both China and Russia unemployment was below 5 percent in part owing to the extensive array of state-owned enterprises that employ workers when the private sector slows.

In a number of European countries including Austria, Denmark, Belgium, and Sweden, the unemployment rate varied between 4.8 and 6.3 percent in 2018. And then there were a number of countries with very high unemployment rates despite a reasonably strong world economy. France's jobless rate stood at 9.1 percent, a tad lower than the 9.2 percent rate in Argentina. Turkey, Iran, and Brazil experienced unemployment rates of 10.9, 12.1 percent, and 12.3 percent respectively. And then there was Greece. With nearly one-fifth of its labor force unemployed in 2018 this country with its ancient history saw its economy unravel and in need of a bailout from the European Central Bank.

While the major cities in each of these countries experienced variance in their job rates, available evidence indicates that with some notable exceptions most large cities in countries with very low unemployment rates experienced relatively low unemployment themselves. We have data for some of those cities for 2018. In high unemployment countries such as Brazil and Greece, their major cities suffered high unemployment as well. In 2018, when the national unemployment rate in Argentina was 9.2 percent, the jobless rate in Buenos Aires was 9 percent. In Japan, Tokyo's unemployment rate was 2.6 percent when all of Japan recorded at 2.4 percent rate. In Canada, Toronto's unemployment rate was 6 percent, just 0.2 percent higher than Canada as a whole.

As such, the national unemployment rates in Figure 6.3 can be used as a pretty good indicator for most large cities and metro areas in these countries.

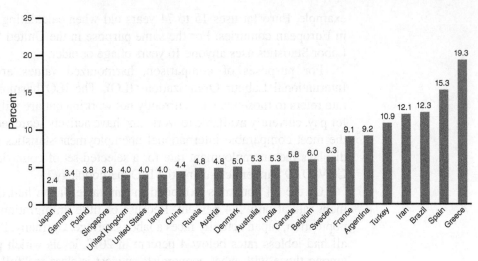

FIGURE 6.3. Unemployment Rates for Selected Nations 2018

Source: International Labour Office. *World Employment Social Outlook: Trends 2018*

https://www.ilo.org/wcmsp5/groups/public/---dgreports/---dcomm/---publ/documents/publication/wcms:615594.pdf

Employment and Unemployment in the United States

Some occupations, such as construction worker or ski lift operator, have seasonal patterns. Others, particularly in manufacturing, are highly susceptible to the national business cycle. By contrast, some seem better insulated from seasonal fluctuations and the business cycle. Public school teachers and nurses are less likely to suffer layoffs than workers in most other occupations. An individual's chances of unemployment also depend on his or her education and skill level. Workers who have less education or training have been subject, at least until quite recently, to more unemployment than those with college degrees or postgraduate training (Mishel et al. 2009).

Because of differences in industrial and occupational composition, the incidence of unemployment varies across metro regions. Relying on the same 25 largest metro areas we have been highlighting, Figure 6.4 provides data on their unemployment rates for 2010, when the economy was just beginning to recover from a deep recession, and January 2020, when the economy was booming just before the COVID-19 pandemic pushed the economy into the worst depression since the 1930s. In 2010, unemployment in the Detroit metropolitan area reached nearly 15 percent and more than 14 percent of the labor force in Riverside, California was unemployed during this deep recession. Detroit's dependency on traditional manufacturing was the leading cause for such a spike in unemployment during the recession. In Riverside, home construction—which was a major industry in the region in the first part of the decade—came to a near stand-still, leading to high unemployment. In 11 of the largest 25 metro areas, unemployment exceeded 10 percent almost regardless of the region of the country. Tampa, Orlando, and Miami, Florida were among these communities. So were San Diego, San Francisco, and Los Angeles.

In many of these metro areas the central cities were hit with even higher unemployment rates in 2010, as Figure 6.5 demonstrates. No city was hit harder than Detroit, which saw unemployment at 26.7 percent, a level not seen since the Great Depression of the 1930s. Motown—once one of the richest cities in America—was now in crisis. Other cities including Riverside, Los Angeles, St. Louis, Chicago, Miami, and Baltimore experienced joblessness in excess of 11 percent. Figure 6.5 points out that some central cities such as St. Louis, Phoenix, Baltimore—and especially Detroit— had unemployment rates higher than the metro areas of which they were a part. But in other cities, including Charlotte, Orlando, San Francisco, and eight others, the central city did not fare quite as badly as the metro area a whole. Smaller communities outside the central city, but inside the metro area, often felt the effects of the 2007–2009 recession and its aftermath more than did the core urban area.

Once this recession was over, the US economy expanded rapidly and unemployment continued to decline. By early 2020, before the outbreak of the COVID-19 pandemic, unemployment across the country was at its lowest level since World War II. Even Detroit and Riverside were experiencing jobless rates of less than 5 percent, as shown in Figure 6.6. And in 9 out of the largest 25 metro areas in the nation, the unemployment rate stood at 3 percent or less—full employment according to economists, and even better than the experience back in 2000. The very lowest rates were in Miami, Denver, San Francisco, and Boston. Only Detroit, Philadelphia, and Washington, DC's central cities experienced unemployment of 5 percent or more.

What Occupations Pay

Workers not only want to find jobs, but they want to find "good" jobs. Suppose you are beginning to think about the type of job you would like to have. No doubt one of the considerations will be how much the job pays. If you are really after a

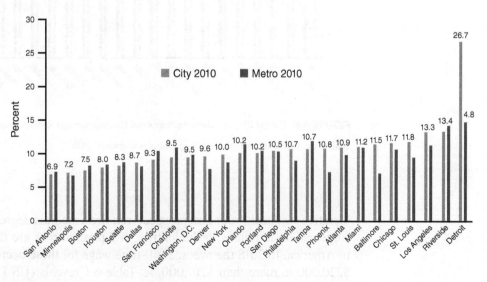

FIGURE 6.4. Central City vs. Metropolitan Area Unemployment Rates, 2010

Source: U.S. Bureau of Labor Statistics *"Employment and Earnings" 2010*

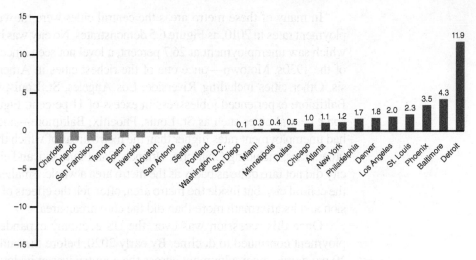

FIGURE 6.5. Percentage Point Difference between Central City and Metropolitan Unemployment Rates, 2010

Source: U.S. Bureau of Labor Statistics. "Metro Area Unemployment Rates" 2010

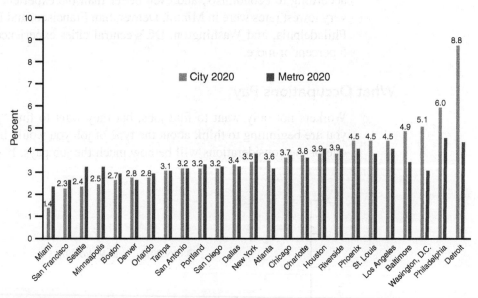

FIGURE 6.6. Cental City vs. Metropolitan Area Unemployment Rates, January 2020

Source: U.S. Bureau of Labor Statistics "Employment and Earnings" 2020

lucrative paycheck, your best prospects require a medical degree. Anesthesiologists, surgeons, obstetricians, orthodontists, and psychiatrists are the best-paid workers in America. In 2018 the average full-time wage for these occupations ranged from $220,000 to more than $267,000, as Table 6.1 reveals (US Department of Labor 2018). Dentists earned an average of nearly $181,000. Outside of the medical sector, chief executives, airline pilots, petroleum engineers, computer systems managers, architects, financial managers, and lawyers are all on the top-25 list of best-paid occupations. Financial managers would have been even higher on this list, but much of their compensation comes in the form of bonuses and stock options, not the wages and salaries measured by the Labor Department.

If possible, you would want to avoid the poorest paid occupations, at least when considering a permanent job. Among the 25 poorest paid occupations are fast food and counter workers, salon shampooers, casino gambling dealers, dishwashers, cashiers, ushers, entertainment attendants, cooks, and agricultural workers. Half are related to the food service industry—fast-food restaurants, cafeterias, and the like. Home health aides and maids also fall into this lowest wage category (see

TABLE 6.1. TOP 25 OCCUPATIONS BY ANNUAL EARNINGS, 2018

RANK	OCCUPATIONS	ANNUAL WAGE FULL-TIME WORKERS
1	Anesthesiologists	$267,020
2	Surgeons	$255,110
3	Oral and Maxillofacial Surgeons	$242,370
4	Obstetricians and Gynecologists	$238,320
5	Orthodontists	$225,760
6	Psychiatrists	$220,380
7	Family and General Practitioners	$211,780
8	Physicians and Surgeons, All Other	$203,880
9	Chief Executives	$200,140
10	Internists, General	$196,490
11	Prosthodontists	$191,400
12	Pediatricians, General	$183,240
13	Dentists	$180,590
14	Dentists, All Other Specialists	$178,800
15	Dentists, General	$175,840
16	Nurse Anesthetists	$174,790
17	Airline Pilots, Copilots, and Flight Engineers	$169,560
18	Petroleum Engineers	$156,370
19	Computer and Information Systems Managers	$152,860
20	Architectural and Engineering Managers	$148,970
21	Podiatrists	$148,220
22	Marketing Managers	$147,240
23	Financial Managers	$146,830
24	Lawyers	$144,230
25	Marketing and Sales Managers	$143,000

Source: U.S. Bureau of Labor Statistics, 2018

TABLE 6.2. BOTTOM 25 OCCUPATIONS BY ANNUAL EARNINGS, 2018

RANK	OCCUPATIONS	ANNUAL WAGE FULL-TIME WORKERS
1	Food Preparation and Serving Workers, Including Fast Food	$22,140
2	Shampooers	$22,160
3	Cooks, Fast Food	$22,650
4	Gaming Dealers	$23,070
5	Dishwashers	$23,190
6	Counter Attendants, Cafeteria, Food Concession, and Coffee Shop	$23,240
7	Cashiers	$23,240
8	Hosts and Hostesses, Restaurant, Lounge, and Coffee Shop	$23,260
9	Amusement and Recreation Attendants	$23,460
10	Ushers, Lobby Attendants, and Ticket Takers	$23,610
11	Dining Room and Cafeteria Attendants and Bartender Helpers	$23,950
12	Pressers, Textile, Garment, and Related Materials	$24,060
13	Lifeguards, Ski Patrol, and Other Recreational Protective Service Workers	$24,420
14	Laundry and Dry-Cleaning Workers	$24,480
15	Childcare Workers	$24,610
16	Food Preparation Workers	$24,830
17	Food Servers, Non-restaurant	$24,980
18	Personal Care Aides	$25,090
19	Hotel, Motel, and Resort Desk Clerks	$25,130
20	Parking Lot Attendants	$25,130
21	Cooks, Short Order	$25,140
22	Home Health Aides	$25,330
23	Food Preparation and Serving Related Workers, All Other	$25,430
24	Maids and Housekeeping Cleaners	$25,570
25	Food Preparation and Serving Related Occupations	$25,580

Source: U.S. Bureau of Labor Statistics, 2018

Table 6.2). On average, an anesthesiologist who puts you to sleep before a nearly equally paid surgeon operates on you earns twelve 12 times what the typical food prep worker makes preparing your burger and fries at McDonalds. Put another way, by the end of January, the former has earned more than what the latter will earn all year long.

Labor Market Earnings by Metro Area

By itself, the occupation you choose does not determine how much you will earn. Where you live matters a great deal. Average hourly earnings differ significantly across regions. Figure 6.7 reveals that earnings, taking into account all 820 occupations, averaged $30.72 an hour in San Francisco in 2019. Washington, DC, Boston, Seattle, and New York had all occupation average hourly wages of at least $26.81 that year. At the other end of the earnings spectrum, the typical worker in Orlando earned less than $18 per hour. San Antonio, Miami, and Tampa were all gathered near the low end of the wage distribution for the largest 25 metropolitan areas in the United States. The average wage in San Francisco exceeded the average in Orlando by nearly 75 percent. Assuming workers spend about 2,000 hours a year in the labor market if they work full-time and work all year long, the typical employee in San Francisco is going to earn in excess of $61,400 per year, roughly $26,000 more per year than the typical employee across the country in Orlando.

Yet before you pack your bags and head out to the Bay Area, consider the living costs you would encounter in each of the metro areas. Given the high cost of housing and other goods and services in San Francisco, you would find your **real adjusted wage** is 15 percent higher in Orlando. Despite the fact that the Detroit metro area has the 12th highest nominal wage among these 25 communities, adjusting for the cost of living makes Detroit the most affordable place to live (see Figure 6.8). Housing costs are the critical factor. In 2019, you would have had to pay more than $875,000 for the median-priced home in the San Francisco Bay Area. If you lived in Detroit, you would have paid about $165,000 to purchase the median-priced home (Kiplinger 2020). Transportation would cost more in the Bay Area, taking into account the price of car insurance, gas, and repairs. California has the 6th highest auto insurance rates in the nation and groceries there run nearly 37 percent higher than the national average (Josephson 2019).

Beside Detroit, the metro areas with the highest cost-of-living adjusted wage are Minneapolis, Houston, Charlotte, and Phoenix. This might help explain why everyone is not moving to San Francisco, Los Angeles, and San Diego, and why a significant number of younger workers are heading to places such as Detroit, despite its reputation as a "poor" city, or not moving at all. As William Frey (2019) has shown, geographic mobility in 2018–2019 reached an all-time low of 9.8 percent of the population, and this decline was most pronounced among young adults aged 18 to 34. Frey attributes this decline to higher housing costs in destinations that would otherwise be attractive, along with underemployment within this age group.

The higher **nominal wages**—that is, before adjusting for cost-of-living—in places such as San Francisco, Washington, DC, Boston, Seattle, and New York reflect the fact that employers in these metro areas often are forced to offer higher pay or better employment benefits to attract a sufficient number of skilled employees to work for them in the face of high living costs. According to these real-wage calculations, it would seem that employers in these high-cost locales would have to pay even higher nominal wages to compensate for their lofty housing prices. Presumably, it is only because these cities have so many natural amenities and

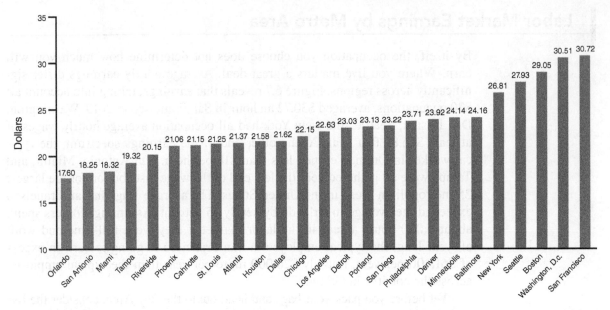

FIGURE 6.7. Metropolitan Area Average Hourly Wage, 2019

Source: Salary Data and Career Research Center (based on U.S. Bureau of Labor Statistics data) 2019 www.payscale.com/US

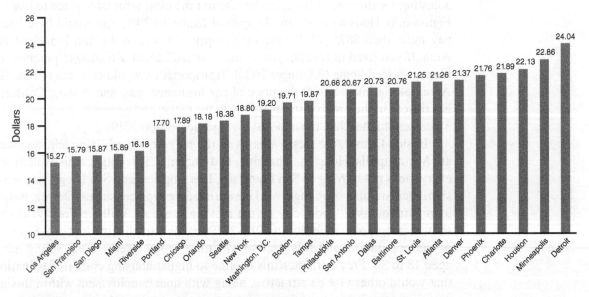

FIGURE 6.8. Metropolitan Average Hourly Wage Median, 2019, Cost-of-Living Adjusted

Source: Salary Data and Career Research Center (based on U.S. Bureau of Labor Statistics data) 2019 www.payscale.com/US and Michael B. Sauter, "Cost of Living in America's Major Cities," 24/7 Wall St., January 2019 www.247wallst.co

cultural and recreational activities that workers are willing to flock there, live in smaller homes or apartments, do without a car, or give up other material possessions in order to survive on low cost-of-living-adjusted wages.

Occupational Wage Differentials Across Metro Areas

Such large wage differentials across urban regions, particularly before controlling for the variation in living costs, can be explained in part by differences in the industrial or occupational composition in each metro area. Cities with a concentration of hospitals, clinics, and highly skilled medical personnel or with corporate headquarters housing a large number of executives and managers enjoy higher average wages than areas or regions where there is a greater concentration of lower-wage industries and occupations. San Francisco, Washington, DC, Boston, Seattle, and New York are the five areas with the highest nominal average hourly wages among the 25 largest metro areas in the United States. These are communities with a rich array of industries known for high wages—financial firms, medical institutions, digital technology, and biotech.

At the other end of the wage spectrum are Orlando, San Antonio, Miami, and Tampa. In these vacation destinations there is an abundance of hotels, fast food outlets, and amusement parks and therefore a large number of workers in the lowest wage occupations—hotel and motel clerks, maids and housekeepers, food preparation workers, lifeguards, and amusement and recreation attendants. As such, these metro areas will have lower overall average wages because of their occupational composition.

Theories About Wage Determination

How can we explain such wide differences in wages across metro areas, across occupations, and within occupations? Economists have thought about this for a long time and have developed a number of theories to try to explain at least some of these differentials. We can begin by introducing a model that relies on the fundamental concept of the *marginal productivity of labor.*

This simple model rests on five key assumptions:

1. *The labor force for any particular type of job is homogeneous.* For the same job, there are no differences between workers in skill level or in motivation.

2. *There are no barriers to labor mobility.* Workers are free to move between firms, offering their services to the highest bidder, no matter where the firm is located.

3. *The product market is competitive.* There are many firms producing exactly the same product at the same price so that consumers are indifferent between purchasing the same product from firm 1, firm 2, or any number of other firms.

4. *Transportation costs are negligible.* A product produced in one region can be shipped at minimal cost to other regions.

5. *Firms are in business with the simple objective of maximizing profit.*

In this economic model of the labor market, free of all kinds of restraints, workers are paid according to their **marginal product** or in simpler terms, the additional output generated for a firm by the last worker in its employ. In this case, the wage for all workers of the same skill level will be equal to the value of output produced by the last worker hired. If a firm would see its output increase by $25,000 a year by hiring one additional worker, all workers who do the same work for the firm and have the same skill would be paid this amount.

Competition *among workers* keeps the wage no higher than the additional output or marginal product of that last worker. Competition *among firms* for workers will keep the wage no lower than marginal product. If the wage paid workers at a particular firm was below their marginal product, another firm would be willing to hire those workers at a higher wage. If workers demanded a wage higher than their marginal product, no firm would hire them. Thus, the wage tends to settle at a particular level across all firms who hire workers with similar skills.

Under this set of assumptions—and the added assumption of no differences in the cost-of-living across cities—firms will be forced to pay exactly the same wage for workers in a particular occupation, no matter where they are located. Plumbers in Detroit will be paid exactly the same as plumbers in San Francisco. If the wages in San Francisco were much higher for some reason, some plumbers in Detroit would move to the Bay Area. Now with a larger supply of plumbers in San Francisco, wages would fall. With a lower supply in Detroit, wages would rise. As long as labor is infinitely mobile in this simplified model, wages for similarly skilled plumbers would tend to equalize everywhere.

Human Capital

The model becomes a little more complicated if we relax the assumption of homogeneous labor meaning that workers have the same skill level and job experience. Now wages can differ among workers, but the wage differentials will reflect different skill levels. A skilled plumber will make more than an unskilled assembly-line worker because presumably the plumber generates a higher marginal product than does the worker on the assembly line. In this case, wage differentials will exist, but they will reflect differences in the **human capital** investment that workers have made in themselves. Those who are better educated or have specialized skills will earn more than those who are less educated and have only general skills that are easy to acquire. Skilled plumbers are like backhoes, while assembly-line workers are more akin to shovels. Since a worker with a backhoe can dig more trench per hour (i.e., have a higher marginal product) than one with a shovel, the better equipped worker is better paid.

Since the other four assumptions still hold in the pure theoretical model, the wages of identically skilled workers should be the same, no matter where they work or where they live. Any differences in wages between workers would be due only to differences in human capital investments that in turn affect marginal productivity. Given the assumption of unlimited mobility and minimal transportation costs, skilled plumbers would still be paid more or less the same whether they work in Baltimore or Charlotte—again assuming no differences in cost-of-living.

Formal schooling, vocational education, and on-the-job training are all types of human capital investment. In the specific occupation of professional baseball player, an investment in batting practice is a human capital investment although it has little monetary value for another occupation, say, the professional accountant—even if taking batting practice may help in the company's Saturday morning softball tournament.

A simple model of earnings can be captured in an equation, as follows:

$$\text{Earnings}_i = a_0 + b_1 * \text{Years of Education}_i + b_2 * \text{Vocational Education}_i$$
$$+ b_3 * \text{On-the-Job Training}_i + b_4 * \text{Health Status}_i$$
$$+ b_5 * \text{Other Human Capital Investments}_i$$

where Earnings_i = the wage rate of individual I, a_0 = return to unskilled, uneducated labor, and b_j = return to an extra unit of a given form of human capital j.

In simple English, the earnings (e.g., hourly wage) of individual i are equal to some base wage rate a_0 plus the sum of the increments in earnings due to each human capital investment times the units of human capital that individual i has accumulated. The increment in earnings—or rate of return—to an additional year of schooling, for example, is b_1. If we were to statistically estimate b_1, we might find, for example, that it is equal to $2.50 per hour. In this case, for two workers who were identical in all other respects, except that one completed college (16 years of school) while the other did not go beyond high school (12 years of school), the college-educated worker would earn $10 ($2.50 × 4) more per hour. This equation would help to explain the difference in earnings between occupations such as surgeon and registered nurse since the two require different amounts of investment in schooling.

Note that in this model, the return to each human capital investment (b_j) is determined in the labor market and is the same across workers. Workers differ only in the amount of human capital investment they have made. An extra year of vocational education in a specific field is worth the same across all workers who have made that investment, no matter where they work. All differences in wages reflect differences in human capital investments, pure and simple. Factors such as gender, race, or ethnicity, for example, should have no effect on earnings if they are determined by the pure human capital model.

By most standards, one of the most important human capital variables is education level. Over time, the return to education has increased because the productivity of skilled workers has climbed, along with an increase in demand for such workers. Table 6.3 provides the median weekly wage for workers with different levels of schooling in 2017. Those with less than a high school degree averaged just $520 a week—or about $27,000 per year. High school graduates earned, on average, $712 per week—about $37,000 per year. Thus, on average, finishing high school provides about a $10,000 increase in annual earning—a 37 percent boost in pay.

Attending college but not completing a degree adds $62 a week, or about $3,200 a year. But completing an associate's degree after two years of college leads to an annual wage of nearly $43,500. Completing a bachelor's degree yields on average nearly $61,000, a 40 percent gain over completing community college. A master's degree takes you to nearly $73,000 and completing a PhD adds still more to your salary—resulting in more than $90,600 on average. If you want to aim for the highest annual salary, going to a professional school such as a School of Law or a School of Business will lead to an average weekly wage of $1,836 and

TABLE 6.3. MEDIAN WEEKLY EARNINGS BY EDUCATION LEVEL, 2017

EDUCATIONAL ATTAINMENT	MEDIAN USUAL WEEKLY EARNINGS
Doctoral degree	$1,743
Professional degree	1,836
Master's degree	1,401
Bachelor's degree	1,173
Associate degree	836
Some college, no degree	774
High school diploma, no college	712
Less than a high school diploma	520

Source: U.S. Bureau of Labor Statistics

an annual salary of nearly $95,500. Such a progression in earnings with respect to schooling is precisely what human capital theory would predict.

Market Power and Barriers to Mobility in the Labor Market

There are still a range of other factors besides human capital and the cost of living that can help explain wage differentials in the real world. If we relax the assumptions of perfectly competitive firms and perfectly competitive labor markets, we begin to see that after controlling for human capital, where someone lives and works actually can make a difference in earnings. Barriers to mobility between firms or between locations can produce wage differentials among workers with identical human capital. A range of sociological and political factors can enter into wage determination by a process known as **labor market segmentation**. This occurs whenever specific groups of workers are restricted by *spatial immobility*: by *discrimination* on the basis of race, gender, sexual orientation, or age; by *occupational licensing requirements*; or by *union rules* (Edwards et al. 1973; Piore 1973; Stevenson 1973; Harrison and Bluestone 1988).

One variant of this model suggests that where there are barriers to entering certain labor market segments, a **dual labor market** can arise with a primary sector composed of higher wage, more secure jobs with certain career paths (often in industries that enjoy some form of monopolistic advantage) and a secondary sector, usually comprised of low-wage, temporary, and dead-end jobs (often in highly competitive industries).

When a firm enjoys a **monopoly** advantage in a particular market or a few firms as part of an **oligopoly** can collude—whether in the formal or informal sector—they are not subject to the same kind of price competition that perfectly competitive firms face. These firms have **market power**, which allows them to increase their prices without losing all their customers to another firm. Depending on the **price elasticity of demand** for their products, they may be able to raise their prices without losing many customers. This will be true in the case of **inelastic demand**, where a commodity (e.g., a life-saving medication for which there is no substitute) is considered so valuable or necessary that consumers will continue to buy it even when its price rises. How can this affect wages?

If the labor market were still perfectly competitive, then the wages paid for a specific type of labor in the monopoly firm would still be the same across all firms using the same kind of labor, regardless of industry. All of the monopoly advantage will show up in the form of higher profits. But if there are some barriers to labor mobility so that the monopolist cannot hire all the workers it wants at the market wage, then the workers in this firm are in a position to win a wage premium without having other workers compete it away. There are many examples where this occurs.

Consider the case of labor unions. If a firm faces little market competition and thus can charge higher prices for its products, then workers in that firm can form a union, bargain for higher wages, and, if successful, attain and keep them. A wage gap will develop between identically skilled workers who differ only by reason of union membership. If some cities are highly unionized and others are not, it would not be surprising to see that the workforce in the highly unionized city is better paid, at least if the unionized employers operate in an industry with monopoly or oligopoly advantage.

This helps to explain the high wages of assembly workers in the Detroit and St. Louis metro areas, where the United Auto Workers (UAW) have organized a large share of the auto industry. In these two communities, the annual wage for production workers is $43,160 and $42,290, respectively. By contrast, production workers in Charlotte, North Carolina and Atlanta, Georgia—where unionization rates are particularly low—earn an annual average wage of only $38,380 and $36,870. Thus, before considering differences in cost of living, the typical blue-collar production worker in Detroit earns 17 percent more than his or her counterpart in Charlotte. In these southern cities, the manufacturing base is generally made up of smaller shops in more competitive industries and unions are either weak or close to nonexistent. The oligopoly power of the auto industry before the onset of foreign competition plus the bargaining power of the UAW explain a good deal of why, back in 1969, Detroit had the highest median household income of the 25 metro areas we have been following.

By contrast, while Georgia as a whole has a large transportation production industry including auto plants and facilities that produce corporate jets (Gulfstream), it has the 3rd lowest manufacturing unionization rate in the United States. Charlotte is known for its many small contract manufacturing shops that produce parts for larger manufacturing corporations. Both Georgia and North Carolina are so-called right-to-work states where unions are not welcome. Although Michigan enacted a right-to-work law in 2012, the law has had a greater impact in reducing union strength in states where unions had no prior foothold.

Geographic regions that have trouble attracting new workers may be forced to pay higher wages as a result of imperfect mobility between locations. If many people want to move to Phoenix, Los Angeles, or Miami to escape the cold winters of the north, even those employers with considerable market power may not need to pay a premium wage to satisfy their labor needs. Convincing workers to move to Chicago or Philadelphia may be more difficult. As we mentioned earlier, the high cost of housing in Greater Boston forces many employers to pay top dollar to have workers remain in the area or to persuade new workers to move in. Thus, we begin to understand the importance of the spatial dimension in explaining wage differentials once we enter a world of imperfect competition between firms and barriers to mobility among workers.

Outside of economic activity in the formal economy where firms pay regular taxes and are tracked in government statistics, there is often an **informal, shadow**, or **underground economy** (Fields 2005). This part of the economy consists of both legal activities (with the exception that taxes are usually not paid on their proceeds) and a range of illegal pursuits, from unsanctioned gambling and prostitution to the sale of illicit drugs. The informal economies in sub-Saharan Africa, Latin America, and Southeast Asia have been in decline over time as more of their economic activities have become part of the regular economy, but as late as 2017 these informal businesses ranged from nearly one-third of the economies in some African and Latin American countries to more than 17 percent in Europe (Medina et al. 2019). Estimates of the size of the underground or informal economy in the United States and Canada are much lower, yet still account for about 6 percent of the national economy.

Racial and Ethnic Discrimination

Still another reason for wage differentials is racial and gender discrimination. When otherwise similar workers are treated differently in the labor market, the assumption of perfect labor mobility is violated and wage differentials can result. At the level of the firm, this can occur when a significant number of companies discriminate on the basis of race or gender when hiring or promoting workers. Those who are discriminated against are harmed by reason of being crowded into the limited number of firms willing to hire them. This increases the supply of workers to these businesses, driving down the wage for those in the group being discriminated against. Meanwhile, those who are favored by employers face less competition for jobs and therefore find their wages driven up. The result is a wage gap between two groups of workers who have the same skills, but differ by skin color, ethnicity, or gender.

The effect of such discrimination can be seen in Figure 6.9 where we have two firms, A and B, with identical demand curves for their products. To make it easy to compare the two firms, we use the same Y axis for both firms, but have rotated the X axis for Firm B so it is the mirror image of Firm A. Let us assume for the sake of argument that Firm A refuses to hire anyone with the exception of White men, while Firm B will hire anyone, regardless of race or gender. As a consequence, the supply of workers to Firm A is limited (E_A) and the intersection of supply and demand is at wage W_A. All the remaining workers are crowded into Firm B, increasing the labor supply to (E_B), which drives the wage down in this company to W_B. The result is the wage differential $W_A–W_B$ favoring White men (Bergmann 1971).

As Becker (1957) demonstrated more than 60 years ago, this type of discrimination will theoretically disappear if firms have no market power and must compete in the product market. His reasoning was quite straightforward. If the owners of Firm A indulge their taste for discrimination they will be forced to pay higher wages, which will increase the firm's **average total cost curve**. Firm B will benefit

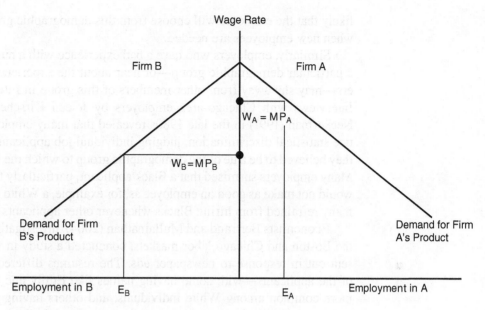

FIGURE 6.9. Employer Discrimination in the Labor Market

from not discriminating because its average total cost curve will be lower. This company will be able to lower its price below what the discriminating Firm A must charge, driving the discriminating firm out of business. This is one of those cases where the free market rewards ethical behavior.

Of course, if Firm A is a **monopolist** or **oligopolist**, it can indulge its taste for discrimination without paying the price of going bankrupt because there is no equivalent of Firm B. Given that many firms have at least a modicum of market power because their products are unique or are sufficiently differentiated to garner consumer demand, the discrimination wage gap can be sustained. Thus, in the days before global competition made even the largest US firms compete for consumers, discrimination could be rampant without its perpetrators paying a price for their behavior.

Employers who discriminated could avoid paying for their discrimination if consumers were the ones who were racially discriminating either by being less willing to buy goods and services from companies who hired employees of a particular racial or ethnic group or gender, or if consumers were willing to pay more for goods and services from firms that did discriminate. Under this circumstance of consumer-led discrimination a wage gap could be sustained and not eliminated through interfirm competition.

A more subtle form of bias is found in what economists call **statistical discrimination,** a practice in which employers judge an individual not on his or her own credentials—which may be difficult, time-consuming, or expensive to ascertain—but on beliefs about the characteristics of the typical or average member of the demographic group to which the individual belongs (Bluestone and Stevenson 2000). If employers experience better performance from a certain demographic group—or even if they just *perceive* or *believe* they will get better performance—then it is likely that the employer will choose from this demographic group again and again when new employees are needed.

Similarly, employers who have a bad experience with a number of members of a particular demographic group—or hear about the experiences of other employers—may shy away from other members of this group in future hiring decisions. Interviews with Chicago-area employers by Joleen Kirschenman and Kathryn Neckerman (1991) in the late 1980s revealed that many employers there did practice statistical discrimination, judging individual job applicants according to what they believed to be true of the demographic group to which the individual belonged. Many employers surmised that a Black applicant, particularly from the central city, would not make as good an employee as, for example, a White immigrant. As such, many refrained from hiring Blacks whenever other applicants were available.

Economists Bertrand and Mullainathan (2004), investigating discrimination in the Boston and Chicago labor markets, conducted a study in which resumes were sent out in response to newspaper ads. The resumes differed only in the names of the applicants—with some having names like Emily and Greg that are much more common among White individuals, and others having names like Lakisha and Jamal that are much more common among Black individuals. The study found that resumes with a White-sounding name were 50 percent more likely to receive a call from an employer than equally qualified resumes with a Black-sounding name.

Sociologists Pager and Quillian (2005), using matched pairs of White and Black job seekers with equivalent resumes, found that Milwaukee-area employers called back to interview 34 percent of White applicants without a criminal background, 17 percent of White applicants with a criminal background, and only 14 percent of Blacks who had *no* criminal record—suggesting that even more information about employees, such as criminal record, did not change the cognitive map of many employers.

Spatial Mismatch

Labor market barriers need not emanate from the explicit discriminatory behavior of firms. Instead, they can be the product of **residential segregation**—where households of different races or members of particular ethnic groups live in separate neighborhoods within a city or metro area—combined with the deindustrialization of central cities. In this case, the barrier is erected not in the firm's employment office, but somewhere between where people live and where the firm is located. The concept of a **spatial mismatch**, where those trapped in inner-city neighborhoods cannot easily access jobs in the suburbs, was first advanced by the Harvard economist John Kain in a seminal paper that appeared in 1968 (Kain 1968). The topic once again gained currency in the 1990s, with a flurry of academic research devoted to testing how much of the unemployment rate differential and the wage gap between Blacks and Whites could be explained by residential segregation (Ihlanfeldt and Sjoquist 1998).

At least until World War II, manufacturing operations were often located in central cities or suburbs close to their company's corporate headquarters. The steel mills in Pittsburgh were not far from the city along the Allegheny and Monongahela rivers; Ford and Chrysler had massive multistory assembly plants in the middle of Detroit; and the stockyards of Chicago were close to the residential neighborhoods where their employees lived. Unskilled and semiskilled immigrant workers and African Americans who had come from the South were able to find jobs in these factories that paid reasonably well.

After the war, many US firms closed operations in central cities and moved to the suburbs, often beyond the reach of mass transit (see Chapter 4). Cheaper land in the suburbs made it cost effective to keep production on a single floor rather than having to move parts and assemblies up and down a multistory building on huge freight elevators, as the Chrysler Corporation had done at its enormous six-story Dodge Main auto assembly operation in downtown Detroit. Improved intracity and intercity trucking made it feasible to be farther away from centralized port facilities and parts depots. As for the workforce, the interstate highway system made it possible for suburban-based residents to travel to their jobs in suburban-based firms along circumferential highways and north–south and east–west freeways.

For Black workers and new immigrants, leaving the central city when the jobs moved out was not always an option. As we will see in **Chapter 14** where we examine housing markets, a variety of practices led to residential segregation, with Whites moving to the suburbs, while Black households were often trapped in the neighborhoods where they had originally come to live in the central cities. For those unable to move to the suburbs, a spatial mismatch evolved whereby the cost and distance of commuting served as a barrier that blocked job opportunities for the central city population (Ellwood 1986).

While the actual quantitative impact of spatial mismatch has been a matter of dispute, there are a range of credible studies that have found inner-city Blacks disadvantaged in terms of both income and employment. Ihlanfeldt and Young (1996) concluded that geographic barriers to suburban jobs explained between 24 and 27 percent of the gap in employment rates between Black and White workers and between 29 and 34 percent of the Latinx–White gap. Not unexpectedly, spatial mismatch was found to be especially important in larger metro areas, where the commuting distances from central city to suburb are greater.

Other researchers have found equally strong evidence of the impact of spatial mismatch, particularly in metro areas in the Northeast and the Midwest (Jencks and Mayer 1990; Holzer 1991; Moss and Tilly 1991; Cutler and Glaeser 1997). Wyly (1996), for example, investigating the impact of an increase in spatial mismatch between 1980 and 1990 in the Minneapolis-St. Paul metropolitan area, concluded that as high-wage manufacturing jobs left the central city, Black workers who could not move to the suburbs were often left with low-wage service jobs and a consequent decline in their incomes. In later work, Glaeser and Kahn (2003) and Stoll (2005) have added to the literature by measuring "job sprawl" as a factor in exacerbating spatial mismatch. Stoll, in particular, finds that metro areas with higher levels of employment decentralization exhibit greater spatial mismatch and this particularly affects Black workers.

So it is not simply that jobs have moved to the suburbs, but the fact that they are moving farther and farther away from the central city that adversely affects workers who still live there. The cities, Stoll finds, with the highest "mismatch index" are generally the ones with the highest "job sprawl index." Detroit, Chicago, Newark, and Philadelphia lead his list. Cities in the South and West generally have less job sprawl and less spatial mismatch.

Skills Mismatch

Not all the intrametropolitan unemployment rate differential or the difference in incomes can be attributed to spatial mismatch per se. As Table 6.4 demonstrates, there are significant differences in the educational attainment of central city and suburban residents, particularly in high spatial mismatch metro areas. In Detroit, according to the 2019 census, nearly 20 percent of central city residents (age 25 and older) had failed to graduate from high school, more than six times the rate in the affluent Detroit suburb of Bloomfield Hills. More than 52 percent of central city adults had no more than a high school diploma while less than 15 percent had completed an undergraduate education or more. In Bloomfield Hills, more than 70 percent of its adult population had a bachelor's degree or more education—including more than 44 percent who had a graduate degree or a professional degree in such fields as law and medicine.

Similar statistics for the City of Los Angeles and its suburb Santa Monica reveal something akin to Detroit's educational attainment, but the differences

TABLE 6.4. CENTRAL CITY/SUBURBAN EDUCATIONAL ATTAINMENT, SELECTED CITIES, 2019 (HIGHEST EDUCATION LEVEL ATTAINED—AGE 25 OR OLDER)

	CITY OF DETROIT	**BLOOMFIELD HILLS**
Less than High School	19.9%	3.2%
High School Grad	32.6%	11.4%
Some College	25.5%	11.8%
Associates Degree	2.5%	3.1%
B.A. Degree	8.7%	26.9%
Graduate/Professional Degree	5.9%	44.1%
	City of Los Angeles	**Santa Monica**
Less than High School	22.0%	5.2%
High School Grad	19.4%	8.3%
Some College	17.8%	13.9%
Associates Degree	6.1%	5.0%
B.A. Degree	22.1%	38.8%
Graduate/Professional Degree	11.6%	28.8%
	City of Boston	**Newton**
Less than High School	11.4%	2.6%
High School Grad	19.1%	8.3%
Some College	12.7%	5.3%
Associates Degree	5.1%	2.7%
B.A. Degree	27.5%	29.9%
Graduate/Professional Degree	24.3%	51.2%

Source: U.S. Census Bureau http://data.census/cedsci

between central city and suburb are not quite as extreme. Of these three cities, the City of Boston had the highest level of educational attainment with more than half of its adults with a bachelor's or higher degree. But even there, its suburb to its west, Newton, could boast of having more than 8 out of 10 of its adults with at least an undergraduate degree.

Given these data, it is clear that even if there were no spatial barriers to suburban jobs, one would expect that many central city workers would have difficulty qualifying for higher-wage jobs. Thus, a significant share of both the intrametropolitan unemployment rate differential and the income differential is likely due to differences in human capital and cannot be attributed solely to a spatial mismatch between where firms and workers are located.

Of course, education is only one form of human capital. Differences in "soft skills," such as work attitudes and work ethic, problem-solving skills, technological competencies, and interpersonal skills and attitudes are important as well, although they are difficult to measure. Nonetheless, if these differ between those who live in central cities and suburbs, differences in formal schooling may explain only some of the central city–suburban unemployment gap and wage differential (Moss and Tilly 2001).

Statistical studies have attempted to determine the share of central city and suburban labor market differences that can be attributed to spatial versus skills mismatch. Most of this research tries to decipher the extent to which Black workers are at a disadvantage because of their central city location. One of the most important early studies in this field found that 56 percent of the average wage difference between Black and White workers was due to the latter's better human capital characteristics, including education and experience (Price and Mills 1985). So the *skills* mismatch was found to be the dominant factor. The remaining 44 percent of the Black–White earning differential was found to be split between outright employer discrimination and spatial mismatch. In estimating how much Black workers would boost their earnings by moving from the central city to the suburbs, Price and Mills concluded that about a third of the remaining wage gap was due to housing segregation.

Over time, one might expect the spatial aspect of employment and earnings differentials to decline, if the degree of housing segregation diminishes and if new technology induces a skill upgrading, even in traditional manufacturing jobs. In this case, space will become even less important relative to skill (Zhang and Bingham 2000). Some evidence of a narrowing during the 1990s in the spatial mismatch between Blacks and jobs has been found in research by Raphael and Stoll (2002).

There is one caveat to this argument. If housing segregation based on race is the reason for the spatial mismatch on the employee side, deliberate relocation to the suburbs by employers to escape the racial composition of the central city should also be considered a form of spatial mismatch. Some circumstantial evidence from a 1995 employer survey in Boston seems to indicate such a motivation on the part of at least some employers. Moss and Tilly argue from their qualitative survey data that "racial composition figures prominently in employers' cognitive maps of space" (Moss and Tilly 2001, p. 347). They argue that information about race combines with the perception of concentrated poverty, crime, and congestion in central city locations to induce some employers to move to the suburbs, exacerbating spatial mismatch.

What has happened to Black–White wage differentials over time? The Economic Policy Institute keeps track of such matters (Wilson and Rogers 2016). They find that Black–White wage gaps are even larger today than they were in 1979, but the increase has not occurred along a straight line. During the early 1980s, rising unemployment, declining unionization, and policies such as the failure to raise the minimum wage and lax enforcement of anti-discrimination laws contributed to the growing Black–White wage gap.

According to the Economic Policy Institute (EPI), during the late 1990s the gap shrank due in part to tighter labor markets which made discrimination more costly and increases in the minimum wage. Since 2000 the gap has grown again. As of 2015, relative to the average hourly wages of White men with the same education, experience, metro status, and region of residence, Black men earn 22 percent less, and Black women earn 34 percent less. Black women receive nearly 12 percent less than their White female counterparts. The widening gap has not affected everyone equally. Young Black women (those with 0 to 10 years of experience) have been hardest hit since 2000.

Employment, Social Networks, and Social Capital

The relationships between housing patterns, neighborhoods, discrimination, and labor markets call attention once again to the interaction of market activity and social contexts. The economic sociologist Mark Granovetter referred to this interaction as "embeddedness" (Granovetter 1985). The economist Glenn Loury advocated for this view stating "in actuality, individuals are embedded in complex networks of affiliations . . . Each individual is socially situated, and one's location within the network of social affiliations substantially affects one's access to various resources. Opportunity travels along the synapses of these social networks" (Loury 1998).

Social networks are the key aspect of social capital, a term that was used by the urban scholar Jane Jacobs in 1961 and re-emerged in writings by Loury and then more broadly articulated and widely popularized by the sociologist James Coleman in 1988. In general, social capital refers to the economic value within a person's relationships with other people. Widespread study of the concept can be found in volumes by Baron et al. (2001), Lin et al. (2002), and Jennings (2007).

Social networks play an important role in labor markets. Numerous studies show that half of all jobs are found through information passed on through friends, family, and other members of an individual's social network.

The value of this labor market aspect of social context depends upon the nature of an individual's social networks, the frequency of interaction found among the individuals in those networks, and the strength of the relationships and exchanges in those networks (Mitchell 1969). An economic rationale for the impact of social networks was presented by Montgomery (1991), who introduced an employer-initiated-employee-referral explanation. The Montgomery model hypothesized that the motivation for using social networks of existing employees begins with employers who are faced with imperfect information about applicants. Knowing that resumes and interviews often do not provide sufficient information about applicants, an employer has an incentive to go to a high-quality existing employee and ask if that employee knows someone who might be appropriate for the job. This referral system can lead to a good match between a job and the new employee because (it is assumed) the existing employee will know individuals who have similar productivity-related attributes and because the existing employee may, in fact, know what is needed for the job better than the employer.

Labor markets reflect social networks and social networks in turn are shaped by childhood neighborhoods, current income levels, housing patterns, and interracial interactions. As such, cities with their dense populations play a critical role in the creation of social networks and therefore are important in providing the labor market with a steady supply of employees and job opportunities for those who seek work.

The Role of Unions

Your job opportunities and your earnings appear to be affected by whether you live in the central city or the suburb, whether you are Black or White, or whether you live in a deindustrializing metro area or one on the forefront of newly evolving high-tech industrial sectors. Being covered by a union contract where wages and benefits are collectively bargained has played a major role in labor market outcomes in a bygone era when trade unionism was in full bloom in the United States. After controlling for differences in the experience, education, region, industry, occupation, and marital status of the working population, it has been estimated that the average union wage premium was close to 16 percent in 2003 (Mishel et al. 2005). That is, nationwide, members of unions earned 16 percent more than comparable workers who were not represented by a union. The union advantage varied by race, ethnicity, and gender with unionization being particularly important for Black and Latinx workers. Overall, the union premium varied from 9.1 percent for White women and 13.8 percent for White men, to 18.2 percent for Black women and nearly 24 percent for Black men. The union wage premiums for Latinx are slightly larger still—19.5 percent for women, 25.5 percent for men.

Metro areas that are more heavily unionized are those where wages are somewhat higher. For metro areas with a union coverage rate below 10 percent, the average hourly wage is $21.33. For those metro areas with unionization rates between 10 and 15 percent, the average wage is a bit higher at $24.15, while the average wage for metro areas with more than 15 percent union rate is $24.72. Hence, the metro areas with the highest level of union collective bargaining generally average a 16 percent wage advantage. With collectively bargained job benefits such as health insurance and pensions, the union–nonunion gap might be even larger. In explaining the metro area wage differentials shown in earlier tables and figures, unionization remains at least something of a contributing factor.

The metropolitan pattern of union density has historical roots. Before the 1930s, only about 10 percent of the total nonagricultural workforce consisted of union members. Most of these were organized into craft unions that were the direct descendants of the medieval guilds in Europe. These were skilled blue-collar professionals, including carpenters, electricians, plumbers, and teamsters—those who drove horse-drawn delivery wagons. With the passage of the National Labor Relations Act (the NLRA, or Wagner Act) in 1935, workers had new protections from unfair labor practices that employers had used to keep their employees from joining unions.

The NLRA provided the legal support for massive union drives among unskilled and semiskilled workers in key manufacturing industries. Thus, by the end of the 1930s, as the result of new union activism, millions of auto, tire, glass, steel, and electrical machinery workers were organized. The percentage of the American nonfarm organized workforce nearly tripled to 29 percent by 1939. Given that the overwhelming majority of traditional manufacturing plants were in the Northeast and the Midwest, these regions and the metro areas within them became unionized. Unionization rates in the South and Southwest were particularly low, with somewhat higher rates on the West Coast where the aircraft industry and the movie industry became bastions of union organizing.

Meanwhile, particularly in the South, there was a business-led movement to make union organizing more difficult. The so-called right-to-work movement has been successful in 27 states in passing laws that banned the **union shop**, which the NLRA had sanctioned. Under the union shop, if a majority of workers in an NLRA-approved bargaining unit within a firm vote to join a union, all workers in that bargaining unit are required to join the union and pay dues. In that way, no workers benefit from union representation without helping to pay for it. Essentially, the union shop borrows from a theory of taxation stating that everyone should pay for the services that are provided to the community.

When the NLRA was amended by the Taft-Hartley Act of 1947, each state was given permission to opt out of this portion of the federal law. Many of the southern states adopted right-to-work laws immediately in 1947, others by the 1950s. More recently, these laws have been adopted in Michigan (2012), Indiana (2012), Wisconsin (2015), West Virginia (2016), and Kentucky (2017). The wage gaps we find between many metro areas in the Northeast and Midwest on the one hand and in the South and Southwest on the other continue to reflect this history.

Today, however, unionization is something of a mixed blessing for workers. While unionized workers are better compensated, many of the private industries with strong unions have been subject to huge layoffs. The sharp cuts in employment in such industries as auto, steel, and electrical goods as well as in apparel and textiles have come as the result of automation and globalization. To the extent that union wage gains and other negotiated benefits have encouraged firms to substitute new technology for workers and to seek cheaper sources of labor in less unionized regions of the country and abroad, many unionized workers have been displaced from their jobs. Heavily unionized cities such as Detroit, Pittsburgh, and Youngstown, Ohio, have been devastated by plant closings, some of which may have been related to the higher labor costs associated with a heavily unionized workforce.

The one bright spot in what remains of the union movement is taking place primarily in central cities, where service-industry unions similar to the Service Employees International Union (SEIU) and UNITE HERE (a merger of the former United Needletrades, Industrial, and Textile Employees union and the Hotel Employees and Restaurant Employees international union) have been aggressively organizing low-wage workers in janitorial services, airport concessions, industrial laundries, hotels, and food services. The United Automobile Workers Union has moved well beyond representing manufacturing workers to organize graduate students in major universities.

Overall, unionization has plummeted in the United States, from representing 35 percent of the labor force in 1954 to only 24 percent in 1973. After 1973, union membership continued to plummet. By 1993 it was down to 12.9 percent of the total US labor force, and by 2019 it was 10.3 percent. As such, unionization plays a much smaller role in wage determination today than in the past.

Indeed, the one place where unionization remains strong is in the public sector. Public school teachers, police officers, and other state and local workers have joined unions to support their needs on the job. By 2020, more than a third (34.8%) of public-sector workers were union members compared with just 6.3 percent of workers in the private sector (US Bureau of Labors Statistics 2021). The largest public-sector unions include the National Education Association (NEA), which represents public school teachers throughout the country along with the American Federation of Teachers (AFT); the Service Employees International Union (SEIU), which represents many municipal employees in various occupations; and the American Federation of State, County, and Municipal Employees (AFSME).

Immigration

Unionization affects wages through labor-management negotiation rather than by permitting the free flow of labor into a firm to set wages according to the laws of supply and demand. Immigration, by contrast, can affect wages simply by increasing the supply of labor in a particular labor market.

Several generations ago, immigrants who came to the United States from abroad generally were less educated and less skilled than native-born Americans. As such, they often went to work in occupations that required little education or training and as a result they earned very little unless they could acquire work in a company with a strong union, such as the International Ladies' Garment Workers Union (ILGWU) in New York or later the United Automobile Workers union (UAW) in a city such as Detroit. Over time, of course, many of the children of these immigrants were able to take advantage of reasonably good public schools and many headed off to college. Within a generation or two, the earnings differentials between those whose families came to America generations ago and those whose grandparents or parents were the first to land on these shores virtually disappeared.

Moreover, over time the education level of immigrants to the United States has increased rather dramatically. In 1960, only 2.5 percent immigrants ages 25 and older had a bachelor's degree and only 2.6 percent had a postgraduate degree. Hence nearly 95 percent of immigrants to America back then had a high school degree or less. As such, immigrants on average earned a good deal less than the native born and much of this was due to having less human capital. Metro areas with large numbers of immigrants back then generally had lower average earnings than communities where there was little immigration.

By 1980, the proportion of foreign born age 25 or older with at least the bachelor's degree represented more than 15 percent of all those new to the United States. By 1990 nearly 25 percent of all the foreign born in the United States were equally well-educated. And by 2016 the percentage rose to 30 percent, just a trifle less than the percentage of similarly aged native born, 32.7 percent (Ryan and Bauman 2016). By far the best educated residents in the United States are of Asian descent. Nearly 54 percent have at least a bachelor's degree.

As such, foreign workers now provide an enormous boost to the human capital stock in many of the metro areas where they have settled. They provide the skills needed in some of the most important industries in the United States: health services, biotech, and architecture.

Explaining Metro Area Earnings Differentials: A Summary

With all this information, we can take a stab at explaining the large wage differences between metro areas, as shown in Figure 6.8. Metro areas such as San Francisco, Washington, DC, Boston, and Seattle were found to have the highest average wages among the metro areas we have been tracking. What do they have in common? All of these are highly unionized cities with relatively little immigration. Cities such as Orlando, San Antonio, Miami, and Tampa have relatively average wages. All have been destinations for a large number of less educated foreign-born immigrant workers who have come to work in the service economies in these communities.

Black and to some extent Latinx workers suffer lower wages because, on average, they have less human capital, because they are often trapped in deindustrializing central cities, and because of continuing outright discrimination.

We have learned that when product markets are not perfectly competitive and mobility within labor markets is constrained, large wage differentials can occur even for workers in the same occupation but who live in different labor markets.

Race and location of residence remain critically important variables even in the twenty-first century. In a detailed study of annual earnings of Black, Latino, and White men in the Greater Boston metro region, all of whom had no more than a high school education, Bluestone and Stevenson (2000) found that Black men earned only 55 percent of what White men received, and Latinos 63 percent. Using a statistical simulation technique, they were able to estimate how the Black–White and Latinx–White earnings ratios would change if Blacks and Latinos had different characteristics. Assigning these two groups the same human capital attributes as White men (i.e., age, education level, word recognition test scores, number of years of specific job experience, health status, and veteran status), they found that the earnings gap for these workers with no more than a high school degree disappeared for Latinx, but Black men still earned only a little more than two-thirds (69%) of White men.

In an alternative simulation, Bluestone and Stevenson assigned the same metro area residential location to everyone and gave Black and Latinx men the same job characteristics as White men. Now Latinx men earned earned only 87 percent as much as whites, but the Black men earned 92 percent as much. They concluded that within at least this one metro area, closing the human capital gap was all that was necessary to bring earnings parity for Latinx. But this would not solve the problem for Black men. Trapped in the inner city and unable to gain admittance to the same jobs as White men because of various forms of discrimination, they were placed at

TABLE 6.5. FACTORS AFFECTING RACIAL AND ETHNIC ANNUAL EARNINGS DIFFERENTIALS: INDIVIDUALS WITH NO MORE THAN A HIGH SCHOOL DEGREE IN GREATER BOSTON

MEN	BLACK/WHITE RATIO	LATINX/WHITE RATIO
Original Earnings Ratio	.55	.63
Equal Human Capital	.69	1.01
Same Residence/Same Job Characteristics	.92	.87
Women	**Black/White Ratio**	**Latinx/White Ratio**
Original Earnings Ratio	.65	.94
Equal Human Capital	.77	.96
Same Residence/Same Job Characteristics	.79	.84

Source: Adapted from Bluestone and Stevenson 2000, figure 8.12, p. 247.

a considerable disadvantage. To close most of the earnings gap, it would be necessary to overcome spatial mismatch and eliminate racial prejudice (see Table 6.5).

For women who had no more than a high school degree in the Boston study, the annual earnings gap between Latinas and Whites was found to be extremely modest. This turned out to be true because Latinas have become the new manufacturing workforce in that metro region and are more likely to have full-time jobs with union benefits. But as in the case of men, the earnings gap between Black and White women was large and could not be closed through infusions of human capital. Indeed, for all women, the key factor that explained annual earnings was related to marital status and the presence of children. Single women with children, no matter their race or ethnicity, were trapped in low-wage, part-time jobs and experienced higher unemployment. As a result, their earnings fell far below those of single women without children and below those of married women with and without children.

Labor Markets and Urban Prosperity

As we have seen, for almost all households, economic well-being is tied closely to how their breadwinners fare in the labor market. At one time, how well they prospered in the labor market was a function of many factors that included whether they were members of trade unions and how much discrimination they might face in the search for employment. While both of these factors are still important, human capital has become increasingly important in a global economy based on sophisticated new information technologies.

What holds for individuals holds for cities and suburbs. Prosperity is now tied increasingly to the human capital of their residents. At one time, a city's location on a key waterway or its proximity to a valuable natural resource was critical to its well-being. While physical location is still important, global competition is now based less on location per se and more on the ability of a metro area to retain and attract the talent that its industries need to remain competitive.

But it is clear that a combination of disparities in human capital and discrimination in labor markets are responsible for the continuing gap in earnings and household incomes across racial and ethnic groups. Because of housing segregation, the pattern of racial and ethnic gaps in labor market earnings is replicated in many metro areas in the disparity of economic well-being between central cities and suburbs. To assure growing prosperity that is more equally shared, we need to explore public policies that help urban areas compete for talent and programs that equalize individual economic opportunity. These are explored in later chapters.

References

Baron, Stephen, John Field, and Tom Schuller, eds. 2001. *Social Capital: Critical Perspectives*. New York: Oxford University Press.

Becker, Gary S. 1957. *The Economics of Discrimination*. Chicago: University of Chicago Press.

Bergmann, Barbara. 1971. "The Effect on White Incomes of Discrimination in Employment." *Journal of Political Economy* 79, no. 2: 294–313.

Bertrand, Marianne, and Sendhil Mullainathan. 2004. "Are Emily and Greg More Employable Than Lakisha and Jamal? A Field Experiment on Labor Market Discrimination." *American Economic Review* 94, no. 4: 991–1013.

Bluestone, Barry, and Mary Huff Stevenson. 2000. *The Boston Renaissance: Race, Space, and Economic Change in an American Metropolis*. New York: Russell Sage.

Coleman, James. 1988. "Social Capital in the Creation of Human Capital." *American Journal of Sociology* 94 (Supplement P. S96): S95-S120.

Cutler, David M., and Edward M. Glaeser. 1997. "Are Ghettos Good or Bad?" *Quarterly Journal of Economics* 112, no. 3: 827–872.

Edwards, Richard C., Michael Reich, and David M. Gordon, eds. 1973. *Labor Market Segmentation*. Lexington, MA: D.C. Heath.

Ellwood, David T. 1986. "The Spatial Mismatch Theory: Are There Teenage Jobs Missing in the Ghetto?" In *The Black Youth Employment Crisis*, edited by Richard B. Freeman and Harry Holzer. Chicago: University of Chicago Press, pp. 147–190.

Fields, Gary S. 2005. *A Guide to Multisector Labor Market Models. Social Protection Unit, Human Development Network*. Washington, DC: The World Bank.

Frey, William H. 2019. "For the First Time on Record, Fewer Than 10% of Americans Moved in a Year: Millenials Are Driving the Trend." *The Avenue*, November 22. Washington, DC: Brookings Institution.

Glaeser, Edward L., and Matthew E. Kahn. 2003. "Sprawl and Urban Growth." NBER Working Paper No. W9733, May. Cambridge, MA: National Bureau of Economic Research.

Granovetter, Mark. 1985. "Economic Action and Social Structure: The Problem of Embeddedness." *American Journal of Sociology* 91, no. 3: 481–510.

Harrison, Bennett, and Barry Bluestone. 1988. *The Great U-Turn: Corporate Restructuring and the Polarizing of America*. New York: Basic Books.

Holzer, Harry. 1991. "The Spatial Mismatch Hypothesis: What Has the Evidence Shown?" *Urban Studies* 28, no. 1: 105–122.

Ihlanfeldt, Keith R., and Madelyn V. Young. 1996. "The Spatial Distribution of Black Employment between the Central City and Suburbs." *Economic Inquiry* 34 no. 4: 693–707.

Ihlanfeldt, Keith, and David L. Sjoquist. 1998. "The Spatial Mismatch Hypothesis: A Review of Recent Studies and Their Implications for Welfare Reform." *Housing Policy Debate* 9, no. 4: 849–892.

Jacobs, Jane 1961. *The Life and Death of Great American Cities*. New York: Vintage.

Jencks, Christopher, and Susan Mayer. 1990. "Residential Segregation, Job Proximity, and Black Job Opportunities." In *Inner City Poverty in the United States*, edited by Laurence E. Lind and Michael McGeary. Washington, DC: National Academies Press, pp. 187–222.

Jennings, James, ed. 2007. *Race, Neighborhoods, and the Misuse of Social Capital*. London: Palgrave-Macmillan.

Josephson, Amelia. 2019. "The Cost of Living in California." *Smart Asset*, May 28.

Kain, John. 1968. "Housing Segregation, Negro Employment, and Metropolitan Decentralization." *Quarterly Journal of Economics* 82, no. 2: 175–197.

Kiplinger Personal Finance Editor. 2020. "Home Prices in the 100 Largest Metro Areas." February 26. https://www.kiplinger.com/article/real-estate/t010-c000-s002-home-price-changes-in-the-100-largest-metro-areas.html

Kirschenman, Joleen, and Katherine Neckerman. 1991. "'We'd Love to Hire Them, But . . .': The Meaning of Race for Employers." In *The Urban Underclass*, edited by Christopher Jencks and Paul E. Peterson. Washington, DC: Brookings Institution, pp. 203–234.

Lin, Nan, Karen Cook, and Ronald S. Burt, eds. 2001. *Social Capital: Theory and Research*. New York: Aldine de Gruyter.

Loury, Glenn C. 1998. "Discrimination in the Post–Civil Rights Era: Beyond Market Interactions." *Journal of Economic Perspectives* 12, no. 2: 117–126.

Medina, Leandro, and Friedich Schneider. 2019. *Shedding Light on the Shadow Economy: A Global Database*. IMF Working Paper. Washington, DC: International Monetary Fund.

Mishel, Lawerence, Jared Bernstein, and Sylvia Allegretto. 2005. *The State of Working America 2004/2005*. Ithaca, NY: ILR Press.Mishel, Lawerence, Jared Bernstein, and Heidi Shierholz. 2009. *The State of Working America 2008–2009*. Ithaca, NY: Cornell University Press.

Mitchell, J. Clyde. 1969. "The Concept and Use of Social Networks." In *Social Networks in Urban Situations: Analyses of Personal Relationships in Central African Towns*, edited by J. Clyde Mitchell. Manchester, UK: Manchester University Press, 1–50.

Montgomery, James D. 1991. "Social Networks and Labor-Market Outcomes: Toward an Economic Analysis." *American Economic Review* 81, no. 5: 1408–1418.

Moss, Philip, and Chris Tilly. 1991. "Why Black Men Are Doing Worse in the Labor Market: A Review of Supply-Side and Demand-Side Explanations." *Working Paper.* New York: Social Science Research Council.

Moss, Philip, and Chris Tilly. 2001. *Stories Employers Tell: Race and Hiring in America.* New York: Russell Sage Foundation.

Pager, Devah, and Lincoln Quillian. 2005. "Walking the Talk? What Employers Say Versus What They Do." *American Sociological Review* 70, no. 3: 355–380.

Piore, Michael. 1973. "Notes on a Theory of Labor Market Stratification." In *Labor Market Segmentation*, edited by Richard C. Edwards, Michael Reich, and David M. Gordon. Lexington, MA: D.C. Heath, pp. 125–150.

Price, Richard, and Edwin Mills. 1985. "Race and Residence in Earnings Determination." *Journal of Urban Economics* 17, no. 1: 1–18.

Raphael, Steven, and Michael A. Stoll. 2002. "Modest Progress: The Narrowing Spatial Mismatch between Blacks and Jobs in the 1990s." December. Washington, DC: Brookings Institution.

Ryan, Camille L., and Kurt Bauman. 2016. "Educational Attainment in the United States: 2015." Current Population Reports, March. Washington, DC: US Census Bureau.

Stevenson, Mary. 1973. "Women's Wages and Job Segregation." In *Labor Market Segmentation*, edited by Richard C. Edwards, Michael Reich, and David M. Gordon. Lexington, MA: D.C. Heath, pp. 243–255.

Stoll, Michael A. 2005. "*Job Sprawl and the Spatial Mismatch between Blacks and Jobs*." February. Washington, DC: Brookings Institution.

US Bureau of Labor Statistics. 2017. *Median Weekly Earnings by Education Level.* Washington, DC: Government Printing Office.

US Bureau of Labor Statistics. 2018. *Occupational Employment Survey.* Washington, DC: Government Printing Office.US Bureau of Labor Statistics. 2019. *Occupational Earnings.* Washington, DC: Government Printing Office.

US Bureau of Labor Statistics. 2021. "Union Members Summary." January 22. Washington, DC: US Bureau of Labor Statistics. https://www.bls.gov/news.release/union2.nr0.htm.

US Department of Labor. 2018. *Metropolitan Area Occupational Employment and Wage Estimates.*" Washington, DC: Government Printing Office.

Wilson, Valerie, and William M. Rogers III. 2016. "Black-White Wage Gaps Expand with Rising Wage Inequality." September 19. Washington, DC: Economic Policy Institute.

Wyly, Elvin K. 1996. "Race, Gender, and Spatial Segmentation in the Twin Cities." *Professional Geographer* 48, no. 4: 431–444.

Zhang, Zhongcai, and Richard D. Bingham. 2000. "Metropolitan Employment Growth and Neighborhood Job Access in Spatial and Skills Perspective: Empirical Evidence from Seven Ohio Metropolitan Regions." *Urban Affairs Review* 35, no. 3: 390–421.

Questions and Exercises

1. Using data from the US Bureau of Labor Statistics website https://www.bls.gov/web/metro.supp.toc.htm, find the unemployment rates for the metro area closest to you and two other metro areas of your choice for a given month in the years 1990, 2000, 2010, 2020, and the most current year. Taking *each metro area* one at a time, how would you describe the change in the unemployment rates from decade to decade in that metro area over the period from 1990 to the present? Do the unemployment rates stay about the same, increase, decrease, or display some other pattern? Next, comparing *across* the metro areas, which of the metro areas had the greatest changes in unemployment rates over this period?

2. The BLS Web page https://www.bls.gov/emp/chart-unemployment-earnings-education.htm provides unemployment rates by educational level for the United States as a whole. The website also provides data on educational attainment for each US metro area. Given the educational attainment in the metro areas you selected in Question 1, how well does educational level appear to predict metro area unemployment rates?

3. Using readily available website data on the industrial composition of the three metro areas you selected in Question 1, describe the industrial landscape of each community. How does the industrial composition in each metro area seem to be correlated with its unemployment rate?

4. The wage for a given occupation can vary considerably across metropolitan areas. Estimates of wages for occupations by metro area can be found in the US Bureau of Labor Statistics website at http://www.bls.gov/bls/blswage.htm.

Go to this website and under "Metropolitan Area Wage Data" click on the link that begins "For 375 metropolitan statistical areas." Click on a metro area of your choice (other than the 20 we follow in the charts in this chapter).

Find the wage estimate ("mean annual") for the following four occupations:

• Registered nurses (located under "Health Care Practitioner and Technical Occupations")

• Civil engineers (located under "Architecture and Engineering Occupations")

- Elementary school teachers, except special education (located under "Education, Training and Library Occupations")

- Machinists (located under "Production Occupations")

Next, find this information for three other metropolitan areas of your choice. In which metro areas is the average wage/salary of each of these occupations the highest? In which metro areas is the average wage/salary the lowest? How would you explain these differences?

PART IV

Current Policy Issues in Metropolitan Areas

The Urban Public Sector

7

LEARNING OBJECTIVES

- ■ Itemize the conditions that are necessary for the private market to produce allocative efficiency and explain why, in their absence, government intervention might be necessary

- ■ Explain how a natural monopoly is different from monopolies achieved by other means and why it often necessitates some form of government intervention

- ■ Explain why a private market would produce too much of an item that has negative externalities and too little of an item that has positive externalities

- ■ Explain how a pure public good is different from a pure private good and what that implies about government provision of goods in this category

- ■ Explain the Tiebout hypothesis and discuss its shortcomings

- ■ Compare and contrast the various political science approaches to public decision-making and explain why it is difficult to create a perfect voting system

The biggest news stories about the public sector often focus on the federal government—the decisions made by the president, the US Congress, or the US Supreme Court. Our daily lives, however, are profoundly affected by the ordinary activities of state and local governments, whose decisions shape our existence in myriad ways, from the time we turn on our water faucets in the morning until the time we turn off our lights at night. Decisions at the state and local level govern the regulation of many public utilities including electricity, water, and cable TV; the provision of health and safety services such as police, fire protection, garbage collection, sewage treatment, and building inspections; the operation of a network of paved and lighted streets and sidewalks, traffic signals and mass transportation; and the offering of educational and recreational services such as schools, libraries, parks, and playgrounds.

From the workers who repair potholes in the streets to the city councilors who deliberate over whether to build a new convention center, public-sector decisions affect our lives in a variety of ways both large and small. If we are to have a full understanding of how metropolitan areas work, we must understand the operation of the urban public sector.

With regard to the political structure of most cities, the residents choose who will serve as mayor—the chief executive officer of the municipality—and who will serve as members of the city council responsible for formulating public policy along with the mayor. In many cities they elect members of the school board. The mayor normally has the responsibility for selecting a staff which will oversee the myriad functions of the city. In most cities, these functions are organized into offices with department heads. Table 7.1 provides a list of departments one will often find in larger cities.

As this list suggests, local city government requires a large civil service comprised of thousands of employees to carry out the myriad tasks in each department. Nationwide, more than 14.7 million people work for local governments (US Bureau of Labor Statistics 2020).

While many of these municipal tasks are designed to provide particular services to city residents, such as elderly affairs, with its range of activities aimed at assisting older citizens, there is a fundamental economic purpose for most of these ranging from negotiating labor contracts for unionized city employees to deciding what kinds of housing and commercial development should be encouraged in which neighborhoods.

As such, it is useful to first step back and ask a fundamental question: What is the economic role of government in metropolitan areas?

Government's Economic Role in Metro Areas

As we pointed out in Chapter 1, population density is the central distinguishing characteristic of metropolitan areas. A large population mass is necessary to support cable TV, municipal trash collection, or public transportation. At low population densities, children might have a short school bus ride to the local elementary school, but they would need to travel longer distances to attend a regional high school. At very low population densities, fire protection services might rely on volunteers, or might even be sold through the market. Street lighting and paved sidewalks would be rare or nonexistent, and a visit to the nearest public library might entail a long journey. While the higher population densities of cities and towns make it *possible* to provide a wider array of public goods and services because of economies of scale, they make it *necessary* to provide some of these goods and services through the public sector because of externalities such as those discussed in Chapter 1 and because of other ways in which private markets fail.

At the local level, the major economic task of government is to change the level of output of certain items from what the market would typically produce so as to increase the output of some items and decrease the output of others. We need, for example, more schooling but less traffic congestion and more fire protection and less pollution than the private market on its own would normally produce.

TABLE 7.1. KEY CITY DEPARTMENTS IN MAJOR MUNICIPALITIES

Elderly Commission
Election Department
Emergency Management
Emergency Medical Services
Emergency Shelter
Emergency Storm Center
Environment Department
Environmental & Energy Services
Fire Department
Human Resources
Innovation and Technology
Inspectional Services
Intergovernmental Relations
Jobs and Community Services
Labor Relations
Law Department
Neighborhood Development
Neighborhood Services
Office of Business Development
Office of the Parking Clerk
Parks & Recreation
Police Department
Planning & Development Department
Press Office
Property & Construction Management
Public Works Department
Purchasing / Bids
Registry Division
Rental Housing Resource Center
Retirement Board
School Department
Small & Local Business Enterprise
Registry of Deeds
Transportation Department
Treasury
Veteran's Services
Women's Commission
Zoning Board of Appeal

Under ideal circumstances, a private-market economy will produce the right items in the required amounts. If these ideal circumstances do not apply, however, the market will produce too little of some goods and too much of others. Correcting these malfunctions comes under the **allocation role of government**, which is an important function of local governments everywhere. The denser the population of an area, the more likely parts of the private market will fail and require public intervention.

The public sector also has a role to play in providing services that only the wealthy might enjoy in the absence of city government. Presumably a rich family could purchase clean water from a private vendor. Those with the means can pay for private schools and books for their children. The public sector exists to make sure such basic services are available to everyone through public water supply, public schools, and public libraries. This can be considered the **distributional role of government**.

How the Private Market Is Supposed to Work

To understand the critical role of the public sector in the local economy, it is useful to begin by understanding how the private sector is supposed to operate. Markets provide a mechanism for exchanging goods and services in a modern economy. The prices that consumers are willing to pay serve as signals to producers, guiding them in their decisions about what to produce and in what quantities.

Ideally, this would lead to an economic system that produces the right items in the correct amounts for people who need and want them and in such a way that the items are channeled to the consumers who value them most. The focus of **allocative efficiency** is on the maximization of each consumer's satisfaction through the market, given the consumer's initial endowment of purchasing power. If resources are not being used in this way, the prices of some goods or services demanded by consumers will rise while others will fall, signaling to business that reallocating resources to fill consumer demand will result in higher profits. In theory, this process of constant reallocation of resources in response to changes in demand and price is an elegant, self-regulating system. Adam Smith, the eighteenth-century founder of modern economics, called this "the invisible hand" of perfect competition, in which the coordination of the activities of many individuals is achieved without any one of them taking control of the market.

This idea of allocative efficiency under perfect competition requires elaboration before we can use it to fully understand the circumstances in which market failure occurs and allocative efficiency is not achieved. Specifically, the ideal world of perfect competition rests on several key assumptions:

1. *No one has market power.* For every good and service in the market, there are many buyers and many sellers.

2. *Output is homogeneous.* For each good or service, each seller produces output indistinguishable from that of all other sellers of the same good or service.

3. *There is perfect information.* All buyers are informed about the price and quality of each product so they can make a rational choice about what to buy.

4. *There are no barriers to entering or exiting the industry.* New producers are free to enter any market for a good or service without impediment, and existing producers are free to leave.

5. *There are no externalities.* Sellers take into account all the costs of producing a particular good or service and only the buyers themselves receive the benefits from purchasing the particular good or service.

As we will explain, under this set of circumstances, the price at which every good and service is sold will equal its marginal cost (the cost of producing one additional unit) and firms will produce the precise mix of goods and services that conform to maximum allocative efficiency.

Assuming there are *no* collective goals in society, but only individual ones, the market *price* for each good and service can be viewed as a proxy for **social benefit** (how much consumers really value each good and service), while *marginal cost* can be viewed as a proxy for **social cost** (the cost to society of using up the resources to produce an additional unit of each good and service rather than using the resources for some other purpose). Under these conditions, the marginal cost is the full opportunity cost of getting the last unit of any given good or service produced.

Supply and Demand in the Private Sector

Let us use an example of a perfectly competitive market in an urban setting—street vendors. In many large cities, you can find vendors who sell everything from handbags to hot dogs. In the busiest parts of the city, there might be a hot dog vendor on nearly every street corner. The National Hot Dog and Sausage Council (2007) estimates that 15 percent of the 20 billion hot dogs Americans consume each year are bought from street vendors. Although the product is not entirely homogeneous—several brands that vary in taste or quality might be available in any given city—the conditions in this market are nevertheless very close to those of textbook perfect competition. Lunchtime strollers can choose to buy pretty much the same hot dog from many different vendors. This assures that the price of a hot dog will not vary much from one vendor to the next.

But how many hot dogs will be prepared and sold in this city? To answer this question, let us say that each vendor's marginal cost of purchasing hot dogs, preparing them, and selling them on the street—including a normal profit of 50 cents a dog—is initially $2 (see Figure 7.1a). If the initial price that consumers are willing to pay to consume all the hot dogs prepared by the vendors is greater than the marginal cost, say $2.50 per dog, vendors could raise their price and make an even greater profit. More likely, in a competitive market, some vendors would prepare more hot dogs to satisfy the demand at a price of $2. But as that happens, marginal cost will normally begin to rise because resources will have to be lured away from other industries and the scarcity of these resources will cause their prices to increase. The vendors will find that their marginal costs are rising as they increase output to satisfy the demand. They can no longer maintain a price of $2 and thus the price will ultimately settle at something above that amount, say $2.25, where the amount supplied, Q_2, just equals the amount demanded and the new (higher) price equals the new (higher) marginal cost.

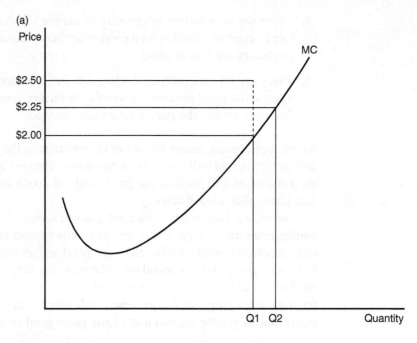

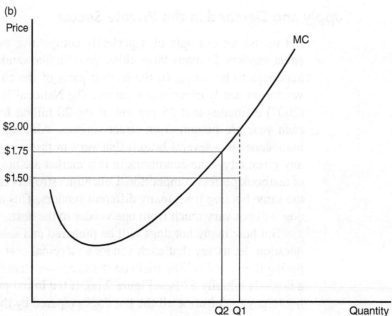

FIGURE 7.1. A Marginal Cost Curve for Hot Dog Stand

What if the initial price that vendors could charge to sell all the hot dogs they prepared was less than marginal cost? In this case, consumers value a hot dog at, say, $1.50, but it uses up $2 worth of resources to produce one more (see Figure 7.1b). If hot dogs are such a low priority for consumers, resources should leave hot dog production in search of better opportunities elsewhere. As hot dog output declines, marginal cost will fall until it equals the price that consumers are willing to pay. Again, at some point, price and marginal cost will balance, let us say at $1.75 at output Q_2.

Accordingly, when the market price is greater than marginal cost, resources generally flow into that use and output will expand. If price is less than marginal cost, resources will flow out of that use and output contracts. If price is equal to full marginal cost, hot dog vendors are producing just the right amount of output consistent with consumer preferences. If every good and service is produced so that price equals marginal cost, there would be no way for some businesses to grow or others to shrink that would make consumers any better off. We would be in a condition of what economists call **Pareto optimality**, where resources are so perfectly allocated that no shift of resources is possible without reducing the satisfaction of at least one consumer.

If consumers are willing to pay a price greater than marginal cost, each vendor will want to increase his output. However, if all hot dog vendors try to produce a larger quantity, their costs for raw materials will increase and the marginal cost of a hot dog will rise for each vendor as he expands output from Q1 to Q2. At Q2, price will equal marginal cost and the vendor will not want to expand output further.

If consumers are not willing to pay a price at least as great as the marginal cost, each vendor will want to reduce their output. However, when all vendors produce less, their costs for raw materials will decrease and the marginal cost of a hot dog will fall for each vendor as they reduce output from Q1 to Q2. At Q2, price will equal marginal cost and the vendor will not want to reduce output any further.

Market Failure and the Public Sector

In the real world, however, conditions for Pareto optimality are rarely attained. Indeed, under normal conditions, markets fail to achieve allocative efficiency because one or another of the five assumptions of the perfectly competitive market enumerated earlier is violated. Indeed, there are four broad conditions under which this is true: market power, imperfect information within the market, negative and positive externalities, and pure public goods. In each of these cases, government intervention may be warranted for society to come closer to an outcome more consistent with Pareto optimality.

Market Power

Perfect competition requires large numbers of buyers and sellers as in the hot dog vendor example. In some markets, however, there is only a handful of producers and, in some cases, only one. Patent protection, access to raw materials, or brand name identification can severely limit the number of producers of a given commodity. In these circumstances of **monopoly** or **oligopoly**—one or only a few producers in the industry, respectively—producers seeking to maximize their profit will artificially restrict output, sending prices higher than marginal cost. The purpose of government-imposed antimonopoly laws—better known as antitrust laws—is to reduce the market power of individual producers in order to expand total output and thereby lower price. Since this kind of market power often exists on a nationwide level, antitrust laws are federal laws, and it is the federal government that enforces them. Using government regulation to break up monopolies and oligopolies in order to allow competing firms to enter the market normally moves the economy closer to the ideal of allocative efficiency.

But one form of market power arises strictly from economies of scale, where the larger the firm the lower its cost. In this case, it is more efficient in the sense of lower cost per unit—**productive efficiency** rather than allocative efficiency—for a single large firm to produce all the output in a particular industry because only the single largest firm can produce at lowest cost. This situation is called **natural monopoly**, and it makes little sense to break up such a monopoly because this will only increase cost per unit and ultimately increase price. As output expands, average cost per unit of production continuously falls along with falling marginal cost.

In this special case, it is better for government to allow the monopoly to exist and regulate the price the monopolist can charge rather than break it up into smaller, less efficient units. Figure 7.2 depicts a natural monopoly. Unlike the traditional U-shaped marginal cost curve where cost per unit rises after a point, this cost curve declines continuously. That means the larger the firm, the lower its costs. All other firms will be run out of business if the largest firm lowers its price below the minimum point on every other firm's average cost curve. The largest firm will still make a profit as long as its price is above its own minimum cost. Here, the large firm makes a profit of AB at the price it sets, while the smaller firm takes a loss of CD. Any small firm trying to compete with the large one will quickly go bankrupt. Knowing this, there is likely to be no upstart to challenge the acknowledged position of the natural monopolist. Note that the cost for a small firm in the natural monopoly industry would be higher than for the large firm. Since only one firm can be the largest and, therefore, the lowest-cost producer, this industry will ultimately have only a single firm.

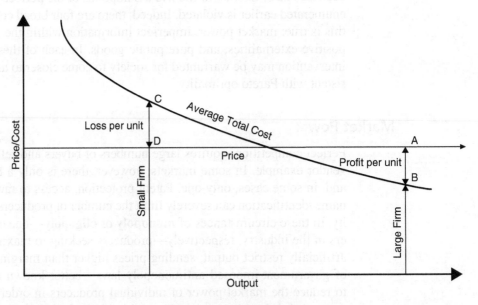

FIGURE 7.2. Natural Monopoly Long-Run Average Cost Curve

Generally, natural monopolies exist where there is a very large fixed cost for providing a service to a community but very low marginal cost of extending the service to each additional customer. Thus, average cost per unit continually declines with an increase in output and sales. Essentially, they have enormous economies of scale, meaning large size allows lower cost. Public utilities such as the natural gas company fall into this category. The natural gas company needs to make an extensive investment in laying gas mains throughout a city. The marginal cost of attaching one more house to the main pipeline is trivial compared to the cost of the original main line. It makes no economic sense for a competitor to spend the enormous resources needed to construct a completely new structure of natural gas mains. Unregulated, the natural gas company could, in the short run, charge relatively high prices and customers would have no choice but to pay the price if they wanted the service. For this reason, state agencies regulate the prices that natural gas companies can charge. Over time, technology might reduce the power of such natural monopolies. The introduction of satellite-based TV, for example, provided a competitor to cable and Digital Subscriber Line (DSL) landlines, keeping prices from rising precipitously even if there is no local government regulation.

Information Problems

The model of perfect competition assumes that buyers and sellers of a good or service have all the information necessary to make a rational choice. However, this is not always the case. Federal truth-in-lending, truth-in-labeling, and truth-in-advertising laws are aimed at improving information as a way of improving consumer decision-making when it comes to banking services and all kinds of consumption. The detailed labeling on prepared foods is regulated right down to the font type used in the ingredients and nutrition information mandated by the federal government so that consumers can presumably make a more rational choice among products. At the city and town levels some local newspapers routinely carry listings of restaurants cited for violating sanitary laws, along with the nature of the violation. Since consumers themselves are not always able to inspect a restaurant's kitchen, they might want to know which restaurants have been cited, and whether the violation is for improper disposal of bacon grease or for evidence of rodent infestation.

The federal government's Home Mortgage Disclosure Act of 1975 is still another example of requiring information disclosure. Banks must report the geographic location of the mortgage loans they make in a city or metro area. In this way, communities gain the information they need to determine whether banks that accept deposits within a neighborhood make mortgage loans within that neighborhood in a fair and unbiased manner. Subsequent passage of the Community Reinvestment Act in 1977 required that this information be taken into account when banks apply for permission to merge or acquire other financial institutions.

Negative and Positive Externalities

The model of perfect competition assumes that all the costs of production are borne by the producer and that all the benefits from the consumption of a given good or service are captured by those who choose to buy it. This is the basis for our previous assertion that price is a proxy for social benefit and marginal cost is a proxy for social cost. In some cases, however, there is a discrepancy between individual and social benefit, or between individual and social cost. If price measures individual but not social benefit, or if marginal cost measures individual but not social cost, then a price equal to marginal cost will no longer represent full allocative efficiency. There will be benefits or costs not accounted for in the price of the good or service. These benefits and costs are called **externalities**.

Externalities can be illustrated with two examples: the case of pollution, in which there are negative externalities, and the case of elementary and secondary education, in which there are positive externalities.

Pollution: A Negative Externality   In the late 1970s, more than a thousand households had to be evacuated and relocated from the Love Canal area of Niagara Falls, New York, because dangerous toxic wastes from chemicals dumped there in the 1940s by the Hooker Chemical Corporation had begun seeping into their basements. Love Canal alerted many cities and towns to the problem of toxic waste and, since then, thousands of other urban toxic waste sites have been discovered. While Love Canal and others date back to industrial processes of the mid-twentieth century and earlier, others, such as those in Silicon Valley, are a product of more recent times and new industries. With 28 hazardous waste sites within a 15-square-mile area, the semiconductor industry of Silicon Valley once had the highest concentration of Environmental Protection Agency Superfund sites in the country. Many have now been cleaned up as a result of government action.

When the owner of a semiconductor plant produces output, he must take into account the cost of capital, labor, and raw materials, along with any other expenses he pays out of pocket in order to calculate his total costs. But in the absence of government intervention, some of the costs of production are not counted in this calculation if the company is not forced to pay for remediating the contamination to the soil or water in the surrounding community. These are called "negative externalities" by economists. In the absence of government intervention, no individual producer will voluntarily take these costs into account because of the need to compete with other producers and keep costs low. Therefore, the community bears these costs rather than the semiconductor firm. In a perfectly competitive market, if one socially conscious producer would choose to cover the cost of an externality related to his production and no other producers were to do the same, the socially conscious producer would be forced out of business because it would face higher costs. As a result, without government regulation, there is no way to cover the cost of the externality.

In a sense, the consumers of the semiconductors gain as a result of lower prices because the cost of environmental remediation does not have to be included in the price. Essentially, the residents of the community and not the consumers of the semiconductors pay for the cost of the toxic waste. In this case, allocative efficiency is not achieved because real resources (i.e., water and soil) are used up in production but not counted as a cost. What is more, equity considerations are violated since the consumers of semiconductors essentially pass on the social cost of production to others who do not purchase them.

Put another way, even if the semiconductor industry were perfectly competitive, and even if the market price were equal to private marginal cost, allocative efficiency would not be achieved because there is a discrepancy between private costs (those the owner takes into account) and social costs (private costs plus the cost of the negative externality). Because price covers only private costs and not social costs, it is too low, and the output of this industry is too high. The purpose of government intervention is to raise the price of the company's product and reduce the output until allocative efficiency is achieved with all costs of production borne by the consumer—in this case, the ultimate consumer of the semiconductors. This can be done by having the government prohibit the release of pollutants, requiring antipollution devices to be installed, mandating the company cleanup of the waste site, or requiring the company to purchase a pollution permit that provides the government with the revenue needed to clean up the site itself. (A graphical analysis of a negative environmental externality is provided in Appendix A.)

Elementary and Secondary Education: A Positive Externality   In other cases, government intervenes because of a positive externality. Households have a stake in the education of their children. The private benefits of another year of education might include the ability of their children to obtain better jobs and perhaps an enhanced ability to contribute toward the support of their parents in old age. However, the benefits of elementary and secondary education accrue to others outside the household. Educated citizens presumably can make better informed choices at the polls, improving the democratic process. Better educated individuals are less likely to be involved in crime, reducing the costs of robbery, burglary, and assault on others. Better educated workers are more likely to invent goods and services such as cancer treatments that benefit all of society. If government did not intervene in this market, households might purchase enough education for their children to cover the private benefits, but not enough to cover the positive externalities. The price in the private market would be too high and output would be too low. The purpose of government intervention in this instance is to expand total output of education by subsidizing it.

As we pointed out in Chapter 1, in the United States, public elementary and secondary education is fully subsidized. The price to the actual consumer of public K–12 schooling is essentially zero. The costs are absorbed by taxpayers, including those who do not have children or whose children do not attend public schools. As Fischel (2001) argues, local property taxpayers without children in the public schools still have a pecuniary motive for supporting good-quality schools because it enhances the value of their homes, usually a major component of their wealth.

Because the positive externalities are considered to be so important, not only do we reduce the price to the consumer to zero, we pass mandatory attendance laws that say children must attend until they reach a certain age—usually 17 or 18. The same logic of positive externalities applies to local public libraries, but we do not force people to use them. (A graphical analysis of education as a positive externality can be found in Appendix B.)

Pure Public Goods

The final category of market failure includes a very small number of goods that have some unusual characteristics. Most goods are **excludable**—if you do not pay the price, you cannot get the good. Most goods are also **rival**, meaning that my consumption reduces what is left for you. **Pure public goods**, on the other hand, are neither; households that do not pay for a public good nevertheless receive the benefit of it, and one household's consumption of such a good does not reduce the amount left over for other households.

To illustrate the difference between pure public goods and ordinary private goods, imagine that you are at a Fourth of July celebration in a municipal park. There are vendors selling hot dogs, ice cream, and soda. These goods are ordinary private goods. You cannot have the hot dog unless you pay for it, and if there are lots of folks lined up ahead of you, the vendor might run out of hot dogs before you reach the front of the line. The hot dogs, therefore, are an excludable and rival good.

By contrast, the fireworks display later in the evening is neither excludable nor rival; once they are set off, they are there for everyone to see. An additional viewer can see the display without using any additional resources. The fireworks display is a pure public good; it would be difficult to charge the consumer a price to see the display since consumers know they can see it whether they pay the price or not. If we tried to charge a price based on how much consumers enjoyed the show, they would have every reason to conceal their true level of enjoyment. By not revealing their true preferences for fireworks, they presumably would have to pay little or nothing for viewing them. When it comes to ordinary private goods, we automatically reveal our preferences every time we buy something. If we choose to spend $14 on a paperback book, we aver our preference for that particular book at that price to any alternative.

For pure public goods, it is difficult or virtually impossible to get people to reveal their preferences. As a result, there is a **free rider problem**. Those who refuse to pay for a pure public good receive its benefits as fully as those who are willing to pay. Knowing this no rational individual would contribute, and a good or service that many would want is not produced at all. In this case, it falls to government or some other nonmarket entity to provide these special goods. In Boston, the Fourth of July fireworks are paid for by a wealthy philanthropist. In most other places, they are paid for from the city or town budget. Other examples of pure public goods in metropolitan areas include public health, sanitation, sidewalks, and street lighting. Free or highly subsidized municipally provided Wi-Fi networks, currently a topic of heated debate, would fall into this category as well.

A good that has the characteristics of a pure *private* good in low-density communities can become a pure *public* good as density increases. This is why the concepts of externalities and pure public goods both take on more significance in urban areas. Take fire protection, for example. Tennessee's Blount County Fire Protection District (2020) states that it receives no tax money for fighting fires and that it has served county residents since 1948 through its subscription program. For $110 a year, a household can buy fire protection for its single-family residence; a nonsubscriber would pay $2,200 to hire the company in the event of a fire. It operates seven fire stations and has 55 firefighters, some of whom work part-time. This good is excludable: if you have not paid $110 for a subscription and your house is on fire, your choice is to pay $2,200 or watch your house burn down. It is also rival: the company has a total of 29 fire and emergency vehicles, but of these, only 10 are engines and only one is a ladder truck. Its capacity to fight multiple fires is limited.

In a rural Tennessee county where houses are far apart this privatized fire-fighting service works reasonably well. If your house burns down, probably mine is safe. But in densely packed cities in most metropolitan areas, a company that is called to protect apartment 4D, which has paid for its subscription, will likely end up protecting apartments 3D and 5D as well, whether or not their owners have paid. The service that was excludable at low density is no longer excludable at high density. Thus, selling subscription fire protection through the private market is not viable in cities and most suburbs. Moreover, given the destruction that fire can cause in densely populated areas, municipalities often have reciprocal agreements with each other so that neighboring fire departments will be called in when necessary, substantially improving their ability to fight multiple fires and reducing the problem of rival goods.

While we can think of goods that fall at either end of the excludable–rival spectrum as pure public goods or pure private goods, there are some goods that fall into a gray area. One example are goods that themselves are excludable and rival, but for which some consumers might have only a "standby" demand—they do not use the good regularly, but place some value on knowing it will be there should they want or need to use it in the future. In essence, the demand for the continued availability of a good on the part of nonusers makes it a public good. This so-called **option value** is the pure public good aspect of a good that is otherwise excludable and rival. Consumers who have never been to Yellowstone National Park, used a public hospital emergency room, or traveled on their city's buses still have a stake in making sure these entities continue to exist, should they want or need to avail themselves of them in the future (Weisbrod 1964). This option value bestows on such services the characteristics of a pure public good. All kinds of urban services fall into this category, from police services to public-sector emergency medical technicians.

Motorists in cities with good public transportation might use the bus or subway only when road conditions are dangerous, if their car is in the shop for repairs, or if they are going downtown where parking is very expensive—or perhaps not at all. While actually using public transportation is excludable (you must pay the fare) and rival (if the trolley is too crowded, you might have to wait for the next one), the continued availability of the service, especially if it would be difficult to start up again once it has been shut down and the tracks have been paved over, is non-excludable and nonrival. The implication of this is that the revenue collected from the fare box does not represent the entire demand for the good, since it does not include the option value or standby demand for the good on the part of nonusers. This option value of keeping the system available even when not fully used is just one reason for subsidizing the public transportation system. You may never need the entire array of urban public services, but having them available if you ever do gives greater security of mind. For this reason, most people will be willing to pay taxes to make sure these public goods are available.

In Chapter 10, where we discuss urban transportation, we shall see that there are at least two other reasons for public subsidies of mass transit—one that has to do with reducing congestion on highways and the other with the negative externalities from automobile exhaust fumes.

Government and the Distribution of Well-Being

While governments within a metropolitan area are primarily concerned with their role in allocation and dealing with market failure, differences in spending patterns from one jurisdiction to another can carry important implications for household well-being. One municipality might subsidize marinas for yachts, while another subsidizes adult literacy programs. The Parks Department in one city might focus on the centrally located facilities visited by tourists, while another emphasizes services within the neighborhoods that are located far off the tourist routes. Likewise, the public library budget might be skewed in favor of the main research library in one city but emphasize the children's rooms in the branch libraries in another. Any given expenditure made for the purpose of allocation will almost invariably have consequences for how the costs and benefits of public services are distributed.

A similar argument can be made at the state level. For example, one state might subsidize higher education primarily through supporting a prestigious flagship campus with its research and graduate programs while another focuses its support at the community college level. Since students from poorer households are likely to attend community colleges and those from wealthier households are likely to attend the flagship campus, the impact of higher education on income inequality will be very different in these two states.

Although the pattern of state and local spending on goods and services has an impact on the distribution of household well-being, most of the programs that are primarily redistributive in nature are the responsibility of the federal government. While markets do some things very well—for example, conveying consumer tastes and preferences to producers—they cannot guarantee that every household will have an income sufficient to support itself. Incomes earned in the market depend primarily on the quantity and quality of productive resources each household owns. A household in which everyone is disabled, old, or poorly educated is unlikely to command many economic resources and will therefore have low (or no) income. As a society we do not expect elderly disabled people to rely solely on income they have earned. We transfer additional income to them through a number of federal programs, from supplementary security income (SSI) to food stamps through the Supplemental Nutrition Assistance Program (SNAP), and housing vouchers primarily through Section 8 of the 1937 Federal Housing Act which provides rent supplements to low-income families. The distribution role of government is to change the distribution of well-being that the market would otherwise produce.

The Debate Over the Scope of Government Intervention

Economists emphasize the degree to which competitive forces influence markets and most would agree that market failure occurs in the case of market power, imperfect information, externalities, and pure public goods. But economists do not agree about what should be done, whether government intervention is always necessary, or what the nature of that intervention should be. Similarly, there is great disagreement as to how much the government should be involved in redistributing well-being through the provision of free or low-cost public services that are funded out of tax revenues.

In this hotly contested area, a few economists believe it is better to suffer some loss in allocative efficiency and higher consumer prices than to resort to the red tape of government bureaucracy. Some believe that strict market regulation is needed, and still others think that carefully constructed regulation, tax, and subsidy programs can deal best with market failure and the distribution of well-being.

Conservative economists, following the lead of the late Nobel Laureate Milton Friedman (2002), concede the need for government intervention on allocative grounds, but only in the case of extraordinarily large externalities or in the rare case of such pure public goods as national defense, local police, and local fire protection. Even when they deem it necessary for government to act, Friedman and others favor reliance on private market forces as much as possible.

Consider the case of elementary and secondary education. Friedman agreed that there are strong positive externalities and that the market left to its own devices will produce too little. He agreed that government needs to subsidize the consumption of education as a way of lowering its price to consumers and expanding the amount of schooling consumed. He did not, however, believe that government needs to—or should—produce education services itself through public schools. Instead, he recommended that families with school-age children be given education vouchers by local school districts that can be used to purchase the education of their choice from what he expected would be a growing cadre of private schools. His goal was to preserve the private-market mechanism in the production of education, even as he acknowledged the need for government intervention in the financing of elementary and secondary schooling.

While conservatives generally endorse strict limits on the scope of government activity, liberals tend to argue that there is an imbalance between the relative affluence we see in private consumption and the relative deprivation we see in the public sector: fancy new cars riding over potholed streets; well-equipped campers staying overnight in poorly maintained national and state parks; and the failure of our society to deal with the chronic problems of poverty, hunger, and homelessness. An eminent liberal scholar, the late John Kenneth Galbraith (1998), a contemporary of the conservative Friedman, often endorsed an expanded role for government, and one that was more actively committed to the redistribution of well-being. He would want to ensure that public schools are well financed, that school resources are equitably shared across school districts, that police and fire services are equally provided in rich and poor neighborhoods, and that other forms of inequality be rectified by appropriate government spending. Liberals who think along the same lines as Galbraith strongly favor universal programs funded by government, such as national health insurance, and believe that government providing public services is the best approach. Thus, they support public schools, public police and fire departments, public housing for the poor, and so forth.

Another controversial area of government intervention involves those instances in which government decision-makers substitute their judgment for the judgment of consumers. Forcing people to put aside money for their retirement through the Social Security system is one example; another was prohibiting the use of marijuana. Until quite recently, the sale and use of marijuana was illegal in every state in the United States because it was feared that some of those who used it would become a burden on society. The same was true of the federal ban on alcohol when the US Constitution was amended in 1920 with the passage of the 18th Amendment. Realizing the unintended consequences of bootlegging and organized crime, the 18th Amendment was repealed in 1933 with the 21st Amendment.

Supporters of Friedman who criticize government intervention as in the case of the prohibition on alcohol and marijuana call it **paternalism**, and argue that adults of sound mind should be free to make their own decisions. Those in opposition who endorse intervention in this category call it **merit wants**, and argue that people do not always know what is good for them, are not always rational actors, and will sometimes choose something that gives them short-term pleasure over long-term prudence.

Recently New York City, Philadelphia, and several other municipalities have banned restaurants from using trans fats (partially hydrogenated oils that contribute to obesity and other serious health problems) that are an easy way to enhance the flavor of food. Other items in this category include local or state laws that mandate the use of helmets for motorcyclists or a local ordinance that prohibits the sale of alcohol within a particular municipality. Not too long ago, some cities and towns had "blue laws" that prohibited stores from opening on Sundays in order to give workers the day off to observe the Christian Sabbath.

Although there is disagreement about the scope and nature of government intervention, and although the preferred size of government might vary according to the political predilections of different economists and political leaders, it is true that even the minimalists would acknowledge the need for government to absorb some tasks that the market cannot accomplish. Moreover, conservatives argue that if government is to be involved in the production of goods or the regulation of markets, it is best to have this occur at the local level rather than state or federal. The argument is that with tens of thousands of municipal governments, the local public sector is akin to the private market. With local governments providing variations in the specific range and extent of public goods, consumers can "vote with their feet" for the public services they want by moving to towns or cities that offer the combination of services they prefer. With only 50 states there is less variation in state policies and only one policy at the federal level. Conservatives would argue that the public sector should be strictly limited and that production or regulation should occur at the lowest possible level of government. With the exception of national defense, a national currency, and perhaps a national highway system, most economic conservatives want to see cities and towns as the focus for whatever services need to be supplied by the public sector.

Market Failure and Alternatives for Providing Goods and Services

As we have seen, if the competitive market mechanism is operating correctly—meaning that no firm has any power to set price, that there are no information problems, no externalities, and that these are pure private goods (excludable and rival)—unregulated private markets will operate effectively. However, in the case of market failure, there are alternatives for how government should intervene. These include:

- allowing a private market to operate, but under regulations set by government
- providing public funding for goods and services produced by the private sector
- having the public sector produce the output itself

Regulated Private Markets

In the case of natural monopoly, where it is more efficient to have one firm produce the entire output because of economies of scale, it is typical for US cities to grant a franchise to a private firm but then place limits on the firm's behavior. Your local natural gas company, for example, would need to seek government approval if it wanted to raise its prices or expand its operations. Earlier in the twentieth century, other public utilities—such as the electric and telephone companies—were also natural monopolies subject to regulation. As the technology changed, however, it was possible to introduce competition into the markets for local and long-distance telephone service.

The market for electricity is in the midst of a transition: the firm that delivers electricity to your home is still a publicly owned company or natural monopoly subject to regulation, but increasingly these distribution monopolies purchase their electricity from numerous private companies that generate the electricity and supply it to the single company in town that owns the local electric power grid. While regulation of private companies has been the norm in the United States, public provision of these services has been more common in Europe. Even in the United States, though, 251 cities and towns still have municipally owned electric companies, including Anaheim, California; Braintree, Massachusetts; Chattanooga, Tennessee; and San Antonio, Texas (Utility Connection 2020).

Public Funding/Private Provision

As we have seen, even most free-market economists who follow in the tradition of Milton Friedman believe that primary and secondary education should be subsidized because of the substantial level of positive externalities they offer. The private market, left to its own devices, would not produce enough education. But as noted before, Friedman and others believe that households should receive **education vouchers** that they can use to purchase education from private companies rather than relying on the public sector itself to produce the educational services.

As is the case for several other services, public vouchers already exist. The SNAP food assistance program and the Section 8 rental voucher system are instances where the public sector provides the monetary resources for the consumption of goods and services by low-income households, but the actual provision remains in the private sector. Recipients of SNAP credit cards use them to buy groceries in local supermarkets. Those who qualify for Section 8 vouchers use them to subsidize their monthly rent. With such programs, low-income individuals, households, and families can eat more nutritionally and live in better housing then they could on the basis of their own income. In 1969 less than 3 million individuals were receiving federal food assistance in the United States. By 2019, the need for such aid had mushroomed to 34.5 million. At the same time, more than 5.2 million American households were receiving some form of housing assistance including apartments in public housing projects run by cities. But of the total, 1.2 million received Section 8 vouchers which permitted them to live in private-sector housing.

In each of these instances, the role of government is to subsidize some form of desired behavior while still allowing consumers to make their choices in the context of competitive markets.

Public Provision

For most of the twentieth century, many municipal services were seen as natural monopolies that should be owned and operated by the city itself and provided by public employees. This was true of sanitation workers, teachers, social workers, police, and firefighters. It was seen as natural and normal that government was responsible for building, operating, and maintaining highways.

Recently, however, the notion of privatization (which we discuss more fully later in this chapter) has been gaining ground. In many cities, the government has signed contracts with private sanitation companies; in a few cases, such as the Chicago Skyway and the Indiana Toll Road (Poole and Samuel 2006), governments have granted long-term leases to private companies who then operate and maintain these highways. Nonetheless, while the ranks of municipal workers might shrink as privatization takes hold, it is difficult to imagine a time when most elementary and secondary schoolteachers, librarians, police, and firefighters would not be employees of local governments. While highways might be operated by private companies that charge tolls, it is unlikely that cities or towns would sell off their local streets and roads—at least until a time when technology might allow every car and truck to have a global positioning system (GPS) enhanced transponder that could keep track of mileage and charge for the use of these public goods.

Local Government Employment and Spending Patterns

To comprehend the size of the municipal sector needed to provide the local public services we enjoy, one can look at the number of workers local governments employ. As Table 7.2 demonstrates, in 2018 the number nationwide was more than 10 million in the areas specified. Of this total number, more than 60 percent work in local schools as teachers, counselors, principals, janitors, and secretaries. On this measure, public education is clearly the number-one task of local governments (US Bureau of the Census 2018). Employment-wise, the other top local government services are police protection, general government administration, and public hospitals.

Information on local employment is only part of the public-sector picture. In addition to those public-sector functions that are largely provided by workers employed by cities and towns, local governments purchase an extensive array of

TABLE 7.2. LOCAL GOVERNMENT FULL-TIME EQUIVALENT EMPLOYEES BY SELECTED FUNCTION, MARCH 2018

Elementary and Secondary Education	6,771,331
Higher Education	330,602
Public Welfare	276,492
Health	259,266
Hospitals	634,940
Highways	280,166
Police Protection	835,900
Fire Protection	363,591
Corrections	265,032
Parks and Recreation	243,387
Government Administration	462,843
Total	**10,723,550**

Source: U.S. Census Bureau, 2018 Annual Survey of Public Employment & Payroll.

services from the private sector. This is illustrated in Table 7.3, which lists the major categories of local government spending. Altogether, between their direct production of services and their purchases from the private sector, city and town expenditures equal about 8.5 percent of the nation's gross domestic product (GDP)—about $1.9 trillion of a nearly $19.5 trillion GDP in 2017.

The structure and function of local governments may vary dramatically within a nation. In the United States elementary and secondary education is primarily a responsibility of state government in Hawaii, but it is the responsibility of local government in the other 49 states. Within states, there may be several layers of government—counties are important units of government in some states, less important in others. Connecticut has abolished counties. Responsibilities that fall to municipalities in some places are assigned to special districts in others (e.g., water supply, vocational education).

It is therefore difficult to compare local governments within a nation. The complexities multiply when trying to compare them across nations whose customs and institutions take very different forms. Wolman (2008) points to the difficulties in creating a framework across nations within which to classify various attributes of local governments. Keeping these caveats in mind, it is nevertheless useful to examine *Subnational Governments Around the World: Structure and Finance,* a report produced by the Organization for Economic Cooperation and Development (OECD) and the United Cities and Local Government (UCLG) in 2016. According to this report covering 101 countries, local governments account for about one-quarter of total government spending on average, the bulk of which is spent on education, general public services related to administration and debt expenses, social protection, health, and transportation. Investment by local governments account for almost 40 percent of all public investment, and local governments account for the majority of public government sector employment. Although there is substantial

TABLE 7.3. LOCAL GOVERNMENT DIRECT EXPENDITURE BY FUNCTION, 2017

(THOUSANDS OF DOLLARS)	
Function	Local Expenditure
Total direct expenditures	**1,895,215,175**
Education services	
Education	696,801,936
Capital outlay	67,568,665
Libraries	12,173,305
Social services and income maintenance	
Public welfare	57,751,711
Cash assistance payments	10,583,068
Vendor payments	6,086,649
Other public welfare	41,081,994
Hospitals	107,228,787
Capital outlay	5,726,874
Health	56,585,568
Employment Security Administration	41,679
Transportation	
Highways	72,060,606
Capital outlays	27,368,746
Air transportation (airports)	23,897,962
Parking facilities	2,065,540
Sea and inland port facilities	4,258,857
Public safety	
Police protection	99,304,262
Fire protection	50,411,660
Corrections	29,880,683
Capital outlay	880,507
Protective inspection and regulation	5,682,396
Environment and housing	
Natural resources	10,375,736
Capital outlay	2,737,970
Parks and recreation	39,021,431
Capital outlay	8,833,370
Housing and community development	43,621,293
Sewerage	55,281,973
Capital outlay	19,129,224
Solid waste management	24,066,255

(THOUSANDS OF DOLLARS)	
Function	Local Expenditure
Capital outlay	2,169,469
Government administration	
Financial administration	19,432,770
Judicial and legal	23,846,139
General public buildings	11,196,821
Other governmental administration	28,405,919
Interest on general debt	62,497,850
General expenditure	
Utility expenditures (water, electricity, gas)	202,176,803
Insurance trust expenditures (unemployment, pensions, etc.)	53,956,719
Miscellaneous commercial activities	5,623,719
Other and unallocated	96,314,093

variability across countries, grants and subsidies from higher levels of government account for over half of local government revenue. In wealthier countries local governments account for a higher share of all government revenue and spending.

The size of local government expenditures varies dramatically across countries. It is as low as 0.4 percent of GDP in the Czech Republic and 0.5 percent in Ireland. But in the Scandinavian countries with much larger public sectors, local government spending amounts to as much as 12 percent in Denmark and 15.6 percent in Sweden (OECD 2018). This great variance is due to two factors. The first is whether local public services are paid for by the federal, state, or local government. The second is the degree to which individual countries have privatized the delivery of public service.

By far, the largest single expenditure of municipal government in the United States is for public education. Across all cities and towns, nearly 39 percent of the budget is spent on public schools, with close to 1 percent allocated for public libraries. Almost 11 percent is spent on social services and specific income maintenance programs for low-income residents. Public safety expenditures comprise about 9 percent of local budgets with more than half of this amount slated for police protection. A little more than 8 percent is for general government administration. The rest is scattered across a range of services that include transportation (5.3%) and environment and housing (7%), and a large general expenditures category that includes spending on utilities and various local commercial activities (17.5%).

Note that in Table 7.3, nearly 10 percent of local government spending on education—more than $67 billion out of $697 billion—was for capital outlay. This was for the construction of new schools and renovations of older ones. About 5 percent of local government hospital expenditures—$5.7 billion out of $107 billion—was spent on capital projects, as were portions of the expenditures on corrections, natural resources, parks and recreation, sewerage, and solid waste management. This investment in new or updated infrastructure is usually contracted out to private construction companies.

Privatization of Public Services

Most local public services such as education are offered by the public sector itself and supplied by public-sector employees. But the case for privatization of public services became a cause celebre in the 1990s, especially after the publication by David Osborne and Ted Gaebler of their influential book *Reinventing Government* (1992). They argued not only that private-sector competition could lead to lower cost and better service freed from political influence, but also made the case that there are actual incentives for inefficiency in public bureaucracies. For example, an agency that can reduce its costs might not do so because it fears that its budget would then be reduced. Therefore, Osborne and Gaebler argue that at least some public services could be produced at lower cost by private firms in a competitive market, and that the size of government in general should be reduced.

The choice and success of service delivery mechanisms appear to be influenced by several factors. In many cases, market competition did not exist because of the small number of possible providers. This indicates that the possibilities for privatization depend upon local-market-specific conditions, including the presence of competition in the private market and the degree of expertise that is available there.

Privatization can take several forms that include not only contracting out for services but eliminating regulations that effectively prevent private firms from competing, subsidizing vouchers for private citizens to use as an alternative or replacement for publicly provided services, eliminating some public-sector service provision so that those who want it must turn to private providers, and selling or leasing public sites to private companies (Starr 1988). The choice of service delivery mechanism also depends upon the degree of in-house expertise and available technology. Warner and Hefetz (2004) note that some governments privatize services that involve new skills or the need to supply a high volume of goods or services beyond the capacity of the local government. They contract out initially and then bring the service delivery in-house when the expertise, technology, or staff training becomes available.

Contracting out, as opposed to cessation of service delivery altogether, requires local government contract management and monitoring, the costs of which need to be weighed against anticipated savings from the service delivery itself. In addition, there are potential problems with private-sector delivery of local public services. Typically, private companies are less transparent than public entities and therefore more prone to bribery and corruption. Private-sector contracts can be lengthy, even spanning decades, and therefore there is some built-in inflexibility. No private company can afford to buy a large fleet of garbage trucks unless it is guaranteed a long-term contract to provide waste services. And once private contractors have a long-term contract, they may be able to increase the cost to the local government so that ultimately there may be little in cost savings to the municipality. For all these reasons, privatization remains a hotly contested topic, especially when public-sector unions raise up their voice to urge public officials to reject further privatization.

Because its impact on local budgets is not always beneficial, the extent of privatization has increased in some municipalities and decreased in others. While the use of for-profit firms to provide local services has increased only slightly in the

United States, it has increased substantially in certain areas. In 1988, for example, 24 percent of city hospitals were operated by private concerns. By 2018, more than 81 percent of local hospitals were in the private for profit and nonprofit sector (American Hospital Association 2019). Even earlier, there was a shift away from local government provision of day-care facilities and homeless shelters as nongovernmental agencies took a greater role in offering these services. Between 1992 and 2002, the operation of day-care facilities increased from 34 percent to 79 percent, while the operation of homeless shelters went from 57 percent operated by public employees to 66 percent operated by for-profit or nonprofit companies (Gerber et al. 2004).

In other areas, however, privatization has been withdrawn because of the poor quality of service rendered under private contracts, failure of anticipated cost savings to materialize, and because of improvements in the internal efficiency of local government.

Paying for Public Services

Earlier in this chapter we explained how prices are determined in the private market under conditions of allocative efficiency. When, as a result of market failure, the good or service is provided by the public sector, resources are used and costs are incurred for which payment must be made.

There are two principles that apply to paying for public services through taxation: the ability-to-pay principle and the benefit principle. A progressive income tax, where the tax payment as a percentage of income rises as income rises, is an example of the ability-to-pay principle. The reasoning is that the last dollar of income is not as important to the wealthy as it is to the poor, and that it is therefore less of a sacrifice for the wealthy to yield that dollar than it would be for the poor.

The benefit principle states that those who use the service are the ones who gain from it, and that those who use more should pay more. In places where there are municipally provided public utilities, metered services such as gas, electricity, and water usage are examples of the benefit principle.

Although the two principles are distinct in concept, any given tax might include elements of both. Local governments rely heavily on property taxes, where the tax bill is higher for more valuable properties. To some extent, the benefit principle applies—households living in more valuable properties gain more from public safety expenditures that minimize the likelihood of loss through crime, vandalism, or fire. However, since property value is a proxy for wealth and since local governments spend the greatest portion of their revenue on elementary and secondary education with its attendant positive externalities, the ability-to-pay principle applies. With these principles in mind, we can further explore the ways in which government services are paid for.

As Figure 7.3 reveals, in fiscal year 2016 a little more than a third of local revenue (36.1%) came from intergovernmental transfers, with the bulk of that local aid coming from the state rather than the federal government. The other two-thirds (63.9%) was raised from local sources, including, on average, nearly 30 percent from local property taxes; nearly 23 percent from a variety of charges and fees for

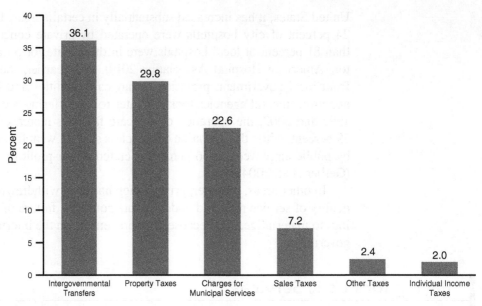

FIGURE 7.3. Sources of Local Government Revenue Fiscal Year 2016

Source: US Census Bureau Annual Survey of State and Local Government Finances.

such things as municipal water supply, municipal parking garages, and traffic ticket revenue; about 7 percent from local sales taxes including restaurant and hotel room taxes; licensing fees; and another 4 percent from other taxes including local income taxes that a few major cities impose.

There is a wide variance in how other countries pay for services provided by local and state governments. Across all cities and states in the United States, about 25 percent of revenue is generated by taxes on income, profits, and capital gains. In countries such as Sweden, Finland, Denmark, Luxembourg, and Israel, more than 90 percent of revenues come from such taxes and little from property. In Turkey, the Netherlands, and in Hungary, local and regional revenue comes mainly from sales taxes on goods and services (OECD 2019).

In the last decades of the twentieth century, the proportion of local general revenue received through the property tax has declined in the United States, as has the proportion received through federal aid. The proportion received through state aid has grown slightly nationwide, and there has been an increased reliance on user charges (fees that vary according to the quantity used by each consumer such as water bills based on meters that gauge actual consumption).

Tannenwald (2001) offers several reasons to explain why the proportion of general revenue received from property taxes has fallen. One is the success of **tax revolt** referenda such as California's Proposition 13 in 1978 and Massachusetts's Proposition 2½ in 1980, which limited the tax rates and amount of revenue that local areas could collect through property taxes. Another is the shift in the composition of business assets, as the economy continues not only to evolve away from the production of goods to the production of services but to evolve within industries toward knowledge-based production. As a result, intangible assets (e.g., patents, databases, software, formulas, and trademarks) are growing both in importance and as a proportion of all business assets. However, intangible assets similar to these are not subject to property taxation. Thus, this shift in the mix of business assets has hampered growth in the property tax base.

Income and Sales Taxes Levied by Local Governments

Whether a municipality will be allowed to impose income taxes or sales taxes is a matter for each state to determine. Some states, including Michigan, New Jersey, New York, and Pennsylvania, allow local governments to levy property taxes, income taxes, and sales taxes. Others, including Arizona, California, Florida, North Carolina, and Washington, do not allow local governments to impose income taxes, but they do allow them to use property taxes and sales taxes. A third group, including Connecticut, Massachusetts, New Hampshire, and Rhode Island, limits local government almost exclusively to the use of property taxes (Bluestone et al. 2006). Cities and towns are chartered by the state government, which normally has the right to decide what types of taxes and sometimes even the tax rates that local governments may charge. As of 2019, only 16 states permitted their cities and towns to levy a local income tax. The rates varied from 1 percent in Birmingham, Alabama to a range of 2.907 percent to 3.648 percent in New York City.

If a municipality can employ income or sales taxes, not only does it have more options for the manner in which to collect taxes, but it can also take advantage of other potential benefits. In periods of economic growth, receipts from income and sales taxes will rise automatically, while property tax receipts might respond more sluggishly or be dependent on periodic reassessments. Using sales or income as a tax base allows the municipality to tax nonresidents who work or shop within its boundaries and thereby benefit from some of the public-sector services it provides. However, if a municipality enacts a local income or sales tax when its neighbors do not, it risks driving residents and businesses to those neighboring jurisdictions (Peterson 1981).

There is one other risk in becoming too dependent on income and sales taxes, and this was proven during the economic collapse that accompanied the COVID-19 pandemic in 2020. Those cities that were most dependent on income and sales tax revenue—as opposed to property tax revenue—experienced a sharp decline in their finances as unemployment soared, incomes fell, and sales declined. The same was true for cities heavily dependent on state aid, which in most states is funded through income or sales taxes. Before the economic downturn, Rochester, New York funded nearly half (49%) of its city services on aid from the state. When New York State's revenue sank, Rochester's annual revenue fell by more than an estimated 20 percent. The same was true for Buffalo and Syracuse.

Other cities such as Detroit, dependent on casino revenue for one-fifth of its municipal budget, experienced more than a 15 percent decline in its municipal budget when those casinos were forced to close due to the pandemic. By contrast, Boston, with 51 percent of its budget from property, experienced less than a 5 percent decline in revenue. Hence, when the overall economy is generally strong, cities more dependent on income and sales taxes find they have more revenue to fund their services. But when the economy falls into recession, the opposite is true. These cities find it more difficult to fund their services while those more dependent on property taxes find it easier to survive the downturn (Badger and Bui 2020).

Pricing in the Public Sector

As we have seen in this chapter, the economic role of government in a market economy is often in response to one form or another of market failure. When the private sector finds it difficult to supply particular goods and services—or to provide them in the needed amounts—the responsibility for their provision often falls to the public sector. The ability of the public sector to solve the inherent problems in providing these goods and services is neither easy nor automatic.

What criteria should be used in determining an appropriate pricing strategy for publicly provided goods and services? It is a complicated question. We will use the example of whether to charge cars a toll for crossing a bridge under three different scenarios to illustrate the kinds of economic questions that must be resolved. But first we need to understand the economics of building the bridge.

A Primer on the Economics of Building and Paying for Bridges

In 1992, Robert Redford directed a movie called *A River Runs Through It*. That title is an apt description of many major cities worldwide, especially those that developed during the centuries of water-based transportation. Some of the bridges in such cities span relatively narrow channels that can be easily crossed on foot like many of the picturesque bridges in the centers of European cities and the famous Ponte Vecchio in Florence, Italy. Others might traverse wider distances, such as the famed Golden Gate Bridge in San Francisco or the Verrazano Narrows Bridge between the boroughs of Brooklyn and Staten Island in New York City.

When a bridge is to be built, the expectation is that it will last for many generations. It is appropriate therefore to raise the revenue to pay for its construction by issuing bonds—that is, by borrowing the money now and paying it back with interest over many decades. The reason bond financing is appropriate in this instance is that if the bridge will be rendering service to future generations, it is fair to have future generations shoulder some of the costs. By contrast, such financing would be inappropriate as a way for a city to pay for treating itself to a lavish 200th birthday bash. If the only ones who benefit from this celebration are those currently alive, it would be unfair to ask future generations to pay for any of those costs. This illustrates the notion of **intergenerational equity** or fairness with respect to how the costs of providing a service are divided across different generations. Costs imposed on future generations should be commensurate with benefits received. Municipal bonds are an appropriate way to finance long-term capital projects, but they are not an appropriate way to finance short-term consumption.

Let us assume we have issued bonds to pay for the bridge, and now we need to raise funds each year to pay for the debt service associated with paying off the bonds. What are our choices? Do we raise the money by charging a toll? Do we take it out of general tax revenue? The conventional wisdom, often seen expressed in letters to the editor, is that tolls are justified when there are bonds to be paid off, but unjustified otherwise. As we will see, the conventional wisdom is wrong. Economic theory tells us that under some circumstances, even if there are bonds to be paid off, it would be better to raise the revenue from general taxation than to charge a toll. Conversely, under other circumstances, it would be desirable to charge tolls even on bridges whose bonds have been paid off long ago. This applies not only to bridges but to tunnels and highways and other large infrastructure projects.

To get a better understanding of why the conventional wisdom is wrong, we will describe three different scenarios regarding the circumstances that affect an automobile about to cross a bridge. In the first scenario, the bridge is not crowded and is used by a cross-section of the population. In the second scenario, the bridge is again not crowded, but it is used primarily by higher-income households. In the third scenario, we look at crowded bridges, a familiar situation in many metropolitan areas.

Scenario 1: Uncrowded Bridge Used by a Cross-Section of the Population As we saw earlier in this chapter, the criterion for allocative efficiency is that price should equal marginal cost. If the cost of allowing one more car to cross the bridge (marginal cost) is zero—ignoring the trivial amount added to the wear and tear on the bridge's road surface—then it follows that the toll (price) should be zero. The rationale is that if the presence of a toll deters even one motorist from crossing the bridge when it does not actually diminish any of society's resources to allow the crossing, a misallocation has occurred. The misallocation might occur because the motorist takes a less direct route, thereby diminishing society's resources by using up more gasoline and putting more pollutants into the air. The misallocation might occur if the motorist's response to the toll is not to make the trip. For example, students with limited resources might decide on less frequent visits to their great-grandmothers, who live in nursing homes on the other side of the bridge. Again, the allocation (efficiency) criterion would say not to charge a toll and pay the debt service on any outstanding bonds out of general tax revenue.

Scenario 2: Uncrowded Bridge Used Primarily by Higher-Income Households On pure allocation (efficiency) grounds, the story remains the same, even if all the cars crossing the bridge are those of wealthy families: if an extra bridge crossing does not use any of society's resources, the toll should be zero and any debt service should be paid from general tax revenue. However, the story becomes more complicated because one might want to take into account how the bridge affects the distribution of well-being. In Michigan, for example, the Mackinac Bridge connects the state's Upper and Lower Peninsulas. The Upper Peninsula is a place of great natural beauty, and many of the Lower Peninsula motorists who cross the bridge are vacationers with incomes above the state's median. To pay for the debt service from general tax revenue would mean that lower-income households who do not use the bridge would subsidize the vacations of the higher-income households who do use it. In effect, the real distribution of income would become more unequal, since taxes would be collected from all segments of the income distribution, but benefits would be concentrated at the high end of the distribution.

The quandary for policymakers is that on allocation and efficiency grounds, the toll should be zero, but on distribution and equity grounds, to pay the debt service from general tax revenue would be inequitable. This is just one of many examples in which the criteria of equity and efficiency conflict. Economic theory gives no guidance as to which criterion should be a higher priority. It becomes a matter of judgment on the part of policymakers, and they are the ones who must decide which of the two criteria is more important in each instance. In the case of the Mackinac Bridge, the Michigan state legislature chose equity over efficiency and imposed a hefty toll.

This lesson does not apply solely to bridges, tunnels, and highways. How much should an individual pay to check out a library book, go to a public college or university, or pay for a rescue service? Often, we think that government redistributes benefits mainly from richer families to poorer ones, but that is not always the case. Take public higher education, for instance. Most of the students who go to public universities and colleges in the United States come from middle- and upper-income families. Yet we subsidize all in-state residents who attend these schools by having the government pay for a large share of higher education costs. This means that many poor people who never take advantage of public universities and colleges end up paying for them through state sales or income taxes or through local property taxes. Similarly, the US Coast Guard rescues thousands of stranded boaters a year, including some on million-dollar yachts. We all pay for this service through our taxes, but only a fraction of us own boats. What is fair? Economics alone does not provide an adequate answer.

Scenario 3: Crowded Bridge   Distribution issues aside, there is still another scenario we need to consider, and in this case economists are more helpful. For those of us who live in large metropolitan areas, the idea of an uncrowded bridge, as posed in our first two scenarios, conjures up a certain quaintness outside of our own everyday experience, but applicable perhaps to the beautiful covered bridges of rural New England. By contrast, our own experience is more likely to include bridges so crowded that traffic generally moves very slowly, except for those times when it comes to a complete standstill. How does our analysis change when the bridge is crowded?

It is no longer true that a car can cross the bridge without using any of society's resources. Once the bridge approaches its capacity—defined here as the number of cars per hour that can travel across the bridge while maintaining some minimum rate of speed, say 25 miles per hour—another car trying to cross will slow things further. As traffic slows to a crawl, individual motorists experience higher costs, including the rush-hour wear and tear on themselves and their vehicles, the value of the extra time spent in traffic, and the extra gasoline used up while idling or driving at very low speeds.

In addition to the costs borne by the individual motorist, there are external costs imposed on others. Nearby residents may suffer higher rates of respiratory disease because of the impact of highly concentrated auto emissions on deteriorated air quality. Employers and coworkers may suffer reduced productivity because of the tardiness of the worker delayed by traffic or the distracted state of mind of the one who arrives after a particularly difficult commute. To the extent that the rush-hour motorist imposes costs on others, the additional cost to society of allowing an extra car to cross the bridge is far above zero, and the price (toll) should be commensurate with that cost. The justification for a congestion toll is that motorists should confront the actual cost of their choices. If the toll deters some motorists from driving during rush hour, it is having its intended impact. Whether the bonds for the bridge have been paid off is entirely irrelevant. Explicit congestion tolls have been implemented successfully in Singapore, Stockholm, and in central London (National League of Cities 2019).

User Fees

In two of the three bridge scenarios sketched in the previous section, there was an economic justification for charging a toll. However, the justifications were very different in Scenarios 2 and 3. In the former, the toll was employed to address equity concerns; in the latter, it addressed efficiency criteria. Tolls are one category of **user fees**. Other examples of user fees are metering the use of water and charging based on usage or structuring trash collection fees on a per-bag basis, rather than a flat household fee. As a growing number of communities find it politically more difficult to increase tax rates to pay for public services, there is greater interest in the employment of user fees.

Pioneers in the field of urban economics such as Wilbur Thompson (1976) and William Vickrey (1963) have long argued that price should play a greater role in the provision of public-sector services. There are some limits: user fees cannot be employed for pure public goods. For example, we cannot pay for national defense through user fees because, as we saw earlier in this chapter, it would be difficult to charge a price for this nonexcludable and nonrival good. Nor can we employ user fees for programs that have a primarily redistributive purpose. We would not want to pay for Supplemental Security Income by charging a price to the elderly poor, since the whole point of the program is to transfer additional income to them.

There are many other instances, however, where the employment of user fees can ameliorate existing income inequalities, promote a better allocation of resources, or do both (Starn 1994). At the local municipal level, most large cities and towns have installed parking meters to ration the number of parking spaces on city streets. Many cities impose a user fee whenever a building permit is issued, presumably to help cover the cost of building inspections. In some states, local communities collect an annual excise tax on the value of automobiles, in part to defray the cost of maintaining city streets and roads. Some local airports charge a departure fee on every ticket to help pay for airport services. The list goes on.

The Tiebout Hypothesis

As we saw in Chapter 2, a metropolitan area describes the boundaries of a labor market, an area that is viewed as a single social and economic entity. However, that same metropolitan area may be comprised of a hundred or more different cities and towns, each with its own local government. Is this situation economically desirable or undesirable? If 100 separate municipalities within a metropolitan area are good, would 200 be even better? If 100 are too many, would the right number be 50, 25, 10, or even 1? The continuing debate over a hypothesis first proposed in 1956 by Charles Tiebout (pronounced *Tee*-bo) sheds some light on these questions though it does not offer definitive answers.

In "A Pure Theory of Local Expenditure," Tiebout argues that it is difficult to get people to reveal their preferences for pure public goods at the national level. Why, for example, should I be forthright in saying how much I value a strong national defense if, as a result, I might be asked to pay more than others to achieve a given level of national security? At the local level, however, he argues that people reveal their preferences for locally provided pure public goods all the time. They do so by voting with their feet—that is, by moving from a jurisdiction whose taxing and spending programs are not a good match for a family's preferences to another jurisdiction, where the match is closer. Ideally, households would keep moving until each found exactly what it was looking for in a jurisdiction's taxing and spending policies. Families seeking high-quality public schools would move to jurisdictions known for their educational excellence, and presumably they would be willing to pay the higher local taxes required to support those schools. Those interested in municipal recreation facilities would move to a place with that emphasis in the municipality's spending pattern. Some households would choose places with higher tax rates to receive a larger and better array of public services, while others seeking to minimize their local tax payments would find places with low tax rates, albeit with limited public services.

Tiebout argues that the more jurisdictions there are within a metropolitan area, and the more different they are from each other, the more likely it is that a household will be able to maximize its satisfaction by choosing where to live. Essentially, access to a large number of diverse cities and towns mimics the array of choices we seem to like so much when it comes to selecting goods and services in the private market.

In addition to Tiebout's economic arguments, others who argue in favor of a large number of small jurisdictions point to the greater likelihood that local government will be more accessible and more accountable to the average citizen. It is the contrast between the traditional New England town meeting that takes place in its smallest villages—perhaps the purest form of direct democracy—versus the complex bureaucracies of large cities, best reflected in that cynical and essentially hopeless phrase, "you can't fight city hall."

Every time you hear someone saying that they moved someplace because the public schools were good or the streets were kept clean, it is confirmation of Tiebout's notion that people do, indeed, vote with their feet.

Limitations of the Tiebout Hypothesis

The controversial aspect of the hypothesis is not that public-sector services have an impact on people's decisions about where to live, but that having a large array of different municipalities within a metropolitan area is desirable. For Tiebout's conclusion to be universally true—the more municipalities the better—he needed to make several rather major assumptions, some of which have been roundly criticized by his opponents.

Several Tiebout assumptions are standard fare in economics. For example, he assumes that people are knowledgeable about the array of choices that are available to them, and that there are many different jurisdictions from which to choose. Because he wants to abstract from other influences on the choice of jurisdiction, he assumes away the need to consider workplace location. In the real world the commute to work is a major factor that affects where households choose to locate.

Tiebout assumes that households have complete mobility and are free to move to the jurisdiction whose public-sector package best matches their preferences. As we saw in our discussion of fiscal and exclusionary zoning in Chapter 4, this is an unlikely outcome, especially for minority households and those at the lower end of the income distribution. If the means, motives, and opportunities to practice fiscal zoning and exclusionary zoning are greater in metropolitan areas with many small jurisdictions, the Tiebout solution may exacerbate inequities based on race, ethnicity, or income. This is particularly true if, in the interest of allowing municipalities the right to offer different packages of services and taxes, they are granted local control that permits them to impose such criteria as one- or two-acre minimum zoning for single-family homes that has the effect of excluding households of modest income from moving into them.

Finally, for the hypothesis to hold, Tiebout must assume that there are no externalities between communities and no economies of scale larger than what can be captured within a single community. If there are externalities, people consume public services in several jurisdictions but express their preferences in only one. Moreover, if there are externalities between communities, rational decision-making becomes more difficult to achieve.

For example, imagine that a town was considering damming up a river that routinely flooded each spring. By damming up the river an artificial lake could be created, and floods could be controlled downstream. The recreational benefits of the lake could easily be limited to town residents—only those who live in the town would be eligible to receive permits to use the lake. However, the flood control benefits could not be limited to town residents. Once the dam is built, all the other towns downstream are protected as well. The flood control benefits are a pure public good. Once the dam is built, no one can be excluded.

The problem is that in deciding whether to build the dam, the town acting rationally will take into account only the costs and benefits to its own residents. The flood-control benefits to the other towns downstream are irrelevant to its decision. The town therefore may decide not to build the dam because the benefits accruing to that individual town do not justify the costs. In that case, it would take a higher level of government to account for all the costs and all the benefits. What is "external" at the level of the town may be "internal" at the level of the county or the state. The proper geographical scope for rational decision-making would encompass an area large enough to "internalize the externalities." Mancur Olson (1969) calls this the "principle of fiscal equivalence," suggesting that for rational decision-making at the local level, the appropriate governmental unit must be large enough to contain all the costs and all the benefits associated with the project.

Hence, the smaller the jurisdiction, the more likely it is that there will be externalities and the shorter the list of projects for which the jurisdiction alone can make rational decisions. Furthermore, the smaller the jurisdiction, the less likely that it will have the critical mass of people necessary to achieve economies of scale. As is currently the case with many small towns, it may have a student population sufficient to support its own elementary school but may have to give up its autonomy and join with other towns to achieve the critical mass of students necessary to support a regional high school.

Thus, there is a tension between the desire to maximize citizen satisfaction by having many jurisdictions and the sacrifice of efficiency when the proliferation of jurisdictions within a metropolitan area increases the likelihood that externalities will be an impediment to rational decision-making and that it will be more difficult to achieve economies of scale in the provision of public services. A 1999 study by the National Research Council concludes that small-scale local governments are more efficient for services that are heavily labor-intensive and that consolidation is more efficient for the highly capital-intensive services that are the most likely to be subject to economics of scale (Altshuler et al. 1999).

Metropolitanism

The realization that jurisdictions in a metropolitan area may have more to gain from cooperating with each other (Orfield 1997; Katz and Bradley 1999) than competing with each other—as in the Tiebout model of competition—has led to a spate of proposals for ways that central cities and their surrounding suburbs could work toward common goals. This has been called **metropolitanism**. While relatively few places in North America have a metropolitan area level of government—metro Toronto and Miami-Dade County are two of the best examples—others have sought to promote greater cooperation, even while preserving traditional units of local government. The Minneapolis-St. Paul area has engaged in tax base sharing for more than two decades. In this framework, some of the tax revenue generated by new economic growth goes to the municipality in which the growth occurred, but some goes into a pool to be distributed among all the other municipalities. By this method, the benefits of growth are more evenly spread throughout the region.

In a similar manner, cities and towns have combined to form region-wide mass-transportation districts, regional water districts, and multijurisdictional sewerage systems. Public transit systems are a good example where there may be an inter-municipal agency responsible for running the system, as is true of the Mass Bay Transit Authority (MBTA) in Greater Boston formed in 1964 by the state that today is responsible for the bus, trolley, subway, and commuter rail system that serves 78 cities and towns in the region. The goal is to link the utility gains from Tiebout's multiple jurisdictions with the efficiency gains from operating large public works projects and rationally internalizing various regional externalities. By moving up in scale and going beyond efficiency, a 1999 National Research Council study argues, state governments should play a larger role in redressing issues within metropolitan areas including economic inequality and racial segregation (Altshuler et al. 1999).

Individuals, Interest Groups, and Values

Once we leave the realm of private markets, where outcomes are presumably the result of the "invisible hand," decisions about production, allocation, and equity need to be made explicitly. Therefore, we need to examine the realm of public decision-making more closely.

This becomes particularly complex because cities and suburbs contain a variety of social classes, racial and ethnic groups, and individuals with a range of political agendas. Further complexity exists because among these social classes, groups, and individuals there are differences in the power to affect public policy outcomes, stemming from economic might or political clout. How public decisions are made under such circumstances is the province of political scientists.

Often we are taught in high school civics class that public decision-making is a democratic process, at least in the United States. Residents of a municipality elect their own mayor and city council, who presumably carry out the will of the majority. This may be generally true, but political theorists find many reasons why the ideal of democratic decision-making diverges from the actual practice.

Public Choice Theory

One of the most widely known theories that questions the democratic nature of public-sector decision-making is **public choice theory**. First developed by James Buchanan (1949; 2003) and Buchanan and Musgrave (1999) and further refined by subsequent writers, public choice theory was designed to provide an alternative to the notion that all public-sector decision-making is done in the interest of the public. Instead, the theory argues, public-sector decisions and other nonmarket decisions could be understood through the assumption that all individuals (including public employees) seek to maximize personal utility—the same set of behavioral assumptions that characterize many economic theories.

Although public employees ostensibly serve the public interest, it can be difficult for citizens to adequately monitor the behavior and choices of civil servants because the citizens who have an interest in the outcomes—who are seen as personal utility maximizers—face opportunity costs. The time and cost spent monitoring could be spent on other important needs. Consequently, there is a likelihood that a number of decisions will be made to benefit public employees' own personal interests and not the interests of the overall public. Examples of the possible effect of the divergence of personal utility from public benefit are a school principal who hires his friends in preference to better qualified job candidates; a school district purchasing agent who buys supplies from a firm that gives him free tickets to the area's professional football games; a superintendent who transfers a good teacher as punishment for having asked a difficult question at a meeting; or a custodian who takes time off to watch the end of a baseball game. Without a good local newspaper or TV station with a mission to investigate possible abuses of public authority, there is every reason to believe that at least some abuse will take place.

Interest Groups and Elites

While public choice theory focuses on individual utility, other theorists argue that public-sector decisions can be most accurately understood by thinking about the effects of interest groups. David Truman (1951) and Earl Latham (1952), two of the pioneers of interest-group theory, believe that people tend to think of themselves as members of groups, and that groups have more power to influence public-sector decision-making than individual citizens. As stated by Latham, groups "concentrate human wit, energy, and muscle . . . for the achievement of ends common to the members, and the means of achievement is the application of the power of the association to the obstacles and hindrances which block the goal." Interest-group theory perceives public-sector decision-makers as subject to the competing pressures and demands of many formal and informal groups of individuals, with each group try-ing to persuade the decision-maker to make decisions in their group's interests.

Another group of public-policy theorists argue that the best way to understand metro area public-sector decision-making is through the study of local elites. While there may be many interest groups, only a few have the power to compel mayors, city councils, and town officials to make decisions consistent with the elite's inter-ests. As articulated by Thomas Dye and Harmon Zeigler (1996), there are two principal components of elite theory. First, elites control more resources: power, wealth, education, prestige, status, and leadership skills, such that elites control public policy, not the will of the people or necessarily their interests. And second, elitism contends that the masses have at best only an indirect influence over the decision-making behavior of elites.

Still other social scientists believe that neither individual interests nor group interests sufficiently explain decision-making in the public sector or private sec-tor. They urge a greater awareness of moral, normative, and ideological influences on public-sector decision-making. In *The Moral Dimension,* economist Amitai Etzioni (1988) argues that the goals that people pursue are determined by a com-bination of individual interest, group interest, and partially internalized norms acquired from their surrounding communities.

Emphasizing that individuals undergo both moral and emotional development, Etzioni focuses on the ways that such ideas shape and constrain decision-making. In *Studying Public Policy,* political scientists Michael Howlett and M. Ramesh (2003) emphasize such influences: "Although efforts have been made by economists, psy-chologists, and others to reduce these sets of ideas to a rational calculation of self-interest, it is apparent that traditions, beliefs, and attitudes about the world and society affect how individuals interpret their interests." The key aspect of moral input into decision-making, as articulated by still other social scientists is that, in contrast to a focus on individual or group well-being, moral values and norms that provide input into decision-making are "held as applicable to everyone" (Kalt and Zupan 1984).

Incrementalism

Finally, two theories of public decision-making emphasize the role of existing policy and the role of nonagreement in constructing policy. Charles Lindblom (1959; 1979) argues that because individuals involved in policymaking typically have neither the time nor money to explore all possibilities, policies emerge from "successive limited comparisons" in which policymakers may disagree about the ultimate ends but agree about particular means or steps to be taken in the short term. Therefore, actual public policies often emerge from incrementalism "build-ing out from the current situation, step-by-step and by small degrees." Carol Weiss (1980), on the other hand, emphasizes that policy can be shaped by numerous small decisions from different offices in an organization without full communica-tion and analysis of the implications of decisions—a process of decision accretion. "A lot of different people, in a lot of different offices, go about their work, taking small steps without consideration of the total issue or the long-term consequences. Through a series of seemingly small and uncoordinated actions, things happen. Precedents are set, responses are generated, and over some period of time these many steps crystallize into a change in direction." The result is not always optimal. That is why conservative economists wish to rely on the private market for many public services, assuming the private market will be less influenced by political actors and will thus deliver optimal outcomes. Unfortunately, the market might provide allocational efficiency, but fail badly in terms of distributional equity.

Regime Theory and Growth Machines

Each of the theories covered so far describes possible decision-making dynamics in urban areas. Furthermore, these dynamics are not all mutually exclusive. The importance of one factor relative to others may vary from one jurisdiction to another, with one municipality being more deeply affected by interest-group dynamics ("this is what would be good for *my* group") and another municipality strongly affected by normative influences ("this is the way we should treat each other"), and still another municipality greatly affected by decision accretion ("this is the way we've always done it"). Variations in the specific ways in which public policy is formulated contribute to differences among cities and suburbs in tax and budgetary priorities.

Political scientists who focus specifically on urban public-sector decision-making have sought to analyze and describe ways in which these theories combine to influence the growth and well-being of urban areas. During the 1980s, Norman and Susan Fainstein and Clarence Stone developed the concept of regime theory as an explanation of decision-making patterns in metropolitan areas (Fainstein and Fainstein 1983; Stone 1989; 2005). Regime theory incorporated awareness of the potential influence of interest groups, elites, public choice theory (self-interested decision-making), and norms.

As conceptualized by these theorists, regimes are coalitions of interest groups dominated by powerful private-sector interests, elected officials, and key public-sector administrators. Regimes form because public-sector officials and private-sector groups need each other to advance their interests. A powerful business may need waivers of various regulations to build a facility; or it may want the public sector to pay for roads, water, or other infrastructure so that the business does not have to incur these costs; or it may want help to control public outcry about a contentious issue (such as damage to the environment). Public officials may need powerful private-sector support for campaign contributions, for favorable news stories in the media, or for employment after leaving office.

After recognizing opportunities for mutual gain, and forming the nucleus of a regime, the initial members of the coalition may widen the coalition to other groups, using the organizational or financial power of the initial members to gain cooperation. Regimes might affect the interests of potential groups or individuals, for example, "through the distribution of selective incentives such as contracts, jobs, facilities for a particular neighborhood, and so on" (Mossberger and Stoker 2001), or by "providing established and familiar ways of getting things done" (Stone 2005). As mentioned by Altshuler and Luberoff (2003), the regime theory literature has "observed that not all cities are governed by cohesive regimes, that regimes can fall apart, and that regimes vary in the degree to which business must share power with other local interests."

Other political scientists studying urban public-sector decision-making focus more narrowly on groups with real estate development interests. Introduced by John Logan and Harvey Molotch in 1987, the concept of "growth-machines" highlights the actions of "place entrepreneurs." These are businesses with significant resources that stand to benefit from real estate development and who in pursuit of this goal form alliances with others who would benefit from the process of development such as construction unions or smaller businesses and property owners who would benefit from increased property values. According to Logan and Molotch, such coalitions often are able to apply significant sustained pressure on public-sector decision-makers to shape decisions about the use and development of urban land to the detriment of less powerful residential residents and neighborhood groups (Logan and Molotch 1987).

The Nature of Voting Systems

Let's say we're voting on whether we like our carrots cooked or raw. Candidate A is a proponent of whole raw carrots. Candidate B is a proponent of overcooked mushy carrots. A clear majority of the group prefers Candidate A. But now Candidate C comes along, and he likes his raw carrots shredded. The raw carrot vote is now split between those who like them whole and those who like them shredded, and Candidate B wins with a plurality of the vote, even though the majority prefer their carrots raw and even though Candidate A would have won in a two-person race. Candidate C is a "spoiler" who upends the rank order of voters' preferences. According to Kenneth Arrow, a Nobel Laureate in Economics, it is impossible to design a voting system that is guaranteed to aggregate individual voter preference into group preference without upsetting that order (Arrow 1950).

In most local jurisdictions, if no candidate receives a majority of the votes, either the candidate with a plurality wins (this is often called a "first-past-the-post" system), or there is a separate runoff election between the two top vote-getters scheduled at a later date. Acknowledging Arrow's conclusion that there is no perfect system, several jurisdictions have adopted a third alternative, *ranked choice voting* (also called instant runoff or proportional representation). In this system, voters rank candidates according to their order of preference. If no candidate receives a majority of first choice votes in the first round of voting, the candidate with the lowest number of first choice votes is eliminated and his or her votes are apportioned to the remaining candidates according to each voter's second choice. If there is still no majority, the process is repeated until a candidate finally receives a majority. New York City recently adopted rank choice voting, joining other major US cities including San Francisco, Minneapolis, St. Paul, Memphis, Santa Fe, and Portland, Maine.

The Challenge of Public-Sector Decision-Making

Overall, public-sector decision-making is the process through which needs and wants are transformed into actual public-sector goods and services. The interplay of the decision-making dynamics discussed here affect public-sector goods and services by shaping how needs are identified, how responses are designed, how taxes are determined, and how resources are channeled to specific uses in the physical and social infrastructure of the urban environment. In the end, these outcomes contribute to the uncontroversial core within Tiebout's outlook—that public-sector services have an impact on people's decisions about where to live.

Public-sector roles and specific outcomes are shaped by needs associated with market failures, but by debates about the appropriate roles of government, by the resources available to pay for government services, by the mobility of households, and by the ways in which public decisions are made.

As we have seen, local governments play a critical role in the everyday life of virtually every individual and household in a city. And the denser the municipality in terms of population and business, the greater the number of externalities and the greater the gain from economies of scale. It is no wonder, then, that as cities grew, more and more services were supplied by the public sector, the number of public agencies expanded, and the number of public employees increased. The modern city owes as much to the public sector as to the private.

But in a highly competitive global economy, city and town officials are faced with more than simply offering services to meet the needs of households and local businesses. Increasingly, they must find a way to maintain economic activity in their jurisdictions and attract business investment in order to keep their citizens employed and public services well financed. In the chapters to come, we turn to the role of the local public sector in promoting economic development and providing for the physical and social infrastructure of cities and suburbs.

APPENDIX A

Negative Externalities

In 1969, the US government identified Chattanooga, Tennessee, as the city with the worst air pollution in the country. Chattanooga at that time was a manufacturing city, where iron foundries and other manufacturers produced a variety of goods and shipped them out by train. While these firms produced jobs for local workers, they created numerous problems for Chattanooga-area residents. The production and distribution activities released high levels of pollutants into the air, which led to heavy smog and a high incidence of pollution-related illnesses that included tuberculosis, bronchitis, and emphysema. While firms paid for the manufacture and distribution of goods, residents paid the additional costs of these spillover effects: the medical bills, the loss of income due to illness or early death, the sacrifice of pollution-free vistas, and the costs of all other deleterious effects caused by the air pollution.

The graph in Figure A7.1 depicts such a situation of divergence of private costs (the costs paid by the firms) and social costs (the sum of the firms' costs and the costs incurred by individuals who experience the firms' production externalities). At each level of output, the marginal social costs are higher than the marginal private costs paid by the firm.

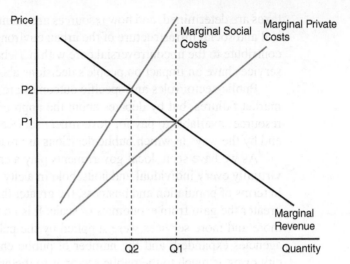

FIGURE A7.1. The Negative Externalities of Pollution

A profit-seeking firm would produce at price P1 and output level Q1, where profits for the firm are maximized. That is where marginal private costs equal marginal revenue. However, at this profit-maximizing level of output for the firm, the marginal social costs are much greater than the marginal private costs that form the basis for the firms' output decisions.

Spurred by the social costs of the worsening pollution and the unflattering national recognition, local and state officials created the Chattanooga-Hamilton County Air Quality Control Bureau, which was empowered to enforce existing regulations, create new guidelines, and take other steps to improve the air quality. One of the steps taken was to confront firms with the likelihood of fines, which essentially raised the firms' costs of production if they continued to produce as they had before. Graphically, this is shown as an upward shift of the marginal private cost curve toward the marginal social cost curve.

Firms would find that their profit-maximizing output level was now lower than the initial Q1. Suppose that fines were imposed at rates such that the marginal private cost curve was brought into correspondence with the marginal social cost curve. Then, the new profit-maximizing level of output would be Q2 at a price of P2, the point of intersection of the marginal social cost curve and the marginal revenue curve. With the full social costs paid for by the firm, the marginal private cost curve would now coincide with the marginal social cost curve. Presumably much of the cost of introducing these environmental controls will be passed onto the utility's residential and business customers in the form of higher prices which represent more closely the private + social costs of producing electricity for the region's consumers.

The goal of imposing fines is often not limited to reducing production. Fines make it relatively more profitable to introduce pollution-control devices or to substitute cleaner technology. This would reduce negative externalities, which would be reflected in a downward shift of the marginal social cost curve, and a new maximizing output greater than Q2.

In Chattanooga, firms rapidly introduced filters and scrubbers, and several firms sought out new technology. Chattanooga was in compliance with Environmental Protection Agency (EPA) standards by 1981, and now prides itself on being a city where many companies have adopted and promoted low-emission technologies.

APPENDIX B

Positive Externalities

In colonial America education was typically private, conducted within families or by a private tutor. After independence, however, many of the nation's leaders believed that effective civic participation depended upon the ability of citizens to read existing and proposed laws. These leaders became strong advocates for publicly provided schools and for compulsory attendance. This position placed them in opposition to some families and industry leaders for whom mandatory school attendance was problematic. In preindustrial times, even the youngest school-age children were old enough to be helpful in the numerous chores and income-producing activities within the home, so the opportunity costs of formal schooling for the family were high. At the dawn of the industrial age, children often were used to work in factories. Taking children out of the textile mill for compulsory schooling limited this source of cheap labor for the early industrialists. Nevertheless, public schools were established and compulsory attendance laws were passed in New England in the mid-1800s. Subsequently, laws were passed by Congress that required the western territories—and ultimately the rest of the country—to establish elementary schools. The social benefits were seen as large enough to warrant using tax dollars to pay for public education.

The divergence between private benefits and social benefits is easily visualized in Figure A7.2. For all quantities of education, the private benefit of education is less than the social benefit, which is the sum of the private benefit plus the added benefit to society. If left to private decision-making alone, the quantity of education would be Q1, obtained at a cost to families of P1. At this level, the private benefits that ensue from that level of education match the private costs that persons acting in their individual interests would be willing to pay. However, because of education's positive social externalities, the private benefit of education is less than the social benefit, as indicated in the graph. Taking into account the social benefits of schooling, public provision moves the quantity of education received out to Q2.

Externalities from education were again a major public policy focus in the late 1800s (particularly in urban areas) as immigration from southern and Eastern Europe accelerated. As noted in Chapter 3, cities were sites where people from different cultures and social allegiances came together. In this context, education held the hope not only of fulfilling the demand for expanding skills but of influencing behavior, creating a base of common expectations, promoting greater cohesion, and thereby reducing social conflict. In the wake of this wave of immigration, compulsory school attendance laws were strengthened and laws banning child

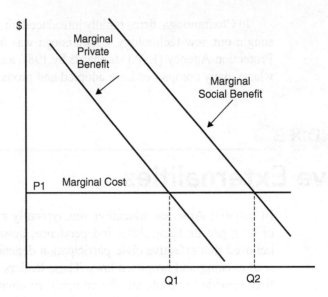

FIGURE A7.2. The Positive Externalities of Education

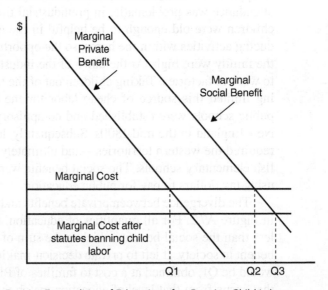

FIGURE A7.3. Positive Externalities of Education after Banning Child Labor

labor—the main source of the opportunity costs that led parents to withhold their children from school—were enacted by many city and state governments.

   The depiction of this development in the graph may not be immediately apparent, but remember that economists are concerned not just with direct out-of-pocket costs but with the relationship of those costs to opportunity costs. The increased enforcement of school attendance laws and the new bans on child labor meant that families would not benefit as much from keeping their children out of school. In effect, this meant that once these statutes were in place, the cost of school attendance (the amount given up when a child was sent to school) was less than it had been before, since now the child could not work. This can be represented as in Figure A7.3 by a downward shift of the marginal cost curve, leading to an even greater increase in the level of education, Q3.

Currently, the rising skill requirements of a postindustrial labor force imply that the positive externalities associated with primary and secondary education are related to the need for metropolitan areas—and the nation as a whole—to have a productive workforce that is capable of competing in a worldwide economy. Increasingly, the prosperity of entire metropolitan areas depends on the skills embodied in each of their workers.

References

Altshuler, Alan, and David Luberoff. 2003. *Mega-Projects: The Changing Politics of Urban Public Investment*. Washington, DC: Brookings Institution Press.

Altshuler, Alan, William Morrill, Harold Wolman, and Faith Mitchell, eds. 1999. *Governance and Opportunity in Metropolitan America*. Washington, DC: National Academy Press.

American Hospital Association. 2019. "1999–2018 Annual Survey." Fall. Chicago: American Hospital Association.

Arrow, Kenneth. 1950. "A Difficulty in the Concept of Social Welfare." *Journal of Political Economy* 58, no. 4: 328–346.

Badger, Emily, and Quoctrung Bui. 2020. "The Recession is About to Slam Cities. Not Just the Blue-State Ones." *New York Times*, August 17.

Blount County Fire Protection District. 2020. "Subscription Form." Blount County, Tennessee. http://www.blountfire.org/.

Bluestone, Barry, Alan Clayton-Matthews, and David Soule. 2006. "Revenue Sharing and the Future of the Massachusetts Economy." Report, January. Boston: Northeastern University, Center for Urban and Regional Policy.

Buchanan, James M. 1949. "The Pure Theory of Government Finance: A Suggested Approach." *Journal of Political Economy* 57, no. 6: 496–505.

Buchanan, James M. 2003. "Public Choice: Politics without Romance." *Policy Magazine*. Centre for Independent Studies 19, no. 3: 3–13.

Buchanan, James M., and Richard A. Musgrave. 1999. *Public Finance and Public Choice: Two Contrasting Visions of the State*. Cambridge, MA: MIT Press.

Dye, Thomas R., and Harmon Zeigler. 1996. *The Irony of Democracy: An Uncommon Introduction to American Politics*, 10th anniversary silver edition. New York: Harcourt.

Etzioni, Amitai. 1988. *The Moral Dimension*. New York: Free Press.

Fainstein, Norman, and Susan Fainstein. 1983. "Regime Strategies, Communal Resistance and Economic Forces." In *Restructuring the City*, edited by Susan Fainstein, Norman Fainstein, Richard Hill, Dennis Judd, and Michael Smith. New York: Longman, pp. 245–282.

Fischel, William A. 2001. *The Homevoter Hypothesis: How Home Values Influence Local Government Taxation, School Finance, and Land-Use Policies.* Cambridge, MA: Harvard University Press.

Friedman, Milton. 2002. *Capitalism and Freedom*, 40th anniversary edition. Chicago: University of Chicago Press.

Galbraith, John Kenneth. 1998. *The Affluent Society*, 40th anniversary edition. Boston: Houghton-Mifflin.

Gerber, Elizabeth, Christianne Hall, and James Hines Jr. 2004. "Privatization: Issues in Local and State Provision." Policy Report No. 1, February. Ann Arbor: University of Michigan, Center for Local, State, and Urban Policy.

Howlett, Michael, and M. Ramesh. 2003. *Studying Public Policy: Policy Cycles and Policy Subsystems*, 2nd ed. Ontario: Oxford University Press.

Kalt, Joseph, and Mark Zupan. 1984. "Capture and Ideology in the Economic Theory of Politics." *American Economic Review* 74, no. 3: 279–300.

Katz, Bruce, and Jennifer Bradley. 1999. "Divided We Sprawl." *Atlantic Monthly* (December), pp. 26–42.

Latham, Earl. 1952. "The Group Basis of Politics: Notes for a Theory." *American Political Science Review* 46, no. 2 (June): 376–397.

Lindblom, Charles E. 1959. "The Science of Muddling Through." *Public Administration Review* 19, no. 2: 79–88.

Lindblom, Charles E. 1979. "Still Muddling, Not Yet Through." *Public Administration Review* 39, no. 6: 517–526.

Logan, John R., and Harvey Molotch. 1987. *Urban Fortunes: The Political Economy of Place.* Berkeley: University of California Press.

Mossberger, Karen, and Gerry Stoker. 2001. "The Evolution of Urban Regime Theory: The Challenge of Conceptualization." *Urban Affairs Review* 36, no. 6: 810–835.

National Hot Dog & Sausage Council. 2007. "Hot Dog Primer." http://www.hot-dog.org/media/consumption-stats

National League of Cities. 2019. "Making Space: Congestion Pricing in Cities." Washington, DC: National League of Cities, Center for City Solutions.

Organisation for Economic Co-operation and Development (OECD). 2018. *Government Spending Survey.* Paris: OECD.

Organisation for Economic Co-operation and Development (OECD). 2019. *Revenue Statistics 2019.* Paris: OECD.

Organisation for Economic Co-operation and Development (OECD)/ United Cities and Local Government (UCLG). 2016. *Subnational Governments around the world: Structure and Finance.* Paris: OECD and Barcelona: UCLG.

Olson, Mancur. 1969. "The Principle of 'Fiscal Equivalence': The Division of Responsibilities among Different Levels of Government." *American Economic Review* 59, no. 2: 479–487.

Orfield, Myron. 1997. *Metropolitics: A Regional Agenda for Community and Stability*, rev. ed. Washington, DC: Brookings Institution Press.

Osborne, David, and Ted Gaebler. 1992. *Reinventing Government: How the Entrepreneurial Spirit Is Transforming the Public Sector*. Reading, MA: Addison-Wesley.

Peterson, Paul. 1981. *City Limits*. Chicago: University of Chicago Press.

Poole, Robert, and Peter Samuel. 2006. "The Return of Private Toll Roads." US Department of Transportation, Federal Highway Administration, *Public Roads* 69, no. 5 (March/April). https://www.fhwa.dot.gov/publications/publicroads/06mar/06.cfm

Starn, Michael. 1994. "User Fees: When Given the Choice, Most Citizens Prefer Service Charges and User Fees over Property Taxes to Fund Municipal Services." *Maine Townsman* (January).

Starr, Paul. 1988. "The Meaning of Privatization." *Yale Law and Policy Review* 6, no.1: 6–41.

Stone, Clarence. 1989. *Regime Politics: Governing Atlanta*. Lawrence: University Press of Kansas.

Stone, Clarence. 2005. "Looking Back to Look Forward: Reflections on Urban Regime Analysis." *Urban Affairs Review* 40, no. 3: 309–341.

Tannenwald, Robert. 2001. "Are State and Local Revenue Systems Becoming Obsolete?" *New England Economic Review* 55, no. 3: 27–43.

Thompson, Wilbur. 1976. "The City as a Distorted Price System." In *The Urban Economy*, edited by Harold Hochman. New York: Norton, pp. 74–86.

Tiebout, Charles M. 1956. "A Pure Theory of Local Expenditures." *Journal of Political Economy* 64, no. 5 (October): 416–424.

Truman, David B. 1951. *The Governmental Process: Political Interests and Public Opinion*. New York: Knopf.

US Bureau of the Census. 2018. *Government Finances*. Washington, DC: Government Printing Office.

US Bureau of Labor Statistics. 2020. Current Employment Statistics Highlights, Washington, D.C. February.

Utility Connection. 2020. http://www.utilityconnection.com.

Vickrey, William S. 1963. "Pricing in Urban and Suburban Transit." *American Economic Review, Papers and Proceedings* (May): 452–445.

Warner, Mildred, and Amir Hefetz. 2004. "Pragmatism Over Politics: Alternative Service Delivery in Local Government, 1992–2002." In *Municipal Year Book 2004*. Washington, DC: International City/County Management Association.

Weisbrod, Burton A. 1964. "Collective-Consumption Services of Individual-Consumption Goods." *Quarterly Journal of Economics* 78, no. 3: 471–477.

Weiss, Carol H. 1980. "Knowledge Creep and Decision Accretion." *Knowledge: Creation, Diffusion, Utilization* 1, no. 3: 381–404.

Wolman, Harold. 2008. "Comparing Local Government Systems Across Countries: Conceptual and Methodological Challenges to Building a Field of Comparative Local Government Studies." *Environment and Planning C: Government and Policy* 26, no. 1: 87–103.

Questions and Exercises

One of the main sources of data about municipal governments is the US Census Bureau's Census of Governments, conducted once every five years (in years ending in 2 and 7). The amount of revenue collected by state and municipal governments within each state and the sources of this revenue are published in the Census of Governments' report *Finances of Municipal and Township Governments*. The latest version at the time of publication (released in 2017) can be found at https://www.census.gov/data/tables/2017/econ/gov-finances/summary-tables.html. Using data from this source for any three states of your choosing, discuss the following issues:

1. What are the relative amounts of revenue generated by various taxes and fees for the state and its local governments as a whole. Within each of these states, what are the three major sources of revenue?

2. Within each of these states, what are the three major sources of local government revenue?

3. What are the total amounts of intergovernmental revenue received by the municipalities from these three state governments?

4. For what purposes was the revenue from state government used?

5. For what purposes was the revenue from local government used?

6. For each of the three states you selected, what is the percentage of municipal government revenue obtained from the federal government and from state government?

7. Do the states you selected allow municipalities to impose local income taxes?

Urban Public Education and Metro Prosperity

8

LEARNING OBJECTIVES

- Explain the justification for government subsidy of elementary and secondary education

- Enumerate the five types of school resource inequalities and give an example of each

- Describe the connection between an area's educational attainment and its median earnings and relate it to the insights of new growth theory

- Explain the concept of an education production function and describe the elements contained in both the simple and expanded versions

- Explain how racial and ethnic discrimination in access to educational resources undermines the notion of meritocracy

- Describe and evaluate alternatives to traditional public schools, including magnet schools, charter schools, and for-profit schools

Since ancient times, education has been recognized as a key component of organized community life. In some societies, the major responsibility for education rested with families and close relatives; in others, there was community-wide training of skills, practices, and rituals; in still others, basic education was regarded as the responsibility of master craftspeople offering apprenticeships; while in some societies, formal schools were established with professional teachers.

Most commonly, ancient education through formal schools was tied to political, religious, and commercial purposes. Access to particular types of education depended upon social class and the perceived future roles of their children. Four thousand years ago, around 2000 BCE, schools were established to provide specialized knowledge for the elite social classes in Egypt's Middle Kingdom (Strouhal 1992), and in China during the Xia dynasty (Lee 1999).

As centuries passed, some cities became renowned centers of knowledge and education as Boston and Paris are today. During the first through the fifth century CE, one of the legendary scholastic centers was Taxila in the Indus Valley of India and Pakistan. During the fifteenth century, among the 100,000 residents of Timbuktu in Mali were 25,000 scholars including many from distant countries who had moved there to study.

As cities grew and developed, education became a focus not only for building specific skills but for the overall benefits of having an educated populace. Who should receive education, how much education should be provided, how would that education take place, and what should be the goals of education? The Chinese philosopher Confucius was a proponent of a basic standard education for all. In *Education in Traditional China: A History*, Thomas H. G. Lee (1999) writes, "Confucius . . . systematically articulated the purpose and meaning of education. He argued that it should be available to anyone seeking education and proposed that its content be regularly revised and rethought." The overall benefits of an educated populace were also recognized by the Aztec Empire of 1345 to 1521, which held mandatory education for its children although there were separate schools for nobles and commoners.

The Greek philosopher Plato (c. 424–c. 348 BCE) is credited with having popularized the concept of compulsory education in Western intellectual thought. Plato's rationale was straightforward. The ideal city would require ideal individuals who would require an ideal education. The popularization of Plato's ideas began with the wider Renaissance and the translation of Plato's works in the fifteenth century, culminating in the Enlightenment. Perhaps taking a clue from Plato, the city-states of ancient Greece developed their first schools, most of them private for the elite. These schools were concerned with the basic socialization and rudimentary education of young Roman children.

Centuries later, the first schools were founded in England. They were private institutions akin to those in early Greece and Rome. The King's School in Canterbury, Kent, is Britain's oldest elementary and secondary school and many consider it the oldest continuously operating school in the world, having been founded in 597 CE by the Catholic Church of England. The Church resisted early attempts for the state to provide secular education. And so it was only in 1811 that the Anglican National Society for Promoting the Education of the Poor was established. The schools founded by the National Society were called National Schools. Most of the surviving schools were eventually absorbed into the state system under the Butler Act in 1944 and to this day many state schools, most of them primary schools, maintain a link to the Church of England reflecting their historic origins. Only in 1833 did the British Parliament finally have government play a role in education, voting sums of money for the construction of schools for poor children (Ensor 1936).

In Germany, Lutheranism had a strong influence on culture, including its education. Martin Luther advocated compulsory schooling so that all people would be able to read and interpret the Bible. This concept became a model for schools throughout Germany. During the eighteenth century, the Kingdom of Prussia was among the first countries in the world to introduce free and generally compulsory primary education consisting of an eight-year course of basic education. It provided not only the skills needed in an early industrialized world (reading, writing, and arithmetic), but also a strict education in ethics, duty, discipline, and obedience. Children of affluent parents often went on to attend preparatory private schools for an additional four years, but the general population had virtually no access to secondary education and universities.

In Asia, Japan has a fascinating history of promoting education dating back to the eighth century. Schools were established in each major city in accordance with the Taihorituryo, or Great Treasure Laws, enacted in 701 CE. Subsequently, various educational systems were established to provide education exclusively for the ruling class—aristocrats, Samurai, and priests. Even though political systems and power structures changed from time to time, these educational systems persisted because the schools were established by the ruling feudal lords or Samurai families. Education for the townsfolk and commoners, though not yet institutionalized, was initiated as early as the thirteenth and fourteenth centuries and continued afterwards in the country's Buddhist temples (Hays 2014).

Not until after 1868, with the ascension of Meiji regime, was the first public education system created to help Japan catch up with the West and form a modern nation. Members of the Iwakura mission were sent abroad to study the education systems of leading Western countries. They returned with the ideas of decentralization, local school boards, and teacher autonomy. After some trial and error, a new national education system emerged. Elementary school enrollments would climb from about 30 percent of the school-age population in the 1870s to more than 90 percent by 1900.

In the new American colonies—only 15 years after the Pilgrims arrived from England—the city of Boston established in 1635 the Boston Latin School, a boys-only public secondary school funded by the municipality. It is still in operation today (Crooks 2020). No one would be a stronger advocate for free universal public education in the United States than Massachusetts' Horace Mann, who called for the establishment of free, nonsectarian, common schools open to all children within the community. In the mid-1830s, with the establishment of the Massachusetts Board of Education, he called for such schools to be placed under public authority and supported by local tax revenue. Such educators as Mann advocated for consolidating local school districts, believing that more centralized decision-making would enhance educational innovations including compulsory school attendance, a longer school year, improved teacher training, a standardized curriculum, and a series of grades based upon age (Kaestle 1983). By 1842, the Detroit Common Council endorsed the idea of the public common school and argued that these could reduce inequality in the city. In their report, the Council praised the value of universal education: "Here the offspring of the rich and poor, seated side by side, will drink in knowledge from the same fountains, and will learn to appreciate each other for their intrinsic values alone. No permanent and transmissible distinction in castes can ever be obtained where such a system exists" (quoted in Euchner and McGovern 2003).

As cities grew during the 1800s, the political, economic, and social impact of education was a focus of considerable discussion. Mandatory education laws spread in response to increased immigration and internal migration. A common primary school education was promoted as a force for social cohesion that brought together immigrants from diverse backgrounds who lived in the burgeoning cities of the United States in the late nineteenth century. By the early twentieth century, comprehensive secondary education was being advocated by an increasing number of influential civic leaders, particularly those associated with the Progressive movement (Wraga 2006). Buoyed by changes in labor markets that reflected changes in technology and office organization, the United States promoted skills well beyond simple literacy in what became known as the "high-school movement." In 1910 only 1 American youth in 10 was a high school graduate; by 1940, more than half (Goldin 2001).

Today, primary and secondary schools exist in all nations and school enrollment for 5 to 17-year-olds is common across the globe. Moreover, in most countries the vast majority of primary and secondary school students attend public schools funded by national, state, or municipal governments or some combination of these.

The benefits from a well-educated population are so great that nearly every country sees education as a **merit good**, an economic concept introduced by Richard Musgrave (1959). A merit good is a commodity or service that is judged to be so important to society that an individual should have access to it on the basis of social need rather than an individual's ability or willingness to pay. Essentially, free schooling is provided because the positive externalities to society as a whole are considered so critically important to the economic well-being and political stability of a nation.

Regardless of how important every country may consider education for its residents, the amount spent per full-time equivalent student in elementary and secondary schools varies enormously across countries, as Table 8.1 reveals. For consistency sake across countries, these dollar values use purchasing power parity (PPP) indices to convert other currencies into US dollars and take into account differences in national consumer prices (US Department of Education 2019).

In 2015, Norway spent more per elementary and secondary student than any other country. At $15,100 per student, Norway spent nearly 60 percent more than the average for all Organisation for Economic Co-operation and Development (OECD) countries of $9,500. The United States ranked second, spending $12,800 per student. Those spending more than $11,000 per student per year included Belgium, the Republic of Korea, Iceland, the United Kingdom, Sweden, Germany, Japan, and France. At the other end of the spending continuum some nations spent as little as $3,300 per student (in Mexico) and $4,500 (in Chile), while Hungary, Greece, the Slovak Republic, Poland, and Estonia, spent less than $7,000 per student—less than three-quarters of the OECD country average.

Some countries increased their spending per student significantly between 2005 and 2015. The Slovak Republic nearly doubled its spending during this 10-year period, while Poland increased its by 70 percent. One of the countries that made the greatest strides in increasing expenditures was the Republic of Korea: from $7,500 in 2005, which gave it a rank of 16th in spending, it ranked 4th by 2015. Not surprisingly, with its emphasis on education, this country is becoming one of the leading exporters of sophisticated manufactured goods, including the Kia and Hyundai automobiles. Across the entire set of OECD countries in Table 8.1,

TABLE 8.1. EXPENDITURES AND PERCENTAGE CHANGE IN EXPENDITURES PER FULL-TIME-EQUIVALENT (FTE) STUDENT FOR ELEMENTARY AND SECONDARY EDUCATION FROM 2005 TO 2015 (IN CONSTANT 2017 U.S. DOLLARS)

	2005	2015	% CHANGE
Norway	$12,600	$15,100	19.8%
United States	$12,300	$12,800	4.1%
Belgium	$9,500	$12,300	29.5%
Republic of Korea	$7,500	$12,000	60.0%
United Kingdom	$10,000	$11,400	14.0%
Sweden	$8.800	$11,400	29.5%
Netherlands	$9,300	$11,100	19.4%
Australia	$9,200	$11,100	20.7%
Germany	$8,300	$11,100	33.7%
Japan	$7,700	$10,200	32.5%
Finland	$8,000	$10,100	26.3%
France	$8,600	$10,000	16.3%
OECD Average	$7,700	$9,500	23.4%
Italy	$8,500	$9,100	7.1%
Portugal	$6,700	$8,700	29.9%
Ireland	$7,300	$8,700	19.2%
Slovenia	$8,600	$8,500	-1.2%
Spain	$7,700	$8,300	7.8%
Czech Republic	$5,200	$7,300	40.4%
Latvia	$4,700	$7,000	48.9%
Estonia	$5,400	$6,900	27.8%
Poland	$4,000	$6,800	70.0%
Slovak Republic	$3,500	$6,800	94.3%
Greece	$6,300	$6,200	-1.6%
Hungary	$5,300	$6,000	13.2%
Chile	$3,200	$4,500	40.6%
Mexico	$3,300	$3.300	0.0%

Source: Organization for Economic Cooperation and Development (OECD), Online Education Database, retrieved January 11, 2019, from https://stats.oecd.org/Index.aspx

education spending increased in real dollar terms by an average of 23 percent, suggesting that education has become an increasingly important component of public spending.

Given these statistics, one might be sanguine about the promise of education in the United States. It is ranked 2nd in school spending and in 2015 was spending nearly 35 percent more per student than the average in the 27 countries listed in the OECD ranking. But as we delve deeper into the US system, we find that critics are now questioning the effectiveness of America's public schools, particularly those in inner cities. The traditional public-school model itself is under attack from competing institutions including charter schools, pilot schools, and voucher systems. If inner cities are increasingly dominated by Black and Latinx families and if the education of inner-city schoolchildren diverges in quality from the schools in the suburbs, what kind of society are we building? Of all the challenges facing cities today, assuring quality education is one of the most important and most vexing. It turns out to be crucial for sustaining the competitive advantage of individual cities and metro areas in an era of global competition.

The Decentralized US Educational System

If the main subject of this book was urban dynamics in France, there probably would not be a chapter or even a section covering urban education. France has a centralized educational system so there is little that distinguishes education in one French city from another. A curriculum set centrally means that much the same math lesson is being taught in every eighth-grade classroom throughout the country, usually on the same day. In Germany, primary and secondary schools are run by its 16 states and not a local authority.

What distinguishes the US school system is its high degree of decentralization. Legal authority for the provision of elementary and secondary education rests not with the federal government but with state governments that have traditionally delegated the actual provision of schooling to local governments. Local school boards, most elected, are responsible for setting kindergarten through twelfth grade (K–12) policy, working within broad regulations set by the state, the federal government, and, in some cases, court orders issued by the state or federal judiciary.

School funding, physical resources, staffing, assignment of students to specific schools, and other important matters are still determined largely at the local level, even as the share of total primary and secondary school funding supplied by local government has declined. As shown in Table 8.2, local authorities provided more than 80 percent of K–12 school funding before 1930, about 50 percent in 1973–1974, and still more than 44 percent in 2017 (US Department of Education 2007; US Census Bureau 2019). Following the dictum that he who pays the piper calls the tune, the still-substantial role that local communities play in funding education means they have a large degree of discretion in setting curriculum and school pedagogy—although their control is somewhat diminished with increased state funding and, to some extent, federal aid.

As of 2018, there were still more than 14,000 individual school districts in the United States—down from nearly 35,000 in 1962 and almost 109,000 in 1942—due to the merger of very small school districts into regional or consolidated districts (US Bureau of the Census 2002a; 2002b; 2019). Their structure varies enormously from state to state, as does the state's financial contribution, as shown in Table 8.3. Both Vermont and Hawaii have what is essentially a state system for elementary and secondary education, with the state funding about 90 percent of total local

TABLE 8.2. PUBLIC FUNDING FOR PRIMARY AND SECONDARY SCHOOLS BY SOURCE, SELECTED YEARS, 1919–2017

SCHOOL YEAR	TOTAL (MILLIONS OF DOLLARS)	LOCAL SHARE (%)	STATE SHARE (%)	FEDERAL SHARE (%)
1919–1920	$970	83.2	16.5	0.3
1929–1930	$2,088	82.7	16.9	0.4
1939–1940	$2,261	68.0	30.3	1.8
1949–1950	$5,437	57.3	39.8	2.9
1959–1960	$14,747	56.5	39.1	4.4
1969–1970	$40,267	52.1	39.9	8.0
1979–1980	$96,881	43.4	46.8	9.8
1989–1990	$208,548	46.8	47.1	6.1
1999–2000	$372,944	43.2	49.5	7.3
2003–2004	$462,016	43.9	47.1	9.1
2017	$739,100	44.5	47.4	8.1

Source: National Center for Education Statistics 2007, table 158, "Revenues for Public Elementary and Secondary Schools, by Source of Funds: Selected Years, 1919–20 through 2003–2004." Data for 2017 are from the U.S. Census Bureau.

school costs. The federal government is responsible for another 6 to 9 percent, with local communities picking up less than 4 percent of the total.

But this system of nearly full funding by the state is fairly rare. In most other jurisdictions the state is responsible for no more than two-thirds of total school spending and in a large number, less than 40 percent. In New Hampshire, the state is responsible for only 32 percent of total school spending, leaving nearly 63 percent to be funded by local communities and a small portion by the federal government. In many other states, there is a more equal sharing of funding responsibility between state and local government. And in most cases, the share from the state takes the form of state aid to local communities based on a formula for individual city and town allocations and comes with only limited strings as to how the revenue is to be used in the schools.

While every state has a number of private elementary and secondary schools, more than two-thirds (68.7%) are traditional local public schools, with another 5.3 percent public charter schools, a new form of school chartered by state government and funded by them, and another 4 percent either local or regional vocational and technical high schools. As such, nearly 80 percent of all schools in the United States are public schools run by a municipality, a regional authority, or by state government.

• Traditional local public schools	91,147
• Local public schools chartered by state government	7,011
• Public vocational and technical schools	5,309
• Private schools	34,576

Source: Schools and Staffing Survey (SASS), "Private School Data File 2015–16"; *Education Data System (IPEDS), "Institutional Characteristics Survey" IPEDS Fall 2016.*

TABLE 8.3. PUBLIC FUNDING FOR PRIMARY AND SECONDARY SCHOOLS BY SOURCE BY STATE, 2017

STATE	FEDERAL SOURCES (%)	STATE SOURCES (%)	LOCAL SOURCES (%)
Vermont	6.1	90.3	3.6
Hawaii	8.9	89.1	2.0
Arkansas	10.9	75.8	13.3
New Mexico	14.4	66.4	19.2
Idaho	9.8	65.0	25.1
Minnesota	5.2	64.9	29.8
Kansas	8.6	64.0	27.5
Alaska	14.0	63.9	22.1
Nevada	9.1	63.2	27.6
Washington	6.8	62.8	30.4
Indiana	7.4	62.6	30.1
North Carolina	11.2	61.5	27.3
Delaware	6.3	59.2	34.5
Wyoming	6.1	59.1	34.7
Michigan	8.1	58.6	33.3
North Dakota	9.2	58.0	32.8
California	8.9	57.3	33.9
Alabama	10.3	55.0	34.7
Kentucky	11.5	54.7	33.8
Iowa	6.9	54.1	39.0
West Virginia	11.6	53.9	34.5
Wisconsin	6.9	53.0	40.1
Oregon	7.3	52.5	40.2
Utah	8.2	51.8	40.0
Mississippi	14.1	50.8	35.1
South Carolina	8.8	47.5	43.7
Montana	12.0	46.9	41.1
Oklahoma	11.1	46.6	42.3
Tennessee	11.5	45.9	42.5
Georgia	9.1	45.2	45.7
Maryland	5.7	43.6	50.7
Colorado	6.7	43.1	50.1
Missouri	8.4	42.2	49.5
Louisiana	12.4	41.4	46.1
Illinois	6.5	41.0	52.4
New Jersey	4.1	41.0	54.9

STATE	FEDERAL SOURCES (%)	STATE SOURCES (%)	LOCAL SOURCES (%)
New York	5.3	40.8	53.9
Rhode Island	7.2	40.5	52.2
Ohio	7.1	40.3	52.6
Arizona	13.7	40.1	46.2
Virginia	6.8	39.7	53.4
Florida	11.0	39.1	49.8
Pennsylvania	6.4	38.7	54.9
Massachusetts	4.3	38.7	57.0
Maine	6.7	38.3	55.0
Connecticut	4.3	38.0	57.7
Texas	10.1	35.6	54.2
South Dakota	12.8	34.1	53.2
Nebraska	7.7	32.7	59.6
New Hampshire	5.4	32.1	62.5

Source: U.S. Department of Education 2017 Annual Survey of School System Finances

There are several significant consequences of having a decentralized educational system. It allows for a wide range of choice by local decision-makers regarding the needs and goals of education in their economic and social environment. Families who can consider moving to different school districts with the means to do so are able to consider differences in educational systems and to include those differences in their choice of residential location. Decentralized systems offer teachers a greater choice about where to work.

Variation in School Spending

To be sure, because of the decentralized school system in the United States, spending per student can vary dramatically from school district to district, both within states and across states. Wealthier cities can afford to spend more on public schools. Even with state aid, poorer cities often are constrained in this regard. As such, children from lower income families who live in poorer communities often find themselves in schools with fewer resources. Richard Rothstein (2004) identifies no less than five types of school resource inequality:

Type I: Disadvantaged children live disproportionately in *states* that spend less money on education than other states.

Type II: Within any state, disadvantaged children may attend schools in *districts* that spend less on education.

Type III: Within any district, disadvantaged children may attend *schools* that command fewer resources than others.

Type IV: Within any school, disadvantaged children may be placed in *classrooms* that have fewer resources at their disposal.

Type V: Within any classroom, disadvantaged children may be offered less adequate *assistance* than others.

As for Type I, Table 8.4 provides strong evidence of the inequality in school spending across the 50 United States. In 2018 New York led all states, with more than $24,000 spent per student in primary and secondary schools. The District of Columbia, Connecticut, and New Jersey each spent more than $20,000 per student per year. At the other extreme, Utah, Idaho, Arizona, Oklahoma, and Mississippi each spent less than $9,000 per student. While there are differences in the cost of living and teacher's salaries across states, these only account for a small portion of these large differences in education spending.

As for Type II inequality, interdistrict gaps within each state are driven by the common reliance on the local property tax to fund schools. Because of differences across cities and towns in property wealth, in the amount of nonresidential industrial and commercial property available to be taxed, and differences in **tax effort**—the tax rate per dollar of assessed property value—differences in per-pupil spending vary *within* states. These gaps persist despite state funding designed to offset the effect of local property tax differences.

As for Types III, IV, and V educational inequalities, Rothstein finds that there is evidence that even within individual school districts, disadvantaged children too often are in particular schools which are underresourced and even within individual schools end up in particular classrooms that are inferior to others and receive less assistance from teachers and staff than their more advantaged and sometimes easier to instruct schoolmates.

One might think that such differences favoring either rich districts or poor would violate the US Constitution, but in a famous 1973 US Supreme Court case (*San Antonio Independent School District v. Rodriquez*), the justices ruled in a 5–4 decision that education was *not* a fundamental right and that states were therefore free to balance the values of local control and equality of educational resources. As late as 2020—nearly 50 years after this court ruling—this decision still holds.

Litigation in individual states has often led to a different conclusion. While equal educational opportunity may not be guaranteed by the Constitution according to the US Supreme Court, some state courts have ruled that extreme inequality across districts violates their state constitutions. As such, in at least 19 states, the courts have invalidated a school finance system that disadvantaged poor cities and towns. To remedy these inequities, a growing number of states have used state funds to partially offset spending gaps across districts and, in some cases, to offset the higher costs of schooling disadvantaged students.

But even with some of these state efforts, Table 8.4 suggests that as late as 2018 there had been little improvement in spending gaps *across* states. Indeed, per pupil spending in New Jersey was still twice as high as Mississippi, and the spending ratio between Connecticut and Alabama increased from 1.45 to 2.13. Some states have increased their spending relative to the US average. By 2018, Alabama was spending 77 percent of the national average, Arkansas 80 percent, and Louisiana 91 percent.

TABLE 8.4. TOTAL SPENDING PER ELEMENTARY AND SECONDARY SCHOOL STUDENT ACROSS THE UNITED STATES, 2018

STATE	SPENDING PER PUPIL
New York	$24,040
District of Columbia	$22,759
Connecticut	$20,635
New Jersey	$20,021
Vermont	$19,340
Alaska	$17,728
Massachusetts	$17,058
New Hampshire	$16,893
Pennsylvania	$16,395
Wyoming	$16,224
Rhode Island	$16,121
Illinois	$15,741
Delaware	$15,639
Hawaii	$15,242
Maryland	$14,762
Maine	$14,145
North Dakota	$13,373
Ohio	$13,027
Washington	$12,995
Minnesota	$12,975
United States	**$12,612**
California	$12,498
Nebraska	$12,491
Michigan	$12,345
Wisconsin	$12,285
Virginia	$12,216
Iowa	$11,732
Montana	$11,680
Kansas	$11,653
Louisiana	$11,452
West Virginia	$11,334
Oregon	$11,290
Kentucky	$11,110
South Carolina	$10,856
Missouri	$10,810

(Continued)

STATE	SPENDING PER PUPIL
Georgia	$10,810
Indiana	$10,262
Colorado	$10,202
Arkansas	$10,139
South Dakota	$10,073
Alabama	$9,696
Texas	$9,606
New Mexico	$9,582
Tennessee	$9,544
Nevada	$9,417
North Carolina	$9,377
Florida	$9,346
Mississippi	$8,935
Oklahoma	$8,239
Arizona	$8,239
Idaho	$7,771
Utah	$7,628

Source: 2018 Annual Survey of School System Finances, U.S. Census Bureau

However, spending per pupil in Oklahoma had actually slipped to just 65 percent of the national average. Hence, the local nature of K–12 schooling in the United States continues to introduce large gaps in primary and secondary school spending.

The Importance of Schooling in Modern Society

Why are these spending differences so important, especially in today's society? Today, most employers demand greater skill from their job applicants. Many look for a high school degree as a minimum either because of the skills required on the job, or because they are using the high school degree as a screening factor for their applicants' motivation or ability to learn new things on the job. For individuals with less than a high school degree, the urban employment experience is no longer what it was in the first half of the twentieth century. Instead of being places of potential economic promise for individuals, many urban areas have become economic quagmires.

The demand for better educated and more highly trained employees has led to a wage premium for skilled workers. Between 2000 and 2019, average hourly wages increased by 0.2 percent per year for high school graduates. For those with a college degree, wages increased twice as much each year (0.4%). For those with an advanced degree, wage growth over this two-decade period was even greater—0.6 percent per year (Gould 2020).

Since the labor market has changed to emphasize the obtaining of higher levels of education, one might expect that individuals would seek greater levels of learning and that elementary and secondary school systems would respond by producing more high school graduates. Indeed, this is the case. Back in 1940, before World War II, only 24 percent of persons age 25 or older in the United States had completed four years of high school or more. By 1970, the percentage had climbed to 80.4 percent and by 2017, nearly 90 percent (Schmidt 2018). The percentage with bachelor's degrees or higher grew from 11 percent in 1970 to 24.4 percent in 2000. By 2019, more than a third (36%) of those 25 years or older living in the United States had completed at least four years of college or an advanced degree (US Census Bureau 2019).

Variation in Educational Attainment Across Metro Areas

There is great variance in the level of schooling completed across metro areas. Across the entire set of 388 metro areas in the United States the percentage of the adult population with a bachelor's degree or more ranges from 60.4 percent in Boulder, Colorado to just 12.3 percent in Lake Havasu City-Kingston, Arizona (State Science & Technology Institute 2019). Even across the nation's 25 largest metro areas, the proportion achieving a bachelor's degree or more education ranges from nearly half (49.9%) in Washington, DC to just one-fifth (20.7%) in Riverside, California, as shown in Figure 8.1. Also at the top of this list are San Francisco, Boston, Denver, and Seattle—all metro areas known for their advanced industries. At the bottom of the list are Riverside, San Antonio, Tampa, and Detroit.

In many of the largest 25 metro areas, the proportion of central city populations with a bachelor's or higher degree exceeds the percentage in their metro areas. By 2014, more than 60 percent (60.4%) of Seattle's central city population was this well-educated. More than half of the residents in the central cities of Washington, DC and San Francisco were equally well-educated. At the other extreme, less than 14 percent (13.8%) of Detroit's central city population had completed a bachelor's degree or higher. This was true also for approximately a quarter of the residents in Philadelphia, San Antonio, Miami, and Riverside.

What do we know about the proportion of the population age 25-plus lacking a high school degree? With so little formal education, many of these residents— particularly younger ones—are at a severe disadvantage in the labor market. In Figure 8.2 one will find the percentage of central city populations in each of the largest 25 US metro areas who have not completed high school. Across the entire United States in 2017, it is estimated that nearly 10 percent of the population lacked a high school diploma. But this percentage varies enormously across central cities. In Seattle, less than 5 percent (4.6%) of its residents had this low level of schooling. Other central cities including Portland, Atlanta, Orlando, Minneapolis, and Charlotte have percentages below 9 percent. By contrast, the urban core of Miami, Dallas, Los Angeles, Houston, Riverside, and Detroit all have close to one-sixth or more of their populations lacking a high school diploma. Many of these central cities have a large number of recent immigrants who may have less education than long-term residents. Detroit and other industrial cities have seen their better educated residents leave for the suburbs.

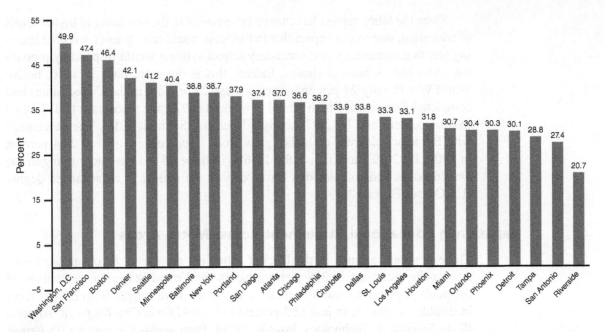

FIGURE 8.1. Percent of Population Age 25+ with a Bachelor's or Higher Degree in 25 Largest US Metropolitan Areas, 2017

Source: US Census Bureau, Quick Facts https://www.census.gov/quickfacts/US

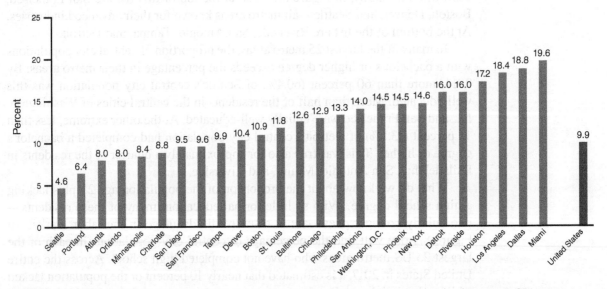

FIGURE 8.2. Estimated Percent of Central City Population Age 25+ with Less than a High School Degree in 25 Largest Metropolitan Areas, 2017

Source: US Census Bureau, Quick Facts https://www.census.gov/quickfacts/US

Educational Attainment and Metro Area Income

Figure 8.3 clearly demonstrates that higher education pays off not only for individual households, but also for entire metro areas and cities. Here we have created a scatter plot of median hourly earnings in each of the 25 metro areas we have been

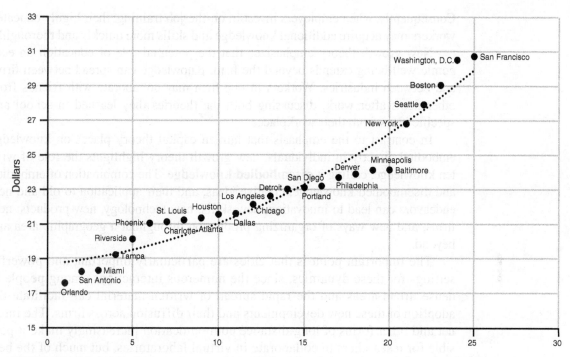

FIGURE 8.3. Relationship Between Percent of Metropolitan Population with a Bachelor's or Higher Degree and Average Metropolitan Area Hourly Wage, 2019

Source: Author's calculations

tracking against the percentage of adults 25 and older who have at least a bachelor's degree. The trend line confirms that those metro areas with more college graduates have significantly higher median hourly wages. San Francisco, Washington, DC, Boston, and Seattle, each with 46 percent or more of its adults having a college education, had median earnings that exceeded $29 per hour. At the other extreme, metro areas with less than a third of their adult residents attaining at least the bachelor's degree earn a median hourly wage of less than $19 an hour.

Education, New Growth Theory, and the Well-Being of Cities and Suburbs

To understand why education has become such an important factor in the well-being of cities and suburbs, it is useful to further elaborate on the **new growth theory** we introduced in earlier chapters. Pioneered first by Robert Solow as noted in Chapter 3, and then by Paul Romer (1986; 1994; 1996) and Robert Lucas (1988), new growth theory considers education to be one of the central factors that determines economic growth at both the metropolitan and national levels not only because of its direct effect on the productivity of individual workers who receive advanced schooling, but because of the spillover effects that enhance the productivity of others who work with them.

Highly educated workers are valued more because they may have gained the advantage of learning *new* things on the job faster than those with less education.

Consequently, when employers invest in on-the-job training, their highly educated workers may acquire additional knowledge and skills more quickly and thoroughly.

New growth theory emphasizes that the potential role of education on economic well-being extends beyond the firm. Knowledge can spread between firms and between industries. Workers in one firm may collaborate with friends from other firms after work, discussing both the theories they learned in school and specific ideas from their workplaces.

In contrast to the emphasis that human capital theory places on knowledge embodied directly in individuals, new growth theory highlights the role of written knowledge, calling it **disembodied knowledge**. The combination of embodied and disembodied knowledge, creative ideas, and their application to old and new endeavors can lead to innovation, new skills, new technology, new products, new firms, and new ways of organizing production throughout a geographic area and beyond.

The important point is that cities are particularly important and powerful settings for these dynamics, since the numerous interactions among people in dense urban areas and the rapid spread of written material can facilitate the adoption of these new developments and their diffusion across firms. The internet and other forms of long-distance communication increasingly make it possible for researchers to collaborate in virtual laboratories, but much of the best research still relies on face-to-face interaction in real ones. Those who study this type of activity sometimes refer to the **bump rate** in a community—the number of times workers bump into each other at work or during leisure time and exchange ideas and new ways to solve problems (Krim et al. 2006). Dense areas are places where the bump rate is unusually high, and therefore unusually productive. That is why places such as Silicon Valley in California; the Boston-Cambridge metro area in Massachusetts, with its rich array of universities, colleges, and teaching hospitals; Raleigh-Durham-Chapel Hill in North Carolina with its Research Triangle; and Austin, Texas with its great research university have become prosperous metro areas with equally prosperous central cities. While it is likely that a higher proportion of skilled individuals can continue to work remotely in the post–COVID 19 era, the value of face-to-face interactions would imply that the bump rate might still matter for those engaged in cutting edge technologies.

Clearly, the educational level of the workforce is critical to the economic and social success of a city or metro area. But the quality of local schools also has an independent effect on the well-being of urban regions for another very important reason. Blair and Premus (1987) have demonstrated that while in the early to mid-1900s, US firms were particularly drawn to sites that minimized transportation costs (as depicted in the Weber graphs of Chapter 4), the educational environment of metropolitan areas has become an increasingly important factor in location decisions since 1960. Indeed, a study of business location dynamics by Natalie Cohen (2000) concludes, "Corporate real estate executives' litany has changed from 'location, location, location' to 'education, education, education.'"

According to Harvard University economist Edward Glaeser, this is especially important for "cold weather cities," which increasingly have trouble competing for young professionals who seek out municipalities with warmer climes. "Cities with average January temperatures under 30 degrees Fahrenheit grew in population only one-third as quickly from 1960 to 1990 as did cities with average January temperatures above 50 degrees" (Glaeser 2005, p. 1). To counteract this population shift, cold-weather cities need to focus on recruiting a high-skilled workforce, and Glaeser argues that highly skilled individuals who are concerned about their children will look for communities with good public schools.

There is evidence for this conjecture. The US Department of Education has reported that in 2003 nearly one in four students (24%) in grades 1 through 12 had parents who moved to their current neighborhoods for the quality of the school system. This suggests that where employers are competing for highly skilled employees, the firm may choose to locate in a community with a well-regarded public-school system. Conversely, a poor school system may be a serious hindrance to the recruitment of skilled young workers. Metropolitan areas that cannot provide high-quality educational facilities might even experience a "brain drain" as talented employees leave in search of a more suitable environment in which to raise their families.

Education Production Functions

Since education has such great significance for metropolitan areas in the twenty-first century, it is important to understand the forces that shape its production. What are the economic, political, and social factors in metropolitan areas that affect the quality and quantity of education? How do the urban dynamics of race, social class, and housing segregation interact to influence—positively or negatively—the production, distribution, and accumulation of schooling?

In Chapter 6 we discussed human capital, the idea that individuals pursue education hoping to receive higher wages in the future. In that initial discussion, we did not discuss variations in the *quality* of education received, but only how the *quantity* of education as measured by years of schooling affects earning. Yet this is an important issue. Families who seek the best schools for their children, businesses that extol the academic reputations of nearby schools, and school system officials who compare test scores or other measures of their students' achievement against test scores from schools in other cities and metro areas all recognize that the quality of education varies from one place to another. School quality is determined by several different inputs.

If we recognize that these inputs comprise (1) school system characteristics, (2) individual student characteristics, and (3) geographically specific socioeconomic environments, it is clear that no two educational outcomes have precisely the same inputs. However, we can try to identify the factors that are most important.

Economists and other social scientists try to do this using the form of an **education production function**. Expressed in mathematical terminology, an education production function is akin to any other production function that tries to explain how inputs are converted into output. In this case, we are interested in the overall process that turns education inputs into educational outcomes measured by, say, graduation rates or test scores.

A simple education production function might be written as follows (King et al. 2003):

$$O = f (C, R, I)$$

where O = Educational Outcome (e.g., graduation rate, test scores) for a single cohort of students

C = Student Characteristics (e.g., family income, parents' education)

R = School Resources (e.g., per-student spending, pupil–teacher ratio)

I = Instructional Processes (e.g., type of curriculum)

and where (f) stands for "a function of."

This simple function states that a measured educational outcome such as the 10th-grade reading scores across tens of thousands of students in hundreds of different schools or school districts is related to the socioeconomic background of the students, the amount of school resources per student, and what is actually taught in each district.

The goal of such research is to reveal how much of the variance in educational outcomes across students is related to each of these factors. This is a critical question for cities and metro areas across the country, for it greatly influences the types of policies that might be used to improve educational outcomes in their school districts. For example, if statistical analysis reveals that the amount of school spending per child is the critical factor in educational outcomes, then one might advocate for boosting spending in the school districts where children are performing poorly on standardized tests. If the pupil-teacher ratio in each class is important to educational outcomes, this information might inform school reform.

Racial and Ethnic Differences in Educational Opportunity and Outcomes

Before the landmark 1954 Supreme Court decision in the case of *Brown v. Board of Education,* states from Maryland and west through Indiana, encompassing the entire South as well as Texas and Oklahoma, had laws mandating that Black and White children were required to attend separate public schools. This example of legally mandated and legally enforced segregation—called **de jure** segregation—had been considered in compliance with the US Constitution based on the 1896 Supreme Court case of *Plessy v. Ferguson*, which sanctioned segregated accommodations on passenger railroad trains.

While de jure segregation was illegal after *Brown*, many of the places where it was practiced actively resisted or at the very least were slow to make the necessary changes despite the fact that the Court directed them to act "with all deliberate speed." Most important was that residential segregation produced school segregation by race and ethnicity given the nature of localized school districts. Most of the states outside of the South did not practice de jure segregation and some along the northern tier from Massachusetts to Minnesota, including Michigan, outlawed it. In many northern cities, however, schools were segregated even in the absence of legal mandates, as a result of segregated housing patterns. In contrast with de jure segregation, this was called **de facto** segregation (Rothstein 2017).

By the late 1960s, schools in the Detroit metropolitan area were overwhelmingly Black inside the central city and overwhelmingly White in the surrounding suburbs. Any meaningful effort toward racial integration of the schools would have required a solution for the entire metropolitan area. However, when the Detroit metropolitan area desegregation plan was brought before the Supreme Court in 1974 in the case of *Milliken v. Bradley*, the Court ruled against integration plans that would cross central city school district boundaries unless it could be shown that suburban jurisdictions or state action contributed to de jure segregation within the central city (Friedman 2002).

This decision made it far more difficult, and often impossible, to implement metropolitan plans for desegregation. As demographic change concentrated higher proportions of Blacks and Latinx inside central cities, the result was a high degree of racial and ethnic segregation of schoolchildren, even in the absence of laws mandating that outcome.

As a result, there remains a high degree of school segregation nearly 70 years after the Brown decision. This is clearly shown in Figure 8.4, which provides the Black–White dissimilarity index for primary and secondary schools in the largest 25 metro areas in the United States during the 2014–2015 school year. Note that in the *most* integrated metro areas such as Riverside, Orlando, and Phoenix, the school dissimilarity index was still nearly 50 percent as late as 2015. That means full racial integration could only occur if up to 50 percent of the Black students moved to predominantly White schools, up to 50 percent of the White students moved to predominantly Black schools or there was some combination of both. In other metro areas school segregation by race was even greater. The dissimilarity index in the St. Louis, Detroit, New York, and Chicago metro areas was 70 percent or higher. There has been little progress since then. As a result of continuing geographic segregation, in his 2020 book, *The Color of Law*, Rothstein reports that "schools are more segregated today than at any time in the last 50 years."

Data on per student spending on K–12 education across the United States reveals that such a high degree of racial segregation among schools has put Black students at a disadvantage in terms of how much is spent per year on their educations. In 2012, across the United States $334 less was spent per year on the schooling of Black students compared to White students (Spatig-Americaner 2012). Over the 13 years of kindergarten through 12th grade, this amounts to a differential of more than $4,300. But the spending differential is even greater in the most segregated schools. Primary and secondary schools with 90 percent or more of Black, Latinx, and Asian students spent a full $733 less per student per year than schools with 90 percent or more White students. For K–12, that amounts to a racial spending gap of more than $9,500.

Most importantly, segregation has had a major impact on school success as measured by high school graduation rates. Historically, graduation rates across school districts have been highly correlated with the racial composition of the student body (Orfield et al. 2004). Among 20 of the largest school districts in the nation, as shown in Table 8.5, the high school graduation rate back in 2000 ranged from just 30.4 percent in Oakland, California and 32.4 percent in Cincinnati, Ohio to 70 percent or more in Sacramento, California; Tucson and Mesa, Arizona; and Portland, Oregon. Of these 20 districts, the predominant racial group for the

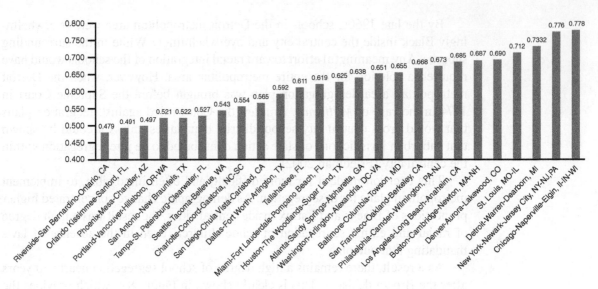

FIGURE 8.4. Black–White/White–Black Dissimilarity Index

Source: Governing analysis of enrollment data from the National Center for Education Statistics, 2015–2016 Common Core of Data

13 districts with the lowest graduation rates were Black or Latinx. Of the remaining 7 districts with the highest graduation rates, none were predominantly Black, 1 was Asian/Pacific, two were Latinx, and the other 4 were predominantly White. As such, school performance gaps have a distinctly geographic dimension due to housing segregation by income and wealth, housing location outcomes—both imposed and self-imposed—and differences in local governments' abilities to fund local schools.

Trends in School Success by Race and Ethnicity

Fortunately, with the recent overall increase in state funding, often with the explicit purpose of reducing local school funding gaps, there has been some closing of the school achievement gap between Black and Latinx students and White students. One measure of this improvement is found in high school graduation rates. As shown in Figure 8.5, in 1975 only 62.2 percent of Latinx aged 18 to 24 graduated from high school. The comparable rate that year for Blacks was 70.2 percent. For Whites the rate was 87.2 percent—a full 25 points higher than the Latinx rate and 17 points higher than the Black rate. Twenty years later in 1995, the Latinx graduation rate had not improved one iota, while the Black–White gap had closed to 5.4 percentage points. By 2015, however, even Latinx had made progress in terms of high school graduation rates closing the gap with Whites to 6.3 percentage points. Black high school graduation rates have increased to nearly 92 percent, less than 3 percentage points behind Whites. One would expect that such progress would begin to show up in terms of better labor market outcomes for both Latinx and Blacks.

Another indication of whether schooling has improved for racial and ethnic minorities in the United States is how well each group succeeds on standardized

TABLE 8.5. HIGH SCHOOL GRADUATION RATES FOR SELECTED LARGE SCHOOL DISTRICTS, 2000

URBAN SCHOOL DISTRICT	BLACK/LATINX ENROLLMENT (PERCENT)	LARGEST RACIAL GROUP	GRADUATION RATE (PERCENT)
Oakland, California	94.4%	Black	30.4%
Cincinnati, Ohio	74.3%	Black	32.4%
Columbus, Ohio	62.9%	Black	34.4%
New York City, New York	84.7%	Latinx	38.2%
Atlanta, Georgia	93.2%	Black	39.6%
Houston, Texas	90.0%	Latinx	40.2%
Denver, Colorado	78.0%	Latinx	40.5%
Philadelphia, Pennsylvania	83.3%	Black	41.9%
Los Angeles, California	90.1%	Latinx	46.4%
Baltimore, Maryland	89.2%	Black	47.9%
Chicago, Illinois	90.4%	Black	48.8%
Dade County, Florida	88.7%	Latinx	52.1%
Minneapolis, Minnesota	72.8%	Black	63.8%
Seattle, Washington	60.0%	White	66.6%
San Francisco, California	88.9%	Asian/Pacific	66.7%
Anchorage, Alaska	36.6%	White	69.4%
Sacramento, California	75.1%	Latinx	70.0%
Tucson, Arizona	58.5%	Latinx	70.6%
Mesa, Arizona	32.2%	White	71.7%
Portland, Oregon	37.8%	White	71.9%

Source: Orfield et al. 2004.

tests. The National Assessment of Educational Progress (NAEP) is the largest nationally representative and continuing assessment of what America's students know and can do in various subject areas. Assessments are conducted periodically in such subjects as mathematics, reading, science, writing, and the arts. Scores on this exam can be used to provide of a measure of racial and ethnic gaps in education performance over time.

In 2005, 29 percent of all eighth graders who took the NAEP scored at the proficient level on the reading exam. White and Asian students scored nearly equally, with 39 percent of Asians and 37 percent of Whites scoring as proficient. By contrast, only 11 percent of Black students and 14 percent of Latinx scored this well. Only 15 percent of economically disadvantaged kids were judged proficient, compared with 38 percent of those who were not disadvantaged.

In math, the scores were similar in rank, but the gaps were even larger. Overall, 28 percent of eighth graders were math proficient. Asians led the pack at 46 percent, followed by Whites at 37 percent, Latinx at 13 percent, and Blacks at only

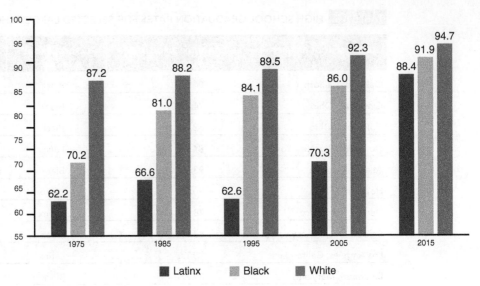

FIGURE 8.5. US High School Graduation Rates by Race and Ethnicity, 1975–2015

Source: National Center for Education Statistics, "High School Completion Rate of 18–24 Year-Olds by Race and Ethnicity, 1972–2016"

8 percent. Economically disadvantaged kids were only one-third as likely to test proficient on the math test as those who were not disadvantaged (13% versus 39%, respectively).

The longer-term trend, however, does suggest that Black and Latinx students have improved their standing on education exams relative to White students. The scores for White 17-year-olds on reading proficiency exams remained roughly constant between 1975 and 2012, while for Black 17-year-olds scores rose sharply by more than 30 points between 1975 and 1990 and have remained more or less constant since then. For Latinx 17-year-olds reading scores have risen by nearly as much, again with the largest gain coming before 1992. Why these test gaps have not closed further is something of a mystery, despite the rising high school completion rates for Blacks and Latinx. It suggests there are still major challenges in the United States in the pursuit of equal educational outcomes across race and ethnic groups.

Understanding Meritocracy

We can define meritocracy as a system in which those who avail themselves of more education and training are rewarded with higher incomes with the implication that this relationship is just and proper. As such, the existing differences in graduation rates and reading scores could be used to justify the fact that on average, Whites have higher incomes than Blacks and Latinx. But what the meritocratic argument fails to account for is how lingering forms of discrimination, including differences in school spending, and the long legacy of residential segregation, all affect a Black or Latinx child's likelihood of completing as much schooling and achieving as well on standardized tests.

As Yale Law School professor Daniel Markovits (2019) suggests in his book *The Meritocracy Trap*, the quantity and quality of the education and skills a child receives today depends very much on the opportunities open to their parents. Lower-income families often have little choice as to where they live and therefore cannot move to neighborhoods with better schools. Residential segregation has made the choice and quality of schools even more constrained for many Black and Latinx parents. The cost of higher education often limits the ability of these families to send their children to elite colleges and universities, even with tuition assistance and scholarships. As such, the strong link between education and income does not necessarily reflect intelligence or effort, but social class inequities. As Markovits notes, existing social class arrangements

> make meritocracy an engine of dynastic privilege, excluding poor and middle-class children from the bases of future income and status. . . . Because training and education work, rich children systematically outperform the rest—again not just the poor, but (increasingly) also the middle class—at each stage of their education. At every stage of childhood, extravagant investments in the human capital of rich children produce exceptional performances by these children. (Markovits 2019, p. 148)

To build a truly meritocratic society, it would be necessary to make it possible for all children, regardless of their background, to have the same opportunity for education and training consistent with their innate intelligence and motivation. In the United States and in many other countries there is a striving for such a system, but much more needs to be done to achieve it. The improvement in high school graduation rates and on standardized tests for Black and Latinx students provides some evidence that at least some of the disadvantages they face are being addressed.

Educational Success: The Role of Preschool

There are many factors that might explain the closing racial and ethnic gap in high school graduation rates. One factor that has surely played a significant role is the now widespread availability of preschool programs for 3- to 5-year-olds. Preschools, both public and private, exist in many nations and across most metro areas in the United States providing early childhood education to children regardless of their family's income or poverty status. With more dual earner families, preschool has become a necessity for many parents. But the benefits to the children themselves may be even more important and this has been particularly important for Black and Latinx children.

Preschool programs were not always available to most students. But as the value of early education became ever more evident, the US federal government launched the Head Start program in 1965 as an effort to break the cycle of poverty, by meeting the social, health, nutritional, and psychological needs of low-income children (ages 3–5) and their families. The program has grown from a brief eight-week summer program for preschoolers in 1965 to a year-round program today serving children from birth to age five. Since 1965 over 160 million children and their families have received Head Start comprehensive services.

Studies of preschool have found this form of early education has an extremely high benefit-cost ratio. Children who attend prekindergarten classes are more ready to take on and benefit from K–12 schooling. They are more likely to succeed in class and to graduate high school.

According to research on the Perry Preschool Program, a two-year intensive early intervention program for disadvantaged Black 3- and 4-year olds, spending time each morning in a preschool with follow-up afternoon visits to the child's home led to increases in measured IQ by age 10, higher achievement scores on standardized tests, higher rates of high school graduation, higher salaries in adulthood, a higher rate of homeownership, a lower probability of being dependent on welfare, and fewer arrests as compared with a control group that was followed until the young children reached age 40 (Schweinhart et al. 2005). In measuring the benefit/cost ratio of this program, Barnett (2004) finds that the total cost of the program averaged $16,514. But the net present value of the benefits was nearly $128,000. Of this total, there were additional earnings in excess of $40,000, a savings in remedial K–12 education of more than $9,000, and a savings to society of $94,000 due to a lower incidence of crime. Altogether, the benefit-cost ratio is 8.74 to 1. Thus, this particular program returned nearly $9 for every $1 invested in these disadvantaged kids.

The value of preschool most likely helps explain the closing gap between Latinx, Black, and White high school graduation rates. According to US census data, as of 2017 non-Latinx Black children ages 3 to 5 were more likely to be attending full-day preschool than either non-Latinx White or Latinx children. More than 42 percent of Black children were in full-day preschool compared with just 29 percent of non-Latinx White children and 23 percent of Latinx children. If you include part-day preschool programs, non-Latinx White children and Black children had virtually identical preschool enrollment rates.

That preschool has become so prevalent in the United States and that lower income households, Black households, and Latinx households have taken advantage of it for many of their children suggests that early childhood education is indeed a great equalizer, at least when it comes to high school graduation rates.

Does the Level of Spending on K–12 Schools Really Matter?

A strong case therefore can be made for expanding preschool to as many children as possible in order to improve educational outcomes. But when it comes to K–12 education, does the amount of per student spending make a difference in educational outcomes? It would seem the answer would be obvious. Despite enormous differences in spending per student across school districts—and one presumes, therefore, differences in the quality of teachers, the size of the average class, the number of high school electives, and the number of extracurricular activities offered through the school—how much these school resources matter in terms of student outcomes is still a matter of empirical analysis.

One of the first and most cited studies of the impact of school inputs on educational outcomes—as measured by standardized tests—was undertaken for the federal government in 1966 by James S. Coleman, a leading education expert from Johns Hopkins University. With President Lyndon Johnson pursuing his declared War on Poverty, there was the need to demonstrate that spending additional money on public schools would improve the educational outcomes of poor children, especially those in inner-city schools. Coleman administered tests to thousands of students across the country, collected data on school resources in hundreds of school districts, and gathered data on the demographic and economic characteristics of the students' families (Coleman 1966).

Having analyzed the data and then reanalyzed them over and over again, Coleman concluded, to his own consternation, that variations in school resources—including teacher–pupil ratios, the number of books in the school library, and the amount of spending per student—had almost nothing to do with explaining the gap in test scores between Black and White children after controlling for such family background variables as parents' education and income (Rothstein 2004). Most of the difference in test scores was attributable to family background and the social and economic conditions of the neighborhoods where students lived.

Since the Coleman report, a plethora of studies have addressed the question of how much school resources matter. The results are extraordinarily mixed depending on the type of sample and the statistical methods used. Take class size as an example. Alan Krueger (1997), using data from Tennessee, found that smaller classes matter, especially for poor and minority children, with kids educated in smaller classes performing significantly better on standardized tests than kids who are in classes with 20 to 25 children. Eric Hanushek (1997a; 1997b), in summarizing the results of many studies, came to nearly the opposite conclusion. He found that class size generally has no effect on test scores. Caroline Hoxby (2000), using data from Connecticut, agreed with Hanushek that class size does not appear to affect students' performance in school. This disagreement regarding the effect of something that should be so simple to measure—class size—is because there are so many variables that affect test performance and no two studies using different data sources hold constant the same set of factors.

The most comprehensive study of the impact of school spending on student outcomes and their future earning capacity has been carried out by researchers at the National Bureau of Economic Research (Jackson et al. 2015). This study focused on the impact of state school reforms that reduced spending disparity across local school districts. The key result of this detailed research, contrary to earlier studies, provides powerful evidence that school spending per student indeed makes a difference in school outputs including years spent in school, student performance on standardized tests, increases in future earnings, and the impact on adult poverty.

While the study found only small effects for children from affluent families, for low-income children, a 10 percent increase in per-pupil spending each year for all 12 years of public school is associated with 0.43 additional years of completed education, 9.5 percent higher earnings, and a 6.8 percentage-point reduction in the annual incidence of adult poverty. To shed light on mechanisms that contributed to these outcomes, the authors document that school spending increases were associated with a reduction in the student–teacher ratio, longer school years, and increased teacher salaries—suggesting that reductions in class size, increases in instructional time, and improvements in teacher quality improve student outcomes.

Still another factor that affects school outcomes is the quality of teachers in each local district. The ideal teacher is knowledgeable about the subject matter being taught, well-versed in the learning process for students in the classroom, skilled and experienced in the ability to convey ideas and maintain a classroom environment that is conducive to learning, relates well to students, and has a sincere interest in the educational development of his or her students. While this is the ideal, teacher quality in fact varies considerably and, as with many other variables that affect metropolitan areas, place matters.

Unlike other inputs for the production of education, teachers have some choice about where they look for work, which job offers they will accept, how much effort to put forth on the job, and whether or not to seek a change in employment after they have been in the job for a while. While there is great variation in the quality of teachers within cities and within suburbs, the overall quality of teachers may differ between central city and suburban schools. For example, a principal in New York City interviewed by education specialist Jonathan Kozol (1992) complained that his school got only the "tenth-best" tier of qualified teachers. This viewpoint has been advanced in more recent studies from researchers who have contributed to a growing literature attesting that schools in central cities may have more trouble recruiting and hiring highly qualified teachers than do suburban schools (Lankford et al. 2002; Buckley et al. (2004).

An Expanded Education Production Function

With children spending more than four-fifths of their time *outside* of school—during summer vacations, holidays, weekends, and evenings—there is a great deal of time for factors other than formal schooling to affect their education. These include the effects of family, peer, and neighborhood. Reflecting these other factors, a slightly more complex specification for the education production function is in order:

$$Ot = f (C, R, I, N, P, Z)$$

where outcome:

O = Educational Outcome (e.g., graduation rate, test scores)
C = Student Characteristics (e.g., family income, parents' education)
R = School Resources (e.g., per-student spending, pupil–teacher ratio)
I = Instructional Processes (e.g., type of curriculum)
N = Neighborhood Characteristics (e.g., crime rate, after-school activities)
P = Peer Influences, and Z = Student Effort

and where (f) stands for "a function of"

Sociologists and psychologists have confirmed that parents of different socioeconomic status—defined by parental education, income, and wealth—tend to raise children somewhat differently. Better-educated parents read to their young children more often and read differently, tending to ask their children questions from the readings that make them think more deeply about the themes of the books. Cross-national studies show that the number of books in a household varies substantially by social class and affects later school performance. Poor students who attend schools with a large number of middle-class students tend to perform better in school than equally poor students who are segregated in poor inner-city schools. Peer pressure, as subtle as it might seem, makes a difference in a young student's motivation toward learning, homework, and earning good grades. Health makes a difference, too, and poorer kids in inner cities tend to be in poorer health and receive poorer medical care. Studies have shown that 50 percent or more of minority and low-income children have vision problems that interfere with their academic performance (Gould and Gould 2003). This is all consistent with the critique of meritocracy we noted earlier in this chapter.

A higher incidence of hearing problems, poor oral health, and lead exposure disproportionately disadvantage children from poor inner-city households. Homes with poor ventilation and mold tend to contribute to higher levels of asthma, which can reduce significantly the number of days a child spends in school. Poor nutrition due to low income or parental neglect can make kids listless in class. Parents who themselves have little education may be hampered in their efforts to help their children learn.

Housing itself can make a big difference as well. Overcrowded housing means that students often do not have a quiet, undisturbed place to do their homework. The level of crime in a neighborhood may affect school performance as well. Kids are more likely to skip school if they are afraid of being attacked on their way there. Worrying about the danger of the street where you live can only make it more difficult to concentrate on your studies. Neighborhoods with lots of clubs, youth sports teams, and other forms of constructive extracurricular activities provide children with the opportunity to be mentored by adults other than their parents or teachers. A good neighborhood basketball coach or dance instructor can do wonders for building the confidence of young people and provide them with good role models.

Hence, the difference between a poor central city and a rich suburb, between a safe neighborhood and a crime-ridden one, and between a home environment that is devoted to reading and learning and one in which there are few adults to engage young minds, is the difference that comprises 83 percent of the waking hours of children. Against this, it is perhaps not surprising at all that inner-city schools in poor neighborhoods, no matter how good they are and no matter how devoted their teachers, can have only a limited impact on reducing the performance differential between poor and middle-class kids and between White, Latinx, and Black children. Only the truly extraordinary inner-city school and access to preschool for 3- to 5-year-olds can compensate for the multiple disadvantages that poor inner-city children often experience.

What happened when the COVID-19 pandemic forced families to self-quarantine for months on end and all schools in the nation were shuttered? According to Rothstein (2020), with schools and most businesses closed, white-collar professionals with college degrees—both parents and grandparents—operated homeschools for their children, often introducing their offspring to advanced subjects that would not be covered until later grades in their schools. Meanwhile, many parents with less education employed as supermarket clerks, warehouse workers, and delivery truck drivers had to work, resulting in their children staying at home with little access to education. And when they were home from work, they may not have had the same tools to educate their children to the same degree as those with more education. Massive social dislocation as the result of tragic events like COVID-19 likely adds to education gaps by social class, race, and ethnicity.

Research into neuroscience and developmental psychology provides still another reason why schools can only partially compensate for the performance differential between advantaged and disadvantaged children. Shonkoff and Phillips (2000) have shown in a pathbreaking study that "virtually every aspect of early human development, from the brain's evolving circuitry to the child's capacity for empathy, is affected by the environments and experiences that are encountered in a cumulative fashion, beginning in the prenatal period and extending throughout the early childhood years." This means that early learning—well before the child enters kindergarten—has a disproportionate impact on acquired skills and leads to self-reinforcing motivation to learn. Once a young child falls behind, there is a tendency for **circular causation with cumulative effect** to set in. This means that a small differential in early childhood education tends to be amplified throughout primary and secondary school and beyond. Small differences when one is young (up to age 4) can lead to large differences when one is an adult. No matter how many resources are devoted to inner-city schools, they simply could not fully compensate for preschool inequality.

A Growing Array of Public Schools

While most students attend traditional local public schools in their city or town, there are in the United States and several other countries a variety of other forms of K–12 education. One alternative is the career and technical high school, which has been in existence for centuries. Over the past few decades, school districts have been turning to such alternatives as magnet schools and charter schools. In addition, private schools flourish for those families that could afford them.

Career and Technical Education Public Schools

Most comprehensive high schools around the world and in the United States offer some courses in technical fields directly related to job readiness in a variety of occupations. And in most countries and most states, there are a handful of specialized career and technical education (CTE) schools that offer specialized training in fields that range from auto repair, allied health sciences, carpentry, and culinary arts to plumbing and welding. The first manual training school, established in St. Louis, Missouri in 1879, set the foundation for modern career and technical education. The school combined hands-on learning with classroom learning. But what was then called **vocational education** did not really come into its own across the country until after World War I. The career and technical education movement expanded to include adult education and retraining citizens to re-enter the workforce. World War II caused a surge in career and technical education as technical skills were needed for defense purposes.

Vocational schools offer training in trades such as carpentry and culinary arts. They also feature programs in fields such as healthcare, technology and graphic design. Advisory committees help focus on programs that provide the most employment opportunities. Most programs include regular academic classes, allowing students to graduate with standard diplomas and provides them the option of going on to two- and four-year colleges.

States differ in how they offer vocational education (Kelly 2020). These include:

- Self-contained schools that are separate from the traditional high school

- Schools that operate in a separate wing within a traditional high school

- Programs where students attend traditional high school in the morning and then take a bus to a technology and career center in their area

Within these technical schools, Science, Technology, Engineering, and Mathematics (STEM) have become critical disciplines in an era dependent upon innovation. By 2017, CTE concentrations in STEM and STEM-related fields including health science, agriculture and natural resources, and information technology represented 35 percent of all CTE high school concentrations.

Magnet Schools, Charter Schools, and For-Profit Schools

The original No Child Left Behind Act was revolutionary for the decentralized US school system because it centralized many rules and sanctions under which local public-school education is provided. At the same time, it enhanced the possibility for school choice by encouraging the establishment of charter schools, magnet schools, and voucher programs.

In contrast to neighborhood schools, **magnet schools** are public schools with a specialized curriculum or a distinctive approach to learning and open to students throughout a school district. The first magnet schools were founded in Tacoma, Washington in 1968, in Boston in 1969, and in Minneapolis in 1970. Sometimes referred to as "pilot schools," they served as laboratories for new approaches to education. The term "magnet school" became popular after Houston opened its performing arts school, stating that it acted like a magnet for interested students (Waldrip 1998).

In the fall of 1990, there were 1,469 magnet schools operating in school districts across the United States. By 2016–2017 the number had swelled to 3,164 magnet schools enrolling more than 2.5 million students. California enrolled more than 580,000 students in such schools. Enrollment in magnet schools exceeded 100,000 in Texas, Florida, Arizona, Michigan, Ohio, New York, Colorado, and Pennsylvania (National Center for Education Statistics 2016). In the District of Columbia, 87 percent of K–12 students were enrolled in magnet schools. In 7 states, magnet schools enrolled at least 10 percent of all elementary and secondary students. These included Arizona with 19 percent, Colorado with 12.6 percent, and Michigan with 11.1 percent.

Magnet schools became more widespread because they offered the opportunity to experiment with new learning techniques, a racially integrated environment, and a promise of high-quality education to attract families who otherwise might leave the city in search of better educational opportunities for their children. In addition, by broadening the area from which students were normally drawn, many magnet schools were able to offer career-related instruction, such as schools for the arts, that may not have had an adequate number of interested students in normal school assignment schemes. Magnet schools were recognized by federal courts as a suitable way to address the impact of residential segregation on the segregation of schools, and most major cities had magnet schools by the early 1980s.

Still another modern alternative to the traditional local district public school and the newer magnet school are the **charter schools**, which were established by private groups that provide publicly funded education under contracts (charters) with designated government authorities, usually at the state level (Finn et al. 2000; Ladd 2002). While magnet schools are a modification of traditional school practices, charter schools are designed to change the management structure and behavioral incentives within schools. The first charter school in the United States opened in St. Paul, Minnesota, in 1992. By school year 2005–2006, there were more than 3,600 charter schools in 41 states (and the District of Columbia), with more than half of all charter schools (51.4%) located in central cities (National Center for Education Statistics 2006). Following the devastation of Hurricane Katrina in 2005, the City of New Orleans—with its schools heavily damaged or destroyed—became the first all-charter-school city in the nation (Harris 2020). By 2016, nationwide there were more than 7,000 such schools in which more than 3 million students were enrolled at the elementary and secondary level (National Center for Education Statistics 2016). Some are established by local nonprofit organizations, while others are established across many cities by for-profit entities.

Because issues involved in public-sector decision-making can be particularly complex and potentially problematic in urban settings, the charter school movement was embraced in many cities. Cutting through all the bureaucratic red tape of the public-school system while still relying on public funding seemed a way to improve public schools without privatizing them. Often, charter school proposals received considerable support from Black and Latinx community leaders who were frustrated by existing inner-city public schools and were seeking new solutions to raise the quality of schooling available to their children.

Charter schools are not without their critics. They argue that on average, these schools do not perform any better than traditional public schools and may harm traditional schools by draining them of needed resources (Carnoy et al. 2005). Since state aid to local public schools is usually tied to the number of students who attend district schools, every time a family chooses to send a child to a state-chartered school, the district loses revenue. If enough students in a district transfer to charter schools, the revenue loss to the local public school district can be severe enough to further undercut the quality of the traditional schools which makes it even more difficult for them to offer a quality education to their students. This effect might be exacerbated if charter schools "skim off" high-achieving students from the traditional public schools, with adverse social and academic effects on the students remaining behind (Wells 1998; Cobb and Glass 1999).

Completing the array of elementary and secondary schools in the United States are private schools. By the 2015–2016 school year, there were almost 34,600 private schools enrolling more than 5.7 million students. Of these private school students, nearly 83 percent attended schools run by religious organizations (National Center for Education Statistics 2018).

School Choice and Voucher Programs

Because of the local nature of public school in the United States, most parents have little choice as to where to send their children to school unless they can afford to send them to private school. As such, some have advocated for introducing a system where parents would have more choice. Broadly speaking, **school choice** includes any system in which parents can choose the school their children will attend. As noted earlier, magnet schools and charter schools are usually open to students from throughout a school district. Many urban school districts have some form of "controlled choice" where families can designate their top choices and enrollment is determined by taking these choices and other factors, such as racial diversity, into account.

There are three basic forms of choice systems. **Intradistrict choice** allows families to select any public school within the boundaries of the school district in which they reside. **Interdistrict choice** allows families to select public schools in school districts other than the ones in which they reside. Such a program in Minnesota, in fact, allows families to choose any public school in the state.

Education vouchers extend choice not only to public schools but to private schools. Vouchers are essentially entitlements to a certain amount of public funding for a child's education, regardless of whether the child attends public, private, or parochial (religiously oriented) schools. Parents of school-age children receive a voucher check that can be used to pay tuition at any school in the voucher system.

Milwaukee is one city noted for implementing a voucher program (Euchner and McGovern 2003). Following a failed desegregation plan, Black parents decided to support a school choice program that provided $2,500 vouchers for each student. The program was targeted to families who earned less than 1.75 times the poverty level. By 2001, 11,000 children in Milwaukee were receiving vouchers that permitted them to choose between public and private schools, including religious ones. Since then, the program has been expanded throughout Wisconsin. In 2019–2020, more than $350 million in taxpayer dollars went to more than 300 voucher schools in Wisconsin. Milwaukee received more than $2.6 billion between 1990 and 2019. In about half the Milwaukee schools, 90 percent of more of the students received a voucher (Miner 2020).

Cleveland followed Milwaukee in implementing a taxpayer-funded voucher plan in which more than 4,500 children from poor neighborhoods took advantage. Florida adopted a statewide voucher program in 1999, such that students in any underperforming public school are eligible for vouchers worth up to $4,000 per year to attend schools of their choice (Euchner and McGovern 2003). By 2020, new forms of vouchers were in effect in Florida and a new law signed in 2020 is expected to expand them rapidly (Solochek 2020).

Around the world, a number of countries have included school vouchers for primary and secondary school as part of their public-school programs. Among these are Belgium, Chile, Estonia, Germany, Israel, Poland, Portugal, the Slovak Republic and Spain (OECD 2009).

Despite the increased interest in voucher programs, its opponents worry about turning education into a market-based system that will still benefit the children of the wealthy more than those of the poor. As such, cities have become the cauldrons in which many school reform initiatives were born and where the complexities and perplexities of the system continue to be debated.

Do School Reforms Work?

In a well-publicized study of charter schools across the country, Caroline Hoxby (2004) compared reading and math scores of fourth-grade students in charter schools with fourth graders in neighboring traditional public schools. On average, she found that the charter school students were 3.8 percent more likely to be proficient on their state's reading exam compared to the children who attended the local district elementary school. On math tests, the charter school students were 1.6 percent more likely to be proficient.

Yet other studies using the same data as Hoxby came to the conclusion that even this small charter school advantage completely vanishes when you control for the income of the children's families as well as their race (Carnoy et al. 2005; Roy and Mishel 2005).

Miron and Horn (2002) come to a somewhat more nuanced conclusion about the success of charter schools. They conclude that there is a slight improvement in average test scores in some states, while research in other states finds a negative impact. Most studies report both positive and negative impacts so that many experts caution against any definitive conclusion for or against charter schools. There are successes where administrators, teachers, and parents are heavily involved and resources are adequate but an equal number, if not more, where students in charter schools fall behind those in traditional public schools on test scores after controlling for family background and neighborhood effects.

Zimmer and Buddin (2006) provide perhaps the best overall analysis of charter schools in their study of the California system. They conclude that charter schools perform about the same as regular public schools and therefore have done little to close achievement gaps. They do, however, provide a different education model that often emphasizes noncore subjects (e.g., art, music, language study) and often uses fewer public resources than traditional schools. As a result, charter schools do not provide a "silver bullet" for school improvement but represent a reform initiative that Zimmer and Buddin consider worth continuing, at least in California.

A similar conclusion seems to be valid for voucher programs. Studies of the Milwaukee system found that parents were more satisfied with the private schools their children attended, but there was little evidence that voucher students scored better on reading and math tests (Witte 2000). A RAND Corporation study (Gill et al. 2001) that surveyed many choice systems found only modest gains for Black children after one to two years in voucher schools, but none for Latinx students. Martin Carnoy (2001) found even less.

What are we left to conclude? The evidence seems to suggest that parental background and community factors play the pivotal role in how kids perform in school and ultimately how they fare in the labor market. Differences between the environments in many central cities and suburbs are critical. Because education plays such a critical role in the labor market and in the earning potential of workers, gaps in central city and suburban school achievement can only lead to greater income and wealth inequality as education becomes more important in determining income. We need to better understand the impact of decent housing, safe neighborhoods, preschool programs, after-school programs, and health disparities to fully comprehend why the achievement gaps by family income, race, and ethnicity are so hard to overcome. As the saying goes, "It takes a village to raise a child." The evidence seems to confirm this conjecture. Essentially, we will need to change a lot about cities and suburbs to make a difference in the success of the children who grow up there.

References

Barnett, W. S. 1993. "Benefit-cost Analysis of Preschool Education: Findings from a 25-year Follow-up." *Am J Orthopsychiatry* 63, no. 4: 500–508. doi: 10.1037/h0079481. PMID: 8267089.

Blair, John P., and Robert Premus. 1987. "Major Factors in Industrial Location: A Review." *Economic Development Quarterly* 1, no. 1: 72–85.

Buckley, Jack, Mark Schneider, and Yi Shang. 2004. "The Effects of School Facility Quality on Teacher Retention in Urban School Districts." National Clearinghouse for Educational Facilities. https://www.semanticscholar.org/paper/The-Effects-of-School-Facility-Quality-on-Teacher-Buckley-Schneider/7afa9727653cb45f09665fef4c711e3c97732e5c

Carnoy, Martin. 2001. *School Vouchers: Examining the Evidence*. Washington, DC: Economic Policy Institute.

Carnoy, Martin, Rebecca Jacobsen, Lawrence Mishel, and Richard Rothstein. 2005. *The Charter School Dust-Up: Examining the Evidence on Enrollment and Achievement*. Washington, DC: Economic Policy Institute.

Cobb, C. D., and G. V. Glass. 1999. "Ethnic Segregation in Arizona Charter Schools." *Education Policy Analysis Archives* 7, no. 1: 1–39.

Cohen, Natalie, 2000. *Business Location Decision-Making and the Cities: Bringing Companies Back*. Washington, DC: Brookings Institution, Center on Urban and Metropolitan Policy.

Coleman, James S. 1966. *Equality of Education Opportunity*. Washington, DC: Government Printing Office.

Crooks, Mary. 2020. "Apr 23, 1635: First Public School in America." *National Geographic*, April 6.

Edwards, Colin. 2019. "Useful Stats: Educational Attainment by Metropolitan Area, 2009–2018." *State Science & Technology Institute*, December 12. https://ssti.org/blog/useful-stats-higher-education-rd-performance-metro-2009-2018

Ensor, Robert. 1936. *England 1870–1914*. Oxford: Clarendon Press.

Euchner, Charles, and Steven J. McGovern. 2003. *Urban Policy Reconsidered*. New York: Routledge.

Finn, Chester E. Jr., Bruno V. Manno, and Gregg Vanourek. 2000. *Charter Schools in Action: Renewing Public Education*. Princeton, NJ: Princeton University Press.

Friedman, Lawrence M. 2002. *American Law in the Twentieth Century*. New Haven, CT: Yale University Press.

Gill, Brian, P. Mike Timpane, Karen E. Ross, Dominic J. Brewer, and Kevin Booker. 2001. *Rhetoric versus Reality: What We Know and What We Need to Know about Vouchers and Charter Schools*. Santa Monica, CA: RAND Education.

Glaeser, Edward. 2005. "Smart Growth: Education, Skilled Workers, and the Future of Cold-Weather Cities." *Rappaport Institute for Greater Boston Policy Briefs*, PB-2005-1, April. Cambridge, MA: Harvard University.

Goldin, Claudia. 2001. "The Human Capital Century and American Leadership: Virtues of the Past." *Journal of Economic History* 61, no. 2: 263–292.

Gould, Elise. 2020. "State of Working America Wages 2019: A Story of Slow, Uneven, and Unequal Wage Growth." February 20. Washington, DC: Economic Policy Institute.

Gould, Marge Christensen, and Herman Gould. 2003. "A Clear Vision for Equity and Opportunity." *Phi Delta Kappan* (December): 324–328.

Hanushek, Eric A. 1997a. "Assessing the Effects of School Resources on Student Performance: An Update." *Educational Evaluation and Policy Review* 19, no. 2: 141–164.

Hanushek, Eric A. 1997b. "Outcomes, Incentives, and Beliefs: Reflections on Analysis of the Economics of Schools." *Educational Evaluation and Policy Analysis* 19, no. 4: 301–308.

Harris, Douglas N. 2020. "How will Covid-19 Change Our Schools in the Long Run?" April 21. Washington, DC: Brookings Institution.

Hays, Jeffrey. 2014. "Education System in Japan: Bureaucracy, Society and International Ranks." *Facts and Details*. https://factsanddetails.com/japan/cat23/sub150/item833.html

Howell, William G., and Paul E. Peterson. 2006. *The Education Gap: Vouchers and Urban Schools*, rev. ed. Washington, DC: Brookings Institution Press.

Hoxby, C. 2004. "Achievement in Charter Schools and Regular Public Schools in the United States." http://www.posteconomics.harvard.edu/faculty/hoxby/papers/charters_040909.pdf. Cambridge, MA: Harvard University.

Hoxby, Caroline. 2000. "The Effects of Class Size on Student Achievement: Evidence from Population Variation." *Quarterly Journal of Economics* 115, no. 4: 1239–1285.

Jackson, C. Kirabo, Rucker C. Johnson, and Claudia Persico. 2015. "The Effects of School Spending on Educational and Economic Outcomes: Evidence from School Finance Reforms." Working Paper 20847:1–81 January. Cambridge, MA: National Bureau of Economic Research.

Kaestle, Carl F. 1983. *Pillars of the Republic: Common Schools and American Society, 1780–1860.* New York. Hill and Wang.

Kelly, Kate. 2020. "Vocational Education in High School: What You Need to Know." https://www.understood.org/articles/en/vocational-education-in-high-school

King, Richard, Austin Swanson, and Scott Sweetland. 2003. *School Finance: Achieving High Standards with Equity and Efficiency,* 3rd ed. Boston: Allyn and Bacon.

Kozol, Jonathan. 1992. *Savage Inequalities: Children in America's Schools.* New York: Perennial Books.

Krim, Robert, David Bartone, Marti Frank, and Colin Rowas. 2006. *Innovate Boston: Shaping the Future from Our Past.* Boston: Boston History & Innovation Collaborative.

Krueger, Alan B. 1997. "Experimental Estimates of Education Production Functions." Working Paper 6051. Cambridge, MA: National Bureau of Economic Research.

Ladd, Helen F. 2002. *Market-Based Reforms in Urban Education.* Washington, DC: Economic Policy Institute.

Lankford, Hamilton, Susanna Loeb, and James Wyckoff. 2002. "Teacher Sorting and the Plight of Urban Schools: A Descriptive Analysis." *Educational Evaluation and Policy Analysis* 24, no. 1: 37–62.

Lee, Thomas H. C. 1999. *Education in Traditional China, a History.* Leiden: Brill.

Lucas, Robert E. 1988. "On the Mechanics of Economic Development." *Journal of Monetary Economics* 22, no. 3: 3–42.

Markovits, David. 2019. *The Meritocracy Trap: How America's Foundational Myth Feeds Inequality, Dismantles the Middle Class, and Devours the Elite.* New York: Penguin.

Miner, Barbara. 2020. "School Vouchers, Black Lives Matter and Democracy." *Wisconsin Examiner,* August 17.

Miron, Gary, and Jerry Horn. 2002. *What's Public about Charter Schools? Lessons Learned About Choice and Accountability.* Thousand Oaks, CA: Corwin Press.

Musgrave, Richard. 1959. *The Theory of Public Finance.* New York: McGraw-Hill.

National Center for Education Statistics. 2006. *"Parental Choice of Schools."* Washington, DC: Department of Education.

National Center for Education Statistics. 2016. *Enrollment in Public Elementary and Secondary Schools, by Region, State, and Jurisdiction.* Washington, DC: Department of Labor.

National Center for Education Statistics. 2018. *Digest of Education Statistics: 1972–2016.* Washington, DC: Department of Labor.

Organisation for Economic Co-operation and Development (OECD). 2009. *Programme for International Student Assessment*. Paris: OECD.

Orfield, Gary, Daniel Losen, Johanna Wald, and Christopher Swanson. 2004. *"Losing Our Future: How Minority Youth Are Being Left Behind by the Graduation Rate Crisis."* Cambridge, MA: The Civil Rights Project at Harvard University.

Romer, Paul. 1986. "Increasing Returns and Long-Run Growth." *Journal of Political Economy* 94, no. 5: 1002–1037.

Romer, Paul. 1994. "The Origins of Endogenous Growth." *Journal of Economic Perspectives* 8, no. 1: 3–22.

Romer, Paul. 1996. "Why Indeed in America? Theory, History and the Origins of Modern Economic Growth." *American Economic Review* 86, no. 2: 202–206.

Rothstein, Richard. 2004. *Class and Schools: Using Social, Economic, and Educational Reform to Close the Black-White Achievement Gap*. Washington, DC: Economic Policy Institute.

Rothstein, Richard. 2017. *The Color of Law: A Forgotten History of How Our Government Segregated America*. New York: Liveright.

Rothstein, Richard. 2020. "The Coronavirus will Explode the Achievement Gaps in Education," *Shelterforce*, April 13.

Roy, Joydeep, and Lawrence Mishel. 2005. *"Advantage None: Re-examining Hoxby's Finding of Charter School Benefits."* Briefing Paper No. 158, April. Washington, DC: Economic Policy Institute.

Schmidt, Eric. 2018. "For the First Time 90 Percent Completed High School or More." July 31. Washington, DC: US Census Bureau.

Schweinhart, Lawrence J., Jeanne Montie, Zongping Xiang, W. Steven Barnett, Clive R. Belfield, and Milagros Nores. 2005. *Lifetime Effects: The High/Scope Perry Preschool Study through Age 40*. Ypsilanti, MI: High/Scope.

Shonkoff, Jack, and Deborah. Phillips. 2000. *From Neurons to Neighborhoods: The Science of Early Child Development*. Washington, DC: National Academies Press.

Solochek, Jeffrey S. 2020. "DeSantis Expands Florida's School Voucher Program." *Tampa Bay Examiner*, June 25.

Spatig-Americaner, Ary. 2012. "Unequal Education: Federal Loopholes Enable Lower Spending on Students of Color." August. Washington, DC: Center for American Progress.

Strouhal, Eugen. 1992. *Life of the Ancient Egyptians*. Norman: University of Oklahoma Press.

US Bureau of the Census. 2002b. "Government Organization, 2002." *Census of Governments* 1, no. 1. GC02(1)-1, US Department of Commerce, Economics and Statistics Administration. Washington, DC: Government Printing Office.

US Bureau of the Census. 2002a. "Government Units in 2002." *GC02-1(P), Census of Governments, 2002*. Washington, DC: Government Printing Office. https://www2.census.gov/govs/cog/2002COGprelim_report.pdf

US Bureau of the Census. 2019. "Educational Attainment in the United States: 2019." Washington, DC: Government Printing Office.

US Department of Education. 2007. *Digest of Education Statistics: 2006*. Washington, DC: National Center for Education Statistics.

US Department of Education. 2019. "Educational Expenditures by Country, May." Washington, DC: National Center for Education Statistics.

Waldrip, Donald. 1998. *"A Brief History of Magnet Schools."* Washington, DC: Magnet Schools of America. http://http://magnet.edu/brief-history-of-magnets

Wells, Amy Stuart. 1998. *Beyond the Rhetoric of Charter School Reform: A Study of Ten California School Districts*. Los Angeles: UCLA Graduate School of Education and Information Studies.

Witte, John F. 2000. *The Market Approach to Education: An Analysis of America's First Voucher Program*. Princeton, NJ: Princeton University Press.

Wraga, William G. 2006. "Progressive Pioneer: Alexander James Inglis (1879–1924)." *Teachers College Record* 108, no. 6 (June): 1080–1105.

Zimmer, Ron and Richard Buddin, "Making Sense of Charter Schools: Evidence from California, Rand Corporation Occasional Papers, 2006.

Questions and Exercises

1. As this chapter discusses, educational attainment within metropolitan areas, and the cities and towns that comprise metropolitan areas, has changed over the years. Using the website: https://ssti.org/blog/useful-stats-educational-attainment-metropolitan-area-2007-2017, find out how educational attainment has changed between 2007 and 2017 in five metro areas of your choice. Array these metro areas from the one with the largest increase in educational attainment to the lowest. Answer the following questions, using data on median household income and racial and ethnic composition from data.gov of each metro area you have selected.

   • How strong does the correlation between educational attainment and median household income appear to be?

   • Does there appear to be any correlation between the racial and ethnic composition of the city and educational attainment?

2. Using US census data for the most recent year for educational attainment for individual central cities found at https://data.census.gov/cedsci/all?q=Education&t=Educational Attainment, consider the educational attainment of the central cities within the metro areas you selected for Question 1.

   - How does the educational distribution of the metro area compare to the distribution in its central city?

   - Of your five metro areas, are there any in which the educational distribution is higher in the central city than the metro area as a whole?

   - How might you explain the educational distribution differences between central city and metro area?

3. Using data for your own metro area or the one closet to you, describe the educational distribution and compare it to the distributions you found in the five metro areas you selected for Question 1.

Urban Physical Infrastructure: Water, Sewer, Waste, and Energy

9

LEARNING OBJECTIVES

■ Distinguish between density and overcrowding and explain why both might contribute to the spread of communicable diseases

■ Explain the principal-agent problem and show how it contributed to the creation of publicly owned waterworks

■ Describe the challenges municipalities face in addressing their sold waste and wastewater disposal needs

■ Define the concept of a prime mover and contrast the ways in which it applies to preindustrial, industrial, and postindustrial eras

■ Describe differences between countries in the ways they generate electricity and discuss the expectations for electricity generation in the near future

Many of the physical features we now take for granted as part of city life—readily available clean safe water, sewers and garbage services that remove waste, sophisticated heating and cooling systems, and easy access to fuel for motorized vehicles—did not exist in the early cities of the United States. Investments in the urban physical infrastructure, particularly water and sewer systems, were made in response to the potentially dangerous health conditions that existed in densely populated areas.

As the late nineteenth century gave way to the twentieth, new insights in physics and engineering, new inventions such as electric street lighting and telephones, and new types of physical networks facilitated the expansion and growing productivity of cities. Each of these required enormous investments in physical infrastructure. Because of the need to deal with urban density, economies of scale, and mounting externalities, this infrastructure has been supplied and managed mostly by municipalities or by private firms licensed and regulated by municipal governments.

In our current information age, where so much seems to be virtual, it is important to remember that cities and suburbs are built environments with "real" roads, highways, and sidewalks and "real" water mains, sewer pipes, electrical transformers, and wiring systems. The physical infrastructure of the city that is made up of bricks and mortar, steel, and concrete provides services so critical that if they did not exist, cities would be virtually uninhabitable. The provision of clean water, waste treatment systems, and power for household appliances may not seem the most scintillating subjects to study, but how these basic services are provided and allocated, and how they are paid for, involves some of the most engaging issues in the field of urban public policy.

Most of us who live in metropolitan areas in developed countries take these public services for granted—until something goes wrong with them. The case of Flint, Michigan suggests that things can go very wrong. In 2014, the Governor of Michigan appointed managers to deal with a financial crisis in this once thriving auto city. To cut costs, the managers decided to switch the city's water supply from the Detroit Water and Sewerage Department (DWSD) to the Flint River. Residents immediately registered their concerns about water quality. Over the following months residents were advised to boil water because of the presence of dangerous levels of bacteria, while General Motors announced that the use of Flint River water at its auto plant was causing corrosion on newly machined engine parts. A spike in the incidence of Legionnaire disease in Flint led county health officials to question whether the outbreak might be connected to contamination of the water supply, but attempts to investigate the matter were met with resistance at the city and state level. In January 2015 the city informed residents that elevated levels of carcinogenic trihalomethanes had been detected in Flint's water yet insisted that it remained safe to drink. Later that month, dangerous levels of lead were detected in two water fountains on the University of Michigan-Flint campus. The DWSD offered to reconnect Flint to its system, but Flint's state-appointed emergency manager declined and internal communications within the state governor's administration revealed that cost remained the primary decision driver. Public health concerns began to mount.

In March 2015 a test of the drinking water in one Flint home uncovered concentrations of lead more than 25 times higher than the level deemed safe by the Environmental Protection Agency (EPA). Subsequent testing found lead levels so high in the water supply that according to standard EPA criteria, the water was now classified as hazardous waste. Despite this, Michigan's Department of Environmental Quality (MDEQ) insisted that no additional steps were necessary to mitigate the levels of lead and copper in Flint's water.

In September 2015 a nationally respected expert on municipal water systems determined that the corrosive nature of insufficiently treated Flint River water was causing lead to leach from aging pipes. Physicians at a Flint hospital warned residents to abstain from drinking the city water after blood tests of area children revealed high levels of lead. Only then—a year and half after the water supply was switched to the Flint River—did Michigan's governor allow Flint to switch back to using safe water from the Detroit system. During the months that Flint residents were forced to use contaminated water from the Flint River, many sustained serious health damage, particularly from lead pollutants (Ray 2016).

Learning of the crisis in Flint led to testing of water in many cities. Experts suggest that in 2016 at least 33 US cities had lead in their water supplies that could be harmful to health (Pierce 2016). The United States is not alone. Experts have found highly contaminated water in many cities around the world. According to one study, the most toxic places on the planet can be found in urban areas in Ghana, Ukraine, Russia, Bangladesh, Zambia, Indonesia, Argentina, and Nigeria (Krunk 2017).

This toxicity persists despite the fact that for centuries, cities have tried to supply clean, safe water for drinking, food preparation, and cleaning.

Combating Disease and Death

Through the early decades of the 1800s, obtaining clear, safe, potable water was regarded as a private matter—not something provided through the public sector. City residents had to obtain water for drinking and bathing by digging wells or by carrying water in buckets and other containers from ponds, streams, lakes, and rivers. Some residents hired people to deliver water to them for a fee. Residents were expected to dispose of their own wastes. This involved digging privy vaults in the ground to dispose of bodily waste or digging trenches to transport such waste to nearby bodies of water. Residents usually threw garbage into streets to be eaten by roaming pigs and dogs. Similarly, businesses were expected to dispose of their own manufacturing byproducts, a task usually carried out by simply discharging untreated byproducts into nearby waterways.

Density and the Spread of Epidemics

These practices and others associated with water, garbage, and waste grew more hazardous as urban populations rose. The population dynamics of urban areas in the 1800s were characterized not just by foreign immigration, internal migration from rural areas, and high birthrates, but by high death rates. Disease, much of it related to polluted water and unsanitary living conditions, caused a massive loss of life. Disease spread like wildfire, given both the density of big-city tenement districts and the overcrowding of each dwelling unit.

While **population density** refers to the number of people per square mile, **overcrowding** refers to the number of people in each housing unit. According to the US government definition, overcrowding occurs when there is more than one person per room in an apartment or home (Myers et al. 1996). Four people living together in a three-room apartment—excluding bathroom—are considered to be living in overcrowded quarters. While it is possible for a household to live in a place that is overcrowded but not dense (a family of four in a rural two-room shack, a mile from their nearest neighbor) or dense but not overcrowded (two people in a four-room apartment, one of 120 such apartments in a 30-story luxury residential building on a one-acre footprint), poor people in the nineteenth century often lived in extremely dense city neighborhoods and in overcrowded buildings.

The typical New York tenement apartment with its 11 x 12' 6" parlor, small kitchen, and one tiny bedroom had a total area of about 325 square feet. In this small space lived households of seven or more people and, in some cases, as many as 18. Many apartments were dark and airless because interior windows faced narrow light shafts. Measles, mumps, cholera, influenza, diphtheria, and tuberculosis could hardly be contained in such an environment. The spread of disease in cramped quarters provides a classic case of a negative externality, where the actions (or inactions) of some have dramatic effects on the well-being of others.

In various years, as noted in Table 9.1, epidemics killed 10 percent or more of the population in such cities as Philadelphia, St. Louis, Cincinnati, and New Orleans. In many cases, epidemics returned to the city frequently. New York City suffered serious outbreaks of cholera in 1832, 1847, and 1849 (Rosenberg 1962), and the city experienced seven serious smallpox outbreaks between 1851 and 1875 (Duffy 1990; Melosi 2000). New Orleans experienced yellow fever epidemics 13 times between 1832 and 1905 (Humphreys 1992; Bloom 1993). Due to the high death rates experienced in cities, the fear engendered by an epidemic could change city life almost overnight. Over the course of 10 days in 1878, yellow fever caused two-thirds of the population of Chattanooga to flee the city. In Memphis, business and government activity came to a halt as three-quarters of all firms and the entire city government shut down.

Illness and death affected the economy in many ways. To avoid epidemics, individuals shut down their businesses, cities barred trade with areas that were

TABLE 9.1.   EXAMPLES OF MAJOR NATIONAL OR REGIONAL EPIDEMICS AND YEARS

1793-1806	Yellow fever hits coastal cities from New Orleans to Boston, with particularly strong outbreaks in 1793, 1798 and 1805. In Philadelphia in 1793, it kills more than 5,000 people (one tenth of the population) in less than four months. In 1805, it strikes hard at New York; one-third of the city population flees the city.
1832-1834	Cholera hits every large city in the U.S. except for Boston and Charleston, S.C. At the same time, yellow fever runs through cities in the South. In New Orleans in 1832, twelve percent of the population (6,700 of the 55,000 residents) is killed by either cholera or yellow fever.
1849-54	Cholera epidemic again strikes cities across the U.S. with Cincinnati, St. Louis, New York and New Orleans suffering the most. In 1849 alone, the epidemic kills more than 5,000 in New York City, more than 7,000 in St. Louis (ten percent of the population), and approximately ten percent of the population of Cincinnati.
1853	Yellow fever hits coastal cities in South, killing 8,100 in New Orleans, and 1,200 in Mobile. Two years later, it kills more than 2,800 in Norfolk, VA.
1866	Cholera returns to many cities. Kills more than 3,500 in St. Louis and more than 2,000 in St. Louis.
1867	Yellow fever is epidemic in Southern coastal cities. 3,100 die in New Orleans and over 1,100 in Galveston, Texas.
1870s	Smallpox kills approximately 1,000 people per year in New York.
1878	Yellow fever again devastates cities in Mississippi Valley. Kills 5-6,000 in Memphis, and 5,000 in New Orleans.
1906	Polio kills 2,500 in New York. New York remains the city hardest hit by polio until the 1950s.
1916	Polio outbreak causes 2,400 deaths in New York, and a total of 7,000 deaths across the U.S.
1918-1919	"Spanish Flu" kills more than 550,000 across the U.S.

Sources: Duffy, John. 1990. *The Sanitarians: A History of American Public Health*, Urbana, IL: University of Illinois Press; Melosi, Martin V. 2000. *The Sanitary City: Urban Infrastructure in America from Colonial Times to the Present*. Baltimore: The Johns Hopkins University Press; Rosenberg, Charles E. 1962. *The Cholera Years*. Chicago: The University of Chicago Press; Bloom, Khaled J. 1993. *The Mississippi Valley's Great Yellow Fever Epidemic of 1878*, Baton Rouge: Louisiana Sate University Press; Crosby, Alfred W., 1989. *America's Forgotten Pandemic: The Influenza of 1918*, New York: Cambridge University Press; Humphreys, Margaret, 1992. *Yellow Fever and the South*. New Brunswick, NJ: Rutgers University Press.

known to harbor infection, and whole families were quarantined if a person in their household became ill. Spouses were lost and children were left without parents. Sick workers lost wages. In addition, epidemic disease was a potential impediment in the competition for economic growth. If they had any choice in the matter, people and businesses were less likely to locate in a city known for severe endemic and epidemic disease. This provided a competitive advantage to cities perceived as relatively healthy, with fewer risks of environmentally caused illness and death.

For the first time since the influenza outbreak in 1917, which affected an estimated 500 million people worldwide and led to the death of an estimated 50 million, the COVID-19 pandemic that began in early 2020 required many of the same responses as the early outbreaks in the nineteenth century—quarantined households, social distancing, and shuttered businesses. Yet back in earlier times with so much density and overcrowding in cities, it was even harder to battle disease.

Successfully addressing the problem back then as now required breakthroughs in science and the subsequent education of city residents about the role of microorganisms as causes of disease. The advances in science occurred gradually in the nineteenth century, with accelerated acceptance of the "gospel of germs" in the scientific and health professions after 1870, and major efforts to educate the populace in the following decades (Duffy 1990; Tomes 1998). But insights without action will not provide solutions to the epidemics. Ultimately, the problem of disease in urban areas could be controlled only by public investment in water and sewer systems and by public regulation of waste disposal.

Water Supply Systems

In 1801, Philadelphia, the largest city in the United States at the time, built the first city waterworks. Reasoning that severe yellow fever in the city in 1793 and 1798 might have been caused by polluted water, the city built a system that pumped water from the Schuylkill River to a central reservoir. From there water was released to the city through a system of pipes. New York acted early after the yellow fever outbreaks of the 1790s, giving a charter to a private company for construction of a reservoir-based system of water supply.

The idea of central water reservoirs dispensing water through pipes was gradually adopted by other cities. By 1860, the 16 largest US cities and many smaller cities had either constructed publicly owned water systems or had granted charters to private waterworks companies (Melosi 2000; Tarr 1984). Though charters to privately owned companies were common through the mid-1800s, over time there was a gradual movement toward public ownership. As early as 1870, nearly half of the waterworks were publicly owned. By 1924, the proportion was up to 70 percent (Melosi 1985; Cutler and Miller 2006).

From Private to Public Operation

The movement from private to public ownership of waterworks was due to the presence of massive fixed costs and huge economies of scale. As cities expanded in the nineteenth century, the costs borne by private water companies in providing service to additional customers was relatively small given excess capacity in the original reservoirs, aqueducts, and water mains. With such low marginal cost, provision of water became a natural monopoly, akin to the electric grid or cable systems of today. Any new competitor to an existing supplier would have to invest huge sums to build an additional set of water works in order to supply water to the residents and businesses in the city. With few customers to begin with, these high fixed costs would drive the average cost of the newcomer well above the average cost of the existing supplier. This condition limited competition to established companies.

As city populations expanded at the end of the nineteenth century and the beginning of the twentieth as a result of immigration, existing private water companies became increasingly incapable of keeping up with demand for water. When it became necessary to seek additional water sources and build additional aqueducts, filtration plants, and water mains, the initial fixed costs often exceeded the scope of what was possible for private firms, even those enjoying a monopoly status. Only the public sector had the resources to build the needed water systems and purification plants. Some private firms sold their existing systems to municipal governments. Other firms tried to continue to operate but failed. According to Schultz and McShane (1978), by the beginning of the 1900s, 41 of the 50 largest cities in the United States had publicly owned water systems.

Some cities moved to create municipally owned water supplies because of poor service by the private companies. The failure to provide adequate water at reasonable price is related to what economists term the **principal-agent problem**—a phenomenon that occurs when the interests of an agent acting on behalf of a client (the principal) diverges from the interests of his or her client. A common example is a CEO (the agent) whose compensation package is written in such a way that it prompts behavior that benefits the CEO and not necessarily the stockholders (the client). Normally, in a competitive market, this problem is solved by the ability of the client to simply choose another agent or revise the nature of the compensation package, so the interests of the agent and the client are aligned. Profit-sharing plans tied to the firm's stock price are often offered top management to mitigate the principal-agent problem.

Where there is **asymmetric information**—where information possessed by the agent is not available to the client—a market malfunction can occur where the interests of the client are harmed. Although charters issued by cities to private companies to provide water and sewer were supposedly granted in the interests of the city's residents, the grantees often acted in their own interests instead, keeping crucial information about the costs of operation from city officials. In one of the most notorious cases, profits from the initial New York charter were used to finance the owners' banking interests at the expense of adequate water service to residents. In order to have all the information they needed to run and benefit from the city water service, the city built its own municipally owned system in 1842. Between 1890 and 1920, efforts to stamp out corruption and graft involving private companies led many residents and activists to support publicly owned systems.

The ability of local governments to sell municipal bonds contributed to the growth of publicly owned waterworks. As Cutler and Miller (2006) note, after the economic "panic of 1893," investors were more willing to buy municipal bonds backed by the faith and credit of the local government than private-sector bonds which had no such assurance.

Finally, the move to municipally owned systems was fueled by a shift in perspective about the responsibility for water. As cities learned more about how disease was spread and recognized the beneficial effects of water and sewer systems on public health, clean water was increasingly seen as a public good with profound positive externalities that *should* be the responsibility of the public sector. By the 1950s, based on the conclusive evidence of the benefits of fluoride for reducing tooth decay, cities began to add small amounts of this chemical to their water supplies. The result has been a dramatic decline in the incidence of tooth decay and greatly improved dental health, although there are still pockets of opposition to the practice.

Solid Waste Management

Wastewater is only part of the problem in large dense regions. Metropolitan areas produce millions of tons of garbage (food waste), trash (paper, plastic and other light weight items), dead vegetation, left-over debris from building construction and repair, and other thrown away materials—collectively known as solid waste.

The removal of solid waste (**refuse**) from residential, commercial and industrial areas is important because uncollected it poses severe problems for metro areas. Uncollected solid waste is a health hazard, providing growth material for harmful microorganisms and breeding grounds for rats, flies, mosquitoes and other carriers of disease. When waste builds up, it can block alleys, sidewalks, streets, and other thoroughfares. If nothing else, it is an annoyance to residents, producing putrid odors and unsightly streets and byways. In 1968, when sanitation workers went on strike in New York City for just one week, a 10-foot wall of garbage grew on many of the city's sidewalks (Wikipedia 2006). Twenty-three years later, when private solid waste haulers in the city went on strike for 17 days, the public works department of the city took over hauling away garbage from the businesses that had contracted for private service. In less than two weeks, the department responded to over 7,600 emergency calls certified by the Health and Fire Departments and collected a total of nearly 12,000 tons of refuse (Finder 1991). The crisis became so severe that some people wrapped their garbage with gift wrapping and left it on park benches, hoping it would be stolen!

The First Municipal Garbage Systems

Picking up the garbage may seem a simple operation, but the provision of solid waste management is not simple nor straightforward. The management of municipal solid waste involves a complex process of collection, transportation, and disposal in which population density, externalities, marginal costs, land use, transportation costs, cost/benefit considerations, political dynamics, and tax incidence all play a role.

To appreciate some of the complexity, imagine that you are camping on a deserted island with some supplies that you had brought with you. How would you dispose of the unwanted materials during your stay on the island? Campers often burn their flammable left-over material. You might throw some of your edible waste into the woods to be eaten by other creatures on the island. Refuse that might be a breeding ground for harmful molds and bacteria you might bury. Waste that was not decomposable might be thrown into the sea—thinking that in the vastness of the ocean they would not present any harm. If the island was large enough and you had enough land on one side for the purposes that were important to you, you might throw much of your refuse onto the other side of the island. If you expected to be there for a long time and needed to grow some of your own food, you might compost some of your leftover organic materials, creating an area where natural biological processes convert the material into nutrient-rich soil.

Now suppose that someone else occupies the other side of the island. There are several things that you might do. You could resign yourself to using only your side of the island for your waste, or you could collaborate with your neighbor to designate one common area for waste disposal. You might strike a deal. You might be willing to accept his or her waste along with your own if they grew extra food and shared it with you. In effect, you would be involved in trade, exchanging the use of your land for dumping purposes for food.

Now suppose that the population on the island grows larger. Space is more limited, and there are more people generating externalities that affect each other. New forms of coordination with your fellow island residents and new methods of disposing of waste may be needed. This hypothetical example captures many of the realities of the history of urban waste management in the United States. In the early nineteenth century, collection of solid waste in cities was handled by individual families who either dumped it onto streets, onto unused land, or into rivers, lakes, and streams. Because there was much land available, people did not think as much as they do today about the externalities of this behavior. As cities grew during the nineteenth century, related problems of waste management continued to grow. Competing uses for land—for homes, businesses, and roads—reduced the availability of vacant dumping areas.

The first calls for the establishment of waste removal by a municipal authority dates to 1751 when a Londoner, Corbyn Morris, proposed that cleaning of the city should be put under one uniform city agency (Centenary History 2013). Before the end of that century, the first organized solid waste management system was established in London. Much of the waste collected from homes and businesses was coal ash from the stoves and heating apparatus of the day which was valuable for brickmaking and soil improvement (Velis et al. 2009). To dispose of other solid waste, the first municipal incinerators were built in the mid-1870s in Nottingham, England (Lewis 2007).

In Asia, Japan introduced its waste management system at the end of the nineteenth century. Waste was treated by private waste treatment operators who collected waste and selected valuables to sell them for profit. Waste was often discarded by waste treatment operators on roadsides or vacant lots and was piled up in unsanitary conditions. As a result, various infectious diseases spread. Consequently, it became important to maintain the cleanliness of entire towns, including waste dump sites that provided breeding grounds for flies, mosquitoes and rats. The Waste Cleaning Act was enacted in 1900 to improve public health. It defined the collection and disposal of waste as the obligation of municipalities and placed waste treatment operators under the supervision of government organizations to establish a waste administration system, and stated that waste should be incinerated if possible. Since waste incineration facilities were not generally available, waste materials were piled up out in the open and continuously burned (Ministry of Environment 2014).

The United States would create its own municipal operated waste management system in the late nineteenth century. By 1880, as documented in the Census Bureau's *Report on the Social Statistics of Cities*, 60 percent of the 149 cities providing information had some municipally sponsored garbage collection either directly or through contracts with private firms. By 1915, municipally sponsored collection had been adopted in virtually all US cities.

Municipally sponsored collection offered some distinct advantages. Centralized collection represented a division of labor within communities. Instead of every family taking time and effort to remove waste, the task was now done by specific workers specializing in this task. Dumping could be concentrated into specific designated areas, aiding efforts to control the use of land. The use of vehicles specifically designed for compacting and transporting waste meant that the disposal of solid waste was more cost and time-efficient. The resulting efficiencies in the use of labor and transportation became more and more important as cities continued to expand and the amount of solid waste to be collected increased dramatically.

Coping with Mountains of Trash

Disposing of solid waste posed additional problems. Many cities turned to covering the waste with soil or setting controlled fires to burn it. Burning solid waste reduced the volume of the waste and thus made it possible for cities to use a site longer. The smell and smoke that accompanied the fires were perceived—at least at that time—as a nuisance not as a health hazard. Soon cities began to adopt a European innovation, the incinerator, where wastes were burned in a large, enclosed furnace before the ashes were transported to a disposal site. Municipal incinerators could be located closer to population centers than open dumps and the combination of nearby incinerators and more remote dumps could lower the total transportation costs of solid waste management. Incinerators provided a weight-losing process where the material collected from households and businesses was heavier and bulkier before incineration than the ashes that remained after incineration. As a result, locating incinerators near solid waste collection sites and transporting the lighter ash to more remote disposal sites minimized transportation costs. Both city-owned and private incinerators became common in metro areas. By the mid-1960s incinerators were handling 40 percent of New York City's refuse (Walsh 2002).

Another way that cities dealt with solid waste involved exporting it to landfills in rural areas under agreements with those communities. This is equivalent to our hypothetical island residents who traded dumping rights for food. Essentially, areas of the United States that have a lot of land with low population density—and therefore where fewer people will be affected by the externalities associated with solid waste—have a comparative advantage in converting some of their land into landfills and take solid waste from cities in exchange for dumping fees.

This follows from what we already know about economic base theory and trade. Remember that economic base theory emphasizes the importance of bringing money into an area. From this standpoint, one can "follow the money trail" and identify the places receiving the fees as the location of an export industry. The solid waste and the dumping fees move in opposite directions. The places receiving the money are exporting the service of their land as landfill sites in return for the payments made by cities who agree to pay them for that service. Both Pennsylvania and Virginia have a comparative advantage in land fill sites because they have many rural areas with low population densities that can be used for waste disposal, and because they are relatively close to many urban areas which desperately need such a service. For the cities that choose to use these landfills, it is cheaper because of transportation costs to send their waste to Pennsylvania and Virginia than it is to send them to sites in Wyoming or Arizona where there is even more land available for such activity.

The issues of land availability and cost-efficiency that were emerging in the late nineteenth and early twentieth centuries highlighted another aspect of waste management. Cities thought about reuse and recycling. From the earliest municipal collection, there was awareness that under some circumstances waste could be reused and that some material could be sold to offset the costs of collection. The 1880 census notes that the City of Boston collected ash and garbage separately, sold the food wastes to farmers for fertilizer, and used ash as fill for low-lying land. Other cities used similar strategies or let pig farmers use the dumps as feeding grounds for pigs. As municipal solid-waste collection further expanded in the twentieth century, the overall solid waste management system became one in which sophisticated pricing was needed to determine what wastes to recycle and which to dispose of in traditional ways. Recycling came into its own during World War II, when paper drives and scrap metal drives were instituted in most high schools to provide raw materials for the war effort.

Municipal strategies were modified as awareness of previously unrecognized types of social costs emerged. Cost-benefit considerations and concern about previously unrecognized social costs shaped many of the changes in solid waste management in the twentieth century. Chief among these has been increasing public awareness of the dangers of air pollution and other environmental hazards and increasing regulation to reduce these hazards.

The primary concern about solid waste management in the twenty-first century arises simply because consumers are generating more waste. According to the US Environmental Protection Agency (EPA), the amount of solid waste generated in the nation increased sharply between 1960 and 2000 on both a per-capita basis and an overall basis (see Figure 9.1). In 1960, solid waste collection in the United States averaged 2.7 pounds per person per day, while in 2000 collection averaged 4.7 pounds per person per day. With both the per capita amount increasing and the population increasing, the amount of solid waste collected in the United States nearly tripled during those 40 years—from 88 million tons to 243.5 million tons. Between 2000 and 2018 per capita waste generation has remained relatively steady, but because the population has increased the total amount of waste generated has also increased. In 2018, the EPA estimated that the total amount of solid waste generated was 292.4 million tons—including a new category to more accurately capture certain types of food waste (see Table 9.2 and Figure 9.2). Cities across the United States have adopted recycling as an integral part of solid waste disposal in order to reduce the amount of material put into landfills, incinerated, or exported to ever more distant locations. In 2018, 24 percent of US municipal solid waste was recycled.

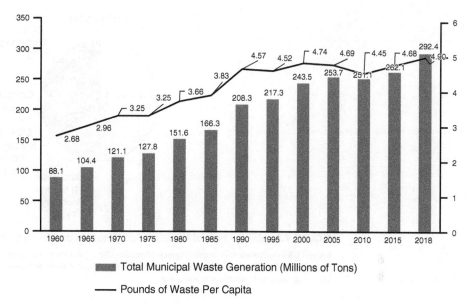

FIGURE 9.1. Municipal Solid Waste Generation Rates, 1960–2018

Source: US Environmental Protection Agency, November 2020 https://www.epa.gov/
facts-and-figures-about-materials-waste-and-recycling/national-overview-facts-and-figures-materials

TABLE 9.2. SOLID WASTE RECYCLING IN THE UNITED STATES

ACTIVITY	1960	1970	1980	1990	2000	2005	2010	2015	2017	2018
Generation	88.1	121.1	151.6	208.3	243.5	253.7	251.1	262.1	268.7	292.4
Recycling	5.6	8.0	14.5	29.0	53.0	59.2	65.3	67.6	67.0	69.0
Composting*	neg.	neg.	neg.	4.2	16.5	20.6	20.2	23.4	27.0	24.9
Other Food Management**	-	-	-	-	-	-	-	-	-	17.7
Combustion with energy recovery†	0.0	0.5	2.8	29.8	33.7	31.7	29.3	33.5	34.2	34.6
Landfilling and other disposal‡	82.5	112.6	134.3	145.3	140.3	142.2	136.3	137.6	140.5	146.2

*Composting of yard trimmings, food and other MSW organic material. Does not include backyard composting.
**Other food management pathways include animal feed, bio-based materials/biochemical processing, codigestion/anaerobic digestion, donation, land application and sewer/wastewater treatment.
Details might not add to totals due to rounding. neg. (negligible) = less than 5,000 tons or 0.05 percent.
†Includes combustion of MSW in mass burn or refuse-derived fuel form, and combustion with energy recovery of source separated materials in MSW (e.g., wood pallets, tire-derived fuel).
‡Landfilling after recycling, composting, other food management and combustion with energy recovery. A dash in the table means that data are not available.
Source: "Advancing Sustainable Materials Management: 2018 Fact Sheet" U.S. Environmental Protection Agency, November 2020.

Urban Wastewater and Sewers

Disposing of liquid waste is still another matter for cities and towns. Sewer systems address two problems in urban areas. First, they move wastewater generated by households and commercial businesses—in today's society, water from sinks, washing machines, toilets, and tubs. Second, they provide a method for directing and removing the excess storm water that runs off streets and land during and after major downpours.

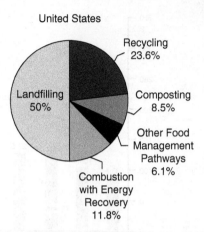

FIGURE 9.2. Management of Municipal Solid Waste in the United States, 2018

Source: US Environmental Protection Agency, November 2020 "Advancing Sustainable Materials Management: 2018 Fact Sheet." https://www.epa.gov/facts-and-figures-about-materials-waste-and-recycling/advancing-sustainable-materials-management

Despite their shared roots in efforts to promote public health and their similar use of underground pipes, the creation of municipal sewer systems lagged many decades behind the creation of water-supply systems. While several cities had already planned and created water systems in the first half of the nineteenth century, the first planned sewer systems were not created until the late 1850s, when Brooklyn and Chicago constructed their systems. The difference in timing occurred for several reasons.

First, effective water works were a necessary preexisting condition for the creation of sewer systems since sewer systems depend upon the existence of a dependable and substantial supply of water that can be relied upon to move the waste from homes and businesses to other areas. Second, in some cities, the previously existing system of privy vaults supplemented by privately built trenches and other disposal methods seemed to be meeting most needs so there was less urgency about creating a new system for household wastewater. Nonetheless, as more people lived in ever closer proximity to each other, the privy vault system began to show its limitations. In most cases there were no standards for construction of the privy vault, and some leaked or occasionally overflowed. The increasing amount of human waste had to be removed periodically and taken elsewhere. Enforcement of standards to dispose of this waste safely proved difficult.

Urban Sewer Systems

As the movement for greater sanitation grew stronger, other cities joined in the construction of planned sewer systems. Providence, Cincinnati, Indianapolis, New Haven, and Boston had extensive sewer systems by 1876. In 1880 the newly created federal public health entity, the National Board of Health, sent a specialist to study the sewer systems that were widely in use in Europe. By the early 1880s, designers and builders of sewer systems were actively marketing their systems to city governments carrying with them the arguments of the now widely accepted germ theory of disease. By the 1920s, the planning and construction of sewer systems was an established role for city governments in most large cities.

As was true of water supply systems, sewer systems were natural monopolies with high fixed costs and huge economies of scale. Accordingly, they were typically built and managed by municipal governments. Sewer pipes carried wastewater to a body of water into which it was then discharged through an open pipe. As the population and spatial dimensions of cities grew, this practice had two problems. The waterways into which the sewers emptied were often the same bodies of water from which drinking water was taken. If a relatively small amount of wastewater flowed into this water, city officials could count on dilution to reduce (but not eliminate) the amount of the raw sewage that returned through water intake pipes. With a growing population, the amount of household and industrial wastewater increased such that satisfactory dilution could not occur.

Many cities dealt with this problem by installing wastewater pipes downstream from the water intake pipes. Unfortunately, as these waterways continued downstream, other cities and towns saw the quality of their drinking water deteriorate. To reduce the impact of sewage on clean water, cities had two alternatives. The cities where the wastewater originated could treat it with filters and other methods of removing potentially harmful material before it was released into waterways. Alternatively, cities could filter water during the intake process between the time that it was removed from the water source and its eventual release into pipes where it flowed to households. One of the major issues of the first half of the twentieth century was whether water would be treated in wastewater treatment plants before being dumped back into waterways, or whether cities would rely upon water filtering of polluted water drawn from those waterways.

Essentially, such sewer systems mirrored the market failure dynamics of some solid waste systems. By sending the wastes to another area, the originating city exported the negative externalities, creating costs for other communities. As long as the originating city did not have to bear the cost of the negative externalities, they had incentives to spend less to correct this problem. Meanwhile, the downstream cities had to bear the higher costs to maintain clean drinking water because of the need to remove the contamination from the raw sewage flowing to them from the upstream cities. Several cities in the United States located downstream from other cities turned to state and federal courts to obtain legal intervention to force upstream cities to initiate or improve sewage treatment processes.

Those who sued often had an important point. With substantial underinvestment in treatment of raw sewage, many waterways became notoriously polluted, filthy, and smelly from the combination of household wastewater, industrial and commercial wastewater, and municipal solid waste. Although sewage treatment techniques were available in the early 1900s, until 1940 more than half of all urban dwellers lived in metro areas with sewage systems that discharged raw sewage into the environment (Melosi 2000; Burian et al. 2000). One of the most widely publicized cases is that of the Cuyahoga River that flows through Cleveland. The river was so filled with solid and liquid waste that it actually caught fire and burned for eight days in 1952, causing damage estimated as high as $1.5 million (Adler 2002). The river caught fire again in 1969, further raising national awareness of the extent of pollution in many of the nation's waterways.

New Challenges to Urban Sewer Systems

The last half of the twentieth century was characterized by urban economic dynamics that presented additional problems for urban sewage systems. The manufacture of new products introduced new chemicals into industrial wastewater (from production processes associated with the new products), household wastewater (from use of products such as modern detergents and cleaning fluids), and runoff water (from pesticides and petrochemicals). The introduction of such chemicals into the wastewater stream ultimately compromised the ability of sewer pipes to withstand the corrosive effect of such materials and challenged the ability of sewage treatment plants to expunge the new chemicals before discharge into waterways. While the federal Water Pollution Control Acts of 1948 and 1956 encouraged the building of sewer treatment plants, understanding the problems inherent in wastewater often outpaced the technology used in the treatment plants. Public attention was brought to the problem by Rachel Carson's widely read book *Silent Spring*, published in 1962 as an environmental call-to-arms, by the creation of the US Environmental Protection Agency in 1970, and by an early study by the EPA, which found that despite sanitation measures taken in earlier decades to deal with bacteria and viruses, major health risks still existed in the form of high concentrations of cancer- causing chemicals in the water of 79 US cities.

The rapid out-migration of central city residents to less dense suburbs added to the problem. When houses and businesses are farther away from each other, it takes more pipe to reach each building, increasing the per unit cost of providing and laying the pipes. Many of the new suburbs constituted political jurisdictions that were too small to finance their own sewage systems and treatment plants. In many metro areas, suburbs dealt with this problem by establishing agreements with central cities under which the central cities would extend their sewage pipes to the suburban communities and charge the suburban communities user fees to cover the costs of constructing and managing the system. In other metro areas, central cities and suburbs agreed to create metropolitan sewer districts—independent of any one municipality—that would finance the expansion of sewers into suburbs and manage both suburban and central city sewer service.

Boston provides a good example of how region-wide sewer systems evolved. The Massachusetts legislature first approved construction of the Boston Main Drainage System in 1876, a project that took seven years to complete. When it was fully in operation it served 18 cities and towns, diverting untreated sewerage to Moon Island in Boston Harbor, where the waste was held for release with the outgoing tide. Expansion to the sewer system continued through the early 1900s, although there was no treatment of the effluent. Not until 1952 was the first regional sewage treatment plant built with a second one constructed in 1968. By the mid-1980s, both proved inadequate leading to rising pollution levels in Boston harbor. A federal court order in 1985 mandated the construction of a modern treatment plant to bring Boston's sewerage system into line with federal environmental protection laws. Only then did Boston and 60 other cities and towns in the region build the state-of-the-art Deer Island treatment facility in Boston harbor. Completed in 2000 at a cost of $3.8 billion, the treatment plant serves 2.5 million residents and 5,500 large industrial users. Even with this Herculean effort, it will still take decades for Boston harbor to be reasonably clear of human-caused pollution.

As the pre-2000 Boston case makes clear, key parts of many sewage systems throughout the country began to reach their maximum capacity well before the dawn of the twenty-first century. Other parts of the older infrastructure reached stages of advanced deterioration due to age or lack of maintenance. Metropolitan area sewage systems faced choices between expansion of existing systems into newer suburbs, augmenting major parts of the system to increase capacity for expected future growth, or replacement of older pipes in central cities. Some cities adopted "fix it first" policies before extending their sewer systems to more distant suburbs.

City sewer systems that were not part of larger sewage districts faced additional challenges. The loss of businesses and the decreasing income profile of residents as more well-to-do families moved to suburbs left cities with decreased business activity and property values, and consequently with little ability to increase revenue because of the lower incomes and property values. For these cities, maintenance, repair, and replacement of deteriorating sewer lines and treatment plants was financially difficult or impossible. Often giving priority to sewage systems was not possible because of large opportunity costs. Providing needed financing for sewers would mean that other basic services such as police, fire, education, and hospitals—many of which might already be underfunded—would have to be cut. The outward movement of urban economic activity, and the consequent increasing poverty within many cities, ultimately affected the ability of older municipalities to provide vital waste treatment services just as the original systems began to wear out or were overwhelmed by demand. If it were not for federal and state courts ordering cities and towns to build modern up-to-date water treatment plants and sewers, it is doubtful that such basic infrastructure would win over the hearts, minds, and purse strings of city leaders faced with so many municipal functions in need of funding.

Urban Energy Infrastructure

A city requires a tremendous amount of energy. Manufacturing activities need to power machinery, communications, transportation, construction and maintenance of facilities. The commercial sector needs illumination within and outside of stores, elevators and escalators, marketing through electronic media, and transportation to bring finished goods to stores. Households need heating and cooling, cooking and cleaning apparatus, communication, entertainment, and transportation to work and shopping. For many other endeavors undertaken for work, fun, or necessity—energy is a fundamental input.

We are aware when a hurricane, tornado, or blizzard causes damage to power lines creating power outages that might last for a few minutes, several hours, or several days. Disruption to our normal activities calls attention to the many ways in which we so heavily depend upon these lines and other components of our energy infrastructures. On a typical day we might not pay attention to the electric power lines connecting houses to poles along the street, be cognizant of the pipes supplying natural gas for heating to homes and businesses, or think about the systems through which gasoline has arrived at our service station from its crude oil sources thousands of miles away.

There are differences in the sources, availability, and uses of energy within and among cities. Economic activity and morphology of those cities have been shaped by changes in energy use. Understanding urban areas entails awareness of the energy infrastructures that support cities and suburbs.

Both historical and comparative understandings across current cities are facilitated by thinking about the following four aspects of energy infrastructure: energy sources, prime movers, distribution systems, and energy utilization devices. Since the eighteenth century each of these has been a focus for discovery and rapid innovation (Hughes 1993; Klein 2008; Smil 2017a; 2017b; Rhodes 2019), leading to the energy infrastructures that exist in cities today. Revolutions in energy technology have been a major aspect of urbanization and industrialization affecting land use, production, population size, and environmental quality. Building knowledge about these systems is particularly important for the future of cities, since, as will be discussed in Chapter 15, the production and uses of energy have many implications for climate change.

Traditional Energy Sources

For millennia, the energy used by humans to accomplish tasks came from a limited number of direct sources. Solar energy is converted through photosynthesis into plant life and the biochemical energy in plants serves as fuel for animals. The movement of wind and water provides kinetic energy that moves things from place to place. Biomass (organic matter from living things, such as wood, other plant life, and dung) can be burned to provide heat. Humans found that fossilized biomass, such as coal, could be burned to provide heat or to obtain purer metals from ores, and coal was used in ancient metallurgy in China, the Middle East, Greece, Rome, Serbia, Africa, and in the Aztec empire of South America. Together, these sources remained the major fuels for energy until near the end of the 1800s (Smil 2017a; 2017b).

Fuels are directly used by prime movers, which are "systems that convert energy into motion"—the primary steps in converting potential energy from an energy source into mechanical motion (Rhodes 2019). Human muscles are prime movers, since they use the biochemical energy stored in human bodies to create work-related motion. The domestication of animals and the invention of various devices (harnesses, plows, turnstiles, etc.) to use their muscular power created another prime mover as the directed activity of horses, oxen, camels, elephants and other large animals was converted into work-related motion. The kinetic energies of wind and water were captured by sails, oars, and rudders—prime movers that aided travel. As centuries passed, windmills and watermills were invented to turn the energy of wind and water into movement of closely placed stones to mill grain into flour to make it more digestible. Windmills were used as well to remove and relocate water for drainage and irrigation (Smil 2017a).

The Impact of New Prime Movers in the Industrial Age

The steam engine, a new type of prime mover with profound implications for the future of energy and the future of cities, was invented in the mid-1700s. Steam engines were first used to help empty water from underground coal mines, where there was a nearly inexhaustible supply of fuel for these early inefficient steam engines. Using coal to heat water into steam (which takes up more space than liquid water) and then rapidly cooling the steam back into water, the first steam engines available commercially (developed by Thomas Newcomen) created vertical motion that could raise buckets of water from underground. The early steam engine designs were improved upon by James Watt in 1769, who created a more efficient model; and then in 1781, in partnership with Matthew Boulton, he introduced a steam engine that converted steam power into circular motion.

By 1800, steam engines were being used not only for mining, but for manufacturing. The new steam engines changed the constraints and opportunities for manufacturing, redirecting urban growth from waterwheel-conducive sites along swiftly flowing rivers to sites with access to water and coal. A wave of innovations and new economic activity ensued in the early decades of the 1800s. The rotary design steam engine was applied not only to manufacturing. It created a revolution in transportation—in the form of steam-powered omnibuses, boats, and trains.

The many uses of steam engine technology and the resulting large increase in the supply of coal created new cities, spurred new manufacturing industry clusters, expanded railroad networks, and raised the importance of interstate and interregional trade. As large coal deposits were found in Pennsylvania, West Virginia, Kentucky, and other states along the Appalachian Mountains, new railroads became an important part of the distribution system in Europe, the United States, and most other developed countries. Coal mining would make resource-rich locations wealthy communities. Coal mining near Pittsburgh began around 1784. For the next 60 years coal from these mines was distributed mainly through the three major rivers that converge in that area. The first railroads linking Pittsburgh with other cities were established in 1852. Since coal is heavy and therefore expensive to transport, coal-rich communities would become the center for the newly developing steel industry. By the mid-1800s, iron and steel production would become Pittsburgh's leading industry (Tarr and Clay 2014).

The creation of the coal-powered steam engine changed urban dynamics by creating a new economic geography for the energy used by cities. Previously, energy sources were to be found mainly in nearby water, vegetation, and animate labor. By the early 1800s there was increasing understanding that the energy sources for manufacturing—and, increasingly, for travel—were to be found in coal mines located often hundreds of miles away. The long-distance delivery of this fuel became part of urban realities and the delivery itself relied upon new forms of transportation for the distribution of this resource. The machinery powered by steam engines spurred larger scale production and created economies of scale. The lowered average production costs increased the geographic market area in which goods could be transported and profitably sold. Thus, in terms of the convergence of energy inputs, new production processes, and the distribution of final products, urban growth was associated with new interdependencies between cities and regions.

Location, Location, Location: The Problem of Distance and the Impact of Electricity

While coal-powered steam engines—and later steam turbines, invented in 1884 by Charles Parsons—provided unprecedented levels of energy for city activities through the conversion of coal to steam and then to motion, they still had a major limitation. They were place-specific devices and had to be at the location of whatever mechanical motion was ultimately needed. The area over which they created motion could be extended through the use of belts, pulleys, and other devices that dispersed or redirected the motion, but the area affected was still limited. Because the prime mover was place-bound, coal had to be transported to the ultimate sites of mechanical motion. As noted earlier, coal is heavy and the costs to transport the coal were significant. Was there a cheaper way to provide needed energy to the machinery that was the ultimate target of the prime movers? Was there a way to reduce the procurement cost of fuel by establishing prime movers near the fuel sources and then distributing the power that was created from them? The solution was ultimately found in electricity.

Solving the problem of distance required theoretical development in the form of what became known as electromagnetic theory. Based on this theory, new inventions based on electric power would revolutionize the economy and cities around the world. Distributing electric power from central power stations would become the major form of energy in the late nineteenth century and would continue to be so right up until the present.

Portable electric power would be important as well. The first batteries were created by Alessandro Volta in 1800. The fact that an electric current caused a magnetic field was discovered by Hans Christian Orsted in 1819, and in 1831 Michael Faraday demonstrated the reverse: that the motion of magnets can create electricity. These findings were put into use on a local basis through various inventions such as the telephone (Alexander Graham Bell) and electric lights (Thomas Edison). Even Edison's structures, which provided light for small areas of a city, were founded on the concept of local neighborhood-specific creation of current (Rhodes 2019). The direct current used in Edison's systems required thick wires, and the practical area that could receive current from prime movers through these wires was only about a quarter mile squared (Smil 2017b). The problem of distance was not solved until William Stanley introduced a lighting infrastructure based on production and distribution of alternating current.

Produced electromagnetically by magnets moving near a rotating coil of wires, alternating current could be sent at high voltages through smaller wires. Although it was a more recent discovery than direct current, its efficacy was enhanced with Stanley's invention of transformers that could raise or lower the voltage of electrical currents sent and received. Stanley demonstrated the usefulness of his system in Great Barrington Massachusetts in 1886 and his system was subsequently backed by the wealthy energy entrepreneur, George Westinghouse. By 1888, just two years later, 100 alternating current generators were supplying electricity to cities and towns in the eastern United States and the first intercity transmission, over a distance of 17 miles, had been established in Italy (Rhodes 2019). A major step forward occurred in 1895 when the kinetic power of the waterfalls at Niagara Falls was harnessed to provide electricity for Buffalo, 30 miles away, and after construction of appropriate transmission lines in 1896, to New York City, 400 miles away. Prime movers could now create electricity that could be transmitted and used hundreds of miles away. From this point forward not only the procurement of fuel, but the production and distribution of power itself, was regional, national, and international.

New Fossil Fuel Sources, Distance, and Pipelines

Innovations associated with electricity also made the long-distance distribution of liquid fuels and natural gas more feasible. Crude oil was initially valued for the kerosene it could provide—a useful substitute for the whale oil that was used in lanterns. The first commercial oil well was built in Russia in 1846; the first in North America was in Ontario in 1858, and the first in the United States was in Titusville, Pennsylvania in 1859. As whale oil became scarcer due to the reduction in the whale population, kerosene and the crude oil from which it was derived became more valuable. But in the United States, the major centers of population were quite distant from the oil fields. Initially, oil was transferred in barrels by wagons to river barges and railroads. Transportation of the quantities demanded by wagon was expensive, and in 1865 the first oil pipeline in the United States was created as an alternative way of moving oil from its point of production closer to urban centers (Johnson 1956). During this time pipes were manually built by blacksmiths, who connected heated sections over coal-based fires. The pipes were costly to make and frequently leaked. The limitations of pipe quality were even more constraining for natural gas.

Natural gas, often found in areas with coal or crude oil, was recognized as being much cleaner to burn than coal, as it does not produce soot. It is more stable in terms of the heat given off. As such, there was a large potential market for it. Transporting natural gas has one major drawback. As a gas, unlike coal (a solid) or crude oil (a liquid that could be transported in barrels), it needed to be transported through pipelines directly from the fields to consumers.

Unfortunately, as already mentioned, the pipeline-building technology of the 1800s was not capable of producing viable nonleaky pipelines. Consequently, because of distance and the impossibility of transportation, even when gas fields were discovered, the discoverers had no economically viable use for the gas.

A new application of electricity—electrical arc welding—solved the pipeline problem. Electrical arc welding, first patented in Russia in 1885 and then in the United States in 1887, used electric current to heat and melt together metal at temperatures much higher than was possible in traditional blacksmithing techniques. The resulting pipes were much stronger and leak resistant. The spread of electrical arc welding was spurred during World War I, when it was widely used for ship repair, and it became common in long-distance pipe construction after the war. Networks of pipelines connecting natural gas fields and cities began to be established and by 1936, 29 large cities across much of the United States had been connected to natural gas lines. The longest single pipeline of this era extended 1,000 miles from Texas to Chicago (Rhodes 2019).

During World War II, to protect delivery of oil to the Northeast, which was threatened by German submarines attacking oil-tanker ships off the East Coast, US oil companies joined together with the government to create a 1,254-mile oil pipeline from Texas to Pennsylvania, with secondary pipelines to Philadelphia and New York. Completed in 1943, the pipeline provided an alternative to the more perilous wartime ocean route. After the war, the pipeline was converted to civilian use and remains a major conduit for natural gas.

Energy Infrastructure in the Early Twenty-First Century

Today, urban life is supported by energy systems that draw upon fuels, prime movers, distribution networks, and final applications that span great distances. Oil and natural gas pipelines traverse the United States and other countries, connecting fossil fuel locations, refineries, and customers. Crude oil use is primarily for electricity generation, and for transportation by road, rail, and air. Distribution of crude oil and the products derived from its distillation are by pipelines, tanker ships, railroad tanker cars, and specially designed trucks.

Natural gas use in the United States is primarily for electricity generation and for heating homes and other buildings. It is distributed by pipelines, and to and from refineries by specially designed pressure and temperature-controlled liquid natural gas (LNG) ships, railcars, and trucks. Throughout the world, many of the pipelines that transport fuel to prime movers are long and international, as shown in Table 9.3.

The most versatile form of power in the United States—electrical power—is now provided by a complex and massive infrastructure system using many fuel sources. These include coal, water (hydro), oil, gas, nuclear, and increasingly, wind and solar. The fundamental transformation that takes place is still the operation of a prime mover that uses steam (or water flow in a hydropower generator or wind in a wind-generator) to turn turbine rotors and magnetic generator rotors. As they spin, the generator rotors create alternating current in coils of wire. The electricity produced is fed into a massive distribution system known as "the grid" that not only sends electricity throughout the United States, but constantly adjusts electrical production to electricity demand in real-time (Blume 2017).

The overall energy infrastructure's systems of fuel sources, prime movers, and distribution networks impact us each time we flip a switch, turn an ignition, adjust a dial on an appliance, or press an on/off button. Our energy-dependent machines, appliances, heating, cooling, lighting, and transportation alternatives make it feasible, efficient, and comfortable for people to live in cities, in transportation dependent suburbs, on farms that produce food for urban areas, and in other rural areas.

TABLE 9.3. PIPELINES IN THE WORLD

PIPELINE	ORIGIN	DESTINATION	LENGTH IN MILES
China Central Asia	Central Asia	Xinjiang,China	6,213
China West-East	Northeast China	Shanghai	5,410
Gasun	Bolivia	Northeastern Brazil	3,100
Ust-Balik-Kurgan-Almetievsk	Russia	Western Europe	2,864
Yamal Europe	Siberia	Germany	2,607
Eastern Siberia-Pacific Ocean	Siberia	Japan	2,597
Trans-Saharan	Nigeria	Northern Algeria	2,564
Druzhba	Russia	Europe	2,500
Keystone	Alberta	Illinois/Oklahoma/Texas	2,150
Rockies Express	Colorado	Ohio	1,679

Source: Husseini (2018)

The sources from which we derive electricity vary dramatically across countries. As of 2013, across the European Union about 24 percent of generated electricity came from the use of such solid fuels as coal. Another 19 percent came from gases, while nuclear power was responsible for fueling 17 percent of electricity generated. Less than 9 percent was powered by petroleum. Renewables in the form of wind and hydro power, were already responsible for nearly 31 percent of total generational capacity.

The leaders in nuclear generation were France, where 74 percent of its electric power came from such power plants. In Slovakia the percentage was nearly 55 percent, while Sweden relied on such power for 43 percent of its total electricity output. The leaders in renewables were Austria, where wind and solar power were responsible for nearly 80 percent of their entire electric generation, followed by Croatia at 65 percent, Portugal at 59 percent, Italy at 57 percent, and Sweden at 54 percent (Desjardins 2015).

By contrast, the United States is still more dependent on fossil fuels, with 61 percent of electricity production generated by coal (23%), natural gas (38%), and petroleum (1%) in 2019. Only 17 percent of total electricity was generated by renewables (US Energy Information Administration 2019).

Cities in Africa, Asia, and South America are expanding their focus on large-grid, micro-grid, and nongrid possibilities as solar and wind technology develop.

The power provided by wind turbines on land and offshore is increasing dramatically as concerns about climate change become more prevalent. Innovations in solar technology and the deployment of solar farms have grown. Solar roof panels have created some houses and buildings that utilize no power from the grid and create excess electricity and feed it into the grid. Researchers continue to investigate the possibilities of cellulosic ethanol—including generation of ethanol from municipal waste. With new technologies, cities will depend less on fossil fuels throughout the world, and this will change the fortunes of communities that are the primary producers of fossil fuels and at the same time increase the fortunes of those that can produce wind power and solar power cheaply and have the natural environment to promote hydroelectric power.

In cities, nothing stands still for very long.

References

Adler, Jonathan H., "Fables of the Cuyahoga: Reconstructing a History of Environmental Protection" (2002). *Faculty Publications.* 191. https://scholarly-commons.law.case.edu/faculty_publications/191

Bloom, Khaled J. 1993. *The Mississippi Valley's Great Yellow Fever Epidemic of 1878.* Baton Rouge: Louisiana State University Press.

Blume, Steven. 2017. *Electric Power System Basics for the Nonelectrical Professional,* 2nd ed. Hoboken, NJ: Wiley.

Burian, Steven J., Stephan J. Nix, Robert E. Pitt, and S. Rocky Durrans, 2000. "Urban Wastewater Management in the United States: Past, Present, and Future." *Journal of Urban Technology* 7, no. 3 (December): 33–62.

Crosby, Alfred W., 1989. *America's Forgotten Pandemic: The Influenza of 1918*, New York: Cambridge University Press

Cutler, David, and Grant Miller. 2006. "Water, Water Everywhere: Municipal Finance and Water Supply in American Cities." In *Corruption and Reform: Lessons from America's History*, edited by Edward Glaeser and Claudia Goldin. National Bureau of Economic Research Conference Report Series. Chicago: University of Chicago Press, 153–184.

Desjardins, Jeff. 2015. "Europe's Electricity Production by Country and Fuel Type." *Visual Capitalist*, October 22.

Duffy, John. 1990. *The Sanitarians: A History of American Public Health*. Urbana: University of Illinois Press.

Finder, Alan. 1991. "New York Sanitation Code for Residents in Building Strike." *New York Times*, April 21.

Herbert, Lewis, 2013 "Centenary History of Waste and Waste Managers in London and Southeast England" *The Chartered Institution of Waste Management*. 1–51 https://www.ciwm.co.uk/Custom/BSIDocumentSelector/Pages/DocumentViewer.aspx?id=QoR7FzWBtitMKLGdXnS8mUgJfkM0vi6KMAYwUqgqau3ztZeoed%252bsdmKIqDzPOm8yAXgBZR%252fn1fYhL%252bTNdjUq9g2xwY63C2g8GcAQQyfpf3SImIrrED%252bTfsUM91bKsogr

Hughes, Thomas P. 1993. *Networks of Power: Electrification in Western Society, 1880–1930*. Baltimore: Johns Hopkins University Press.

Humphreys, Margaret. 1992. *Yellow Fever and the South*. New Brunswick, NJ: Rutgers University Press.

Johnson, Arthur M. 1956. *The Development of American Petroleum Pipelines 1862–1906*. Ithaca, NY: Cornell University Press

Klein, Maury. 2008. *The Power Makers: Steam, Electricity, and the Men Who Invented Modern America*. London: Bloomsbury.

Krunk, Kid. 2017. "Ten Most Toxic Place on the Planet." *Archuup*, March 1.

Melosi, Martin V. 1985. *Coping with Abundance: Energy and Environment in Industrial America*. New York: Knopf.

Melosi, Martin V. 2000. *The Sanitary City: Urban Infrastructure in America from Colonial Times to the Present*. Baltimore: Johns Hopkins University Press.

Ministry of Environment. 2014. "History and Current State of Waste Management in Japan." April. Tokyo: Ministry of Environment.

Myers, Dowell, William Baer, and Seong Yoon Choi. 1996. "The Changing Problem of Overcrowded Housing." *Journal of the American Planning Association* 62, no. 1 66–84

Pierce, Charles P. 2016. "The Nation's Poisonous Water Problem Is Far Worse than You Think." *Esquire Magazine*, June 2.

Ray, Michael. 2016. "Flint Water Crisis." *Brittannica*. https://www.britannica.com/event/Flint-water-crisis.

Rhodes, Richard. 2019. *Energy: A Human History*. New York: Simon & Schuster.

Rosenberg, Charles E. 1962. *The Cholera Years*. Chicago: University of Chicago Press.

Schultz, Stanley K., and Clay McShane. 1978. "To Engineer the Metropolis: Sewers, Sanitation, and City Planning in Late-Nineteenth-Century America." *Journal of American History* 65, no. 2: 389–411.

Smil, Vaclav. 2017a. *Energy and Civilization: A History*. Cambridge, MA: MIT Press.

Smil, Vaclav. 2017b. *Energy: A Beginner's Guide*. London: OneWorld Publications.

Tarr, Joel A. 1984. "The Evolution of the Urban Infrastructure in the Nineteenth and Twentieth Centuries." In *Perspectives on Urban Infrastructure*, edited by Royce Hanson. Washington, DC: National Academy Press, 110–142.

Tarr, Joel, and Karen Clay. 2014. "Pittsburgh as an Energy Capital: Perspectives on Coal and Natural Gas Transitions and the Environment." In *Energy Capitals: Local Impact, Global Influence*, edited by Joseph A. Pratt, Martin Melosi, and Kathleen Brosnan. City: Publisher, 5–29.

Tomes, Nancy. 1998. *The Gospel of Germs: Men, Women, and the Microbe in American Life*. Cambridge, MA: Harvard University Press.

US Energy Information Administration. 2019. "Electricity in the United States is Produced with Diverse Energy Sources and Technologies." Washington, DC: Department of Energy.

Velis, Costas A.; David C. Wilson, and Christopher R. Cheeseman. 2009. "19th Century London Dust-Years: A Case Study in Closed-Loop Resource Efficiency." *Waste Management* 29, no. 4 (April): 1282–1290.

Walsh, Donald C. 2002. "Urban Residential Refuse Composition and Generation Rates for the 20th Century." *Environmental Science and Technology* 36, no. 22 (October): 4936–4942.

Wikipedia. 2006. "John Lindsay." http://en.wikipedia.org/wiki/John_Lindsay.

Questions and Exercises

As we noted in Chapter 7, one of the main sources of data about municipal governments is the US Census Bureau's Census of Governments, conducted once every five years (in years ending in "2" and "7"). The amount of revenue collected by state and municipal governments within each state and the sources of this revenue are published in the Census of Governments' report "Finances of Municipal and Township Governments." The latest version (released in 2017) can be found at https://www.census.gov/data/tables/2017/econ/gov-finances/summary-tables.html.

Using data from this source for any three states of your choosing, discuss the following issues—first for the state government and then for local governments in those states:

1. What percentage of the state revenue is spent on

   - highways and roads
   - air transportation
   - parking facilities
   - sea and inland port facilities

2. What percentage of local government revenue is spent on

   - highways and roads
   - air transportation
   - parking facilities
   - sea and inland port facilities

3. What percentage of state government revenue is spent on

   - sewerage
   - solid waste management
   - parking facilities
   - sea and inland port facilities
   - water supply
   - electric power
   - gas supply

4. What percentage of local government revenue is spent on

   - sewerage
   - solid waste management
   - parking facilities
   - sea and inland port facilities
   - water supply
   - electric power
   - gas supply

5. Do you find large differences in these percentages across the states you selected and local governments within them? What might explain these differences if you find them?

Urban Area Transportation

10

LEARNING OBJECTIVES

- ■ Describe the externalities that accompany the transportation of goods and people in metropolitan areas and explain the nature of government intervention that derives from them

- ■ Explain in what sense there is a high cost to free parking and describe the remedy

- ■ Define congestion pricing and explain the consequences

- ■ Define induced traffic and explain its implications

- ■ Explain how conflicts between the criteria of equity and efficiency might apply to transportation investment decisions

As we saw in Chapter 3, during the age of waterborne transportation, virtually all the first cities around the world were located along rivers and harbors. In Europe, think of London on the Thames, Paris on the Seine, and Berlin on the Spree. In the United States it was the completion of the Erie Canal early in the nineteenth century that vaulted New York City into its position of preeminence among US cities—a position it has held unchallenged for nearly two centuries. Later, in the mid-nineteenth century, during the age of railroad construction, the location of railway routes was critical to the growth of such places as Chicago. Rail transportation first connected one city with another; later, it became an important means of transportation within cities. In both instances, land values along the routes rose as those locations became more accessible and therefore more valuable for development. In the case of the intracity lines, entrepreneurs prospered from the sale of land adjacent to the tracks more than from the transit lines themselves.

Transportation routes helped to channel the path of subsequent economic development. As cities grew, the need for improved transportation between established population centers influenced subsequent patterns of investment in transportation. In New York State, for example, many of the largest cities including Albany and Buffalo originally grew because of their location along the Erie Canal. In later eras railroad and highway routes connected these existing population centers, following the route of the canal. In this example, we can see both the interaction of public policy (the decision by New York State to build the canal (and market forces (the decisions of thousands of households and firms to locate in a place with good transportation and the interaction between transportation decisions and land-use options). In an iterative process, decisions regarding transportation affect patterns of land use and land-use patterns then affect the siting of transportation routes.

As a result, a metropolitan area's transportation network is a crucial part of its physical infrastructure. If we were designing a city on a blank slate, our initial choices about where to place our investments in transportation infrastructure and how to balance rail networks with highways would have a profound impact on the shape of the resulting city. Yet once the city is built, our choices about subsequent transportation investment is constrained by the existing patterns of land use. A transportation project such as a subway that would make sense in a highly centralized metropolitan area such as New York is less likely to work in a more decentralized metropolitan area such as Houston.

Unless we are building a fresh new city, we will need to take the "dead hand of history" into account. As the saying goes, "all roads lead to Rome." In the days of the Roman Empire, that is what the emperors wanted. More than 2,000 years later, many of the routes originally laid out by the Romans are still in use throughout Europe. That is a "dead hand" that extended its influence over two millennia.

In looking at the transportation problems that arise in metropolitan areas, we need to concern ourselves with short-term issues (getting transportation prices right) versus long-term issues (guiding future transportation investment), externalities (pollution, congestion, and accidents), and conflicts between the criteria of efficiency and equity. For example, a new commuter rail link might reduce highway congestion in a metropolitan area, but would do nothing to solve the mobility problems of the area's poor.

What Consumers Want: The Demand Side of Metropolitan Transportation

Aspiring journalists are told that their news stories must include the *who*, *what*, *when*, *where*, *why*, and *how* of the situation. Similarly, regarding the demand for transportation, we can ask: *Who* is doing the traveling, *at what time* and *for what purpose*, *from what origin to what destination*, and *by what means*? How can a metropolitan area's transportation system for moving goods as well as people—a network that might include airports, highways, heavy rail, light rail, ferries, buses, cars, trucks, and streets that might or might not be attractive to pedestrians and bicyclists—serve the varied needs of out-of-town business travelers or tourists and the parcel deliverers as well as the needs of residents who might be journeying to work or to a doctor's appointment, shopping for groceries, or venturing out for entertainment or for visits with friends and relatives? How does the demand for transportation differ between households who own cars and those who do not, and between individuals who can drive cars and those who cannot?

What we do know is that transit mode for daily commuters varies enormously across cities. In Zurich, Vienna, and in Budapest, somewhere between 70 and 75 percent of commuters rely on public transit—buses, subways, and streetcars. Commuters are much more bike-friendly in Copenhagen and Amsterdam, where over 50 percent ride to work each day by bicycle. Similarly, in the United States, commuting patterns differ dramatically depending on where you live. In New York City, more than 55 percent of commuters use public transit, although this is a decrease from 70 percent in 1960. In Boston, more than a third take the bus, subway, streetcar, or ferry to work. But in Kansas City, the public transit system is so limited that only 2 to 3 percent use the bus system. Most commuters use their private automobiles. More than 90 percent of commuters in Detroit and Indianapolis can be found driving alone in their cars to work or carpooling.

Travel Trends

The US Department of Transportation has been collecting data on personal travel through periodic surveys, starting with the 1969 *Nationwide Personal Transportation Survey* (*NPTS*). Most recently, the *National Household Travel Survey* (*NHTS*) was first conducted in 2017. Overall, the data reveal a nation ever more reliant on the private automobile to serve its transportation needs. Even as average household size in the United States has declined from 3.16 people in 1969 to 2.55 in 2017, the number of vehicles per household has increased, from 1.16 to 1.88, so that by 2017 there was a vehicle for every licensed driver in the household. We rely heavily on automobiles not just for trips to work but for all trips, as indicated by the growth in the number of vehicles per worker, from 0.96 in 1969 to 1.42 in 2017 (see Table 10.1).

TABLE 10.1. MAJOR TRAVEL INDICATORS BY SURVEY YEAR

	1969	1977	1983	1990	1995	2001	2009	2017
Persons per house-hold	3.16	2.83	2.69	2.56	2.63	2.58	2.50	2.55
Vehicles per house-hold	1.16	1.59	1.68	1.77	1.78	1.89	1.86	1.88
Licensed drivers per household	1.65	1.69	1.72	1.75	1.78	1.77	1.88	1.89
Vehicles per licensed driver	0.70	0.94	0.98	1.01	1.00	1.06	0.99	1.00
Workers per house-hold	1.21	1.23	1.21	1.27	1.33	1.35	1.34	1.33
Vehicles per worker	0.96	1.29	1.39	1.40	1.34	1.39	1.39	1.42

Note: The 1969 survey does not include pickups and other light trucks as household vehicles.
Source: U.S. Department of Transportation, Federal Highway Administration

TABLE 10.2. TRENDS IN THE PERCENT OF PERSON TRIPS BY MODE OF TRANSPORTATION AND TRIP PURPOSE

PRIVATE VEHICLE

	To/From Work	Work-Related Business	Shopping and Errands	School or Church	Social and Recreational	Other	Total
1990	91.2%	90.3%	92.7%	61.9%	86.3%	81.4%	87.8%
1996	92.8%	91.9%	92.6%	69.6%	87.6%	83.2%	89.3%
2001	92.4%	91.2%	90.9%	71.3%	80.7%	67.2%	86.3%
2009	91.4%	88.1%	87.8%	70.7%	76.9%	71.0%	83.4%
2017	88.2%	80.1%	88.5%	70.5%	77.1%	72.6%	82.6%

PUBLIC TRANSIT

	To/From Work	Work-Related Business	Shopping and Errands	School or Church	Social and Recreational	Other	Total
1990	4.0%	2.6%	1.0%	3.8%	1.2%	1.7%	1.8%
1996	3.6%	1.3%	1.2%	2.6%	1.5%	1.9%	1.8%
2001	3.7%	1.8%	1.1%	2.1%	1.0%	4.2%	1.6%
2009	3.7%	2.2%	1.4%	2.2%	1.3%	5.9%	1.9%
2017	5.5%	3.4%	1.8%	2.5%	1.6%	3.2%	2.5%

WALK

Year	To/From Work	Work-Related Business	Shopping and Errands	School or Church	Social and Recreational	Other	Total
1990	4.0%	4.4%	5.6%	12.8%	9.9%	13.2%	7.2%
1995	2.3%	2.4%	5.0%	8.8%	7.3%	7.6%	5.4%
2001	2.8%	4.2%	7.1%	9.6%	14.5%	15.9%	8.6%
2009	3.0%	5.7%	9.1%	9.4%	17.5%	12.6%	10.4%
2017	3.9%	8.4%	8.1%	10.3%	18.1%	11.8%	10.5%

OTHER

Year	To/From Work	Work-Related Business	Shopping and Errands	School or Church	Social and Recreational	Other	Total
1990	0.8%	2.7%	0.8%	21.4%	2.6%	3.6%	3.2%
1995	1.3%	4.2%	1.0%	18.1%	3.1%	6.0%	3.2%
2001	1.0%	2.7%	0.9%	16.9%	3.7%	12.3%	3.4%
2009	1.9%	3.9%	1.7%	17.7%	4.2%	10.5%	4.2%
2017	2.4%	8.0%	1.7%	16.7%	3.3%	12.4%	4.4%

Note:
- Totals in all tables can include cases that were not included in any table subcategory, for instance people who did not report their age are included in the total persons, but not in any age category.
- 1990 NPTS data were adjusted to make them more comparable with later surveys.
- In 1995, VMT and vehicle trips with "To or From Work" as a trip purpose are believed to be overstated
- 2001 NHTS sample included children 0 to 4 in the survey. The data shown here exclude them to be comparable with other survey years.
- 2009 NHTS sample did not include households without landlines telephones (CPO households).
- 2017 NHTS sample was address-based and included more urban and CPO households. This and other methods changes in the data series are outlined in Appendix B.
- Changes in walk trips throughout the data series could be a result at least in part, to questionnaire changes: Recent NHTS surveys explicitly prompt respondents to include walk and bike trips, which was not the case in prior surveys. The 2017 NHTS changed the definition of a trip to allow walk and bike trips to and from home (loop trips).
- "Other" trip purpose includes trips for work-related business and trips not categorized.

Source: U.S. Department of Transportation, Federal Highway Administration

Where were we going and how did we get there? In the United States, the private automobile dominates for nearly all purposes from commuting to work and traveling for work-related business to shopping, running errands, attending school or church, and for recreation (see Table 10.2).

As shown in Figure 10.1, there is a strong relationship between vehicle ownership and population density. In areas with the sparsest amount of population per square mile, households are heavily reliant on multiple vehicles; in the densest settlements, single-vehicle households are more common and there are nearly as many households with no vehicles as there are with multiple vehicles.

In a nation so reliant on private vehicles, what does it mean to live in a household without one? A small number of these households might be car-free by choice—for example, relatively prosperous Manhattan residents who could afford to own a car but choose not to because of the hassles of traffic and parking. These households have many other travel modes easily available to them, including limousine services, taxicabs, and Uber or Lyft. They have the option of renting a car occasionally should the need arise. For most households without vehicles, however, it is not a matter of choice. These are households too poor to own a car. In an era when a good deal of job growth has occurred outside the central city in the suburbs, these households confront serious employment problems. Many of those who must commute to jobs in the suburbs often find their transportation needs are not adequately addressed by existing public transit routes.

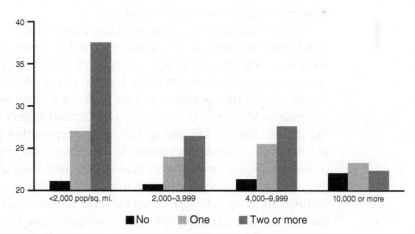

FIGURE 10.1. Distribution of the Number of US Households by Vehicle Ownership and Population Density, 2017 NHTS Millions of Households

Notes:
- Totals in all tables can include cases that were not included in any table subcategory.
- 2009 NHTS sample did not include households without landlines telephones (CPO households).
- 2017 NHTS sample was address-based and included more urban and CPO households. This and other methods changes in the data series are outlined in Appendix B.
- In 1969, household vehicles did not include pickups or other light trucks.
- SUVs were added as a vehicle class in the NHTS survey in 1995.
- In 2009 the survey included Light Electric Vehicles (LEV) as a separate classification.
- Motorcycle, moped, LEVs and other POV are excluded from the calculation of vehicle age.

Source: US Department of Transportation, Federal Highway Administration

The Journey to Work

Although the demand for transportation encompasses far more than the journey to work, it is there that some of the thorniest problems arise. Traveling from point A to point B involves costs including the expense of owning and operating a car, paying fares to access public transportation, and the opportunity cost of one's time. If you are relocating from one metropolitan area to another for a new job, you might look for housing conveniently located to reduce your commute time. Conversely, you might look for a new home in your current metro area in order to reduce drive time.

Still, there are likely to be trade-offs between your housing preferences and commute time. You might have to accept a longer commute to be able to afford a larger house with more land in a metro area where housing is cheaper on the fringes of the region. In metropolitan areas with tight housing markets, you might need to move to a more distant suburb to be able to afford anything. Alternatively, you might opt for a long commute to accept a job with better wages and working conditions or greater chances for promotion. If there is more than one worker in the household, a delicate process of triangulation might ensue—a balancing act between home and two or more job destinations. With the typical family now having two working adults, this balancing job is more difficult than ever. It is even more complicated if the commute includes dropping off kids at school, picking them up at day care, and stopping to get the groceries or the dry cleaning. In this case, most commuters will opt for the use of their private automobiles even if a bus, subway, or other mass transit is available.

In their pathbreaking book on urban transportation, Meyer, Kain, and Wohl (1965) point out that decentralization in mid-twentieth-century US metropolitan areas was occurring as rapidly in places with well-developed public transportation systems as in places without them. Even in places where consumers had a choice between public transportation and the automobile, they overwhelmingly chose the automobile. Moreover, they argued, as decentralization affected not only residential location but the location of businesses, commuting patterns would continue to shift away from job destinations in the central city. Instead, a growing share of commuters would be cross-commuting (traveling from one suburb to another) or they would be reverse-commuting (traveling from homes in the central city to job destinations in the suburbs). Given the large economies of scale required to justify the creation of a fixed rail system, the authors argue that the shift in commuting patterns would make new investment in fixed rail systems undesirable and that it would be a poor use of resources.

As we saw in Table 10.1, the automobile is by far the dominant mode of commuting in the United States. Although the data for 2017 show a modest decline in automobile reliance and a modest increase in public transportation use since 2009, public transportation has accounted for less than 10 percent of work trips in all but the very largest metropolitan areas: New York, San Francisco, Washington, DC, Boston, and Chicago. Nevertheless, the primacy of driving to work should not be taken as a pure expression of consumer preferences. Changes in the location and types of workplaces, as well as the location and structure of households, have also played an important role in determining the transportation we select. The continued decentralization of residences and workplaces has made it less possible for workers to find alternatives to commuting by private vehicle. This explains at least part of the decline in the use of public transit in many US cities. The changing demographics of the workforce and the workplace—including the increase in the proportion of women workers since 1960 and the variability in work schedules—make carpooling less feasible for many. The more dispersed the location of firms and families, the less likely that mass transit will have the ridership to support regular bus service, let alone commuter rail or subway service.

Externalities and the Movement of Goods

An area's transportation network moves goods as well as people. The NHTS added a question about online shopping and home delivery starting with its 2009 survey. Overall, the estimated number of purchases delivered to a household in a month more than doubled between 2009 (2.4 purchases) and 2017 (4.9 purchases). While the growth in purchases was greatest in households without children, the number of purchases was highest in households with teenagers and young adults.

Similarly, data from the US Postal Service shows that while first class mail volume declined steadily from 2009 to 2018, the volume of shipping and package services doubled over that time period (US Postal Service 2019). Such dramatic growth in package deliveries, much of which was direct to consumers rather than businesses, has led to greater interest in the impact of parcel deliveries. During the COVID-19 pandemic in 2020, purchases from Amazon and other e-commerce retail firms grew by 35 percent. The result was that package delivery services including United Parcel (UPS) and FedEx had more trucks on the road than any time in their history. Such increases in package delivery bring their own concerns about congestion and pollution, as do the large number of Uber and Lyft vehicles. As of 2020, Uber was operating in 76 countries and in 473 cities around the world.

Externalities and Mass-Transit Subsidies

If commuting motorists paid the full cost when using their private autos for transit, we could leave the story here, noting simply that driving to work alone is an increasingly popular choice. But it is not as simple as that. An individual who drives to work alone imposes costs on other drivers and on the larger community. The more people who choose to use this transportation mode, the higher the external costs imposed on others. These externalities arise chiefly in the form of traffic congestion, time-delayed trips, air and water pollution from the use of automobiles, and a growing incidence of accidents on congested highways. As is true of any negative externality, too many drivers will choose to drive during periods of congestion unless the cost of the externalities is factored into the price of driving.

Essentially, the social cost of solo driving is higher—perhaps significantly higher—than the private cost. The private costs to the individual motorist, no matter how much it costs to own a car, do not include the spillover costs to other motorists or to the residents of the area. The denser the region, the higher the social cost. Those who live in rural areas impose much lower social costs than those who drive their vehicles in downtown Manhattan or any large central city.

One interesting corollary of this phenomenon concerns the question of subsidies for mass transit. It is highly unlikely that a public transit authority would be able to charge a price that would cover the average cost of operating buses or subway systems. As the price of a bus or subway ride rises, the ridership normally declines, which would be the case for most goods or services. The higher the price, the lower the number of rides demanded. The new higher price multiplied by the new lower ridership yields a revenue that is below the full cost of providing the service. Yet given the enormous fixed cost of operating a mass-transit system, charging a low price to attract more riders will not usually generate enough new ridership to cover total costs.

The reason for this is that for almost any mass-transit system the revenue from fares is not sufficient to cover the cost of building and operating the system. This is depicted in Figure 10.2. With the price of gasoline at $2.25 per gallon, the demand curve for mass transit lies everywhere below the average total cost curve for mass transit. If the transit authority sets the transit fare at A, a subsidy of AB per passenger is needed to cover the transit system's average total cost. If the authority were to raise the transit fare, the number of mass-transit passengers would decline further reducing total fare revenue. Given the nature of ridership demand, at no mass-transit fare can the system survive without a subsidy. Given the relatively low cost of gasoline, the transit demand curve at $2.25 per gallon lies below the average total cost curve at all points on the curve.

Essentially, the authority must consider how many mass-transit riders it would want to subsidize in order to encourage people to leave their cars at home. Note that it is possible to operate the mass-transit system without a subsidy (at point C on demand curve 2), but only if taxes on gasoline are raised so high as to discourage drivers from using their cars. In this case presumably many more commuters would choose to use urban bus, trolley, and subway transport as the cheaper option, even at a transit fare that covered the entire average total cost of the public transit system.

Because gasoline prices (including federal and state taxes) are still at levels that do not force auto drivers to shift to mass transit, virtually all mass-transit systems in the United States require some form of subsidy from local, state, and federal government. These subsidies are quite large. According to data from the National Transit Database, revenue from fares covered only only one-third of the operating expenses of transit systems in 2004 (Federal Transit Administration 2019).

Normally, this would suggest that automobile drivers are subsidizing mass-transit riders. But given rising congestion costs on highways and roads and the added time and frustration needed to proceed from point A to point B by car, it can be argued that the real subsidy may go in the opposite direction. Those who use private cars to drive to work or to do chores, especially during rush hour, are subsidized by

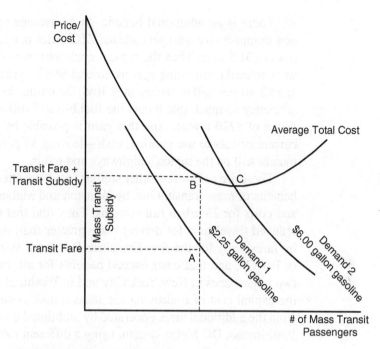

FIGURE 10.2. Mass Transit Subsidy

mass-transit riders. The subsidy does not take the form of a cash allowance, but in the form of less congestion and less time to get to work. In our busy lives, time is money. The commuters who leave their cars behind and rely on mass transit reduce the amount of congestion and drive time for those who continue to use cars. In this case, a subsidy goes from the mass-transit user to those who commute by auto.

The potential direct benefits to auto commuters of reducing highway congestion as a result of some current drivers switching their commute to mass transit has been estimated for the Greater Boston metropolitan area (Bluestone 2019). Because of the region's population growth and strong economy, there are now more than 2.25 million commuters in Greater Boston on a typical workday. Of these, two-thirds or 1.5 million wend their way to work in their private vehicles. These highways were never constructed to handle such crowds, nor an additional projected 50,000 by 2030.

Overall, the average morning commute speed on all the region's highways is now 18.4 miles per hour (mph), with the afternoon commute hardly better at 18.8 mph. That means the typical commuter is spending around 15 hours a week in their autos simply to get to and from work. On an annual basis, this amounts to 720 hours spent in their cars. If you were to count that commute time as work time, a typical workweek is now approaching 55 hours.

But if by improving mass-transit options just 13 percent of these daily highway commuters were now to select public transit for their daily commute, highway flow analysis suggests that the average speed during commuting hours could be doubled to more than 37 mph—still well below the highway speed limit. That improvement would save the typical commuter about 7.5 hours per week in commuting time, or 360 hours per year. For most, this time could be put to much better use.

There is an additional benefit. At an average speed of 18.6 mph, the typical new compact-size auto gets around 21.2 miles per gallon (mpg). At 37.2 mph, this rises to 31.5 mpg. Thus the typical commuter who drives 6,000 miles per year in work-related commuting spends around $680 a year in fuel when gas prices average $2.40 per gallon where they live. Doubling the average speed increases fuel efficiency so much that it cuts the fuel bill to $460 a year—a direct savings to the driver of $220 a year. And this gain is possible by just persuading 13 percent of current drivers to use public transit—leaving 87 percent of Greater Boston's commuters still on the region's highways and roads.

There are only a few other studies that have attempted to measure these social benefits of mass transit. One, by Winston and Maheshri (2006), examines benefits and costs for 25 urban rail systems. They find that the social benefits—including reduced travel time for drivers—are greater than the subsidies (costs not covered by fares) only for the San Francisco Bay Area system (Bay Area Rapid Transit, or BART), and that costs exceed benefits for all the other systems, including the two largest ones in New York City and in Washington, DC. Their argument is that the capital cost of improving the mass-transit system exceeds the added revenue from the additional fares generated by additional transit users. Another study of the Washington, DC Metro system, using a different methodology, found the opposite: net social benefits were positive, with congestion-reduction benefits of the system far larger than the subsidies (Nelson et al. 2007). This occurs when there is a good deal of excess capacity in the mass-transit system and thus little additional cost to improve and expand the system.

The controversy continues. But before we examine the various policy alternatives available for addressing the externalities caused by the movement of people and goods, as well as the mobility needs of those without access to automobiles, we need to explore the supply side of urban transportation markets. How have past decisions affected the array of transportation options available to us today?

The Supply Side of Metropolitan Transportation

If transportation was similar to most other goods, we would have a highly competitive market in which there were many producers, each accounting for only a small amount of total output. It would be relatively easy for new producers to enter the market on a small scale if they were attracted by profitable opportunities. Economist Adam Smith's "invisible hand"—the assertion that many independent producers interacting in a market with many independent buyers results in a socially optimal outcome—would ensure that the result of each producer acting in their own self-interest would be low prices and a large array of choice.

But the transportation market is different. As is true of other components of a metropolitan area's physical infrastructure, transportation networks are subject to large economies of scale. Transportation networks are another example of a natural monopoly in which it is more efficient for one large supplier to produce the entire output. In this case we can refer to the highways, roads, and metro rail systems that have enormous economies of scale as natural monopolies. In most cases, but not all, federal, state, or local government pays for their construction and maintenance. Therefore, in looking at the supply side of metropolitan area transportation, we are really examining the decisions about infrastructure investment made by the public sector.

Before the steam engine, the first large-scale transportation systems took the form of canals, the most famous being the Erie Canal in New York State, first proposed in 1808 and completed in 1825. The canal systems of the early nineteenth century gave way to the railroads, with their construction beginning in the middle of that century. By the late nineteenth and early twentieth centuries rail lines were built not only to facilitate transportation between cities, but most importantly, within them. Before the advent of the automobile and truck and the construction of hardened road surfaces, rail was the fastest and most convenient form of transportation for passengers and freight within the city. Early photos of major cities throughout the world show trolleys and their rail tracks running through their streets.

Because of the extraordinarily high fixed costs and large scale of these systems, state and local governments played a crucial role in their creation. In some instances, these were government projects; in others, private developers received franchise rights as well as some financial support from state and local governments. Eventually, most of these private systems were no longer profitable and were taken over by government agencies. The same transformation from private ownership to public we saw in the case of water and sewer systems applied to transportation.

Although state and local governments were building roadways from the 1920s through the early part of the 1950s to accommodate the increasing popularity of the automobile, the passage of the federal government's 1956 National Interstate and Defense Highways Act profoundly changed the transportation and land-use patterns of US metropolitan areas. This legislation created the Highway Trust Fund (HTF). All proceeds from the federal gasoline tax would go directly into this earmarked fund. Until the early 1970s, the fund could be used for one purpose only: to build interstate highways.

As the highway network grew, automobile travel became ever more attractive and feasible. With more drivers on the road and more miles driven, gasoline tax revenues continued to grow and the highway trust fund coffers were filled, and so it became easy to finance round after round of highway construction. Subsidies increase the demand for whatever is subsidized. Highways are perhaps America's best example.

The flip side of this positive reinforcement loop for motorists was that as commuters abandoned public transit for private automobiles, revenues from fare collections fell, transit agencies faced budget problems that necessitated cuts in service, and poorer-quality service drove more commuters away from transit and toward automobiles. The United States became more reliant on highways and on the low-density suburban expansion they spawned.

Issues in Contemporary Metropolitan Transportation Policy

In the twenty-first century, we live with transportation infrastructure decisions that were made 50, 100, and even 150 years ago. How can we make the best use of what we currently have, and how can we make wise decisions about transportation infrastructure investment now so that future generations will have a more reliable, environmentally friendly system for their use? These are not easy questions to answer, and even in instances where there is substantial agreement about the nature of the problem, there is no clear agreement among policymakers about the best solution.

Short-Run Issues: Getting Prices Right

Tomatoes are cheap and delicious in the summertime, when they are easy to grow in many parts of the country. They are more expensive and often not as tasty in the winter, when many are grown with greater effort and expense inside special hothouses. Consumers will buy more tomatoes when they are cheaper, fewer when they are more expensive. In the tomato market, the lower summer price and the higher winter price reflect the actual difference in production costs. The market works the way it is supposed to work. Prices, which reflect underlying production costs, send the right signals to consumers who change their buying behavior accordingly.

In a market system, prices can play an extremely useful role in guiding consumer choice but only if they reflect accurate cost information. If the price a consumer faces does not accurately reflect the cost of making that choice, decisions will be distorted. When the cost to drive one's own car does not reflect the full cost to society of making that choice, those who drive will tend to make too many car trips, drive too many miles, and drive during the "wrong" time of day. One issue for getting prices right is that automobile transportation is generally priced too low, and the underpricing is more extreme during the rush-hour commute. Another, as noted earlier, is that the actual—though often unacknowledged and implicit—subsidy to the rush-hour motorist is often greater than the explicit subsidy given to transit riders, thereby distorting the choice between automobile and transit. What would we need to do to get prices right?

Although the federal gasoline tax is often referred to as a "user tax" because motorists' payments are correlated with the amount of driving they do and the tax revenues are earmarked for transportation projects, it does not actually fit that description. A true **user tax** requires consumers to pay the full cost of their activity. In the case of the federal gasoline tax, there are many **cross-subsidies**. Drivers in some states receive more from the Highway Trust Fund (HTF) than they contribute. Over the period from 1956 to 2002, for example, Alaska received six and a half times as much funding from the HTF as its drivers contributed (Wachs 2005). Other cross-subsidies are said to favor drivers of heavy trucks over lighter vehicles.

Cross-subsidies affect state gasoline tax receipts and expenditures as well. In Ohio, some of the funds received from state fuel taxes are distributed equally across the state's 88 counties so that motorists in dense urban areas end up subsidizing the roadways of the state's rural areas. Funds generated in urban areas with greater road maintenance requirements are often siphoned off to rural areas with less pressing needs (Hill et al. 2005). As in the case of the HTF before the 1970s, Ohio's receipts from fuel taxes may be used only for highways and not for public transit. These constraints occur in many other states as well and are barriers to a more efficient use of transportation revenues and resources.

Economists are fond of reminding people that there is "no free lunch," meaning that everything has an opportunity cost and that it is being paid by someone, somewhere, even if the good is provided free of charge to the consumer. Consider the case of free parking provided to employees who drive to work. There were costs involved in acquiring the land and in building the parking structures or paving the parking lots. If businesses deduct these costs from their taxes as business expenses, it means that taxpayers in general are subsidizing those employees who drive to work. As Donald Shoup argues in *The High Cost of Free Parking* (2005, p. 2), "If drivers don't pay for parking, who does? Everyone does, even if they don't drive. Initially the developer pays for the required parking, but soon the tenants do, and then their customers, and so on, until the cost of parking has diffused everywhere in the economy."

Shoup argues that ubiquitous free parking distorts the consumers' choice of travel mode because of its implicit subsidy to motorists. In the case of employers' subsidizing parking for their workers, Shoup estimates that the total variable cost per day for a typical commuter, including operating costs plus parking cost, would be $8.09; with employer-provided free parking, it is only $2.32. Free parking subsidizes the commuting motorist for more than two-thirds of the variable costs of driving to work.

The externalities of congestion, pollution, and accidents are other ways that the motorist fails to confront the actual cost of his behavior. As we demonstrated in Chapter 7, the question of what, if any, toll to charge for a car crossing a bridge depends in part on whether the bridge has reached its capacity. Once the bridge is congested, another driver trying to cross increases travel time not only for themselves but for other drivers as well.

There are many instances in which consumers will face higher prices for a given product depending on the timing of their demand. In-season rates for airplane travel or resort hotels are higher than they would be for those who are willing to travel offseason. Movie theaters charge higher prices for evening shows than for matinees. Restaurants might offer "early bird specials" for diners who are willing to come in before the evening rush. In all these instances there is a fixed seating capacity, and building additional capacity would be difficult and expensive. There are times when the demand is higher than can be easily accommodated and other times when there is a good deal of excess capacity. Charging different prices for the peak load versus the off-peak demand helps to make better use of the existing capacity by shifting some of the demand to a time when it can more easily be handled.

Although peak-load pricing is common in the private sector, it has not been used as much in the public sector. Many economists argue that it should be, and that is their basis for endorsing **congestion pricing** for highways. During times of low off-peak demand when there is excess capacity, the cost of allowing one additional driver on the road is minimal and therefore there is no need to charge a congestion toll. Once the road has reached its capacity, the cost of adding each additional driver rises. Some of these costs are borne by the driver, but others are spillover costs that the driver does not consider. The purpose of the congestion toll is to have the driver take these spillover costs into account.

As Figure 10.3 shows, there is a greater and more inelastic demand (D_1) for highway travel during the morning and evening rush hour, as going to and from work cannot be avoided or postponed. At other times of the day, the demand for highway use is much smaller and more elastic (D_2)—say, two to four o'clock in the morning. The marginal cost of allowing one more car on the highway in the wee hours of the morning is trivial, since the highway is not likely to be congested. Once congestion begins and cars slow down during rush hour, the marginal private cost (MPC) of having one extra car traveling on the highway begins to rise and continues to climb as more cars try to travel at the same time. The individual driver experiences the increase in marginal private cost. It takes commuters more time to get to work, they use more gasoline, they bear the frustration of crawling along in traffic, and they are aware that this stop-and-go driving will mean extra maintenance expenses to keep their cars in good working order.

In addition to the increasing marginal private cost as congestion increases, there is an even more sharply increasing marginal social cost (MSC): the sum of marginal private cost and the external cost imposed on others. For instance, the concentration of automobile exhaust fumes pollutes the neighborhoods in which the congestion is occurring and hence their residents may suffer higher levels of respiratory illnesses. In addition, employers will not operate as efficiently when workers are delayed by traffic, and emergency vehicles will not be able to make their way through traffic jams in a timely fashion.

The idea of congestion pricing is to charge a toll equivalent to these external costs. If solo motorists face a higher price for traveling during congested times, they might have the incentive to change their behavior—to carpool or to select a different mode of transportation. New York City is the first US city to adopt

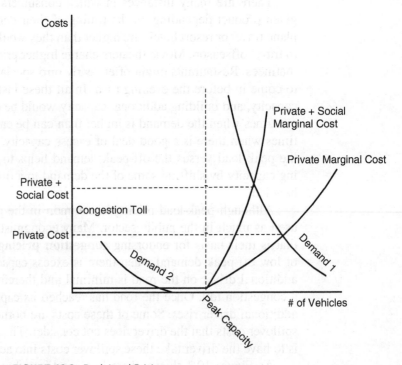

FIGURE 10.3. Peak Load Pricing

congestion pricing in the form of fees to enter the central business district. A limited program applying only to yellow taxis and ride-hail services such as Uber and Lyft began in February 2019. A much more comprehensive program was to have started in 2021 but was delayed. These initiatives build on successful experiences with congestion pricing in Singapore, London, and Stockholm.

Singapore has had congestion pricing since 1975, when it instituted a flat fee for vehicles entering the congestion zone at certain hours of high demand. The program has been modified several times, including expansion of the size of the zone and extension of congested time periods. Starting in 1988, electronic road pricing with the use of in-vehicle transponders has allowed for varying fees by time of day, location, and vehicle type. As the program expanded, so have improvements in public transit options. London's congestion pricing started in 2003. The zone has expanded, and as a result public transit options have been improved. The system charges a flat fee and relies on closed-circuit cameras. Stockholm introduced a six-month trial of congestion zone pricing in early 2006 and reintroduced it on a permanent basis in mid-2007. The system uses overhead gantries and transponders with license plate photos for vehicles without transponders. While the Singapore and London initiatives were originally focused on reducing congestion, newer initiatives in Stockholm, Madrid, and other European cities give more explicit attention to the reduction of greenhouse gases by targeting high-emission vehicles (US Dept. of Transportation 2017).

Congestion pricing can take many specific forms. On some toll roads in the United States, higher tolls are charged during rush hours. Most recently, some areas have been expanding the use of special carpool lanes—high-occupancy vehicle (HOV) lanes developed to encourage carpooling. In some cities, these lanes have been renamed HOT (high-occupancy plus toll) lanes. In the case of Interstate 15 in San Diego, for example, the price for single-occupancy vehicles to enter the HOT lane changes every few minutes with the level of congestion. Single-occupancy motorists then have a choice of whether to spend more time or more money to get to their destination. As the number of cars equipped with transponders continues to grow, it will be feasible to use congestion pricing in a wider variety of situations.

Even if automobile travel occurs under free-flow circumstances where there is no congestion, every additional driver adds to air pollution and the emission of greenhouse gases unless they are driving a fully electric vehicle, and even then the need for more electric generating capacity to fuel auto needs contributes something to greenhouse gas emissions. These are externalities generated by motorists for which they are generally not forced to pay, and therefore another way that automobile travel is underpriced. As we have seen during periods of gasoline price spikes, consumers will respond to higher prices with efforts to change their behavior. Sales of gas-guzzling vehicles fall off dramatically. Newspapers run feature articles about motorists switching to bicycles or public transit. There have even been reports of increased ridership on school buses as growing numbers of parents forgo the usual practice of driving their children to school. Yet unless gasoline prices are high, there is little incentive to switch to these modes of transit.

All this implies that raising gasoline taxes would be an effective way to counteract the underpricing of automobile travel. Following good market principles, higher gasoline prices would do all the following:

- More commuters would use mass transit, which produces fewer emissions per passenger.

- Motorists would purchase more fuel-efficient cars reducing the amount of emissions and greenhouse gases per mile.

- Households would consider living closer to the central city or closer to their jobs in order to reduce the cost of commuting, thereby reducing emissions.

And yet even as most automobiles and trucks continue to spew pollution from the combustion of fossil fuels, a growing segment of motorists in the future will be driving less-polluting vehicles such as hybrids or electric-powered. This has led to interest in replacing the gasoline tax altogether and shifting to a vehicle-miles-traveled (VMT) tax. As Langer, Maheshir, and Winston (2017, p. 45) note, "a major potential efficiency advantage in the long run of the VMT tax over the gasoline tax is that it could be implemented to vary with traffic volumes on different roads at different times of day. And it could be implemented to vary with pollution levels in different geographical areas at different times of the year and with the riskiness of different drivers to set differentiated prices for motorists' road use that could accurately approximate the true social marginal costs of automobile travel." Getting prices right would encourage motorists to change their behavior and thereby lead to a more efficient use of existing resources.

While the focus of congestion pricing has been the central business district, we are now finding that public thoroughfares are scarce commodities in residential districts. The increased volume of package deliveries described earlier has created its own problems of congestion and pollution both inside central business districts and beyond. How can we address the problem of "the last mile"—the final, most challenging phase of delivering parcels to the customer's front door? One solution is to switch from delivery trucks to electric cargo bikes that are more maneuverable, take up less space, and are nonpolluting. UPS introduced cargo bikes in Hamburg, Germany in 2012. They are also used in Paris, London, Dublin, and other cities. New York has adopted such a program, as has Seattle (Hu and Haag 2019). Another solution is to impose a surcharge on e-commerce delivery, something already proposed in Paris (O'Sullivan 2019). Now there are experiments with drones delivering packages.

Even if electric cargo bikes and drones can reduce the negative externalities caused by delivery trucks, we still need to address the problem of city streets as scarce commodities where the needs of pedestrians, bicyclists, and motorists often clash. Policy interventions might include areas where cars are excluded, such as bus-only thoroughfares or areas that are reserved for pedestrians and bicyclists, or the use of variable pricing for parking meters to ration the limited number of parking spaces during peak times.

While we often rely on new technology to solve some of our most pressing problems, some technological developments might ultimately exacerbate the problem of congestion. A study by McKinsey & Company (Joerss et al. 2016) predicts that in the not-too-distant future, while drones can be used for delivery in areas with low population density, the solution for urban areas is likely to involve autonomous ground vehicles including **droids**, similar in concept to autonomous vehicles for passenger use. Sam Schwartz, a former New York City traffic commissioner and coauthor of *No One at the Wheel: Driverless Cars and the Road of the Future* (2018), acknowledges that autonomous vehicles are likely to reduce traffic deaths dramatically, a strong argument in their favor. Yet he warns that progress toward shared streets could be undone if autonomous vehicles are given primacy over pedestrians and bicyclists.

Long-Run Issues: Deciding on Future Transportation Infrastructure Investment

What about the future? What factors should policymakers consider in making decisions about new investment in transportation infrastructure?

The Interstate highway system has been substantially complete since 1991, and a new agenda for transportation infrastructure investment is the subject of continuing debate. Should we continue to encourage dependence on private vehicles? How do we address the mobility and access needs of those who are unable to drive because of age, infirmity, or poverty? If we are to encourage other transportation modes including public transit, bicycles, and walking, what does that imply for changes in land-use policy?

One fundamental question is whether it is possible to solve traffic congestion problems by building more highway capacity. In his biography of Robert Moses, *The Power Broker: Robert Moses and the Fall of New York*, Robert Caro (1974) describes Moses's enthusiasm for highway construction during the several decades that he wielded extraordinary power in shaping the New York City metropolitan area's transportation network. Each time a new highway experienced congestion, Moses's solution was to build another. Decade after decade, new capacity was added but congestion did not diminish. Caro reports that Moses resisted the extension of public transit to the developing suburbs by rejecting proposals to build highway median strips that were capable of accommodating rail transit and by designing highway overpasses that were too low to allow clearance for buses.

Why does it seem so difficult to build our way out of congestion? The tendency of new road capacity to generate additional traffic is called "induced traffic." According to Anthony Downs (2004) of the Brookings Institution, it is the result of a "triple convergence." First, when the new road opens, if it seems to offer a faster way to travel, commuters will be induced to shift the time they travel during the day. Off-peak travelers will return to traveling during peak hours. Second, commuters will switch their route from the road they are currently using to the new one. And third, some mass-transit commuters will shift their mode to highway use. In the end, congestion will occur soon after the additional highway is built. Supply creates its own demand.

In 1991, Congress made a dramatic change in federal transportation policy when it passed the Intermodal Surface Transportation Efficiency Act (ISTEA, pronounced "ice tea"). With the substantial completion of the Interstate highway system, the new legislation focused on metropolitan transportation planning, development of alternatives to automobile transportation, linking transportation modes such as bus-rail links, and making changes in transportation investment that would promote greater compliance with the Clean Air Act. It allowed flexibility in how metropolitan areas used their federal transportation dollars and shifted the focus of lessening traffic congestion by reducing the necessity of travel via private automobile (Vuchic 1999).

Two subsequent federal laws, including the 1998 Transportation Equity Act for the 21st Century (TEA-21) and the 2005 Safe, Accountable, Flexible, Efficient Transportation Equity Act: A Legacy for Users (SAFETEA-LU), have preserved these policy shifts, but this remains a contentious area. Proponents of automobile transportation and highway construction oppose this new approach. They argue that most public transit requires high-density development along transportation corridors and that such investment is not justified in a nation that has voted with its feet for low-density development.

To the extent that an increase in auto and truck use is associated with adverse health, environmental, economic, and community cohesion consequences, we can learn from efforts elsewhere to design denser multiuse developments. While the total amount of miles has increased by nearly 10 percent in the United States since 2010, the comparable figures are much lower in other countries that have found alternatives to the private automobile. Total mileage has increased over the past decade by only 1.4 percent in the United Kingdom, 6.4 percent in France, and 6.7 percent in Germany, while total highway and road miles traveled have actually declined in Denmark (-0.1%), Spain (-3.8%), and Finland (-9.7%) (Kane 2020).

Given the environmental concerns about greenhouse gas emission from air travel, intercity rail transportation is another area where the experience of cities outside the United States is instructive. Within the United States, it is only along the densely packed Northeast Corridor that rail transportation is competitive with air transportation. In Europe and Asia planes and high-speed trains are competitive on routes under 600 miles, including Rome–Milan, Tokyo–Osaka, and Paris–London. For routes less than 300 miles the train is often preferable, for the total travel time by rail is less than that involved in traveling to an airport, waiting for your plane to depart, and then having to travel to your ultimate destination from the airport in that city (Grabar 2019).

Transportation Equity Issues

Finally, aside from the longer-term efficiency issues, there are additional equity issues that surround transportation planning. How do we provide mobility for those who are too young, too old, too infirm, or too poor to drive? There is a growing interest in fare-free public transportation. Estonia made public transportation free in their capital city of Tallinn in 2013 and extended it nationwide in 2020. Kansas City, Missouri became the first major city to offer fare-free public transit in 2020.

Even free fares along existing routes may not be enough to solve the problem if they do not go from the desired point A to the desired point B. If there is a spatial mismatch between the poor who are concentrated in the central cities and the availability of new jobs located on the periphery of the metropolitan area, there are three logical alternatives for reducing the severity of the problem: (1) move jobs closer to the areas where poor people are concentrated (this is the aim of the enterprise zone and empowerment zone programs that provide incentives for firms to locate in low-income areas); (2) move people closer to where the new jobs are located (this is one of the aims of the Moving to Opportunity program that helps low-income families move to affordable housing in the suburbs); or (3) improve the transportation options available to the poor so that they can more easily overcome the barrier of spatial separation between home and workplace.

Because commuter rail systems were designed to transport suburban residents to jobs in the central city, the stations are in residential areas. Therefore, these systems do not work well to satisfy the needs of reverse commuters—those who commute from central city homes to widely dispersed suburban job locations. Programs that subsidize car ownership for inner-city residents have been viewed with promise. Other alternatives to solving the mobility needs of those who cannot drive focus on "para-transit," which involves the use of small vans that are responsive to demand and whose dispatchers devise flexible routes that depend on the origins and destinations of those who wish to travel at any given time on any given day. Developing Uber- and Lyft-type transport from suburban commuter rail stations to places of employment might make it possible for more reverse commuters to avail themselves of mass transit.

Moreover, as life expectancies increase and as baby-boom drivers age, we need to pay more attention to the mobility needs of the elderly. As Rosenbloom (2005) notes, we do not understand these needs very well because as some elders might become too infirm to drive, paradoxically many others with limited ability to walk or climb steps are still fully capable of driving. For this latter group, driving is what allows them to maintain their independence.

Ultimately, for all the reasons we have explored in this chapter, if we are to meet the transportation needs of cities and towns in the future, we will need to have a better understanding of externalities, subsidies, commuting needs, and land-use patterns, and how each of these affects mobility and independence not just for the poor, the elderly, and infirm, but for all of us. With changing demographics, growing environmental concerns, and changing life styles, what kind of urban transportation system will be best for individual households as well as the entire planet in the years to come?

References

Bluestone, Barry. 2019. "Who Benefits from Public Transit? Count Auto Commuters as Potential #1 Beneficiaries." Unpublished OpEd. Boston, Massachusetts.

Caro, Robert. 1974. *The Power Broker: Robert Moses and the Fall of New York.* New York: Knopf.

Downs, Anthony. 2004. *Still Stuck in Traffic*. Washington, DC: Brookings Institution Press.

Federal Highway Administration. 2017a. *Lessons Learned From International Experience in Congestion Pricing.* Washington, DC: Department of Transportation.

Federal Highway Administration. 2017b. *Summary of Travel Trends.* Washington, DC: Department of Transportation.

Federal Transit Authority, U.S. Department of Transporation. 2019. *National Transit Database–2018 National Transit Summaries and Trends: Appendix*, December.

Grabar, Henry. 2019. "There's Nothing Ridiculous About Trains Replacing Planes." *Slate*, February 12.

Hill, Edward, Billie Geyer, Kevin O'Brien, Claudette Robey, John Brennan, and Robert Puentes. 2005. "Slanted Pavement: How Ohio's Highway Spending Shortchanges Cities and Suburbs." In *Taking the High Road: A Metropolitan Agenda for Transportation Reform*, edited by Bruce Katz and Robert Puentes. Washington, DC: Brookings Institution Press, pp. 101–138.

Hu, Winnie, and Matthew Haag. 2019. "Park It, Trucks: Here Come New York's Cargo Bikes." *New York Times*, December 4.

Joerss, Martin, Jurgen Schroder, Florian Neuhaus, Christoph Klink, and Florian Mann. 2016. *Parcel Delivery: The Future of Last Mile.* September. New York: McKinsey & Company.

Kane, Joseph W. 2020. "Banning Cars Won't Solve America's Bigger Transportation Problem: Long Trips." January 6. Washington, DC: Brookings Institution.

Langer, Ashley, Vikram Maheshri, and Clifford Winston. 2017. "From Gallons to Miles: A Disaggregate Analysis of Automobile Travel and Externality Taxes." *Journal of Public Economics* 152, August: 34–46.

Meyer, John R., John F. Kain, and Martin Wohl. 1965. *The Urban Transportation Problem.* Cambridge, MA: Harvard University Press.

Nelson, Peter, Andrew Baglino, Winston Harrington, Elena Safirova, and Abram Lipman. 2007. "Transit in Washington, DC: Current Benefits and Optimal Level of Provision." *Journal of Urban Economics* 62, no. 2: 231–251.

O'Sullivan, Feargus. 2019. "Paris Wants a Tax to Cover Amazon Delivery Impacts." *Citylab*, November.

Rosenbloom, Sandra. 2005. "The Mobility Needs of Older Americans: Implications for Transportation Reauthorization." In *Taking the High Road: A Metropolitan Agenda for Transportation Reform*, edited by Bruce Katz and Robert Puentes. Washington, DC: Brookings Institution Press, pp. 227–256.

Schwartz, Samuel I., and Karen Kelly. 2018. *No One at the Wheel: Driverless Cars and the Road of the Future.* New York: Public Affairs.

Shoup, Donald. 2005. *The High Cost of Free Parking.* Chicago: American Planning Association.

US Postal Service. 2019. "A Decade of Facts & Figures." February 26. Washington, DC: US Postal Service.

Vuchic, Vukan R. 1999. *Transportation for Livable Cities.* New Brunswick, NJ: Rutgers University, Center for Urban Policy Research.

Wachs, Martin. 2005. "Improving Efficiency and Equity and Transportation Finance." In *Taking the High Road: A Metropolitan Agenda for Transportation Reform,* edited by Bruce Katz and Robert Puentes. Washington, DC: Brookings Institution Press, pp. 77–100.

Winston, Clifford, and Vikram Maheshri. 2006. "On the Social Desirability of Urban Rail Transit Systems." *Journal of Urban Economics,* 62, no. 2: 362–382.

Questions and Exercises

1. As Chapter 10 articulates, one of the major issues facing metropolitan areas is the heavy traffic on their roadways, particularly during certain hours of the day. Data on traffic congestion for US cities can be found in the Texas Transportation Institute's *Urban Mobility Report,* available at http://mobility.tamu.edu. Included in the report is a table of the annual delays during peak period travel from 1982 through a most recent year.

   • Select 10 cities of your choice and discuss what was the change in the annual delay per traveler for each of those cities between 1982 and the latest year available.

   • Did most of this change occur between 1982 and 1995, or after 1995?

2. For each of the 10 urban areas you selected, how much excess fuel was consumed due to congestion delays? According to this table, what was the cost of congestion for travelers in each of those urban areas? Examine the explanation of the congestion cost estimates found in the notes at the bottom of the table. How, if at all, does the estimation consider each of the following types of costs: opportunity costs, private costs, and social costs? Explain.

   As Chapter 10 discusses, public transportation is typically subsidized by local, state, or federal governments. The extent to which the operating expenses are subsidized varies from one metropolitan area to another. The pertinent data on the recovery rate—the percentage of operating funds that are recovered from fare revenues—are published by the Federal Transit Administration in its National Transit Database (NTD). These data can be accessed through the NTD's website at https://www.transit.dot.gov/sites/fta.dot.gov/files/docs/ntd/data-product/134406/2018-ntst-appendix_0.pdf

3. Select three metro areas of your choice and then for each select a public transit agency.

- For each of these three metro area transit agencies, examine its operational characteristics including types of vehicles used in each region.

- How do the operational characteristics vary across the three metro areas you are examining?

- How do the performance measures in terms of operating expenses stack up in the three metro areas you are following?

- Using data for various years for one of the three metro areas you selected, examine the trend in operational characteristics and performance measures. Is this public transit system expanding or contracting in terms of vehicles in service and operating expenses?

Urban Social Infrastructure: Public Health, Welfare Policies, and Public Amenities

LEARNING OBJECTIVES

- Identify three major indicators of a population's health and describe how the United States fares on these indicators compared with other nations

- Explain the role of public health departments in dealing with infectious diseases as well as with chronic health conditions

- Describe the concept of "deaths of despair" and identify which demographic groups are the most affected by it and explain why

- Describe the elements of urban public amenities and apply them to the creation of public libraries and pastoral parks

- Explain how the original purpose of public libraries and pastoral parks have evolved from their nineteenth-century origins

As we have seen in previous chapters, in rural areas where there may be no more than a few people per acre or per square mile, externalities are not a major factor. Yet as population density increases and people live near each other, spillover effects—both positive and negative—can grow exponentially. As a result, metropolitan areas are where we need to be most concerned about reducing the negative externalities of density, such as when the COVID-19 pandemic swept across the globe in 2020. Public health policies dominated all others during that tragic period. By contrast, during normal times the provision of such urban public amenities as parks and playgrounds where social gatherings can take place provide more sanguine externalities.

These elements of urban social infrastructure provide valuable contributions to both the economic vitality and the quality of life in metropolitan areas. The social dynamics of cities and suburbs, as well as the specific location decisions of businesses and families, have been significantly shaped by health and welfare issues and by the effectiveness of the public infrastructure developed to deal with them. In addition, social infrastructure itself has spillover effects. The ways and extent to which cities provide public services affect the cohesiveness of communities, their norms and values, and their residents' sense of the opportunities available to them.

Public Health Indicators

Three important measures of a population's health are life expectancy, **infant mortality**, and access to health insurance. By these measures, the United States lags far behind other developed nations. Table 11.1 shows that in 2019 the United States ranked 27th out of 34 developed countries in life expectancy, with an average life expectancy of 79.1 years compared, for example, with Japan's 84.6 years.

Life expectancy varies across metropolitan areas. Wealthier Americans have life expectancies comparable to, or even longer, than Japan's. Poorer households

TABLE 11.1.   LIFE EXPECTANCY AT BIRTH - 2019

Japan	84.6
Switzerland	83.8
Spain	83.5
Italy	83.4
Australia	83.4
Iceland	83.0
Israel	83.0
South Korea	83.0
Sweden	82.8
France	82.7
Norway	82.4
Canada	82.4
Ireland	82.3
Netherlands	82.3
New Zealand	82.3
Luxembourg	82.3
Greece	82.2
Portugal	82.1
Finland	81.9
Belgium	81.6
Austria	81.5

Germany	81.3
United Kingdom	81.3
Slovenia	81.3
Denmark	80.9
Czech Republic	79.4
United States	79.1
Cuba	78.8
Poland	78.7
Turkey	77.7
Hungary	76.9
China	77.5
Argentina	76.7
Brazil	76.7

Source: World Health Organization

fare worse. Yet even here, place matters. Within the bottom income quartile, life expectancy is higher in wealthier metropolitan areas. Lower income individuals have a life expectancy of 81.8 years in the New York City metropolitan area, compared with only 77.4 years in the Gary, Indiana metro area (Chetty et al. 2016). Researchers attribute this 4.4-year difference in part to public health policies enacted by these wealthier, more highly educated metropolitan areas, including smoking bans and greater funding for public services. Note that taking income into account plus location, there is a better than 10-year difference in mean life expectancy. This is by no means trivial.

The United States lags many other developed countries in its infant mortality rate—ranking 29th out of 35 countries, as shown in Figure 11.1. In this instance, variation by race and level of urbanization matter. Infant mortality rates, while still higher than in most developed countries, are lowest for Whites in large urban counties. Latinx in large urban counties have rates similar to Whites. Blacks, however, have rates more than double the rates for the other two groups at every level of urbanization. The rate for Blacks in nonmetropolitan rural areas is more than 12 per 1,000, a rate comparable to that of Turkey or Mexico (see Figure 11.2).

Across racial and ethnic lines, residents of nonmetropolitan areas tend to have worse health outcomes than those in metro areas. The higher infant death rates are associated with risk factors that are more common in nonmetropolitan areas including smoking, obesity, and poverty, all of which tend to be more common in rural areas across all racial/ethnic groups. Nonmetropolitan areas have fewer healthcare providers and residents often live farther away from healthcare resources, making it difficult to access care (Womack et al. 2020).

Part of the explanation for the poor outcomes on life expectancy and infant mortality is that unlike most other developed countries, the United States does not

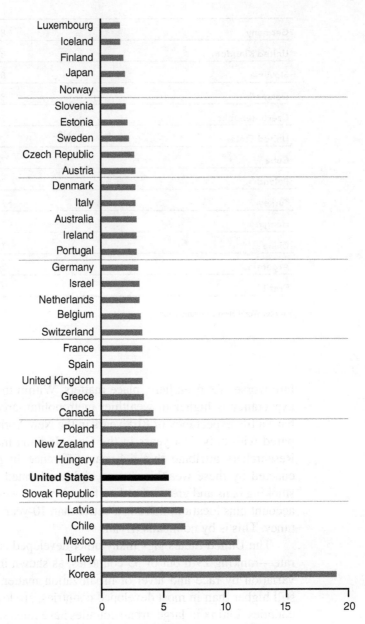

FIGURE 11.1. Infant Mortality Rate Among OECD Countries, 2015

Source: United Health Foundation, America's Health Rankings Annual Report, 2016, p. 24. https://assets. americashealthrankings.org/app/uploads/ahr16-completerev.pdf

have universal health insurance coverage. Although the Affordable Care Act of 2010 (ACA) increased coverage nationwide, there is still significant variation by states and localities. The ACA gave states financial incentives to expand **Medicaid** coverage for lower-income households and while most of the states did so, other states chose not to. As shown in Table 11.2 the variation in uninsured rates across metropolitan areas is sizeable. No more than 3 percent of the population lack health insurance in the five MSAs with the lowest rates. Four of these MSAs are

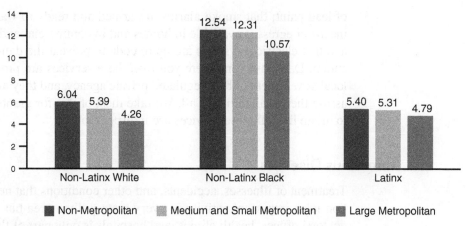

FIGURE 11.2. Infant Mortality Rates by Urbanization Level and Race and Latinx Origin of Mother, 2014–2016 (per 1,000 Live Births)

Source: Womack et al. 2019

| TABLE 11.2. | HIGHEST AND LOWEST RATES OF HEALTH INSURANCE BY METRO AREA, PERCENT NOT COVERED BY PRIVATE OR PUBLIC INSURANCE, 2017 |

HIGHEST AND LOWEST UNINSURED RATES BY MSA, 2017			
MSAs with Lowest Uninsured Rates	Uninsured Rate	MSAs with Highest Uninsured Rates	Uninsured Rate
1. Pittsfeld, MA	2.1%	1. McAllen-Edinburg-Mission, TX	30.0%
2. Springfeld, MA	2.6%	2. Laredo, TX	28.9%
3. Ann Arbor, MI	2.7%	3. Brownsville-Harlingen, TX	27.6%
4. Worcester, MA	2.9%	4. Odessa, TX	21.1%
5. Boston-Cambridge-Newton, MA	3.0%	5. El Paso, TX	20.6%

Source: State Health Access Data Assistance Center. 2018. "Health Insurance Coverage: Uninsurance by Metro Areas in 2017." November 16, p. 3.

in Massachusetts, which adopted a precursor to the ACA in 2006. Ann Arbor, Michigan, a university town with a highly educated population, ranks third best in terms of its insurance coverage. By contrast, five MSAs in Texas, one of the states that did not expand Medicaid coverage, have uninsured rates of 20 percent or more, with the McAllen-Edinburg-Mission MSA having the highest rate of 30 percent.

The Provision of Public Health Services

Most metro areas rely on a variety of local agencies to provide a battery of health-related services. As discussed in Chapter 9, water and sewer systems are essential parts of the health system. In addition, local health boards regulate eating and drinking establishments to give us some reasonable assurance that the food we eat will not make us ill. Emergency medical technicians (EMTs) and ambulance service are available 24/7 in the case of an accident or major illness. Local housing inspection services exist to make sure that children are protected from the dangers of lead paint; that smoke alarms are armed and ready to warn of fire; that a safe means of egress is available in homes and in commercial and industrial buildings; and that electrical systems are up to code to prevent the danger of fire or electrocution. Depending on where you live, these services are provided directly by the local government or by a regulated private agency, and they are often subsidized to assure their availability to all. We take most of this for granted but when it comes to urban life, all these services are indispensable.

Infectious Diseases

Treatment of illnesses, accidents, and other conditions that need medical intervention is an important activity in every metropolitan area but medical treatment at doctors' offices, health clinics, and hospitals is only part of the urban health infrastructure. The other part focuses on keeping people healthy. This is the province of municipal health departments and other public health agencies.

By the early nineteenth century it was recognized that many diseases were **contagious** and passed from one person to another, although the exact means by which the diseases were transmitted had not been determined (Tomes 1998). While the wealthy could try to flee from cities that were in the early stages of **epidemics**, this was not an option for most residents. To protect the health of residents and the activities within cities, one of the early functions of city government was the quarantining of people with **communicable diseases** (Duffy 1990). This applied to city residents and their families as well as to crew members from the ships and boats that frequently arrived in city ports (Humphreys 1992). Quarantining as an urban public health measure continued to be the basic defense against potential epidemics throughout most of the nineteenth century.

The establishment and enforcement of quarantines provided the genesis of modern municipal health departments. During the widespread outbreak of yellow fever between 1793 and 1805, volunteer health committees, the precursor to local health departments, enforced quarantines (Duffy 1990). Recognizing the need to establish legal authority for such efforts, state legislatures in Massachusetts and New York gave municipalities within their borders the authority to appoint local **boards of health** that had the unquestioned power to enforce quarantines during epidemics. Similar authority was subsequently given to local boards of health in the other states.

After the cholera epidemic of 1849–1854 raised public concern regarding sanitary conditions, many city governments commissioned surveys and reports on conditions that affected health in their cities. Subsequently, between 1870 and 1890, they created permanent boards of health (Rosenberg 1987). These initial boards typically served in an advisory role to city government rather than having direct administrative authority for action. Support for the safety of water and sewer systems was one of the key responsibilities of these boards.

It was during this period that the first urban public health programs were created. According to historian Victoria Hallas (2014), the growth of the public health movement and the subsequent Healthy Cities Program in Great Britain gained much of its support from the Health of Towns Association, which was founded in 1844 in Exeter, England. In that same year Frederick Engels published his landmark report,

Conditions of the Working Class, to bring attention to how differences in class and wealth were responsible for health disparities.

In the United States at nearly the same time there were two noteworthy reports related to health in New York City. In 1845 John H. Griscom, New York City's sanitary inspector, published *Sanitary Conditions of the Laboring Population of NYC*, which drew upon health recommendations from the Health of Towns Report that had recently been published in England. Around the time of the US Civil War, a New York City survey of the distribution of infectious diseases by neighborhood revealed the connection between the level of economic prosperity and environmental health. This likely marks the beginning of public health activists making the connection between physical and social planning, with the early public health goals of assuring sanitary conditions and containing infectious diseases.

Public health officials were not the only ones concerned about making their cities healthier. City planners and landscape architects led by Frederick Law Olmstead were concerned with designing cities that would support health. Central Park in Manhattan and Prospect Park in Brooklyn, and the Emerald Necklace of parks in Boston, were designed by Olmstead in the mid-nineteenth century as part of the movement for healthy cities. To Olmstead, public parks were considered the "lungs of the city" where residents could enjoy life in open fields and breathe clean air (Scheer 2001). The planning for public parks within cities was the first step to accepting how design could alter the health of the city.

In the late nineteenth and early twentieth centuries, a deeper understanding emerged about the role of microorganisms in disease. In addition to promoting parks within urban centers and the development of citywide water and sewer systems, local health boards were made responsible for preparing laboratory testing for evidence of bacteria and viruses and educating the populace about the need for sanitary practices in and around the home. With these new roles, both municipal and state boards of health received additional administrative powers and achieved new prominence, not only influencing the response of local government and individual families during outbreaks of major diseases but acting as a constant presence and source of action for public health education, inspection, and research (Duffy 1990).

With the introduction of the first polio vaccine in 1955 and the measles-mumps-rubella (MMR) vaccine in 1963, along with the near eradication of smallpox worldwide by 1980, the perception through much of the late twentieth century—at least in the developed world—was that attention could be shifted from infectious diseases to a new focus on chronic health problems. That perception turned out to be premature. Misguided beliefs about the supposed dangers of the MMR vaccine led to geographically localized epidemics of measles when immunization rates fell below the level required for **herd immunity**—a situation in which high levels of immunization protect not only those who have received the vaccine but those who have not, primarily because they are infants or because their specific health circumstances make vaccination inadvisable. Herd immunity is an example of a pure public good where everyone benefits and has become an important element of public health. Without herd immunity, there are avoidable deaths both among those who are eligible for vaccination and those who are not. In response, some local health agencies rescinded religious exemptions and required proof of vaccination for all children enrolling in schools whether public, private, or parochial.

In 2020, normal life in much of the world was halted by the COVID-19 pandemic. With public health services overwhelmed by this global outbreak and the need to quarantine in place to prevent the further spread of this deadly virus, the world's economy went into recession and **unemployment rates** hit levels not seen since the Great Depression of the 1930s. Particularly in places where precautions to slow the spread of the disease were not enacted early enough, the rapid rise in total cases and in cases severe enough to warrant hospitalization led to local health services being overwhelmed with needs they could not meet. Nothing in our lifetimes could have made us better understand the need for public health and political leaders—in the United States mostly state governors and city mayors—who stepped in to help stop spread this deadly outbreak.

Chronic Illnesses and the Expansion of Public Health Initiatives

While early public health boards advocated for the development of hospitals and other institutions to provide for the care of the sick and injured, over time public health officials have focused on an ever-broader set of policies and programs to keep people healthy and safe. For more than 150 years they have dealt with the quality of water and food being provided in their jurisdictions. They were originally concerned with how health was related to the physical and social environment, particularly in poor neighborhoods where thousands of families were crowded into tenements. More recently, they have drawn attention to lead paint poisoning, asthma, pollution, and violence—recognizing that place matters for health as it does for so many other urban issues (Kawachi and Berkman 2003). They address lifestyle issues contributing to illnesses including high blood pressure, diabetes, lung cancer, obesity, and kidney failure. Their concerns include the problems that are associated with substance abuse, the mentally ill, and individuals being released from prison (Cohen 2007). Today, the purview of public health covers ten different functions that can be grouped into four general categories (Institute of Medicine of the National Academies 2002), as follows.

Assessment

1. Monitor health status to identify community health problems.

2. Diagnose and investigate health problems and health hazards in the community.

Policy Development

3. Inform, educate, and empower people about health issues.

4. Mobilize community partnerships to identify and solve health problems.

5. Develop policies and plans that support individual and community health efforts.

Assurance

6. Enforce laws and regulations that protect health and ensure safety.

7. Link people to needed personal health services and assure the provision of healthcare when otherwise unavailable.

8. Assure a competent public health and personal healthcare workforce.

9. Evaluate effectiveness, accessibility, and quality of personal and population-based health services.

Serving All Functions

10. Research for new insights and innovative solutions to health problems.

What are the elements of a healthy city that current public health boards might promote? The Partnership for Healthy Cities describes itself as "a prestigious global network of cities committed to saving lives by preventing noncommunicable diseases (NCDs) and injuries" (Partnership for Healthy Cities 2020). It is a collaboration of Bloomberg Philanthropies, the World Health Organization, and Vital Strategies (a nonprofit public health organization), and it includes cities across every continent except Antarctica. Currently, 70 cities participate and are supported for implementing one of the following 14 interventions:

- create a smoke-free city

- ban tobacco advertising

- raise tobacco taxes or levies/fees

- tax sugary drinks

- set nutrition standards for foods served and sold in public institutions

- regulate food and drink marketing

- create healthier restaurant environments

- reduce speeding

- increase motorcycle helmet use

- reduce drunk driving

- increase seat belt use

- promote active mobility

- prevent opioid-associated overdose deaths

- enhance public health data and monitoring systems

The first 12 items on the preceding list encompass efforts to alter personal behavior to encourage healthier lifestyles. We have known for decades that smoking causes lung cancer and other illnesses that shorten life expectancy. Similarly, we have known for decades that deaths from automobile accidents can be reduced by driving at lower speeds and wearing seat belts while motorcycle fatalities can be reduced by wearing helmets. More recently, there has been growing concern about increased rates of obesity and the accompanying increase in rates of Type II diabetes, heart disease, and stroke. Hence the encouragement of healthy eating and more physical exercise.

TABLE 11.3. AVERAGE ANNUAL PERCENT CHANGE IN MORTALITY FOR AGE 50–54 BY CAUSE, 1999–2015

COUNTRY OR RACIAL OR ETHNIC GROUP	ALL-CAUSE	DRUGS, ALCOHOL, OR SUICIDE	HEART DISEASE
U.S. White non-Latinx	0.5	5.4	−1.0
U.S. Black non-Latinx	−2.3	0.1	−2.7
U.S. Latinx	−1.5	1.0	−2.5
United Kingdom	−2.1	1.0	−4.0
Ireland	−2.6	3.0	−5.1
Canada	−1.1	2.5	−3.0
Australia	−1.0	2.5	−2.8
France	−1.3	−1.2	−2.9
Germany	−1.9	−2.3	−3.5
Sweden	−2.1	0.8	−3.1
Switzerland	−2.5	−2.6	−4.0
Denmark	−1.8	0.1	−4.7
Netherlands	−2.3	−0.0	−5.5
Spain	−2.1	−0.3	−3.2
Italy	−2.1	−2.2	−4.7
Japan	−2.2	−2.1	−1.4

Sources: National Vital Statistics System; Human Mortality Database; WHO Mortality Database; authors' calculations.

The 13th item, with its focus on opioid-related deaths, is an example of recent interest in "deaths of despair." Case and Deaton (2017) observed that mortality rates for middle-aged non-Latinx Whites have increased over the course of the twenty-first century in the United States in contrast with the pattern in other developed nations and for other groups within the United States. As shown in Table 11.3 these deaths caused by drug overdoses, alcohol abuse, or suicide increased for many demographic groups in the United States as well as in other English-speaking nations including the United Kingdom, Ireland, Canada, and Australia. These deaths were counterbalanced by long-term declines in mortality due to heart disease and cancer for all groups other than non-Latinx Whites in the United States. Only for them was the increase in mortality from deaths of despair large enough to outweigh the improvement from mortality declines in heart disease and cancer.

Further examination by Case and Deaton shows that the incidence of deaths of despair is highest among less-educated groups, particularly those with a high school degree or less. The authors introduce the concept of "cumulative disadvantage" to describe conditions in which economic and social circumstances have changed dramatically over the course of decades. As they noted, "This process, which began for those leaving high school and entering the labor force after the early 1970s—the peak of working-class wages, and the beginning of the end of the 'blue-collar aristocracy'—worsened over time and caused, or at least was accompanied by, other changes in society that made life more difficult for less educated people, not only in their employment opportunities but in their marriages, and in the life and prospects for their children. Traditional structures of social and economic support slowly weakened; no longer was it possible for a man to follow his father and grandfather into a manufacturing job, or to join the union and start on the union ladder of wages. Marriage was no longer the only socially acceptable way to form intimate partnerships, or to rear children" (Case and Deaton 2017, p. 429). They cite shifts away from the mainstream religion of their parents as another source of discontinuity. They acknowledge that the overprescription of opioid drugs exacerbated a problem that would have existed in any case.

The final item on the Partnership for Healthy Cities list—enhance public health data and monitoring systems—refers in part to monitoring the environment to recognize and mitigate sources of pollution. In addition to the lifestyle factors and long-term economic and social changes that affect peoples' health, there is a new focus on the need for urban planning to take such public health factors explicitly into account (Owens 2016). The promotion of walking and biking and other forms of physical activity is seen as a strategy to reduce reliance on automobiles and their concomitant pollution. Environmental sustainability includes transit-oriented development projects to further reduce the need for automobile travel. It includes efforts to reduce single-use plastic bags, a measure first adopted country-wide by Bangladesh in 2002. In the United States, California adopted the first statewide ban in 2014. These efforts seem to be most effective in inducing consumers to use their own bags or go without a bag when combined with a small fee for any bag provided by the store (Zeitlin 2019). Food waste is another focus and in this category South Korea is a leader, recycling 95 percent of its food waste (Galchen 2020).

One critical role for city public health officials is assuring that restaurants are providing their services in a manner that does not undermine the health of their customers. A high-profile case of the need for local regulation occurred in Los Angeles in 1999. According to that city's director of public health, the local news channel KCBS-TV aired an investigative report that used hidden cameras to reveal egregious food safety violations in Los Angeles restaurants. The resulting news coverage inspired strong public support for holding restaurants more accountable for food safety. A visible restaurant grading system, previously unfeasible due to almost certain opposition by the politically strong restaurant association, was now possible. The city's public health department was able to develop a system that both changed the incentives for retail food establishments and protected the public's health. Restaurant letter grades (A, B, C), prominently posted at the entrance of all food establishments, quickly became an identifiable trademark of public health (Fielding 2015).

Personal Healthcare: Hospitals and Health Centers

In ancient cultures, religion and medicine were linked. Egyptian temples were the earliest documented institutions to provide healthcare. In ancient Greece, temples dedicated to the healer-god Asclepius functioned as centers of medical advice, prognosis, and healing (Risse 1990). Around 100 BCE the Romans constructed buildings for the care of sick slaves, gladiators, and soldiers. Healthcare facilities appeared early in India, dating back to the sixth century BCE (Tabish 2000). By 1123, St Bartholomew's Hospital was founded in London and is still an active hospital to this day. Founded in 1751 by Benjamin Franklin and Dr. Thomas Bond, Pennsylvania Hospital in Philadelphia would become the earliest established public hospital in the United States. It is home to America's first surgical amphitheater and its first medical library (Lemay 2008).

Unlike in many countries, personal healthcare in the United States is handled, for the most part, by the private sector. Visits to private hospitals and other health centers are now a familiar part of life. Most births take place in hospitals and most routine physical examinations are done in smaller clinics or in the clusters of doctors' offices that are an intrinsic part of the urban health infrastructure. Physicians who make house calls are very rare.

This system of care would have astonished residents of early US cities. Births, illnesses, and deaths typically occurred at home rather than in clinics or hospitals, and that is where doctors treated their patients. Institutions for the sick were mainly places for terminally ill poor people or took the form of quarantine stations during outbreaks of major diseases. There were some exceptions that served temporarily ill individuals, such as Massachusetts General Hospital in Boston, Bellevue Hospital in New York, and Charity Hospital in New Orleans, but these were largely seen as places to treat travelers to the city rather than the residents of these cities (Duffy 1990).

The first major expansion of hospital services occurred between 1840 and 1860 as a result of federal government interests in the ship- and boat-based trade. To serve the crews of ships and boats engaged in trade and military activities away from their home ports, the US Congress authorized the construction of 27 hospitals in cities along the Mississippi and Ohio Rivers and on the Great Lakes. Further expansion of hospitals occurred during and after the Civil War (Duffy 1990). After antiseptic techniques and anesthesia were introduced, hospitals developed a new role as centers for surgery. As methods of fighting communicable diseases were developed, the number of hospitals in the United States increased from 100 in 1870 to more than 6,000 in 1920. Most of these were in urban areas (Cassedy 1991). Several them were "city hospitals," built and operated by municipal governments under the auspices of the new municipal health agencies.

The first federal funding for local health facilities was provided during the 1930s as part of the **Social Security** Act of 1935 (Encyclopedia.com 2019). Further increases in the number of urban hospitals occurred in the late 1940s when Congress included federal funding for the construction of public and nonprofit hospitals in smaller cities under the National Hospital Survey and Construction Act, better known today as the Hill-Burton Act (Waagen 1948).

With these twentieth-century developments, hospitals became mainstays of the urban landscape and their role within the health infrastructure continued to grow as centers that contain and treat communicable disease, repair injuries, provide surgery, and address other medically treatable conditions. Today, within metropolitan areas, one is likely to find city hospitals (built and operated under the auspices of the local government), for-profit private hospitals, university-based nonprofit hospitals (built and operated by the medical schools of major universities), and nonprofit hospitals (built and operated by religious groups or other organizations).

While we tend to take hospital care for granted, such economic factors as **fixed costs**, economies of scale, and agglomeration economies are critically important to their existence. Hospitals and health centers have developed as important sites compared to medical treatment in the home because they provide a common location for the aggregation of various health professionals who together can treat illnesses and injuries, and as a centralized setting for costly medical devices such as X-ray machines and CAT scanners. It is a more efficient use of medical expertise to have patients visit the hospital than to have doctors and nurses spend enormous amounts of time traveling from one patient to another.

The activities conducted within hospitals involve high fixed costs for diagnostic and surgical equipment. Other medically related facilities, including doctors' offices and medical laboratories, tend to cluster around hospitals because of agglomeration economies (specifically, localization economies) that are associated with health services. The population density within metropolitan areas provides a stream of patients and revenue that permit health providers to specialize in specific diseases or procedures, thus contributing to the level of expertise in each specialty. For this reason, the quantity of medical facilities and the array of medical specialists available in major urban medical centers greatly exceed those available outside metropolitan areas. As shown in Table 11.4 the physician-to-population ratio, and especially the specialist-to-population ratio, is much lower in rural areas compared with urban ones, despite their having a population with poorer health status.

TABLE 11.4. COMPARISON OF PHYSICIAN RESOURCES AND NEEDS BETWEEN URBAN AND RURAL AREAS, UNITED STATES, 2015

NATIONAL RURAL HEALTH SNAPSHOT	RURAL	URBAN
Percentage of population	19.3%	80.7%
Number of physicians per 10,000 people	13.1	31.2
Number of specialists per 100,000 people	30	263
Population aged 65 and older	18%	12%
Average per capita income	$45,482	$53,657
Non-Hispanic white population	69-82%	45%
Adults who describe health status as fair/poor	19.5%	15.6%
Adolescents who smoke	11%	5%
Male life expectancy in years	76.2	74.1
Female life expectancy	81.3	79.7
Percentage of dual-eligible Medicare beneficiaries	30%	70%
Medicare beneficiaries without drug coverage	43%	27%
Percentage covered by Medicaid	16%	13%

Source: National Rural Health Association, 2020, "About Rural Health Care," p.2. https://www.ruralhealthweb.org/about-nrha/about-rural-health-care

Healthcare for the Poor

Because the prevention of communicable disease is a major goal of the healthcare infrastructure and because disease prevention is a public good, public interest in the provision of a safety net of health services for those who cannot afford to pay the full cost of healthcare is of prime importance. As such, at the beginning of the twentieth century many medical services for the poor were provided through "dispensaries" specifically established to provide medical aid and through **settlement houses**, which were established to deal with a range of health and related issues faced by new immigrant populations. By the 1930s, with the support of local health boards, the American Red Cross, and other health advocacy organizations, most of these facilities had been replaced by more than 1,500 health centers across the United States that combined health treatment with outreach and health education (Duffy 1990). Such health centers continue to provide direct care and many other important services in urban communities.

Municipal health centers derive their mandates and funding from city governments. Nonetheless, to address the confluence of poor healthcare and poverty, Congress authorized the creation of federally funded **comprehensive community health centers** in low-income neighborhoods as part of the War on Poverty in 1965. These health centers, funded through the Office of Economic Opportunity, were called "comprehensive" because they were intended to offer a wide range of medical services that extended beyond those provided by local health centers. The federally funded Community Health Center Program expanded rapidly between 1965 and 1980 and became another mainstay of health service in urban environments. In 2020, there were more than 1,400 such health centers providing services to more than 29 million patients. Fully 55 percent of these were located in urban communities, with the remaining 45 percent serving rural populations (National Association of Community Health Centers 2020).

Health Disparities in the Metro Region

The provision of basic healthcare to all residents in urban areas is still a major issue. **Low birth weight** (infants weighing less than 5.5 pounds), infant mortality, asthma, high blood pressure, tuberculosis, and other medical diseases and conditions are much more prevalent in central cities than in suburban areas and much greater among Blacks and Latinx than among Whites. The Center on Society and Health at the Virginia Commonwealth University (VCU) has mapped differences in life expectancy across several US metropolitan areas including Atlanta, Denver, Detroit, Cleveland, El Paso, Las Vegas, Miami, New York, Philadelphia, Phoenix, Raleigh-Durham, Richmond, St. Louis, Trenton, Tulsa, and Washington, DC. Their map for Chicago shows that life expectancy varies greatly across the city and that locations just a few miles apart along one of Chicago's transit lines can mean a difference in life expectancy at birth of as much as 12 years.

According to the VCU Center on Society and Health (2016), the organization that produced this Chicago map, there are several factors that contribute to variations in neighborhood health. They include education and income, inadequate housing, unavailability of healthy food options, unsafe neighborhoods that limit residents' ability to walk outside, location close to sources of pollutants, poor

TABLE 11.5. LIVES THAT COULD BE SAVED BY REDUCING DISPARITIES				
TYPE OF CANCER	# OF DEATHS IN 2008 AMONG WHITE, BLACK, HISPANIC AND ASIAN NEW YORKERS	LOWEST DEATH RATE PER 100,000 POPULATION	HIGHEST DEATH RATE PER 100,000 POPULATION	# OF LIVES SAVED IF ALL RACE/ETHNICITIES HAD THE LOWEST DEATH RATE
Colorectal	1419	Asians: 9	blacks: 15	638
Breast	1095	Asians: 9	blacks: 27	227
Cervical	138	whites: 2	blacks: 5	86
TOTAL	2652			

Source: Myers et.al. 2011

access to primary care physicians, poor transportation options, and residential segregation and isolation.

A New York City study of health disparities in breast, colorectal, and cervical cancers describes a continuum of prevention, screening, diagnosis, treatment, and survival or death. Prevention strategies reduce risk factors by encouraging healthy lifestyles. Screening strategies refer to tests for early detection. Diagnosis refers to interpreting test results and determining how far the cancer has progressed. Treatment options require access to medical care. Success of treatment determines survival or death. Disparities by race and income arise at every step along the continuum. Black New Yorkers have higher cancer mortality rates, which the researchers attribute to multiple causes including higher risk factors, greater life stress, poorer access to healthcare, delayed or inadequate diagnosis and treatment due to distrust and discrimination within the healthcare system, and a higher incidence of other health problems that worsen outcomes. As shown in Table 11.5 the researchers conclude that removing health disparities in outcomes for these three types of cancers (if every group was subject to the lowest death rate for that type of cancer) would have saved 951 out of 2,652 deaths, a 36 percent reduction in mortality (Myers et al. 2011).

Urban Public Health in a Global Context: Epidemics, Bioterrorism, and Homeland Security

Previous chapters have discussed changes in the speed and cost of transportation and communication that make urban issues of the twenty-first century unlike those of the twentieth. This applies to public health as well. The simple fact of increased business and tourist travel between countries means that there is more frequent contact between individuals from different countries who may have communicable diseases. The increased speed of transportation makes it more likely that people may be exposed to a disease and then travel to new destinations before the incubation period is over and the first noticeable symptoms appear. Consequently, urban areas are now more susceptible to the spread of international epidemics. In addition, as the devastating experience of Hurricane Katrina's impact on New Orleans in 2005 reveals, cities and their surrounding suburbs may be subject to major natural disasters with substantial public health impacts.

As we have seen with the COVID-19 pandemic, disaster might strike at any time. The spread of AIDS around the globe in the last two decades of the twentieth century, the international concern about avian flu in the early twenty-first century, the dissemination of anthrax-contaminated letters through the mail in 2001, the release of nerve gas in a subway in Japan, and other events show that public health officials face new challenges unlike any in the past. While the exact probability and timing of natural and human-caused disasters may be unknown, it is certain that local public health institutions play an important role in preparing for such events, assessing them, providing immediate response, and communicating with the public and other government agencies about them.

Even the rise of global terrorism is a new concern for cities since most of the presumed terrorist targets are urban based. Bioterrorism experts have emphasized that cities bear the brunt of any response to emergency disasters and that the main federal role is to fund state and local health agencies to prepare and to respond to such events (Institute of Medicine of the National Academies 2002; Noji et al. 2005).

Efforts to increase the emergency disaster capacities of state and local public health agencies continue with financial support from the Department of Homeland Security. Still, the challenge of preparing for major disasters remains one of the most important tasks of cities and their surrounding suburbs in the early twenty-first century. Experience with the coronavirus pandemic shows that preparations in the United States and many other developed nations were inadequate causing an appalling number of avoidable deaths. Disaster preparation in the twenty-first century has become a priority as it joins other ongoing efforts of the overall health system—to provide medical intervention when needed and to protect our surroundings and our activities in ways that keep us healthy.

Urban Social Welfare: Poverty, Unemployment, and Living Conditions

As we saw in Chapter 3, the development of steam power in the middle of the nineteenth century allowed factories to relocate from the fall lines of powerful rivers to the large cities where they could more easily assemble a workforce from the hordes of new arrivals. As a result, the social problems inherent in industrialization became specifically urban problems. The economic insecurity of the late-nineteenth-century factory age—the risk of unemployment as well as the risk of death or disability from industrial accidents—was felt most acutely in the cities where the industrial workforce was concentrated. As city populations continued to swell, the problem of urban poverty intensified.

Even before the late nineteenth century, local communities had provided almshouses, orphanages, charity hospitals, and insane asylums (Chudacoff and Smith 2000). These institutions developed during an era in which poverty was viewed primarily as a personal failing. In the wake of the dramatic business-cycle fluctuations that produced the Panic of 1873 and the massive economic depression of the mid-1890s, the notion that poverty and unemployment were primarily the result of individual failings was challenged. One aspect of that challenge was the recognition that economic insecurity was a byproduct of the industrial age and was endemic to a capitalist system.

The recognition that a family could become poor through no fault of its own—that a worker could become unemployed as a result of adverse economic conditions causing massive layoffs and that industrial accidents causing death or disability could deprive a family of its breadwinner—led to a spate of state legislation intended to protect families from the grimmer side of industrialization. In the late nineteenth and early twentieth centuries, several industrial states created programs that included unemployment insurance and workmen's compensation to provide at least a partial replacement for workers' wages.

At a time when married women were generally expected to engage in unpaid work within the home rather than paid work in the labor force, states created pensions for widows and mothers to transfer income to households lacking an adult male breadwinner. They enacted protective legislation that regulated working conditions for those women who did enter the workforce, as well as laws that prohibited child labor. In the wake of the 1911 Triangle Shirtwaist Factory fire in the heart of New York City in which 146 workers died, most of whom were young immigrant women, states enacted workplace safety codes.

Early twentieth-century Supreme Court justice Louis Brandeis referred to the states as "laboratories of democracy" for their willingness to enact innovative solutions to the problems of an industrial society. With the advent of the New Deal in the 1930s—in another period of severe economic depression—the federal government took over major responsibility for many of these state obligations and greatly expanded their scope. These included Social Security providing retirement income and income for surviving spouses and children of deceased workers; **Supplementary Security Income (SSI)** providing income support for the elderly and disabled poor; Aid to Dependent Children (ADC), the forerunner to today's **Temporary Assistance for Needy Families (TANF)**, providing some income support mainly for single-parent, mostly female-headed families; and **unemployment compensation** providing partial wage replacement for workers who lose their jobs. Federal legislation for regulating wages and hours, establishing a **minimum wage** rate, and defining a standard work week of 40 hours originated with the New Deal as well. Federal responsibility for workplace safety began in 1971 with the passage of the **Occupational Safety and Health Act**.

Ameliorating Living Conditions in Poor Neighborhoods

In the late nineteenth and early twentieth centuries, as the notion took hold that individuals were poor not primarily because of personal failings but because of the dire conditions in which they lived, the role of private philanthropy evolved from focusing on individuals to focusing on communities. This is best exemplified in the settlement house movement in which young, idealistic, well-educated volunteers from the middle class moved into community centers in poor neighborhoods and lived there in an effort to reach out to residents and help them improve their circumstances.

Similarly, as the focus shifted from the individual to the neighborhood, a greater emphasis on the documentation of living conditions and systematic data collection emerged. The publication in 1890 of Jacob Riis's *How the Other Half Lives* had a profound impact on public awareness of slum conditions not only because of Riis's narrative, but also from his use of photography that provided compelling documentary evidence. Settlement house workers collected systematic data on living conditions in their neighborhoods. In 1907–1908 the Russell Sage Foundation funded *The Pittsburgh Survey*, a comprehensive pathbreaking examination of social and economic conditions in that steelmaking city. The development of sociology as a field of study in the United States and the development of social work as a profession have their origins in this period of intense urbanization of the very late nineteenth and early twentieth centuries.

Earlier in the nineteenth century, reformers including Charles Loring Brace and his Children's Aid Society tried to improve the lives of urban poor children by removing them from their environment and sending them to live with other families in small towns and rural areas. By the early twentieth century, through the efforts of the settlement houses and other child welfare agencies, the focus shifted to improving the urban environment in which these children lived. Efforts to create more nurturing environments for children were pursued through the movement to establish community playgrounds and other urban outlets for healthy recreation. Some of the services first created through the settlement house movement such as playgrounds, public baths, and kindergartens were then taken on as responsibilities of local government. Yet as the historian Jon Teaford (1984) suggests, US cities lagged far behind those of Germany and Britain in the municipal provision of several types of services including public bathhouses and lodging houses for the poor.

Early in the twentieth century, **municipal public welfare departments** were established to coordinate with private agencies in funding and delivering social services to the poor. Such arrangements continue to the present day and are the method for dealing with such contemporary social service needs as sheltering those who are homeless or who are victims of domestic violence. In January 2019, the best estimate for the total homeless population in the United States was just under 568,000 (National Alliance to End Homelessness 2020). Given the size of the US population, this means that there are about 1,700 homeless per 100,000 in the population—or a rate of 0.17 percent.

The largest concentrations of homelessness were in New York City and Los Angeles. In these two cities alone, nearly one-fourth (23.8%) of the nation's homeless could be found (McCarthy 2020). The high cost of housing in these cities is one reason so many homeless are found there. It is true that these are among the largest cities in the country and therefore not surprisingly have more homeless.

To adjust for city population, Table 11.6 lists rates of homelessness per 10,000 residents in the five highest continuums of care (CoCs)—a city, a county, a group of counties, or a state, depending on the level of coordination of services for the homeless—as well as the five highest rates for those who stay overnight in a shelter and the five highest rates for those who sleep in public areas such as parks or sidewalks. Most of the cities on the list, such as New York and Los Angeles, are areas where the cost of housing is high and where it is difficult to increase housing supply. Adjusted in this way, the highest overall homelessness rate is in Washington, DC followed by Boston, New York, and San Francisco. Some CoCs have done a much better job of providing shelters for their homeless. In Boston, more than

TABLE 11.6. RATE OF HOMELESSNESS PER 10,000 IN CONTINUUMS OF CARE (COCS) WITH TOP FIVE HIGHEST RATES, 2018

OVERALL		SHELTERED		UNSHELTERED	
CoC	Rate	CoC	Rate	CoC	Rate
Washington, DC	103.3	Boston, MA	99.1	San Francisco, CA	59.8
Boston, MA	101.8	New York, NY	96.7	Los Angeles, CA	40.4
New York, NY	101.5	Washington, DC	94.3	Santa Rosa, CA	38.5
San Francisco, CA	94.3	San Francisco, CA	34.4	Seattle, WA	30.9
Santa Rosa, CA	59.8	Baltimore, MD	32.2	SanJose, CA	30.3

Sources: U. S. Department of Housing and Urban Development, Point-in-Time Counts and Shapefiles, 2018; American Community Survey 2013-2017; Council of Economic Advisers, "The State of Homelessness in America," September 2019, p.10. *Note:* Excludes CoCs with population below 500,000 and "balance of state" CoCs.

97 percent of the homeless find a city-provided or nonprofit provided shelter where they can sleep at night and have some meals. In other CoCs nearly two-thirds of the homeless will be found on the streets.

The Organization for Economic Cooperation and Development (OECD) emphasizes the difficulty in comparing rates of homelessness across countries because definitions of homelessness and data collection methods vary substantially. In Austria, Chile, France, Hungary, Ireland Italy, Japan, Latvia, Lithuania, Portugal, Slovenia, Spain, and the United States, the definition of homelessness includes only those who sleep in a shelter and those who sleep in public spaces. In Australia, Canada, the Czech Republic, Finland, Germany, Greece, Luxembourg, New Zealand, Norway, and Sweden, it also includes those who are living in hotels or staying with friends or family. Nevertheless, having stated these caveats, the OECD estimates that homelessness affects less than 1 percent of a nation's population, ranging from a high of 0.9 percent in New Zealand where they include those staying in hotels and with friends, to less than 0.1 percent in Chile, Iceland, Israel, Japan, Poland, and Portugal. Several OECD countries, including Canada, Chile, the Czech Republic, Denmark, Finland, France, Ireland, Japan, Luxembourg, Norway, New Zealand, Poland, and the United States, have adopted "housing first" policies providing permanent supportive housing to alleviate chronic homelessness (OECD 2020).

In the United States, private charities that deal with homelessness and domestic violence continue in the tradition of their early-twentieth-century forebears in which middle-class professionals seek to ameliorate the problems of the poor. Over the last 40 years, they have been joined by another type of nonprofit—**the community-based organization** (CBO)—working on a different model of community change. In CBOs, residents of poor neighborhoods are themselves the decision-makers who guide the policies that will affect the environment in which they live. **Community development corporations (CDCs)**, to which we give greater attention in Chapter 16, have played an integral role in neighborhood improvement in many cities. Their activities range from cleaning up neighborhood eyesores (such as vacant lots and illegal dumping sites) to developing jobs, housing, and retail establishments needed in the community.

Thus, by the early twenty-first century the public health department and the social welfare infrastructure of the modern city continued to evolve from the forms and functions they first were assigned in the nineteenth and early twentieth centuries. As the nature of the city changes and as the demographic composition of urban areas evolves, other new social services undoubtedly will be needed to assure that urban residents are well-protected in terms of health, physical security, and the vagaries of the modern economy.

Urban Public Amenities: Pastoral Parks and Public Libraries

As early as 1637, the first public parks for the enjoyment of the outdoors in crowded urban centers were created. In that year, Hyde Park in London was carved out from private lands owned by royalty. In 1789 the English Garden Park was developed in Munich, and in 1852 Bois de Boulogne was developed in Paris. Today, most large cities in the world have somewhere where its residents and visitors can go to escape the bricks and mortar of the built environment.

The reason that many parks were built began with a darker purpose. With the expansion of water, sewer, and sanitation systems in the nineteenth and early twentieth centuries, the threat to cities from disease and contagion began to subside even if pollution continued to threaten the environment in many regions. Business leaders were often equally concerned about a different kind of threat, one posed by social upheaval and labor activism. The development of public libraries and municipal parks was a response to this threat against the existing social order.

Public libraries and pastoral parks are part of a broader category of municipal services that may be called **urban public amenities** and includes municipally owned museums, zoos, swimming pools, tennis courts, golf courses, and skating rinks. Urban public amenities share these characteristics:

1. They developed during the latter half of the nineteenth century or early in the twentieth century, during the period of explosive urban growth.

2. Though these services may share with public education a purpose of moral, physical, and intellectual development—each may be seen as contributing to the ideal of *mens sana in corpore sano* (a sound mind in a sound body)—their use is entirely voluntary, in contrast with mandatory school attendance.

3. These services are relevant primarily to people's leisure time in contrast with services that provide support to individuals and businesses in their roles as earners of income.

4. Compared with such public health and safety services as police, fire, and sanitation, private-sector substitutes readily exist for these leisure-time amenities and are available for purchase by those who can afford them.

5. Private philanthropy often preceded and may have stimulated municipal funding, helping to redefine the boundary between private and public.

The public libraries established by Andrew Carnegie, the nineteenth-century Pittsburgh steel magnate, are familiar examples of this last point. Carnegie Library funds essentially were matching grants for which municipalities, in order to be eligible, had to agree to spend annually on their libraries a sum no less than 10 percent of the amount of Carnegie's grant (Bobinski 1969). That sum had to come from tax revenues, not from other gifts. The late-nineteenth-century journalist Finley Peter Dunne (1906) has his fictional alter ego, the inestimable Mr. Dooley, mimic Andrew Carnegie expounding on this requirement:

> All I ask iv a city in rayturn f'r a fifty thousan' dollar libry is that it shall raise wan millyon dollars to maintain th' buildin' an' keep me name shiny, an' if it won't do that much f'r lithrachoor, th' divvle take it, it's onworthy iv th' name iv an American city. What ivry community needs is taxes an' lithrachoor. I give thim both. Three cheers f'r a libry an' a bonded debt! Lithrachoor, taxation, and Andhrew Carnaygie, wan an' insiprable, now an' firiver!

Social Unrest and the Provision of Urban Public Amenities

The provision of urban public amenities was a response to the explosive growth of cities and the concomitant growth of urban unrest during the late nineteenth century. This was Lewis Mumford's Paleotechnic era: an economy powered by iron and coal, a period of intense industrialization and growth of manufacturing. Schlesinger's 1933 study of this period in US history is aptly named *The Rise of the City*. It was a period of dramatic demographic change as newcomers poured into the cities, the result of internal migration from rural areas as well as immigration from abroad. It was a period of vast improvements in infrastructure including transportation and public works.

It was as well a period characterized by severe class conflict. There was a high degree of inequality, most pronounced in cities, where the richest of the rich and the poorest of the poor resided. Rising land values made housing expensive and created a housing crisis for the poor. Business cycles and periodic depressions amplified economic insecurity. In 1877, there was great labor unrest focused on the railroads and by 1886 there was a nationwide wave of strike activity. In addition, it was an age of gross municipal corruption. James Bryce (1888), in an influential book of the time, made the pronouncement that "the government of cities is the one conspicuous failure of the United States."

In response to the corruption within cities, the late nineteenth century spawned a number of reform movements. Some were aimed at moral uplift and spearheaded by leaders within Protestant churches. These included the proliferation of the Young Men's Christian Association (YMCA), children's aid societies, and anti-vice and anti-prostitution movements.

The historian Melvin Holli (1969) has distinguished between two categories of late-nineteenth-century municipal reformers: the structural reformers and the social reformers. The structural reformers focused their efforts on achieving "good government": efficient, businesslike procedures; economical government; nonpartisan citywide elections to abolish the influence of parties and wards; shorter ballots; secret ballots; and an emphasis on professional expertise. These structural reformers, including Seth Low of New York City, were the forerunners of the Progressive Era reformers who began to gain influence across the United States in the early twentieth century.

In contrast with the structural reformers, such social reformers as Mayor Hazen Pingree of Detroit advocated for lower utility rates and shifting taxes to corporations. They promoted municipal ownership of streetcar lines and public utilities to address what they saw as the true source of corruption—bribery and graft in the awarding of public franchises to private transportation and utility companies. They tended to dismiss legislation that regulated morals as a distraction from the true problem of corruption, the awarding of municipal franchises. They advocated for free public baths and the expansion of parks, schools, and public relief. The expansion of the economic role of local government thus came out of this milieu of industrialization, urbanization, corruption, and reform.

While the establishment of urban public amenities was one response of the nineteenth-century elite to the turmoil of the cities, it was not the only response. Carnegie donated funds for libraries, but he hired the infamous Pinkerton Agency to put a bloody end to a strike by his workers. The era that witnessed the development of libraries and parks also saw the construction of armories, those quintessential urban structures of the late nineteenth century (Fogelson 1989). The armories, which often resembled medieval fortresses up to their crenellated tops, were built as staging areas for the troops that were called in to quell urban unrest. Both the armory, on the one hand, and the public library and pastoral park, on the other, were responses to class tensions that emerged in the cities of the late nineteenth century. Each was a presumed solution for the unease with which the elite viewed the lower classes. The public libraries and parks could be seen as the velvet glove, the public armories as the iron fist.

The privileged classes of the late nineteenth century could not isolate themselves from the lower classes in the city. Many of the elite lived inside city limits and even those who moved their residences to the early upper-class suburbs continued to depend on the city and its workers for their livelihood. There were common themes in the way the privileged classes thought about the public libraries and pastoral parks they were providing for the lower classes. These were envisioned as large-scale single citywide units that were available to all but meant especially for adult males of the lower classes. Ideally, the laboring husband would take his family to the park on a Sunday for a day to spend together in leisure, enjoying fresh air and relaxation away from their cramped hovel. The laboring man would use the library to teach himself the skills and knowledge necessary for self-improvement. Indeed, at the beginning of the public library era, one had to be over age 14 to use the library. The expectation was that parks and libraries would serve as alternatives to the saloon. The parks provided water fountains but prohibited alcohol; claims were made that where libraries were available, saloons lost business.

There were contradictions. Advocates wanted to attract the lower classes yet not be overrun by them. They wanted to serve the lower classes yet insisted on middle-class standards of behavior. Initially, Central Park allowed middle class activities including cricket, horseback riding, and carriage rides but did not provide for baseball fields or other active pursuits favored by the working class (Taylor 1999). Large areas of vacant land were expensive, so parks were often built at the outskirts of the city, requiring streetcar rides that were prohibitively expensive for poor families.

In the case of the public libraries, middle-class librarians could and did enforce strict rules for silence and cleanliness and harsh punishment for petty thievery. Early librarians debated whether to stock fiction at all and whether to stock foreign language books for non-native speakers of English. As a result, the use of parks and libraries by the lower classes was disappointingly sparse. Much to the chagrin of reformers, the lower classes chose more lively amusement parks and beer gardens over pastoral parks. Instead of using the library, they read newspapers, dime novels, and various publications of ethnic, labor, religious, and political groups.

Failure of Expectations and a Repurposing for the Twenty-First Century

As such, the public libraries and pastoral parks built in the late nineteenth century—no matter their grandiose and stately design—did not fulfill the expectations of their creators. It seems almost quaint now to think that the nineteenth-century elite believed in the power of these institutions to reduce class tensions and rechannel dissatisfaction into individual upward mobility. At the dedication of the multiple-purpose institution comprised of a library, gymnasium, and music hall that Andrew Carnegie donated to Homestead, Pennsylvania in 1898—six years after he broke a strike and destroyed the union there—he said, "How a man spends his time at work may be taken for granted but how he spends his hours of recreation is really the key to his progress in all the virtues" (Carnegie 1920). Similarly, Frederick Law Olmsted's expectations for Central Park in New York City are characterized by the historian Geoffrey Blodgett (1966), as follows: "The natural simplicity of pastoral landscape would, he hoped, inspire communal feelings among all urban classes, muting resentments over disparities of wealth and fashion. For an untrusting, watchful crown of urban strangers, the park would restore that 'communicativeness' which Olmsted prized as a central American need."

Failure to accomplish their original goals led to similar changes in both institutions: the emphasis shifted to a more active policy of outreach centered on smaller, neighborhood-based units that included branch libraries and neighborhood playgrounds. Similarly, with inspiration from the example of the settlement house workers, the focus shifted away from adult males to concentrate more on children, providing organized activities run by trained personnel including children's librarians and recreation workers. Now, in the twenty-first century, investment in large pastoral parks, as well as the refurbishing and expansion of museums, seems to be inspired as much by their potential contributions to an area's tourist economy as they are by a desire to improve the well-being of the resident population. They have as well become part of the economic development strategy of cities trying to retain and attract young workers to the central city.

A twenty-first century perspective on these urban public amenities sees their value not in exerting social control over an unruly working class but in providing critical public services that improve the ways in which cities function. Using a somewhat broader concept of social infrastructure that encompasses the roles of the private and nonprofit sectors as well as the role of government, Eric Klinenberg (2018) defines it as "the physical places and organizations that shape the way people interact." He describes a branch library in a low-income Brooklyn neighborhood that sponsors a virtual bowling league for the neighborhood seniors who might otherwise be isolated. They compete via X-Box with teams from other branch libraries. The library offers children's programs, computers for public use, classes in English as a second language, and a learning center for adults who cannot read at a high school level.

The portrait of the library as a vital community center is the antithesis of the late-nineteenth- and early-twentieth-century Carnegie Libraries, with their narrowly focused emphasis on individual self-improvement. A recent book about the Los Angeles Public Library by Susan Orlean (2018) reinforces the role of the library as community center. She describes the important role that libraries play as a daytime destination for homeless people, its role as a community resource in crisis response, and its offering of an online accredited high school degree program for adults. Both Klinenberg and Orlean note the commitment to openness and inclusivity among modern librarians, again a far cry from the punitive behaviors of the early librarians.

Frederick Law Olmstead was prescient in his belief that time spent in nature would have a beneficial effect on one's mind and body. As Florence Williams (2017) shows, those benefits can now be affirmed and measured. In Japan, *shinrin yoku*, or "forest bathing," is used as preventive medicine to reduce stress and its concomitant illnesses. She cites research showing that forest walks, compared with urban walks, are more effective in reducing cortisol levels (cortisol is a hormone produced by stress), sympathetic nerve activity, blood pressure, heart rate, and anxiety. South Korea has programs to promote well-being by encouraging the use of official healing forests. Evidence from South Korea shows improved immune response and reduction in symptoms of depression and anxiety. Beneficial results are the product of fresh air and calming visuals as well as the stimulation of the sense of smell. Coastlines have similar effects.

Williams acknowledges that multiday nature immersions are not an option for everyone, but exposure to at least a few hours of nature can become more universal. She uses Singapore as an example of a dense urban environment that provides nearby opportunities for exposure to nature. It has a network of parks, "green" walls, and vertical farming. Its Botanical Garden is expansive, open for extended hours, and free, unlike many of its counterparts in the United States. Seventy percent of Singapore residents live within 400 meters (less than five football fields) of a green space, and the goal is to improve that figure to 80 percent.

In the United States, the Trust for Public Land is working toward the goal of guaranteeing access to a quality park within a ten-minute walk from one's home. Currently, 100 million Americans (nearly one-third) lack this access. The group ranks cities according to access, acreage, spending, and facilities at parks. In 2019, the top five cities providing greater access to high-quality neighborhoods parks were Washington, DC; St. Paul, Minnesota; Minneapolis, Minnesota; Arlington, Virginia; and Portland, Oregon.

Singapore is also cited by Klinenberg as an example of a place that is using investment in physical infrastructure not only to provide a natural environment for their residents but to simultaneously protect against climate change. Their Marina Barrage and Reservoir project provides public spaces to attract residents and tourists. Rotterdam created a public square that is designed to collect rainwater. Bangladesh uses a "floating infrastructure" of schools and libraries on boats.

New York City is developing a plan for its flood-prone Lower East Side to build protective walls that serve as sloped parkland and recreational areas (Klinenberg 2018). As the population of cities continues to grow worldwide, our need for urban public amenities will grow apace.

As this chapter and others suggest, we now ask our cities to perform an amazing array of activities day in and day out. Most residents have little idea of the wide range of these services or the positive impact they have on their lives. It is sometimes easier to enumerate cases where government performs badly or where there is some corruption in government process. But we should never forget how life might be without government services that generally keep us safe, educate our children, and provide us with amenities that we often take for granted.

References

Blodgett, Geoffrey. 1966. *The Gentle Reformers: Massachusetts Democrats in the Cleveland Era*. Cambridge, MA: Harvard University Press.

Bobinski, George. 1969. *Carnegie Libraries: Their History and Impact on American Public Library Development*. Chicago: American Library Association.

Bryce, James. 1888. *The American Commonwealth*. New York: Macmillan.

Carnegie, Andrew. 1920. *The Autobiography of Andrew Carnegie*. Republished in 2010 in Houston, Texas: The Halcyon Press Ltd.

Case, Anne, and Angus Deaton. 2017. "Mortality and Morbidity in the 21st Century." *Brookings Papers on Economic Activity* (Spring): 397–476.

Cassedy, James H. 1991. *Medicine in America: A Short History*. Baltimore: Johns Hopkins University Press.

Center on Society and Health. 2016. "Mapping Life Expectancy." September 26. Richmond: Virginia Commonwealth University.

Chetty, Raj, Michael Stepner, Sarah Abraham, Shelby Lin, Benjamin Scuderi, Nicholas Turner, Augusin Bergeron, and David Cutler. 2016. "The Association Between Income and Life Expectancy in the United States, 2001–2014." *Journal of the American Medical Association* 315, no. 16: 1750–1766.

Chudacoff, Howard, and Judith Smith. 2000. *The Evolution of American Urban Society*, 5th ed. Upper Saddle River, NJ: Prentice Hall.

Cohen, Bruce. 2007. E-mail communication with the authors, June.

Duffy, John. 1990. *The Sanitarians: A History of American Public Health*. Urbana: University of Illinois Press.

Dunne, Finley Peter. 1906. *Dissertations by Mr. Dooley*. New York: Harper & Brothers.

Encyclopedia.com. 2019. "Public Health 1929–1941." https://www.biblio.com/dissertations-by-mr-dooley-by-dunne-finley-peter/work/930816

Fielding, Jonathan. 2015. "Public Health in Big Cities: Looking Back, Looking Forward." *Journal of Public Health Management* (January): S20–S23.

Fogelson, Robert. 1989. *America's Armories: Architecture, Society, and Public Order.* Cambridge, MA: Harvard University Press.

Galchen, Rivka. 2020. "Complete Trash." *New Yorker,* March 9.

Hallas, Victoria. 2014. "The History of Public Health." Medium.com, May 25. https://medium.com/a-new-era-of-urban-planning/the-history-of-public-health-1f816bae38ab

Holli, Melvin. 1969. *Reform in Detroit: Hazen S. Pingree and Urban Politics.* New York: Oxford University Press.

Humphreys, Margaret. 1992. *Yellow Fever and the South.* New Brunswick, NJ: Rutgers University Press.

Institute of Medicine of the National Academies. 2002. *The Future of the Public's Health in the 21st Century.* Washington, DC: National Academies Press.

Kawachi, Ichiro, and Lisa Berkman, eds. 2003. *Neighborhoods and Health.* New York: Oxford University Press.

Klinenberg, Eric. 2018. *Palaces for the People: How Social Infrastructure Can Help Fight Inequality, Polarization, and the Decline of Civic Life.* New York: Crown.

Lemay, J. A. Leo. 2008. *The Life of Benjamin Franklin, Volume 3: Soldier, Scientist, and Politician, 1748–1757.* Philadelphia: University of Pennsylvania Press.

McCarthy, Niall. 2020. "The U.S. Cities with the Most Homeless People." *Statista,* January 12.

Myers, C., A. Hakenewerth, C. Olson, B. Kerker, M. Krauskopf, A. Tavares, S. Perlman, C. Greene, and T. Farley. 2011. *Health Disparities in New York City: Health Disparities in Breast, Colorectal, and Cervical Cancers.* New York: New York City Department of Health and Mental Hygiene.

National Alliance to End Homelessness. 2020. "State of Homelessness: 2020 Edition." https://endhomelessness.org/homelessness-in-america/homelessness-statistics/state-of-homelessness-2020/.

National Association of Community Health Centers. 2020. "About Health Centers; Chartbook." https://www.nachc.org/wp-content/uploads/2020/01/Chartbook-2020-Final.pdf.

National Rural Health Association. 2020. "About Rural Health Care." https://www.ruralhealthweb.org/about-nrha/about-rural-health-care.

Noji, Eric, Tress Goodwin, and Michael Hopmeier. 2005. "Demystifying Bioterrorism: Misinformation and Misperceptions." *Prehospital and Disaster Medicine* 20, no. 1: 3–6.

Organisation for Economic Co-operation and Development (OECD). 2020. "Better Data and Policies to Fight Homelessness in the OECD." *Policy Brief on Affordable Housing*. Paris: OECD. http://oe.cd/homelessness-2020.

Orlean, Susan. 2018. *The Library Book*. New York: Simon & Schuster.

Owens, Cassie. 2016. "Reconnecting Urban Planning and Public Health." *Next City*, January 29.

Partnership for Healthy Cities. 2020. "When Mayors and Local Leaders Help Their Citizens Live Healthier and Safer Lives, Cities Are More Prosperous." https://partnershipforhealthycities.bloomberg.org.

Riis, Jacob. 1890. *How the Other Half Lives*. New York: Charles Scribner's Sons.

Risse, G. B. 1990. *Mending Bodies, Saving Souls: A History of Hospitals*. New York: Oxford University Press.

Rosenberg, Charles E. 1987. *The Cholera Years: The United States in 1832, 1849 and 1866*, 2nd ed. Chicago: University of Chicago Press.

Scheer, Roddy. 2001. "Parks as Lungs: America's Urban Forests Make Environmental and Economic Sense." *The Environmental Magazine* 12. no. 1 November/December https://www.fs.fed.us/ne/newtown_square/news/NE_news/2002/articles/e_magazine_lung.pdf.

Schlesinger, Arthur M. 1933. *The Rise of the City, 1878–1898*. New York: Macmillan.

State Health Access Data Assistance Center. 2018. "Health Insurance Coverage: Uninsurance by Metro Areas in 2017 (Interactive)." November 16. https://www.shadac.org/news/health-insurance-coverage-uninsurance-metro-areas-2017-interactive.

Tabish, Syed. 2000. "Historical Development of Health Care in India." In *Hospital & Health Services Administration: Principles & Practice*. New York: Oxford University Press, pp. 23–28.

Taylor, Dorceta E. 1999. "Central Park as a Model for Social Control: Urban Parks, Social Class and Leisure Behavior in Nineteenth-Century America." *Journal of Leisure Research* 31, no. 4: 420–477.

Teaford, Jon C. 1984. *The Unheralded Triumph: City Government in America, 1870–1900*. Baltimore: Johns Hopkins University Press.

Tomes, Nancy. 1998. *The Gospel of Germs: Men, Women and the Microbe in American Life*. Cambridge, MA: Harvard University Press.

Waagen, Louise O. 1948. "The Hospital Survey and Construction Act." *American Journal of Nursing* 48, no. 6 (June): 361–363.

Williams, Florence. 2017. *The Nature Fix: Why Nature Makes Us Happier, Healther, and More Creative*. New York: Norton.

Womack, Lindsey, Lauren Rossen, and Ashley Hirai. 20202019. "Urban–Rural Infant Mortality Disparities by Race and Ethnicity and Cause of Death." *American Journal of Preventive Medicine* 58, no. 2: 254–260.

Zeitlin, Matthew. 2019. "Do Plastic Bag Taxes or Bans Curb Waste? 400 Cities and States Tried It Out." *The Highlight by Vox*, August 27.

Questions and Exercises

1. As mentioned in the exercises for Chapters 9 and 10, the US Bureau of the Census conducts a Census of Governments every five years. One of the reports generated from this census is "Finances of Municipal and Township Governments." The current version of this report is available online at https://www.census.gov/data/datasets/2018/econ/local/public-use-datasets.html.

Select three US states you wish to study and examine the finances for local governments within those states.

- For each state you selected, what is the amount (if any) local governments spend on public welfare, health and hospitals, and police protection? You will find these data beginning on Line 54, "Expenditures."

- What is the percentage of total local government expenditures devoted to each of these categories for your three states?

- How do these percentages vary from one state to another?

2. The National Association of County and City Health Officials (NACCHO) publishes "Big Cities Health Inventory," a compilation of health data covering the 54 largest cities in the United States. This report is available at https://www.bigcitieshealth.org/city-data. Go to this report and scroll down to the map titled "Cities Represented in This Report." Select eight of the cities shown. Then scroll down through the tables and, for each of these cities, determine whether they are above or below the city average for:

- heart disease

- mortality rate

- lung cancer mortality rate

- diabetes mortality rate

- infant mortality rate

3. Now examine how these rates of disease vary within each city by race, ethnicity, and median income. How large are these disparities? Do some of the cities you selected demonstrate less inequality in these health outcomes?

Urban Public Safety

12

LEARNING OBJECTIVES

- Describe the basic questions regarding who, what, how, and from whom the police are expected to "serve and protect"
- Explain and contrast the traditional approach to maintaining law and order with its alternatives
- Describe the crime index and its relationship to economic conditions across cities
- Describe the competing explanations offered for the general reduction in cities' crime indices since the mid-1990s
- Describe the rise of private policing and explain the challenges it poses
- Explain the twenty-first-century challenges to law and order posed by internet crime and terrorism

Urban life requires coordination for everyday activities such as transportation. It also requires coordinated response to naturally caused emergencies, accidents, and for protection against others who have ill intent. In urban settings today, much of the responsibility for such matters is delegated to professional "first responders." These include members of the city police forces, firefighters, and emergency medical technicians (EMTs). Each play an important role in assuring the well-being of the community, particularly when they are well-trained and are committed to treat everyone in a fair and equitable fashion.

Urban Police

In 2016, as shown in Table 12.1, there were 12,261 local police departments in the United States with a total of 599,548 full-time employees, including 468,000 sworn officers and 131,274 civilians (Hyland and Davis 2018). Typically, these departments have a broad range of responsibility including crime prevention, apprehension and detention of crime suspects, crime scene analysis and follow-up detective work, intervention in traffic problems and vehicular accidents, substance abuse crises, domestic violence incidents, mental health crises, and other issues of public safety. As shown in Table 12.2, New York City has the largest municipal police force with over 52,000 employees and an annual budget of $6 billion, followed by Chicago with more than 14,000 employees and an annual budget of $2 billion and Los Angeles with more than 13,000 employees and an annual budget of $2 billion (Sullivan and Baranaukas 2020).

The task which most people commonly associate with municipal police is crime prevention—a mission that has economic and an array of public policy implications. If you ask residents of an area what should be done to reduce crime, you are likely to get a variety of answers. Some residents may advocate hiring more police so that potential crimes are deterred and the likelihood of repeated crimes by the same person is reduced. Some residents may advocate longer sentences, with the thought that if individuals face the prospect of longer jail terms, they are less likely to commit crimes. Others may advocate helping poor people find jobs, reasoning that a significant number of crimes are related to the economic desperation of individuals who find themselves in difficult economic circumstances. Still others may want the creation of more substance abuse treatment programs, noting that a number of crimes are committed by individuals who are addicted. Still others may want funding for community groups, arguing that decreasing anonymity among neighbors is the most effective way of decreasing crime.

In a world without budget constraints, these approaches would not be mutually exclusive. However, given constraints, cities face two important issues. The first is

TABLE 12.1.   LOCAL POLICE DEPARTMENTS AND FULL-TIME EMPLOYEES, BY SIZE OF POPULATION SERVED, 2016

POPULATION SERVED	DEPARTMENTS	FULL-TIME EMPLOYEES	FULL-TIME SWORN OFFICERS	% SWORN OFFICERS	FULL-TIME CIVILIANS	% CIVILIANS
All Sizes	12,261	599,548	468,274	78%	131,274	22%
1 million or more	16	133,178	100,837	76%	32,341	24%
500,000 to 999,999	34	67,426	52,995	79%	14,431	21%
250,000 to 499,999	57	48,401	37,395	77%	11,006	23%
100,000 to 249,999	207	69,898	52,955	76%	16,943	24%
50,000 to 99,999	429	66,714	50,327	75%	16,387	25%
25,000 to 49,999	915	69,317	54,889	79%	14,428	21%
less than 25,000	10,603	144,614	118,876	82%	25,738	18%

Source: U.S. Bureau of Justice Statistics, Law Enforcement Management and Administrative Statistics Survey, 2016

| TABLE 12.2. | MUNICIPAL POLICE DEPARTMENT BUDGETS, EMPLOYEES, AND VIOLENT CRIMES REPORTED |

CITY	POPULATION 2018	TOTAL POLICE BUDGET 2020 (IN MILLIONS)	TOTAL POLICE DEPARTMENT EMPLOYEES	TOTAL OFFICERS	TOTAL CIVILIAN EMPLOYEES	POLICE DEPARTMENT EMPLOYEES PER 100,000 POPULATION	POLICE OFFICERS PER 100,000 POPULATION	VIOLENT CRIMES REPORTED PER 100K POPULATION IN 2018
Atlanta	498,073	205	1,987	1,535	452	399	308	769
Baltimore	602,495	536	2,935	2,488	447	487	413	1,833
Boston	695,926	375	2,715	2,122	593	390	305	622
Chicago	2,705,988	2,000	14,086	13,138	948	521	486	1,006
Dallas	1,345,076	517	3,581	3,007	574	266	224	765
Denver	716,492	426	1,824	1,517	307	255	212	730
Detroit	672,681	317	3,019	2,398	621	449	356	2,008
Houston	2,326,090	965	6,258	5,229	1,029	269	225	1,026
Los Angeles	3,990,469	2,000	13,010	9,974	3,036	326	250	748
Miami	470,911	266	1,741	1,309	432	370	278	630
Minneapolis	425,395	193	1,037	849	188	244	200	793
New York	8,398,748	6,000	52,278	36,134	16,144	622	430	541
Philadelphia	1,584,138	760	7,366	6,577	789	465	415	909
Phoenix	1,660,272	721	3,902	2,919	983	235	176	733
Portland	652,573	245	1,177	922	255	180	141	520
San Antonio	1,532,212	479	2,991	2,352	639	195	154	627
San Diego	1,425,999	566	2,332	1,731	601	164	121	373
San Francisco	883,305	696	2,913	2,306	607	330	261	691
Seattle	744,949	409	1,954	1,420	534	262	191	680
Tampa	392,905	163	1,206	946	260	307	241	407
Washington, DC	702,455	544	4,520	3,841	679	643	547	941

Source: Sullivan and Baranaukas, "Here's how much money goes to police departments in largest cities across the U.S." USAToday, June 26, 2020.

weighing the importance of budget levels for crime prevention against other types of expenditures. The second is *how* local public funds can be efficiently spent on the range of services that can prevent crime or increase the likelihood of apprehending criminals once a crime has been committed.

As residents and city officials consider public safety expenditures and strategies, their potentially different perceptions of the effectiveness of various crime-reducing strategies are important. But also important are the ways in which residents, officials, and other stakeholders view the fundamental roles and practices of police. Police are not only charged with prevention of crime, but as the phrase "law and order" indicates, they are also charged with maintenance of order—a concept that may have different meanings for different stakeholders and different interest groups.

Police, Public Safety, and the Public: Some Basic Questions

"To protect and to serve." This is how the title of a popular television show and a history of police in America (Wadman and Allison 2004) referred to the functions of police. But while this is a simple idealized slogan, the slogan conveys issues that are far more complex, particularly in urban settings.

Among the questions raised by this slogan are: To protect and to serve *whom*? Protection *from what* and *from whom*? Protection *by whom*? To protect and to serve *how*? Serving and protecting with *accountability to whom*? These five questions and their implications for law and order are particularly important given a unique characteristic of police departments when compared to other municipal services—the authorization of police to use force and, at times, violence to enforce the law.

There are a host of answers to these questions. Are police officers in service to the general public, to a particular race or ethnic group (or perhaps more to one race or ethnic group than another), to the interests of a particular political party, to political or economic elites, or to a particular powerful person? Is their focus the protection of those they serve from physical harm, from loss of power, or from political dissent? Is the membership of the police force representative of the residents of communities or are they recruited from particular political parties, neighborhoods, or racial groups? What strategies are condoned, and what strategies are practiced even if they are not officially condoned? To whom do police report, and by whom are they held accountable? These questions are pertinent to police forces around the world. In practice, the possibility of various answers to the five primary questions at the beginning of this section implies that the dynamics between police and their social, political, and economic environments can manifest in different ways from country to country, from city to city, and within individual metropolitan areas. In recognition of the complexities of international public safety comparisons, the specific issues discussed in this chapter will focus only upon the United States.

The presence, actions, and accountability of police are often experienced differently by neighborhood and race. They may engender confidence in one community and distrust in other, reliance in one and fear in the other, with reactions spanning from the images sought by the "Officer Friendly" programs funded in 200 US cities by the Sears Roebuck Foundation between 1966 and 1986 (Easter 2016), to the sentiment of "Our Enemies in Blue," the title of a book by Kristian Williams (Williams 2015).

The form of policing practices in any community shapes the expectations and beliefs of neighborhood residents, government officials, the public at large, and police personnel themselves. The results are far-reaching. Because public safety and police practice are intertwined with so many aspects of city life, they command social, political, and economic interest often far more so than other aspects of urban policy. The issues associated with public safety and police practice are also important because they can contribute to problematic fissures in the potential political, social, and economic collaboration of urban residents and institutions.

In too many unfortunate cases, policy practice has generated a public outcry. A prime example of the impact of overzealous police action is the 2020 arrest and death of George Floyd at the hands of police officers in Minneapolis. A cell phone videorecording of the incident made by a bystander sparked massive protests across the country and around the world. This shocking video, one of many documenting police-related deaths of unarmed Black men and women, led to a stream of protests not only demanding appropriate charges to be filed against the police officers involved, but also insisting on reforms in public safety personnel recruitment, training, practice, deployment, and accountability.

As we move through the first half of the twenty-first century, the possibility of reimagining public safety and reforming police practice are an important subject of debate within cities as well as at the level of the state and the nation. An overall perspective of US municipal police forces is aided by insight into the historical development of this important municipal service.

The Origins of Municipal Police Forces in the United States

Like many other functions of local government, municipal police forces originally arose in response to the challenges arising from population density and urbanization (Monkkonen 1981). The scope of their responsibilities—and the ways in which they have addressed these responsibilities—have been shaped by the economic and social issues discussed throughout this book.

If you lived in cities in the United States before 1825, the question "protection by whom?" was fairly simple, but varied by region. In the cities of the Northeast and the growing Midwest, the general needs of the populace for public order and protection were provided by an appointed constable with arrest powers who relied on volunteers to carry out his orders (Monkkonen 1981; Gaines et al. 1999; Wadman and Allison 2004; Walker and Katz 2005). Typically, able-bodied males were expected to voluntarily serve "on watch" on a rotating basis, maintaining order through their capacity to summon the local militia (armed volunteers) in cases where force was needed, and—in less serious circumstances—through their familiarity with disorderly individuals. Major property owners addressed their specific needs by hiring private guards to watch and protect their property (Hahn and Jeffries 2003).

In the slave-holding cities of the Southeast and Deep South, civilian structures were also utilized but the system was strongly tied to protection of the system of slavery in opposition to the aspirations of the large numbers of enslaved and the smaller number of free African Americans. Protection of the status quo was provided by urban slave patrols appointed by local officials from lists of able-bodied White males whose primary functions were to discourage slave rebellions, to prevent runaways, and to prevent destruction of property (Wadman and Allison 2004; Walker and Katz 2005). The use of extreme violence was often exercised and condoned as a deterrent to efforts to escape or to overturn the slavery system. Permanent paid forces were established in Charleston, South Carolina in 1783 as an alternative to the slave patrols and similar municipally established groups were created in Savannah, Mobile, and Richmond by the early 1800s (Williams 2015).

The watch system of self-policing continued in northern US cities until mid-century. Advocates of self-policing rotating watch systems considered the social embeddedness of watch members was an important aspect of law enforcement. They believed that watch members were a part of the community of citizens, affected by the social context of the community, and could therefore be expected to appropriately apply the authority with which they had temporarily been entrusted. But as cities became larger, the watch systems became more unwieldy. Moreover, the social cohesion and close communication upon which the watch systems were based began to fray. In the 1830s and 1840s ethnic, racial, and workforce conflict led to serious urban riots in Boston, Philadelphia, Cincinnati, New York, Detroit, Indianapolis, and other cities in the Northeast and Midwest (Monkkonen 1981; Gaines, et al. 1999; Wadman and Allison 2004; Walker and Katz 2005). Expanding urban population and growing demographic diversity in the nineteenth century instigated a change in the role of law enforcement in society. In many cities, familiarity, trust, and other social ties between residents across the city became more tenuous and the interaction between the police and the population became more anonymous (Monkkonen 1981; Hahn and Jeffries 2003).

In response to these challenges, cities in the northern half of the United States began to establish formal municipal police forces containing full-time employees paid by city governments from municipal revenue. Boston created a centralized force in 1838—widely regarded as the first formal municipal police force in the United States—followed by New York in 1845 and Albany, New York and Chicago in 1851. By the late 1800s, municipal police forces existed in cities throughout the United States (Monkkonen 1981; 1992). In establishing these forces, cities melded the US experience with civilian watches and slave patrols with the example of municipal police forces that had recently been established in England.

By the time that regular municipal police forces were formed in the cities of the Northeast and Midwest, there was already antipathy toward the large number of immigrants arriving from Ireland and Germany and suspicion about their culture and religion. Ethnic and class interests played increasingly larger roles in urban policing. For the native born, the motivation for establishing formal police forces shifted from self-policing a common community to helping protect "us" against "them"—a conception that already existed in a more intense racial form in the cities of the South (Hahn and Jeffries 2003).

Police departments were embroiled in sociopolitical power conflicts throughout the twentieth and early twenty-first centuries. The decisions of whom to serve and whom to protect became strongly intertwined with political and economic power in many cities. As Douglas Blackmon detailed in the Pulitzer-prize winning book *Slavery By Another Name* (2008), among the roles of southern police and sheriffs were enforcing the political disenfranchisement of Black men and women, arresting Black residents for "vagrancy" and other vague crimes, and then forcing those who were jailed to provide free labor to private companies (often under harsh conditions) through "convict-leasing" programs.

Twentieth-Century Transformation of Urban Police Departments

To understand the key issues facing urban law enforcement today, it is important to understand the genesis of what is now regarded as the twentieth-century **traditional approach to urban crime**. In the early twentieth century, reformers set out to build a revised concept of the role of the police force focused on creating professional crime-fighting specialists. These changes were part of a larger civic reform movement of the early century to reduce patronage in public administration

(Walker and Katz 2005). Exams for hiring and promotion were introduced to reduce the number of politically motivated appointments and nepotism. Civil service status was granted to provide police with job security and reassure officers against arbitrary or sudden unwarranted loss of employment. Many inspection tasks were shifted to departments of health or other municipal offices. Most importantly, the new training was designed to reorient police away from service to powerful individuals—ward bosses and mayors—and to emphasize apprehension of criminals and the solving of criminal cases (Greene 2000).

These reforms became the dominant approach to policing for the rest of the century. Aided by improvements in automotive transportation and communication—including radio communication between police headquarters and patrol cars—and assisted by advances in investigation techniques including the creation of police department crime laboratories, this approach to crime emphasized protection by rapid response and deterrence by raising the probability of arrest.

The Role of Civilian Employees in Police Departments

As cities continued to expand, the increased scale of police operations and innovations in policing technology encouraged a growing division of labor within police departments. Some paperwork and communications tasks could be efficiently handled through centralized offices by individuals without extensive training. On the other end of the spectrum, the growing scientific sophistication of investigatory functions required centralized laboratories and more specialized expertise. Popular television shows frequently convey these roles of specially trained law enforcement personnel. Decades ago, investigators used fingerprints to identify possible culprits; DNA labs are used for this purpose today.

Due to this growing division of labor and specialization, the composition of law enforcement personnel has changed. By the last decades of the twentieth century, the typical urban police department included not only police officers but also numerous civilian employees working as telephone responders for the emergency 911 system, computer data entry workers, and laboratory technicians.

Crime Prevention in Urban Settings: From Twentieth- to Twenty-First-Century Paradigms

In the twentieth century, debate in the United States over the use of police tactics focused on the viability of various approaches to urban crime prevention—among them, the traditional approach of cracking down on crime, the broken-windows/zero tolerance approach of making repairs and sprucing up a neighborhood along with apprehending anyone who degrades it, and community-oriented policing.

Some law enforcement personnel and city officials start from the premise that crime originates with the inclinations of individuals who are outlaws by nature. In the early twentieth century, due to the influence of widespread racism, this idea was often combined with the scientifically discredited notion that some ethnic or racial groups were inherently more predisposed to crime than others (Hahn and Jeffries 2003; National Advisory Commission on Civil Disorders 1968). But whether linked to race or not, these beliefs in the importance of apprehending people who are inherently "criminals" or "bad guys" has had and continues to have in some cases strong resonance in public thought today. Through this perspective, crime-fighting is seen as protection *against* individuals. From the standpoint of those who emphasize this interpretation of the origins of crime, an effective crime reduction strategy focuses on identifying and controlling the activities of those individuals. The traditional approach to crime that depends on rapid response, gathering information about specific individuals, and apprehension is strongly tied to this concept of individual criminal motivation (Greene 2000).

The major alternatives to this approach to urban crime and crime reduction began by trying to understand various aspects of the urban environment. Drawing upon the work of the early-twentieth-century Chicago School of Sociology, which emphasized the relationship between human behavior and the socioeconomic environment, a number of studies have focused on the relationship between crime and such social conditions as overcrowding, poverty, and rapid residential turnover. Rather than focusing on the origin of crime as the work of "criminal minds," this approach argues that while crime is committed by individuals, a substantial amount of crime is spawned by socioeconomic conditions and that levels of crime are best understood as manifestations of social conditions. At the core of the policy prescriptions arising from such studies is the idea that reductions in crime can best occur by improving the socioeconomic environment (Cahill 2004).

Within this approach, some interpretations of the possibilities for crime reduction emphasize the direct relationship between crime and economic circumstances. Reduce poverty and unemployment, the proponents of this view say, and you can substantially reduce crime. Another type of socioeconomic explanation emphasizes noneconomic variables. Many studies tie the incidence of crime to the absence of the social capital that would have provided formal and informal control of individual behavior through the intervention of parents, teachers, coaches and other community personnel. This approach explains why urban neighborhoods with similar levels of poverty or unemployment may have greatly divergent crime levels.

Included among the factors examined within this **systemic social disorganization approach** are neighborhood characteristics that create problems in the individual household's ability to nurture and guide the behavior of children and adolescents such as family disruption; factors at the community level that inhibit the growth of shared norms, trust, communication, and neighborhood involvement; and lack of access to resources from public institutions that could contribute toward solutions to neighborhood problems (Wilcox et al. 2004). The social disorganization approach implies that crime can be substantially reduced by measures that change the pattern of social interaction among families and between families and public institutions within a community.

Another widely adopted perspective on urban crime argues that the key to crime reduction is to be found in the relationship between criminals' preexisting desire to commit crimes and urban circumstances that provide opportunities for crime to be committed including isolated pedestrian pathways and the design of buildings. According to this view, urban crime can be substantially reduced by making changes in the urban environment that increase criminals' perceptions that their crimes will be observed and that attempted escapes from the site of the crime will be impeded. One variation on this approach is the **broken windows/zero tolerance** form of policing, enacted with much media attention in New York

City in the 1990s. This policy follows the reasoning that if the public report broken windows and other signs of vandalism and disorder and the police assure that the problem will be taken care of, criminals are more likely to believe that the residents and the city care about what happens in that location and that residents in the neighborhood are more likely to take note, quickly report, and physically react if a crime occurs (Wilson and Kelling 1982; Greene 2000; Sampson and Raudenbush 2001).

Community-oriented policing is a reform first formally introduced in the mid-1980s (Forst 2000; Greene 2000). It built upon studies of crime as well as riots in major cities, concluding that the magnitude and intensity of poor relationships between urban police and urban residents constituted a real urban crisis. Proponents of community policing have argued that the emphasis on apprehension rather than other forms of crime prevention, the growing racial separation within urban areas, and police hiring practices that tended to draw police recruits primarily from White neighborhoods and suburbia all led to police behavior characterized by alienation from and disrespect for the residents in many of the areas they patrolled, little understanding of neighborhood dynamics, and an overemphasis on force as the first response to many incidents (Forst 2000).

Community policing advocates argued that the focus and operations of police could be changed in ways that could create a better relationship between police and neighborhood residents, create more public support for law enforcement departments, help build a neighborhood's capacity to prevent crime, and strengthen the community's ability to recover from criminal activity when it occurs. As part of community policing, law officers emphasize crime prevention rather than simply response and apprehension. They interact frequently with community residents in a problem-solving context, strengthen and utilize their own communication and interaction skills, and link crime-prevention efforts more closely with other municipal services.

Recognized by some as one of the most significant shifts in the nature of police work in the twentieth century (Greene 2000), community policing received a major boost in 1994 with federal funds for community police training and for allowing police departments to hire additional officers for this specific purpose. By 2003, more than half of all local police departments serving populations of over 100,000 had formal written community policing plans and 75 percent of the local police departments in these larger cities were training their new recruits in these practices.

While the general concept of community-oriented policing focuses on the relationship between residents and the police, another approach focuses upon changing the relationship between police and the events that get their attention. This approach, termed **problem-oriented policing**, stipulates that instead of thinking in terms of responding to incidents, police should think in terms of the underlying factors that lead to such events (Scott 2000; Greene 2000). Rather than reacting to individual events, police forces are encouraged to identify recurring problems, to analyze them systematically, and then have police officers use problem-solving, planning, mediating, and neighborhood organizing skills—along with the improved relationship with the community developed through community-oriented policing—to develop and implement specific strategies to address the underlying factors that cause or contribute to criminal activity. The results are then evaluated to determine their efficacy (Scott and Kirby 2012). Problem-oriented policing was first applied in 1981 in Madison, Wisconsin. Among the urban police departments to first explore this approach were Baltimore County, Newport News, San Diego, Tampa, and Jersey City (Scott 2000).

Reimagining Public Safety for the Twenty-First Century

In 2013, after the killing of a Black teenager, Trayvon Martin, by a neighborhood-watch volunteer and the controversial acquittal of Martin's killer, three Black women started an online social media movement with the hashtag #BlackLivesMatter. As the number of videotape-documented deaths of unarmed Blacks by police and vigilantes mounted in subsequent years, Black Lives Matter became an organization with a global network of chapters. But even more so, it became a phrase that united the efforts of civil rights groups, community groups, and individuals protesting against police atrocities.

Outrage about police malfeasance and lack of accountability also grew through a parallel social media movement, #SayHerName, initiated in 2015, which specifically raised awareness of Black women who died in disturbing police cases. Motivated by tragedies such as those of Yvette Smith in 2014 and Sandra Bland in 2015, #SayHerName's calls for change resonated among wider audiences at the end of the decade as information emerged about the police shootings of Atatiana Jefferson in 2019 and Breonna Taylor in March 2020.

Subsequently, after the death of George Floyd in 2020 at the hands of clearly callous police officers, protest demonstrations occurred in 2,000 cities and towns in the United States (Burch, et al. 2020) and in numerous other cities around the world (Cave, et al. 2020). The words "Black Lives Matter" were now being chanted globally along with the admonition, as stated by author Kristian Williams, that "the slogan represents . . . not simply a fact, but more importantly a challenge. If we believe it, we must make it real."

In August 2020, the US Conference of Mayors, an organization representing 1,400 cities in the nation, recognizing "the urgent need to reset the relationship between our police and our residents," issued a formal *Report on Police Reform and Racial Justice*. According to Chicago Mayor Lori Lightfoot, the "comprehensive bipartisan report . . . provides cities and police departments with strong, actionable steps to build trust and legitimacy between officers and the communities they serve over the coming years." Among the major points in the UCSM report were the following:

- Reform and public safety are not mutually exclusive. The two goals can and should complement each other.

- [Past public safety practices] that devolved into a militarized and aggressive policing model . . . resulted in deepening historic divides, particularly between police and communities of color and other marginalized individuals and populations. By acknowledging this past, we can be effective in addressing inequalities in how we police and ensuring that police treat those they serve with fairness and respect.

- Another important step in this journey is reckoning with our de facto public policy choices that have compelled police to take on some roles that are better played by community-based social services providers. This moment compels us to ask, "who should respond," instead of reflexively sending the police when our residents are in need. These are serious questions that require thoughtful engagement.

- We need to both support our police through better training and supervision and hold accountable those who cross the line, delegitimizing policing. The job of a police officer is often dangerous and difficult and the vast majority perform to the best of their ability and in good faith. But the improper use of force can affect the perceptions of police everywhere. . . . we cannot ignore that there are police departments with systemic problems and that reform, transparency, and accountability have too often been elusive.

- If we want action, we need to empower the leadership of our police departments and hold those leaders accountable for delivering the results that our communities want and deserve.

- We do not have the luxury of inaction and we must act now. Our residents rightly demand concrete solutions. Working together, we—mayors, residents, police chiefs, officers, police unions, and community leaders—can meet this urgent challenge and make this agenda a reality. (UCSM 2020)

Indeed, spurred by widespread concern and protests, several cities initiated reforms in 2020. Amendments to city charters to create new police oversight committees were placed on the ballot and passed in Seattle, San Francisco, San Diego, and Portland, Oregon. New accountability structures and other reform programs were adopted by mayors and city councils in Boston, Philadelphia, Minneapolis, and New York, while task forces to recommend reforms were established in many other cities. Statewide police reform bills were under consideration by the end of 2020 in Massachusetts, Washington, Colorado, and other states.

Insights from the Data

City crime statistics suggest a large variance in the incidence of major criminal offenses across US cities. Using data on murders, rapes, robberies, assaults, burglaries, thefts, auto thefts, and arson, City-Data.com has created a combined crime index for nearly all cities in the United States. Figure 12.1 provides this crime index for the major cities we have been following. Nationwide, across all cities both large and small, the index was 273.5 in 2018, but across these cities the range is enormous. In such large cities as Tampa, San Diego, and New York, the crime index that year was below the national average for all cities. Tampa's index was only 72 percent of the US average. By contrast, St. Louis, Detroit, and Baltimore all had crime indices at least three times the national average.

There are many factors that might explain this variance in crime rates, but clearly one of them is economic. While the correlation between crime rates and median household income tells only part of the story, the relationship shows clearly that those cities with the lowest incomes have some of the highest crime rates while

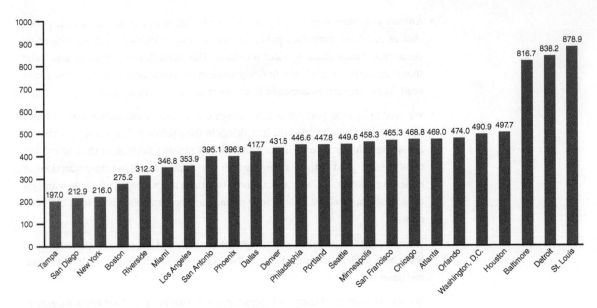

FIGURE 12.1. Crime Index for Largest US Cities, 2018

those with higher income have much lower ones. This is shown in Figure 12.2. The three cities with the highest crime rates also had some of the lowest household incomes—again Detroit, St. Louis, and Baltimore.

Nonetheless there are anomalies that depart from this pattern. While Miami has a relatively low median household income, its crime rate was well below the correlation line. While New York has been the site of many crime shows and movies, it actually has one of the lowest crime rates of these large cities.

If you were to watch the 6 p.m. local TV news station in nearly any city, you would likely believe that crime is increasingly rampant in your community. But as Figure 12.3 demonstrates, the incidence of urban crime has been falling since at least 2005. In many cases, the decline in the crime index is quite substantial. Between 2005 and 2018, the index fell by 33 percent in Philadelphia. In other cities the index was down by 40 percent or more and in Tampa 71 percent. Of the major cities in this figure, only Baltimore has seen an increase in its crime index. More generally, crime rates have plunged across the United States since the mid-1990s (Howe 2015). Even some of the most crime-ridden neighborhoods, such as Bedford-Stuyvesant in New York and South Central Los Angeles, areas once known for drug lords and drive-by shootings, have seen their murder rates fall by two-thirds—in part as a result of these communities beginning to gentrify.

As for explaining the sharp decline in crime rates in most urban areas, there is substantial disagreement among experts. The economic prosperity thesis argues that crime rates fall when economic conditions improve and rise when unemployment and household incomes fall. But despite the modest correlation we see in Figure 12.2 and the fact that crime rates fell during the economic boom of the late 1990s, this thesis cannot explain why crime rates continued to fall during the recession that lasted from 2007 through 2009.

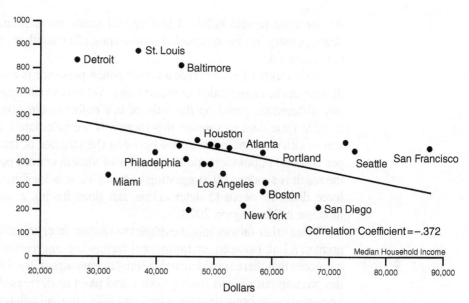

FIGURE 12.2. Relationship Between Median Household Income and Crime Rates for Largest US Cities, 2018

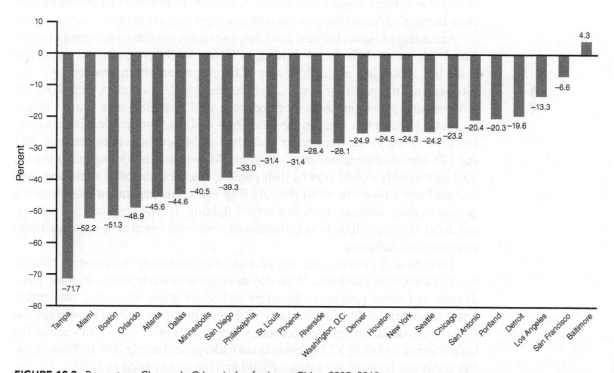

FIGURE 12.3. Percentage Change in Crime Index for Large Cities, 2005–2018

As mentioned earlier in this chapter, some people credit crime-level changes primarily to the criminal justice system. The incarceration theory suggests that crime has declined because more potential offenders are in prison. But data reveal that crime continued to decline in states that have reduced their prison rates.

At one time people believed that capital punishment reduced crime, but as the death penalty has been repealed in one state after another crime rates have fallen, not increased.

Still another thesis is that a larger police presence is responsible for the sharp decline in the crime index in major cities. Yet this would suggest dramatic city-by-city differences based on the ratio of law enforcement officers to population but there is little data to support this theory. If we calculate a correlation coefficient across cities for the relationship between the number of law enforcement officers per 100,000 population and the number of violent crimes per 100,000 population, the result is a paltry .09, suggesting virtually no relationship. Having a larger police force does not seem to deter crime, nor does having a smaller force appear to increase it (Harrington 2020).

What other factors might explain the decline in criminal activity? Some experts point to a link between environmental factors and aggressive social behavior. Howe has noted that there is evidence that links the passage of the 1970s Clean Air Act and the phasing out of lead from gasoline and paint to decreased crime levels. Lead is known to cause brain damage which can affect human behavior. Others suggest that the decreased consumption of heroin, crack, and alcohol could be responsible for less violent behavior and criminal activity. Even a decline in unwanted pregnancies following *Roe v. Wade* might explain some of this downward trend for this resulted in fewer births of children who grow up with less supervision (Levitt and Dubner 2006).

According to Howe, the best candidate to explain the downward trend in crime rates is generational change. According to Howe, youth crime rates started to rise in the late 1960s, just as the first wave of baby boomers (born between 1946 and 1964) entered the youth age bracket. For the next couple of decades, these boomers and first-wave generation Xers (born between 1961 and 1981) took youth violence to spectacular heights. Only in the late 1990s and the first decade of the twenty-first century did crime rates begin to decline as Millennials (born between 1981 and 1996) became the dominant youth group. Millennials, according to this theory, were increasingly looked after by their parents, teachers, and other adults and were sheltered and advised to avoid risk. As they aged, this generation experienced a decline in risky behavior including school fighting, teenage pregnancy, smoking, and drunk driving. All these risky behaviors have been found to be correlated with more criminal behavior.

There is also evidence that the decline in overall crime accelerated with the onset of the Covid pandemic. With stay-at-home quarantine orders in some jurisdictions and fewer people on the street and fewer going into work, researchers found substantial reductions in many cities beginning in 2020. *The Washington Post* (Jackman, 2020) reported decreases in 911 calls in 29 of 30 cities across the United States including a 25% reduction in Chicago and nearly 20% in Washington and Baltimore between the spring of 2019 and the same period in 2020.

While burglaries and larcenies were down because more homeowners were at home and shops were closed reducing shoplifting, one form of crime did increase with the onset of the pandemic – homicide (Corley, 2021). While there is no definitive explanation for the spike in murder in 2020, it appears to have occurred across nearly all major U.S. cities. Overall, homicides were up nearly 37 percent between 2019 and 2020. In Milwaukee, the number of murders increased from 98 to 191, an increase of nearly 95 percent. In a range of cities from New Orleans, Boston, Minneapolis, Chicago, Atlanta, Memphis, and Fort Worth to Seattle, Louisville, and Phoenix, the homicide rate increased by more than 50 percent during Covid.

According to the Mayor of New York, Bill de Blasio, the 39 percent spike in the murder rate in his city may have been related to the fact that the criminal justice system was on pause given the limited numbers of police on the streets and the closing of courts of law. Clearly the pandemic made people already suffering poverty even more desperate and this could have led to a spike in violence.

One can expect that theories about crime levels and explanations of changes in crime will continue to be debated. The question of how best to protect and serve the community continues to be a major topic of discussion, and both police practices and the relationship between police and residents continue to be modified in law enforcement forces across the country. As reforms in concepts, practices, and accountability occur, it will be important for public officials and residents to remember that public safety and police practice are multidimensional elements of society and the success of neighborhoods, cities, and metropolitan areas require interdisciplinary insights and multidisciplinary approaches.

New Issues of the Twenty-First Century: Private Security, Internet Crime, and Homeland Security

Just as public safety in the early 1900s was faced with new challenges as cities grew rapidly with new migrants from rural areas and immigrants from many parts of the world, urban public safety in the twenty-first century is faced with new challenges that did not exist throughout most of the twentieth century.

Today, if you go to a shopping center, a hospital, a sports stadium, a large concert, or many other kinds of activities open to the public, you are likely to see uniformed security guards hired as employees by the business directly or as contract workers from firms specializing in security services. They provide a range of services in such public places, and also in many **gated communities**. These include screening at the entrances to buildings or neighborhood entry points and the monitoring of behavior through direct observation and the use of closed-circuit television cameras. The number of security guards and others engaged in private policing has outgrown the number of public-sector police—an increase beginning in the 1970s that has been dubbed the "quiet revolution" in public safety (Stenning and Shearing 1980).

Summarizing the literature on private policing, Bayley and Shearing (2001) suggested that the rapid growth of this phenomenon constitutes a basic "restructuring of policing." While they note that private policing is generally more focused upon prevention rather than the apprehension of criminals, the growth of market-provided security has many implications for justice, equity, and political stability. The reason for this is that the restructuring of policing through markets distorts the distribution of security in favor of those who can afford it, and runs the risk of creating a dual system of policing where the poor are protected by the public police while the rich are protected by private security officers.

The US Bureau of Labor Statistics reports that in May 2019, there were over 1.1 million individuals working as **private security guards**. Articles about this phenomenon have raised issues about violations of civil liberties and a lack of public accountability (Joh 2006). Yet given the rapid growth in private security forces, such policing has become a subject of intense study (Button 2019), while authors of articles addressed to police professionals have argued for "skillful management of the relationships between public and private policing" (Sparrow 2014).

Another important issue for twenty-first century public safety is the increasing use of the internet and information technology by predators and perpetrators of crime. The Federal Bureau of Investigation (FBI) established the Internet Crime Complaint Center (IC3) in 2000 to gather reports of crimes carried out or facilitated through the internet. In 2019, the IC3 had 467,361 complaints—up from 288,012 in 2015. The total amount of money reported lost due to these crimes in 2019 was $3.5 billion—three times the amount in 2015. Among the types of crimes proliferating through internet capabilities are credit card fraud, identity theft, and ransomware. According to a 2018 report from the Police Executive Research Forum, "The United States is experiencing a transformation in how criminals are using technology to invent new types of crime and are creating new methods for committing traditional crimes. . . . Police departments will need to make significant changes to address these developments but most agencies have not yet begun the process." The PERF report suggests that addressing these crimes will require new skills (such as experience with digital evidence), new training (in social media platforms, "dark web" investigations, Internet of Things applications, and other internet interactions), and possibly reorganization of police departments (Morison & Sloan 2018).

Since the September 11, 2001 attack on the World Trade Center in New York and the Pentagon just outside of Washington, DC, there has also been greater awareness of the need to prevent terrorism. The National Institute for Justice defines terrorists as "those individuals who commit or provide support for the commission of ideologically motivated violence to further political, social, or religious goals" (Qureshi 2020). According to the University of Maryland's National Consortium for the Study of Terrorism and Response to Terrorism (START), there were 856 attacks classified as terrorist in the United States in the 25 years from 1995 to 2019. These include 310 attacks within the five years from 2015 to 2019 that cost 316 people their lives.

In 1996, a year after the Oklahoma City bombing of federal office buildings, the US Department of Justice began its State and Local Anti-Terrorism Training Program to provide terrorism prevention training to state, local, and tribal law enforcement personnel. As an assessment of this program in 2016 noted:

> Although the FBI and other federal law enforcement are responsible for investigating terrorist threats, they rely on the information-sharing about terrorist threats and the detection and response by state and local law enforcement. State and local law enforcement play an important role in detecting and preventing terrorist attacks. . . . 80 percent of foiled terrorist plots in the United States were discovered because of observations by state and local law enforcement or by the general public. (Davis et al. 2016)

According to police experts, the threat of terrorism not only presents a physical threat to cities but also challenges police departments to think through their approaches to policing. Murray (2005) noted the tendency among some police officers and some politicians to abandon community-oriented policing and instead revert to traditional policing models in order to prevent terrorist acts. This is despite the fact, Murray argued, that the community-police relationship, based on mutual trust, is more likely to help identify prospective terrorists.

The challenges discussed in this last section—of the relationships between municipal police forces and private security forces, the impact of the internet and other powerful information technologies, and the need to prevent terrorist attacks—add to the urgency to improve police–community relationships and related reforms in recruitment, training, deployment, and accountability. These issues highlight the need for effective and adaptive urban police departments that can effectively consider, analyze, and appropriately address current and future public safety concerns.

Fire Departments

Earlier chapters have emphasized that density is one of the primary characteristics of cities, and with this density comes many externalities. One of the most fear-raising of externalities is the possibility of fire spreading from an initial source to destroy homes, workplaces, and other structures. Throughout the nineteenth century and into the twentieth, the threat of fire was one of the greatest fears of urban residents. The crowded wood-frame housing in which most people lived made it easy for flames to pass quickly from one residence to another, while the use of woodstoves and open fireplaces for warmth and cooking provided the opportunity for wayward sparks to ignite. "Great fires" that left many dead and hundreds or thousands homeless occurred in many cities including Boston (1760, 1787, and 1872); New York (1776 and 1835); New Orleans (1788 and 1794); Pittsburgh (1845); San Francisco (1851 and 1906); Portland, Maine (1866); Chicago (1871); Seattle (1889); Jacksonville (1901); Baltimore (1904); and Atlanta (1917).

As was the case with policing, the threat of fire in early US cities was initially addressed by volunteers, some of whom acted as lookouts, while others responded to emergencies when summoned (Rothenberg and Giglierano 2006). However, by the mid-nineteenth century, as increasing city size reduced the efficacy of volunteer systems, cities turned to full-time municipally paid fire departments (Hashagan 2006). Cincinnati began its paid firefighting force in 1853, Chicago in 1858, the New York boroughs in 1865, and Philadelphia in 1870.

Successful firefighting has relied upon speedy response and the availability of water. Advances in city water systems and steam engine technology during the nineteenth century moved firefighting from human lines of bucket brigades in the early 1800s to horse-drawn steam-powered pumps tapping water from city hydrants by the late 1800s. The invention and increasing affordability of motorized vehicles in the early twentieth century allowed fire stations to utilize trucks specifically designed for quick response (Calderone 2006). Fire departments in the United States are well-known today, even to little children, for their iconic red pumper and ladder trucks.

Fire continues to be a major threat to cities, suburbs, towns, and wilderness areas. According to the National Fire Protection Association (NFPA), local fire departments in the United States responded to 1.3 million fires in 2019. Total losses that year included 3,700 civilian deaths, 16,600 civilian injuries, and nearly $15 billion in property damage (Ahrens and Evarts 2020).

In 2018, according to the NFPA, among the 29,705 local fire departments in the United States, there were 2,292 departments serving populations of 25,000 or more. New York City has the nation's largest fire department with approximately 11,000 uniformed firefighters, 4,300 emergency medical service staff, and 2,100 civilians, followed by Los Angeles County and Houston. While the nation's largest cities use mainly career firefighters, a number of cities use a mix of careerists and volunteers. Nationwide there were more than 1.1 million firefighters, with 370,000 career firefighters and 745,000 volunteers (Evarts and Stein 2020).

As was the case with police departments, in many cities the social context of firefighting and the racial composition of fire departments became an issue. In the early twentieth century, fire departments were frequently part of the political machinery of urban areas, providing patronage jobs and support for political figures. Race and ethnicity also played a direct part in firefighting. By the mid-twentieth century recruitment practices and fire department racial composition became—and in many cases, continue to be—an area of contention for cities that are increasingly Black and Hispanic. According to the US Bureau of Labor Statistics, in 2019 only 8.5 percent of career firefighters were Black, 11.6 percent were Latinx, and 1.3 percent were Asian (BLS 2020).

Fire Safety Regulations

Today's fire departments not only extinguish fires but enforce fire-prevention regulations, respond to emergencies involving hazardous materials, handle numerous rescues from dangerous conditions, and provide **emergency medical services (EMS)**. The distribution of situations to which fire departments responded in 2015 is depicted in Figure 12.4.

The damage fires cause cannot be addressed by quick response alone, for the damage caused by fires often occurs before fire departments can arrive on the

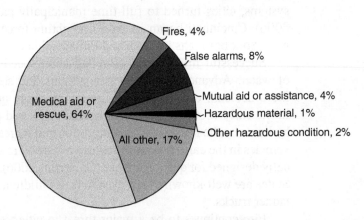

FIGURE 12.4. Fire Department Responses by Incident Type, 2015

Source: National Fire Protection Association. 2021. "Fire Department Calls," https://www.nfpa.org/News-and-Research/Data-research-and-tools/Emergency-Responders/Fire-department-calls

scene. Fire *prevention* is therefore a key aspect of public safety. Although it may not be apparent to everyone, virtually every part of every building in urban areas must comply with city, state, and national regulations designed to reduce the threat of fire, smoke, and other hazards. In addition, many levels of government have fire-safety education programs to teach the public how to avoid creating dangerous conditions and how to respond in the initial stages of a fire or chemical emergency.

Development and recommendations of fire prevention standards is led by the National Fire Protection Association (NFPA), an international nonprofit organization which in 2020 had 60,000 members from more than 100 countries (NFPA 2020). The NFPA was established in the last years of the nineteenth century and grew out of a recognition that water sprinkler systems connected to city water systems could be highly effective in reducing the damage and spread of a fire. The technology for water delivery through pipes for firefighting had been a focus of invention and innovation in the United States since the 1850s, and the first automatic sprinklers (releasing water when high temperatures melt fusing material within the sprinkler design) were patented in the early 1870s (Grant 2020). The proliferation of municipal water systems described in Chapter 9 created opportunities to install sprinklers widely. However, in the early 1890s there were no uniform standards for pipes, fixtures, and other elements needed for general adoption of sprinklers. In 1895, sprinkler manufacturers and insurance companies took the lead in convening conferences in Boston to establish standards for this important fire control technology. These conferences led to the creation in 1896 of the National Fire Protection Association "to promote the science and improve the methods of fire protection and prevention, electrical safety and other related safety goals; to obtain and circulate information and promote education and research on these subjects; and to secure the cooperation of its members and the public in establishing proper safeguards against loss of life and property" (NFPA 2020a). Since 1896, the NFPA has carried out this mission "by advocating scientifically based consensus codes and standards, research, and education for fire and related safety issues" (Grant 2000).

To be set in place, potential standards need to be adopted by government and enforced by government employees and this focuses attention once again on public-sector decision-making. Tragedy was often the direct impetus for government adoption of new regulations incorporating codes and standards or for enhanced enforcement (Brannigan and Carter 2006). In 1903 a fire in Chicago's Iroquois Theater, a venue with poorly marked exits, left 602 dead. In 1911, despite pleas by the New York Fire Chief for more regulation of conditions in factories, the Triangle Shirtwaist Company caught fire, killing 146 workers. In 1942 a fire broke out at Boston's Cocoanut Grove Nightclub, killing 491. More recently, a fire at the Station Nightclub in West Warwick, Rhode Island on February 20, 2003 resulted in 100 deaths and more than 200 injuries (Boston Globe 2003). Studies of each of these fires pointed to the importance of **building construction guidelines**, occupancy limits, clear unfettered paths to exits, and overall fire safety plans that could be taken to decrease the toll from fire, smoke, and trampling as people rush toward the exits.

The NFPA reports that today it has developed more than 300 safety standards dealing with a myriad of subjects related to fire, electrical, chemical, building, and life safety, and that its codes and standards are reviewed and updated every

3 to 5 years (NFPA 2020c). NFPA members include national, state, and local government officials; fire department representatives; healthcare professionals; representatives from business, industry, and insurance companies; engineers; and other constituencies interested in fire prevention. The organization includes research and public education divisions, and provides certification programs and documentation of competency for numerous technicians, inspectors, and other specialists (NFPA 2020b). Through NFPA efforts to develop standards, undertake research, encourage public-sector adoption of regulations, and provide certification of enforcement professionals, the interaction between municipalities and the NFPA is an important component of public safety in urban areas and to nations around the world.

Structural and Chemical Fire Hazards

While new regulations could be incorporated into the construction of new buildings, the renovation of older buildings to include such measures is more complicated. In many cities some older buildings were renovated, some were demolished, some were abandoned, and others became targets of arson. As the stock of central city housing and commercial buildings aged, fighting fires in such older buildings presented special hazards for firefighters and for nearby residents.

During the twentieth century and into the twenty-first, changes in manufacturing also affected firefighting. New types of plastics and new chemicals created numerous situations in which water alone was not effective in extinguishing flames, and others in which hazardous fumes are released during fires. In some cases, such incidents require not only extinguishing the fire but also evacuation of the nearby population. These developments challenged firefighting techniques and led to an expansion of expertise within fire departments. Firefighting training expanded to include treatment of hazardous materials, with many large cities equipped with **hazmat trucks** fully equipped to deal with a range of hazardous materials.

Today, fire departments are more highly trained than they were half a century ago. However, they face new challenges in the twenty-first century. Continual changes in industrial inputs, the presence of abandoned and structurally unsound buildings, the threat of arson and terrorism, the expanding number of high-rise office towers, and other urban features make metro areas ever-more dependent on fire regulations and effective firefighting as essential contributors to public safety and the quality of life.

Emergency Medical Services (EMS)

One of the key responsibilities of firefighting is rescuing individuals who might be trapped, rendered unconscious, or injured by flame, smoke, or lack of oxygen. This was a major factor in the creation of Emergency Medical Services (EMS) in the 1960s (National Highway Traffic Safety Administration 1996). Previously, ambulance drivers and the attendants who rode with them to transport people in need of immediate medical care were relatively unskilled. Public health officials in that era thought that more lives could be saved if effective intervention could be done before patients reached hospitals.

In 1960 studies showed that cardio-pulmonary resuscitation (CPR)—a combination of mouth-to-mouth breathing assistance and rhythmic chest compressions—could help save lives. The first systematic implementation of CPR occurred among firefighters during rescues, and the positive results from this use led Congress to approve funds for the development of regional emergency medical services as part of the Highway Safety Act of 1966 (National Highway Traffic Safety Administration 2006). Federal funding for further development of EMS and for the training of EMTs was expanded in 1973 with the Emergency Medical Services Systems Act. Today, emergency medical systems and the professionals who staff this important first-responder service have become a basic part of public health and safety infrastructure across the United States—a fact that was made even more salient in 2020 by the increased visibility of EMS services in the course of the COVID-19 pandemic.

The funding, base of operations, and organizational structure for EMS varies from place to place, and within the same city one may find activities operated by fire departments, hospitals, and private ambulance services. According to a 2007 report from the Institute of Medicine, 45 percent of EMS services nationally were fire-department based (Institute of Medicine 2007).

According to data collected in 2019 and early 2020 by the National Association of EMS Officials, there are over one million licensed EMS professionals in the nation. Their certification levels adhere to the following classifications established by the National Registry of Emergency Medical Technicians: emergency medical responders (EMRs) are certified to perform basic immediate interventions with minimal equipment while awaiting other EMS resources. **Emergency medical technicians (EMTs)** are certified to stabilize and transport patients and to provide interventions using the basic equipment found in ambulances. Advanced emergency medical technicians (AEMTs) are certified to provide basic and limited advanced medical care using the basic and advanced equipment found in ambulances. Paramedics are certified to provide advanced medical care using basic and advanced equipment found in ambulances. Table 12.3 shows their distribution by skill level.

TABLE 12.3. EMERGENCY MEDICAL SERVICES STAFF IN THE UNITED STATES

CLASSIFICATION BY SKILL-LEVEL	TOTAL NUMBER IN US	PERCENTAGE OF EMS STAFF
Total EMS Staff	1,052,082	100%
EMD—Emergency Medical Dispatchers	21,514	2.0%
EMR—Emergency Medical Responder	113,973	10.8%
EMT—Emergency Medical Technician	583,608	55.5%
AEMT—Advanced Emergency Medical Technician	39,294	3.7%
Other Level between EMT and Paramedic	17,634	1.7%
Paramedic	268,420	25.5%
Level above Paramedic	8,399	0.8%

Source: 2020 National EMS Assessment. May 2020, National Association of State EMS Officials, Table 30, p. 47-2

TABLE 12.4. FIRE DEPARTMENTS PROVIDING EMERGENCY MEDICAL SERVICE BY COMMUNITY SIZE, 2016-2018

POPULATION PROTECTED	NO EMS	BLS	ALS	TOTAL
1,000,000 or more	0%	0%	100%	100%
500,000 to 999,999	0%	26%	74%	100%
250,000 to 499,999	2%	27%	72%	100%
100,000 to 249,999	3%	34%	63%	100%
50,000 to 99,999	6%	39%	55%	100%
25,000 to 49,999	17%	37%	46%	100%
10,000 to 24,999	27%	42%	32%	100%
5,000 to 9,999	38%	43%	19%	100%
2,500 to 4,999	41%	47%	12%	100%
Under 2,500	45%	49%	6%	100%
Nationwide	38%	45%	17%	100%

BLS refers to fire departments providing basic life support, and ALS refers to fire departments providing advanced life support.
Source: "U.S. Fire Department Profile 2018, Supporting Tables", Table 20. National Fire Protection Association.

According to the National Fire Protection Association, all fire departments serving populations of a million or more provide advanced life support EMS through staff with certifications at AEMT, paramedic, or the level above paramedic. The percentages for smaller populations is given by Table 12.4.

The importance of fire departments, fire regulations, and the provision of emergency medical services underscore not only the many human-to-human interdependencies in urban life but also several ways in which the urban life built by humans interacts with biological, chemical, and physical sciences. The spread of the COVID-19 pandemic in 2020 called our attention not only to our reliance on EMS, but also to the danger of microscopic pathogens and the realities of our biochemical world. The dependence of first responders on the complexities of urban water, electrical, and communication infrastructures highlights the importance of the engineers who design such systems. The need for new fire suppression techniques to address new potentially dangerous chemicals released by fire directs us to the work of chemists and other material scientists. The interdependence of emergency medical services, hospitals, and other parts of urban health system infrastructures increases our awareness of the roles of doctors, nurses, epidemiologists, and other health professionals in modern society. In turn, the new capabilities, processes, and potential interventions created by scientists and health professionals shape the goals, activities, and effectiveness of fire, EMS, and other first responders.

The interdisciplinary insight gained by scholars and practitioners, and further cross-disciplinary teamwork, will be major factors in the effectiveness of first responders—and therefore for the quality of urban life—in the future.

References

Ahrens, Marty and Ben Evarts. 2020. "Fire Loss in the United States in 2019." *News and Research*, September. Quincy, Massachusetts: National Fire Protection Association.

Bayley, David, and Clifford D. Shearing. 2001. "The New Structure of Policing: Description, Conceptualization, and Research Agenda." *National Institute of Justice Research Report NCJ 187083*. Washington, DC: Department of Justice, Office of Justice Programs.

Blackmon, Douglas A. 2008. *Slavery By Another Name: The Re-Enslavement of Black Americans from the Civil War to World War II*. New York: Anchor Books.

Boston Globe. 2003. "First Victims ID'd; Tales of Lives Lost for Families, Show Slowly Fades to a Grim Reality." *Boston Globe*, February 23.

Brannigan, Francis, and Harry Carter. 2006. "Fire Disasters: What Have We Learned." http://www.firefightercentral.com/history/learned_from_fire_disaster.htm.

Burch, Audra, Weiyi Cai, Gabriel Gianordoli, Morrigan McCarthy, and Jugal Patel. 2020. "How Black Lives Matter Reached Every Corner of America." *New York Times*, June 13, 2020.

Button, Mark. 2019. *Private Policing*, 2nd ed. London: Routledge.

Cahill, Meagan E. 2004. "Geographies of Urban Crime: An Intraurban Study of Crime in Nashville, Tennessee; Portland, Oregon; and Tucson, Arizona." PhD dissertation, University of Arizona.

Calderone, John. 2006. "Fire Apparatus: Past and Present." Firefighter Central. www.firefightercentral.com/history/fire_appartus_past_and_present.htm.

Cave, Damien, Livia Albeck-Ripka, and Iliana Magra. 2020. "Huge Crowds Around the Globe March in Solidarity Against Police Brutality." *New York Times*, June 13, 2020.

Corley, Cheryl. 2021. "Massive 1-Year Rise in Homicide Rates Collided with the Pandemic in 2020. *National Public Radio*, January 6.

Davis, Lois M., Todd Helmus, Priscillia Hunt, Leslie Adrienne Payne, Salar Jahedi, and Flavia Tsang. 2016. "Assessment of the State and Local Anti-Terrorism Training (SLATT) Program." Santa Monica, CA: RAND Corporation.

Easter, Eric. 2016. "Whatever Happened to Officer Friendly?" Urban News Service, August 12, 2016. https://www.ebony.com/news/police-relations-officer-friendly/.

Evarts, Ben, and Gary Stein. 2020. "US Fire Department Profiles 2018." February. Quincy, Massachusetts: National Fire Protection Association.

Forst, Brian. 2000. "The Privatization and Civilianization of Policing." U.S. Department of Justice, Office of Justice Programs, Washington, D.C., September, 1–61

Gaines, Larry K., Victor Kappeler, and Joseph Vaughn. 1999. *Policing in America*, 3rd ed. Cincinnati: Anderson Publishing Company.

Grant, Casey Cavanaugh. 2000. "History of NFPA." https://www.nfpa.org/About-NFPA/NFPA-overview/History-of-NFPA.

Greene, Jack R. 2000. "Community Policing in America: Changing the Nature, Structure, and Function of the Police." U.S. Department of Justice, Office of Justice Programs, Washington, D.C., January, 1–72.

Hahn, Harlan, and Judson Jeffries. 2003. *Urban America and Its Police*. Boulder: University Press of Colorado.

Harrington, John. 2020. "Cities with the Most Police Per Capita." *Wall Street Journal*, July 24. https://247wallst.com/special-report/2020/06/24/cities-with-most-police-per-capita/

Hashagan, Paul. 2006. "Firefighting in Colonial America." http://www.firefighter-central.com/firefighter_history.htm.

Howe, Neil. 2015. "What's Behind the Decline in Crime?" *Forbes*, May 28.

Hyland, Shelley, and Elizabeth Davis. 2019. "Local Police Departments, 2016: Personnel." NCJ 252835, October. Washington, DC: Bureau of Justice Statistics, Department of Justice.

Institute of Medicine 2007. *Emergency Medical Services: At the Crossroads*. Washington, DC: The National Academies Press.

Jackman, T. (2020, May 19). "Amid Pandemic, Crime dropped in many U.S. Cities, but not all." Retrieved May 28, 2020, from https://www.washingtonpost.com/crimlaw/2020/05/19/amid-pandemic-crime-dropped-many-us-cities-not-all/

Joh, Elizabeth. 2006. "The Forgotten Threat: Private Policing and the State." *Indiana Journal of Global Legal Studies* 13, no. 2 (Summer): 357–389.

Levitt, Stephen D., and Stephen J. Dubner. 2006. *Freakonomics: A Rogue Economist Explores the Hidden Side of Everything*. New York: Harper Collins.

Monkkonen, Eric. 1981. *Police in Urban America, 1860–1920*. New York: Cambridge University Press.

Morison, Kevin and Madelone Sloan. 2018. "The Changing Nature of Crime and Criminal Investigations," National Training and Technical Assistance Center, Police Executive Research Forum, Occasional Paper, November 28. https://www.policeforum.org/assets/ChangingNatureofCrime.pdf.

Murray, John. 2005. "Policing Terrorism: A Threat to Community Policing or Just a Shift in Priorities?" *Police Practice and Research* 6, no. 4: 347–361.

National Advisory Commission on Civil Disorders, 1968. *Report of the National Advisory Commission on Civil Disorders*. Washington, DC: National Advisory Commission on Civil Disorders.

National Association of State EMS Officials. 2020. *National EMS Assessment*, May. Falls Church, Virginia: National Association of State EMS Officials.

National Consortium for the Study of Terrorism and Reponses to Terrorism (START). 2020. "American Deaths in Terrorist Attacks, 1995–2019." October. College Park: University of Maryland.

National Fire Protection Association (NFPA). 2020a. "History of the NFPA Codes and Standard-Making System." https://www.nfpa.org/-/media/Files/Codes-and-standards/Standards-development-process/HistoryNFPACodesStandards.ashx. Accessed December 13.

National Fire Protection Association (NFPA). 2020b. "NFPA Overview." December 13. https://www.nfpa.org/About-NFPA/NFPA-overview.

National Fire Protection Association (NFPA). 2020c. NFPA Standards Directory. https://www.nfpa.org/-/media/Files/Codes-and-standards/Regulations-directory-and-forms/NFPA_Standards_Directory_2020.ashx.

National Highway Traffic Safety Administration. 1996. "The EMS Agenda for the Future." Washington, DC: National Highway Traffic Safety Administration.

Qureshi, Aisha J. 2020. "Understanding Domestic Radicalization and Terrorism: A National Issue Within a Global Context." *National Institute of Justice Journal* 282. https://nij.ojp.gov/topics/articles/understanding-domestic-radicalization-and-terrorism

Rothenberg, Peter, and Geoff Giglierano. 2006. "A Quick History of the FDNY." http://www.nycfiremuseum.org/education/history/chapter1.php.

Sampson, Robert, and Stephen Raudenbush. 2001. "Disorder in Urban Neighborhoods—Does It Lead to Crime." *National Institute of Justice Research in Brief*. February. Washington, D.C.: National Institute of Justice.

Scott, Michael S. 2000. "Problem-Oriented Policing: Reflections on the First 20 Years." Washington, DC: Department of Justice, Office of Community Oriented Policing Services.

Scott, Michael S., and Stuart Kirby. 2012. "Implementing POP: Leading, Structuring, and Managing a Problem-Oriented Police Agency." September. Tempe: Center for Problem-Oriented Policing, Inc., Arizona State University.

Sparrow, Malcolm K. 2014. "Managing the Boundary Between Public and Private Policing." *New Perspectives in Policing Bulletin*, NCJ 247182. Washington, DC: US Department of Justice, National Institute of Justice.

Stenning, Philip, and Clifford Shearing. 1980. "Quiet Revolution: The Nature, Development and General Legal Implications of Private Security in Canada." *Criminal Law Quarterly* 22: 220–248.

Sullivan, Carl, and Carla Baranaukas. 2020. "Here's How Much Money Goes to Police Departments in Largest Cities Across the U.S." *24/7 Wall Street Journal*, June 26. https://www.usatoday.com/story/money/2020/06/26/how-much-money-goes-to-police-departments-in-americas-largest-cities/112004904/.

US Bureau of Labor Statistics. 2020. "Employed Persons by Detailed Occupation, Sex, Race, and Hispanic or Latino Ethnicity." https://www.bls.gov/cps/cpsaat11.htm, accessed December 13.

Wadman, Robert, and William Allison. 2004. *To Protect and To Serve: A History of Police in America*. Upper Saddle River, NJ: Pearson/Prentice Hall Publishers.

Walker, Samuel, and Charles Katz. 2005. The *Police in America*. New York: McGraw-Hill.

Wilcox, Pamela, Neil Quisenberry, Debra Cabrera, and Shayne Jones. 2004. "Busy Places and Broken Windows?: Toward Defining the Role of Physical Structure and Process in Community Crime Models." *Sociological Quarterly*. Berkeley: University of California Press. 45. No. 2 Spring. 285–307.

Williams, Kristian. 2015. *Our Enemies in Blue: Police and Power in America*, 3rd ed. Chico, California City: AK Press.

Wilson, James Q., and George Kelling. 1982. "Broken Windows: The Police and Neighborhood Public Safety." *Atlantic Monthly*, March.

Questions and Exercises

Comprehensive crime data for US cities is collected can be found at http://www.city-data.com/crime.

1. Select five cities of your choice and examine data on the following crimes:

   - murder
   - robberies
   - assaults
   - arson

For each of these cities track these crime rates over the most recent 10-year period.

   a. What is the trend for each of these crimes in each of these cities?
   b. Which type of crime is on the rise? Which type is in decline?
   c. Does the trend vary from one city to the next?
   d. Using your browser, try to find data on crime prevention activities for one or more of these cities that might explain what factors are responsible for this trend.

2. This same data set provides information on a range of demographic characteristics for each of the cities you selected. These data include:

- median household income

- race and ethnicity

- median age

Across the cities you have selected, examine whether there appears to be any relationship between these demographic characteristics and the crime rate trends you found in answering Question 1.

3. In the wake of the Black Lives Matter movement, some cities have instituted new policies and programs in an attempt to reduce policing activities that appear to be overzealous or possibly racist. Using your browser investigate whether any of the cities you have been tracking has taken such action. What is the nature of policing reform you may have identified?

13

Land-Use Controls, Sprawl, and Smart Growth

LEARNING OBJECTIVES

- ■ Explain the power of eminent domain and how its application in the United States has expanded over time

- ■ Distinguish between the four principal motives for zoning and provide an example for each

- ■ Explain the Coase theorem and show how it can be used as an alternative to zoning

- ■ Explain the concepts of underzoning and overzoning and give an example of each

- ■ Explain the concept of urban sprawl and the arguments for and against it

- ■ Explain the relationship between urban sprawl, density, and initiatives such as smart growth and transit-oriented development

Industrial age cities were never pleasant places in which to work or live. The smell, the smoke, and the noise; the foulness that permeated air and water; the filth in the streets; and the soot and grime that defeated even the most vigorous attempts to maintain a clean home were not only an assault on the senses but a danger to health and life itself. Urban historian Lewis Mumford (1961) describes nineteenth-century cities, dominated by factories and the railroads that ran through them, as places where smoke billowed throughout residential areas and rivers served as open sewers for the byproducts of the cotton, chemical, and iron industries. In *The City in History,* he points out:

> Workers' houses, often those of the middle classes, too, would be built smack up against a steelworks, a dye plant, a gas works, or a railroad cutting. They would be

built, often enough, on land filled in with ashes and broken glass and rubbish, where even the grass could not take root; they might be on the edge of a dump or a vast permanent pile of coal and slag; day in and day out the stench of the refuse, the murky outpouring of chimneys, the noise of hammering or of whirring machinery, accompanied the household routine.

In 1906 Upton Sinclair published his muckraking novel *The Jungle,* an indictment of the living and working conditions of the immigrant workforce in Chicago's meatpacking plants. The "Back-of-the-Yards" neighborhood adjacent to these factories that reeked of packinghouse decay, overflowing garbage, and sewage had high rates of deadly infectious diseases including tuberculosis and numerous cases of infant mortality.

As industrial cities grew throughout the nineteenth and early twentieth centuries, the completely unfettered land market contributed to sanitation and public health ills that ultimately threatened further growth. One response to these negative externalities was the development of municipal sanitation systems; another was the movement for public health reform that we discussed in Chapters 9 and 11. Another, as this chapter details, was the development of land-use controls.

Land-Use Restrictions and Zoning

While location restrictions of some economic activities—particularly those officially recognized as posing a threat to the well-being of the general populace—extend back to colonial periods, citywide planning through land-use restrictions is of more recent vintage.

A growing awareness of the need for city planning emerged during the explosive urban growth of the late 1800s and early 1900s, when factories were being built in cities at a feverish pace. In the span of one year alone (1906–1907), New York saw 3,060 new factories established, most in Manhattan and in close proximity to where hundreds of thousands of residents lived (Boyer 1994).

There were a number of problems with unregulated location. Newly established industries with offensive aromas or with water and air pollution as byproducts could harm nearby retail businesses. Crowded tenement housing in the alleys of industrial areas contributed to crime and disastrous fires. The uncertainty of the future uses of adjacent land could preclude investment in a business or create unwanted risk for real estate speculators. Families who sought to remove themselves from the central city might find their new locations encroached upon by the same social and economic ills they had sought to escape.

With the growth in cities and the water and air pollution that accompanied early factories constructed within them, Europe would lead the way in city planning to put distance between industrial and residential neighborhoods. By the 1860s, Italy and France had already adopted rules to protect residential neighborhoods from factories (Hirt 2010). German reformers in the 1870s and 1880s introduced the idea of zoning an entire city into residential and industrial districts (Platt 2004). From its inception, the goals of such German zoning were control of noxious industry, relief from overcrowding, and in some cases protection of the countryside. In 1891, Frankfurt became one of the first large cities to have citywide zoning (Logan 2007).

In Germany, planners rarely prohibited all industry from locating in residential neighborhoods but instead permitted some which met strict performance standards regarding air and water emissions. The Frankfurt planning code had six zones. Two were exclusively for residential use and two were exclusively industrial, but two permitted mixed use as long as industrial enterprises met emission standards (Logan 2007).

By the early 1900s, US cities were beginning to adopt their own planning systems as various residential, business, real estate, environmental, social reform, and public-sector interests began to coalesce into a widespread movement for the adoption of citywide regulations to control land use (Boyer 1994). William Fischel (1999), a Dartmouth College economist who has written extensively about government-imposed land-use controls, offers the possibility that they were necessary, like sewer systems, for industrial era cities to continue to take advantage of agglomeration economies and counteract the disadvantages hazardous to health and to life. Unlike the German system that predated them, zoning in the United States seldom allowed residential and industrial uses in the same neighborhood.

In the early 1990s, Los Angeles would be the first city in the United States to zone its entire area into residential and industrial districts. New York would enact its own comprehensive zoning system in 1916, which banned all industrial and most commercial operations from residential neighborhoods. In the process, the new zoning would force hundreds of factories to move from central Manhattan and reserved two-thirds of the city for residential purposes. The new law regulated building heights throughout the city. The practice quickly spread. After their adoption in New York, zoning regulations spread to 76 US cities by 1926 and to more than 1,300 cities by 1936 (Boyer 1994).

In northern Europe, the Scandinavian countries, the Netherlands, and Great Britain would take planning seriously introducing their own stringent forms of zoning (Nivola 1999). In Southern Europe, cities including Belgrade in Serbia, Salonica in Greece, and Sofia in Bulgaria adopted zoning of their own making with general city plans and multiple binding building use plans. Yet in each of these cities, the level of mixed use would exceed that in Germany and more than in the United States (Hirt 2010).

The Power of Eminent Domain

In the United States, the legal authority for local governments to exercise some control over the use of private property includes the rights of **eminent domain** and **police power**. The former refers to the power of local government to take private land for public use, the latter to the local government's right to protect the health, safety, and general well-being of its citizens by imposing enforceable regulations. The legitimacy of zoning—essentially the imposition of government restrictions on how private (and public) land can be used in order to limit negative externalities and in some cases enhance positive externalities—derives from these local government police powers.

In the legal tradition followed by the United States, real estate exists as a right conferred to individuals and to private entities by government under an ownership classification called **fee simple**. The right to own property is transferable to other parties but remains fundamentally a right conferred by government. This is why deeds ensuring the ownership and the right to transfer privately owned real property are handled by a government agency, usually at the municipal level.

But it has long been established that a local government has the right to take private land to serve a public purpose so long as the owner is paid the property's fair market value. Through the middle of the twentieth century, the power of eminent domain was used to transfer land from the private sector back to the public sector in order to build public schools, courthouses, and highways. Under the Housing Act of 1949—which, among other provisions, established the nation's urban renewal program—the definition of public purpose was expanded to include slum clearance. The urban renewal program often used the power of eminent domain to transfer property from one group of private owners to another, who would then agree to erase blighted areas by redeveloping the land. Based on the expectation at the time that private developers would shun the city and instead build only in the suburbs, the program subsidized these developers by buying the land, clearing it, and then selling it to them far below its cost.

The Supreme Court in June 2005 ruled in *Kelo v. City of New London* that local economic development was itself a legitimate public purpose for which a city could use eminent domain even when an area was not a slum or blighted area. The court opined that improving the climate for private investment and job creation in a municipality hard hit by disinvestment and job loss could serve as a legal rationale for a local community to seize land under eminent domain as long as the owners were fairly compensated.

For the plaintiffs, fair compensation was beside the point. The issue for them was not about their homes' objective value—their **market value**—but about their homes' subjective value—their **use value**. Even with fair compensation for her house, it would have been difficult for Susette Kelo, one of the plaintiffs, to replicate the distinctive water views she cherished. But it would have been impossible for Wilhelmina Dery, another plaintiff, to replicate what she lost. Her house had been in her family for more than a hundred years, she herself was born there in 1918, and she had lived there ever since. As Logan and Molotch (1987) point out, those who acquire land for its potential future market value are often more savvy about the uses of political power than those who want to retain the land for its use value.

The *Kelo* case was decided by a vote of 5–4 and has generated enormous controversy. Ultimately, the land was mostly cleared but to date nothing has been built there. In response to the *Kelo* decision, many states have sought to pass their own laws that restrict the use of eminent domain especially in those instances when the local government transfers land from one group of private owners to another. In her dissenting opinion, Justice Sandra Day O'Connor wrote, "The specter of condemnation hangs over all property. Nothing is to prevent the State from replacing any Motel 6 with a Ritz-Carlton, any home with a shopping mall, or any farm with a factory."

O'Connor's statement raises an intriguing puzzle. In a market economy such as ours, where land is usually sold to the highest bidder, why would the state need to intervene at all? Why would the market itself not replace a Motel 6 with a Ritz-Carlton? That is indeed the logic behind the bid rent curves we discussed in Chapter 4. We see the result of that bidding process every time a drive-in movie theater gives way to an industrial park or an apple orchard is sold off to become a residential subdivision. The concept of **highest and best use** refers to the normal situation in which the market mechanism itself determines the most productive use for any given plot of land. Therefore, why would the state need to use its power of eminent domain?

If you have ever played the famous board game, Monopoly, you learned something about the buying and selling of property. Players can buy property they land on, but they can build houses and hotels only if they own all the properties of the same color. Say you own two of the three yellow properties—Atlantic and Ventnor—but another player owns Marvin Gardens. Maybe you can negotiate to buy it from him. He might hold out for a high price, but the price still might be worth it to you to be able to build and collect higher rents. That other player might be your kid brother and he might refuse to sell just because yellow is his favorite color or maybe just to spite you. Now you have a **site assembly problem**. In Monopoly, the site assembly problem means you cannot build at all. In the real world, the site assembly problem—the prospect of dealing with holdouts who believe they can ransom their properties or those who just plain refuse to sell—is a powerful deterrent to redevelopment. A municipality's ability to use eminent domain solves the developer's site assembly problem.

The Legalization of US Zoning Regulations

Like eminent domain, zoning may involve a change in circumstances for the landowner. In this case, the government places limits on how a parcel of land may be used. But unlike the power of eminent domain, the land is not taken from its owner, and zoning does not normally require that the owner be compensated for any loss in value. The power to zone was ultimately affirmed in a 1926 US Supreme Court decision, *Village of Euclid, Ohio v. Ambler Realty Co.* Although some large cities already had zoning ordinances prior to 1926, as seen earlier, these regulations proliferated among municipalities of all sizes after the Supreme Court made its ruling. Today, because of the Standard State Zoning Enabling Act passed by the US Congress two years later, in 1928, there is a good deal of uniformity in zoning laws nationwide.

While recent cases have reaffirmed the court's decision in the *Euclid* case—arguing compensation for loss in value is not required if a legitimate public purpose is being served, it remains an area of great legal contention. The Fifth Amendment to the US Constitution states, in part, "nor shall private property be taken for public use, without just compensation." The issue in contention is whether loss in property value as a result of zoning or other environmental regulation such as wetlands protection is a "taking" under the Fifth Amendment that requires compensation for the owner. According to Jerold Kayden (2001), an expert on property rights, the Supreme Court established the broad principle that "although owners are not entitled to the most profitable use of their property, they are entitled not to be denied all economically viable use." Beyond that, the Supreme Court has left it to lower courts to adjudicate the issue on a case-by-case basis.

Types of Zoning Regulations

There are four principal motives for zoning. **Externality zoning** separates land uses to deal with the fact that land used for some purposes creates negative externalities for other uses, as we noted earlier. Today, externality zoning is typically addressed through one of three means: (1) prescriptive approaches to externality zoning that identify a specific use for each plot of land in a city, (2) cumulative approaches that identify a range of specific allowable uses for each plot, and (3) performance approaches that focus on the intensity of the externality—for example, the amount of noise, glare, or fumes allowed. In performance approaches, standards are set for the externality and instead of restricting a particular type of use, land may be used by any entity that produces externalities below the maximum intensity permitted.

Design zoning restricts land use to promote the efficient use of the city's infrastructure or the conservation of open spaces. Through the zoning process, new development can be limited to areas that have compatible transportation, water, and sewer systems. Green spaces that include parks, riverfronts, and other open spaces for plazas and fields can be preserved in this way.

Fiscal zoning attempts to bar changes that would have an adverse effect on a city's municipal budget. The central motivation for this form of zoning is to assure that any additional municipal costs associated with a change in land use should not be greater than the additional revenues coming from that change. For example, some cities and towns may want to discourage increased population density because the additional tax revenues would be less than the cost of providing city services, especially schooling, to the increased population.

While externality, design, and fiscal zoning may provide some real benefits for a city, there is a fourth type of zoning that can be quite pernicious and often implemented as an explicit racist policy. **Exclusionary zoning** attempts to bar one or more racial or ethnic subgroups from sections of the city. Efforts to exclude on the basis of race represented one of the primary goals of early citywide zoning. In the 1880s, San Francisco adopted laws that segregated its Chinese population. In 1910, Baltimore adopted a citywide regulation that mandated the separation of White and Black residences. By 1914, racial zoning regulations had been adopted in nine southern cities—Richmond, Norfolk, Portsmouth, Roanoke, Winston-Salem, Greenville, Atlanta, Louisville, and Birmingham. The US Supreme Court ruled such laws unconstitutional in 1917, but many southern cities attempted to establish new racial zoning laws in the decades that followed. Birmingham enforced a racial zoning law until 1951, despite the Supreme Court ruling. Throughout the 1900s, some cities in both the North and the South engaged in "racially informed zoning," in which goals of racial separation were not explicitly mentioned, but were nonetheless advanced through the use of externality, design, and fiscal zoning (Silver 1997).

Exclusionary zoning has also been used to maintain the social class character of some suburban areas contributing to income and wealth segregation. Minimum lot sizes, for example, may be set forth as a form of fiscal zoning when the underlying motivation that drives the regulation is to prevent the development of housing for families with more moderate income who cannot afford large lots. In practice, it is often difficult to disentangle the legitimate role of zoning to reduce the negative externalities that would accompany incompatible land use from its "hidden agenda" of promoting exclusion on the basis of race, ethnicity, or income (Boyer 1994; Silver 1997). Often such "snob" zoning prohibits multifamily housing in a particular city or town and has the effect of maintaining social class divisions.

Land-use regulations are often a source of conflict in metropolitan areas because citywide and suburban zoning affect the entire metropolitan economy, because various interest groups within metropolitan areas may be in conflict over specific zoning plans, and because exclusionary motives can often be presented as externality or design zoning. Zoning plans pit developers against local communities, businesses against homeowners, and often one race or social class against another. Whenever limits are placed on land use through zoning, there is bound to be some conflict. Indeed, in many communities, battles over zoning are often the most contentious issues facing city or town councils. But without some forms of zoning, one can imagine that cities might be much more unpleasant places in which to live and work.

Houston's Alternative to Zoning

There are alternatives to zoning and Houston, Texas is a city with no zoning at all. One would think that Houston would have a hodgepodge of activities throughout the city and would therefore experience a high level of adverse outcomes. Yet there is no stark contrast between land-use patterns in Houston and other cities. In the absence of zoning, one might ask how Houston has avoided a return to the nightmare landscapes of an earlier age such as those with which we began this chapter. Although land in Houston is not zoned, its use is nevertheless regulated through private arrangements called deed restrictions or restrictive covenants (Siegan 1972).

For example, two individuals purchasing property in Houston, Smith and Jones, have to decide whether to buy into a subdivision with restrictive covenants. Smith decides that restrictions on his own property, such as the color he is allowed to paint the exterior of his home or the type of fence he can erect in his yard— regulations that limit his ability to impose negative externalities on his neighbors— would reduce its value to him by $10,000. But Smith also calculates that restrictions on what his immediate neighbors can do—which limit their ability to impose negative externalities on him—would increase the value of his own home by $15,000. Smith therefore buys the property. By contrast, Jones might calculate that the restrictions on him would reduce his value by $20,000 while restrictions on his neighbors would increase it by only $10,000, in which case he does not buy the property. To the extent that more households see the situation in the same way as Smith, the subdivision will be successful.

Much of Houston's land was built up in big subdivisions owned by large-scale developers. These developers established rules, enforceable by the city, that governed the use of the property through its sale and resale to subsequent owners. This ability to avoid negative externalities through negotiations in the private market is consistent with the limited-government orientation of the noted economist Ronald Coase, recipient of the 1991 Nobel Prize in Economics.

In his landmark 1960 article "The Problem of Social Cost," Coase argues that externalities do not necessarily require government intervention and that private bargaining will lead to the optimal outcome if three conditions hold: (1) property rights are clearly specified, (2) the number of parties involved is small, and (3) the costs of bargaining (transaction costs) are negligible. Using this line of argument, the **Coase theorem** begins from the presumption that the problem of externalities is reciprocal. For example, I might be harmed if you add another story to your house casting a shadow that causes my landscaped garden to wither, but you might be harmed if I prevent you from doing so, even though your family is expanding and you need another bedroom.

Coase argues that as long as property rights are completely specified, it does not matter who initially possesses them. If the garden owner possesses the property right and thus the power to veto a building project, the builder and the garden owner should be willing to arrange compensation for the externality that affects the garden owner as long as the value to the builder exceeds the value of the garden owner's loss. An outcome that maximizes total value to the parties taken as a whole will occur in either case.

Say the new room will add $10,000 to the value of your house above the cost of building it. Moreover, assume that it would cost me $6,000 for alternative landscaping with shrubs that thrive in shadow and are as pleasing to me as my current landscaping. If *you* have the property right to build, you will do so since I will not be willing to pay you enough to get you to change your mind. I will not pay you $10,000 to save my garden which is worth only $6,000 to me. However, if *I* have the right to prevent you from building, you can still negotiate a side payment of $6,000 to me that pays for the new landscaping thereby compensating me for my loss. Whether or not I receive compensation will be determined by which of us possesses the property right, but it will not determine whether the bedroom is built. In either case, you wind up building your new bedroom: in the first case, without having to pay me; and in the latter, by making the $6,000 side payment. In both cases, the total value to the two parties together is $10,000. If you have the right to build, you will gain the total $10,000 benefit. If I have the right to prevent you from building, you can pay me the $6,000 and you have a net gain of $4,000—a total benefit again of $10,000.

On the other hand, if the new room adds $10,000 to the value of your house but causes $20,000 in damages to my landscaping, the optimal outcome in terms of our total benefits would be not to build, and that is what will occur. In this case, if I have the right to prevent you from building, I will, since it would not be worth it for you to try to compensate me for the value of my loss. If you have the right to build, I will negotiate a payment that makes it worth your while not to do so. You could use that payment to purchase a larger house elsewhere or figure out some other way to create more space, perhaps by waterproofing your basement. Whether or not you get paid (for not building) depends on which of us possesses the property right but in either case the additional story will not be built.

Where it can be applied, the Coase theorem is an elegant private-market solution to the problem of externalities. But in many real-world instances of externalities, property rights cannot be completely specified, a large number of parties are affected, or transaction costs are significant. If the pattern of land development in Houston had not involved big subdivisions developed by a small number of large companies that had the right to specify the terms of purchase, it is unlikely that such a nonzoning alternative would have been possible. No other major US city has even attempted this. Moreover, although Houston does not have a zoning board, it does have a planning department as well as a deed restriction enforcement team within the city's legal department. Though more reliant on private markets to determine land use, Houston is still a significant departure from the notion of an unfettered free market where property owners can do as they please in terms of the the unrestricted use of their land.

Underzoning and Overzoning

It is one thing to say that the justification for zoning is the reduction of negative externalities that result from incompatible land uses and quite another to determine the optimal amount of zoning. Under what circumstances do zoning laws fail to effectively reduce negative externalities? Under what circumstances do zoning regulations go beyond the point of meeting the efficiency criteria for which they were intended?

In Niagara Falls, New York, land was excavated for a canal in the 1890s, but the Love Canal (the builder, Love, named it after himself) was never completed. Beginning in the 1920s and continuing until 1952, several chemical companies used the site as a waste dump. The area was covered over in 1953 and was subsequently the site of an elementary school and many homes. The water table in the area rose throughout the 1960s and 1970s, causing contaminated groundwater to come to the surface. By 1978 air samples showed dangerously high levels of toxic waste including benzene, a known human carcinogen. The area was found to have a higher than normal incidence of cancer, miscarriages, and birth defects. Ultimately, all the residents in a ten-square-block area were relocated and the elementary school was demolished (Beck 1979).

In 1980, in response to the environmental tragedy at Love Canal, the US Congress enacted the Superfund program to clean up hazardous waste sites. Under the terms of this law the US Environmental Protection Agency (EPA) had, by April 2004, relocated more than 45,000 people who were living on or near Superfund cleanup sites and provided alternative sources of drinking water to more than 600,000 people living on or near these sites (US Environmental Protection Agency 2004). In many instances the nature and severity of the hazard was not known until long after the damage was done and therefore would not have been prevented by zoning. The *Washington Post* reported in 2002 that hundreds of public schools are located within one-half mile of Superfund sites and that while many had been built decades earlier, some were relatively new (Pianin and Fletcher 2002). They described instances in which parents and other community members were successful in blocking attempts to site new schools on former waste sites. Zoning regulations do not necessarily deal with such environmental hazards. Land formerly used for waste sites is relatively cheap and therefore attractive, from a cost perspective, for development.

The issue of **underzoning**, or failure to prevent negative externalities that arise from incompatible land use, is central to the concept of **environmental justice**. The EPA's definition of environmental justice includes this criterion for fair treatment: "No group of people, including racial, ethnic, or socioeconomic groups, should bear a disproportionate share of negative consequences resulting from industrial, municipal, and commercial operations or the execution of federal, state, local, and tribal environmental programs and policies" (US Environmental Protection Agency 2007).

Yale Rabin (1989), an urban planning expert, argues that many municipalities have used zoning ordinances to protect White residential areas from incompatible land uses but have denied Black residential areas the same protection. He uses the term **expulsive zoning** to describe local governments' use of zoning ordinances to protect White residential areas, while zoning Black residential areas for industrial or other **locally unwanted land uses (LULUs)**.

A study completed for the EPA by the National Academy of Public Administration (2003) reports that even though minorities were far more likely than White residents to live near hazardous waste sites, enforcement of the law was stronger in White areas. The study found that the penalties imposed on environmentally compromised sites were greater in White areas and it took longer to place sites in minority areas on the hazardous waste site National Priorities List. It took one to three and a half years longer for the EPA to begin cleanups at sites in minority neighborhoods and it chose containment rather than permanent treatment more often in minority areas while choosing permanent treatment more often in White areas.

The issue of environmental justice combines problems of efficiency (the failure to prevent negative externalities) and equity (the disparate treatment of various racial and ethnic groups) that arise when areas are underzoned. As we shall see, other equity issues arise from instances where areas are subject to **overzoning** rather than being underzoned, with the explicit goal of keeping any further development from occurring in the community.

Equity Issues in Zoning

As Fischel (2000) points out, "Zoning is the product of a political process and it serves the interests of those who control that process." In many jurisdictions, those interests are served through the use of fiscal zoning, as noted earlier in this chapter, in which land uses that bring in more property tax revenue than they cost in local expenditures are sought after, while land uses that do the opposite are excluded. Similarly, in those jurisdictions that collect local sales taxes, there is a powerful incentive to zone land for retail use.

As we saw in Chapter 7, municipalities are heavily dependent on the property tax as a source of revenue to fund local public-sector functions, the largest category being primary and secondary education. Existing property owners within a jurisdiction know that they will be able to attain more or better-quality public services in return for their own contribution to tax revenues to the extent that they are successful in practicing fiscal zoning. Attracting office parks, regional headquarters, or other forms of clean, nonpolluting business activity will generate high property tax revenue more than sufficient to pay for the additional roads and public safety expenditures they might require. On the other hand, allowing the construction of homes worth less than the current median house value will dilute the public-sector benefits that existing property owners receive in return for their property tax payments. If those homes contain school-age children, the town will often incur additional expenditures that are not fully offset by additional revenues. Therefore, it is in the interest of existing residents to repel low- or moderate-income families with children while welcoming higher-income families and older households without children.

If current residents want to ensure that the value of new homes will be above that of the existing housing stock, they can use zoning laws to exclude trailer parks, garden apartments, multiunit housing, and even single-family homes on small lots. Large-lot, single-family zoning ensures that the area will be low density and therefore beyond the price range of families who would cost local government more than they contribute.

While low- and moderate-income families are shunned, clean industry is sought for its contribution to the fiscal health of a community. The motives for fiscal zoning are economic but the result is exclusion based on income. Since minorities tend to have lower incomes than Whites, exclusion on the basis of income will exclude a disproportionate number of minority families.

In addition to the economic motives behind fiscal zoning, there may be other motives to exclude households not simply on the basis of income but on the basis of race and ethnicity. In Chapter 6, we saw how employers who practice statistical discrimination would exclude qualified minority workers from desirable jobs. Similarly, White property owners who believe that the incidence of crime is higher among low-income minority households with young adults can use carefully constructed exclusionary zoning to bar such households from the area. Zoning for age-restricted housing where only those over age 55 are allowed to rent or buy is just one type of such zoning. In the end, residential segregation by income results in fiscal disparities between communities. The winners in the fiscal zoning competition are able to provide high-quality public-sector services at relatively low tax rates. The losers are forced to tax themselves more heavily, but even then are often unable to fund public-sector services of comparable quality.

Edwin S. Mills (1979), a noted urban economist, points out that exclusion based on race or ethnicity was the hidden agenda behind some of the nation's earliest zoning laws. As mentioned earlier in this chapter, in the 1880s, during a time of virulent discrimination against Asians, San Francisco passed a law excluding them from living in some parts of the city. California courts judged that law unconstitutional, so the city passed a law that excluded laundries from those areas. Since many laundries were operated by Asians who lived close to where they worked, the new law served the same purpose as the old, but without running afoul of the state's constitution. Similarly, New York City's early twentieth-century zoning laws used districting and height limits to keep garment manufacturers and their low-income Eastern European immigrant female workforce segregated from the city's fashionable shopping areas and their more prosperous clientele. Mills argues that the ability to determine their own zoning laws was an important motivation for suburban jurisdictions to reject central city attempts at annexation.

In a similar vein, urban economist John M. Levy (1985) argues that the powers of local zoning boards to rezone or to grant **variances** can be applied selectively to enforce exclusionary goals without blatantly violating the law. Rezoning changes the land-use restrictions in a given area. Granting a variance keeps the restrictions in place but gives permission to a nonconforming use that would otherwise be in violation of the ordinance. An area zoned for single-family housing might be rezoned if a company wanted to build its corporate headquarters there or if a developer wanted to build apartments for affluent retirees but not if the developer wanted to build **affordable housing** for young families. Levy notes that many of the corporate headquarters in Westchester County, New York (the county just north of New York City), have been built on land that was originally zoned for large-lot, single-family homes.

In the face of these economic and discriminatory motives, efforts to encourage suburban jurisdictions to accept even small amounts of affordable housing have had very limited success. Judicial decisions such as in the 1975 New Jersey case, *Southern Burlington County NAACP v. Township of Mount Laurel (Mount Laurel* I) and the subsequent 1983 ruling *(Mount Laurel* II) and such legislative efforts as in the 1969 Massachusetts passage of Chapter 40B, the "anti-snob-zoning" act, require that every jurisdiction in each state provide some affordable housing units as a proportion of its total housing stock. While these requirements have led to the construction of a modest number of affordable units in the suburbs, the overall impact has been relatively small leading to a continuation of income and racial/ethnic segregation.

Thus, while the fundamental economic justification for zoning to reduce negative externalities is still widely accepted, concerns about the motives behind its implementation in many municipalities raise important issues of social equity. From a public policy perspective, the conundrum is how to craft zoning laws that limit true adverse externalities but do not blatantly or even subtly create insurmountable hurdles to those who are striving for a better place to live.

Zoning and Informal Settlements

Despite the existence of laws protecting private property and regulating land use, the worldwide growth of urbanization has been accompanied by the growth of informal settlements where residents do not have property rights, their neighborhoods often lack such basic services as running water and electricity, and their housing may violate **building codes** or may be located in environmentally unsafe areas. By the mid-2010s, an estimated 25 percent of the world's urban population lived in such places (Avis 2016).

In the developing world, these informal settlements are often on land near the outskirts of cities. In her award-winning 2012 book about a shantytown near the Mumbai airport in India, Katherine Boo describes the poverty and disease-ridden lives of those who live there hoping to find a better life for themselves and their families (Boo 2012). Similar settlements to the *favelas* of Brazil and the *asentimientos humanos* of Peru exist in other developing nations. Only in some cases, for example El Alto near La Paz, Bolivia and Villa El Salvador, near Lima, Peru, are these settlements acknowledged by their municipal governments allowing public services and infrastructure to be extended to them (Brunn et al. 2016).

Informal settlements are not limited to the developing world. Vasudevan (2017) describes squatters' movements in London, Berlin, Amsterdam, New York City, Frankfurt, Hamburg, Bologna, Milan, Rome, Turin, and Vancouver. Christiana, an informal settlement in Copenhagen, has been in existence since 1971.

Within the United States, informal housing can take many forms, from the *colonias* that spread along the Texas–Mexico border during the mid-twentieth century, where developers built housing on subdivided land in unincorporated areas but did not provide such basic services as running water, paved roads, or electricity, to other forms in which housing originally contructed to building code specifications is allowed to fall into noncompliance. The latter includes partitioning existing living space into tiny units that violate code, or simply allowing extreme overcrowding in violation of occupancy laws. This is in addition to the people who live in their vehicles, in tent cities, or as squatters on abandoned property (Durst and Wegmann 2017).

Zoning and Metropolitan Sprawl

Particular forms of suburban development raise an additional set of efficiency and equity issues. If you walk out the front door of your house and you do not have access to an automobile, what opportunities are available to you? Can you borrow a cup of sugar from a neighbor? Can you walk to the store to buy a container of milk? Can you bicycle down to the local coffee shop? Can you board a bus, light-rail, or other "fixed guideway" vehicle (e.g., a trolley, subway, or monorail) that will take you to another part of town? If you live inside a city or in one of the older suburbs built before World War II, it is likely that at least some of these options will be available to you. But if you live in a newer suburb at the edge of the metropolitan area, exclusive-use zoning and the complete separation of land use make it more likely that you will depend on an automobile for most, or even all, of these activities. The tendency to build newer suburbs at lower density, to segregate land use more completely, and to be more dependent on automobiles is part of the phenomenon called **urban sprawl**. It is one reason for our love–hate relationship with cities and suburbs that we described in Chapter 1.

William H. Whyte is credited with coining this term in a 1958 essay in which he warns, "Already huge patches of once green countryside have been turned into vast, smog-filled deserts that are neither city, suburb, nor country, and each day— at a rate of some 3,000 acres a day—more countryside is being bulldozed under." Although there is no commonly accepted definition of sprawl, figuring prominently in many descriptions are low density, separation of land uses, and automobile dependency. A relatively dispassionate discussion of the costs and benefits of sprawl is available in Burchell et al. (2002).

As we saw in Chapter 4, decentralization has been occurring since the late nineteenth century. Its pace increased after the 1920s and accelerated further after the 1950s. Sprawl is not synonymous with decentralization, although it is sometimes used this way, sowing much confusion. Sprawl refers to a specific form of decentralization that is characterized by much of the late-twentieth-century metropolitan growth in which single-use developments—housing subdivisions, shopping malls, office parks, and industrial parks—are segregated from each other and accessible primarily by automobiles traveling on arterial roads. This pattern of land use differs not only from that of cities but from that of older suburbs. In the debate over sprawl, the dichotomy is not between city and suburb, but between pre–World War II patterns of city and suburban growth and development patterns adopted after World War II. The concern is not primarily about the continuation of decentralization per se, but the form that decentralization has taken in recent decades.

What's Wrong With Sprawl?

Critics of sprawl raise a number of concerns. Some architectural critics find it aesthetically undesirable. For example, Dolores Hayden (2003) of Yale University describes the quintessential edge city of Tyson's Corner, Virginia as resembling "a model with all the building blocks for both suburb and city thrown on the ground by a two-year-old having a tantrum."

Other criticisms of sprawl fall more comfortably into the economists' domain of efficiency and equity. The list of efficiency concerns includes those that are specifically related to environmental degradation as well as a more general set of negative externalities that affect various subgroups of the population.

A sprawling pattern of growth consumes large areas of land. Figure 13.1 shows US Geological Survey maps for the Washington, DC–Baltimore area that track urban growth over more than 200 years and projects possible scenarios by 2025. The expansion of metropolitan area boundaries is disproportionate to the area's population growth. Similar expansion occurs even in metropolitan areas whose populations are shrinking.

Large-lot, low-density development may contribute to the pollution of soil and groundwater through the use of septic systems instead of sewers as well as through the use of pesticides and fertilizers on large expanses of lawn. In some regions of the country, the use of scarce water supplies to nourish parched lawns and other nonindigenous plants and shrubs places further strain on natural resources. Moreover, new infrastructure including streets and highways, communication networks, and other public utilities are extended out to the fringe of the metropolitan area only at great expense while some of the existing infrastructure in depopulated areas within the central city remains underutilized.

Urban Sprawl and Commuting Times

Average one-way commuting times have been inching up from less than 22 minutes in 1980 to more than 27 minutes in 2018. This is nearly an hour a week or about a full-time workweek over the course of a year (Ingraham 2019). As we pointed out in Chapter 10, reliance on the automobile for virtually all trips to all destinations raises its own set of concerns, only some of which are related to environmental issues. Increases in gasoline consumption as automobile ownership rises and an increase in total per capita miles driven accelerate the depletion of a nonrenewable resource. With increased road congestion due to the total number of trips

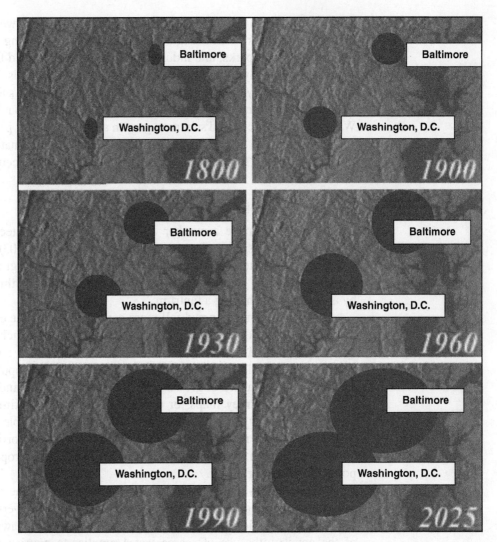

FIGURE 13.1. Washington, DC–Baltimore Metropolitan Growth

Source: US Department of the Interior, US Geological Survey.1999. "Analyzing Land Use Change in Urban Environments," USGS Fact Sheet 188-99. Washington DC: US Government Printing Office.

taken each day, overall travel times continue to grow, which reduces the amount of time people can spend at work, with family, or simply enjoying leisure. This can represent a huge opportunity cost in terms of an individual's time and for society in terms of revenue. The resources used in highway construction could potentially have been used for other purposes including the building of schools and parks.

Moving farther away from central cities explicitly involves decentralization. The specific manner in which a suburban development is designed can turn well-intentioned decentralization into expensive and inhumane sprawl. In *A Better Place to Live*, Philip Langdon (1994) demonstrates how the design of many modern residential subdivisions not only makes it impossible to provide public transportation, but actually discourages residents from walking or riding bicycles. The development of residential "pods" that are accessible from an external arterial road and contain long, curving internal routes and cul-de-sacs that lack easy connections between sites makes it difficult to navigate even *within* the pod by any means other than automobile. The result for residents is that the automobile is indispensable for even the simplest of errands. The corollary for nondrivers—the young, the old, and some of the disabled—is that there is a significant loss of autonomy, since even the simplest of errands requires dependence on someone else who can drive them to their destinations.

The reliance on automobiles and the disappearance of opportunities to walk simply as part of one's normal way of being out in the world has been linked to increases in obesity and other illnesses related to sedentary lifestyles (Frumkin et al. 2004). Health experts tell us that we should be pursuing exercise equivalent to walking 30 minutes each day. A generation or two ago this could be achieved effortlessly in the course of living one's life: going to work or school, stopping for a container of milk, making it to a doctor's appointment, mailing a letter, or stopping in for a haircut or manicure. Nowadays, for many of us, that exercise has to be deliberatively scheduled because it no longer occurs in the normal course of our daily lives. In a real sense, the rise of the modern health club can trace its roots to urban sprawl.

The Debate About Sprawl

Critics of sprawl argue that it is undesirable because of its concomitant inefficiencies and inequities. They support a range of public policies at the federal, state, and local levels that would curb sprawl. By contrast, defenders of sprawl argue that current land-use patterns reflect consumer choice. If the fastest-growing counties in the United States are characterized by large houses on large lots and populated by adults who drive SUVs, it is simply a reflection of people voting with their feet and evidence that a growing number of households have been successful in achieving the American Dream of single-family homeownership.

The defenders of sprawl maintain that the automobile has allowed an unprecedented degree of geographic mobility which has expanded the range of choices for household members in their roles as workers, consumers, and citizens. They argue that suburb-to-suburb commuting patterns reduce the pressure on downtown roads and relieve congestion. Concerns over the loss of farmland and open space are misplaced or overblown. After all, productivity per acre has increased dramatically so that less farmland is needed, and areas of open space are increasing in the United States as the rural population continues to dwindle.

Moreover, defenders of sprawl, including Gordon and Richardson (1998), point out that the Los Angeles metropolitan area, the proverbial "poster child" of sprawl, actually has a higher population density than many eastern metropolitan areas such as Boston or Philadelphia. They argue that the critics of sprawl tend to be intellectuals who prefer to live in cities and who are imposing their own tastes on an unreceptive population. In this view, policies to curb sprawl would be unwise, unwarranted, and unworkable.

Robert Bruegmann (2005), an art historian, argues that current decentralization is simply the continuation of a worldwide process that has been going on for centuries, facilitated by economic growth and affluence that give people more choice about where to locate their homes and businesses. In comparing older and newer US metropolitan areas, he argues that settlement patterns seem to be converging as density falls in older, higher-density locations and rises in the newer, lower-density ones. While a desire for mobility, privacy, and choice will cause some households to choose the high-density core of the metropolitan area, many will seek lower densities as a way to achieve these goals. Ultimately, he argues, sprawl is the product of increasing affluence and political democracy.

Jan Brueckner (2000), an urban economist, observes that while sprawl could be accompanied by several types of market failure, remedies should address those specific forms of market failure rather than deterring sprawl itself. He recognizes that market failure could arise in three ways: (1) failure to account for the social value of open space near cities, in which case, at least theoretically, a development tax could be imposed on agricultural land that is being converted to urban use; (2) failure to account for the social costs of highway congestion, in which case a congestion toll could be charged; and (3) failure to fully account for the infrastructure costs of new development, in which case impact fees could be assessed on the developer who would then need to take these costs into account. Glaeser and Kahn (2004) concur with Brueckner's arguments. They add that the major social problem caused by sprawl is the inability of poor families without cars to participate in an automobile-based economy. The remedy, they say, is not to enact a policy to limit sprawl but to subsidize automobile ownership for the poor.

To get a better handle on this debate, we need to understand how current land-use patterns developed, and the extent to which they were shaped by market forces and public policy. But first, we need a way to measure sprawl and to assess its effects. As we shall see, even this seemingly straightforward task turns out to be controversial.

Measuring Sprawl

Some attempts to measure sprawl focus solely on population density; others account for a set of additional attributes. In a study based on the 2010 census, researchers tried to refine the notion of population density beyond a simple measure of population per square mile. They defined population-weighted density as the average of densities across every census tract within the metropolitan area. This allows for a more precise indication of how centralized an area's population is. Recall from Chapter 2 that as metropolitan areas grow, additional counties are added at the periphery. Those additional counties have areas that are largely rural so simply measuring population per square mile means the denominator, land area, can be artificially large, and that the rural components may vary across metropolitan areas. Population-weighted density gives a more accurate indicator of the proportion of the area's population that lives closer to the center of the city. The difference in the two measures can be seen in Table 13.1. Using the standard measure of population density, the New York and Los Angeles areas are first and second highest, with similar population values per square mile. They are followed by the metropolitan areas surrounding San Francisco, Trenton, New Jersey, and Honolulu. By contrast, using population-weighted density as the measure, the difference in density between the highly centralized New York metropolitan area and the others on the list stands out. Moreover, the San Francisco area now takes second

TABLE 13.1. U.S. CONSOLIDATED METROPOLITAN STATISTICAL AREAS (CMSA) WITH HIGHEST POPULATION DENSITIES - 2010

CONSOLIDATED METROPOLITAN STATISTICAL AREA (CMSA)	POPULATION	LAND AREA SQ. MI.	POPULATION DENSITY PER SQ. MI.
New York-Northern New Jersey-Long Island NY-NJ-PA	18,897,109	6,686.9	2,826.0
Los Angeles-Long Beach-Sana Ana CA	12,828,837	4,848.5	2,646.0
San Francisco-Oakland-Fremont CA	4,335,391	2,470.5	1,754.8
Trenton-Ewing NJ	366,513	224.6	1,632.2
Honolulu HI	953,207	600.7	1,586.7
CONSOLIDATED METROPOLITAN STATISTICAL AREA (CMSA)	POPULATION	LAND AREA SQ. MI.	POPULATION WEIGHTED DENSITY
New York-Northern New Jersey-Long Island NY-NJ-PA	18,897,109	6,686.9	31,251.4
San Francisco-Oakland-Fremont CA	4,335,391	2,470.5	12,144.9
Los Angeles-Long Beach-Santa Ana CA	12,828,837	4,848.5	12,113.9
Honolulu HI	953,207	600.7	11,548.2
Chicago-Joliet-Naperville IL-IN-WI	9461135	7,196.8	8,613.4

Source: U.S. Census Bureau Special Reports 2010

place, Los Angeles drops to third, and the Chicago area replaces Trenton on the list (Wilson et al. 2012).

Others who have attempted to measure sprawl argue that population is not by itself an accurate indicator of sprawl (Galster et al. 2001; Lopez and Hynes 2003). Ewing et al. (2002) present a more extensive approach to measuring sprawl. They created an index score based on four factors: (1) residential density; (2) neighborhood mix of homes, jobs, and services; (3) strength of activity centers and downtowns; and (4) accessibility of the street network. Using a variety of data sources, they define 22 variables to operationalize the components of their four-factor sprawl index. A score of 100 on the sprawl index represents the average while scores over 100 represent less-than-average sprawl and scores under 100 represent greater-than-average sprawl. Their results for 83 metropolitan areas in 2000 were updated and expanded by Ewing and Hamidi (2014) for 221 metropolitan areas in 2010. They present information for large, medium, and small metropolitan areas. Their findings for the large metropolitan areas are presented in Table 13.2.

Generating Sprawl: Market Forces and Public Policy

Recently, the fastest-growing counties in the United States have been those outside of major cities in the South and West. If households can be said to vote with their feet, the vast majority are voting in such a way as to exacerbate sprawl. As we saw in Chapter 4, land values often decline with distance from the center of the metropolitan area. Hence, households that locate at the edge of the metropolitan area benefit from cheaper land prices that make bigger homes on larger lots more affordable than they would be if they were closer to the urban core. To the extent that these communities practice fiscal zoning, the consequent exclusion of

TABLE 13.2. MOST COMPACT AND MOST SPRAWLING LARGE METRO AREAS, | 2010

LARGE METRO AREAS ARE DEFINED AS HAVING A POPULATION MORE THAN ONE MILLION.		
Rank	Metro area	Index score
1	New York/White Plains/Wayne, NY-NJ	203.4
2	San Francisco/San Mateo-Redwood City, CA	194.3
8	Miami/Miami Beach/Kendall, FL	144.1
10	Santa Ana/Anaheim/Irvine, CA	139.9
12	Detroit/Livonia/Dearborn, MI	137.2
15	Milwaukee/Waukesha/West Allis, WI	134.2
21	Los Angeles/Long Beach/Glendale, CA	130.3
24	San Jose/Sunnyvale/Santa Clara, CA	128.8
25	Oakland/Fremont/Hayward, CA	127.2
26	Chicago/Joliet/Naperville, IL	125.9
MOST SPRAWLING LARGE METRO AREAS		
LARGE METRO AREAS ARE DEFINED AS HAVING A POPULATION MORE THAN ONE MILLION.		
Rank	Metro area	Index score
182	Houston/Sugar Land/Baytown, TX	76.7
184	Richmond, VA	76.4
189	Rochester, NY	74.5
192	Birmingham-Hoover, AL	73.6
196	Memphis, TN-MS-AR	70.8
197	Charlotte/Gastonia-Rock Hill, NC-SC	70.5
201	Warren/Troy/Farmington Hills, MI	67.0
215	Riverside-San Bernardino/Ontario, CA	56.3
217	Nashville/Davidson/Murfreesboro/Franklin, TN	51.7
220	Atlanta-Sandy Springs/Marietta, GA	41.0

Source: Ewing, Reid and Shima Hamidi. 2014. *Measuring Sprawl 2014.* Smart Growth America. Making Neighborhoods Great Together. pp. 5 & 7.

lower-income households means the exclusion of lower-income children from the community's public schools.

Consumer sovereignty, the notion that the consumer is "king" and knows best what goods and services will yield the most satisfaction, implies that suburban sprawl has occurred because it best satisfies consumers' desires for low-density living along with the flexibility and convenience of automobile-based transportation. The decentralization of jobs makes it desirable for households to move to the edge of the metropolitan area without necessarily increasing commuting time. Thus, market forces have played an important role in promoting sprawl, especially for families with children—the quintessential suburbanites.

A variety of public policies at the federal, state, and local levels have contributed to this pattern of development. Chapter 4 discussed how the federal government subsidized the migration of households to the suburbs through the Federal Housing Administration (FHA) mortgage insurance program, the deductibility of mortgage interest and property taxes from the federal personal income tax, and the construction of the interstate highway system.

At the state level, the infrastructure to support households moving into new developments at the periphery is heavily subsidized. Residents of these areas do not pay the full cost of the new roads, schools, and water and sewer systems that are required to serve them. At the local level, the ability to zone out small-lot, single-family housing, or any other land use that is perceived to require a higher expenditure on public services than it generates in tax revenues ensures that the density in new areas will be low while older urban jurisdictions will bear the burden of housing the region's lower-income households.

As we saw in Chapter 7, proper allocation of resources requires that individuals and households take into account all the costs and all the benefits of their choices. While proponents of sprawl place their emphasis on the degree to which this outcome is a result of consumer choice, critics argue that consumers do not face the full cost of their choice and that the subsidies given to households at the periphery are unwarranted. Consumer sovereignty only yields an efficient outcome when all the costs of consumption including externalities are fully borne by the consumer. With a bevy of tax and subsidy programs explicitly or implicitly encouraging sprawl, one cannot be assured that consumer sovereignty will lead to an efficient use of land.

Reducing Sprawl: Market Forces and Public Policy

Recent demographic changes in the United States may have reduced the attractiveness of large-lot single-family homes in automobile-dependent suburbs, at least among some growing subgroups of the population. An increasing proportion of households do not have school-age children. Some empty nesters with grown children no longer want to maintain large homes and lawns. The very old among the elderly are no longer willing or able to drive and many recent college graduates find better job opportunities and better entertainment options closer to or within the central city. Many new immigrants value access to their community's institutions including churches, cultural centers, ethnic restaurants, and food stores more highly than they value low-density living.

Growing numbers in all these segments of the population would indicate an increasing demand for higher-density patterns of development found in central cities and older suburbs. Moreover, the sustainability of sprawling development has been called into question by physical and geographical limits. As we noted earlier, some metropolitan areas in the West have already encountered natural limits to continued low-density development because of topographical features including coastlines or mountain ranges, federally owned land not available for development, or limited water supplies already strained to capacity.

If sprawl has been caused in part by public policies that have subsidized this form of development either directly or indirectly, then its reduction requires that these policies be altered. Implicit subsidies would need to be removed whether in the form of below-cost extension of infrastructure or gasoline prices that do not reflect the full costs of driving, including the social costs of pollution and congestion.

States might finance a larger share of per-pupil spending as a way to remove one of the strongest incentives for localities to practice fiscal zoning. Higher-density patterns of development would need to be encouraged on efficiency grounds and this is what the **smart growth** initiatives in several states have tried to do. Essentially, consumers respond to incentives. When the incentives provide the appropriate pricing of public services their decisions about where to live change.

Smart Growth

The suburbs that were developed *before* World War II exhibit many of the characteristics admired by smart growth proponents. Compared with newer developments, the older suburbs tend to be served by mass-transit routes, rely on mixed-use development, and are more conducive to walking and bicycling. A variety of housing options existed in close proximity to each other. Apartments were built over storefronts. Accessory apartments—sometimes called "mother-in-law" apartments—were built into single-family homes. These places reflect the human scale and the lively streets that Jane Jacobs (1961) wrote about so eloquently.

Today, smart growth initiatives try to replicate some of these features rather than prohibiting them as most current zoning laws would do. **Transit-oriented development (TOD)** emphasizes alternatives to the exclusive reliance on automobiles by locating higher-density housing and mixed-use development near transit routes. Peter Calthorpe (1993), one of its original proponents, argues that a minimum density of ten households per acre is necessary to achieve the critical mass to support transit routes. A social concept known as **new urbanism** places emphasis on architecture and design elements that restore the importance of lively streets, front porches, and higher-density housing in order to recreate more vibrant civic life. In their 2007 book *Visualizing Density*, Campoli and MacLean emphasize that density need not mean ugly tenements, overcrowding, or congestion. They try to overcome the negative connotations of higher density with myriad examples of well-designed dense neighborhoods.

Location-efficient mortgages—currently available in Seattle, San Francisco, Los Angeles, and Chicago—allow households that locate in areas where driving is less necessary to qualify for larger loans on the theory that more of the household's income can be used for housing. If an expanding municipality wishes to change its current zoning practices of 100 acres of farmland zoned for 100 single-family homes each on a one-acre lot, it can instead use **transferable development rights (TDRs)** to preserve a portion of that farmland while granting the owners the ability to sell those rights to developers who will use them to build at higher density within only a portion of the area that is set aside for new construction. An **urban growth boundary** can be used to contain development within a certain radius of the core city. Keeping density constant, places with growth boundaries would find that limiting the supply of land would make housing more expensive than in places without such a boundary. Yet one of the purposes of the boundary is specifically to encourage higher-density development so that the land is used more intensively and permits more affordable housing.

Many of these tools are being considered by communities across the country. Other initiatives to increase density include changing zoning laws to eliminate areas restricted exclusively to single-family housing and removing specifications for minimum square footage of apartments. The former, adopted in recent years by the cities of Minneapolis and Seattle and the state of Oregon, would increase density per acre. Wegmann (2020) justifies this on grounds of efficiency (combatting climate change) as well as equity (reducing inequality by making housing more affordable). The latter can be justified on both efficiency and equity grounds, recognizing that household size has fallen and that prescribing minimum square footage for an apartment housing four or five people is not as necessary when a substantial number of households consist of a person living alone (Greenspan 2016).

Density, Crowding, and Pandemics

Reducing sprawl requires increases in population density. Therefore, we need to have a clearer understanding of the relationship between density, crowding, and pandemics. In the early days of the COVID-19 pandemic, some observers expected that the United States would fare better than the first two nations to be severely affected by the outbreak—China and Italy. These two countries are noted for their urban high density and their more intense use of public transit. Since a higher proportion of the US population lives at low density in single-family homes in sprawling suburbs and relies more on private automobiles for their transportation needs, experts thought the United States might not suffer as much as these countries. When New York City, the most densely populated city in the nation, became the epicenter of the US pandemic, it confirmed their belief that dense cities would suffer but suburbs, smaller cities, and rural areas would come through relatively unscathed (Olsen 2020; Kotkin 2020). The reality turned out to be far more complex for six important reasons, detailed in the following sections.

Density Per Se Is Not the Problem The spread of communicable diseases often starts in international travel hubs and these are typically located in dense cities. So it is not surprising that the earliest cases of COVID-19 occurred there. It does not follow that these cities are necessarily doomed to suffer calamitous outcomes. High-density East Asian cities in Taiwan and South Korea, as well as the city of Hong Kong, were able to contain the virus through early testing, tracing, and isolation, the practices for which US epidemiologists have been advocating. Many of these areas suffered through previous epidemics, such as SARS in 2003 and MERS in 2015 and learned from those experiences how to be better prepared this time around (Thompson 2020; Beech 2020).

Timing Matters Both in the United States and around the world, municipalities that acted quickly to shut schools and announce stay-at-home orders were more successful in controlling the spread of the virus. Within the United States other cities and states acted more quickly than New York. San Francisco closed its schools when the city had 18 confirmed cases; Los Angeles when it had 40. Ohio closed its schools when the state had only five confirmed cases. New York City already had 329 cases by the time the schools were closed. California issued a statewide stay-at-home order when it had 675 confirmed cases. By the time the state of New York acted, it had over 7,000 (Goodman 2020).

Communication Matters According to the Epidemic Intelligence Service (EIS), a program of the Centers for Disease Control that trains epidemiologists on how to manage epidemics, effective gathering and distribution of information is crucial, especially since advice to the public may shift as more information about the disease becomes known. They recommend that there be a lead spokesperson who is a scientist and whose job it is to convey empathy, establish trust, and convey information frankly, explaining what is already known and what is still to be established. That person must lead by example adhering to the recommendations being announced to the public. In Seattle, the mayor, the governor, and the health agencies coordinated the efforts recommended by the spokesperson scientists. In New York, long-standing tensions between the governor, the mayor, and the city health agency, as well as conflicting statements issued by the mayor and the governor, made coordination more difficult and sent a muddled message out to the public. Seattle followed the EIS protocol, while New York did not. As a result, Seattle's compliance occurred earlier and more fully, and the city was better able to subdue the outbreak (Duhigg 2020).

Density and Overcrowding Are Not Synonymous As we pointed out in Chapter 9 in our discussion of the water and sewer systems that were created in response to earlier epidemics, density refers to population per square mile, while overcrowding refers to the number of people in each dwelling unit and is defined as more than one person per room. The likelihood of contagion increases when people are confined together in close spaces, and this can occur at any level of density. In the vast reaches of the Navajo Nation in the Southwest, there are only six people per square mile, yet the death rate from COVID-19 has been devastating. Families living under crowded housing conditions with poor access to healthcare and a high incidence of underlying health conditions have suffered tragic losses (PBS News Hour 2020). Wherever groups of people are near each other for an extended period, whether in workplaces such as a meatpacking plant or a call center—or for social gatherings including weddings and funerals—disease transmission is most likely to occur (Burdick 2020).

Variation Within Areas Is Not Correlated with Density New York City and Chicago have both been seriously impacted by COVID-19, but the neighborhoods most affected have not been the ones most densely populated. In Chicago, a low-income minority neighborhood on the South Side with a population density of 2,800 households per square mile has a high infection rate; a high-income White area on the North Side, with 16,000 households per square mile, has a low infection rate. The low-income neighborhood has multigenerational and extended families sharing living space as a consequence of the 2008 financial crisis, and it also faces other health challenges (Coryne 2020). Similarly, the incidence of COVID-19 in New York City is higher in areas with lower population density but more overcrowding and where residents are low-income minorities with a greater likelihood of underlying health conditions, many of whom are essential workers who cannot work from home (The Stoop 2020).

Climate Change Will Outlive the Consequences of the Coronavirus While it is likely that some city households, especially those containing workers who expect to be able to work from home indefinitely, will search for lower-density housing options in areas with cheaper land values, such practices leading to greater sprawl will conflict with practices necessary for sustainable growth. The constraints of climate change will continue to make smart growth policies necessary.

Barriers to Smart Growth Implementation

As urban expert Anthony Downs (2005) points out, even when there is sentiment in favor of smart growth initiatives, these programs are often difficult to implement. He argues that the pressure to adopt smart growth policies typically comes from environmentalists, urban planners, local public officials, and some innovative real estate developers, rather than from ordinary citizens. Some of the obstacles encountered in persuading ordinary citizens to support smart growth policies include: (1) a shift in the distribution of the costs and benefits of development which creates new categories of winners and losers, (2) the need to shift power from local to regional authorities that is often resisted because of the loss of local autonomy, and (3) an increase in residential density that might threaten the property values of existing homes in the face of Fischel's homevoter hypothesis (Fischel 2001) that homeowners' primary motivation is to protect the value of their single most important asset. Although these latter fears might be mitigated to the extent that limits on growth might actually raise housing prices, this possibility is at odds with one of the oft-stated goals of smart growth—to increase the supply of affordable housing.

In a similar vein, political scientist David Luberoff (2007) argues that strict policies to enforce smart growth goals such as Portland, Oregon's growth boundary are more likely to create a backlash that ultimately undermines those goals. Policies that merely offer incentives are less apt to cause a backlash, but they are less prone to have a dramatic impact on changing settlement patterns.

In the Portland case, the state of Oregon adopted urban growth boundaries for its cities in 1973. The boundary around Portland was intended to provide enough undeveloped land to accommodate 20 years of future growth and has been successful in confining growth to areas within the boundary. Since land outside the boundary could not be developed, there was as a consequence a huge discrepancy in land value between the land just inside versus the land just outside. In a hotly contested election in 2004, voters approved Measure 37, which allowed landowners outside the boundary to request full compensation from their local government for the loss in value caused by the growth boundary's restrictions on development. Local governments could choose either to pay full compensation or to grant a waiver that allowed development in accordance with whatever use would have been permitted before the boundary went into effect.

Equity and Efficiency Considerations in Alternative Metropolitan Growth Scenarios

In an article written for a Federal National Mortgage Association (Fannie Mae) publication in 2000, architecture and planning professor Lance Freeman asked the question of how metropolitan areas would be structured in the year 2020 and outlined four possible scenarios: (1) *Sprawlville*, a continuation of current practices with regard to sprawl and social equity; (2) *Smart Town*, adoption of practices to combat sprawl without thought to equity implications; (3) *Equitopia*, programs to address equity issues such as affordable housing but without any attention to sprawl; and (4) *Milleniumburg*, smart growth initiatives that include a concern for social equity.

In Sprawlville, the relocation of workplaces to the expanding metropolitan fringe, along with total reliance on automobiles and their attendant traffic jams, make workplaces inaccessible to a growing proportion of the potential labor pool. Poor central city and inner-ring suburban residents are unable to relocate closer to jobs because of the continuing lack of affordable housing and because of zoning laws that effectively exclude the poor. Income segregation increases, as do fiscal disparities between communities. Differences in the quality of public-school systems reinforce existing inequalities and perpetuate them through the next generation.

Smart Town establishes an urban growth boundary so that farmlands and woodlands outside the boundary are preserved. As the area grows, underutilized land within the boundary is developed through infill projects. Transit-oriented development projects are undertaken, and the resulting new urbanism-style higher density and mixed land-use patterns attract high-earning professionals. An **unintended consequence** of this success is the disappearance of affordable housing as neighborhoods become gentrified. With few alternatives available to them, families of the low-paid service workers in the area double or triple up in units that were meant for one family while single individuals live in overcrowded conditions in rooming houses.

Equitopia is in the forefront of enacting affordable-housing initiatives, and it has been able to implement its plans because it has a single government for the entire metropolitan area. It scatters affordable housing throughout the metropolitan area, avoiding concentrations of the poor in any single location. However, the lack of a workable transit system that is necessary to improve job opportunities for the poor and the competing demands to use funds to finance the infrastructure required by unabated sprawl undermine support for affordable housing.

In Milleniumburg, attention is given both to smart growth initiatives and to equity issues. There is a regional authority with responsibility for planning. Open space is set aside to protect the most ecologically sensitive lands but there are greenbelts and watersheds that meander through the region rather than a fixed growth boundary. Transit-oriented development is encouraged as is central city redevelopment—the latter through the expediting of permits and reducing red tape. Zoning is based on performance standards to encourage mixed land use while preventing negative externalities. Inclusionary zoning requires that 10 percent of the units in new developments are affordable. Location-efficient mortgages help to bring homeownership to families who would not be able to afford the combination of transportation and housing expenses required of exurbanites.

Freeman's scenarios remind us that current patterns of metropolitan growth are inefficient and inequitable. Alternative scenarios that focus only on efficiency without regard to equity or vice versa are problematic as well. The challenge is to find ways to promote metropolitan growth that are both equitable and efficient and make Milleniumburg more than just an imaginary place.

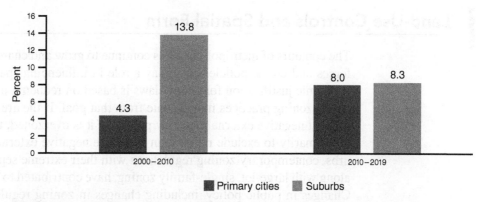

FIGURE 13.2. Growth Comparisons 2000–2010 and 2010–2019 (Primary Cities and Suburbs of Major Metropolitan Areas)

Source: Frey, William H. 2020. "American Cities Saw Uneven Growth Last Decade, New Census Data Show," Brookings Institution. https://www.brookings.edu/research/new-census-data-show-an-uneven-decade-of-growth-for-us-cities/

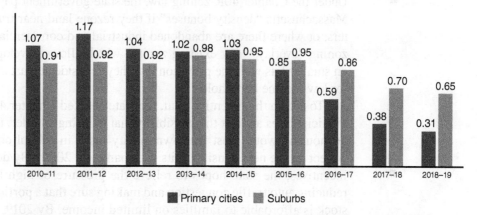

FIGURE 13.3. Primary Cities and Suburbs Within Major Metropolitan Areas (Annual Growth, 2010–2019)

Source: Frey, William H. 2020. "American Cities Saw Uneven Growth Last Decade, New Census Data Show," Brookings Institution. https://www.brookings.edu/research/new-census-data-show-an-uneven-decade-of-growth-for-us-cities/

Freeman was writing in 2000. How does it appear from the vantage point of 2020? Demographer William Frey examined city and suburban population growth rates of major metropolitan areas across two periods: 2000–2010 and 2010–2019. Compared with the first decade in which suburbs grew far faster, in the more current period primary cities grew as fast as the suburbs (see Figure 13.2). Frey's research covered 53 metropolitan areas with populations greater of one million or more.

When Frey examined the 2010–2019 period more closely, he found that although primary cities in major metropolitan areas grew faster than their suburbs in the earlier years, growth declined dramatically in the later years as suburbs outgrew their central cities (see Figure 13.3). Frey argues that as the nation recovered from the financial crisis of 2008 and as housing market revived, suburbs once again attracted large numbers of households. So Sprawlville remains a dominant pattern of development.

Land-Use Controls and Spatial Form

The contours of metropolitan areas continue to grow and change over time. Market forces and public policies each play a role in influencing spatial form. While the economic justification for zoning laws is based on reducing negative externalities, actual zoning practices may deviate from that goal. If the area is underzoned, significant negative externalities may persist. If it is overzoned, the motivation might be primarily to exclude rather than to reduce negative externalities. In many suburbs, contemporary zoning regulations with their extreme separation of land uses, along with large-lot, single-family zoning, have contributed to metropolitan sprawl. Changes in public policy, including changes in zoning regulations are important elements in smart growth efforts to promote higher-density development.

Massachusetts's Chapter 40R Smart Growth Overlay Zoning Law, enacted in 2005, provides just one example of how smart growth and affordable housing can be encouraged through well-engineered public policy (Carman et al. 2004). Under the Chapter 40R zoning law, the state government pays towns and cities in Massachusetts "density bonuses" if they rezone land near transit stops, town centers, or where there are abandoned industrial and commercial buildings. The new zoning "overlays" any existing zoning, which allows developers to build housing on smaller lots with the provision that they set aside at least 20 percent of the units for low-income households.

To add to the incentive plan, the state enacted Chapter 40S in 2006 to insure municipalities against the possibility that building smaller, more affordable family housing would cost the town or city more in school costs than they would collect on the new housing units (Carman et al. 2005). By developing the correct incentives, the state hopes to relieve the pressure of high housing prices while reducing auto traffic congestion and making sure that a portion of the new housing stock is affordable to families on limited income. By 2019, 42 of Massachusetts 351 municipalities had applied for Chapter 40R/40S. Other states—including Connecticut and New Jersey—are now considering following Massachusetts's lead toward using a range of incentives that encourage municipalities to alter their zoning laws and permit denser, smarter growth with guaranteed affordable housing. In this way, regions desperate for housing may be able to obtain it while reducing urban sprawl.

It will not be easy to overcome the combination of market forces and public policy that has produced sprawl over the last 60 years of US metropolitan growth, but with a combination of innovative public policies, sprawl can be contained over the next 60 years.

References

Avis, William R. 2016. *Urban Governance* (Topic Guide). Birmingham, UK: Governance and Social Development Resource Center, University of Birmingham.

Beck, Eckardt C. 1979. "The Love Canal Tragedy." *Environmental Protection Agency Journal* 5, no. 1 (January): pp. 16–19.

Beech, Hannah. 2020. "Tracking the Coronavirus: How Crowded Asian Cities Tackled an Epidemic." *New York Times*. March 17.

Boo, Katherine. 2012. *Behind the Beautiful Forevers: Life, Death, and Hope in a Mumbai Undercity*. New York: Random House.

Boyer, M. Christine. 1994. *Dreaming the Rational City. The Myth of American City Planning*. Cambridge, MA.: MIT Press.

Brueckner, Jan. 2000. "Urban Sprawl: Diagnosis and Remedies." *International Regional Science Review* 23, no. 2: 160–171.

Bruegmann, Robert. 2005. *Sprawl: A Compact History*. Chicago: University of Chicago Press.

Brunn, Stanley D., Maureen Hays-Mitchell, Donald J. Zeigler, and Jessica K. Graybill, eds. 2016. *Cities of the World: Regional Patterns and Urban Environments*, 6th ed. Lanham, MD: Rowman & Littlefield.

Burchell, Robert W., George Lowenstein, William R. Dolphin, Catherine C. Galley, Anthony Downs, Samuel Seskin, Catherine Gray Still, and Terry Moore. 2002. *Costs of Sprawl—2000*. Washington, DC: Transportation Research Board, National Research Council.

Burdick, Alan. 2020. "Monster or Machine? A Profile of the Coronavirus at 6 Months: Our 'Hidden Enemy' in Plain Sight." *New York Times*, June 2.

Calthorpe, Peter. 1993. *The Next American Metropolis: Ecology, Community, and the American Dream*. Princeton, NJ: Princeton Architectural Press.

Campoli, Julie, and Alex S. MacLean. 2007. *Visualizing Density*. Cambridge, MA: Lincoln Institute of Land Policy.

Carman, Ted, Barry Bluestone, and Eleanor White. 2004. *Building on Our Heritage: A Housing Strategy for Smart Growth and Economic Development*. Boston: The Boston Foundation.

Carman, Ted, Barry Bluestone, and Eleanor White 2005. *Chapter 40R School Cost Analysis and Proposed Smart Growth School Cost Insurance Supplement*. Boston: The Boston Foundation.

Coase, Ronald. 1960. "The Problem of Social Cost." *Journal of Law and Economics* 3 (October): 1–44.

Coryne, Haru. 2020. "In Chicago, Urban Density May Not Be to Blame for the Spread of the Coronavirus." *ProPublica Illinois*, April 30. https://www.propublica.org/article/in-chicago-urban-density-may-not-be-to-blame-for-the-spread-of-the-coronavirus

Downs, Anthony. 2005. "Smart Growth: Why We Discuss It More than We Do It." *Journal of the American Planning Association* 71, no. 4 (Autumn): 367–380.

Duhigg, Charles. 2020. "Seattle's Leaders Let Scientists Take the Lead. New York's Did Not." *New Yorker*, April 26.

Durst, Noah J., and Jake Wegmann. 2017. "Informal Housing in the United States." *Inernational Journal of Urban and Regional Research* 41, no. 2 (February): pp. 282–297.

Ewing, Reid, Rolf Pendall, and Don Chen. 2002. *Measuring Sprawl and Its Impact*. Washington, DC: Smart Growth America.

Ewing, Reid, and Shima Hamidi. 2014. *Measuring Sprawl 2014*. Washington, DC: Smart Growth America.

Fischel, William A. 2000. "Zoning and Land Use Regulation." *Encyclopedia of Law and Economics*, pp. 403–442. https://reference.findlaw.com/lawandeconomics/2200-zoning-and-land-use-regulation.pdf

Fischel, William A. 2001. *The Homevoter Hypothesis: How Home Values Influence Local Government Taxation, School Finance, and Land-Use Policies*. Cambridge, MA: Harvard University Press.

Freeman, Lance. 2000. "Fair Growth 2020: A Tale of Four Futures." *Housing Facts & Findings* 2, no. 4: 1, 6–14.

Frumkin, Howard, Lawrence Frank, and Richard Jackson. 2004. *Urban Sprawl and Public Health: Designing, Planning, and Building for Healthy Communities*. Washington, DC: Island Press.

Galster, George, Royce Hanson, Hal Wolman, Stephen Coleman, and Jason Freihage. 2001. "Wrestling Sprawl to the Ground: Defining and Measuring an Elusive Concept." *Housing Policy Debate* 12, no. 4: 681–717.

Glaeser, Edward L., and Matthew E. Kahn. 2004. "Sprawl and Urban Growth." In *Handbook of Regional and Urban Economics*, vol. 4, *Cities and Geography*, edited by J. Vernon Henderson and Jacques F. Thisse. New York: Reed Elsevier, pp. 2481–2527.

Goodman, J. David. 2020. "How Delays and Unheeded Warnings Hindered New York's Virus Fight." *New York Times*, April 8.

Gordon, Peter, and Harry W. Richardson. 1998. "Prove It: The Costs and Benefits of Sprawl." *Brookings Review*, September 22, pp. 23–26.

Greenspan, Elizabeth. 2016. "Are Micro-Apartments a Good Solution to the Affordable -Housing Crisis?" *The New Yorker*, March 3.

Hayden, Dolores. 2003. *Building Suburbia: Greenfields and Urban Growth*. New York: Pantheon.

Hirt, Sonia. 2010. "To Zone or Not to Zone? Comparing European and American Land-Use Regulation." PND|online II, https://vtechworks.lib.vt.edu/bitstream/handle/10919/48185/hirt_to_zone_or_not_to_zone.pdf .

Ingraham, Christopher. 2019. "Nine Days on the Road. Average Commute Time Reached a New Record Last Year." *Washington Post*, October 7.

Jacobs, Jane. 1961. *The Death and Life of Great American Cities*. New York: Random House.

Kayden, Jerold S. 2001. "National Land-Use Planning and Regulation in the United States:Understanding its Fundamental Importance." In *National-Level Spatial Planning in Democratic Countries: An International Comparison of City and Regional Policy-Making*, edited by Rachel Alterman. Liverpool: Liverpool University Press, pp. 43–64.

Kotkin, Joel. 2020. "The End of New York: Will the Pandemic Push America's Greatest City Over the Edge?" *Tablet Magazine*, March 27.

Langdon, Philip. 1994. *A Better Place to Live: Reshaping the American Suburb.* Amherst: University of Massachusetts Press.

Levy, John M. 1985. *Urban and Metropolitan Economics.* New York: McGraw-Hill.

Logan, John R,, and Harvey L. Molotch. 1987. *Urban Fortunes.* Berkeley: University of California Press.

Logan, Thomas. 2007. "The Americanization of Germany Zoning." *Journal of the American Institute of Planners* 42, n. 4 (November): pp. 377–385.

Lopez, Russ, and H. Patricia Hynes. 2003. "Sprawl in the 1990s, Measurement, Distribution, and Trends." *Urban Affairs Review* 38, no. 3: 325–355.

Luberoff, David. 2007. "Getting Smart." *Commonwealth Magazine* (Winter), https://commonwealthmagazine.org/economy/smart-growth-may-not-be-as-effectiveor-as-popularas-its-proponents-claim/.

Mills, Edwin. 1979. "Economic Analysis of Land Use Controls." In *Current Issues in Urban Economics*, edited by Peter Mieszkowski and Mahlon Straszheim. Baltimore: Johns Hopkins University Press, pp. 511–541.

Mumford, Lewis. 1961. *The City in History.* New York: Harcourt Brace Jovanovich.

National Academy of Public Administration. 2003. *Addressing Community Concerns: How Environmental Justice Relates to Land Use Planning and Zoning.* Washington, DC: National Academy of Public Administration.

Nivola, Pietro. 1999. "Are Europe Cities Better?" Washington, DC: The Brooking Institution.

Olsen, Henry. 2020. "The United States Might Have a Secret Weapon Against Coronavirus." *Washington Post*, March 19.

PBS News Hour. 2020. "'The Grief Is So Unbearable': Virus Takes Toll on Navajo." May 12.

Pianin, Eric, and Michael A. Fletcher. 2002. "Many Schools Built Near Toxic Sites, Study Finds." *Washington Post*, January 21, p. A2.

Platt, Rutherford. 2004. *Land Use and Society: Geography, Law, and Public Policy* Washington, DC: Island Press.

Rabin, Yale. 1989. "Expulsive Zoning: The Inequitable Legacy of Euclid." In *Zoning and the American Dream: Promises Still to Keep*, edited by Charles Harr and Jerold Kayden. Washington, DC: American Planning Association Press, pp. 101–121.

Siegan, Bernard H. 1972. *Land Use Without Zoning*. Lexington, MA: Lexington Books.

Silver, Christopher. 1997. "The Racial Origins of Zoning in American Cities." In *Urban Planning and the African American Community*, edited by June Manning Thomas and Marsha Ritzdorf. Thousand Oaks, CA: Sage Publications, pp. 23–42.

Sinclair, Upton. 1906. *The Jungle*. New York: Doubleday.

Thompson, Derek. 2020. "What's Behind South Korea's Dovid-19 Exceptionalism?" *The Atlantic*, May 6.

The Stoop. 2020. "Covid-19 Cases in New York City, a Neighborhood-Level Analysis." NYU Furman Center Blog, April 10, https://furmancenter.org/thestoop/entry/covid-19-cases-in-new-york-city-a-neighborhood-level-analysis

US Environmental Protection Agency. 2004. "Populations Protected." Superfund Environmental Indicators Guidance Manual, September. pp. 8–9, http://www.epa.gov/superfund/accomp/ei/ind_a.htm.

US Environmental Protection Agency. 2007. "Environmental Justice," http://www.epa.gov/compliance/environmentaljustice.

Vasudevan, Alexander. 2017. *The Autonomous City*. London: Verso.

Wegmann, Jake. 2020. "Death to Single-Family Zonong . . . and New Life to the Missing Middle." *Journal of the American Planning Association* 86, no. 1: pp. 113–119.

Whyte, William H. 1958. "Urban Sprawl." In *The Exploding Metropolis*, edited by William H. Whyte. New York: Doubleday, pp. 133–156.

Wilson, Steven G., David A. Plane, Paul J. Mackun, Thomas R. Fischetti, and Justuna Goworowska (with Darryl T. Cohen, Marc J. Perry, and Geoffrey W. Hatchard). 2012. *Patterns of Metropolitan and Micropolitan Population Change: 2000 to 2010*. 2010 Census Special Reports. Washington, DC: Department of Commerce, Economics and Statistics Administration, Census Bureau.

Questions and Exercises

1. Imagine that a supermarket chain announces plans to open a store very near where you live, drawing customers from a wide area. What externalities, positive and negative, would this store impose on you? How might the issues of eminent domain, design zoning, fiscal zoning, and exclusionary zoning appear in discussions by neighbors or in city government as they discuss the store's plans?

2. Microsoft Bing has a large set of maps and images of urban sprawl in many metro areas around the world. You will find a website with these maps by typing into your browser "Maps of Urban Sprawl" or go directly there using the following link: https://www.bing.com/images/search?q=maps+of+urban+sprawl&qpvt=Maps+of+Urban+Sprawl&form=IGRE&first=1&tsc=ImageBasicHover. There are maps for many metro areas. Take a look at a number of them and

describe the visual images of the spatial growth of each area. Note the variety of forms that urban sprawl can take.

3. University of Utah's Metropolitan Research Center and Smart Growth America, an organization that advocates for sustainable growth have produced a report that measures 221 metropolitan areas and 994 counties using 2010 statistics in four key areas:

- residential and employment density

- diversity of land use

- the proportion of people and businesses located near each other

- measures of physical infrastructure, such as the average length of street blocks and the percentage of four-or-more-way intersections

Researchers weighed the four factors equally, producing an index with an average of 100. Metro areas that scored above 100 tend to be more compact while those scoring below 100 are more sprawling. The data for these rankings can be found at https://www.governing.com/news/headlines/gov-study-ranks-metro-areas-by-sprawl.html. Analyzing the data on these 221 US metropolitan areas, find the ten metro areas with the highest sprawl index and the ten with the lowest. Is sprawl more intense in certain regions of the United States and particular states?

14

Urban Housing Markets, Residential Location, and Housing Policy

LEARNING OBJECTIVES

■ Explain the attributes theory of consumer behavior and show how it can be embodied in a hedonic price index for housing

■ Enumerate the incentives for homeownership under US federal tax policies

■ Describe the dissimilarity index and show how it is used to compare the degree of racial segregation across metropolitan areas

■ Explain the filtering model of housing and give examples of downward and upward filtering

■ Describe the three pillars of European housing policies

■ Describe the ways in which the US federal government has intervened to affect both the supply side and the demand side of housing markets

It should now be clear that how well you live depends in part on where you live. Some urban areas have plenty of jobs while others are losing them when employers close down or lay off employees. Some cities and suburbs have better schools than others and therefore you or your children have a better chance of acquiring the human capital needed to succeed in the labor market.

How well you live also depends on a city or suburb's physical and social infrastructure. Better city services and transportation, better healthcare, and safer streets can make life more pleasant. Housing is important not only because it affects residents' living standards but its price and quality may affect the municipality's ability to attract workers and their families, as well as business investment.

To understand the housing market, we need to examine a range of important issues. Why do housing prices and apartment rents vary so much within and across metropolitan areas? What determines whether a family will rent rather than own a home? How do housing prices affect a metro area's ability to attract young families and new business ventures? And how have federal, state, and local government policies affected the housing market over time?

The Size of the US Housing Market

To begin with, it is important to note that a great deal of our wealth is in the form of housing. In 2019 there were 124 million housing units in the United States, of which 80.7 million units were owner-occupied while the remaining 43.3 million housed renters. Hence about two-thirds of the total residential housing stock was owner-occupied.

The total value of all wealth in the United States in 2019 was nearly $123 trillion. Of this nearly 72 percent took the form of financial assets such as stocks and bonds, bank deposits, and noncorporate small business. But more than $29 trillion was in the form of residential real estate, nearly one-quarter of total assets. By contrast, the total value of household durables including automobiles, furniture and appliances represent less than 5 percent of household assets. Moreover, the total value of the housing stock is more than 50 percent higher than the value of all factories, commercial buildings, retail establishments, and other nonresidential structures combined.

The value of the US housing stock has increased dramatically over the past two decades. In the year 2000, the asset value of the total US housing stock was a little less than $11 trillion, three-fourths of this in owner-occupied housing and a quarter in rental units. In just two decades the value of residential assets has nearly tripled. For those who were able to purchase housing in the hottest housing markets in the country—in such metro areas as New York, San Francisco, Boston, Seattle, Chicago, and Denver—ownership has been a boon as the value of real estate has appreciated in these communities more rapidly than most other assets.

What may surprise many is that the homeownership rate is much lower in the United States than in most other countries. As Table 14.1 reveals, among the top 47 countries in terms of homeownership in 2018, the United States ranks #35 with an owner-occupied units to total residential units rate of 65.1 percent. At the top of the list are Romania, with a rate of 96.4 percent. Singapore ranks #3 with 91 percent. In Russia nearly 90 percent of households own their own homes. Across the European Union, the average homeownership rate is slightly higher than that in the United States. In Switzerland, however, the nationwide homeownership rate is only 42.5 percent and in its major cities even lower. In Geneva, the homeownership rate is less than 10 percent. More than 90 percent are tenants in rental homes and apartments.

Why do these homeownership rates differ so much across countries? Much is due to different cultures, demographics, and public policy (Goodman et al. 2018). In some countries such as Romania, Slovakia, and Croatia owner-occupied housing is often as inexpensive as renting because of favorable tax policy and mortgage markets. Moreover, with few tenants' rights in many of these countries, many families have taken the opportunity to become homeowners to be free of landlords. After the fall of the Soviet Union, a good deal of state-owned property including

TABLE 14.1. HOMEOWNERSHIP RATES BY COUNTRY – 2018

RANK	COUNTRY	%
1	Romania	96.4
2	Slovakia	91.3
3	Singapore	91.0
4	Croatia	90.1
5	China	90.0
6	Lithuania	89.9
7	Russia	89.0
8	Macedonia	88.3
9	Hungary	86.0
10	Nepal	85.3
11	Serbia	84.4
12	Poland	84.0
13	Bulgaria	83.6
14	Estonia	82.4
15	Latvia	81.6
16	Malta	81.6
17	Norway	81.3
18	Czech Republic	78.7
19	Spain	76.3
20	Slovenia	75.1
21	Portugal	74.5
22	Greece	73.5
23	Belgium	72.7
24	Italy	72.4
25	Finland	71.6
26	Luxembourg	71.2
27	Ireland	70.3
28	Cyprus	70.1
29	European Union	69.3
30	Netherlands	69.0
31	Israel	66.5
32	Canada	66.3
33	Euro Area	66.2
34	France	65.1
35	United Kingdom	65.1

RANK	COUNTRY	%
36	United States	65.1
37	Australia	65.0
38	New Zealand	64.8
39	Sweden	64.1
40	Japan	61.7
41	Denmark	60.5
42	New Caledonia	60.0
43	Turkey	59.1
44	South Korea	57.7
45	Austria	55.4
46	Germany	51.5
47	Hong Kong	49.2
48	Switzerland	42.5

Source: Trading Economics "Homeownership Rates by Country" 2018

housing was privatized permitting residents in these former Soviet countries to access the home buying market. With a mortgage down payment rate of just 5 percent in countries such as Romania, homeownership became highly affordable (Simeleviciene 2018).

In China, there is a strong cultural norm that parents should help their sons purchase a home so that they can more easily marry. The relatively low home-ownership rate in Germany is due in part to its policy of protecting renters from skyrocketing rental prices and hence renting is often considerably less expensive than owning. In Switzerland and Germany this is due in large measure to an array of benefits accorded renters. In these countries, laws protect tenants from eviction and a sudden or large rent increase. You can check their city's websites to see if your rent is reasonable. Since cities in both of these countries have high residential property taxes and steep mortgage requirements, it is often much less expensive to rent than buy a home.

Likewise, in the United States the credit environment is such that it makes it difficult for households with less than excellent credit ratings to obtain a mortgage, and therefore many are consigned to the rental market. Until recently it was quite difficult for many people of color to obtain a mortgage almost regardless of their income.

US Homeownership Rates Over Time

It was not until after World War II that a majority of American households owned their own homes. From 1890 until 1940, the homeownership rate remained between 44 and 48 percent (see Figure 14.1). A slight long-term decline during this period is partially due to the huge number of immigrants who came to the United States after

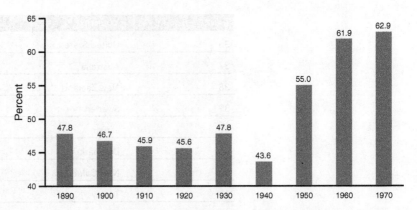

FIGURE 14.1. US Homeownership Rate, Proportion of Households Owning Homes, 1890–1970

Source: DQYDJ, "Historical Homeownership Rate in the United States, 1890-Present," https://dqydj.com/historical-homeownership-rate-united-states/

1890. Many lived in tenement housing when they first arrived and rented homes until they had accumulated enough savings to afford a down payment. During the Great Depression, families were forced to rent after they lost their homes and their farms due to foreclosure. Consequently, by the end of the 1930s, the homeownership rate had fallen to 43.6 percent, the lowest rate of the twentieth century (Berson and Neely 1997, US Bureau of the Census 2017).

It was during the brief period between 1940 and 1960 that the proportion of households owning their own homes increased by nearly half (from 43.6% to 61.9%), much of this occurring in the decade after World War II when federal housing policies encouraged homeownership for returning servicemen. Since then, the ownership rate has varied from under 63 percent to about 68 percent.

The percentage of US households who own their homes varies enormously by household income. Among the poorest households—those with total incomes of less than $30,000—only 36% are homeowners. About two-thirds (64%) of all households with incomes of $30,000 to $75,000 are homeowners, while the homeownership proportion of those with incomes of $150,000 or more exceeds 84 percent.

Variance in Home Prices and Rents Across Metro Areas

In 2019 the median value of a unit of single-family and condominium housing in the United States was approximately $253,000, but as shown in Figure 14.2 housing prices vary enormously across metro areas. The median price ranged from $163,000 in St. Louis, to five times that amount in San Francisco, where half the housing units had prices exceeding $875,000. The most expensive housing is found on the West Coast and the East Coast, with Los Angeles in second place with a median of $650,000 and San Diego at $568,000, followed by Seattle at $460,000. On the East Coast Boston and New York were close to Seattle, with median prices of $421,000 and $418,000, respectively. These are all metro areas with booming economies attracting a large number of new households from other parts of the nation and from abroad.

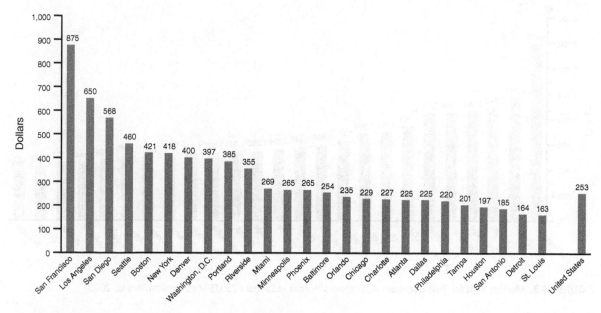

FIGURE 14.2. Median Price of Single-Family Homes and Condominiums in 25 Largest US Metropolitan Areas, 2019 (in Thousands)

The metro areas with the lowest housing prices are found in two types of locations. Older industrial cities such as Detroit and St. Louis saw their populations decline sharply since the heyday of manufacturing in the 1950s and 1960s. As a result, a large percentage of their housing stock has been vacant and in such a market prices fall. But there are other metro areas where the economy is strong, but housing prices have remained low or moderate. Consider Atlanta, Dallas, Tampa, Houston, and San Antonio. In these metro areas the population has increased, but these metro areas are spread out across large geographies and developers have built sufficient housing to supply increased demand.

Median monthly rents for two-bedroom apartments and homes also vary substantially across metro areas, as shown in Figure 14.3. In 2020, the San Francisco metro area topped the chart with a median rent of nearly $3,500 per month—nearly 3.6 times the median rent in the St. Louis metro area and 3.3 times as expensive as in Detroit. To put this in context, to rent the median priced two-bedroom apartment in the San Francisco Bay Area costs nearly $42,000 per year. Median household income in this metro area is quite high. At $115,300 it is nearly 50 percent higher than the national median income. Nonetheless, the median household needs to spend more than a third of its annual income on rent in this high cost-of-living metro area (36.4%).

In St. Louis, median household income was estimated at $65,300 in 2020. Yet because median rent is so low, the annual rent for the typical two-bedroom apartment in this metro area is only $11,652. Hence, the median household only needs to spend about 18 percent of its income on rent.

Along with San Francisco, the next four most expensive metro areas in terms of housing rents are Boston, Seattle, San Diego, and New York—all metro areas with booming economies based on such powerful industries as high-tech, bioscience, and financial services. According to a Brookings Institution report on the concentration of "innovation sector" jobs across the United States, 90 percent of

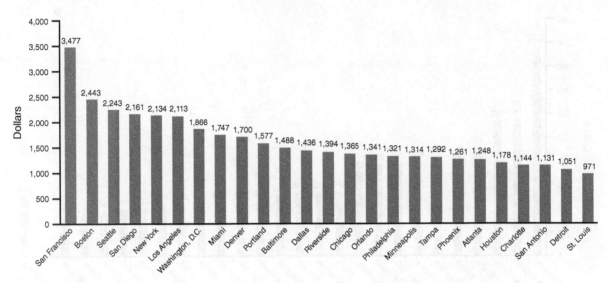

FIGURE 14.3. Median Rent for Two-Bedroom Apartments/Homes in Largest 25 US Metropolitan Areas, 2020

the nation's jobs in such fields as digital technology and biotechnology are found in just five metro areas: Seattle, Boston, San Francisco, San Diego, and San Jose (Atkinson et al. 2019). With such an industrial revolution, these metro areas have seen soaring housing prices and rents.

What Drives Metro Area Housing Prices: Supply and Demand

Demand for housing in a particular city or suburb is determined by many factors. Families with children might care about the quality of the public schools. Communities with many amenities ranging from public parks and museums to a wealth of recreational activities will attract families. Cities situated in a warm climate will attract retirees and others who are weary of wintry months of snow and ice. But as we noted earlier, perhaps the most important factor that drives housing demand is the state of a region's economy.

The supply of housing is likewise a function of many factors. An area that experiences rapid population growth because new jobs are being created or because older households are seeking a retirement home will be a prime location for housing developers. But the ability of developers to acquire land for housing construction is often constrained by the amount of vacant land available, zoning restrictions imposed by cities and towns to limit the type or amount of new housing, and environmental considerations.

We can summarize the impact of a range of factors on the direction of home prices and rents in the following way. On the one hand:

- With a *stronger economy* and rising household incomes, there is good reason to believe home prices will *rise* as a result of an increase in housing demand.

- With a *growing population*, the demand for housing will increase putting *upward pressure* on home prices and rents.

- A *limited supply* of new single-family homes, condominiums, and rental apartments will lead to *higher* prices and rents.

- *Low mortgage rates* will lead to more housing demand and therefore *upward pressure* on home prices.

On the other hand:

- With *delayed family formation and childbearing*, home prices might *fall* as home buying is postponed, reducing demand.

- An *aging population* might signal a *decline* in prices as the supply of existing homes on the market increases.

- Increased individual or family *indebtedness* can lead to *lower* home prices as a result of difficulty in procuring mortgage financing.

- A *shift from home buying to renting* should put *upward* pressure on rents as the demand for rental housing increases.

In the short run—which can last a number of years if any of the preceding factors hold—the supply of housing in a given city or suburb is relatively fixed and even modest increases in demand can lead to a sharp increase in housing prices and rents. This condition is depicted in Figure 14.4. With supply fixed in the short run, an increase in demand results in the average house price rising sharply from A to B. When an increase in demand elicits no change in supply, economists refer to this

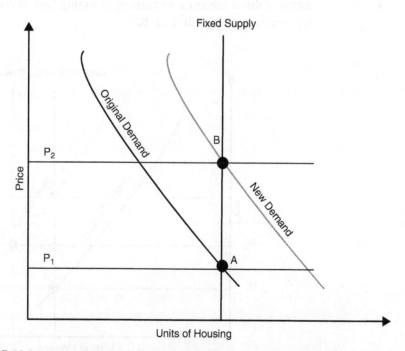

FIGURE 14.4. Housing Prices with Fixed Housing Supply Curve A represents the original demand for housing. When the demand increases to curve B, the price of housing rises sharply from P_1 to P_2 due to a fixed housing supply in the short run.

as a zero **price elasticity of supply**. Given the time it takes to develop new plans for housing and then construct it, prices can rise for some period of time before demand leads to greater supply.

In the long run, if developers can produce the housing demanded, supply increases, as in Figure 14.5, and housing prices tend to moderate. With the increase in supply, the new price is found at C rather than at B. In newer cities, particularly those where there is undeveloped land and few zoning restrictions, developers have been able to build housing almost as soon as it is demanded and sometimes in anticipation of increased demand. In these metro areas, housing prices have risen at a rate little more than overall inflation—3 to 4 percent a year. In those metro areas where barriers to new development are high, housing prices have often risen by more than 10 percent a year.

The Greater Boston metropolitan statistical area is a good example of a region with high barriers to new development. Recall from Figure 14.2 that by 2019, the Greater Boston region had the fifth highest median home prices among the largest 25 US metro areas. Between 2001 and 2020, it experienced the fourth largest increase in apartment and home rents. In the face of a strong economy with a substantial increase in employment, there was little new housing construction in the region. Glaeser et al. (2006) found that the sluggish growth in housing development was due primarily to local land-use regulations, and not a lack of land per se. Minimum lot sizes of one acre or more under strict local zoning laws, extensive wetlands regulations, and the ability to use the court system to delay building permits all contributed to forestalling further housing construction in the region. The median lot size for a new single-family home rose from an average of .76 acres between 1990 and 1998 to an average of .91 acres between 1998 and 2002, with much of this a response to municipal zoning (Jakabovics 2006). As a result, housing prices increased dramatically.

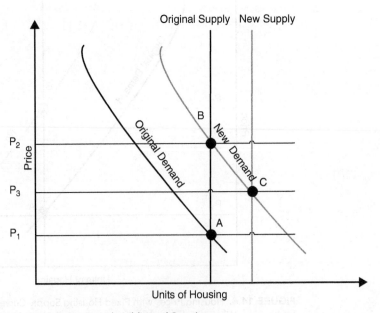

FIGURE 14.5. Housing Prices with Additional Supply

Eliminating these barriers to new housing construction is no simple matter because existing residents raise many objections whenever a new development is planned. Some fear more housing means more traffic congestion. The possibility of young families with children moving in means the municipality may have to raise additional revenue to finance additional schooling. Deeper fears, often not expressed, have to do with the value of their homes and possible changes in their perceptions of the character of their neighborhoods (Fischel 2001). If sufficient housing is built, a sellers' market—where the seller has pricing leverage over potential buyers—can turn into a buyers' market where sellers must consider reducing their asking price. Politically, those opposed to liberalized zoning and deregulation often have power over local municipal leaders, making it difficult for any reform to occur. Existing residents exert the equivalent of monopoly power in the housing market, eliminating much of the competition that would come from additional housing production. As in any monopoly, this results in higher prices and lower output than would occur in a competitive market.

Pricing Housing and the Hedonic Index

From the point of view of the individual homeowner or renter, there are many factors that contribute to the value of a housing unit and ultimately its market price. The characteristics of both the dwelling itself and its site are important so that the full value of a home is not exclusively internal to the house. The value of the house comes from its use in *conjunction* with external goods and services including the quality of the local school and the neighborhood's access to highways and mass transit. As such, municipal government plays a major role in housing prices.

Recognition of such **complex goods** as housing has led to the development of the **attributes theory of consumer behavior**. As articulated by one of the pioneers of this approach, Kelvin Lancaster (1972), the theory eschews the idea "that goods are the direct objects of utility" and instead states that "it is the properties or characteristics of the goods from which utility is derived." This might seem obvious, but it has profound implications for how we value things.

Because housing has numerous attributes providing an array of value, consumers' choices almost always involve trade-offs. It is rare that a single home will provide the absolutely ideal dwelling for a household. A consumer may have to consider the size of the backyard, access to transportation, and ideas about the quality of the neighborhood over the size of the kitchen or the design of the house. Importantly, the attributes theory recognizes that utility obtained from a good (the house, in this case) may change over time as the internal characteristics of the good change (e.g., as the house gets older) or as the external attributes change (e.g., if the city decides to discontinue the nearest public transit route, or if homes nearby are either renovated or left to deteriorate).

Because of the many attributes considered in the choice of housing, economists often resort to a **hedonic price index** to measure the value of one house against another. In theory, any given house can have hundreds of attributes, each of which can be given a value.

In developing a hedonic price index for housing, researchers usually generate an equation where price is on the left-hand side and all the relevant characteristics of housing are on the right. This is somewhat analogous to the human capital equation shown involving urban labor markets discussed in Chapter 6. The equation here might look as follows:

$$Price_i = a_0 + b_1 * Sq. Ft._i + b_2 * Year Built_i + b_3 * Number of Bedrooms_i$$
$$+ b_4 * Garage_i + b_5 * Central Air_i + b_6 * Number of Bathrooms_i$$
$$+ b_7 * Average High School SAT Score_j$$
$$+ b_8 * Number of Burglaries per 100,000 in neighborhood_j$$

where a_0 refers to the value of an undeveloped piece of land with no house on it

and

$b_1, b_2 \dots b_8$ refers to the difference in price due to each characteristic, and i refers to an individual housing unit and j refers to a particular neighborhood

For instance, if we ran this equation on a set of 1,000 house sales in a metro area, the coefficient (b_i) on Sq. Ft might be 61, meaning that a home with 3,000 square feet would sell for $61,000 more than a 2,000-square-foot home, all else equal. Similarly, if the coefficient on Year Built was positive, this would show that newer homes were more highly valued than older ones. The value of the coefficient would tell us whether the age of the house contributed a great deal to its price or if it was relatively unimportant. If the coefficient were negative and statistically significant, it would tell us that in this community, ceteris paribus, older homes are valued more highly.

Note that other factors—such as the perceived quality of the school district j where house$_i$ is located (measured here as the average SAT score of high school students)—enter the equation as well. One suspects that this coefficient would be positive while the coefficient on number of burglaries per 100,000 residents in the neighborhood would be negative.

Just such an analysis was carried out by Kain and Quigley (1975) using data from St. Louis. In the 1970s when housing was much less expensive, they found that a home with four extra years of roof life was worth $400 more, a longer commute time was worth $2,000 less, and being in a neighborhood with relatively low pollution added $1,200 to the value of a home.

If one had all this information and it was up to date, it could be used for house hunting. One could estimate the value of a particular house based on the equation, check it against the asking price and conclude that the price was too high, just about right, or a real steal. You could counteroffer based on this analysis. In real life, it is rare that someone has so much information. But each rational home buyer does a mental back-of-the-envelope calculation that mimics this process when deciding whether to purchase a particular home.

Budget Constraints and Housing Preferences

The reason why trade-offs are almost always important is that everyone with perhaps the exception of few billionaires faces a **budget constraint** when it comes to buying a home. We can see how preferences as represented by **indifference curves** and a budget constraint interact to determine what type of home someone will buy.

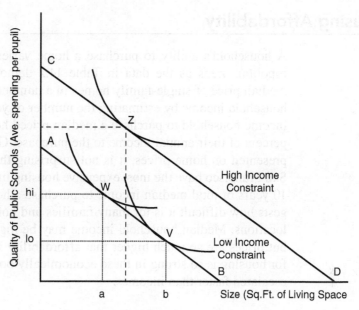

FIGURE 14.6. Housing Choice: Budget Constraints and Indifference Curves

Figure 14.6 depicts the trade-off between house size and the quality of its neighborhood schools. It suggests that if there is a given budget constraint—a fixed amount of money to purchase a home—as shown by either of the angled lines in the drawing, you can choose to buy a small home in a high-quality school district or a larger home in a district where the schools are reputed to be less stellar. The line AB represents the combination of size and school quality that a low-income family can buy or a family that wishes to spend no more than what a low-income family could afford.

The lines AB and CD represent the income constraints for low- and high-income households, respectively. Each point on these lines represents a combination of school quality and size of home that can be purchased given the budget constraint, revealing the trade-off between these two housing attributes. The two indifference curves, W and V, show the preferences of two different households with similar budget constraints but where the former chooses to buy a smaller home in a district with better schools and the latter chooses a larger home in a district where less is spent per pupil. Compared with household W, household Z is able to purchase a larger home in a district that spends more on its students because of its higher income.

Because of the large array of factors that influence home buying and renting decisions, the wide variety of preferences for different housing attributes, and the great variance in household incomes, we can begin to appreciate the diverse pattern of housing one finds in any city or metropolitan area. The distribution of housing—where it is located and its style and size—reflects this diversity. As we will see later in this chapter, other factors play a role including racial discrimination and the business practices of mortgage companies and real estate agents. These factors affect the way households are distributed by community and neighborhood across a metropolitan area's stock of housing.

Housing Affordability

A household's ability to purchase a home varies dramatically across US metropolitan areas as the data in Table 14.2 demonstrate. Here we compare the median price of single-family homes in a number of metro regions with median household income by estimating the number of years it would take for a median income household to purchase a median priced home if they were to devote 100 percent of their annual income to the purchase. Given the previous data we have presented on home prices, it is not surprising that Los Angeles, San Jose, and San Francisco have the most expensive housing markets. That it takes nearly 9 to 10 years of total median income to purchase a home in these communities suggests how difficult it is for many families and households to buy homes in these locations. Median household income may be higher in these areas than others, but prices are so much higher that affordability is a serious challenge. Demand for housing is so strong in these economically booming regions that prices have escalated faster than incomes.

TABLE 14.2. YEARS OF MEDIAN HOUSEHOLD INCOME TO BUY MEDIAN HOME BY METRO AREA

MOST EXPENSIVE		LEAST EXPENSIVE	
Los Angeles	9.6	Harrisburg, PA	2.7
San Jose	9.5	Cincinnati	2.6
San Francisco	9.2	Cleveland	2.6
San Diego	7.9	Pittsburgh	2.6
Honolulu	7.6	Buffalo	2.5
Ventura, CA	7.2	Akron, OH	2.5
Sacramento	5.9	Toledo, OH	2.5
Stockton, CA	5.9	Dayton, OH	2.3
Riverside, CA	5.9	Scranton, PA	2.0
Portland	5.6	Youngstown, OH	1.9
Seattle	5.6		
New York	5.4		
Fresno, CA	5.4		
Denver	5.4		
Boston	5.2		
Miami	5.0		
Sarasota, FL	4.5		
Stamford, CT	4.5		
Las Vegas	4.5		
Salt Lake City	4.5		

At the other end of the income/price spectrum are such communities as Youngstown, Akron, Toledo, and Dayton, Ohio; Scranton, Pennsylvania; and Buffalo, New York, where the price to income ratio is 2:5 or less. Note these are all older industrial communities where home prices have remained more affordable as a result of weaker demand given either slowly growing populations or in many cases a decline in population and thus a ready supply of available housing.

The home price to household income ratio is particularly high where housing supply is constrained by zoning restrictions and construction costs. The US Department of Housing and Urban Development (HUD) considers housing to be affordable if a family needs to spend no more than 30 percent of its gross annual income to cover its mortgage payments, real estate taxes, and homeowners' insurance or to pay their rent and utilities. Families who spend more than this are considered **cost-burdened** in the sense that they need to skimp on other necessities including food, clothing, transportation, and medical care (US Department of Housing and Urban Development 2007a).

Nearly one-third of all US households pay more than 30 percent of their incomes for housing, according to a study from Harvard's Joint Center for Housing Studies (2018). And approximately half (47%) of all renter households nationwide bear a "severe burden," which means they are spending 50 percent or more of their gross income on housing.

Whether they own or rent, most low-income households pay outsized shares of income for housing. Fully 80 percent of renters earning less than $30,000 were cost burdened in 2016 including 55 percent with severe burdens. Owners earning less than $30,000 have a cost-burden rate of 63 percent with 42 percent **severely** burdened. Among low-income owners with mortgages, a staggering 93 percent are cost burdened. Cost-burdened shares are much higher among Black (45%) and Latinx households (43%) than among Asian and other minority households (36%) or White households (27%). The nation's 10 largest metros have the highest concentrations of cost-burdened households with nearly 40 percent of households cost burdened. Median housing costs in small metros were generally lower, so that the cost-burdened rate across all these regions is 26 percent.

Housing costs are so high in many US cities that individuals and families cannot afford any housing and they end up homeless. According to the US Department of Housing and Urban Development, there were nearly 568,000 persons homeless in early 2020 living temporarily in shelters or on the street (McCarthy 2020). Three-quarters of the homeless are found in central cities; one-quarter are found on suburban streets. Of the total nationwide, more than 30 percent are found in just six locations: New York City, Los Angeles County, Seattle County, San Jose County, San Diego County, and the city of San Francisco. These places have extraordinarily high housing costs for both homeowners and renters.

Affordability has also become a problem in many European cities. According to Eurostat's 2015 Urban Europe report, European big city residents feel that affordable housing is increasingly hard to come by. Across all of Europe, only in Athens and Greater Manchester in England did more than half of citizens surveyed agree that affordable housing was easy to find. Not unexpectedly, it is in wealthy northern

European cities where people feel that finding affordable housing is most difficult. Less than 19 percent of respondents in London, Paris, Berlin, Hamburg, Vienna, Munich, Stockholm, and Oslo thought such housing was easy to find (O'Sullivan 2016). Overall in Europe, housing costs were highest in Greece, Denmark, the Netherlands, Germany, Romania, the Czech Republic, and Sweden. In Europe, spending more than 40 percent of household income is considered an "overburden." In 2013 the overburden rate across the European Union was 11 percent, but 37.4 percent among those with an income below 60 percent of median national income (Housing Europe 2015).

In 2020, the cost of housing relative to family income ranges dramatically across countries. In Table 14.3, this relative cost is expressed in terms of how many years of family disposable income it would take to buy the median priced apartment. In poverty-stricken Venezuela, it would take more than 133 years of median income to purchase an apartment in Caracas. In Damascus, Syria, it takes more than 69 years and in the City of Hong Kong nearly 47 years. For most major cities around the world, the time required is between 10 and 20 years. And in some, the cost in terms of years of income needed to purchase is considerably lower. In Denmark the time required is 7.45 years, and in Puerto Rico, only 3.93 years. In Hanover, Germany it would take 7.91 years of purchasing power; in Valencia, Spain it would take 7.16 years. Across the United States the time required is 3.52 years, with some cities having considerably cheaper housing stock. In Houston, it takes just over 2 years of median family disposable income to purchase the median priced apartment and in depressed St. Louis and Detroit just 1.77 and 1.43, respectively.

TABLE 14.3. RATIO OF MEDIAN APARTMENT PURCHASE PRICE TO MEDIAN FAMILY DISPOSABLE INCOME EXPRESSED IN YEARS OF INCOME NEEDED TO PURCHASE - TEN HIGHEST COST CITIES IN THE WORLD, 2020

RANK	CITY	PRICE TO INCOME RATIO
1	Caracas, Venezuela	133.8
2	Damascus, Syria	69.34
3	Hone Kong, Hone Kong	46.94
4	Shenzhen, China	43.81
5	Tehran, Iran	43.64
6	Beijing, China	42.89
7	Mumbai, India	40.94
8	Phnom Penh, Cambodia	37.49
9	Taipei, Taiwan	37.25
10	Shanghai, China	37.03

Housing Prices and Vacancy Rates

In labor economics, there is a well-known relationship between the rate of unemployment and inflation. This relationship is captured in the notion of the **Phillips curve**, first discovered by the British economist A. W. Phillips (1958) in the late 1950s. Phillips observed that in England over the period 1861–1957 there was a nonlinear inverse relationship between the rate of increase in money wage rates and the unemployment rate. He found that inflation increased at an ever faster rate the further unemployment fell below 2.5 percent. Above that rate, money wage rates would decline, at least modestly. When there was a lot of "excess demand," wages were bid up. When unemployment was high, indicating an absence of excess demand, wages stabilized or fell.

We can apply this same logic to the housing market, using housing **vacancy rates**—the percentage of housing stock available to new owners or tenants—as a measure of excess demand for homes. Here, one must distinguish between vacancies and excess supply. Vacancy rates will always be greater than zero because of housing market friction and imperfect information (Belsky 2006). Renters and potential home buyers take time to search for housing that meets their needs and their budget. Landlords and home sellers attempt to maximize the rent or price they receive, and therefore often set prices above what the market will absorb immediately. A vacancy exists until a buyer and a seller (or renter and landlord) can come to terms. As Belsky (2006) points out, the landlord (or home seller) is in much the same position as a retailer who receives periodic shipments of goods. It is more profitable for him to maintain an inventory than to set prices so low that the merchandise is sold as soon as it is placed on the shelves. Testing the waters to see "what the market will bear" requires time, and therefore creates vacancies in the short run. But just as introductory economics teaches, when there is excess demand in the market there is upward pressure on prices, and when there is excess supply there is downward pressure on prices.

We would expect that when vacancy rates are in the normal range for owner-occupied housing—about 1.5 to 2 percent—housing price appreciation will not be much greater than general inflation. The normal range for rental unit vacancies is considered to be between 5 to 6 percent. As vacancy rates rise above the normal range, prices will tend to stabilize and ultimately may decline. In the short run housing prices will not decline very much, as sellers either hold out for the price they had hoped to receive or perhaps take their homes off the market altogether. As vacancy rates fall below the normal rate, housing prices will tend to rise at a faster and faster rate the more the vacancy rate falls below normal. The home market becomes a sellers' market, much like the game of musical chairs with people running ever faster to find an empty chair and bidding prices up in the process. Ultimately, this leads to a housing price spiral.

We find this relationship holds for owner-occupied housing when applied to the 75 largest metro areas in the United States (see Figure 14.7). The fitted curve provides just the kind of Phillips curve relationship expected. At vacancy rates below

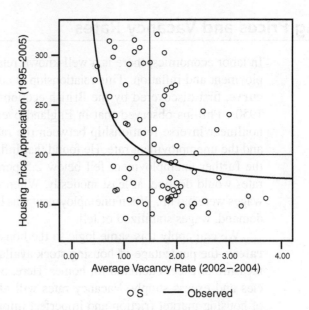

FIGURE 14.7. Housing Price Appreciation vs. Vacancy Rates At very low vacancy rates (below 1%), housing prices rise sharply. At vacancy rates above 1.5%, prices fall slowly.

1.5 percent, home prices appreciated at higher and higher rates, depending on how low the vacancy rate declined below normal.

Refitting the same data using a more complex statistical function provides some insight as to what happens when vacancy rates rise to even higher levels (see Figure 14.8). Note that at vacancy rates above 3.5 percent, price appreciation falls off more rapidly. This suggests that when the number of housing units available far outstrips the number that households want to buy, there can be a housing bubble effect and prices deflate quickly.

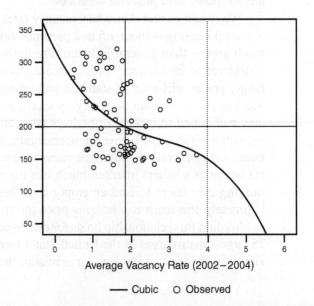

FIGURE 14.8. Housing Price Appreciation vs. Vacancy Rates With Greater Range

The Impact of Accelerating Home Prices and Rents on Household Location

In some of the nation's most expensive metro areas, home prices and rents have skyrocketed so much that middle-income and working-class families can no longer afford to live in them and have had to move further and further away to distant towns and suburbs. A case in point is Greater Boston where a booming economy led to such high housing costs by 2015 that those who wished to buy a home or find a way to reduce their rent had to search further and further away from the region's central core. This has led to a "flattening" of the **housing price gradient**, which relates average home prices and rents to distance from the city center.

In most cities with a vibrant central city, home prices and rents are usually highest at the very center of the region near the central business district and decline with distance from the core. This is because those who can afford higher priced housing often prefer to live near work and where there are many cultural amenities. This is especially true for young professionals and older empty-nesters.

A statistical analysis undertaken based on housing price data in the Greater Boston metropolitan area provides evidence of the change in housing prices over time as prices in the central city grew sharply at the beginning of the twenty-first century (Bluestone and Huessy 2017). The analysis was based on the prices of single-family homes sold in each of the region's 147 communities and the distance from the center of the city of Boston to each of these cities and towns. The result is the home price gradient shown in Figure 14.9. The vertical axis measures the appreciation rate for single-family homes for two periods: 2009–2017 and within this period 2015–2017. The horizontal axis measures the distance in miles of each community from central city Boston.

Note that over the entire period 2009–2017 the price gradient was very steep, falling from 59 percent appreciation inside the City of Boston to an average of just 20 percent for communities that are 35 miles from the central city. However,

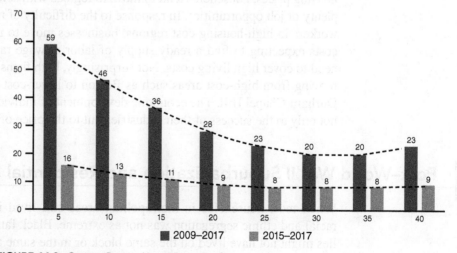

FIGURE 14.9. Greater Boston Home Price Gradient

Source: Bluestone and Huessy, 2017

for the more recent period 2015–2017, the gradient has flattened considerably ranging from 16 percent to 8–9 percent the further one moves away from Boston itself. Essentially, over this very short period the ratio of central city to distant location home price appreciation has fallen from nearly 3 to 1 to no higher than 2 to 1.

What caused this dramatic shift in the home price gradient? Further analysis of the Greater Boston home price data revealed that middle-class and working-class households frustrated by the high prices in and near the central city began to buy homes in the outer ring—including in older industrial cities and towns that had earlier lost population as jobs disappeared. In some cases, home prices actually rose faster over the 2015–2017 period in these older industrial communities than in some of the wealthier suburbs of Boston.

This trend was revealed in household income data for the City of Boston. Over this period, the proportion of the city's population with incomes of two times the **poverty rate** or less increased modestly (because of the existence of public housing and rental subsidies for poorer households). The proportion of higher-income households with incomes of five times the poverty rate increased even more. The number of households with incomes in the range of 2 to 5 times the poverty rate actually declined, as these households did not have incomes that allowed them to buy into the high-priced housing in Boston but had incomes too high to be eligible for public housing or rent subsidies.

A related analysis investigating internal net population migration across the United States had been carried out in earlier research involving 304 metropolitan statistical areas in the United States (Bluestone 2006). What this research revealed was that the highest housing price metro areas lost population due to the out-migration of a portion of their residents, presumably seeking more reasonable cost housing. The big migration losers in addition to Boston are San Francisco, Stamford-Norwalk, San Jose, Oakland, and Nassau-Suffolk, New York—metro areas with among the highest housing costs in the nation.

In a powerful way, this analysis underscores the more general economic notion of how prices affect both consumer and business behavior. Responding to high housing prices, households tend to move to regions with somewhat lower costs and plenty of job opportunities. In response to the difficulty of retaining and attracting workers in high-housing-cost regions, businesses move to metro areas with lower costs expecting to find a ready supply of labor at wage rates not inflated by the need to cover high living costs. Not surprisingly, both firms and people seem to be moving from high-cost areas such as Boston to lower-cost areas akin to Raleigh-Durham-Chapel Hill. The economic development of individual metro areas is tied not only to the success of their industries but to the price of their housing.

Post–World War II Suburbanization and Residential Segregation

When most households in metropolitan areas still lived inside the central city, racial and ethnic segregation was not as extreme. Black families and White families might not have lived on the same block or in the same neighborhood, but they lived in the same municipality. With the growth of suburbs after World War II, residential segregation became more prevalent.

Part of the reason for residential segregation by race was related to social class and income. In many cases, White families could afford to move to the suburbs where housing prices were higher while Black families remained economically segregated in highly dense neighborhoods within the central city where rents and home prices were lower. Despite the second wave of the Great Migration of Black families to cities from the rural South, the flow of White families to the suburbs created a net decrease in the populations of central cities and a surplus in central city housing stock. White flight to the suburbs was reinforced as central cities lost population and therefore municipal revenue, making it more difficult for them to support good public services including public schools and well-equipped police forces. In a matter of decades, many American metro areas became "chocolate cities with vanilla suburbs," to use the phrase coined by demographer Reynolds Farley and his colleagues (1978).

Measuring Segregation

Residential or housing segregation is normally measured using the **dissimilarity index**, which reflects the proportion of one racial or ethnic group that must relocate to achieve a spatial configuration where each census tract or neighborhood replicates the racial composition of the metropolitan region as a whole. There are as many as 20 different indicators of segregation as identified by Massey and Denton (1988) that measure the evenness of a distribution; exposure or isolation from other groups; or the concentration, centralization, or clustering of a particular subgroup of a population. Nonetheless, the dissimilarity index is the measure most widely used.

According to the US Bureau of the Census (2005), across 300 metropolitan areas, the average dissimilarity index in 1980 for African Americans was 0.727. Back then in the average MSA, nearly 73 percent of African Americans would have had to relocate to census tracts where other racial and ethnic groups dominated— particularly White neighborhoods—in order to achieve full racial integration. Slow progress occurred over the next two decades, but even by 2000 almost two-thirds (64%) of African Americans would have had to move to non-Black areas for racial parity. By the period 2014–2017, progress toward desegregation had continued. Nevertheless, more than half (52%) of Black metropolitan area residents would have had to relocate to White census tracts to achieve full racial integration. For the Latinx population, there was less segregation, but the dissimilarity index remained .41 during this latest period.

Segregation varies dramatically across the largest 25 metropolitan areas in the United States. Table 14.4 reveals the degree of segregation between Blacks and Whites in these metro regions. Table 14.5 provides the same information for Latinx versus non-Latinx populations. The highest degree of Black–White residential segregation is found in New York, Chicago, Detroit, St. Louis, and Philadelphia—all metro areas in the Northeast and Midwest regions of the country. These are large communities that attracted a substantial number of Black jobseekers from the South decades ago. When these migrants arrived in Northern cities, they were settled in "Negro" neighborhoods and the legacy of that enforced segregation continues to exist today. White flight to the emerging

TABLE 14.4.	WHITE-BLACK/BLACK WHITE DISSIMILARITY INDEX FOR LARGEST 25 U.S. METRO AREAS (1980-2017)					
	WHITE-BLACK/BLACK-WHITE DISSIMILARITY INDEX					**% CHANGE**
METROPOLITAN STATISTICAL AREA	**1980**	**1990**	**2000**	**2010**	**2017**	**1980-2017**
New York-Newark-Jersey City, NY-NJ-PA	0.813	0.809	0.795	0.769	0.768	−5.5%
Chicago-Naperville-Elgin, IL-IN-WI	0.881	0.844	0.804	0.752	0.753	−14.5%
Detroit-Warren-Dearborn, MI	0.879	0.876	0.849	0.740	0.737	−15.9%
St. Louis, MO-IL	0.816	0.772	0.734	0.706	0.717	−12.1%
Philadelphia-Camden-Wilmington, Pa-NJ-DE-MD	0.772	0.752	0.703	0.670	0.670	−13.2%
Los Angeles-Long Beach-Anaheim, CA	0.810	0.728	0.681	0.652	0.668	−17.5%
Boston-Cambridge-Newton, MA-NH	0.798	0.737	0.714	0.678	0.650	−18.5%
Baltimore-Columbia-Towson, MD	0.794	0.714	0.676	0.643	0.639	−19.5%
Miami-Fort Lauderdale-Pompano Beach, FL	0.821	0.740	0.685	0.640	0.639	−22.2%
Denver-Aurora-Lakewood, CO	0.691	0.649	0.620	0.594	0.624	−9.7%
Washington-Arlington-Alexandria, DC-VA-MD-WV	0.697	0.655	0.630	0.610	0.614	−11.9%
San Francisco-Oakland-Berkeley, CA	0.720	0.671	0.637	0.593	0.610	−15.3%
Houston-The Woodlands-Sugar Land, TX	0.737	0.655	0.651	0.606	0.603	−18.2%
Atlanta-Sandy Springs-Alpharetta, GA	0.769	0.663	0.639	0.584	0.588	−23.5%
Dallas-Fort Worth-Arlington, TX	0.782	0.628	0.590	0.555	0.566	−27.6%
Minneapolis-St. Paul-Bloomington, MN-WI	0.677	0.623	0.578	0.502	0.551	−18.6%
Tampa-St. Petersburg-Clearwater, FL	0.782	0.697	0.635	0.543	0.548	−29.9%
Charlotte-Concord-Gastonia, NC-SC	0.580	0.547	0.540	0.531	0.531	−8.4%
San Diego-Chula Vista-Carlsbad, CA	0.644	0.682	0.538	0.484	0.522	−18.9%
Seattle-Tacoma-Bellevue, WA	0.648	0.565	0.497	0.456	0.516	−20.4%
Portland-Vancouver-Hillsboro, OR-WA	0.687	0.632	0.474	0.409	0.513	−25.3%
Orlando-Kissimmee-Sanford, FL	0.710	0.591	0.552	0.493	0.498	−29.9%
Phoenix-Mesa-Chandler, AZ	0.614	0.500	0.433	0.413	0.492	−19.9%
San Antonio-New Braunfels, TX	0.614	0.561	0.519	0.477	0.491	−20.0%
Riverside-San Bernardino-Ontario, CA	0.527	0.438	0.455	0.440	0.464	−12.0%

Source: Logan, John, ed. 2014. *Diversity and Disparities: America Enters a New Century.* Russell Sage Foundation.

suburbs in these metro areas after World War II reinforced the high degree of segregation.

Note that the lowest dissimilarity index scores are found in Western metro areas, which were settled much later than those in the Northeast and Midwest. Black families moving there were more likely to find housing in less segregated neighborhoods.

Progress against segregation has varied substantially across metro areas as shown in the last column of Table 14.4. Between 1980 and 2017, the White–Black/Black–White

TABLE 14.5. LATINX/NON-LATINX DISSIMILARITY INDEX FOR LARGEST 25 U.S. METRO AREAS (2014-2017)

MSA	LATINX/NON-LATINX DISSIMILARITY INDEX
Boston-Cambridge-Newton, MA-NH	0.530
Chicago-Naperville-Elgin, IL-IN-WI	0.524
Miami-Fort Lauderdale-Pompano Beach, FL	0.521
Los Angeles-Long Beach-Anaheim, CA	0.507
New York-Newark-Jersey City, NY-NJ-PA	0.479
Philadelphia-Camden-Wilmington, PA-NJ-DE-MD	0.469
Detroit-Warren-Dearborn, MI	0.466
Phoenix-Mesa-Chandler, AZ	0.446
Denver-Aurora-Lakewood, CO	0.444
San Diego-Chula Vista-Carlsbad, CA	0.423
Dallas-Fort Worth-Arlington, TX	0.422
Atlanta-Sandy Springs-Alpharetta, GA	0.418
Houston-The Woodlands-Sugar Land, TX	0.405
San Antonio-New Braunfels, TX	0.405
Washington-Arlington-Alexandria, DC-VA-MD-WV	0.404
San Francisco-Oakland-Berkeley, CA	0.401
Minneapolis-St. Paul-Bloomington, MN-WI	0.391
Charlotte-Concord-Gastonia, NC-SC	0.391
Baltimore-Columbia-Towson, MD	0.385
Orlando-Kissimmee-Sanford, FL	0.378
St. Louis, MO-IL	0.368
Riverside-San Bernardino-Ontario, CA	0.362
Tampa-St. Petersburg-Clearwater, FL	0.349
Portland-Vancouver-Hillsboro, OR-WA	0.331
Seattle-Tacoma-Bellevue, WA	0.305

Source: U.S. Census American Community Survey (2014-2017)

Dissimilarity Index has fallen by nearly 30 percent in metro areas such as Tampa and Orlando, Florida. In Miami, Atlanta, Dallas-Ft. Worth, Seattle, and Portland, Oregon the index has declined by at least 20 percent.

By contrast, there has been little movement toward residential desegregation in the older cities of the Northeast and Midwest where segregation was already substantial. Note that in New York, Chicago, Detroit, and St. Louis, the Dissimilarity Index has declined by less than 20 percent since 1980.

In general, the degree of Latinx/non-Latinx residential segregation is much less than for Blacks and Whites. The highest Dissimilarity Index is .53 in Boston, followed by .524 in Chicago and .521 in Miami—all metro areas with fast growing

Latinx populations. Around Boston one will find several communities that have been open to Latinx migration and immigration and have become home for many Latin Americans. Miami has a large number of Puerto Ricans and Cubans, while Los Angeles has become home to many Mexican immigrants. The lowest level of Latinx/non-Latinx residential segregation is found in such metro areas as Seattle, Portland, Tampa, and Riverside, where the few Latinx live in integrated neighborhoods.

The Causes of Housing Segregation

Housing segregation has many causes. Social class as measured by income is one, but it is surprisingly less important than one might think. Using data from Los Angeles County for 1990, Camille Charles (2000) calculated the predicted index of dissimilarity for Black, Latinx, and Asian and compared it with the actual index. The predicted index controls for household income and household structure including family type, age of head of household, and number of household members. The predicted index for Blacks was 0.110, more than five and half times lower than the actual index. For Latinx, the predicted index was 0.191, less than half the actual 0.458. For Asians, the predicted dissimilarity index was a mere .087, one-fourth the actual 0.344.

This suggests that other factors besides income and family structure must be responsible for much of the segregation we find in major metro areas. One factor is racial preference. In Los Angeles, more than 70 percent of White express comfort with a neighborhood that is one-third Black. When asked to consider living in a neighborhood that is 53 percent Black and 47 percent White, the percentage of Whites expressing comfort drops to 46 percent. Using a similar technique for assessing preferences, Bluestone and Stevenson (2000) found that in the Boston metro area, Whites felt the ideal neighborhood was one in which they represented 62 percent of the households, Blacks represented 15 percent, Latinx 10 percent, and Asians 13 percent. This would make for a fairly integrated neighborhood. When Blacks were asked the same set of questions about their preferences, their ideal neighborhood turned out to be 41 percent Black, 23 percent White, 19 percent Latinx, and 17 percent Asian—also a fairly integrated neighborhood. The same was true for Latinx, whose ideal community was 40 percent Latinx, 25 percent White, 19 percent Black, and 16 percent Asian. It seems nearly everyone is in favor of living in a racially and ethnically diverse neighborhood.

But there is one problem. The math simply does not add up. Combining the three ideals from the perspective of each racial/ethnic group, the perfect community is 62 percent White, 41 percent Black, and 40 percent Latinx. Unfortunately, a community cannot have more than 100 percent population. Therefore, part of the reason segregation persists is that few Whites, Blacks, Latinx, and Asians want to live in a community where they are a distinct minority. As a result, there appears to be a good deal of self-segregation as well as segregation due to income differentials.

Beyond income and personal preferences is the role of government policy in encouraging residential segregation. In 1938, the Federal Housing Administration (FHA) explicitly asserted in its underwriting manual that "if a neighborhood is to retain stability, it is necessary that properties shall continue to be occupied by the same social and racial classes. A change in social or racial occupancy generally contributes to instability or a decline in values" (Squires 1994). The agency encouraged the use of racially restrictive covenants in sales contracts and deeds and this view was emphasized in real estate textbooks and training manuals (Mohl 1996). While the Supreme Court ruled that such covenants were unenforceable in 1948, it was not until 1968, when Congress passed the 1968 Fair Housing Act, that the inclusion of racial covenants in property deeds became illegal. By building public housing almost exclusively in central cities, the federal and state governments concentrated poorer families—many of them racial and ethnic minorities—into central city locations. In his powerful history of government-sponsored segregation, Richard Rothstein documented all the ways in which the federal government, as well as state and local government, implemented policies and regulations that kept Black households from living in White neighborhoods (Rothstein 2019).

As late as 1973—nine years after the passage of the landmark Civil Rights Act—the US Supreme Court in *Milliken v. Bradley* ruled that the White suburbs of Detroit could not be included in Detroit's school desegregation plan because no evidence existed to show that segregation in the region's schools or neighborhoods was "in any significant measure caused by governmental activity." The justices concluded Black students were concentrated in Detroit because of "unknown and perhaps unknowable factors." Essentially the court ruled that segregation existed de facto, implying that segregation's origins were not in government policy but in the collective psyche of Americans. As such, the court ruled there was no legal remedy for segregation.

Even after the civil rights laws of the 1960s barred the federal government from outright racial discrimination, real estate brokers and banks contributed to racial and ethnic segregation by deliberate racial **steering**—showing White families housing only in White areas and showing Black families housing only in Black areas. Commercial banks and mortgage companies discriminated against Black families who were trying to obtain mortgages, as shown in matched-pair studies where a Black borrower in the same financial position as a White borrower approached the same bank for a housing loan. In many cases, the White borrower was more likely to obtain the mortgage. The courts did not consider any of this outright discrimination that violated the new civil rights law.

The combination of unequal incomes, racial and ethnic preferences, and the legacy of implicit as well as explicit government policies is powerful enough to have kept segregation indices at well over 50 percent for most US metropolitan areas. Adding to this problem is that it has proven difficult to maintain integrated neighborhoods once they achieve a low dissimilarity index. As a racial or ethnic minority begins to move into a neighborhood that was previously nearly all-White, there is normally only a small change in the racial or ethnic composition of the community. But in many cities, as more minority members move in, there appears to be a **tipping point** when the pace of White flight suddenly accelerates and a neighborhood becomes majority minority in just a few years. This is consistent with the residential preferences mentioned earlier, which revealed that White residents are satisfied with having some minority neighbors, but prefer not to live in a neighborhood where they no longer comprise at least three-fifths of the residents.

Segregation and Social-Class Structure

In some cities, as the racial or ethnic composition of a particular neighborhood changed, there was a change in the social-class structure of the community. The first African Americans who moved into the northwest section of Detroit in the 1960s—an area that had been comprised overwhelmingly of middle-class Whites—were solidly middle class themselves and often had incomes equal to or greater than the Whites who sold them their homes. However, communities were subject to both financial and demographic dynamics. Beginning in 1934, the federal government and private banks engaged in a practice called "redlining"---drawing color-coded maps depicting the racial composition within a city. Areas that were predominantly Black or which seemed to be in transition to greater percentages of occupancy by Black families were colored in red (Domonoske 2016). For decades, the FHA and private banks refused to make mortgage loans or home-improvement loans to those areas. With less money available for householders to make repairs, the housing stock often began to deteriorate. The FHA continued to redline or refuse mortgage insurance to minority-dominated inner-city areas until 1965 (Colman 1975). Also, over time, as both middle-class White and middle-class Black families moved to the suburbs, lower-income Black families moved in behind them. The result of the loan constraints and the changing income profiles of residents was **downward filtering**, with the housing stock moving from medium quality to lower quality. In some cases this was true because the new families had less money to maintain these properties, but in other cases because banks refused to offer loans in redlined areas, refused to provide loans to Black borrowers in nonredlined neighborhoods, and in other cases approved loans to Black borrowers only at very high interest rates.

The opposite can occur as well. As we saw in Chapter 4, in a number of metro areas, central city neighborhoods have been rejuvenated as middle-class "pioneers" choose to move back to the city to take advantage of short commutes to downtown office jobs and the cultural and social amenities offered in dense communities. When these upper-income households begin to move into a dilapidated inner-city neighborhood, they bring resources that can help improve the community. But as more middle-class households choose to buy into the community, they bid up rents and home prices, which leads to the displacement of the original residents. Such gentrification leads to **upward filtering**, and the consequent loss of affordable housing units is difficult to stop once a neighborhood's property values begin to rise.

The passing of the tipping point in previously White neighborhoods that transition toward a majority or almost exclusive minority presence and the gentrification of formerly rundown inner-city locations to White middle-class enclaves help explain why the dissimilarity index in most metro areas declined only slightly between 1980 and 2000.

Concentrated Poverty in the Inner City

The combination of upward and downward filtering combined with racial segregation has intensified the spatial dimension of poverty in most metro areas. By the 1960s, social scientists were using the term **urban ghetto** to refer to sections of the city that contained high proportions of desperately poor households, most of them people of color. The term **urban slum** was also used to describe these neighborhoods where the concentration of poor people leads to a concentration of social ills that cause or are caused by poverty. Between 1970 and 1990, the number of people living in high-poverty areas doubled, as we noted in Chapter 2. The probability that a poor Black child would be trapped in a high-poverty neighborhood increased from one in four to one in three (Jargowsky 2003). This occurred during a time when the poverty rate—the proportion of families living under the official US poverty threshold—did not increase at all. What changed was the growing physical isolation of the poor in America. The social distance between the poor inner city and the more prosperous suburbs grew dramatically.

Family poverty rates in the central cities of the largest 25 metro areas in the United States are found in Table 14.6. What is noticeable is that many of these

TABLE 14.6. FAMILY POVERTY RATES IN CENTRAL CITIES IN 25 LARGEST U.S. METRO AREAS

	2000	2017
Detroit	26.1%	37.9%
Miami	28.5%	25.8%
Philadelphia	22.9%	25.8%
St. Louis	24.6%	25.0%
Atlanta	24.4%	22.4%
Baltimore	22.9%	22.4%
Dallas	17.8%	21.8%
Houston	19.2%	21.2%
Phoenix	15.8%	20.9%
Minneapolis	16.9%	20.7%
Chicago	19.6%	20.6%
Boston	19.5%	20.5%
Los Angeles	22.1%	20.4%
Tampa	18.1%	20.0%
New York	21.2%	19.6%
Orlando	15.9%	19.1%
San Antonio	17.3%	18.6%
Washington, D.C.	20.2%	17.4%
Riverside	15.8%	16.6%
Portland	13.1%	16.2%
Denver	14.3%	15.1%
Charlotte	10.6%	14.9%
San Diego	14.6%	14.5%
Seattle	11.8%	12.5%
San Francisco	11.3%	11.7%

cities have poverty rates that hover in the 20 percent range, and that there has been little reduction in concentrated poverty between 2000 and 2017. Indeed, in many of these cities, poverty has increased since the beginning of the twenty-first century and eradicating poverty is difficult for a number of reasons.

As we noted in Chapter 5, with jobs moving to the suburbs there is a tendency for **spatial** mismatch to occur, where those trapped in the city are unable to reach the jobs that are increasingly located in more distant suburbs. The lack of good public transportation to the suburbs makes this problem even worse. In studying Atlanta, Katz and Allen (2001) found that three-fourths of new entry-level jobs were located at least 10 miles away from the inner city where many poor unemployed workers live. Ihlanfeldt and Sjoquist (1990) estimate that about a quarter of the gap between Black and White youth employment rates can be explained simply by the lack of access to employment opportunities afforded those living in inner-city poor neighborhoods.

There is at least one apparent anomaly in the poverty data. Detroit has among the lowest housing costs among large cities, yet its poverty rate is nearly double the average rate for the other 24 central cities in this analysis. In San Francisco, the cost of housing exceeds the other 24 cities. One might think that Detroit should have a low poverty rate because of relatively inexpensive housing and San Francisco a very high one given its high-priced housing market. But just the opposite is true. The reason is that family incomes in Detroit are very low due to the loss of good jobs in that city and the fact that families with higher incomes have escaped to the suburbs. In San Francisco, the cost of housing is so high and the amount of public housing and subsidized housing is so low that few poor families can afford to live there.

The Suburbanization of Poverty

A new trend in poverty has been experienced in the United States over the past 50 years: the suburbanization of poverty. Poverty rates across the suburban landscape have increased by 50 percent since 1990. The number of suburban residents living in high-poverty areas has almost tripled in that time. Between 2000 and 2015 the overall number of people in poverty in the United States grew by 11.5 million, with suburbs accounting for roughly 5.7 million or 48 percent of that growth. By 2015, there were roughly 3 million more poor people in suburbs than in cities (Maher 2017–2018). Some of the outstanding examples of rising suburban poverty are found in metro areas that are generally better off, as well as those that have suffered deindustrialization and job loss. In Oak Park, Michigan, a close-in suburb of Detroit, the poverty rate has increased from 9.4 percent to 13.3 percent between 2000 and 2017. In Southfield, Michigan, another of Detroit's suburbs, the rate has increased from 7.4 percent to 13 percent. In Brockton, Massachusetts, a close-in suburb of economically strong Boston, the poverty rate has increased from 14.5 to 16.8 percent over this period.

There are many reasons for this phenomenon. Population growth in suburbs has been faster than in central cities and the slow growth of wages, especially for low-skill jobs, has left an increasing number of suburban workers below the poverty line. In most suburbs, unemployment rates were twice as high in 2014 as in 1990. Good-paying jobs that do not require advanced training have started to disappear in suburbs, just as they did in central cities in decades past.

In some high-cost cities, including San Francisco, poverty rates are generally higher outside the central city. Recall that the poverty rate in San Francisco's central city was 11.7 percent in 2017. But in two of its suburban communities, Oakland and Richmond, the rates were 16.2 percent and 18.7 percent, respectively. Unable to find affordable housing in the city itself, lower-income families have relocated to these outlying suburbs, and this has led to the divergence in poverty rates between the central city and its suburbs.

Housing Policy Across the Globe

In virtually every country in the world and in every city, there are public policies to deal with housing. The reason why government is involved at all in housing is that shelter is considered a merit good, a commodity whose consumption is deemed to be intrinsically beneficial and therefore worth encouraging. Decent shelter is seen as important to a household's well-being not only for keeping its members warm and dry during inclement weather, but because it contributes to better health, likely improves the chances of educational success for young children, and provides a place for families to have quiet refuge from the rest of the community. Just as they are encouraged to pay attention to proper nutrition and healthcare, families are encouraged to live in decent homes.

Even before the advent of the twentieth century, European governments were deeply involved in housing programs beginning with direct control of housing quality. Most European countries had undertaken demolition programs and introduced building standards legislation to address the adverse public health effects of slum housing. Rent controls introduced in some countries during World War I were extended more widely in the 1930s and became near ubiquitous throughout Europe after 1945. Only in the second half of the 1980s did many countries abolish them.

Social housing in Europe—or what in the United States is called public housing—was first introduced in Sweden, Denmark, Austria, Germany, France, the Netherlands, and Britain at the beginning of the twentieth century. In these countries, subsidies of up to 50 percent were provided by government to reduce housing development costs so that they could be offered at below-market rents. Housing quality was ensured by government regulated building standards. Since the start of the 1980s programs to support low-income homeowners have become more widespread, partly in response to dissatisfaction with the upkeep and conditions in public housing projects. By the first decades of the twenty-first century, subsidizing the cost of homeownership or rent of low-income households had become a more critical component of European housing policy. This is done either by providing capital subsidies to enhance supply and restricting rents or by subsidizing the incomes of residents (European Parliament 1996).

Today, in Europe, there are three pillars of housing policies. The first and most important is to promote homeownership. The second is the construction of public housing and the third is direct rental subsidies to households, especially those of low income. There are, however, very large differences between countries. In Ireland, Spain, and the United Kingdom housing policy is focused primarily on expanding owner occupancy, and that is why we found that ownership occupancy rates in Europe are often higher than in the United States. Homeownership is encouraged through the provision of direct subsidies and mortgage-tax relief. In other European countries including the Netherlands, Sweden, and Austria, there is more emphasis on public or so-called social housing operated by local authorities for lower income households.

In many Asian countries, government is even more invested in the provision of housing. While Singapore is not generally regarded as a welfare state, the provision of housing on a large scale has been a defining feature of its welfare system. Hong Kong has a large public housing sector, as well. The Korean government entered the housing market in a major way at the beginning of the twenty-first century, establishing the Construction Plan for One Million Rental Housing Units from 2003–2012. The aim was to ensure a supply of good quality affordable rented housing for low-income families. Additionally, in 2004 the Korean government established the Korea Housing Finance Corporation to promote homeownership for low- and middle-income families by providing long-term mortgages. The main pillar of housing policy in Japan is to encourage the building of owner-occupied housing by means of government loans. Loans are available for rental housing construction, but the subsidies involved are much smaller (Zenou 2011).

In China, before 1949 and the communist revolution, most urban housing in such cities as Beijing and Shanghai was private rental, provided by landlords. But beginning in the 1950s, a majority of these properties were nationalized under the socialist transformation. Public housing was built by government owned enterprises and institutions and distributed directly to their employees as part of a comprehensive welfare provision system. New housing reforms in all cities and large towns were implemented in the 1980s, including a public housing provision. By the 1990s, China turned to commercial developers rather than public-sector employees for the production of housing and housing privatization became a main element of these reform programs. By 2002, 80 percent of the public housing stock had been sold to the households who lived in them. As such, private housing has become the norm in much of China, despite its socialist form of government (Zenou 2011).

US Federal Housing Policy

Over time, the United States has developed its own policies. While housing would seem to be the quintessential local good, an array of national policies dictated by the federal government has an enormous influence on the supply of housing, the type of housing demanded, and the price households pay to live where they do.

The great postwar homeownership boom in the United States was spurred by several factors. During World War II, families had built up large savings accounts. Virtually everyone who wanted to work during the war could find a job and often earned overtime pay. Since there was wartime rationing, there was little to buy, including housing. Thus, at the end of the war, households were flush with savings and had—often for the first time—the wherewithal for a down payment.

Adding to the housing momentum were federal government policies explicitly aimed at encouraging ownership. The Federal Housing Administration (FHA), first established in 1934 as part of President Franklin Roosevelt's New Deal, provided insurance to mortgage lenders that permitted them to lower the down payment for potential homeowners and extend home loan repayment for up to 30 years. The longer term allowed lower monthly payments and provided homeowners with the ability to pay back some of the principal as well as interest so that they owned their homes outright at the end of the mortgage period. These are fully **amortized** mortgages. When mortgage rates were higher, mortgages were often **nonamortizing**, meaning that only the interest on the loan was paid during the mortgage period. At the end of the mortgage a family had to secure another mortgage if they wanted to continue to live in their home, or they could pay for the entire cost of the house if they wanted to buy it outright. The Veterans Housing Administration (VHA) provided mortgage insurance that served the purpose of substituting amortized mortgages for those that were nonamortized.

Equally important for fostering homeownership was the mortgage deduction under the federal personal income tax. By making all the interest charges on a home mortgage fully deductible on the homeowner's federal personal income tax return and thus reducing taxable income, the effective monthly cost of buying a home was often less than the monthly cost of renting. If a household pays $1,400 per month in mortgage interest payments and is in the 25 percent federal income tax bracket, the household's $1,400 monthly mortgage interest payment is equal *after-tax* to a monthly payment of only $1,050. Being able to deduct the full cost of local residential property taxes in addition to mortgage interest against the federal tax gave an added incentive to buy rather than rent. No other consumer good was as tax-favored as homeownership. The full deductibility of mortgage interest on mortgages of up to $1 million and the full deduction of all state and local property taxes against one's federal income tax essentially meant that the federal government was encouraging homeownership by lowering the after-tax cost of housing.

This full deductibility of most mortgage interest and all state and local property taxes was in effect for decades until the Tax Cuts and Jobs Act enacted by Congress in 2017. Under this act, mortgage interest on mortgage amounts exceeding $750,000 were no longer eligible for a federal tax deduction. For states and local governments with high property taxes, the limitation of the state and local government property tax deduction to $10,000 from 2018 through at least 2025 is potentially an even greater disincentive to homeownership. By limiting the federal income tax deductions on large mortgages and high state and local property taxes, the decision to rent versus buy shifts, at least to some extent, toward renting.

But even the reduced value of federal tax deductions cannot fully explain the low homeownership rate in the U.S relative to many other nations. A large part of the answer is that low-income households do not have the means for a down payment, nor possibly a credit rating that permits them to obtain a conventional mortgage. As a result, they are forced to rent rather than become homeowners. Another factor has to do with the competitiveness of the rental market. If there is a sufficiently high vacancy rate to keep landlords' **economic profit** close to zero, some of the benefits that homeowners receive are received by renters as well. Since landlords can deduct their mortgage interest on rental property, this will translate into lower rents in a competitive rental market.

In addition, landlords can use **accelerated depreciation** to deduct maintenance expenses from their federal income tax. Under the accelerated depreciation provision of the federal income tax, landlords can deduct a large proportion of the cost of mainte-nance in the early years of such an investment rather than spreading out the deduction in equal shares over the full expected life of the property-improvement investment. This reduces their after-tax costs, which, in a competitive market, will be passed along to renters. Using our example, this might translate into a rent of $800 per month, not $1,050. In this case, for equal amounts of housing, renting can be competitive with buying. This is particularly true if the renter can invest the monthly savings in an asset that is appreciating faster than housing. So while there are advantages to buying a home in the United States, there are also advantages to remain a renter.

Subsidizing Housing Demand

Before 1962, the federal government played only a minor role in providing housing assistance. Even accounting for inflation, total federal spending in 1962 was less than $1 billion. It was in the period between 1973 and 2004 that real federal spend-ing on housing assistance increased rapidly. Since then, the rate at which spending has increased (in real dollars) has slowed, but in FY2018 it reached $49.5 billion.

Direct housing assistance is provided by the federal government through a variety of programs. The largest is tenant-based rental subsidies through the gov-ernment's Section 8 program which provides low-income families with help in paying their monthly rent when they find a place to live. In FY2018, this program was funded at a level of nearly $21 billion. Section 8 takes the form of a **voucher** provided to local public housing agencies that distributes these to tenants who use them to pay rent on single-family homes, townhouses, or apartments. The voucher amount is calculated based on a standard rental price in the specific city or town. The end result of the voucher program is to limit a family's rental expense to 30 percent of their income. To qualify a tenant must have income below 50 percent of the median income for the county or metropolitan area where they live although most participants are at 30 percent or less of the median.

Project-based assistance is tied to particular units and does not travel with individual tenants. This means that project-based rental assistance can be a source of long-term affordability as such housing can be preserved as more affordable over time. This assistance is particularly helpful in rapidly gentrifying areas where the loss of project-based rental assistance would likely result in the displacement of low-income families. In FY2018, the federal government spent $11.5 billion on such assistance. In addition, the federal government supplied more than $6 billion in FY2018 to help local public housing authorities maintain public housing for low-income individuals and families and an additional $2.3 billion for programs to assist the homeless, subsidizing homeless shelters throughout the United States.

Despite the spending on low-income housing, the federal government pro-vides even more housing assistance—more than four times as much—through **tax expenditures**, most of which benefit middle- and upper-income homeowners. Tax expenditures are defined by the government as "revenue losses attributable to provisions of the federal tax laws which allow a special exclusion, exemption, or deduction from gross income or which provide a special credit, a preferential rate of tax, or a deferral of tax liability" (US Congress Committee on Ways and Means and the Committee on Finance 2003).

In FY 2015 tax expenditures for housing amounted to $133 billion, including $70 billion for the tax deductibility of home mortgage interest, $33 billion for the residential property tax deduction, and $30 billion for the exclusion of capital gains on the sale of a homeowner's principal residence (Fischer and Sard 2017). The higher the tax bracket of the homeowner and the greater the value of the home, the more valuable the deduction. As noted earlier, in 2019, the value of these exclusions was reduced a small amount by limiting the amount of mortgage interest and state and local taxes eligible for the federal tax exclusion.

Also, as we noted earlier, the creation of the Federal Housing Administration (FHA) in 1934 has played a critical role in increasing the homeownership rate in the United States. Under FHA, the Federal National Mortgage Association, better known as Fannie Mae, was created to help reduce mortgage risk by assisting financial institutions to diversify their portfolios. Fannie Mae runs a **secondary mortgage market** so that private banks can sell a portion of their primary mortgages sold to homeowners in return for other types of securities. Fannie Mae and its newer federal mortgage cousin, Freddie Mac, aid the homeowner by providing funds for mortgage lending and permitting local banks to limit their default risk and therefore offer lower interest rates. Freddie Mac claims that it saves the typical homeowner $18,000 in interest charges over the 30-year life of a $150,000 mortgage (Freddie Mac 2007).

Tax expenditures and the expanded availability of mortgage money increase the consumption of housing by augmenting the demand side of the housing market. The same has been true of a number of federal mortgage and rent subsidy programs. The Section 221(d)(3) program, introduced in 1961 under President John F. Kennedy, provided a mortgage subsidy for low-income home buyers, increasing their demand for housing.

For many decades Fannie Mae and Freddie Mac, along with the mortgage banking industry made homeownership easier for middle income households to buy a home. After 2000, mortgage banks trying to add to their profits from mortgage lending loosened their credit standards making it possible for many lower income households with tenuous employment histories to borrow funds to become homeowners. Some banks would be accused of making "no doc" mortgages, asking borrowers for little or no documentation of their income and debt. This would lead to a housing and financial crisis as a result of these **predatory private mortgage lending practices** made possible by federal deregulation of the banking industry. When the economy began to weaken in 2006, many of these new homeowners could not maintain their mortgage payments. Between 2007 and 2016, 7.8 million households faced foreclosure and the loss of their homes. This, in turn, led to a sharp reduction in home prices because of the millions of homes that flooded the market.

Across the country, the median price of a single-family home fell by an average of 18 percent. In metro areas which had sustained an earlier housing construction boom, prices fell even more precipitously. In Phoenix and Las Vegas, home prices plummeted by more than 30 percent in 2008 alone. Miami, Los Angeles, and San Diego recorded one-year price declines in that year of 29, 28, and 27 percent, respectively (CNN Money 2008). It would take a number of years for prices to regain their pre-2008 highs.

Subsidizing Housing Supply

If we are concerned about improving housing conditions for low-income families, the irony of federal government intervention on the demand side is that, as we have just seen, more than 80 percent of the demand-side subsidies go to better-off families through the tax expenditures that result from the deductibility of mortgage interest. What about the federal government's interventions on the supply side of the housing market? There is an irony here as well. As we demonstrated earlier, increasing the supply of housing is one way to reduce its price. Therefore, the logic of a supply-side intervention to improve housing conditions for low-income families would require that we increase the number of housing units. However, neither of the two major federal supply-side interventions of the mid-twentieth century actually resulted in an expansion of the housing stock. How can that be?

The Public Housing Act of 1937 provided federal subsidies to local housing authorities that wanted to clear out slums. It is the program under which many of the large-scale high-rise projects were constructed, including the notorious and since-demolished Pruitt-Igoe homes in St. Louis and the Cabrini Green homes in Chicago. These projects tended to exacerbate the social isolation of the poor. This proved to be a disastrous social experiment where the concentration of poverty in these projects often led to dilapidation and high crime rates. Based on this adverse experience, very few new units of public housing have been built since the 1970s.

According to the noted urban historian Kenneth Jackson (1985), the purpose of the 1937 law was primarily to create construction jobs as a way of stimulating economic activity during the Great Depression of the 1930s. In order to protect real estate interests at a time when private housing markets were already weak, the law required that one housing unit—presumably a unit of low-quality slum housing—be destroyed for every new housing unit created by the program. Thus, on net, this intervention left the total supply of housing units unchanged.

The next major federal intervention on the supply side occurred with passage of the Housing Act of 1949. The preamble of this law stated that every American family deserves a "decent home and a suitable living environment" (Lang and Sohmer 2000). This act established the urban renewal program that cleared large swaths through many low-income urban neighborhoods and often used the cleared land to house a smaller number of higher-income households (as in the development of the upscale Charles River Park in the old working-class West End of Boston) or converted it to a nonresidential use (as in the Lincoln Center Performing Arts complex that replaced a Latinx neighborhood on Manhattan's West Side). As Rothenberg (1972) points out, the many goals of the urban renewal program were often incompatible with each other. Efforts to revitalize cities and bring back middle- and higher-income residents often played a greater role than improving housing standards for the poor. The program destroyed more housing units than it created, and many of those who were displaced wound up paying higher rents for poorer-quality units—the outcome we would expect knowing that the program actually reduced the number of housing units available.

What is left of public housing provision by the federal government is the HOPE VI (Housing Opportunities for People Everywhere) program, which provides government funds to rehabilitate existing housing projects that are badly in need of renovation and repair. Under this program that began in the early 1990s, older high-rise buildings have been razed and in their place the government has constructed low-rise units and town houses. Public housing tenants are given temporary housing while the new units are built and then have an opportunity to establish residency in the new units.

A more recent federal housing supply program, begun in 1986, is the Low Income Housing Tax Credit (LIHTC) targeted at encouraging affordable housing construction by private developers. By 2000 nearly one million housing units had been built under this program, which offers federally tax-exempt bonds to lower interest rates plus tax credits equal to 70 percent of the construction costs for privately developed housing projects that include a proportion of units reserved for low-income households. Developers can use the tax credits to offset losses to their after-tax profit that occurs as a result of offering housing to low-income households at below-market prices or rents. Today, the LIHTC is used to build more low-income housing than any other single federal program.

Finally, the Department of Housing and Urban Development administers a broad set of Community Planning and Development programs. These include block grants to communities to support a wide range of unique community development needs. The grants can cover homeless shelters and programs, rent subsidy and support, community studies, information gathering, and other purposes. The grants generally are made to the communities to support low-income housing and low-income living standards in some manner.

State and Local Housing Policy

While the federal government has played a substantial role—albeit one that has its paradoxes—on both the supply and demand sides of the housing market, states and local communities are still responsible for most housing policies. As we noted earlier, the zoning decisions of local municipalities can reduce the supply of land available for housing, which increases the cost of producing new housing units. Without spending a penny, local jurisdictions can exert a powerful influence on both the rental and the homeownership markets through such land regulation. For example, Glaeser et al. (2006) estimate that increasing minimum lot size by one acre results in anywhere from an 11.5 to 13.8 percent increase in median home prices after controlling for the size, age, and number of rooms in the house.

As state governments begin to better understand the impact of high housing prices on their own economic development, a number of states have begun to develop policies to influence local land regulations and to provide incentives for housing construction, particularly aimed at building housing for low- and moderate-income households. A number of states have created **housing trust funds** that provide developers with low-cost loans if they agree to set aside a minimum number of units in their projects that can be rented or sold at below-market prices.

Some cities, including Boston and Cambridge, Massachusetts, have passed **inclusionary zoning laws** which encourage builders to include a number of affordable housing units in their developments in return for the municipality permitting them to construct more units per acre and therefore lower their land costs. Alternatively, the developer of such a dense housing project can pay into a municipal fund that is then used to underwrite the housing trust fund, which can encourage the building of affordable units in other locations within the community.

Other municipalities have instituted **linkage programs** that require developers of commercial and industrial property to pay into a housing fund to offset pressure on the housing market caused by the hiring of new employees in the businesses that occupy these properties and who need housing.

In a unique program, Massachusetts passed a Smart Growth Overlay Zoning law in 2005 that provides its cities and towns with monetary incentives if they rezone land around town centers, transit stops, and where abandoned industrial property is located so that denser, more affordable housing can be built (Carman et al. 2004). The new law complements older legislation passed in 1969, which required cities and towns to assure that 10 percent of their housing stock is affordable to low- and moderate-income households. If municipalities under the 10 percent threshold balk at permitting developers to build new housing in their communities, the developer can bypass local zoning and obtain a "comprehensive permit" from the state. In Massachusetts, where local home rule is so powerful in terms of zoning, this state law has been the single most potent instrument for assuring the production of low- and moderate-income housing.

This Massachusetts law enacted in 1969 spawned action in other states. In 1975, the New Jersey Supreme Court held every city and town in the state has the constitutional obligation to provide for the "regional general welfare" by, in part, helping to meet the region's affordable housing needs (Haar 1996; Kirp et al. 1996). The state court's now famous *Mt. Laurel* decision came in response to a group of low-income Black residents in that New Jersey town who tried to replace a local slum with 36 units of modestly priced garden apartments. The town refused to permit the small development by maintaining zoning only for single-family houses. The court struck down the use of zoning to exclude low-income housing, but in the ensuing years, Mt. Laurel and virtually all other suburbs in the state found ways to evade the court's intent by establishing other barriers to development that included minimum lot sizes, building setback rules, and extraordinarily rigid environmental regulations.

Angered by the municipal response to its original ruling, the state supreme court came back in 1983 in *Mt. Laurel II* with a much more powerful set of sanctions similar to those in Massachusetts permitting a "builder's remedy" such that developers could circumvent local town regulations. While the state legislature in New Jersey, under great pressure from suburban voters, weakened the impact of *Mt. Laurel II* by permitting municipalities to meet their obligations through age-restricted housing for the elderly and through regional contribution agreements, the court's rulings have brought some positive results. In the town of Mt. Laurel itself, 140 town houses for low- and moderate-income renters were constructed and throughout the state more than 15,000 units of affordable housing were produced in the decade following the court's reaffirmation of the original *Mt. Laurel* decision.

Rent Control

In the face of escalating housing prices and rents, increasing the supply of housing should eventually bring the cost down and make decent shelter affordable to more families. But because of the range of barriers to producing more housing units, some advocates for low-income families have suggested the need to go back to some form of price control on rents. During World War II, as factory after factory switched from the production of civilian goods to military products, the US Office of Price Administration established wage and price controls to combat inflationary pressure in the civilian sector. At the same time, to prevent landlords from gouging renters on what were now fixed incomes, it instituted a national system of rent control. After the war, New York City retained the controls and during the 1970s a number of cities including Boston and Cambridge in Massachusetts and Los Angeles, Berkeley, and Santa Monica in California reinstituted various forms of rent stabilization. In a state-wide referendum in 1994 in Massachusetts, voters overthrew by a tiny margin (51% to 49%) the state law permitting rent control so no longer is there rent control anywhere in the state. Still to this day, there are advocates for rent control in the most pricey communities in the nation.

The Unintended Short-Run Consequences of Rent Control

On the surface, such controls seem warranted and low-income households who find rent-controlled apartments benefit from them. Nonetheless, there is considerable evidence that while rent control may provide some price relief in the short run, there are consequences that build up over time and prove counterproductive to prospective tenants, perhaps even more so than to landlords. There are at least six reasons for this:

1. By reducing the profitability of rental housing and increasing the possibility of expensive, time-consuming litigation over rent increases or evictions, the supply of rental housing tends to shrink in the long run.

2. Owners of existing rental housing are less likely and, in some cases, unable to afford to maintain their properties which accelerates the *deterioration* of existing rental stock.

3. If not explicitly prohibited from doing so, landlords will *convert* their rental units to condominiums or other land uses, further reducing the supply of rental property to those who cannot afford to buy.

4. The existence of rent controls *discourages* developers from building new housing, even if the new housing is initially exempt from the rent-control statute. Possible future control of these properties is factored into the calculation of the rate of return, which reduces the expected value of the development.

5. Where only one municipality passes rent control, there is every inducement for developers to go elsewhere if they wish to remain in the housing production business.

6. In the long run, deterioration of the existing housing stock and the discouragement of new production leads to lower property tax revenue for the city and greater difficulty in funding city services including those for low-income households.

These unintended consequences are not simply theoretical. An early study of rent control in New York City conducted by the RAND Corporation found that between 1960 and 1967, the inventory of "sound" housing increased by only 2.4 percent, while the inventory of "dilapidated" housing increased by 44 percent and the inventory of "deteriorating" housing increased by 37 percent. The same RAND study found that between 1965 and 1967, 111,400 units in the city were retired from the housing stock by landlords, converting them to other uses or abandoning them (Lowry et al. 1971). A more recent study in Cambridge, Massachusetts, found that maintenance expenditure per rental unit declined by $50 per year as the result of rent control that led to growing deterioration over time (Navarro 1985).

In practice, because of these unintended consequences, municipalities with rent control were often forced to consider "vacancy decontrol" in order to maintain some incentive for developers to build new units and for existing landlords to maintain their properties. Rent-control statutes were amended so that rents remained fixed only as long as the current tenant lived in the unit. When the tenant moved out of the apartment, the landlord was allowed to seek the market rate rent for the next tenant, where the rent would be fixed again. This, however, created a strong incentive for landlords to evict tenants in order to hike the rent periodically. To counter this response, rent control needed further tinkering, which created rent-control boards where tenants could appeal their evictions. In order to evict a tenant, the landlord would have to prove that the tenant violated the lease.

As rent control became increasingly burdensome with more and more rules to follow, landlords sought other ways to avoid it. By turning their rental units into condominiums and selling these units to home buyers, the supply of rental property declined even faster. In a number of municipalities, this led in a continuing series of legal gambits and countergambits to the inclusion of anti-condominium conversion amendments in the rent-control statutes. In trying to deal with the landlords' ability to circumvent rent control, the entire rent-control machinery became more and more complex and difficult to implement.

Beyond the deleterious effect on housing supply, rent control often ended up with unintended "distribution" effects. Those who are most in need of affordable rental housing are not the ones who always obtain it when rent control is instituted. Landlords have every incentive to select higher-income tenants who have the means to maintain their properties and perform the routine upkeep that normally would be the responsibility of the owner. This means that landlords are less likely under rent control to lease units to low-income families, especially those with children, and once in a rent-controlled unit, renters are less likely to move even when "overhoused." In this case one- and two-person households end up living in units that would be much better suited to larger families.

Essentially, rent control or "stabilization" creates a form of rationing that benefits those already in controlled housing yet harms those who need it most, exacerbating inequity in the housing market. In addition, if rent control lasts long, it is common for a "black market" to be established in which landlords may ask for—or be urged to accept from potential tenants who are desperate for a rent-controlled apartment—illegal or quasi-legal, under-the-table payments. Without a great deal of monitoring, this activity will take place along with renter subletting that allows the renter to charge a fee in excess of the rent-controlled price. The longer rent control is in force, the greater the certainty that all these unintended consequences will arise, undermining the stated objective of rent control. Not surprisingly, by the late 1990s, rent control had disappeared in most cities.

Indeed, there are only a few rare circumstances when economists conclude that the benefits of rent control can outweigh its adverse consequences. During World War II, when nearly everything was rationed or subject to price controls, it made sense to impose temporary limits on rent increases. It probably made sense during the oil boom in Alaska, but only as a short-term measure where it was expected that after construction of the pipeline there would no longer be the need for a large permanent housing stock. In these cases, there was no concern about the impact of rent control on discouraging future supply or of displacing low-income families in favor of richer ones.

Intervening in Housing Markets: A Word of Caution

Given the importance of housing to social well-being, only those who hold the strongest free-market conservative philosophy are against any and all interventions in the housing market. For those who favor deliberate policy, it is critical to understand that the variety of interventions confer a range of benefits and costs and produce both winners and losers. The federal tax deductions for mortgage interest and local property taxes costs the federal government forgone tax revenue that could be used for all manner of other public goods and services. These tax expenditures benefit homeowners while conferring little advantage to renters and almost surely lead to the "overconsumption" of housing in the form of bigger and plusher accommodations than would be the case if such tax forgiveness did not exist.

Public subsidies to developers of affordable housing increase the supply of housing, particularly for lower-income households, making it possible for such families to afford better places to live. But once again, these housing subsidies have an opportunity cost because the revenue for such publicly provided subsidies could be used for other public goods and services or returned to the taxpayers for their own use. Public subsidies that are provided to renters—and in some cases, homeowners—permit low-income households to move into better housing. But in expanding the demand for housing, these vouchers may raise the rents for those who do not qualify for them.

Rent control provides immediate relief for low-income renters and others who somehow can take advantage of rent-controlled unit but the long-term implications for housing supply and prices are often adverse.

Programs to limit zoning restrictions or to provide incentives for zoning reform that favor more housing probably have the fewest unintended consequences but even here there are winners and losers. Increasing the supply of housing reduces the rate of housing price appreciation which benefits those entering the housing market but reduces the price premium that existing homeowners can charge.

There is a simple lesson here. As long as we believe that a particular good is a merit good, there can be a case for subsidizing its production and consumption. However, care must be taken to assure that both efficiency and equity are served by intervention in the market. This takes a thorough examination of various policies and even more careful implementation.

References

Atkinson, Robert D., Mark Munro, and Jacob Whiton. 2019. "The Case for Growth Centers: How to Spread Tech Innovation across America." Washington, DC: Brookings Institution.

Belsky, Eric S. 2006. "Rental Vacancy Rates: A Policy Primer." *Housing Policy Debate* 3, no. 3: 793–813.

Berson, David and Eileen Neely. 1997. "Homeownership in the United States: Where We've Been; Where We're Going." *Business Economics* 32 (3): 7-11

Bluestone, Barry. 2006. "Sustaining the Mass Economy: Housing Costs, Population Dynamics, and Employment." Boston: Federal Reserve Bank of Boston and Cambridge, MA: Rappaport Institute for Greater Boston, Harvard University.

Bluestone, Barry, and James Huessy. 2017. *The Greater Boston Housing Report Card 2017*. Boston: The Boston Foundation.

Bluestone, Barry, and Mary Huff Stevenson. 2000. *The Boston Renaissance: Race, Space, and Economic Change in an American Metropolis*. New York: Russell Sage.

Carman, Ted, Barry Bluestone, and Eleanor White. 2004. *Building on Our Heritage: A Housing Strategy for Smart Growth and Economic Development*. Boston: The Boston Foundation.

Charles, Camille Z. 2000. "Residential Segregation in Los Angeles." In *Prismatic Metropolis: Inequality in Los Angeles*, edited by Lawrence Bobo, Melvin Oliver, James Johnson, and Abel Valenzuela Jr. New York: Russell Sage, pp. 167–219.

CNN Money. 2008. "Home Prices Post 18% Drop." December 30.

Colman, William G. 1975. *Cities, Suburbs and States: Governing and Financing Urban America*. New York: Free Press.

Domonoske, Camila. 2016. "Interactive Redlining Map Zooms In On America's History Of Discrimination." *NPR Digital Media*. https://www.wbez.org/shows/npr/interactive-redlining-map-zooms-in-on-americas-history-of-discrimination/3b0d970d-b8f7-4293-841c-c7a2118e9c1a.

European Parliament. 1996. *Housing Policy in the EU Member States*. Report No. W-4. Brussels: European Parliament.

Farley, Reynolds, Howard Shuman, Suzanne Bianchi, Diane Colasanto, and Shirley Hatchett. 1978. "Chocolate City, Vanilla Suburbs: Will the Trend toward Racially Separate Communities Continue?" *Social Science Research* 7 (December): 319–344.

Fischel, William A. 2001. *The Homevoter Hypothesis: How Home Values Influence Local Government Taxation, School Finance, and Land-Use Policies*. Cambridge, MA: Harvard University Press.

Fischer, Will, and Barbara Sard. 2017. "Chart Book: Federal Housing Spending is Poorly Matched to Need." March 8. Washington, DC: Center for Budget and Policy Priorities.

Freddie Mac. 2007. "Just the Facts: How We Make Home Possible." September. McLean, VA: Freddie Mac.

Glaeser, Edward L., Jenny Schuetz, and Bryce Ward. 2006. "Regulation and the Rise of Housing Prices in Greater Boston: A Study Based on New Data from 187 Communities in Eastern Massachusetts." January. Cambridge, MA: Rappaport Institute for Greater Boston, Harvard University.

Goodman, Laurie, Christopher Mayer, and Monica Clodius. 2018. "The US Homeownership Rate has Lost Ground Compared with Other Countries." March 12. Washington, DC: The Urban Institute.

Haar, Charles M. 1996. *Suburbs Under Siege*. Princeton, NJ: Princeton University Press.

Housing Europe. 2015. *A Housing Europe Review: The State of Housing in the EU*. Brussels, Belgium: Housing Europe.

Ihlanfeldt, Keith, and David Sjoquist. 1990. "Job Accessibility and Racial Differences in Youth Employment Rates." *American Economic Review* 80, no. 1: 266–276.

Jackson, Kenneth. 1985. *Crabgrass Frontier: The Suburbanization of the United States*. New York: Oxford University Press.

Jakabovics, Andrew. 2006. "Housing Affordability Initiative: Land Use Research Findings." http://web.mit.edu/cre/research/hai/land-use.html.

Jargowsky, Paul. 2003. *"Stunning Progress, Hidden Problems: The Dramatic Decline of Concentrated Poverty in the 1990s."* May. Washington, DC: Brookings Institution.

Joint Center for Housing Studies. 2018. *The State of the Nation's Housing*. Cambridge, MA: Harvard University Press.

Kain, John, and John Quigley. 1975. *Housing Markets and Racial Discrimination: A Microeconomic Analysis*. Cambridge, MA: National Bureau of Economic Research.

Katz, Bruce, and Katherine Allen. 2001. "Cities Matter: Shifting the Focus of Welfare Reform." *Brookings Review* 19, no. 3 (Summer): 30–33.

Kirp, David L., John P. Dwyer, and Larry Rosenthal. 1996. *Our Town: Race, Housing, and the Soul of Suburbia*. New Brunswick, NJ: Rutgers University Press.

Lancaster, Kelvin. 1972. *Consumer Demand: A New Approach*. New York: Columbia University Press.

Lang, Robert E., and Rebecca R. Sohmer. 2000. "Legacy of the Housing Act of 1949: The Past, Present, and Future of Housing and Urban Policy." *Housing Policy Debate* 11, no. 2: 291–298.

Lipsey, Richard. 1960. "The Relation between Unemployment and the Rate of Change of Money Wage Rates in the United Kingdom, 1862–1957: A Further Analysis." *Economica* 26, no. 105 (February): 1–31.

Lowry, Ira S. 1982. *Rental Housing in the 1970s: Searching for the Crisis.* Santa Monica, CA: RAND Corporation, https://www.rand.org/pubs/notes/N1833.html.

Maher, Will. 2017–2018. "Suburban Poverty." No. 14. Madison: Institute for Research on Poverty, University of Wisconsin.

Massey, Douglas S., and Nancy A. Denton. 1988. "The Dimensions of Residential Segregation." *Social Forces* 67, no. 2: 281–315.

McCarthy, Niall. 2021. "The U.S. Cities with the Most Homeless People." Statista, April 16, 2021. https://www.statista.com/chart/6949/the-us-cities-with-the-most-homeless-people/

Mohl, Raymond A. 1996. "The Second Ghetto and the 'Infiltration Theory' in Urban Real Estate, 1940–1960." In *Urban Planning and the African-American Community: In the Shadows*, edited by June Thomas Manning and Marsha Ritzdorf. Thousand Oaks, CA: Sage Publications, pp. 58–74.

Navarro, Peter. 1985. "Rent Control in Cambridge, Massachusetts." *Public Interest* 91 (Spring): 83–100.

O'Sullivan, Feargus. 2016. "Which European Cities Have the Most Affordable Housing." Bloomberg *CityLab*, September 9, https://www.bloomberg.com/news/articles/2016-09-09/the-european-cities-with-the-most-affordable-housing

Phillips, A. W. 1958. "The Relation Between Unemployment and the Rate of Change of Money Wage Rates in the United Kingdom, 1861–1957." *Economica* 25, no. 100 (November): 283–299.

Rothenberg, Jerome. 1972. "The Nature of Redevelopment Benefits." In *Readings in Urban Economics*, edited by Matthew Edel and Jerome Rothenberg. New York: Macmillan, pp. 215–226.

Rothstein, Richard. 2019. *The Color of Law: A Forgotten History of How Our Government Segregated America.* New York: Liveright.

Simeleviciene, Jurgita. 2018. "Why Romania Is a Nation of Homeowners While Switzerland—a Nation of Tenants." *Business Fondue*, September 7. http://www.businessfondue.com/2018/09/07/why-romania-is-a-nation-of-homeowners-while-switzerland-a-nation-of-tenants/#more-1652

Squires, Gregory. 1994. *Capital and Communities in Black and White: The Intersection of Race, Class and Uneven Development.* Albany: State University of New York Press.

US Bureau of the Census. 2005a. *Racial and Ethnic Segregation in the United States: 1980–2000.* Washington, DC: Government Printing Office.

US Bureau of the Census. 2017. "Historical Census of Housing Tables: Homeownership Rates" https://www2.census.gov/programs-surveys/decennial/tables/time-series/coh-owner/owner-tab.txt Accessed August 1, 2021.

US Congress. Committee on Ways and Means and the Committee on Finance. 2003. *Estimates of Federal Tax Expenditures for Fiscal Years 2004–2008*. December 22. Washington, DC: Government Printing Office.

US Department of Housing and Urban Development. 2006. *Fiscal Year 2006 Budget Summary. Appendix A*. Washington, DC: Government Printing Office.

US Department of Housing and Urban Development. 2007a. "Affordable Housing." https://www.hud.gov/program_offices/comm_planning/home/cpd/affordablehousing.

Zenou, Yves. 2011. "Housing Policies in China: Issues and Options." *Policy Paper No. 24*, February. Bonn, Germany: Forschungsinstitut zur Zukunft der Arbeit (IZA) Institute for the Study of Labor.

Questions and Exercises

1. As Chapter 14 discusses, the housing market is a key aspect of the metropolitan economic and social environment. What is the housing market like in the metropolitan (or micropolitan) areas of interest to you? To explore this question, let's look first at how housing in those areas is divided among owner-occupied housing, renter-occupied housing, and vacancies in three metro areas of your choice and in one central city within each of those three metro areas. To access housing data, go to the following website: https://www.huduser.gov/portal/datasets/socds.html. Within this dataset, go to "Principal Cities" and select data for the most current census year. Then select five different states and within each one a large city. Finally, check off the box for "Housing Units."

   - Calculate the percentage of owner-occupied and rental housing units in each city. How much difference is there in the rate of homeownership?

   Now do the same thing for the same set of principal cities for an earlier census year.

   - After calculating the percentage of owner-occupied units in each city, compare and discuss the trend in homeownership in each city.

2. Using the same data source, calculate the vacancy rate for housing units (= 100 − Percent of Occupied Units).

   - Among the cities you chose, which have the highest vacancy rates?
   - Which factors might account for the variation in the vacancy rates?

3. Using the same data source, check the box for "Household Rents/Owners Values" in order obtain statistics on median rents and home values.

   - Among the cities you chose, which has the highest and lowest home values?
   - Among the cities you chose, which has the highest and lowest rents?
   - Which factors might account for this variation in rents and home values?

To answer this last question, you might consult other data in this website regarding race and ethnicity, educational attainment, and poverty and income.

15

Urban Resilience and Adaptation to Climate Change

LEARNING OBJECTIVES

- Enumerate the major sources of greenhouse gas emissions and describe their effects

- Enumerate the forms of renewable energy and describe efforts to encourage their use

- Explain how an emissions trading system works

- Explain the elements of adaption and resilience as they apply to combatting climate change

- Define LEED and explain its role in combatting climate change

- Identify two environmental problems other than greenhouse gas emissions and discuss efforts to reduce these problems

Well before the first humans walked the earth, our planet was subject to massive environmental disruptions in the form of hurricanes, tropical storms, typhoons, earthquakes, floods, tornadoes, and droughts.

An international team studying storm development from the Pliocene era, roughly three million years ago, found an increase in the average intensity of ancient storms. They reached their peak intensity at higher latitudes of the northern and southern hemispheres following a warming trend that led to an increase in tropical conditions. These findings turned out to be fully consistent with smaller changes in the same patterns that have been observed over recent decades and are projected to continue over the next 100 years (Science Daily 2016).

With the development of human societies and the rise of densely populated cities, the cost of tropical windstorms became immense. In 1896, a hurricane that came on shore near Cedar Key, Florida, killed more than 200 residents and left nearly $10 billion in property damage in today's dollars. A typhoon that struck Galveston, Texas four years later in 1900 left a much greater death toll of between 6,000 and 12,000 souls.

Late in the twentieth century, a massive series of hurricanes wreaked death and destruction across the southern United States. In 1989, Hurricane Hugo hit South Carolina, causing 21 deaths and $7 billion in property damage. In 1992, Hurricane Andrew came on shore in Florida, killing 62 and causing $27 billion in property damage. And then in the twenty-first century, the United States was hit by some of the deadliest storms in the country's history. The most violent was Hurricane Katrina, which struck New Orleans in 2005 in the early morning hours of August 29. The levees that had been built in that city to avoid storm surge buckled and the city was submerged in sea water. More than 1,800 residents perished, and property damage mounted to $100 billion.

Earthquakes have also wreaked untold damage on human society. In Aleppo on Oct. 11, 1138, the ground under this Syrian city began to shake. The magnitude of the quake is lost to time, but contemporary chroniclers reported that the city's citadel collapsed and houses crumbled. The death toll of this quake is estimated at around 230,000. Even more deadly was the earthquake that struck Shaanxi, China on January 23, 1556, killing an estimated 830,000 people.

Earthquakes have struck around the world and caused loss of life and inflicted massive damage in more modern times as well. In 1906, the Great San Francisco earthquake left more than 3,000 dead. In 1989 another quake hit San Francisco, killing 69 and destroying at least $6 billion in property. On July 28, 1976, the Chinese city of Tangshan and its surroundings were rocked by a magnitude 7.8 earthquake. An industrial city with a population of about one million people, Tangshan saw a staggering 255,000 of its residents perish. Another 700,000 people were injured and many of the city's buildings were completely destroyed (Yong et al. 1988). More than 150,000 needed to find new residences in the six years following the quake. In Haiti, the 7.0 magnitude quake on January 12, 2010 killed 220,000 and left 300,000 injured.

Tornados have also taken their toll on cities. In 1896, a tornado struck St. Louis, Missouri, killing as many as 400 and causing, in today's dollars, $2.9 billion in property damage. Massive tornados caused loss of life and extensive property damage in 1925 in Missouri, Illinois, and Indiana. Eleven years later, a twister in Tupelo, Mississippi killed more than 400 in a matter of hours. More recently, these vicious storms caused massive damage and destruction in Flint, Michigan; Joplin, Missouri; and throughout the Midwest.

Fires spread by high winds killed as many as 300 in the 1871 "Great Chicago Fire" and more recently in a 2016 forest fire that spread to Paradise, California, bringing death to 85 of its residents. Just four years later in 2020, fires raged in Oregon, California, and Washington for three weeks, burning millions of acres of land and destroying thousands of homes. Tens of thousands of people were forced to flee. In just a matter of weeks, these wildfires scorched an area of land the size of New Jersey. In Oregon, where firefighters were battling 16 large blazes, 40,000 people were under mandatory evacuation orders after these fires had already killed 10 people, with the final death toll expected to be much higher. At the same time, in Washington State, firefighters were tackling 15 large fires. In California, where the blazes were most pronounced, some of the summer's 28 major fires lasted a month or more despite the best efforts by nearly 15,000 firefighters. According to experts, this is the legacy of climate change with western temperatures rising, diminished rains, and howling winds (Thorner 2020).

Heat waves and smog produce casualties as well. In 1980, a severe heat wave in the central and southern states in the United States killed 1,700. In the summer of 2003, the heat wave that spread across Europe caused more than 70,000 deaths. Dense smog itself can cause fatalities. In 1966 unhealthy air left nearly 170 dead in New York City.

Floods have often caused equal or greater damage. The Yellow River (Huang He) in China was precariously situated far above most of the land around it in the late 1880s, thanks to a series of dikes built to contain the river as it flowed through the farmland. Over time these dikes silted up, gradually lifting the river in elevation. When heavy rains swelled the river in September 1887, it spilled over these dikes into the surrounding low-lying land, inundating 5,000 square miles and killing an estimated 900,000 (Gunn 2007).

When a dam broke because of flooding in Johnstown, Pennsylvania in 1889 more than 2,200 drowned. In 1913 more than 360 died because of flooding in Dayton, Ohio. And in 1936, a flood in Pittsburgh, Pennsylvania killed 69 and caused over $3 billion in property damage. More recently, there was the massive flooding in 2018 caused by Hurricane Florence. Although the hurricane landed in North Carolina as only a mild hurricane in terms of wind speed (Category 1), it brought torrential rain to the area—up to nearly three feet in some towns—causing 54 deaths and more than $24 billion in property damage.

The Human Causes of Climate Disasters

While these stories tell us that harsh weather has always had consequences, what we know now is that part of climate change and its consequent damage is human-caused. Massive carbon emission is leading to increases in global temperatures and sea-level rise while extensive urban, suburban, and rural development has led to various forms of environmental calamity in many regions. Between 1940 and 1970 developers dredged and filled tens of thousands of acres of wetlands along the back bays of New Jersey. In Ocean County alone, more than 400 communities and 13,000 lagoons were built along the adjacent Barnegat Bay. More than 100,000 houses were built on or near the water, and these are now prime targets for hurricanes and rising sea levels.

Developers in coastal communities in South Carolina, Florida, Mississippi, and Texas filled thousands of acres of salt marsh along the coast in order to provide land for millions of homes and cottages. Many of these developments now flood routinely in storms such as Hurricane Harvey in 2017 and Florence in 2018 (Gaul 2019).

This litany of environmental disasters reminds us of how much we need to reduce the underlying causes for such events and find ways to become more resilient in the face of those over which we have little control. This will be particularly true as global warming leads to additional sea-level rise and the possibility of many cities located on rivers, lakes, and oceans becoming inundated with flood waters.

That cities are already subject to higher surface temperatures because of the concentration of industrial activities and the extensive use of fossil-fueled vehicles suggests that all aspects of the urban built environment are at high risk (The Climate Report 2018).

What will be needed are worldwide efforts to reduce **greenhouse gases** to slow temperature rise and extensive efforts by national, state, and municipal governments to assure that their citizens and their built environments are more secure against future storms and flooding. In this effort cities will have to play a major role, since they cover about 3 percent of the earth's land area but produce 72 percent of all global greenhouse gas emissions (Fitzgerald 2020).

Rising Global Temperatures and the Potential Impact on Cities

Given the capacity of the world's oceans to store heat, it takes an immense amount of heat to raise Earth's average yearly surface temperature. The 2-degree increase in global average surface temperature that has occurred since the preindustrial era (1880–1900) might seem small, but it means a significant increase in accumulated heat. That extra heat is driving regional and seasonal temperature extremes, reducing snow cover and sea ice, intensifying heavy rainfall, and changing habitat ranges for plants and animals.

According to the National Oceanic and Atmospheric Agency (NOAA) *2019 Global Climate Summary* and the National Aeronautics and Space Administration (NASA), two-thirds of the combined land and ocean temperature rise since 1880 has occurred since 1975 (see Figure 15.1). In 2019 record high annual temperatures over land surfaces were measured across parts of central Europe, Asia, Australia, southern Africa, Madagascar, New Zealand, North America, and eastern South America. Record high sea surface temperatures were observed across parts of all oceans, including both the North and South Atlantic, the western Indian Ocean,

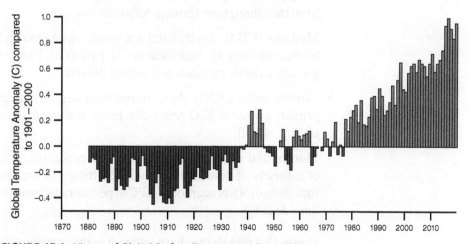

FIGURE 15.1. History of Global Surface Temperature Since 1880

Source: NOAA. 2021. "Climate Change: Global Temperature," https://www.climate.gov/news-features/understanding-climate/climate-change-global-temperature

and areas of the northern, central, and southwestern Pacific. No large land mass or ocean experienced cooler temperatures that year, and the only substantial pockets of cooler-than-average land temperatures were in central North America (National Centers for Environmental Information 2019). Most of the scientific evidence now points to human activity as the main cause of this rapid increase in the mean temperature of the earth.

The global temperature record in Figure 15.1 represents an average over the entire surface of the planet. The temperatures we experience locally can fluctuate due to predictable cyclical events (night and day, summer and winter) and hard-to-predict wind and precipitation patterns. But the global temperature mainly depends on how much energy the planet receives from the Sun and how much it radiates back into space—quantities that change very little.

The amount of heat radiated by the Earth depends significantly on the chemical composition of the atmosphere and particularly the amount of heat-trapping gases within it. These particular gases are called greenhouse gases (GHG) because they function in much the same way as glass does in a botanical greenhouse. The glass in greenhouses lets light in but does not allow the heat produced by the plants' photosynthesis of the light to escape, thus creating a warmer environment. Atmospheric greenhouse gases act similarly. They interfere with the ability of heat from the earth to radiate into space. While the presence of some amount of greenhouse gases is necessary to keep the earth warm enough to sustain life, large increases in the amount of GHG can raise earth temperatures with many detrimental effects (Denchak 2019). This is the crisis that we face today. Human activity is changing the composition of gases in the atmosphere, increasing the amount of greenhouse gases, and thus causing temperatures around the world to rise. Greenhouse Gases contributing to this phenomenon, according to the US Environmental Protection Agency (EPA), include:

- **Carbon dioxide (CO2).** Most CO_2 is generated from the combustion of fossil fuel, and less of it is absorbed from the atmosphere because of deforestation and land clearing for agriculture. The good news is that CO_2 can be removed from the atmosphere through reforestation.

- **Methane (CH4).** Agricultural activities, waste management, energy use, and biomass burning all contribute to CH_4 emissions. Farm animals breathe in oxygen and exhaust methane and carbon dioxide.

- **Nitrous oxide (N2O).** Agricultural activities including fertilizer use are the primary source of N_2O emissions. Fossil fuel combustion generates a measure of N_2O as well.

- **Fluorinated gases (F-gases).** Industrial processes, refrigeration, and the use of a variety of consumer products contribute to emissions of F-gases, which include hydrofluorocarbons (HFCs), perfluorocarbons (PFCs), and sulfur hexafluoride (SF_6)

Figure 15.2 reveals the sharp increase in the concentration of greenhouse gases (GHG) over the past 2,000 years. Only with the beginning of the twentieth century and the period of rapid industrialization did the amount of carbon dioxide,

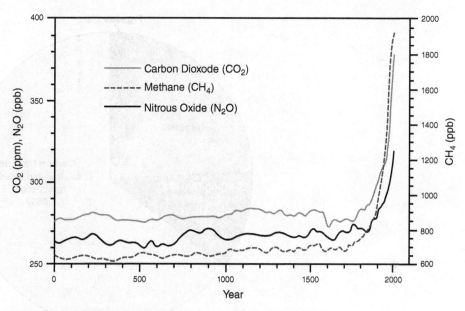

FIGURE 15.2. Concentrations of Greenhouse Gases Over Two Millenia

Source: Healing Earth, "Concentrations of Greenhouse Gases from 0 to 2005," https://healingearth.ijep.net/climate/photo/concentrations-greenhouse-gases-0-2005

methane, and nitrous oxide increase dramatically. According to virtually all climate scientists, this increase in greenhouse gases plays a significant role in the current rise in world temperatures we saw in Figure 15.1, and suggests that the earth will continue to heat up for decades if not centuries.

The relative amount of these greenhouse gases in the environment is shown in Figure 15.3. By far, carbon dioxide is the gas most prevalent in the atmosphere, making up more than three-quarters (76%) of the total. Another 16 percent is accounted for by methane, with the remainder being nitrous oxide and fluorocarbons. While methane emission is a fraction of carbon dioxide, it turns out that it is much more hazardous because it has stronger heat-trapping qualities, so that it contributes fully 25 percent of the current rate of global warming (Beradelli 2020). And while fluorinated (F-gases) only account for 2 percent of total emissions, they are especially dangerous because they, along with nitrous oxide, directly contribute to another atmospheric danger -- the thinning of the ozone layer in the atmosphere.

The ozone layer in the stratosphere acts as the Earth's sunscreen absorbing about 98 percent of the ultraviolet rays (UV) emitted from the sun. UV helps in the human production of vitamin D but in larger doses UV causes skin cancer and can damage the human immune system. The protection provided by the ozone layer is therefore essential to human life. A significant decrease in the ozone layer—at a rate of 5% to 7% per decade—occurred in the 1980s and the early 1990s prompting international concern and calls for immediate action (World Meteorological Association 2018). In 1987, an international agreement, the Montreal Protocol On Substances That Delete The Ozone Layer, was established to take steps to reduce threats to the ozone layer and to monitor progress toward ozone layer recovery. There has been some improvement in ozone levels since 2000, but concern remains.

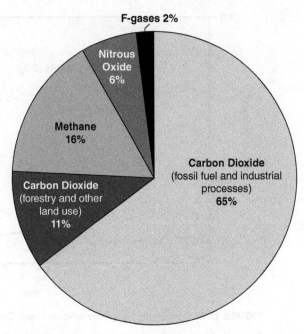

FIGURE 15.3. Global Greenhouse Gas Emissions by Gas

Source: US Environmental Protection Agency, "Global Greenhouse Gas Emissions Data," https://www.epa.gov/ghgemissions/global-greenhouse-gas-emissions-data

Because nitrous oxide and hydrofluorocarbons contribute to both greenhouse gas effects and ozone depletion, the future of global warming and the mitigation of ozone depletion are intertwined (Ravishankara et al 2009, World Meteorological Association 2018).

Major Sources of Greenhouse Gas Emissions

For cities, regions, and nations to reduce GHG emissions, it is first necessary to better understand which sectors of the economy are responsible for producing them. Here, in order of importance, are the key sectors responsible for these emissions.

1. **Electricity and Heat Production**

   The oil, coal, and natural gas used to generate electricity and produce heat for homes and commercial operations are responsible for more than 25 percent of global greenhouse gas emissions (EPA 2020b). Carbon dioxide and nitrous oxide are released by burning coal, oil and gas. Even though oil is considered one of the most harmful fossil fuels, it remains the main energy source worldwide and responsible for producing 46 percent of global carbon dioxide emissions (Greentumble 2018).

2. **Transportation**

   The transportation sector accounts for almost 14 percent of the carbon dioxide released into the atmosphere (EPA 2020a). While developed countries are making efforts to increase low-carbon public transportation and developing countries are implementing initiatives to reduce both freight transport and personal transportation, emissions remain high.

3. **Manufacturing and Construction**

Manufacturing and construction account for over 21 percent of emissions (World Bank 2014). Legislative attempts to curb the use of high carbon and high sulfur are often opposed by industry leaders who argue that moving too quickly to enforce such laws will result in the shutdown of industry and widespread unemployment.

4. **Agriculture, Forestry and Other Land Uses**

While energy generation, transportation, and industry are major emitters of greenhouse gases, there are other ways in which humans have contributed to the increase of greenhouse gases. Livestock farming produces large amounts of methane when animals digest their food. Fertilizers used in agriculture produce nitrous oxide. As such agriculture and forestry are responsible for over 24 percent of GHG emissions globally and 9 percent of carbon emissions in the United States (IBioMASS Lab 2017). If one adds in the spraying of pesticides and fertilizers, the GHG share from agriculture and forestry jumps to 30 percent of total emissions in the United States. Moreover, deforestation for agriculture land use means the forests can no longer absorb carbon dioxide to the degree it has in the past.

5. **Commercial and Residential Buildings**

Additional greenhouse gas emissions, accounting for 6 percent of the global total, arise from on-site energy generation and burning fuels for heat in buildings or cooking in homes. This is in addition to the emissions that arise from the use of electricity for all kinds of devices in residential and commercial buildings which we included in the Electricity and Heat Production sector.

6. **Other Energy**

The final source of greenhouse gas emissions, accounting for the remaining 10 percent of the total, refers to all emissions from the Energy sector which are not directly associated with electricity or heat production such as fuel extraction, refining, processing, and transportation.

Figure 15.4 provides a summary of the sources of greenhouse gas emissions by economic sector.

Cities vary in terms of the specific sources of greenhouse emission, as Joan Fitzgerald has shown in her 2020 book *Greenovation*. Within most cities today, buildings are responsible for the greatest amount of GHG. In Amsterdam and Paris, where driving is less common, commercial and residential buildings produce nearly four-fifths or more of carbon dioxide, methane, and smog emissions. In such cities as Oslo and Seattle, auto and trucks play a much greater role in emissions. Hence, if cities can find ways to reduce GHG emissions from both buildings and from transportation, they could play a critical role in meeting global environmental challenges.

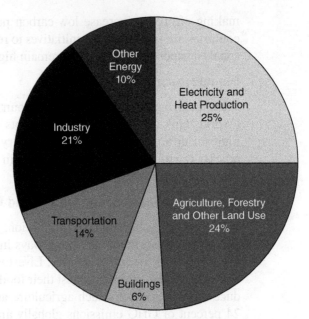

FIGURE 15.4. Global Greenhouse Gas Emissions by Economic Sector

Source: US Environmental Protection Agency, "Global Greenhouse Gas Emissions by Economic Sector," https://www.epa.gov/ghgemissions/global-greenhouse-gas-emissions-data

The Cities Most Likely to Experience the Impact of Climate Change

Working with climate change experts from around the World, Nestpick—an aggregator website for furnished apartments operating worldwide—decided that their clients needed to know more about how climate change might affect the livability of cities around the world (Nestpick 2020). The results of their detailed research reveal the specific destinations which may face the biggest shifts by 2050 in terms of temperature change, water shortages, and rising sea levels. All of these will almost surely affect livability. The temperature shift predicted in this exhaustive study are found in Table 15.1 for the 50 most affected cities. No part of the world appears to be exempt from this warming trend, but some cities will be affected more than others.

As this table suggests, the city with the largest projected increase in average annual temperature is Ljubljana, in Slovenia. Between 2020 and 2050, the Nestpick projections suggest that the residents of this city will experience a 6.35 degree increase in Fahrenheit temperature. The average daily high temperature in the city in July would increase from its current 83 degrees to nearly 89.4. Cincinnati, Ohio on the Kentucky border could expect to see its average daily high temperature in July increase from today's 87 degrees to more than 93 while Rome could see its August high rise from 89 to nearly 94 degrees. These averages mean that for these cities summer temperatures are expected to exceed 100 degrees for a good number of days. In Doha, Qatar, the average high temperature in July will top 110 degrees.

There is ample scientific evidence that increases in the earth's temperatures will increase both the incidence of severe hurricanes and tornadoes, as well as

TABLE 15.1. PROJECTED TEMPERATURE RISE BY 2050 IN WORLD CITIES

CITY	COUNTRY	TEMPERATURE SHIFT (DEGREES F)
Ljubljana	Slovenia	6.35
Cincinnati	United States	6.08
Baltimore	United States	6.03
Jerusalem	Israel	5.85
Philadelphia	United States	5.78
Montreal	Canada	5.76
Chicago	United States	5.60
Nashville	United States	5.60
Ottawa	Canada	5.49
Stockholm	Sweden	5.49
Budapest	Hungary	5.47
Toronto	Canada	5.44
Washington	United States	5.40
Kiev	Ukraine	5.38
New York	United States	5.31
Marrakesh	Morocco	5.17
St. Petersburg	United States	5.15
Helsinki	Finland	5.09
Boston	United States	4.68
Seattle	United States	4.61
Rome	Italy	4.57
Athens	Greece	4.50
Barcelona	Spain	4.50
Milan	Italy	4.48
Warsaw	Poland	4.34
Atlanta	United States	4.27
Vienna	Austria	4.19
Zagreb	Croatia	4.18
Doha	Qatar	4.18
Nairobi	Kenya	4.16
Kuala Lumpur	Malaysia	4.14
Oslo	Norway	4.05
Reykjavik	Iceland	3.94
Delhi	India	3.92
Houston	United States	3.87
Calgary	Canada	3.85

(Continued)

TABLE 15.1. CONTINUED

CITY	COUNTRY	TEMPERATURE SHIFT (DEGREES F)
Denver	United States	3.83
Seoul	South Korea	3.82
Istanbul	Turkey	3.76
Beijing	China	3.74
London	England	3.73
Madrid	Spain	3.73
Orlando	United States	3.6
Copenhagen	Denmark	3.58
Tokyo	Japan	3.58
Jacksonville	United States	3.55
Osaka	Japan	3.49
Auckland	Australia	3.44
New Orleans	United States	3.38
Shenzhen	China	3.33

Source: Nestpick https://www.nestpick.com/2050-climate-change-city-index-usa/

cause serious drought in other locations. Most critically, rising temperatures accelerate melting of the world's glaciers leading to rising sea levels.

The impact of rising temperatures varies according to the physical features of individual regions and specifically cities. Where water is already scarce, rising temperatures can put an added strain on a city's water supply. Cities that lie close to the sea are prone to a variety of severe consequences as sea levels rise as a result of melting ice caps in the Arctic and Antarctic. Since 2009, satellite recognizance reveals that Greenland has doubled its annual rate of ice loss to 375 cubic kilometers per year. As such, 90 cubic miles of ice is melting each year in Greenland alone adding to sea-level rise (Room 2018).

Nestpick created an index based on three measures: sea-level rise, climate shift, and water stress. Sea-level rise is measured in centimeters. The climate shift score is based on an amalgamation of the change in annual precipitation, changes in annual temperature, the change in the temperature of the warmest month and coldest month, and change in precipitation in the wettest month between 2021 and 2050. Water stress is defined as the ratio of demand for water by human society divided by available water. The overall Nestpick index is the total score based on these three measures, where rank #1 indicates the city which is expected to encounter the most extreme climate change impact over the next three decades and where rank #85 indicates the city that is least likely to encounter a dramatic shift by 2050, relative to the other 84. These rankings are based on a business-as-usual assumption. That is, if nothing is done to reduce climate change and cities do nothing to protect themselves, this is how severely they could be affected.

Table 15.2 provides a list of the 50 cities that are expected to be affected the most by one or more of these climate change stressors over the next 30 years.

TABLE 15.2. CLIMATE CHANGE SEVERITY – 50 TOP CITIES

RANK	CITY	COUNTRY	CLIMATE CHANGE SEVERITY
1	Bangkok	Thailand	100.00
2	Ho Chi Minh City	Vietnam	85.27
3	Amsterdam	Netherlands	84.28
4	Shenzhen	China	62.21
5	Melbourne	Australia	49.53
6	Cardiff	UK	47.03
7	Seoul	South Korea	45.75
8	Boston	US	44.80
9	Nairobi	Kenya	44.80
10	Marrakesh	Morocco	44.64
11	Manila	Philippines	40.79
12	Chicago	US	40.71
13	Hong Kong	Hong Kong	40.68
14	Toronto	Canada	39.33
15	Istanbul	Turkey	39.31
16	Beijing	China	39.30
17	Kiev	Ukraine	37.98
18	Santiago	Chile	37.97
19	New Orleans	US	36.13
20	Helsinki	Finland	34.53
21	St. Petersburg	Russia	33.69
22	London	UK	33.61
23	Philadelphia	US	32.91
24	New York	US	29.02
25	Oslo	Norway	28.82
16	Ljubljana	Slovenia	27.00
27	Hamburg	Germany	25.64
28	Belfast	UK	23.11
29	Jerusalem	Israel	22.71
30	Baltimore	US	22.56
31	Dubai	United Arab Emirates	22.35
32	Seattle	US	22.21
33	Ottawa	Canada	20.28
34	Montreal	Canada	20.06
35	Dublin	Ireland	18.47

(Continued)

TABLE 15.2. CONTINUED

RANK	CITY	COUNTRY	CLIMATE CHANGE SEVERITY
36	Budapest	Hungary	17.49
37	Jacksonville	US	16.47
38	Cincinnati	US	16.35
39	Washington	US	14.97
40	Osaka	Japan	14.44
41	Copenhagen	Denmark	14.28
42	Stockholm	Sweden	14.00
43	Rome	Italy	12.93
44	Nashville	US	12.79
45	Zagreb	Croatia	12.48
46	Delhi	India	11.96
47	San Francisco	US	11.93
48	Vienna	Austria	11.83
49	Auckland	New Zealand	11.55
50	Prague	Czechia	11.42

Source: Nestpick https://www.nestpick.com/2050-climate-change-city-index-usa/

As the table suggests, these cities are in nearly every corner of the globe. The two cities that are expected to be affected the most by climate change are both in Southeast Asia. Sea-level rise will affect low-lying Bangkok, Thailand and Ho Chi Minh City, Vietnam, with severe flooding in both communities. Amsterdam is #3 on the list, given that it lies below sea level already and remains above water only because of its extensive set of dikes. Number four is Shenzhen, China. While it may be affected moderately by sea-level rise, its location will make it a prime target for an increase in tropical monsoons that could periodically inundate the city. At #8 is Boston, Massachusetts, the US city ranked highest in this climate change study. Situated on the Atlantic Ocean and literally at sea level, rising seas could begin to flood the city, especially at high tide. Rising temperatures and increasing humidity could make outdoor summer activity ever more uncomfortable.

The authors of the study note that Venice, Italy—already under water for part of each year—would have been high on the list, but lack of complete climate data for this city left it off the rankings.

The Impact of Climate Change on US Regions and States

Across the United States, the influence of increased greenhouse gas emissions on the environment will take on different manifestations, as Table 15.3 suggests. Across the states of New England, environmental degradation will lead to early snow melt, urban heat islands, heat waves, drought, flooding, and sea-level rise. The same is true in the Middle Atlantic states, but these five states and many of the cities within them may face as well increased damage from tropical storms.

TABLE 15.3. THE IMPACT OF GREENHOUSE GAS EMISSIONS AND CLIMATE CHANGE ON U.S. REGIONS

	EARLY SNOWMELT	DEGRADED AIR QUALITY	URBAN HEAT ISLAND	WILDFIRES	HEAT WAVES	DROUGHT	TROPICAL STORMS	EXTREME RAINFALL WITH FLOODING	SEA LEVEL RISE
New England ME VT NH MA RI CT	X	X	X		X	X		X	X
Middle Atlantic NY PA NJ DE MD	X	X	X		X	X	X	X	X
East North Central WI MI IL IN OH	X	X	X		X	X		X	
West North Central ND MN SD IA NE KS MO	X		X		X	X		X	
South Atlantic WV VA NC SC GA FL DC		X	X	X	X	X	X	X	X
East South Central KY TN MS AL		X			X	X	X	X	X
West South Central TX OK AR LA		X	X	X	X	X	X	X	X
Mountain MT ID WY NV UT CO AZ NM	X	X	X	X	X	X		X	
Pacific AK CA WA OR HI	X	X	X	X	X	X	X	X	X

Source: US Environmental Protection Agency.2009. "Analyses of the Effects of Global Change on Human Health and Welfare and Human Systems (SAP 4.6)," https://cfpub.epa.gov/ncea/risk/recordisplay.cfm?deid=197244

The East North Central and West North Central states from the industrial midwestern region, including Michigan, Ohio, Indiana, Wisconsin, and Illinois and the Farm Belt states, including North Dakota, South Dakota, and Nebraska, will likely face all these climate change challenges with the exception of tropical storms and sea-level rise.

The South Atlantic states along the Atlantic Ocean face more climate challenges than any aside from the Pacific region. Except for early snowmelt, they face many dangers including an increased number of wildfires in their interior. The same is true for the West South Central region, including Texas, Oklahoma, Arkansas, and Louisiana.

In the mountain states ranging from Montana and Idaho in the north to Arizona and New Mexico in the south, climate change can wreak havoc in every way but tropical storms and sea-level rise. Finally, the Far West, including Alaska, Hawaii, California, Oregon, and Washington, may see everything from a heightened incidence of degraded air quality to urban heat islands, and wildfires near dense urban areas. At times, they may face drought, extreme flooding at others, and heat waves at still others.

As this table reveals, all regions of the United States can be affected by either sea-level rise, tropical storms, or flooding. The cost of such environmental disasters can be immense.

Sea-Level Rise and Ground Water Loss

If global temperatures rise by 1.5° Celsius (2.7 degrees Fahrenheit) above preindustrial levels—the ideal temperature limit set by the 2016 Paris Climate Accords signed by 194 nations—global sea levels will rise by approximately 15.7 inches by 2100. If the temperature increase tops 2 degrees Celsius (3.6 degrees Fahrenheit), sea-level rise will be approximately 20 inches by century's end, according to reporting on the Accord by Olivia Rosane (2018). This could be devastating to coastal cities around the world that are already vulnerable to storms and flooding. What many may not know is that two factors compound the problem of sea-level rise. One is that so much water has been pumped out of underground aquifers under major cities to supply fresh water for households and commercial activities that the land mass under these urban areas is actually being compressed and sinking. The second factor is that the mass of buildings in these dense urban cores depresses the land mass upon which they sit.

As such, the combination of rising sea levels and sinking land mass is speeding up the number of cities around the world that are facing the prospect of being underwater. Venice has already reached that point several times each year. With the water line so close to the land surface, especially in seacoast regions, hurricanes and typhoons become even more dangerous because of accompanying storm surges that can overflow human-made barriers and repeatedly flood downtown neighborhoods and even suburban communities. Cities that lie low against rivers are in danger of a similar plight. The report by Rosane quotes an unidentified sea-level researcher who notes that "these global metropolises may look strong and stable, but it is a mirage. As sea levels rise, they are increasingly under threat and under water" (Rosane 2018).

Because of urban development, the eight cities facing the greatest danger from sea-level rise and sinking land mass, according to this report, are the following:

>**Jakarta, Indonesia**: At a rate of approximately 10 inches per year, Jakarta is the world's fastest sinking city. Because more than 97 percent of the city is covered in concrete, the groundwater is not replenished by rain and rivers. The city is also sinking due to the weight of its buildings. In addition, such natural flood barriers as mangroves have been cut down to clear space for housing, increasing the city's vulnerabilities.
>
>**Bangkok, Thailand**: Bangkok faces a similar problem of skyscrapers pushing down on water-depleted soils. A study released by the city government in 2015 predicted that it could be underwater within 15 years. The city is sinking now at a slower rate than before, as water is being pumped back into the ground, but it is not enough to save the city from rising seas.
>
>**Lagos, Nigeria**: Lagos is built on the coast and incorporates a series of islands. Poor drainage worsened the impact of devastating floods in 2011, and just 8 inches of

sea-level rise could render 740,000 people across Nigeria homeless. There are concerns that new development in the city could worsen flooding for the rest of coastal and island Lagos by pushing flood waters their way.

Manila, Philippines: Manila is sinking due to groundwater extraction at a rate of approximately 4 inches per year, 10 times the rate of climate-caused sea-level rise.

Dhaka, Bangladesh: Dhaka is sinking approximately 0.55 inches per year and sea-level rise in the Bay of Bengal is around 10 times the global average. About 1.5 million people have already migrated from coastal villages to the city's slums, which will be the most vulnerable to flooding.

Shanghai, China: Shanghai is another major city sinking under the weight of its own development as groundwater extraction and increased construction cause it to subside. It is losing sediment that would naturally protect it because its rivers are dammed and because this resource is used for building materials.

London, England: The south of the United Kingdom is sinking, particularly affecting London. The Thames Barrier, opened in 1984 to protect London from a 1-in-100-year flood, was expected to be used at most two to three times a year to prevent the city from flooding. Already the barrier is needed six to seven times each year.

Houston, Texas: Houston sits on the Buffalo Bayou and is naturally flood-prone for that reason, but in addition it is sinking due to groundwater extraction and from the extraction of oil and natural gas from the ground beneath it. The Houston-Galveston area has sunk by approximately 9 feet, and the northwest section of this area is sinking by two inches a year.

These are the cities that will be hit hardest by sea-level rise and sinking land mass. But cities all along coastal regions are in trouble. Of all the US cities facing climate-related challenges listed in Table 15.2, the following are especially susceptible: Boston, New Orleans, New York, Baltimore, Seattle, Jacksonville, and San Francisco. Miami could easily be added to this endangered list along with Galveston, Charlestown, Los Angeles, and San Diego.

While sea-level rise and tropical storms are the biggest danger to coastal cities around the world and flooding affects inland cities on rivers as well, other parts of the globe suffer from drought. Dependable and safe water supplies are critical for cities, and these supplies are threatened by rising temperatures, sea-level rise, saltwater intrusion, and increased risks of drought. Rising temperatures that lead to algae blooms in lakes can result in restrictions to water usage for drinking and recreation. In some regions, intensifying droughts and reduced snowpack are combining with groundwater depletion to reduce the future reliability of water supplies. In other regions where power is supplied by hydroelectric dams, drought can be expected to reduce power supplies to nearby urban areas (The Climate Report 2018).

A Tale of One City

To consider the potential costs of climate change on cities, it is useful to look at an example. In 1904 Dania Beach was the first city to be founded in Broward County, Florida—seven years before the incorporation of adjacent Ft. Lauderdale and only eight years after the founding of Miami in adjoining Miami-Dade County. By most standards it is a small city of just 8 square miles and a 2019 population of less than 32,000. Ft. Lauderdale's population is nearly six times larger on a land mass approximately four times that of Dania Beach.

Strategically, though, Dania Beach is in a prime location. It is situated near the Ft. Lauderdale-Hollywood International Airport and the Port Everglades Seaport with easy access to interstate highway I-95, which runs the length of the entire US eastern coastline. As such, Dania Beach's location provides an ideal place for businesses to locate, and the city is becoming the prime location for South Florida's maritime industries. What makes this small city special for this chapter—despite the fact that few outside the southern Florida region have ever heard of it—is that in 2018 Dania Beach was awarded funds from the US National Oceanic and Atmospheric Administration for a comprehensive assessment of its susceptibility to the consequences of climate change. The study was carried out by AECOM, an established consulting firm (AECOM 2018). As such, it provides a superb case study of what climate change and sea-level rise could mean for urban areas.

The report provides reasonable estimates of the economic costs that could occur from failing to take action to protect Dania Beach's business community from future storm surge and sea-level rise, as well as the economic benefits from adaptation actions that could mitigate future coastal hazards to the city's commercial core. In addition to consideration of the costs and benefits of protective investments to reduce future hazard risks, this study considered more broadly the opportunities for advancing economic resilience in communities similar to Dania Beach. Resilience is generally framed as the ability to recover from or adjust quickly to changing circumstances.

For Dania Beach, like so many coastal cities, the greatest danger is from sea-level rise. The potential for sea-level rise on the southern Florida coast has been estimated by several agencies. By 2060, the estimates run from a low of 14 inches to a high of 34 inches—nearly three feet. Two feet of sea-level rise will affect $109 million of existing commercial property in this small Florida city. And this is simply the sway of sea-level rise itself. The greater damage to property on the coastline itself and inland occurs not simply because of the resulting flooding in the lowest-lying coastal area, but because of the increased damage caused throughout the region by storm surges, especially at high tide.

The model assumed that in each decade from 2030 through 2070 there will be three serious storms that could hit Dania Beach. In addition, the model assumes one colossal hurricane in the year 2050. The cost of the damages from these storms present a worst-case scenario in which no action is taken to make the city more resilient to sea-level rise and storm surge. Results are broken out for each category of damage evaluated. The impacts of the storms intensify over the 40-year period, based on the assumption that there will be continued increases in sea levels over time. As such, a storm of given intensity in 2060 is expected to have higher flood depths than a similar storm in 2030. Losses are assumed to only occur in the year of the storm. The damages of the modeled storms were discounted and summed to arrive at an estimate of cumulative net present damages over the 2030–2070 time period in 2020 dollars.

According to the AECOM model, under this worst-case scenario, the small city of Dania Beach would sustain nearly $719 million in damages. Of this total, nearly $165 million would be in the form of damaged buildings and homes. More than half a billion dollars would be in the form of destroyed building contents and business inventory losses. More than $11 million would be due to sales losses and foregone taxes due to reduced sales and tourist activity, and $4.5 million would result from the costs of residents having to spend their incomes on alternative housing and shelter.

While these losses might seem small compared with the hundreds of billions that might be the cost of damages to larger cities, on a per capita basis these costs are enormous. Given the population of Dania Beach in 2018, the total amount is equivalent to nearly $50,000 per household. A series of equivalent storms that hit the much larger city of Miami not far from Dania Beach would have a total cost of nearly $39 billion dollars.

To put this in perspective, in 2018 total state tax revenue in the entire state of Florida was $46 billion. Given the state's population of 21.7 million at that time, only 2.1 percent of the state's population live in the City of Miami. On a per capita basis, the total share of the annual state tax revenue generated in Miami amounts to $966 million. As such, the $39 billion price tag for possible climate change storm damage in Miami would be roughly 40 times the amount of state tax revenue generated from Miami's residents and businesses each year. Given the 40-year AECOM model (2030–2070), it would take the equivalent of the total amount of Miami-generated state tax revenue over the 40-year period to cover the projected cost of expected climate-related storm damage to the city.

But even these enormous costs assume that coastal storms hit Dania Beach and other coastal cities and then subside, and that sea-level rise itself does not permanently flood the city. If there is a permanent rise in sea level and Dania Beach becomes essentially uninhabitable, the economic costs are even greater. Of the total $1.167 billion in cumulative losses, about $1.04 billion is due to the loss of sales in the city as businesses are forced out of business or forced to move elsewhere. Another $56.4 million is lost in sales tax revenue as result of this loss in sales.

The impact on Broward County from a permanent sea-level rise based on the same model used to evaluate Dania Beach concluded that overall there would be 36,400 fewer jobs and a nearly $5 billion loss of GDP in Broward County. While Dania Beach is a community of less than 32,000, larger cities, including Charleston, South Carolina, with a population of more than 130,000, are facing similar climate impacts. In 1950, Charleston averaged five days of "nuisance flooding" where water levels were high enough to interfere with traffic and shut down business. By 2016, the number of such days swelled to 50 and by 2050 experts forecast that such flooding will occur at least 180 days a year. Moreover, climate scientists believe that by the end of this century upward of 80 million Americans could be forced to flee the coasts. In this scenario, Amtrak's popular Northeast Corridor Service, serving 12 million passengers along the route from Boston to Washington, DC, could be continually inundated (Gaul 2019).

Combatting Environmental Disaster by Reducing Greenhouse Gases

To avoid these extraordinarily costly effects of climate-related challenges, scientists are in near full agreement that it is necessary to accelerate the pace of reducing greenhouse gas emissions. Fortunately, they argue, there are many approaches to cutting carbon emissions that can partially mitigate projected adverse climate-related disasters.

A good place to begin such efforts starts far from the city. Agriculture can play a prominent role in efforts to address climate change if farms and ranches undertake activities that reduce GHG emissions or take greenhouse gases out of the atmosphere (Horowitz and Gottlieb 2010). These activities include shifting to conservation tillage, reducing the amount of nitrogen fertilizer applied to crops, changing livestock and manure management practices to reduce emissions, and planting trees or grass to absorb CO_2. Farmers can contribute to reducing GHG emissions by growing the feedstocks used for biofuels or by installing wind turbines or solar panels on their land.

While agriculture can play a critical role, most human-caused climate change occurs in industrial areas and in densely populated urban areas. To reduce the level of greenhouse gases that contribute to climate change, environmentalists urge the replacement of most of the energy sources now used to power factories and provide energy for homes. According to experts, new technologies could substitute for the oil and gas now used for heat and power. They include the following sources and the percentage of electricity consumed globally that could be generated by these means by the year 2050 (Hawkin 2017):

- wind turbine power: 21.6%
- geothermal (heat from underground): 4.9%
- solar farms: 10%
- rooftop solar: 7%
- wave and tidal: 0.28%
- nuclear: 12%
- hydroelectric: 3.7%

If all these sources are deployed they could meet nearly 60 percent of the world's energy needs, reducing carbon emissions from existing coal, oil, and gas electric generating stations. One method for encouraging the reduction in carbon emissions is to adopt a **carbon tax**. Essentially, putting a price on carbon dioxide emissions is necessary in order to encourage utilities and others to switch electricity production from coal and oil-fired plants to more efficient and lower emissions forms of energy generation. A carbon tax is a fee imposed on the burning of carbon-based fuels. Utilizing existing tax collection mechanisms, a carbon tax is paid "upstream" at the point where fuels are extracted from the Earth or paid as an import fee when brought into a nation. Fuel suppliers and processors are free to pass along the cost of the tax to customers to the extent that market conditions allow. Placing a tax on carbon gives consumers and producers a monetary incentive to reduce their carbon dioxide emissions. The Canadian province of British Columbia introduced a carbon tax, and today nearly all the province's electricity is produced by hydro and biomass.

A second method encouraging the reduction in carbon emissions and related pollutants is known as **emission trading**, or better known as **cap and trade**. In contrast to command-and-control environmental regulations that require businesses to take specifically defined measures to reduce pollution, cap and trade is a flexible regulation that allows markets to decide how to best meet policy targets usually set by national governments (EPA 2014).

In an emissions trading system, the government sets an overall limit on emissions and then provides each business with a permit so that all businesses combined emit no more than the overall limit. The government may sell the permits, but in many such schemes the government gives permits to regulated private-sector firms equal to each participant's base emissions assessed through historical records on emissions for each company. Because permits can be bought and sold, a company can choose to use its permits by reducing its own emissions, sell to other companies excess permits that it does not need to meet pollution standards, or buy permits from other companies if it is more profitable for the company to continue to pollute above their own permitted level. Over time, the government can reduce the overall level of pollution in the environment by reducing the number and value of permits, forcing companies to increase their pollution abatement efforts.

While the United States has no such cap and trade system, Europe has introduced such systems since 2005. The European Union Trading Scheme (EU ETS) is the largest multinational greenhouse emissions trading system in the world. It is the EU's central policy for meeting the emissions caps set in the International Kyoto Protocol signed by 84 nations in 1997 and in full implementation after ratification in 2005. Using cap and trade, by 2012 carbon dioxide emissions had been reduced across Europe by 12.5 percent compared to 1990 levels. In the EU, the program caps the amount of carbon dioxide that can be emitted by large power plants but allows these utilities to trade permits in order to meet the protocol's goals (Jones 2007). Under the Protocol, nations can trade permits with other nations in order to advance the global goal of CO_2 emissions. The United States is the only industrialized nation that has not ratified the Kyoto Protocol, but it did establish one of the first cap and trade policies on sulfur dioxide emissions as part of the nation's Acid Rain Program in the 1990 Clean Air Act. Oher countries that have established their own cap and trade programs are Australia, New Zealand, Japan, South Korea, China, and India.

While there is no national program within the United States, a number of state and regional cap and trade programs have been established. In 2003, New York State proposed and attained commitments from nine Northeast states to form a carbon dioxide emissions program to regulate power generators. In 2006 California passed the California Global Warming Solutions Act, which uses cap and trade to regulate carbon dioxide emissions (Center for Climate and Energy Solutions 2016), while the State of Illinois adopted a trading program for the Chicago metro area to regulate the emission of volatile organic compounds (Illinois EPA 2007).

Reducing Pollution of Varied Types

Greenhouse gas emissions are not the only form of pollution affecting the quality of life. Plastics pollution has become a major problem. Millions of tons of plastic end up in the oceans and in landfills every year. Scientists believe that about 8 million metric tons of plastic enter the ocean every year—the equivalent in weight to nearly 90 aircraft carriers, the largest ships on the sea (National Ocean Service 2020). Unlike other kinds of waste, plastic does not decompose. Plastic can remain indefinitely in the sea, wreaking havoc on marine ecosystems for decades to come.

While plastics do not completely decompose, they can form microparticles that are found in drinking water in many countries including the United States.

A 2017 study found that 83 percent of tap water samples taken around the world contained plastic pollutants (Lui 2017). With a contamination rate of 94 percent, tap water in the United States was the most polluted, followed by Lebanon and India. In Europe, the United Kingdom, Germany, and France had the lowest contamination rate, although still as high as 72 percent. It is currently unclear if this contamination affects human health, but scientists are concerned that it could.

Some countries have taken action to reduce such pollution. Kenya initiated a strict plastic bag ban in 2017 with heavy penalties for those who flout it. Outdoor markets provide nonplastic tote bags for customers who have not brought their own reusable ones. Before the ban was introduced, grocery stores in the country were handing out over 100 million bags per year despite a lack of waste disposal infrastructure to keep them out of the environment. The capital city of Nairobi was plagued by them. Plastic bags clogged waterways and drainage systems, which made flooding worse during the rainy season.

Kenya's plastic ban followed in the footsteps of Rwanda and Morocco, and these initiatives have led other East African countries such as Tanzania to introduce a complete ban on lightweight plastic bags. In total, according to a United Nations December 2018 report, there are 34 bag bans or taxes across the African continent. These countries join dozens of others around the world in their efforts to tackle pervasive plastic pollution. Across the United States, more than 400 cities and states have bag bans or taxes on plastic bags and in 2021 the European Union's ban on such single-use plastic items as straws, forks, spoons, and plates went into effect (Mbugna 2020).

Climate Adaptation Activities and Climate Resilience

Even with all these efforts, climate change will continue to be a serious problem for decades to come. As such, cities need to adapt to environmental challenges and find ways to become more resilient.

Climate **adaptation** refers to the actions taken to manage the effects of climate change by reducing vulnerability and exposure to its harmful effects and exploiting any potential benefits. Adaptation takes place at international, national, and local levels. Subnational jurisdictions and entities, including urban and rural municipalities, are key to developing and reinforcing measures for reducing weather- and climate-related risks (Allen et al. 2018).

Environmentalists have developed a terminology for the various aspects of approaches to safeguard against climate change.

adaptation	Adjustment in natural or human systems to a new or changing environment that exploits beneficial opportunities or moderates negative effects.
adaptive capacity	The ability of a system to adjust to climate change to moderate potential damage or to cope with the consequences.
resilience	A capability to anticipate, prepare for, respond to, and recover from significant multihazard threats with minimum damage to social well-being, the economy, and the environment.

| risk | A combination of the magnitude of the potential consequences of climate change impacts and the likelihood that the consequences will occur. |
| vulnerability | The degree to which a system is susceptible to, or unable to cope with, adverse effects of climate change and is a function of the character, magnitude, and rate of climate variation to which a system is exposed. |

Adapting to climate change can take many forms, as Table 15.4 reveals. To deal with sea-level rise, federal, state, and local governments can make sure that future public works projects are located safely above predicted sea levels. They can eliminate any subsidies for future development in high hazard areas and strengthen building codes. They can retrofit existing public buildings to be sea-level resilient. Where sea-level rise is expected to be especially high, public authorities can facilitate inland migration and the relocation of communities and neighborhoods facing the most hazardous conditions.

Some US cities began their climate adaptation activities in the first decade of the twenty-first century. King County, Washington, where Seattle is situated, funded a district-wide study of the implications of climate change on both water quality and the amount of clean water in the region. Working with the University of Washington, the county conducted an infrastructure assessment to prioritize spending on climate resilience projects. In 2006 Seattle passed a Climate Action Plan that outlined strategies for reducing dependence on cars, increasing the use of biofuels, and achieving higher energy efficiency in residential and commercial buildings. The county's transit authority inaugurated the world's largest fleet of hybrid buses and entered into contracts to purchase biodiesel fuel for its fleet (Fitzgerald 2010).

In 2008 Chicago developed its own Chicago Climate Action Plan, which provided a detailed assessment of the city's vulnerabilities and prioritized planning strategies to address their impact. It shared all these strategic plans with community groups in the city. Miami used Federal Emergency Management Agency (FEMA) funds to strengthen buildings and develop hurricane shelters. And Milwaukee, Wisconsin prepared for more intense flooding by targeting zero stormwater overflow to protect water quality in Lake Michigan. It did this by constructing a deep tunnel for increased stormwater storage (National Research Council 2010).

New York City is one of the most vulnerable cities in the United States, as became clear in October 2012 when Hurricane Sandy struck the region. The storm wreaked havoc on much of the mid-Atlantic coast between New Jersey and New York. Across the five boroughs of New York City and Long Island 72 people were killed and total damage was in excess of $62 billion dollars. The New York City subway system was flooded, along with all road tunnels entering Manhattan except the Lincoln Tunnel. The floodwater depth in certain parts of Staten Island reached 12.5 feet above sea level, damaging 80 percent of all structures in the borough plus public buildings, including schools.

To reduce the potential for such devastation occurring again, the United States Army Corps of Engineers is slated to begin construction of a $616 million seawall to protect Staten Island. Local and federal officials hope the seawall will prevent

TABLE 15.4. POSSIBLE OPTIONS FOR ADAPTING TO CLIMATE CHANGE

CLIMATE CHANGE	IMPACT	POSSIBLE ADAPTATION ACTION	FEDERAL	STATE	LOCAL
Accelerated Sea Level Rise and Lake Level Changes	Gradual Inundation of Low-Lying Land; Loss of Coastal Habitats especially Coastal Wetlands	Site and Design All Future Public Works Projects to take into account Projections for Sea Level Rise	X	X	X
	Saltwater Intrustion into Coastal Aquifers and Rivers	Eliminate Public Subsidies for Future Development in High Hazard Areas along the Coast	X	X	
	Increased Shoreline Erosion and Loss of Barrier islands; Changes in Navigational Conditions				
		Develop Strong, Well-Planned Shoreline Retreat or Relocation Plans and Programs (Public Infrastructure and Private Properties), and Post-Storm Redevelopment Plans		X	X
		Retrofit and Protect Public Infrastructure (Stormwater and Wastewater Systems; Energy Facilities; Roads, Causeways, Ports, Bridges, etc.	X	X	X
		Adapt Infrastructure and Dredging to Cope with Altered Water Levels	X	X	
		Use Natural Shorlines, Setbacks, and Buffer Zones to allow Inland Migration and Short Habitats and Barrier Islands over time (e.g. Dunes and Forested Buffers mitigate Storm Damage and Erosion	X	X	X
		Encourage Alternatives to Shoreline "Armoring" through "Living Shorelines"	X	X	X
		Develop Strategic Property Acquisition Programs to discourage Development in Hazardous Areas, Encourage Relocation, and/or Allow for Inland Migration	X	X	X
Changes in Sea Ice	Changes in Ecosystem	Plan and Manage Ecosystems to encourage Adaptation		X	X
	Exacerbate Coastal Erosion; Severe Storms reach Coast	Facilitate Migration and Relocation of Coastal Communities		X	X
Increased Intensity/ Frequency of Coastal Storms	Increased Storm Surge and Flooding; Increased Wind Damage; Sudden Coastal/Shorline Alterations	Strengthen and Implement Building Codes that make Buildings more Resilient to Storm Damage along Coasts		X	X
		Identify and Improve Evacuation Routes in Low-Lying Areas	X	X	X
		Improve Storm Readiness for Harbors and Marinas		X	X
		Establish Marine Debris Reduction Strategy	X	X	X
		Establish and Enforce Shoreline Setback Requirements		X	X

Source: National Research Council. 2010. *Adapting to the Impacts of Climate Change.* Washington, DC: The National Academies Press. https://doi. org/10.17226/12783.

such devastating events in the future once the project is completed (Smithson 2019). According to the US Army Corps of Engineers and the office of New York's governor, the seawall system will include several components known collectively as the Staten Island Multi-Use Elevated Promenade. Nearly 4.5 miles of buried seawall, topped by a walkable promenade, will protect the area against up to 21.4 feet of seawater rise. In addition to the wall and gates that can be closed in anticipation of storm surge, there will be 300 acres of natural water storage to manage surge and over 226 acres of tidal wetlands and ponding areas. The latter two components will have the capacity to absorb an immense amount of floodwater, forming a robust natural barrier against major storms.

Regardless of these ongoing steps to reduce climate change and sea-level rise affecting the Greater New York City region, the city is planning a still much larger sea wall to protect Manhattan and Brooklyn. The city has a plan to spend $119 billion to build a massive structure six miles long and 20 to 30 feet high to keep the ocean out when hurricanes and storm surges strike. The idea involves constructing human-made islands with retractable gates that would stretch from the borough of Queens to a strip of land in New Jersey, south of Staten Island. The gates would be set to swing shut as a storm surge approaches (Barnard 2020).

Those who support this barrier miles from Manhattan's coast say it would be the best solution for protecting the most people, properties, and landmarks, including the Statue of Liberty, from a storm surge swelling the East and Hudson Rivers without cutting off the city from its waterfront. Opinion suggests that the use of locally tailored, onshore solutions alone, similar to berms, wetlands restoration, and raised parks, would likely benefit wealthy areas first, not the low-income communities that suffered disproportionately from Hurricane Sandy.

But despite its boldness and cost, the Army Corps of Engineers design for New York City barrier would address only storm surges. It would not counter two other climate-related threats—flooding from high tides and storm runoff. Moreover, the Corps estimates it would take 25 years to build the barrier. Even if construction went smoothly, opponents say the sea wall could be obsolete within decades because they believe the Corps' estimates of future sea levels are too low.

The conundrum on how to best protect New York reflects the challenges other major cities face in deciding how best to respond to climate change. Coastal areas not only power much of the world's economy; they also house 40 percent of its population.

No one is sure if the most ambitious and costly engineering solutions will work in the long run, nor what their impact could be. A five-mile-long swinging-gate structure in the Netherlands, built after a deadly storm in the 1950s, has curbed flooding but has also caused environmental damage, changing the ecology of estuaries and marshlands. The same is true of the Thames Barrier in London. Russia has credited a nearly 15-mile barrier completed in 2010 with protecting St. Petersburg from a catastrophic storm a year later.

The City of Boston is another urban community bracing for sea-level rise and storm surges. Boston was ranked the world's eighth most vulnerable to floods among

136 coastal cities by a 2013 study produced by the Organization for Economic Cooperation and Development.

Boston is raising streets, building berms, and even requiring that new high-rise condominium developments on its harbor acquire "aqua fences"—portable metal barriers that can be dragged to the street and anchored to the pavement to deflect incoming waves (Mufson 2020). Already rising sea levels have increased the frequency of flooding from relatively normal tides and rainfalls. In 2017, Boston saw a record 22 days with high-tide flooding and it is likely the city could experience more "blue sky" flooding as seawater laps onto streets during high tides on sunny days. The sea that surrounds Boston crept up nine inches in the twentieth century and is advancing ever faster toward the heart of the city. As climate change accelerates, the pace of sea-level rise in Boston is expected to triple, adding eight inches over 2000 levels by 2030. If there is no cessation in climate warming, the ocean could climb as much as three feet above 2013 levels by 2070, inundating large parts of the city.

The University of Massachusetts at Boston and the Woods Hole Group, an environmental and scientific consulting firm, have studied the possibility of building a massive harbor barrier for the city similar to those in the low-lying Netherlands or the one across the River Thames in London. They estimate that construction would cost $11.8 billion.

In the meantime, many engineers are suggesting that modest scale environmental projects are no less crucial. In the Charlestown neighborhood of Boston, the city plans to raise Main Street by about two feet at an estimated cost of just $3 million. When completed, the higher structure would block the main flood pathway and protect more than 250 residences and 60 businesses. The Massachusetts Bay Transportation Authority (MBTA), which oversees all of Boston's subways, buses, and streetcars, is spending $22 million to build watertight steel doors that can be closed at the entrance of a rail tunnel near Fenway Park where the Boston Red Sox play. The transit authority plans to tear out a heavy glass-brick cube protecting an underground rail ventilation system near its Aquarium stop on Boston Harbor and replace it with brick and steel-reinforced concrete. In South Boston, adjacent to the harbor, there is a park that floods regularly, forcing the cancellation of sporting events at its playing fields. With rising sea levels, the park will be underwater before too long. So the city is considering the construction of a flood protection berm as high as 10 feet along the shore, raising the level of the park and installing large chambers beneath the playing fields to hold 5 million cubic feet of storm water. Similar plans have been drawn up for other parks near the harbor along the city's Mystic River.

In making plans to safeguard cities and their neighborhoods from the potential ravages of climate change, equity considerations must be a key component of any adaptation investment strategy. When paying for resilience investments, there are a few equity principles to consider. As we described in Chapter 7, one is the **benefit principle** in which those who benefit the most from an investment should pay a disproportionate amount of the total cost. Another is the **ability-to-pay principle** in which regardless of direct benefit, those who are better off should pay a larger share of such investments.

Relocation as a Response to Climate Change

Resilience is one method for meeting environmental challenges. Relocation can be another. In the summer of 2019, Hurricane Dorian struck the Caribbean and the US coastline. It was one of the most powerful hurricanes ever recorded in the Atlantic Ocean with sustained winds peaking at 185 mph. Dorian was the third hurricane to strike North Carolina in four years. Many of the places inundated, such as Ocracoke Island in the Outer Banks, had been hit by one of the earlier storms only to rebuild and then flood again. In some places along the Carolina coast homes have been flooded as many as five times only to have their owners rebuild in place. Aiding these property owners is flood insurance offered by the US Department of Housing and Urban Development (HUD). Accordingly, when a property is located in an area designated by the Federal Insurance Administrator as a special flood hazard area and is available for sale, HUD requires that the mortgagor and mortgagee must obtain and maintain, where available, National Flood Insurance to cover the property when the mortgage is insured. Such insurance has been required by law for decades under the Flood Disaster Protection Act of 1973 with respect to FHA insured properties. The amount of flood insurance must at least equal either the outstanding balance of the mortgage or the maximum amount of NFIP insurance available with respect to the property (US Department of Housing and Urban Development 2020). As such, in trying to protect property owners from storm and flood damage these regulations inadvertently encourage homeowners and businesses to remain in flood-prone areas.

Canada has been testing a very different approach to disaster recovery: forcing people to move (Flavelle 2019). Unlike in the United States, where the federal government has historically helped pay for people to rebuild in place often repeatedly, Canada is now responding to severe climate change by limiting aid after disasters and telling people who live on the edge of riverbanks and coastlines to leave their homes. Gatineau, a city across the river from the Canadian capital of Ottawa, has been hit by two massive floods since 2017. Instead of helping these residents rebuild in place, the Canadian government sent out notices to homeowners whose losses exceeded 50 percent of their home value that they would be offered some compensation in return for relocating away from the river's edge.

By most accounts, Canada's experiment began in the summer of 2013 when floods in southern Alberta caused more than $5.7 billion in damage, the most expensive disaster in the country's history. The toll was particularly great in High River, a town of 14,000 about an hour south of Calgary, where floods affected 80 percent of homes. Rather than pay to rebuild them all, officials issued mandatory buyouts for two particularly exposed neighborhoods. Not all residents were on board. Still, the homes came down.

In 2019, the Canadian federal government went further still, warning that homeowners nationwide would eventually be on their own. If people deliberately rebuild in danger zones, at some point they would be notified that they were going to have to assume their own responsibility for the cost burden.

No part of the country has been more aggressive than Quebec. Since 2005, the province, Canada's largest in area, has prohibited building new homes or rebuilding flood-damaged ones in the 20-year floodplain—areas with a particularly high risk of inundation. It limited disaster aid setting an upper threshold for assistance at $100,000 over the lifetime of the house. After that, homeowners face a choice: they can sell to the government, which will pay no more than $250,000 regardless of market value. Or they can obtain money to rebuild one last time—but in doing so, they forfeit any future financial assistance.

In forcing people off their property, Canada's policymakers have an advantage over the United States. Canada's constitution contains no explicit protection for private property, unlike its neighbor to the south. While the government is unlikely to seize someone's home without compensation, it faces fewer constraints. This collision between the individual and collective good—between what is fair and what is safe—is playing out across Canada in areas subject to the harshest climate change. As for the City of Gatineau, its mayor must now navigate a landscape that is emotionally and financially precarious: helping people who want to leave, working with those who refuse to go, and trying to prepare the city for a future that might look very different from its past.

Despite the historical US resistance to relocation, there have been recent steps in that direction. The recognition that some communities simply cannot be saved after repeated rounds of rebuilding has led to new initiatives by FEMA, the Department of Housing and Urban Development, and the Army Corps of Engineers to emphasize required relocation of communities, now referred to as "managed retreat." Some state governments, including California and New Jersey, have moved in this direction (Flavelle 2020 b).

Other researchers now believe that climate change will lead to massive migration—not simply modest relocation—in the United States and elsewhere. The result could completely reshape urban society. Some go so far as to suggest that a warming planet along with pandemics has the potential for moving hundreds of millions of "climate refugees" across the globe. In much of the developing world, according to some demographers, vulnerable people will attempt to flee global warming, seeking cooler temperatures, more fresh water, and safety.

Similarly, megafires such as those in the western United States in 2020 could force millions of residents to leave rural areas for the safety of cities. Paradoxically, it was high housing costs in California cities that prompted housing construction in these wildfire danger zones (Weil and Simon 2020). Millions of others may migrate north from such desert west cities as Phoenix and such humid southern cities as Atlanta to seek a more comfortable environment. New York, Boston, Chicago, Detroit, and Duluth, Minnesota could once again see a large influx of refugees. For Detroit, this could reverse decades of out-migration. Matthew Hauer, a sociologist, has modeled American climate change and his research suggests that as many as 13 million Americans will be forced to move away from submerged coastlines. This would reverse the migration to such places as Florida, which has experienced in-migration for decades (Hauer 2017).

Adding to this new migration trend may be an increased reluctance of property insurers to issue policies in areas where climate change leads to damaged homes and businesses. Florida and California have passed laws mandating that insurance remain available even in vulnerable locations. But with climate change-related destruction rising, insurance companies are forced to increase insurance premiums to a point where many homeowners may choose to relocate rather than pay a sky-rocketing price to insure their homes. Similarly, banks may become more unwilling to write mortgages in environmentally endangered locations (Flavelle 2020a).

Steps Toward an Urban Resilience Plan

To avoid de-population, it will be necessary for cities to develop comprehensive adaptation and resilience plans (Fitzgerald 2020). These include the following:

- **Prioritize phased adaptation investments with an eye toward long-term risk**. Often it is too costly to pay for projects that mitigate for long-term impacts, but full life-cycle cost assessments may help to inform which projects are better suited to address long-term risk.

- **Establish an accessible data platform** for businesses to identify their potential vulnerabilities to both existing and future climate conditions.

- **Develop business continuity plans to prepare for disaster** and establish local partnerships to understand how other businesses are addressing adaptation.

- **Expand assessment of projected damages beyond the local business community** to include residential and public infrastructure to improve an understanding of shared strategies by different groups of beneficiaries.

- **Create eco-innovation districts** within cities to concentrate sustainability efforts at the neighborhood or district level. The eco districts can serve as test beds for experimenting with new technologies to limit environmental damage and increase environmental resilience.

Tools for Comparing and Selecting Adaptation Options

There are scores of methods cities can use to become more resilient and adaptive. But each of these methods has economic costs and often social and political costs as well. As such, it is useful to have a set of analytic tools to consider which options are most beneficial and have the least adverse side effects. This is particularly true when there are multiple competing options for addressing a climate change risk. Cities need to consider the relative effectiveness of adaptations, whether a particular adaptation has some benefits which others lack, and whether some adaptations have fewer undesirable side effects.

One such analytic tool is **cost-effectiveness analysis**. This method is used to compare alternatives that are expected to achieve the same or similar benefits. Alternatives are compared based on their relative costs to find the most efficient approach—the approach that meets the same or higher level of adaptation at lowest cost.

Cost-benefit analysis is a second tool. This method searches for the climate adaptation approach that yields the greatest net benefit—the difference between benefits and costs—or the highest ratio of benefits to costs. In using this tool, researchers include a **discount rate** that considers the timing of when a mitigation effort takes effect. Those that take many years or decades to implement are essentially worth less than those that take effect soon. (Appendix A provides more information on cost-benefit analysis.)

Risk management is a third analytic tool used to consider cases where there is a need for information about the relative likelihood of a variety of possible events or variation in the intensity of an event. When it is difficult to determine which event or events will occur or the intensity of the event, planners focus on worst-case scenarios to ensure they are prepared.

Decision analysis (DA) or **statistical decision theory** is similar to cost-benefit analysis, but focuses on a decision made by a specific interested party such as a homeowner, an industrial firm, or a government department or division rather than society as a whole. DA often constructs a "decision tree" indicating what steps might be taken given an adverse climate change event. With increased information, the decision tree becomes more robust permitting a focused response.

What makes the use of these analytic methods important is the high degree of uncertainty about future climate impacts. A city or metro area can spend an enormous amount of resources to prevent an event that never occurs. In this case there are potentially large opportunity costs, because funds spent on climate change adaptation or resilience cannot be spent on something that may be quite valuable itself including better schools and safer streets.

Because the cost of climate change resilience is so high, it is often difficult for city leaders to make the case for spending these large sums to prevent an environmental event that may only occur in the distant future or not at all, when there is such a large need for spending these resources on public activities that will have an immediate value.

In the United States, the political struggle over climate change has been a highly charged issue at the federal level. While a number of US presidents have championed legislation to reduce the nation's dependence on coal and oil, increase vehicle fuel efficiency, and expand the purview and budget of the nation's EPA, other administrations have been less active in this realm and at least one has worked to reverse attempts to rein in environmental damage. Many members of President Donald Trump's administration did not believe in sea-level rise or human-induced global warming, including President Trump himself. During his presidency that lasted from 2017 through 2020, Trump's EPA chief administrator spent a good deal of effort on undoing the climate-control efforts of President Obama's EPA director. What is more, the Trump administration proposed rolling back Obama's landmark 2012 legislation to increase fuel efficiency standards for cars, trucks, and SUVs in order to cut greenhouse gas emissions (Gaul 2019). And in June 2017, the Trump administration announced that the United States would cease all participation in the 2015 Paris Agreement on Climate Change Mitigation—once again proving the importance of understanding and navigating the political environment when dealing with many of the critical issues we face globally, in each of our nations, and in virtually every community.

Urban Measures to Cut Greenhouse Gas Emissions

According to Joan Fitzgerald, one of the leading researchers on urban sustainability and economic development, the global response to climate change begins with cities and the buildings within them and the transportation systems they employ (Fitzgerald 2010). Buildings consume about 70 percent of the electric power in the United States and 39 percent of all power. Because of this heavy use, buildings are responsible for nearly 40 percent of the nation's carbon dioxide emissions. As such, reducing greenhouse gas emissions requires making urban buildings more energy efficient. Reducing gasoline and diesel-powered vehicle travel through the encouragement of hybrid and electric cars and trucks, expansion of public mass transit, and increased bicycle use are critical to reduce the personal reliance on fossil fuels.

Looking to other countries as models for what can be done in cities to become more environmentally friendly is helpful in this regard. Germany has been particularly successful at retrofitting older buildings and reducing vehicle emissions. Beginning in 1999, according to Fitzgerald, Germany initiated a program with the twin goals of increasing energy efficiency and stimulating employment in the building construction industry. With a government investment of €5.2 billion ($5.7 billion) over ten years that stimulated another $16.6 billion in private investment, more than 342,000 apartments and houses were retrofitted to conserve energy use. Earlier in 1975, the small university city of Freiberg, with a population of around 215,000, became one of the world's leading communities addressing climate change with a comprehensive program to reduce the use of autos through free public transit and encouraging the use of solar arrays on public buildings and schools to generate electricity. By 1989, Freiberg became one of 40 German cities implementing a "feed in tariff" through which residents and businesses that install solar arrays can sell power back to the utility grid (Fitzgerald 2010). Germany's Green Party has become a major political force throughout the country, encouraging such activity as well as the deployment of wind energy.

Stockholm, Sweden has a record as good or better than Germany in the environmental arena. Beginning in the 1970s, the city worked diligently to reduce auto use through increasing public transit and making it more affordable. It has encouraged bicycle commuting by introducing more than 185 miles of separate bike lanes and imposing congestion fees where drivers are charged a fee that varies with time of day for entering the city's center.

In the United States by 2010, several cities had introduced "green building ordinances" to encourage construction of new energy efficient buildings or retrofit existing structures. In each case the goal was to reach Leadership in Energy and Environmental Design (LEED) standards. The LEED standard was first introduced in the United States in 1993 by the Natural Resources Defense Council (NRDC) and now is used in many nations around the world. LEED standards exist for new construction of commercial buildings and homes, school buildings, retail establishments, and healthcare facilities. The highest level of LEED certification is platinum, followed by gold and silver.

According to Fitzgerald's early research, by 2007 a number of US cities were already applying LEED standards.

- **Portland, Oregon** introduced one of the first LEED sustainable building policies in 1999 requiring all municipally owned or occupied new construction and renovation projects and all new city-funded private construction and renovation projects to meet LEED silver standards. By 2007, nearly 1,400 building permits were issued to developers complying with the ordinance.

- **Seattle** introduced its own green building policy in 2000 requiring all city-funded projects and renovations over 5,000 square feet in area to comply with LEED silver standards.

- **Chicago** followed suit in 2002, requiring all new and renovated city-funded building projects to comply with LEED silver standards. By 2007, the city had issued nearly 1,700 building permits under this ordinance.

- **Boston** required all new larger municipal buildings constructed after 2004 to meet the same LEED standard.

- **Oakland, California; New York City; Austin, Texas, and San Francisco** quickly followed suit. In 2009, New York City pioneered in developing building-disclosure ordinances requiring building owners to submit to city departments annual data on their energy and water use, making it mandatory for building owners making renovations to upgrade their systems to meet current city code, and requiring nonresidential building owners to install high-efficiency lighting to reduce energy use.

- **Los Angeles** passed its GREEN LA building ordinance on Earth Day, April 22, 2008. The goal is to reduce greenhouse gas emissions by 35 percent below 1990 levels by 2030. A year later the city passed its Green Retrofits Ordinance, which commits the city to installing energy efficient upgrades in all large city-owned building built before 1978 in order to bring them up to the LEED silver standard.

On average, the buildings that comply with at least LEED silver standards deliver 25 to 35 percent energy savings over comparable buildings that do not comply. Many climate scientists argue that buildings could be constructed that are even more energy efficient than the original LEED gold standard and in some cases even the LEED platinum standard. In response, LEED increased the requirements to meet its highest standards first in 2005 and then again in 2009. The challenge now, according to Architecture 2030, an organization for advocating strict reductions in emissions, is to have newly constructed buildings reduce their fossil fuel consumption by 90 percent by 2030 from 2000 levels and be carbon neutral by 2030—using no fossil fuel at all (Architecture 2030).

In Europe, the equivalent to LEED is Building Research Establishment's Environmental Assessment Method (BREEM), which is also in use in some US cities. BREEM goes beyond energy efficiency to include measures of sustainability and toxicity in construction materials, water management, waste handling, health and well-being, and energy consumption (Fitzgerald 2020). The city of Malmö in Sweden has led the way in meeting BREEM standards by altering a 395-acre site in an abandoned shipbuilding district into a mixed-use eco-neighborhood that integrates all of the city's sustainability goals: building efficiency, renewable energy adoption, stormwater management, green space for recreation, bike paths, and biogas-fueled buses. The entire site is completely powered by renewable energy.

Reducing Waste and Recycling Trash

Beside energy use and its concomitant contribution to greenhouse emissions, sea-level rise, and other environmental hazards, cities pollute the landscape with all forms of waste and trash. More than two-thirds of the materials we use are ultimately incinerated or dumped in landfills (Platt et al. 2008). Landfills themselves are the single largest human-made producer of methane gas contributing to rising earth temperatures.

The most effective way to deal with the wide range of waste is recycling. By separating forms of waste, it is possible for industry to reuse some of these materials including scrap metal and glass and therefore reduce the need for producing as much new material and ultimately filling landfills even further. By 2007, waste reduction and recycling regulations in California reduced carbon dioxide emissions in the state by over 2 million tons per year and saved enough energy to power 400,000 homes for a year. San Francisco had a recycling rate of 72 percent by 2007 (Fitzgerald 2010).

As late as 2000, few US cities had full-scale recycling programs. But since then, recycling has become more commonplace. Across Massachusetts cities, 94 percent of the population reports that they mostly or always recycle. By 2016, surveys suggest that 53 percent of the US population reported they have automatic recycling provided to their homes. The average amount of curbside recycled materials amounted to 357 pounds per household per year. Across states the average amount of materials recycled varies with top records of 541 pounds per household in Washington, 507 pounds per household in California, and 483 pounds in Oregon (Recycling Partnership 2017).

Other nations are working toward waste reduction and recycling as well. By 2010 in the United Kingdom, 10,000 companies were participating in the National Industrial Symbiosis Program (NISP). Using a tax imposed on businesses and municipalities of nearly $10 per ton on waste sent to British landfills, the British were able to divert 3.4 million tons of business waste from landfills, reduce carbon emissions by 4.4 million tons per year, and eliminate 342,000 tons of hazardous waste—and in the process create or save more than 1,700 jobs.

Creating Urban Energy Systems

Another approach to reducing carbon emissions is for cities to create a district-wide Combined Heat and Power system (CHP) so that buildings can be heated from a central plant in ways that substantially reduces or eliminates the use of fossil fuels. Copenhagen, Denmark has been a leader in this realm for more than a century. In 1903, the city created a steam system powered by a waste generator. A more modern system was introduced in 1984 which uses four CHP plants, three waste incinerators, and more than 50 boiler plants that now provide nearly 100 percent of the heating throughout the city. Solar arrays have now been added to generate heat and store it in a lined and lidded water basin during the warm summer months until the heat is needed. The network can switch plants and fuel source to provide energy at lowest cost. This system has replaced all older coal-fired boilers in the city and reduces by more than 200,000 tons a year the amount of oil once used for heat generation, and Copenhagen's system has reduced annual carbon emissions by more than 665,000 tons (Fitzgerald 2020).

While district central heating systems are one way that cities can reduce carbon emissions, another are federal and state subsidies to encourage residents and businesses to install solar panels on their roofs to reduce their need for obtaining electricity from fossil fuel dependent utilities. From 2007 through 2021, the US federal government allowed homeowners and businesses to deduct a percentage of their costs of installing solar in their homes and businesses (Energy Sage 2020). When the federal rebate declined in value from 30 percent to 10 percent, individual states and cities took up the environmental challenge. As of 2020, a majority of states in the United States provided tax credits or rebates for such installations. In addition, a number of US cities have created programs to encourage their residents and businesses to install solar to produce their own electricity and, in some cases, to sell surplus current to their utilities.

New York City offers a 100 percent local sales tax exemption on solar installations. Boulder, Colorado provides grants for solar installations as part of their affordable housing program. Honolulu, Hawaii offers 0 percent loans for this purpose and Anne Arundel County in Maryland offers a 50 percent tax credit. Other cities offer cash rebates to help underwrite the cost of solar for their residents and commercial businesses. These include Rochester, Minnesota; Kansas City, Missouri; and Ashland, Oregon (Darcey 2017).

Reducing Vehicle Emissions

Still another way that cities are trying to meet greenhouse gas emissions is to encourage the use of electric vehicles (EV). Oslo has led by installing an extensive charging infrastructure in the city and providing incentives for purchasing EV. Amsterdam is transitioning to electric taxis, buses, and delivery vehicles. Incentives in a number of US states, including California and Georgia, allowed the cities of Los Angeles and Atlanta to move aggressively toward electrifying its vehicles. Los Angeles provides residents and owners of commercial properties rebates when they install 240-volt chargers in their homes or businesses for charging EVs (Fitzgerald 2020).

To combat pollution, particularly in the form of nitrogen dioxide, London was one of the first cities to impose congestion pricing so that vehicles entering central London during the day are charged a daily fee of $15. The policy has reduced traffic by 34 percent, reduced emissions substantially, and encouraged bicycle use. Such congestion zones are now being used in at least 200 cities throughout Europe, and New York City became the first US city to do so in its central business district beginning in 2021. It had already boosted bridge and tunnel fees to reduce the number of cars entering the city (Santora 2017). As one might expect, such congestion pricing schemes have their critics—particularly central city businesses that fear such plans will adversely affect their revenue. Few issues generate more political struggle than those that involve restricting American's use of personal vehicles.

Increasing city parking fees is another way cities are trying to discourage the use of automobiles in the city. Improving mass transit with dedicated bus lanes is another. Curitiba, Brazil, a city of more than 1.8 million, has perhaps the most extensive use of dedicated busways. Large articulated (double or triple cabin) buses run in separate lanes with local traffic on either side. The system has special high-speed express bus lanes and five radial busways that run from the suburbs into the central city. With such a robust system, these buses carry about 2 million passengers a day (Godfrey and Hays-Mitchell 2016; Fitzgerald 2020).

Can Cities Be Good for the Environment?

All the foregoing might suggest that cities are to blame for climate change, and indeed people often tend to picture cities, particularly in the developing world, as urban wastelands belching out pollution, breeding sickness, promoting endless consumption, and driving population increases. But it needs to be recognized that cities have the potential for reducing the pace of climate change. Well-designed cities, with dense housing and efficient mass transit, can reduce energy use and emissions per person (Dickie 2019).

Urbanization concentrates people and activities and therefore conserves both land and resources, and in doing so reduces the amount of resources used per person. A 2011 report from the office of the Mayor of New York found that the average New Yorker consumes 74 percent less water, uses 35 percent less electricity, and produces 45 percent less garbage per person when compared with the average American.

That urban dwellers on a per capita basis pose less danger to the environment is obviously advantageous in meeting a wide array of environmental challenges. But if cities can increase their success at becoming resilient to climate change and find ways to reduce environmental damage, they will play a critical role in enhancing global sustainability. With urban areas now housing more than 55 percent of the entire world's population and with the expectation they will be home to 68 percent by 2050, they will become ever more important in the front lines of the battle for environmental sustainability.

APPENDIX A

Cost-Benefit Analysis

A city councilor introduces a bill under which the city would create a riverfront park. Should the other councilors vote for or against this bill? Issues involving the expenditure of public funds arise frequently. Assuming that the goal is to do something good for the city, how do we determine whether a particular project is worthwhile? This is the question that cost-benefit analysis attempts to answer.

As its name implies, the evaluation undertaken in cost-benefit analysis is not just a matter of determining whether benefits ensue from a project. We would probably not want to gain $10 worth of pleasure from something that cost $100 to obtain. Benefits must be weighed against the costs incurred to gain those benefits.

Cost-benefit analysis differs from cost-effectiveness analysis because the latter does not include any evaluation of whether the ultimate benefits of the project are worthwhile. Instead, cost-effectiveness analysis simply takes a given objective and asks how it can be achieved at least cost.

Doing a full cost-benefit analysis is not easy. It first involves trying to make sure that all the benefits from a particular project are actually measured. The same is true for costs. In terms of public policy, there are often hidden benefits and costs that are easily overlooked. If these turn out to be important, the cost-benefit analysis can give policymakers the wrong answer when they are deciding to proceed or reject a particular a project. Moreover, since the stream of costs and the stream of benefits of most projects extend over time and the two streams are often not coterminous, it is necessary to "discount" both of them because benefits and costs incurred now are typically considered more important than those experienced later.

The general mathematical framework in which cost-benefit analysis occurs is

$$\Sigma(\text{Benefits}_t - \text{Costs}_t) / (1 + r)^t$$

which is evaluated over the meaningful life of the project with t representing time and r representing a discount rate for time. To elucidate the ideas behind this mathematical expression, we can examine a number of issues involved in the conceptualization and measurement of this form of project analysis.

Time Discounts in Cost-Benefit Analysis

One of the most important characteristics of a major project is the time span over which costs and benefits occur. In many initiatives, costs and benefits extend over years, decades, or longer. Most school buildings may last for decades, while some infrastructure may last indefinitely—such as San Francisco's Golden Gate Bridge, constructed in 1937, and the Brooklyn Bridge, completed in 1883. Cost-benefit analysis must be prepared not only to identify specific costs and benefits but to specify when they can be expected to occur and to evaluate how the timing of the costs and benefits affect the overall value of the project.

The most common way to evaluate future costs and benefits builds upon the idea that a benefit in the present is perceived as more valuable than the same benefit in the future. Consequently, under this approach, future benefits must be discounted to establish their present value. Arguments in support of the present value approach include the ideas that:

- people are "myopic," that is, predisposed to value things that are experienced now more highly than things that are in the future;

- the future is more uncertain than the present. The longer that one extends expectations of costs or benefits into the future, the less certain they are. It is appropriate, therefore, to weight expectations about the future less heavily because of this factor; and

- benefits obtained should be weighed against the returns that would have occurred in the financial market from lending the money at market interest rates rather than spending it on the project.

Typically, the present value is calculated by determining the net benefits (benefits minus costs) expected in each time period, discounting each period's net benefits to its value in the present, and then summing the net benefits over the meaningful life of the project. It is easy to see how discounting works mathematically.

Suppose that an individual, who we shall call Elaine, has the choice of spending a sum of money now or in the future. If she does not spend the money, it can earn interest so that at the end of the year, she would have a greater sum than at the beginning of the year. The sum at the end of one year, S_1, would be the original sum, P, plus the interest earned on that sum iP. Thus, $S_1 = P + iP$. Stated another way, $S_1 = P(1 + i)$.

If Elaine continues to invest this sum of money at a given interest rate, the sum builds up over time. Since the interest rate is now applied to the amount she has accumulated going into the second year, the sum at the end of the second year would be $S_2 = P + iP + i(P + iP)$ or $S_2 = P + 2iP + i^2P = P(1+ 2i + i^2)$.

Noting that $1 + 2i + i^2 = (1 + i)^2$, we can rewrite the equation as

$$S_2 = P(1+i)^2.$$

Similarly, at the end of the third year, the returns through the financial market would be

$$S_3 = P + iP + i(P + iP) + i[P + iP + i(P + iP)].$$

Simplifying this equation, we obtain

$$S_3 = P + iP + iP + i^2P + iP + i^2P + i^2P + i^3P = P + 3iP + 3 i^2P + i^3P$$

which can be expressed as

$$S_3 = P(1+i)^3.$$

In fact, generalizing for the returns through any time period, t,

$$S_t = P(1+i)^t.$$

This equation can be reorganized in the following simplified form:

$$P = S_t / (1+i)^t.$$

In this form, P is the **present discounted value** of the sum S_t at time t.

This example uses the interest rates faced by individuals in the financial market as the source of the time discount rate. Several other sources of time discount have been proposed for cost-benefit analysis. They include the interest rate faced by producers (which may not be the same as the interest rate faced by consumers) and a weighted average of the interest rates faced by producers and consumers.

Measuring Benefits and Costs

We can return to our initial mathematical expression for cost-benefit analysis:

$$\Sigma(\text{Benefits}_t - \text{Costs}_t) / (1+r)^t,$$

and focus upon the numerator of this expression. Within the cost-benefit framework, there are several aspects of benefits and costs that should be considered. Among these are:

1. Benefits may accrue to some people but not to others. Alternatively, benefits to one part of the public may be substantial while another segment of the population receives little benefit. Therefore, an important part of cost-benefit analysis is determining which groups benefit, to what degree each benefit, and how to compare benefits for different groups. For example, should benefits for one group be weighted more heavily than benefits for another group?

2. Benefits may not be all the same type. For example, residents' access to recreation is a different type of benefit than a change in businesses' access to customers. Cost-benefit analysis seeks to identify the different types of benefits and costs and to place a dollar valuation on each.

3. The valuation of benefits and costs cannot rely strictly upon market values in all cases, since various forms of market failure may result in market values differing from their social costs and social benefits.

Once costs and benefits have been determined and appropriate adjustments have been made for the time periods in which they occur, the task of cost-benefit analysis is still not complete. For an economically acceptable analysis, another key aspect remains to be taken into consideration: opportunity costs. The economic costs that are incurred in creating the benefits are not just the direct costs associated with the project but the opportunity costs (forgone benefits) from other projects that could be undertaken with the same money. Accordingly, once it is determined whether benefits outweigh costs for a project, this project must be weighed against other projects that could be undertaken with the same resources. The relevant question for decision-makers is not simply whether this project's benefits outweigh their costs. Instead, given our limited resources, the question is: Does this project provide greater benefits than any of the alternatives we could pursue?

Thorough cost-benefit analysis involves skilled use of time discounting, calculation of costs and benefits, aggregation of different types of benefits and different types of costs, a consideration of various groups that might be affected, and a weighing of opportunity costs. Because of these complexities, some critics argue that a flawed cost-benefit analysis is worse than none at all and therefore should be used with great caution. Supporters note that despite its potential flaws, this tool provides greater transparency about the reasoning and assumptions that contribute to the conclusion regarding a project's worth.

References

Adler, Matthew, and Eric Posner, eds. 2001. *Cost-Benefit Analysis: Economic, Philosophical and Legal Perspectives*. Chicago: University of Chicago Press.

AECOM. 2018. "Dania Beach: Economic Impact of Sea Level Rise and Coastal Storms." November. https://www.remi.com/wp-content/uploads/2019/07/567-Dania-Beach-Economic-Impacts-of-Sea-Level-Rise-and-Coastal-Storms.pdf

Allen, Myles R., Opal P. Dube, and William F. Solecki. 2018. *Global Warming of 1.5°C*. IPCC Special Report on the Impacts of Global Warming. Geneva: Intergovernmental Panel on Climate Change.

Architecture 2030: How to Build a Better World, August 10. 2018 https://architecture2030.org/?s=Architecture+2030%3A+How+to+Build+a+Better+World

Barnard, Anne. 2020. "The $199 Billion Sea Wall That Could Defend New York City . . . or Not." *New York Times*, January 17.

Beradelli, Jeff. 2020. "Satellite Images Reveal Huge Amounts of Methane Leaking from U.S. Oil Fields." *CBS News*, April 25.

Borunda, Alejandra. 2019. "Methane, Explained." *National Geographic*. January 23, 2019 https://www.nationalgeographic.com/environment/article/methane

Darcey, Melissa. 2017. "The Solar Incentives and Financing Available in Every State." *Solar Power Authority*, March 29. https://www.solarpowerauthority.com/solar-incentives-and-financing-available-in-every-state/

Denchak, Melissa. 2019. "Greenhouse Effect 101." *Natural Resources Defense Council*. July 16. https://www.nrdc.org/stories/greenhouse-effect-101.

Dickie, Gloria. 2019. "The Surprising Ways Big Cities are Good for the Environment." *Impact*, The Huffington Post July 8. https://www.huffpost.com/entry/big-cities-benefit-environment_n_5d1b99c2e4b07f6ca5851593

Energy Sage, "Investment Tax Credits for Solar Power," March 11, 2020.

Fitzgerald, Joan. 2010. *Emerald Cities: Urban Sustainability and Economic Development*. New York: Oxford University Press.

Fitzgerald, Joan. 2020. *Greenovation: Urban Leadership on Climate Change*. New York: Oxford University Press.

Flavelle, Christopher. 2019. "Canada Tries a Forceful Message for Flood Victims: Live Someplace Else." *New York Times*, September 10.

Flavelle, Christoper. 2020a. "Rising Seas Threaten an American Institution: The 30-Year Mortgage." *New York Times*, June 19.

Flavelle, Christopher. 2020b. "U.S. Flood Strategy Shifts to 'Unavoidable" Relocation of Entire Neighborhoods." *New York Times*, August 26.

Gaul, Gilbert M. 2019. *The Geography of Risk: Epic Storms, Rising Seas, and the Cost of America's Coasts*. New York: Farrar, Straus and Giroux.

Godfrey, Brian L., and Maureen Hays-Mitchell. 2016. "Cities of South America." In *Cities of the World: Regional Patterns and Urban Environments, 6th edition*, edited by Stanley Brunn, Maureent Hays-Mitchell, Donald Ziegler, and Jessica Graybill. Lanham, MD: Rowman & Littlefield, pp. 137–185.

Greentumble. 2018. "The Greatest Contributors to Climate Change." June 14. https://greentumble.com/the-greatest-contributors-to-climate-change.

Gunn, Angus (ed). 2007. *Encyclopedia of Disasters: Environmental Catastrophes and Human Tragedies*. Westport, CT. Greenwood Press.

Hauer, Mathew. 2017. "Migration Induced by Sea-Level Rise Could Reshape the US Population Landscape." *Nature Climate Change* 7, no. 5: 321–325.

Hawkin, Paul, ed. 2017. *Drawdown: The Most Comprehensive Plan Ever Proposed to Reverse Global Warming.* New York: Penguin.

Horowitz, John, and Jessica Gottlieb. 2010. "The Role of Agriculture in Reducing Greenhouse Gas Emissions." *Economic Brief Number 15*, September. Washington, DC: US Department of Agriculture.

IBioMASSLab. 2017. "What Has Climate Change Done?" February 2. https://publish.illinois.edu/lfr/2017/02/02/what-has-climate-change-done/

Illinois EPA. 2007. "Emissions Reduction Market System: What Is ERMS?"

Johnson, Ben. "The Spanish Flu Pandemic of 1918." Historic UK. www.historic-uk.com/HistoryUK/HistoryofBritain/The-Spanish-Flu-pandemic-of-1918.

Jones, Benjamin. 2007. "Climate Change: Economic Impact and Policy Responses." October. Washington, DC: International Monetary Fund.Layard, Richard, and Stephen Glaister, eds. 1994. *Cost-Benefit Analysis.* Cambridge, MA: Cambridge University Press.

Lui, Kevin. 2017. "Plastic Fibers Are Found in 83% of the World's Tap Water." *Time*, September 15.

Mbugna, Sophie. 2020. "2 Years Ago, Kenya Set the World's Strictest Plastic Bag Ban. Did It Work?" January 23. https://www.huffpost.com/entry/plastic-bag-ban-works-kenya_n_5e272713c5b63211761a4698.

Mufson, Steven. 2020. "Boston Harbor Brings Ashore a New Enemy: Rising Seas." *Washington Post*, February 19.

National Centers for Environmental Information. 2019. *Global Climate Report—Annual 2019.* Asheville, NC: National Centers for Environmental Information.

National Ocean Service. 2020. "A Guide to Plastics in the Ocean." Washington, DC: National Oceanic and Atmospheric Administration.

National Research Council. 2010. *Adapting to the Impacts of Climate Change.* Washington, DC: National Research Council.

Nestpick. 2020. "2050 Climate Change City Index." https://www.nestpick.com/2050-climate-change-city-index-usa.

Platt, Brenda, David Ciplet, Kate M. Bailey, and Eric Lombardi. 2008. *Stop Trashing the Climate.* Washington, DC: Institute for Local Self-Reliance.

Ravishankara, A. R., John S. Daniel, and Robert W. Portmann 2009. "Nitrous Oxide (N2O): The Dominant Ozone-Depleting Substance Emitted in the 21st Century". *Science* 326(5949):123–125.

Recycling Partnership. 2017. "The 2016 State of Curbside Report." January 31. Falls Church, VA.

Room, Joseph. 2018. *Climate Change: What Everyone Needs to Know.* New York: Oxford University Press.

Rosane, Olivia. 2018. "8 World Cities that Could be Underwater as Oceans Rise." *EcoWatch*, October 5. https://www.ecowatch.com/cities-vulnerable-sea-level-rise-2610208792.html

Salman, Sarah. 2020. "Top 10 Major Disasters of the World." *Wonderlist*.

Santora, Marc. 2017. "Cuomo Calls Manhattan Traffic Plan an Idea 'Whose Time has Come.'" *New York Times*, August 13.

Texas A&M University. *Science Daily*. 2016. "Hurricanes from Three Million Years Ago Give Us Clues About Present Storms." *ScienceDaily.*, November 1. https://www.sciencedaily.com/releases/2016/11/161101093850.htm>.

Smithson, Aaron. 2019. "Army Corps of Engineers Will Erect Miles of Sea Walls Along Staten Island." August 26. *The Architect's Newspaper*. https://www.arch-paper.com/2019/08/army-corps-engineers-seawalls-staten-island/

The Climate Report. 2018. *The National Climate Assessment—Impact, Risks, and Adaptation in the United States.* Brooklyn: Melville House.

Thorner, Nancy. 2020. "Western Forest Fires Hijacked to Promote Global Warming." *Illinois Review*, September 16. https://www.illinoisreview.com/illinoisreview/2020/09/thorner-western-forest-fires-hijacked-to-promote-global-warming.html

US Energy Information Administration. 2021. "Frequently Asked Questions (FAQS)". Updated July 8, 2021. https://www.eia.gov/tools/faqs/faq.php?id=84&t=11. Accessed on August 1, 2021.

US Environmental Protection Agency (EPA). 2014. "Cap and Trade 101." October 27.

US Environmental Protection Agency (EPA). 2020a. "Fast Facts on Transportation Greenhouse Gas Emissions." www.epa.gov/greenvehicles/fast-facts-transportation-greenhouse-gas-emissions.

US Environmental Protection Agency (EPA). 2020b. "Global Greenhouse Emissions Data." www.epa.gov/ghgemissions/global-greenhouse-gas-emissions-data.

Weil, Elizabeth, and Mollie Simon. 2020. "California Will Keep Burning. But Housing Policy is Making it Worse." *ProPublica*, October 2. https://www.propublica.org/article/california-will-keep-burning-but-housing-policy-is-making-it-worse

World Bank. 2014. "CO2 Emissions for Manufacturing Industries and Construction." http://data.worldbank.org/indicator/EN.CO2.MANF.ZS.

World Meteorological Association. 2018. "Scientific Assessment of Ozone Depletion: 2018" *Global Ozone Research and Monitoring P:roject – Report No. 58.* https://csl.noaa.gov/assessments/ozone/2018/

Yong, Chen, Kam-Ling Tsoi, Chen Feibi, Gao Zhenhuan, Zou Qijia, and Chen Zhongli, eds. 1988. *The Great Tangshan Earthquake of 1976: An Anatomy of Disaster.* Oxford: Pergamon Press.

Questions and Exercises

1. Cities of the world differ substantially in how well they are adapting to climate change and taking remedial action. CDP is a global information center that keeps track of such matters. You can access their data on carbon dioxide emissions for a large number of cities at https://data.cdp.net/Emissions/2016-Citywide-Emissions-Map/iqbu-zjaj.

   - Go to the world map and select 10 cities from around the world.
   - Measure the number of metric tons of CO_2 emitted in each of these cities per person, by dividing metric tons by population.

   Which of these cities have the highest emissions? Which the lowest among the cities you have selected?

   - Which of these cities has seen an increase in per capita emissions? Which have seen a reduction?
   - Using your browser, try to discover what environmental measures have been taken by the cities with a reduction in CO_2 emissions.

2. Now go to the CDP data on renewable energy for cities, using

   https://data.cdp.net/Renewable-Energy/2015-Renewable-Energy-in-Cities-USA/qqp5-vmdm.

   - Which cities listed depend the most on nonfossil fuel? Which cities are most dependent on fossil fuels?
   - Using your browser, try to discover why some cities have moved so aggressively to use nonfossil fuel.
   - What nonfossil fuel sources do each of these cities use?

3. Now go to the CDP data on the various energy sources around the world at https://data.cdp.net/Renewable-Energy/City-wide-Electricity-Mix/ycef-psus/data.

   - Select ten cities of your choice (and make sure that no four are from the same continent), and set up a spreadsheet in which you enter the percentage of energy generated by each source.
   - Calculate the share (percentage) generated by each source.
   - Which three of these cities is still most heavily dependent on oil and gas?
   - Which three of these cities relies the most on hydroelectric power?
   - Have any of your ten cities moved in the direction of using solar or wind power?

Urban Economic Development Strategies

16

LEARNING OBJECTIVES

- Define industrial policy and explain its role in US economic history
- Explain the concept of creative destruction and apply it to the United States in the early 1970s
- Explain the three goals of economic development and describe the criteria for evaluating their implementation
- Enumerate three strategies aimed at reducing capital costs and explain how each operates
- Explain the five arguments that have been used to advocate for stimulating economic activity by reducing state and local taxes
- Explain the prisoner's dilemma and show how it applies to local decision-making

What is the proper role of government in promoting business? Essentially, that is the question of **industrial policy**: the strategic effort by a federal, state, or local government to encourage the development and growth of a particular sector of the economy, a particular industry, or business. According to Pack and Saggi (2006) industrial policy refers to *any type* of selective intervention or government policy that attempts to alter the structure of production toward sectors that are expected to offer better prospects for economic growth than would occur in the absence of such intervention.

At the federal level, the United States has entertained such a strategy since the earliest days of the Republic. In 1791, Alexander Hamilton, the first Secretary of the United States Treasury, outlined an industrial policy to Congress arguing for targeted subsidies to manufacturing industries to help the new nation compete economically and militarily with England (Stensrud 2016). To help win the War of 1812, Henry Clay and other members of the Whig Party devised an explicit industrial policy consisting of tariffs to protect domestic industry, a national bank to foster commerce, and federal subsidies for roads and canals to help develop profitable agricultural markets (Bingham 1998). Under Abraham Lincoln, between 1861 and 1865, agriculture was supported by the federal government; science, research, and technological development was aided financially; and the first direct federal grants for private railroads were implemented.

At the beginning of the twentieth century the nation's emerging aircraft industry was aided by the US Post Office, which subsidized airlines with lucrative air mail contracts. All this government intervention was taken to a much higher level when the Franklin Roosevelt administration battled the Great Depression of the 1930s by supporting private industry with massive infrastructure projects and direct aid to agriculture.

In the aftermath of Sputnik, the federal government invested billions of research dollars to perfect solid-state guidance systems and software for rockets and missiles, helping to create what today is the high-tech universe of cell phones, the internet, iPads, GPS, and a dizzying array of gadgets based on the integrated circuit and the software that run them. By 1982, the Department of Defense and other government agencies were purchasing more than half of all aircraft, radio, and television communications equipment, and one-third of all electron tubes and nonferrous forgings manufactured in the United States (Reich 1982).

Yet as a recent Center for Economic and Policy Research working paper noted, "For the past generation, the dominant view among economists was that giving businesses a free hand—that is, little regulation and low taxes—was the most important contribution governments could make to encourage productive investment. The corollary to this view is that as much as possible overall investments in the economy should be undertaken by the private sector as opposed to any sort of government entity" (Pollin and Baker 2009).

The case *against* public-sector industrial policy is that governments are not capable of picking winners, and therefore too often waste tax dollars in their attempts to do so. The libertarian Cato Institute claims that government subsidies inevitably distort economic activity and "create even larger failures than might have existed in the marketplace" (DeHaven 2012). By aiding some businesses, according to the Institute, government places others at a disadvantage either by reason of having to pay higher taxes or having to compete with subsidized firms. Hence, diverting resources from businesses preferred by the market to those preferred by policymakers leads to losses for the overall economy.

The case *for* such public investment in the private sector is that public investment, rather than "crowding out," actually can "crowd in" private investment by incubating new technologies and helping private businesses bring these innovations to where they can be effective in the marketplace. In brief, well-placed public funds in the private sector can yield large, long-term gains at relatively modest short-term cost.

But what makes for well-placed public funds? Can the government really invest in the private sector in ways that accelerate economic growth and create good private-sector jobs? Is there a reasonable position, halfway between government's never investing and government's investing indiscriminately? What kinds of investments in what industries makes sense?

What is true for industrial policy at the federal level takes on even greater significance at the state and local level. Just for a moment, consider that you are the mayor or city manager of a midsized city that has been hemorrhaging jobs and revenue for some years. The unemployment rate in your community is double the state average, some of the commercial and industrial buildings in town have been closed and boarded up, and younger people are beginning to move to other locations to find work. You have read about what happened to such older industrial cities as Detroit and Flint, Michigan; Youngstown, Ohio; and Wilkes-Barre, Pennsylvania during the 1960s and 1970s and worry that the same kind of deindustrialization and economic deterioration could happen to yours. What do you recommend to the city council? What economic development tools should you use to keep businesses from moving out, and how can you attract new ones to set up shop? These questions are faced every day by mayors, city managers, and city planners across the country.

While the provision of public services and the drafting and enforcement of city and town laws and regulations constitute the chief functions of local government, state and municipal officials also face the task of keeping companies and jobs in their communities and attracting new ones. Because of the continual turnover in business enterprise in any one city or town, few metro areas can rest on their laurels celebrating the investments they attracted yesterday. Local leaders try to promulgate a "good business climate" by resorting to a range of policies from property tax abatements and public subsidies to government investments in infrastructure, worker training, sports facilities, and cultural amenities. It is a high-stakes game that few cities can choose not to play. In doing so, they have to work with private developers, bankers, and neighborhood associations trying to balance the demands of the business community with the needs of the broader population.

Firm Relocation in the United States

To provide some idea of just how much business turnover exists during a relatively short time period, we can turn to the period between 1969 and 1976 throughout the United States. This was a period that began with a buoyant national economy for the first four years, followed by a recession in 1975 and the beginning of a recovery in 1976. Nationwide, between 1969 and 1976, investment in brand-new private-sector facilities—from large manufacturing plants to small retail establishments—was responsible for creating 25 million jobs, an average of 3.6 million new jobs each year. Over the same period, 22 million jobs or 3.2 million per year disappeared as a result of establishment closings. This "churning" of employment is part of a process the early twentieth-century economist Joseph Schumpeter termed **creative destruction**—out with the old, in with the new.

During this same time period, firms created more than 19 million jobs in existing facilities in the cities, towns, and rural areas where they already had establishments. Offsetting this good news for workers and communities was the loss of more than 13 million jobs due to the downsizing of companies.

Overall, between new facilities and expanding ones, the nation could boast of nearly 9 million more jobs in 1976 than had existed just seven years before. But certain states and metro areas were great winners in the job game and others were big losers. The biggest net losers were states in the Northeast—the six New England states plus New York, New Jersey, and Pennsylvania. More than 4.9 million new jobs were created in these nine states through establishment openings and through firms moving into the region from other places in the country or from abroad. But this gain was more than offset by the loss of nearly 5.9 million jobs as thousands of establishments closed or relocated across state lines. Many of these Snowbelt jobs went to the Sunbelt states in the South and the West. Even though expansions of existing facilities created more jobs than contractions destroyed, on net across the entire national labor market the Northeast lost more jobs than it created. The states of the Midwest fared somewhat better than those in the Northeast with a net addition of 2.4 million jobs, but there too millions of jobs were lost to plant closings and contractions. Auto plants were closing or moving to the South. Some companies were beginning to experiment with plants in Mexico. Similarly, steel mills were closing, along with all kinds of other manufacturing concerns. When these anchor institutions moved, thousands of local smaller plants, retail shops, and service companies went out of business as part of a ripple effect throughout the region.

Even the emerging South and West were not immune to business contraction and the consequent massive loss of jobs. Throughout the South almost 7 million jobs were lost to shutdowns, with another 3.8 million lost through cutbacks in existing operations. Altogether, the West lost more than 6 million jobs. What made these Sunbelt regions so successful is that for every job lost, more than 1.4 new jobs were created. In the Snowbelt regions, for every job lost, only 1.1 new jobs took its place.

The Trend in Manufacturing Employment

The loss of manufacturing jobs in the United States was at the center of business contraction from at least 1989, when total manufacturing firms employed nearly 20.7 million workers, until 2010, when manufacturing employment had plummeted to just 13.3 million. During this two-decade period, employment in this sector declined by more than 56 percent. Only after 2010 did this important sector in the economy begin to recover, so that by 2019 employment was back up to 15 million. Much of this new manufacturing employment was due to the creation of new high-tech firms in industries that produced everything from mini-computers to cell phone parts. The introduction of new automation techniques allowed some firms to produce manufactured products in the United States that otherwise would have been produced in lower-cost countries such as China and Vietnam. The establishment of auto assembly plants in the United States by such foreign producers as BMW, Mercedes, and Toyota added to the growth in US manufacturing employment.

The Geographic Dispersion of Jobs

In the great scheme of things, a job lost in one location (if it stays in the United States) can be a job gained somewhere else. But the addition of a job in Springhill, Tennessee at the expense of a job lost in Flint, Michigan is certainly a cause of concern for the mayor of Flint, while the job gained in Springhill is cause for celebration among local officials there. If the loss or gain is numbered in the hundreds or thousands, it is a major political issue and not just an economic one.

Because job turnover affects every region of the country, no community can expect that its industries will continue to create jobs for its citizens automatically and generate tax revenues to pay for public services. At one time Detroit felt that its economic success was assured by the presence of the auto industry. Pittsburgh felt the same way because of steel.

Between 1995 and 2003, when the nation as a whole saw the creation of more than 13 million jobs, a gain of nearly 11 percent, the Springfield, Massachusetts metro area lost 3 percent of its job base while the Youngtown, Ohio region lost 5 percent. Today, even the cities and regions that are leaders in growth industries, including information technology, know that they could suddenly lose their **economic base** because of changing technology, changes in demand, or the opening of new competing firms elsewhere in the United States or abroad. Even California, with its burgeoning population, lost one out of six of its existing manufacturing jobs between 1990 and 2002 (State of California 2003).

Consequently, cities and towns find themselves in the business of constantly trying to attract new capital in order to secure jobs and revenue, and striving just as hard to hold on to the businesses they have. In this competitive battleground for jobs and investment, municipalities and states have relied on an arsenal of economic development strategies, instruments, and tools. By one estimate, state and local governments spend at least $45 billion a year on tax breaks and other incentives to lure or keep job-producing businesses and plants in their jurisdictions (Pianin 2017). Other estimates put the total as high as $95 billion a year when all state and local incentives are included in the total (Parilla and Liu 2018).

Goals of Economic Development

Local public officials have three major objectives when they consider ways to encourage economic investment in their municipalities. The first is to produce jobs that can provide wages, salaries, and benefits for local citizens (Blair et al. 1984; Furdell 1994). Obviously, if the number of jobs in a locale is declining quickly or not keeping up with population growth, there will be an increase in unemployment. If joblessness is prolonged, the result can be increased poverty and ultimately out-migration as the unemployed seek work elsewhere. This can lead to a **vicious cycle** in which an initial increase in unemployment leads to a loss in prime-age workers, making the community less likely to attract new investment and more likely to sink ever further into decline and disrepair. This was the story of many Rustbelt cities in the Northeast and Midwest in the last few decades of the twentieth century, with the most extreme case being the old-fashioned western "ghost town" abandoned when the gold mine went bust or the railroad passed it by.

The second objective for local officials is to maintain or increase the local tax base by attracting private-sector investment (Jones and Bachelor 1993; Pagano and Bowman 1995). To provide for roads, parks, libraries, public schools, and other public services, towns and cities must have sufficient tax revenue. Some of this can be raised from homeowners through the local residential property tax. In a limited number of larger cities revenue also comes from a general sales tax, levies on specific services (e.g., hotel or meal taxes), or a local income tax. Most municipalities rely on the taxation of industrial and commercial properties to help pay for local public services. A suburban strip mall or downtown commercial district teeming with office towers, restaurants, hotels, and a bevy of service firms can often provide tax revenues in excess of the expense incurred from the municipality's requirement to supply these business ventures with police and fire protection, road maintenance, and other public services. The surplus can be used to improve local schools, provide subsidized housing for low-income families, beautify a park, or improve a city's waterfront. Likewise, a large factory can generate property tax revenue that can be used for the same purposes.

The third objective is to raise the local economic multiplier by substituting local services and production for imported ones. If municipal leaders can encourage entrepreneurs to set up local operations, dollars that would have quickly left the community can be recirculated, increasing the incomes of residents and thereby producing greater local prosperity. For these reasons—jobs, tax revenue, and an increased local multiplier—most local public officials work hard to attract private-sector investment to their own towns and cities. The question is, what options are available to them?

Location from the Business Perspective

Whether a firm will choose to locate in a particular city or town depends on a wide array of factors, some of which are susceptible to influence by state and local public policy. To understand this variety of factors, it is useful to look at a simple model of the firm. We can assume that the primary objective of a firm is to make a profit. The profit of a firm over any discrete period of time is the difference between its total revenue and its total costs, as we noted in Chapter 4 when we looked at the basic Alonso model. The equation for a firm's profit is therefore:

$$\pi = TR - TC \qquad (16a)$$

where π = profits, TR = total revenue, and TC = total cost.

Total revenue (TR) is equal to the price of each of the products or services that the firm sells times the quantity sold, or $p \times Q$, where p = price and Q = quantity. Total costs are a bit more complicated but can be reduced to the cost of the three primary inputs used in production: physical capital (K), labor (L), and raw materials (N). Thus, rewriting equation 16a, we obtain the following equation:

$$\pi = (p \times Q) - (r \times K) - (w \times L) - (p_n \times N) \qquad (16b)$$

where r = interest rate on capital, K = plant and equipment, w = wage and benefit cost per worker, L = number of employees, p_n = price of raw materials, and N = raw materials.

In a world with transportation costs, taxes, and regulations, this equation becomes even more complex. Since firms are interested in maximizing their *after-tax* profits, we need to subtract out their transportation costs, as well as any taxes they pay and any regulatory costs they face. That makes our final equation the following:

$$\pi_{AT} = (p \times Q) - (r \times K) - (w \times L) - (p_n \times N) - C_s - T - R \qquad (16c)$$

$$\underbrace{\begin{bmatrix} \text{Total} \\ \text{Revenue} \end{bmatrix}}_{} \quad \underbrace{[\ldots\ldots\ldots\ldots\ldots\ldots\text{Total Costs}\ldots\ldots\ldots\ldots\quad]}_{}$$

Where π_{AT} = after-tax profits
C_s = shipping/transportation costs
T = taxes and public fees
R = costs of complying with public-sector regulations.

Based on this equation, we can begin to see what firms must do to maximize profits and how municipal officials might try to influence companies to remain in their communities, expand their operations, or entice new companies to move in.

In a reasonably competitive marketplace, firms can only increase their total revenue by improving their product or differentiating it from others so that they can sell a larger quantity. Highly competitive firms have little leeway to change the price they charge. If they raise their prices above the level set by their competitors, they lose customers. In this case p might go up, but Q falls so much in response that the product of the two, TR, actually declines. This is the case where the price elasticity of demand has a value smaller than negative 1. A 1 percent *increase* in price leads to more than a 1 percent *decrease* in quantity sold.

On the other hand, if a firm lowers its price a great deal in an attempt to attract customers, it may not even be able to cover its costs and will likewise take a loss. Moreover, if its competitors lower their prices in response, this reduces any price advantage. The only thing a firm in a competitive market can do to raise revenue is try to differentiate its product from those of its competitors. This is what drives most firms to continually attempt to innovate and advertise in order to stay one jump ahead of the competition. This takes investment and time.

Because of the short-term barriers to increasing total revenue, most firms are in a constant battle to find ways to reduce their total costs. Given the fact that the interest rate (r) on loanable funds used to purchase plant and equipment (K) is set by banks or other lending institutions, most firms can do little about lowering their capital costs—unless they can obtain an interest-subsidized loan through some government program. Finding cheaper sources of labor (L) is possible, especially if the firm can move its operations to lower wage regions of the country or to lower wage countries abroad. During the nineteenth century, textile manufacturers in the highly competitive market in New England turned to one immigrant group after another seeking out workers who were willing to accept ever-lower wages (w). When Irish immigrants who fled the potato famine demanded higher wages, the textile mill owners turned to French Canadians and, in rapid succession, Italians, Russian Jews, Poles, and other Eastern Europeans to keep their wage costs down.

At the end of the nineteenth century and throughout the first half of the twentieth, the mill owners found they could find even cheaper labor by moving their operations to the South. By 1922, the majority of US textile production was found outside New England. Other industries, including steel and auto, followed suit and left their original midwestern locations for cheaper labor in the South and later in Mexico. With cheaper transportation available via rail and interstate highway, it was possible to move industrial inputs to wherever they were needed and ship final products to wherever they were demanded.

As for raw materials (N), which range from agricultural products, minerals, and energy sources to finished inputs purchased for assembly into final products, firms scout out different locations to assure lowest cost. The early textile mills were built in such cities as Lawrence and Lowell, Massachusetts because there was a ready supply of low-cost waterpower in towns situated along rivers. With the introduction and perfection of the steam engine, companies no longer needed to be situated in riverside towns. Many landlocked towns and cities became cost-effective options for industrial production. Today, with low-cost, high-speed communications and transportation (C_s) available by telephone and the internet, permitting economically efficient management of far-flung industrial empires, an ever-expanding number of locations have become viable alternatives for production. All of this reduces labor cost for US producers, but it means the export of jobs from American cities and towns and real concerns for mayors and other municipal officials.

The final factors on the cost side of any firm's financial accounts are taxes (T) and regulatory costs (R). While usually small in relation to capital, labor, and natural resource costs, firms try to find locations for their operations that, other things being equal, impose lower taxes and a smaller regulatory burden. City and town officials often try to influence firm location by offering favorable tax treatment but there are a host of other economic development strategies they can pursue in an effort to provide jobs for their citizens, augment local tax revenues, and increase the local multiplier.

Public Policy, Economic Development, and Firm Location

A review of equation 16c helps us to develop a taxonomy of local economic development strategies. There is not a great deal that local or state governments can do to attract or retain investment by assisting firms in their drive to increase their total revenue (p × Q). There are no simple direct ways to increase the price of a firm's products or services or increase the quantity sold, short of the local community or state guaranteeing the purchase of a share of the firm's output. In a few cases, it might be able to influence where a bank places its branches if the local or state government agrees to use the bank to hold its deposits, but this is extremely rare. When Michael Dukakis was governor of Massachusetts, he helped keep open a General Motors assembly plant in his state by agreeing to buy cars built in that plant to replace older vehicles in the state's agency fleet.

More common is the use of lobbying by local and state government officials to encourage the federal government to contract with firms in their communities (Leonard and Walder 2000). This is especially true with regard to defense procurement and spending by the National Aeronautics and Space Administration

(NASA). Local government officials in Seattle have long helped lobby members of Congress and procurement officers at the Department of Defense to assure that Boeing receives contracts for military aircraft built in the state of Washington. President Lyndon Johnson was famous for steering business to firms in his home state of Texas with contracts to build equipment for NASA and the space program. Such lobbying pays off in terms of local jobs and increased local tax revenue, although the overall result can be thought of as a **zero-sum game**. What cities including Houston received in the way of federal contracts simply reduces the amount of revenue that could have flowed to localities with less political clout.

Reducing Capital Costs (r × K)

Much more can be done by government with respect to assisting firms to reduce their total costs rather than by trying to boost their revenue. We can begin with the cost of capital. States have a variety of tools available to them to help reduce the cost of capital for firms that consider relocating or starting up new operations (Maguire and Hughes 2018). A state can issue **industrial revenue bonds**—also known as **industrial development bonds (IDBs)**—which offer a critical source of low-cost financing for small manufacturers. Such IDBs can support expansion and investment in existing manufacturing facilities, as well as the development of new facilities and the purchase of new machinery and equipment. These bonds carry a lower interest rate than can be obtained in the private sector because their interest is exempt from federal and state taxes and because the bonds are considered low risk, backed by the full faith and credit of the state. As such, they are valuable assets in the investment portfolios of individuals in high tax brackets, since the interest they earn is not subject to federal taxes. Offering capital to firms at these discounted interest rates can make a particular community location more appealing.

In 2018 a total of $152.8 million in IDBs was issued, although in previous years the amount was as high as $3.1 billion (Council of Development Finance Agencies 2019). The Commonwealth of Massachusetts issued the most IDBs in 2018 with $30.3 million, and continued to be among the top issuers of this form of finance over a number of ensuing years. Wisconsin was the second-highest issuer of IDBs at $28 million, followed by Pennsylvania at $25.8 million, Georgia's $18.4 million, Indiana's $14.4 million, and Iowa's $13.3 million.

An alternative development tool to industrial revenue bonds was established by the Urban Development Action Grant (UDAG) program enacted into federal law in 1977 as part of President Jimmy Carter's urban policy (Stephenson 1987; Pelissero 2003). The purpose of UDAGs was to alleviate central city decay by offering local communities direct subsidies for real estate development that they could use in combination with private capital to redevelop distressed neighborhoods. The ratio of private capital to UDAG subsidy was set at 2.5 to 1, and the locality was required to prove to the federal government that the development project would be financially infeasible without the subsidy.

Research on economic development policies undertaken by Richard Bingham (2003) provides a good example of the use of a UDAG. In redeveloping its riverfront in an effort to become a prime location for conventions, the mayor and city council of San Antonio wanted a 600-room luxury convention hotel built along its projected Riverwalk. Using the lure of a $14 million UDAG grant to restore nearby historic properties, develop a small commercial shopping mall, and construct a 500-car parking garage, the city was able to coax the Hyatt Corporation to build the luxury hotel it wanted at a cost of $37 million in private funds, which satisfied the federal government's 2.5:1 private capital–subsidy ratio. Without the federal grant, it is unlikely that any private developer would have taken the gamble of putting up such a hotel in a community whose convention potential was not readily apparent. Today, San Antonio boasts a $4 billion per year visitor industry based on national and regional conventions and tourism.

UDAGs were not without their critics, and the program was canceled by Congress after 12 years in operation. Conservatives claimed that the program was simply a new form of **pork barrel politics**—awarding billions of federal dollars to city mayors to dole out on the pet projects of private developers in return for their political support. Community activists often criticized the UDAG program for focusing development on downtown office projects rather than on projects that would serve the neighborhoods. Clearly, many UDAG projects served the broader interests of the community, while some no doubt ended up mainly serving the profit needs of locally influential developers. The real key to their success was in the ability of city leaders to bargain aggressively with private developers to assure that the community benefited from the projects underwritten with public subsidies (Sagalyn 1997).

One of the most creative development tools available to local communities to affect capital costs is **tax increment financing (TIF)** (Bingham 2003). Unlike economic development programs funded by the federal government, TIF emanates from state government. Under a TIF, a city designates a specific neighborhood for improvement, making it a "TIF district." The central idea behind this development instrument is to use all or a substantial share of expected *future increments* in local property tax revenue to underwrite *currently* issued general obligation bonds. Essentially, new development in TIF districts should increase property values and therefore property tax revenue. Future increments in property tax revenues made possible by a TIF-backed development can then be used to pay the principal and interest on the original bonds. The amount of property tax revenue that goes to the local community over the period of the TIF-backed bonds is fixed at or just above its predevelopment level. Then, all or at least most of the increase in real estate taxes tied to increased property values in the TIF district go to pay off the bonds until the full principal and interest is paid off. Only then can the community use increased property tax revenue inside the TIF district to pay for city services.

The biggest risk that cities run when engaging in tax increment financing is that the expected tax revenue will never materialize or will be insufficient to cover the money spent on the project. TIF has been used to redevelop blighted areas and encourage new or expanded manufacturing, where it can contribute to job creation and income generation in economically distressed community.

Reducing Labor Costs (w × L)

State and local communities have weighed in on labor costs hoping to attract firms by helping to keep wage costs down or contributing to the cost of training employees so as to improve the productivity of the workers hired by firms. To keep wages low, many southern states have long supported so-called right-to-work statutes that make it difficult for unions to organize workers. They have done this so as to signal to firms that they are more likely to avoid unionization if they locate in communities within these states.

Besides attempting to influence the actual price of labor, state and local communities have tried to attract firms by promising to pay for the training of their employees. This directly reduces the cost of labor by substituting publicly provided training for what would have been paid for by the private sector. This training presumably improves the quality of the labor force, boosts a firm's productivity, and likely increases its profits. Of course, providing excellent public schools including vocational and technical high schools and community colleges is the most widespread method municipalities use to assure employers a well-trained labor force.

Reducing Raw Materials, Natural Resources, and Transportation Costs $(p_n \times N)$, C_s

Not much opportunity exists for municipalities to affect the quantity or price of raw materials or natural resources that private firms use, except for the provision of water and sewerage and of land. However, by using bond financing to pay for this basic infrastructure, local communities can help to reduce company costs. To coax new large developments into their regions, cities and towns will often underwrite the cost of making changes to existing roads and highways to accommodate a company's needs.

Many cities and suburbs have developed industrial parks, providing subsidized land to private firms in the hopes of attracting new investment. In older cities, this often means assembling parcels of land large enough for industrial or commercial use. One of the most spectacular examples of this strategy once again involved General Motors, this time with the city of Detroit. With auto factories closing down and fleeing the Motor City in the early 1980s, GM informed Detroit's mayor that it would agree to build a new ultramodern, single-story Cadillac assembly facility right in the middle of the city in an area called "Poletown" (due to its once-heavy Polish immigrant population). But to get the company to do this rather than move out of state, the city would have to meet its demands for land assembly, site preparation, and a substantial property tax abatement. With little bargaining power, Detroit ultimately agreed to use its power of eminent domain to clear more than 400 acres of land, in the process displacing 3,200 residents, dozens of churches, nursing homes, and 160 community businesses. It paid for the relocation of on-off ramps for two of the city's expressways, paid for clearing the land to the point where it was ready for construction, and then added a $240 million, 12-year property tax abatement into the bargain. In return, the city retained about 3,000 autoworker jobs (Bluestone and Harrison 1982).

Reducing Taxes (T)

Two factors that states and municipalities have the greatest control over are taxes and business regulation. Many states use an array of tax exemptions in an attempt to attract industry to a particular state or community including low taxes on business, providing abatements on taxes in the form of lower rates or tax holidays for new businesses, and limiting taxes on highly paid executives.

Robert Lynch (2004) noted that there are five common arguments that politicians and special-interest groups make for cutting state and local taxes to induce economic development. The first is the tax burden argument. Simply stated, lowering the tax burden on companies increases their after-tax profits. All else being equal, communities that help companies improve the bottom line are the communities where businesses want to set up operations. If this works, this could mean more jobs.

Second, the supply-side argument is actually a variant of the tax burden claim. It holds that tax cuts for individuals and for businesses provide incentives that encourage people to work more and to increase their savings and investment, thereby stimulating economic activity. A reduction in the individual income tax, for example, supposedly will encourage workers to work harder and longer because they can keep more of every dollar they earn. Workers substitute more work for leisure because the opportunity cost—the implicit price—of leisure goes up when the after-tax value of an hour's work goes up. For businesses, a tax cut provides an incentive to invest both because it boosts their after-tax profit rate, which makes investment more profitable and because it leaves them with more funds for investment.

The third argument, this one on the demand side, is another variant of the tax burden claim. When taxes are reduced, consumers and businesses will spend part of their tax savings on goods and services, leading to a higher volume of business sales. This, in turn, will help create jobs and additional income.

Still a fourth argument rests on the effect of taxes on the so-called business climate. A state, a metro region, or a city's business climate is usually defined in terms of a combination of factors that makes an area a good place in which to invest. This includes everything from the area's social and physical infrastructure and the quality of life for employees to indicators of how local government deals with business in terms of zoning, building codes, and taxes—essentially, how the local government accommodates the needs of business. Those who promote tax cuts suggest that businesses judge the business climate first and foremost on the basis of the local tax burden. The tax burden here is seen as less important in terms of after-tax profit per se and more important as a general indicator or sign of a local community's attitude toward business. Thus, even if the tax burden is a tiny fraction of a company's costs, a lower tax is seen as beneficial to economic development because it sends a signal that a local community is hungry for business and is working hard to attract it.

Finally, there is the competitiveness argument. Even if taxes have little impact on corporate profits and even if companies do not explicitly demand lower taxes or special tax treatment, cities and towns must offer tax relief to compete with other locales that do. Those communities that refuse to play the tax-cut game are presumably doomed to lose. Jurisdictions that actively court business with low taxes and other monetary incentives will allegedly have a leg up when it comes to attracting footloose industry.

In practice, states, cities, and towns have a broad array of tax weapons to use as part of an economic development strategy. Tax cuts generally refer to reductions in income, sales, or property tax rates. Tax revenue can be manipulated by changes in the tax base. For example, excluding certain forms of capital from the property tax can reduce the property tax burden without changing the tax rate. A local property tax can be changed by deciding to include or exclude physical equipment inside a plant as property. In addition, changes in tax burdens can be accomplished by manipulating income thresholds on a graduated income tax or by changing the level and types of exemptions.

Local tax policy can also be targeted. **General tax incentives** are "**entitlements** automatically provided to all firms meeting qualifications specified in the tax law" (Lynch 2004, p. 14). Alternatively, a city or town might provide a **special tax break** or a tax credit to specific firms, keyed to the number of new workers they hire. Such incentives can be targeted geographically so that only specified neighborhoods within a municipality are eligible for favorable treatment. There are many cases where special tax treatment is offered to a single firm in order to encourage it to stay in town, move to town, or expand its operations. The problem, of course, is that by reducing taxes on selected firms, a wedge is driven between their tax burden and that of all other firms in the area. This may appear to be inequitable and may dissuade, or at least not encourage, other firms from increasing their employment levels.

Streamlining Regulations (R)

The other factor over which states and municipalities have direct control is the set of business regulations that govern zoning, building code enforcement, pollution control, and local minimum wage rates. These regulations were put in place to control the use of land, to assure that buildings are safe for occupancy, to control air and water contamination, and to limit downward pressure on wages and family incomes. These objectives of government policy are now widely accepted.

To be sure, each of them imposes costs on business. As is true of taxes, if they are too onerous they can dissuade firms from establishing operations in a city or town, and in some cases may encourage companies to close up shop and move to a location where the regulatory burden is lower. Moreover, it is not simply the level of regulation that matters but the uncertainty that sometimes attends its implementation. A firm that needs a zoning variance to construct its building may be frustrated for months as its request works its way through the local bureaucracy and any community review process that is stipulated in the zoning law. Fulfilling the letter of the law with regard to building codes and passing muster with the local building inspector can add a great deal of uncertainty to the investment process. Developers refer to the legal costs and time delays due to regulation as **soft costs**, but these can be as much a burden as the **hard costs** of capital, labor, and taxes.

In making investment decisions, firms differentiate between **risk** and **uncertainty**, and worry particularly about the latter. Risk involves the calculation of probabilities. A developer may not know for sure whether it will receive a municipal zoning variance that will permit it to build on a specified site, but if it knows that in 80 percent of cases in this city or town zoning relief is granted, it can take this risk into account in making its location decision. Uncertainly exists where the probabilities of something occurring are not known because the process is truly random or arbitrary. A city that develops a reputation for making zoning decisions that seem haphazard or indiscriminate will soon find that few businesses are willing to locate there.

Soule et al. (2004) found anecdotal evidence—from developers and location specialists who are charged with the responsibility of finding appropriate sites for business development—that regulatory costs are generally more burdensome in older industrial cities where the volume of zoning laws and building codes tend to be greater because they have evolved over many decades. Similarly, there is a widespread belief that communities in older cities have a stronger network of organizations that can resist new development through social pressure and legal action. This often presents an unacceptable level of uncertainty to firms and developers. As such, establishing a business in the suburbs, especially in younger areas farthest from the central city, is seen as less costly on regulatory grounds and on the basis of less uncertainty. Nonetheless, as newer suburbs mature with more residents and more firms, they too often add regulations that, according to some developers, are nearly as burdensome as those in older cities. This is especially true when it comes to zoning and the granting of building permits.

One particular approach to reducing the tax and regulatory burden in distressed areas is found in the concept of the **enterprise zone (EZ)**. The original idea was borrowed from the Margaret Thatcher government in Britain and gained adherents in the United States under the Reagan administration during the 1980s. Businesses that agree to locate in an economically distressed area designated as an enterprise zone are eligible for tax and regulatory relief. This relief can take many forms, including state sales tax exemptions, real estate assessment freezes, local property tax waivers, and waivers of building permit fees. In some cases, subsidies are provided to firms that hire workers in designated EZs. Although a federal enterprise zone law was not enacted until 1993 under the Clinton administration's **empowerment zone** program, at least 40 states have implemented some form of the legislation beginning as early as 1981 (Bingham 2003). Theoretically, other things held constant, firms can increase their after-tax profits by choosing to locate in an enterprise zone. In doing so, jobs are supposedly created where they are most needed—in depressed communities with high unemployment.

Increasing Social Amenities

Beyond what municipal leaders can do to augment the profits of companies that are willing to remain or settle in their city or town is a set of policies aimed at making their communities physically and culturally attractive to business leaders and employees. Most business leaders would rather live in communities where there is a bevy of cultural attractions, natural beauty, a wide availability of retail services, and sports franchises. A city rich in museums and parks, professional sports teams, and close to recreational areas often can use these amenities to attract businesses. That is why cities often bid for major-league teams by offering free land and subsidies for stadium construction. Since 1991, Phoenix, Arizona, has spent almost $1 billion on the construction of cultural and sporting attractions in the downtown area with the explicit goal of increasing business investment and boosting tourist trade (Bogart 1998). Phoenix is not alone. Since 1985, 71 major performing arts centers and museums have been built, renovated, or substantially expanded in cities that range from Baltimore, Newark, and Pittsburgh in the east to Atlanta, Charlotte, Miami, Nashville, and New Orleans in the South to Albuquerque, Denver, Dallas, and Seattle in the West. In 2001 alone, nearly $450 million was allocated by states across the country to help subsidize the construction of museums and art galleries, performing arts centers, and symphony halls (Strom 2002). In 2012, about 24 percent of the total annual funding of museums across the United States emanated from government coffers, the vast majority from state and local sources (Bell 2012).

There is still another way of looking at cultural amenities as a spur to regional economic growth. Richard Florida has argued that at one time, cities and towns grew prosperous because they were located near transportation routes or because they were endowed with valuable natural resources. Today modern business turns less on physical forms of capital and more on human capital. The human capital theory of economic development argues that "the key to regional growth lies not in reducing the costs of doing business, but in endowments of highly educated and productive people" (Florida 2002, p. 221). Even cities with a high cost of doing business such as Boston and San Diego survive and prosper because they can attract members of the **creative class**—those who work in such fields as science and engineering, computers and mathematics, education, arts and design, and entertainment.

Presumably, those metro areas that can attract a disproportionate share of the creative class are destined for greater prosperity in very much the same way that older industrial cities in the late nineteenth and early twentieth centuries grew prosperous if they had access to transportation and natural resources. According to Florida, what draws the creative class to places such as Washington, DC, Raleigh-Durham, Boston, Austin, San Francisco, Minneapolis, Denver, and Seattle is lifestyle, diversity, and social interaction. The best places offer a combination of a built environment and a natural environment conducive to indoor cultural attractions and outdoor recreation; culturally diverse neighborhoods that offer a variety of food, entertainment, and lifestyle; and a "vibrancy of street life, café culture, arts, music, and people engaging in outdoor activity—altogether a lot of active, exciting, creative endeavors" (Florida 2002, p. 232).

If this model of the new economy is roughly correct, then cities can do little to attract business by helping it to boost revenue or to cut the costs of capital, labor, raw materials, transportation, or taxes and regulations. Instead, a region that wishes to attract business must find ways to attract the creative class. This involves sizable investments in cultural amenities and improvements in the natural ecology of a region. In Florida's words, the winning municipalities of the future are going to be the ones that develop a world-class *people climate* rather than simply trying to create the best *business climate*. The former requires significant public-sector investments; the latter has historically required significant cuts in the revenues needed for those very investments.

What Works?

So far, we have laid out an extremely broad array of possible public policies to help attract investment and jobs. Table 16.1 summarizes all these policies in a simple taxonomy. But which of these work best and what are the costs of implementing

TABLE 16.1.   A TAXONOMY OF LOCAL AND STATE ECONOMIC DEVELOPMENT STRATEGIES

Assisting Firms in Boosting Their Total Revenue	
	Direct purchases of firm's product or service by local or state municipality
	State or local lobbying of federal government for federal contracts for local firms to produce goods or service for the federal government
Assisting Firms in Reducing Their Capital Costs	
	State issuance of tax-exempt industrial revenue bonds with the proceeds used to provide low-interest loans to private firms
	Urban Development Action Grant (UDAGs) to subsidize private capital investments in distressed neighborhoods
	State provision of venture capital to new start-up firms
	Tax increment financing to underwrite cost of infrastructure in neighborhoods
Assisting Firms in Reducing Their Labor Costs	
	State passage of right-to-work laws
	State and local investments in primary, secondary, and postsecondary education
	State and local investments in community colleges and technical training
	State subsidies for specialized training for individual firms or industries
Assisting Firms in Reducing Their Raw Materials, Natural Resources, and Transportation Costs	
	Local provision of water and sewer systems
	State or local investment in highways and on-off expressway ramps to meet individual company needs
	State and local investment in airports, seaport facilities
	Local development of industrial parks for the sitting of new business
Reductions in State and Local Taxes	
	Limit the number and type of state and local taxes on business
	Reductions in income and sales tax rates
	Local property tax abatements
Streamlining Regulations	
	Reduce the time for zoning variances
	Speed up the building code review process
	Create enterprise zones/empowerment zones in economically distressed areas within which the tax and regulatory burden is reduced
Increasing Social Arsenities	
	Subsidize construction of cultural venues and sports stadiums
	Public investment in parks, waterfronts, and festival areas

them? Let us take a look at what we think we know about the efficacy of all these strategies aimed at retaining or attracting businesses to a local community.

Once again, the concept of opportunity costs is central to any evaluation of these strategies. Pursuing a given strategy almost always reduces the funds available for pursuing something else. If implementing a particular strategy were truly costless—and it was not inherently counterproductive—then there would be little reason not to implement that strategy, even if the payoff in terms of investment and employment were minimal. But since every strategy has at least some opportunity costs, it needs to be weighed in some form of cost-benefit analysis.

Without taking into account the direct costs (and opportunity costs) of a particular development strategy as well as its benefits, it is possible and even likely to engage in strategies that are quite inefficient. By this, we mean that the goals of the strategy could have been met using fewer resources.

Those who have studied public policy have developed what has been called the "rational model" of policy implementation (Howlett and Ramesh 2003). It assumes that a "rational individual," in this case a mayor or city manager or a designated city planner or policy analyst, undertakes the following sequential set of activities:

1. *Establish* a goal for solving a problem.

2. *Explore all* alternative strategies of achieving the goal.

3. *Estimate* the probability of all significant consequences of each alternative strategy.

4. *Select* the strategy that most nearly solves the problem or offers the least costly solution.

For various reasons, the pure rational model is seldom followed. The Nobel Prize-winning economist Herbert Simon (1997) has studied the problem of public administration and policy implementation and concludes that "pure comprehensive rationality" is impossible because of two primary factors. First, there are cognitive limits to the decision-makers' ability to consider all options, forcing them to consider alternatives selectively. The number of possible options facing a city or town that wishes to attract investment and jobs is so great that only a few options can actually be analyzed with any rigor.

Second, each policy entails a bundle of favorable and adverse consequences that makes comparisons among them difficult. One policy may create more jobs than another, but the jobs may pay lower wages. Another may be more efficient but have distribution implications that are not favored. Therefore, there is no unambiguous best policy. No matter what strategy is contemplated by a mayor or city manager, one will find both winners and losers among his or her constituencies, especially when there are large opportunity costs attached to any single strategy.

As a result, it is nearly impossible in practice to pursue the pure rational model. At best, we get public decisions that do not necessarily maximize benefits over costs but merely tend to be satisfactory outcomes given the goals and criteria established by decision-makers. Simon concludes that this "satisficing" criterion is a realistic one given the bounded rationality with which human beings are endowed. It represents the best we can do.

With this as prologue, let us finally turn to examining the benefits and costs of the local development strategies outlined earlier.

Increasing a Firm's Total Revenue

As noted, there is little a municipality can do to add to corporate profitability on the revenue side of the company's accounts. What appears from anecdotal evidence is that this strategy only works as a sweetener when a company has already come close to selecting a location. Its cost to the government may be quite small if the product would have been purchased in any case.

More important, perhaps, is the belief on the part of corporate executives that local and state leaders will take an active role in lobbying for federal contracts. Economic advantage often has deep political roots. Knowing that a mayor, a governor, or a House or Senate member can be counted on to use political leverage to win contracts can help attract certain firms to a particular state or city. That is one reason why, regardless of political party, incumbents in the Congress, in state legislatures, and on city councils have an inherent advantage in elections. Their seniority is seen as giving them political clout when it comes to the allocation of federal, state, and municipal contracts. Local political leaders understand that in the real world, successful economic development strategies rely on many tactics.

Most local development strategies focus on the cost side of the company's ledger. Here we can look at the existing evidence regarding the efficiency and efficacy of these strategies. Again, returning to equation 16c, we can review these in order, beginning with incentives to assist a firm with its capital investments.

Reducing a Firm's Capital Costs

The evidence regarding public subsidy of private-sector capital costs is hardly conclusive despite the widespread use of industrial development bonds and, for at least a decade, UDAGs. Little is known about how important such subsidies have been for increasing the level of capital investment or redirecting investment into depressed cities, towns, older suburbs, and neighborhoods. It seems clearer that such subsidies are an expensive way to generate new jobs.

One example is provided by economic journalists Donald Bartlett and James Steele (1998), who have chronicled what has been dubbed **corporate welfare**—direct and indirect subsidies to corporations. They note as one example that in 1997 the city of Philadelphia and the state of Pennsylvania provided $307 million in incentives, including capital subsidies, to a Norwegian company to encourage it to reopen a portion of the closed Philadelphia naval yard. The project was a success from the point of view of restoring an important business in the city. However, given the level of incentives, the 950 jobs that were created "cost" $323,000 each. For the most part, these were good jobs that paid around $50,000 a year. Yet given local and state tax rates, it will take 48 years for the city and state to earn back its investment.

The question one should ask is whether that $307 million could have been spent in another way that would have created just as many or more good jobs at less than $323,000 each. In theory, there may have been a lot of possibilities for using that pool of public funds, but in practice the city fathers of Philadelphia were presented with a company willing to reopen the city's naval yard, and the decision had to be made whether to take the bird in hand or wait for the two that might be hidden in the bush. City managers would love the opportunity to make choices among a set of equally viable strategies, but they rarely have a chance to compare one strategy against another given the sequencing of available options and the fear that passing up one option to pursue another eliminates the possibility of coming back to the first if subsequent options prove illusory or more expensive. So despite the fact that public-sector subsidies of private-sector investment often appear economically inefficient, city and town officials find themselves in the political bind of being obligated to offer them, especially if jobs are desperately needed for their unemployed citizens.

Public venture funds, in theory, should be more cost efficient. If the private venture assisted through public investment proves profitable, the state or local venture capital program should earn back its investment plus a capital gain. The return could be used as part of a revolving credit system to assist additional start-ups or used to pay for normal public services. MassDevelopment is the quasi-public agency charged with this responsibility in Massachusetts. In 2003, this statewide development agency financed $860 million in projects across the state using development funds, tax-exempt bonds, and a variety of loan and guarantee programs. These ventures ranged from a $75,000 loan to a Boston-based community development corporation to conduct a brownfield site assessment for a possible new retail business establishment in the inner city to a $4 million tax-exempt bond refinancing for a manufacturing company in the middle of the state (MassDevelopment 2003). By 2018, MassDevelopment was either financing or managing 384 projects generating investment of more than $4.1 billion in the Massachusetts economy. The agency expected that these investments in the private sector would create or support nearly 11,000 jobs (MassDevelopment 2018).

MassDevelopment has a fine reputation, yet existing evaluations seem to show that public venture funds are likely to be effective only in a very limited number of metropolitan areas. These are locations where there is already a supply of the other inputs needed to make such risky new enterprise successful: a rich array of technologically savvy entrepreneurs and a technologically skilled labor force such as is found in Silicon Valley in California, the neighborhoods around Harvard University and MIT in Massachusetts, or the Research Triangle of Durham, Chapel Hill, and Raleigh, North Carolina. In most other cases, few jobs are generated as a result of public investment and the gains tend to be of a zero-sum variety where jurisdictions compete for investment in a manner that benefits private investors with little return to the community (Florida and Smith 1992).

Local communities that offer such capital subsidies and then carefully negotiate with private businesses over the conditions governing their granting are more likely to attain public benefits that would not otherwise be forthcoming. Robert Meir (1984) notes that one of the early UDAGs used by the city of Oakland, California garnered gains for inner-city businesses and minority residents. In return for providing 12.5 percent of the development costs of a new Hyatt Hotel in that city, the city council required the private developers to assure that at least a quarter of the construction expenditures went to minority contractors, that half the construction workforce should be minority, and that at least two-fifths of the professional work associated with the construction (e.g., architecture, engineering, legal) should be with minority firms.

The difficult questions that need to be answered by city leaders in deciding whether to grant a capital subsidy or other investment incentive should be: How many jobs will the project actually produce? Are they permanent or temporary? Who gets the jobs—city residents or suburbanites, the technically skilled or the unskilled (Krumholz 1984)? Without having answers to these questions and reasonable assurance from the private venture that certain job goals will be met, it is likely that any form of public subsidy to a private concern will end up failing a straightforward cost-benefit test.

Tax increment financing (TIF) seems to be a better targeted and more efficient investment instrument, particularly in blighted areas, but it is not without its costs or risks. Chicago provides a good example (Fitzgerald and Leigh 2002). In the 1990s, the Windy City created more than 110 TIF districts that cover a total land area with a 1995 assessed property tax value of more than $2 billion—nearly 7 percent of that year's total assessed property valuation of the entire city. Chicago used TIF financing to float bonds that were used to underwrite both private and public investment in these deteriorating areas. It combined up-front financing for public infrastructure with a pay-as-you-go system for private development whereby the private developers put up the initial cash for investment but then were partly reimbursed by the city over time as the tax revenues were realized. Essentially, this links public-sector investment in infrastructure to a property tax rebate for firms that invest in TIF districts. In just three of these Chicago TIFs, the city estimated that between 5,750 and 8,000 new jobs would be created on property that would rise in value to $315 million by 2015 from the undeveloped value of $135 million in 1998. What the city risked was that an increasing share of future tax revenues would be diverted to paying off bonds or reimbursing businesses rather than being available for improving public schools, repairing roads, cleaning up parks, and doing the thousands of other things cities need to do. Despite these concerns, TIFs continue to be one of the most used business incentive programs across the country.

Reducing Labor Costs and Increasing Skills and Education

Public investment in people rather than enterprises is generally considered a much better use of city or town resources. This is particularly true in an information age when a larger proportion of a firm's workers need an advanced education in order to perform their jobs. As such, the leaders of local communities with good public schools trumpet this fact when they are trying to attract new investment. Nonetheless, the best research into the impact of public school spending levels on employment growth yields mixed results. Of 19 research studies reviewed by Luce (1994) regarding the impact of various forms of public-sector spending on local employment growth, only six revealed a significant positive relationship between education spending and employment creation. Hence, while everyone will acknowledge that education is important, it is not clear that spending an additional $10 million or $100 million on schooling will result in more companies remaining in a community or additional companies choosing to locate there. Public spending on schools may be absolutely crucial to attracting private investment, but differences in spending among communities does not seem to be critical, at least in a preponderance of studies.

College and university education may be much more important in attracting industry. Given the emergence of an information-age society, one would think that state governments and local municipalities would be moving aggressively to expand their two-year community colleges and their state colleges and universities. These are training grounds for local workers and crucibles for developing new technology and they seem to pay off in terms of local output and employment. Timothy Bartik (1996), who has evaluated a variety of state incentives aimed at increasing local development, finds that public-service spending in general provides only a modest boost to economic development. But spending on public universities and colleges pays off handsomely. He found that an increase in higher education spending equal to 1 percent of a state's personal income and financed by an increase in property taxes increased state manufacturing output in the long run by 8.3 percent. In earlier research that compared education spending across 48 states between 1973 and 1980, Michael Wasylenko (1986) found that a 1 percentage point increase in the ratio of public education spending to state personal income was associated with a 0.72 percent increase in total employment.

Nonetheless, state funding for public higher education as a percentage of state tax revenue has been on a roller coaster, especially after 1990 (Feller 2004). In 1980, states spent 9.82 percent of their revenue on higher education; by 1990, they were spending 8.85 percent; and by 2000, only 6.94 percent—before recovering to 9.3 percent in 2004–2005 (US Bureau of the Census 2007) and remaining at that level through at least 2018 (Selingo 2018). That funding for public higher education has not grown any further, as a share of state budgets reflects the fact that public university officials have to compete with the growing demands on state budgets for elementary and secondary education, Medicaid and prisons, and shifting perspectives regarding whether the benefits from public universities and colleges accrue to society as a whole or just to the students who take advantage of subsidized higher education. If students and their families are willing to pay ever higher tuitions and fees, why should the state subsidize higher education at all? In this case, the private benefits are apparently so high that state and local communities receive the public benefits from advanced education at little or no public cost.

When one looks at the metropolitan regions growing the fastest, a common denominator seems to be the presence of one or more nationally prominent universities. Boston, Austin, Ann Arbor, Durham-Chapel Hill, and the region around Stanford University are the most noteworthy of these communities. What is likely true is less the pedagogical value of these schools per se than their research value. Each of these regions boasts universities that are heavily research-based with powerful laboratories and graduate programs producing scientific, engineering, and medical technology that can be transferred to viable private-sector firms in the community or provide the core ideas for new start-up ventures. Unfortunately, for those communities without such institutions of higher education, there is little that can be done on this front.

Programs that are directly aimed at reducing labor cost by providing job tax credits and specific training receive mixed reviews in the evaluation literature. Cost-benefit studies often show that tax credits linked to hiring and retraining disadvantaged individuals are not efficient or particularly effective. A US General Accounting Office (1991) study of the federal Targeted Jobs Tax Credit (TJTC) that compensated employers for hiring and retraining young workers, welfare clients, and the disabled found that more than half (55%) of employers actually hired a disadvantaged worker first and then found out they were eligible for a tax credit. Similarly, a US Department of Labor (1993) audit of the TJTC program found that for every dollar in program costs, there were only 37 cents in benefits to recipients and the public sector.

These high cost-benefit ratios are apparently commonplace. Ultimately, they may point to the weakness in existing job credit and training programs rather than the failure of a link between human capital investment and local economic development. Better and more finely targeted programs with real performance criteria might yield greater benefits.

Public Provision of Transportation and Land

As in the case of the support for public investment in education and training as a local economic development strategy, most economists and policy planners agree that metropolitan regions must supply an adequate amount of public infrastructure to meet the needs of business enterprise. This includes provision of sufficient water and sewerage capacity; roads, highways, rail, air, and mass transit to transport goods, workers, and customers; fair-priced electric and gas utilities; and land suitably zoned for industrial or commercial uses.

Separate research completed in the late 1980s and early 1990s by David Aschauer (1989) and Alicia Munnell (1990; 1992) suggested that public infrastructure investment was so critical to economic development that much of the decline in US productivity experienced in the 1970s could be traced to declining rates of public capital investment. According to Aschauer, a $1 increase in public capital stock raises private output by 60 cents. Munnell found a smaller impact, but by no means trivial: a 1 percent increase in public-sector capital investment yields a .34 percent increase in national output. While these precise estimates have been challenged by other economists (Holtz-Eakin 1993), there is no doubt that businesses demand high-quality infrastructure to remain in a location and they are especially demanding when choosing a new location.

Industrial Parks and Eminent Domain

Providing land for business enterprise is still another matter. In the case of public subsidies to build industrial parks, the use of eminent domain for private enterprise is a departure from its earlier use. Originally, states and cities used their eminent domain powers to secure land for public use, most importantly for obtaining the rights of way for new roads and highways. Clearly, such a purpose could be justified. From an equity perspective, the justification for taking land from one set of private citizens (with presumably fair compensation) to reallocate to other private parties is not as obvious. Moreover, even from an efficiency perspective it is not necessarily true that the new uses of the land will yield a higher return than the original uses.

Again, measuring the opportunity costs is critical. If the area to be turned into an industrial park is essentially vacant, then the cost to the city is equal to the price of securing the land from the current owners and rehabilitating the space for new tenants. City leaders need to calculate whether these direct costs will be recouped in the long run. This will depend on whether business tenants will set up operations in the new industrial park, how many jobs will be created and at what wages, and how much additional property tax will be generated by these new businesses. When a municipality begins to consider such an investment, it is unlikely that they have all the information they need to make a fully rational choice.

Reducing State and Local Taxes

More than 60 years of economic research has been devoted to assessing the impact of state and local taxes on the business location decision since the early work of Due (1961); Mueller et al. (1961); and Greenhut and Goldberg (1962). Nearly all this research concludes that state and local taxes are not a significant factor affecting firms' location decisions. Once a firm is satisfied that a community offers it a cost-effective combination of labor, transportation, raw materials, and quality-of-life factors, state and local taxes have little significance. Interview studies during the 1970s and early 1980s confirmed the early research in this regard.

Yet more recent surveys taken as markets have become more competitive both nationally and internationally suggest that while other factors remain more important, tax rates and tax incentives can sometimes be decisive factors in firm location decisions. A survey by Walker and Greenstreet (1991) found that 37 percent of new manufacturing plants that had accepted tax and financial incentives to locate in Appalachia would not, according to their owners, have set up operations in this region without them. Similarly, a study of firms that moved into a New Jersey enterprise zone found the zone's tax incentives were the sole or major factor in their location decision (Rubin 1991).

From the confusing array of tax-incentive studies, policymakers receive little guidance in what to do in any particular case. As Terry Buss has concluded, "Taxes should matter to states (and local communities), but researchers cannot say how, when, and where with much certainty. Firms may need tax incentives to increase their viability in some locations, but researchers cannot definitively say which businesses or which locations" (Buss 2001, p. 101). We need to ask whether the job gain to the locality that offers a tax incentive is offset by the loss of jobs to another municipality. When firms are induced to move from more viable locations to less viable ones in response to tax incentives, the result, even if beneficial to the winning locality, may well be a society that uses its resources less efficiently.

Streamlining Regulations and Enterprise Zones

Anecdotal evidence from developers and location specialists who advise firms on where to locate their operations suggests that with the spread of other incentives across so many jurisdictions, firms are looking now to such factors as the speed of building inspections and the difficulty of obtaining zoning variances in order to differentiate among possible sites. How important such bureaucratic factors are varies from industry to industry based on the complexity of the building inspection process (e.g., for biotech firms using dangerous microorganisms versus a plastics extrusion plant) and the market necessity for a speedy transition from building a new plant to actual occupancy and production.

Much more evidence exists regarding the efficacy of enterprise and empowerment zones. The establishment of an enterprise or empowerment zone would seem to provide obvious benefits to a community. In practice, it is harder to make a strong case for them. When an EZ is limited to a small, severely depressed area, as was the original intent, the economic limitations of such areas—locations with high crime, poor schools, and environmental distress—render it unlikely that private investment will respond to tax or regulatory relief. There are simply too many other factors that make such locations a high cost from the firm's point of view.

If, on the other hand, the EZ covers a large area, then the tax and regulatory relief is likely to be diluted, providing little incentive to firms. In either case, unless the EZ actually induces additional economic activity rather than redistributing existing activity from outside an EZ into it, then the overall result is a zero-sum game (Erickson 1992). In addition, if the incentives induce capital-intensive firms to enter the EZ, the result may be very little job creation in areas with high unemployment (Jacobs and Wasylenko 1981). Alternatively, if the EZ permits local minimum wage laws to be circumvented, more jobs may result, but at sweatshop wage levels.

In his assessment of enterprise zones at the beginning of the 1990s, Rodney Erickson concluded that while EZ programs were not a panacea for economic distress, notable economic improvement occurred in many zones (Erickson 1992). On average, nearly nine new establishments were developed in each zone with another nine firms expanding operations. According to Erickson's analysis, the mean investment in a zone exceeded $23 million and created or saved an average of 464 jobs. More than 60 percent of the jobs went to EZ residents and more than half went to low-income persons. On the other hand, the cost was not trivial: in excess of $106,000 per job created or saved. The added local tax revenues derived from greater EZ investments were sufficient apparently to offset the estimated tax losses.

Other researchers have come to less optimistic conclusions about the efficacy of empowerment zones. A 1999 study by the US Department of Housing and Urban Development (HUD) claims that EZs and so-called enterprise communities (ECs) have created 20,000 new jobs based on $4 billion of new private-sector investment (US Department of Housing and Urban Development 1999). But when University of Michigan planning professor Margaret Dewar (2000) reviewed the HUD study, she found that the assumptions behind this research were hard to maintain. Essentially, the study assumed that all new development in a zone was due to the EZ or EC incentives. This was in sharp contrast to the results in Dewar's own more detailed studies of employer behavior in three business districts in the Detroit EZ, where she found that the official EZ incentives had no impact on business investment, enterprise expansion, or firm location decisions.

Building Convention Centers and Sports Stadiums

Cities desperately compete to be prime destinations for conventions and trade shows and even more for professional sports franchises. Any mayor who sat back while his baseball, football, or basketball team was snatched away to another city would certainly find local fans cursing his name. Yet virtually every study evaluating the economic gains from public underwriting of convention centers and public subsidies to sports franchises has concluded that the economic benefits fall far short of the public costs.

For convention arenas, the problem lies in the number of cities that rely on this development strategy. With so many cities building convention centers and expanding them, total convention capacity exceeds total convention demand. As a result, convention and hotel occupancy rates are almost always lower than the rosy predictions conjured up by the consultants hired by cities to justify spending public dollars on convention center construction, expansion, and remodeling (Sanders 2002). The only big winners in the convention game appear to be Las Vegas, Orlando, and pre-Katrina New Orleans. The gambling capital (Las Vegas) has seen its number of top 200 trade show events increase from 17 in 1989 to 34 in 1999, while the city known as the Big Easy (New Orleans) hosted 17 of these massive trade shows and conventions, up from eight. Based on the successes of Walt Disney World, Universal Studios, and SeaWorld, Orlando parlayed its reputation as a tourist destination into a tourist plus conventioneer city, hosting 18 major trade shows in 1999.

Over the same period, Chicago was down from 29 to 23 conventions; New York, despite its massive investment in the Jacob Javits Convention Center, was down to 16 from 28; and Dallas was down from 20 to 11 (Sanders 2002). The story seems to be that if you are not already a tourist-based city, the chances of attracting major convention traffic is very low.

More recent data suggest that city subsidized convention centers are paying off even less (Sanders 2014). Between 1989 and 2011, the number of convention exhibition square feet nearly doubled from 36 million to 70.5 million. While the supply was close to double, demand for convention space remained virtually flat. As such, the actual number of convention visitors by local convention authorities fell well short of projections.

The data on state and municipal funds to help underwrite the development of sports stadiums do not provide much evidence of successful public investment. According to Noll and Zimbalist (1997), who have examined virtually every stadium project in recent history, "building a stadium is good for the local economy only if a stadium is the most productive way to make capital investments and use its workers." But the opportunity costs almost always exceed the benefits. They find that no recent facility, including the extremely popular Camden Yards in Baltimore, has earned anything that approaches a reasonable rate of return on public investment.

The problem is that a sports stadium does not have the export base potential of a convention arena. Most of the fans who come to games are from the locality and therefore do not generate any new revenue in the community. Essentially, stadiums serve the purpose of redistributing income from fans to owners and players but produce little new output or tax revenue.

Why Do Cities Pursue Economic Development Strategies with Such Low Payoffs?

If most of the economic development strategies pursued by state governments and local communities have benefit–cost ratios that are less than one, why do most states, cities, and towns pursue them? There are a number of answers to this question.

The first is simply that governments are run by politicians who need to demonstrate to their constituencies that they are working hard to solve such problems as unemployment and the poverty that afflicts disadvantaged groups within their jurisdictions. If issuing a tax-exempt industrial revenue bond, subsidizing a training program, building a new on-off ramp to a freeway, providing a business property tax abatement, creating an enterprise zone, or subsidizing the construction of a convention center provides some jobs or targets some of those jobs for disadvantaged workers, the subtleties of a poor cost-benefit ratio will often be overlooked. This is particularly true in communities that have long suffered deindustrialization. Because "something has to be done" to arrest economic decline and deterioration, many mayors, city councils, and governors grasp at straws to assuage their constituencies.

A closely related second reason is found in the literature on stakeholders. Even if the real cost-benefit ratio associated with a particular incentive is greater than one and even if a majority of constituents, if mobilized, would urge denial of the development scheme, a small group of powerful stakeholders can carry the day because of the real gain accruing to them. Thus, for example, team owners, local business leaders, and sports fans can exert so much pressure on local political leaders that mayors and city councilors find it difficult not to support an exorbitant demand for a publicly subsidized stadium.

A third reason has to do with what is known as the **prisoner's dilemma**. Cities are not in isolation when they are urged to consider stakeholder requests for location subsidies. In practice, a firm will play off one city against another in an attempt to win the best set of incentives it can muster. For example, let us say that a firm has considered three cities for a new branch office, and City A is found to be the lowest-cost option. The firm will still pursue City B and City C—or at least communicate to City A that it is considering doing so—to see what these cities will offer in the form of a property tax abatement or some other subsidy or to see if City A will make an offer itself. Not knowing definitively about any possible secret negotiations with B and C, City A will often offer a subsidy itself, fearing it could lose the firm to one of its competitor municipalities. Instead of being the exceptional case, this type of prisoner's dilemma is routinely faced by local governments. Individual cities would all fare better in this game if they could trust each other not to offer cost-ineffective subsidies. But the pressure to attract investment and jobs is so great that cities and states rarely trust each other in this high-stakes game.

Finally, there is the question of how to measure the opportunity costs of any given location incentive. In the best of all possible worlds, a city would be faced simultaneously with a large array of economic development policy options and then have the time and resources to make a careful assessment of the costs and benefits of each one. But this is rarely the case. Individual firms approach a municipality one at a time, which forces local leaders to make choices without having the full array of options. If you pass up pursuing a given firm that is considering the possibility of locating in your community, you have no idea when the next opportunity will arise and whether this opportunity is better or worse than what the first firm offered in terms of investment and jobs. Essentially, firms contemplating a location decision benefit from being in a monopoly position vis-à-vis cities and towns. Monopolists win when they can play one customer off against another.

In addition, simply measuring the opportunity costs is not at all easy. If a firm demands the equivalent of a $1 million tax subsidy, it is not easy to measure what the benefits would be if, instead of offering the subsidy, the city were to use these funds to improve their public schools, add an addition to a branch library, or invest in a public health program. The benefits from all these investments seem amorphous when compared with the alleged benefits that take the form of promised real investment and real jobs. Therefore, although most mayors and city managers will tell you that they know the location subsidy game is rigged against them, they will nevertheless play the game because they feel they have little economic or political option.

What Are the Most Powerful Ways for Cities to Attract Private Investment and Jobs?

Given what we know about all the ways urban communities might try to attract firms and jobs, what seems to work best? One part of the answer comes from a unique study carried out at Northeastern University between 2005 and 2015 (Bluestone 2014). At the beginning of this study, the research staff at the university's Dukakis Center for Urban and Regional Policy began developing a software instrument—the Economic Development Self-Assessment Tool (EDSAT)—that would make it possible for leaders of local government to assess more accurately their communities' capacity to attract business investment and create job opportunity.

The initial step in this process was to convene several focus groups, each consisting of about a dozen location and professional site specialists in Massachusetts, many of whom help firms find sites for new business establishments. These focus groups helped the Center develop a detailed survey about the factors that can influence business locations. The specialists differentiated between what they considered to be "deal breakers" and those they considered "deal makers." This survey was then distributed nationally to members of professional organizations whose members include real estate agents who work for large companies.

More than 230 members of these organizations completed the survey, ranking 39 different factors in the business location decision-making process using a four-point Likert scale (1 = unimportant; 4 = very important). The survey items covered a broad range of topics including rental rates, transportation access, infrastructure, labor market needs, municipal processes (e.g., zoning appeals and building code inspection practices), local tax rates, local business incentives, economic development marketing, crime rates, and school quality. The respondents ranked the following factors as most important in their assessment of a municipality's business environment:

FACTOR	MEAN LIKERT SCORE
On-site parking for employees	3.52
Building rental/lease rates	3.48
Availability of appropriate labor	3.37
Timeliness of approvals/appeals	3.33
Quality/capacity of infrastructure	3.22
Traffic congestion	3.21
State tax/financial incentives	3.17

Predictability/clarity in permitting	3.15
Competitive labor costs	3.15
Access to major highways	3.15
Property tax rates	3.13
Crime rates	3.13
Fast track permitting	3.07
Physical attractiveness of area	3.01

The following factors were ranked as less important in the location decisions:

FACTOR	MEAN LIKERT SCORE
Municipal minimum wage law	1.95
Access to railroads	2.16
Informative municipal website	2.18
Existence of strong trade unions	2.24
Sports/cultural amenities	2.35
Proximity to research/universities	2.37
Customized workforce training	2.51

According to the survey, location specialists consider the absence of on-site parking for employees and customers to be a major deal breaker. Similarly, rental/lease rates are a critical factor in whether a particular development site will be attractive to potential business investors. The quality of the labor pool is a major consideration as well, along with several measures of the speed with which a municipality deals with site approvals, zoning appeals, and building inspections. "Time to market" was a catchphrase heard often in the original focus groups with near total agreement that in the new, globalized, high-speed economy, firms need to have assurance that they can get up and running quickly so they can outrun the competition to the marketplace and thereby successfully market their products or services. Any municipal process that appreciably slows the pace of business development is considered a deal breaker. Property tax rates and local tax incentives were considered somewhat less important. Most of the focus group members agreed that many firms request a tax abatement or other development incentive only once they are satisfied with the other attributes of a particular municipality.

Among the factors considered relatively unimportant were several that might have been critical a generation or two ago. With the real value of minimum wage rates falling, few of the survey respondents considered that a local minimum wage would be a deal breaker for most firms, especially as most firms pay well above such levels. Given the sharp decline in union density and union power, few considered the presence of organized labor in a municipality to be a major barrier to business investment. Access to railroads, once critical to business, has been eclipsed by access to highways and airports. Even the quality of local schools and the proximity of universities and research institutions are seen as relatively unimportant factors in most business location decisions as firms are able to draw on a workforce from a broader region than the particular municipality in which the firm locates. The one major exception was for those industries that depend on a close working relationship with scientists and engineers (e.g., firms in the life sciences and other highly advanced technology-based industries), which still value highly a location near universities and research institutions (Bluestone and Clayton-Matthews 2013).

Based on the list of location factors identified by the expert focus groups and the Likert scores obtained from the survey of site specialists, the Center developed a questionnaire to be completed by municipal officials regarding their own city or town's ability to attract business investment and jobs. The process was enhanced when the municipal leaders invited others to answer the questionnaire including members of the local Chamber of Commerce, local bankers, educators from local community colleges or vocational schools, and other community organizations.

Using the municipal responses from more than 80 cities and towns in Massachusetts, it was possible to develop a correlation analysis between the change in employment between 2001 and 2013 in each community and how much each municipality pursued a given economic development strategy. That is, how large was the correlation between a community scoring high on an economic development factor and its growth in total employment in the community over the period 2001–2013.

Figure 16.1 reveals the study's highest zero-order correlation coefficients between individual economic development factors and employment growth.

By far, the measure most highly correlated with employment growth is available development sites, with a zero-order correlation coefficient of +.59. According to this measure, cities that have publicly owned sites available for economic development, protect industrial land from residential encroachment, have an active strategy for reclaiming vacant shopping centers and tax-delinquent properties, have up-to-date lists of existing commercial and industrial sites, or work actively with property brokers and developers to identify appropriate properties are substantially

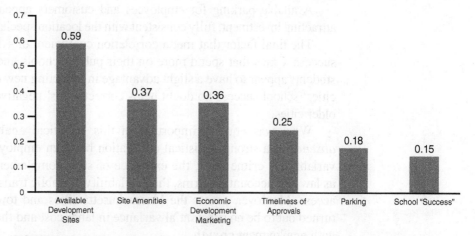

FIGURE 16.1. Working Cities: Factors Most Highly Correlated with Percentage Change in Employment, All Private Sector Industries 2001–2013

Source: Bluestone, 2014.

more likely to attract new employment to their communities. Clearly, if cities want to be in the running for new investment, they need to make development sites available.

Site amenities, with a correlation coefficient of +.37, are very important for attracting new employers. Firms are more likely to opt for sites with nearby fast-food restaurants for their employees, along with fine-dining facilities, retail shops, and day care centers.

Economic-development marketing has the third-highest positive correlation coefficient, just one point lower than the coefficient for site amenities. The EDSAT variables that comprise this measure include whether the city has a marketing strategy keyed to specific industry needs, whether it maintains a rapid-response team to cater to the concerns raised by the local business community, whether within municipal government there is a designated spokesperson for economic development, and whether the city engages its own populace in encouraging local business investment. Those municipalities that have more comprehensive marketing campaigns appear to do better in attracting business investment and jobs possibly in part because a comprehensive marketing campaign helps change the negative impressions—or what the location specialists call the **cognitive maps**—that location specialists and firms may have of older industrial cities. For this reason, development marketing may be much more important for cities that have experienced some degree of deindustrialization than for locations that have not suffered from this phenomenon and its oft-related urban decay.

Timeliness of the municipal approval process has the fourth-highest correlation coefficient (+.25). This measure is a composite of responses to 10 EDSAT questions regarding the time it takes a municipality to complete a site plan review, make a decision on a zoning variance, and grant a special permit or building permit, as well as the duration of the appeals process for new and existing structures. This measure's reasonably strong correlation with improved employment seems to confirm the importance of time to market which location specialists insist is a critical factor in today's global economy. Anything that slows this process puts a city at a disadvantage in its competition for business investment.

Available parking for employees and customers appears to be important for attracting investment, fully consistent with the location specialist survey results (+.18).

The final factor that met a correlation coefficient of +.15 or better was school success. Cities that spend more on their public schools and have more successful students appear to have a slight advantage in attracting new employers. Learning of cities' school success no doubt helps correct firms' negative preconceptions about older cities.

What was equally important in this statistical analysis was the apparent *absence* of a strong statistical correlation between employment growth and such variables as crime rates, the existence of such complementary business services as law and accounting firms, the availability of public transit, and nearby highway access. Moreover, across the Massachusetts cities and towns in this study, there turned out to be no substantial variance in labor cost and therefore zero correlation with employment growth.

Perhaps even more interesting was relatively large *negative* coefficients on such measures as high traffic congestion, low local tax rates, the level of reputed citizen opposition to development, the quality of available development sites, and the physical attractiveness of the city.

Apparently, being less physically attractive does not put a city at a disadvantage when it comes to attracting new businesses. Indeed, most surprising was that *higher*, not lower local tax rates, contributed to *better* employment outcomes between 2001 and 2013, suggesting the possibility that higher tax levies provide the possibility of better public services that are conducive to business.

Essentially, the results suggest that cities need to concentrate on readying sites for development and marketing the municipality so as to make these cities' positive attributes abundantly clear to location specialists and prospective firms. Assuring that firms will be able to obtain timely approval of their development plans appears to sway firms' decision on where to locate.

What was most encouraging for municipal officials in this analysis was the relatively high positive correlations for measures over which municipal leaders have some control. Timeliness of approvals and economic development marketing are factors that enlightened city government can implement if the will is there to do so. Making development sites available for business and equipping those sites with a range of amenities are steps municipal leaders can take that appear likely to attract business and employment. Many of the cities that have abandoned mills can be converted for new commercial and industrial uses.

It is more difficult to rapidly improve school quality or provide for adequate water, sewer, electric, gas, and communications infrastructure in cities that have deficits in these areas but if this analysis is accurate, these factors turn out to be somewhat less important for successful employment growth in working cities. Cities that have experienced severe deindustrialization in the past and are struggling to provide good schools and safe streets can affect their own economic destiny by focusing on improving municipal processes and using economic development marketing to change obsolete negative preconceptions about themselves. The key seems to be effective municipal leadership especially when it forges a strong working relationship with the local business community.

Innovation Districts

As we have noted at several points throughout this book, the "new growth theory" first developed by the Nobel prize-winning economist Robert Solow in the 1950s (Solow 1956), with expansions on this theory by a number of other economists, placed technological progress at the very epicenter of growth dynamics. According to this theory, while capital and labor are critical for economic growth, advances in technology and interdependencies between new ideas and new investment provide the basis for entire new industries and products that can be extremely useful to the public and highly profitable to the firms that adopt it. Moreover, the new growth theory posits a strong connection between skill acquisition among workers and the growth dividend society obtains from the new capital and new inventions that government can help to sponsor. As such, programs that combine incentives for innovation along with government or private resources to augment human capital can fuel rapid economic growth more than anything else society can do to promote prosperity.

This theory has been the basis for the creation of a relatively new approach to economic development—the creation of **innovation districts** that bring together in close proximity within a city all the ingredients needed to spawn new industry. With the emergence of digital technology and with the growth in biotechnology even before the onset of the COVID-19 pandemic in 2020, there has been a push by many states to develop innovation districts within their communities, centered around research universities, teaching hospitals, and research and development centers. The idea is to foster increased research and development (R&D), workforce development, capital availability, and face-to-face social networking where new high-tech products and services can be developed and marketed. Encouraged by municipal or state authorities, these new districts provide "collaborative environments that facilitate R&D innovation and promote the development, transfer, and commercialization of technology by providing a bounded and branded location in which companies, entrepreneurs, and research institutions and their highly skilled talent base operate in close proximity" (Tripp 2020).

By conservative estimates, there were already more than 100 innovation districts emerging around the world by 2020. In the United States alone, according to Wagner et al. (2020), roughly 20 districts have reached a high level of sophistication, concentrating in close proximity a mix of research institutions, mature companies, start-ups and scale-ups, coworking spaces, and supportive intermediaries. They find that such districts are emerging as powerful economic engines in their cities and metropolitan areas, serving as platforms for research commercialization, firm formation, and often transit-oriented development, as well as enhancing state and municipal tax revenues.

One example cited by Wagner et al. is the Pittsburgh Innovation District which has emerged as a global leader in robotics, machine learning, and immunology thanks to the research prowess of Carnegie Mellon University and the University of Pittsburgh and the consistent support of well-endowed philanthropies. They note that in Europe more than 40 districts are emerging, including those in the United Kingdom, Denmark, Sweden, and the Netherlands. With strong public and private support, new innovation districts are advancing quickly in cities in Germany, Italy, and France. The existing districts have been so successful that other nations such as Finland, Poland, and Ireland are considering investment in some of their key cities. Not to be left out, cities in Australia, Latin America, the Middle East, and Asia are observing the rise of innovation districts and are attempting to develop them based on their own specific innovation and research capacities.

Playing Industrial Policy Right: The Case of the Massachusetts Life Sciences Center

As we have noted, industrial policy has a mixed record of success. Too often cities desperate for investment and jobs have pursued individual firms with gifts of outright grants, tax-exempt bond financing, a promise of low or no taxes, and free land. The cost of many of these attempts outruns the benefits—or the benefits come at a price of hundreds of thousands of dollars per job.

There are some good examples of when industrial policy has been done effectively and efficiently. One of these involves the creation of the Massachusetts Life

Sciences Center (MLSC) (Bluestone 2020). In June 2006, the Massachusetts legislature created the new quasi-public agency to promote the life sciences within the Commonwealth. The then-governor, Deval Patrick, led this effort and he quickly gained legislative support for the concept of the new Center. By suggesting a plan to support not only pharmaceutical startups and new medical device manufacturers as well as university life science programs and local public infrastructure related to this emerging sector, the governor found widespread support for this new endeavor—from industry, the academic community, and local political leaders.

The MLSC was tasked with investing in life sciences research and economic development by making financial investments in public and private institutions. Its mandate was broad: to encourage basic research, development, and commercialization in the biosciences; ensure the preparation of a skilled workforce to meet the needs of the state's bioscience industry cluster; and build stronger collaboration between the sectors of the local and international life sciences community.

Instead of simply providing funds to individual companies, the MLSC was tasked with carrying out a broad array of industrial policies—from tax credits to the support of bioscience training—all aimed at assisting the development of an entire industrial sector, not just a few individual firms. Essentially, the goal was to create a statewide all-inclusive **ecosystem** for the life sciences—a statewide system of industries and institutions sharing common characteristics and complementary processes, technologies, needs, and outlooks within which the newly evolving life science industries could flourish.

To support the mission of the Life Science Center, Governor Patrick unveiled in May 2007 an ambitious plan for a ten-year $1 billion public investment in the new center that could be used for the range of initiatives developed by the Center. In June 2008, the legislature approved the governor's budget request with the aspiration of building on the existing strengths of the state's research universities, its world-renowned healthcare sector, and its emerging private-sector life sciences firms. The immodest goal was to make the Commonwealth the foremost location for life sciences in the world.

The MLSC took as its strategic mission the role of pulling together all the parts of the biotech sector, creating a dense, highly connected community of scholars, entrepreneurs, industry leaders, venture capitalists, and government officials dedicated to the success of the life sciences cluster of industries and institutions in the Commonwealth. As such, the Center has a wide spectrum of strategic priorities geared to enhance *all* aspects of this evolving sector. These include funding translational research (research that commercializes basic research into marketable products and services); investing in promising new technologies; ensuring worker-skill acquisition that aligns with the needs of the life sciences industries; creating new infrastructure that provides such needed resources as a ready supply of clean water for pharmaceutical manufacturing; and building partnerships between sectors of the local and international life sciences communities.

The critical element is how the MLSC functions. The MLSC operates under a Board of Directors that includes state government officials but also includes industry CEOs, leaders from academia and academic medical centers, bioscience researchers, and other nongovernmental leaders who have extensive life science experience. Investments are reviewed by a panel that draws from more than 200 experts who send their recommendations to the Center's Scientific Advisory Board (SAB), which itself is dominated by academic researchers, industry scientists, and private venture capital experts who together can judge the scientific and economic potential of an MLSC investment.

Most importantly, the Center insists on accountability in terms of private-sector investment matches and specific job creation goals and retains the power to "claw back" tax incentives and other investments when these employment goals are not reached by grant recipients. Accordingly, firms that receive MLSC tax incentives are required to report to the Center so that it can determine whether the awardee's job targets have been met. Companies that fail to achieve at least 70 percent of their job targets at the end of any annual reporting period are subject to an investigation to determine the cause of this "material variance." In cases where it is found that the company cannot meet its requirements, the Center notifies the Massachusetts Department of Revenue so that the department can initiate procedures to recover the tax value of any award provided.

As such, by relying on scientists and engineers to decide where best to place MLSC funds and by utilizing the claw-back provision when necessary, the MLSC not only provides a broad array of support to the biotech cluster, but insulates the entire process from political manipulation and possible corruption. As such, in its report on creating fiscally sound state tax incentives, the Pew Center on the States singled out the Massachusetts Life Sciences Tax Incentive Program for its focus on annual cost controls and its reliance on scientific merit in making awards (Pew Center on the States 2012).

The creation of the Mass Life Sciences Center as a comprehensive industrial policy in an evolving industrial sector has paid off handsomely for the state. Between 2001 and 2017, the number of life science jobs in the state increased by 45 percent, much of this after the MLSC was introduced. What makes this rapid growth in life sciences employment stand out even more since the creation of the MLSC is how this sector has grown relative to this sector in the rest of the United States. Nationally, employment in the cluster of life science industries increased by 7.5 percent between 2007 and 2017. In Massachusetts the growth was more than three times as great—23 percent.

There appear to be five main lessons to be drawn from the experience of MLSC to date.

1. Long-term success in the use of tax incentives and business loans is most likely to occur when funds are focused on a group of firms and a set of technologies in a given industry rather than a single firm, thus helping to create an industrial ecosystem that in turn attracts and nurtures new firms in the state.

2. The use of expert panels to determine loan and grant awards significantly increases the likelihood that these funds will be well-utilized. The concomitant use of claw-back provisions to recapture funds from companies that fail to meet stated employment goals is an important motivational tool and safeguard.

3. The focus on encouraging firms in their early-stage innovation activity is central to promoting economic growth and prosperity.

4. Helping fund workforce development efforts for critical industries as part of the mandate helps assure a pipeline of skilled workers for the industry and this activity in and of itself helps attract new firms to the region.

5. Taking a "portfolio" approach to the entire range of activities in the life sciences helps sustain all elements of that particular industrial/economic sector and creates a self-reinforcing **virtuous cycle** of discovery, innovation, investment, and employment.

6. Whether this model can work in other sectors is still to be determined. But as small firms lead technological revolutions in future products and services, one could imagine the creation of federal and state industrial policies aimed at supporting the entire ecosystems of these yet-to-be-developed industries.

What Should City Leaders and Policymakers Do to Play the Economic Development Game Better?

In Chapter 5 we concluded that the quality and quantity of an area's productive resources are the real key to its long-term prosperity. To the extent that local policymakers are able to augment and improve their social and physical infrastructure through investment in education as well as in transportation and communication networks, they can create places that are attractive to businesses because of their inherent productivity—their ability to generate external economies. Nevertheless, for cities that face job loss and economic stagnation, the pressure to offer location incentives can be overwhelming. While few cities can opt out from actively encouraging economic development to retain firms and attract new ones, there are at least some basic principles that local officials and state agencies should follow. Terry Buss (2001, pp. 101–102) provides an excellent summary of them:

1. Require cost-benefit studies prior to making large incentive awards to individual firms or inaugurating new or revised tax incentive programs.

2. Require periodic evaluations of all tax incentive programs.

3. Require sunset provisions for all economic development legislation and terminate programs after a set period of time unless explicitly reauthorized by new legislation.

4. Require truth and disclosure in financing provisions rendering all aspects of a public subsidy program transparent to all constituencies.

5. Require legally binding performance contracts and penalize firms for not meeting the goals established in exchange for incentives.

6. Embed specific incentive programs within broader cohesive strategic plans so that any incentives offered have maximum impact.

7. Eliminate entitlements to just any business that wants incentive programs. Do not be overgenerous and be sure to carefully negotiate with firms to reduce unneeded public expenditures.

8. Award incentives only if they do not put other businesses in a less competitive position.

9. Avoid redistributing wealth by using incentives. Be careful not to tax low-income families in order to award wealthy interests with large economic gains.

10. Encourage public participation in debates over the issuing of location incentives.

All of these are good suggestions for when you decide to run for mayor; the hard part will be putting them into practice once you win.

References

Aschauer, David Alan. 1989. "Is Public Expenditure Productive?" *Journal of Monetary Economics* 23, no. 2 (March): 177–200.

Bartik, Timothy J. 1996. *Growing State Economies: How Taxes and Public Services Affect Private-Sector Performance*. Washington, DC: Economic Policy Institute.

Bartlett, David, and James Steele. 1998. "Corporate Welfare." *Part One. Time*, November 8 (reprint).

Bell, Ford W. 2012. "How Are Museums Supported Financially in the United States." March. Washington, DC: US State Department.

Bingham, Richard D. 1998. *Industrial Policy American Style: From Hamilton to HDTV*. New York: M. E. Sharp.

Bingham, Richard D. 2003. "Economic Development Policies." In *Cities, Politics, and Policy*, edited by John P. Pelissero. Washington, DC: CQ Press, pp. 237–253.

Blair, John P., Rudy H. Fictenbaum, and James A. Swaney. 1984. "The Market for Jobs: Locational Decisions and the Competition for Economic Development." *Urban Affairs Quarterly* 20:1 (September): 64–77.

Bluestone, Barry. 2014. "What Makes Working Cities Work? Key Factors in Urban Economic Growth." *Community Development Brief No. 3*, May. Boston: Federal Reserve Bank of Boston.

Bluestone, Barry. "The Massachusetts Life Sciences Center: An 'Ecosystem' Approach to Industrial Policy." In *Understanding Industrial Policy*, edited by Ian Fletcher 2022.

Bluestone, Barry, and Alan Clayton-Matthews. 2013. *Life Sciences Innovation as a Catalyst for Economic Development: The Role of the Massachusetts Life Sciences Center*. Boston: The Boston Foundation.

Bluestone, Barry, and Bennett Harrison, 1982. *The Deindustrialization of America: Plant Closings, Community Abandonment, and the Dismantling of Basic Industry*. New York: Basic Books.

Bogart, William Thomas. 1998. *The Economics of Cities and Suburbs*. Upper Saddle River, NJ: Prentice Hall.

Buss, Terry. 2001. "The Effect of State Tax Incentives on Economic Growth and Firm Location Decisions: An Overview of the Literature." *Economic Development Quarterly* 15, no. 1 (February): 90–105.

Council of Development Finance Agencies. 2019. *CDFA Annual Volume Cap Report*. October. Columbus, OH: Council of Development Finance Agencies.

DeHaven, Tad. 2012. "Corporate Welfare in the Federal Budget." *Policy Analysis No. 703*, July 25. Washington, DC: Cato Institute.

Dewar, Margaret. 2000. *The Detroit Empowerment Zone's Effect on Economic Opportunity: Employers' Responses to the Zone's Programs and Incentives*. Ann Arbor: University of Michigan Urban and Planning Program.

Due, John. 1961. "Studies of State and Local Tax Incentives on Location of Industry." *National Tax Journal* 14:2 (June): 163–173.

Erickson, Rodney A. 1992. "Enterprise Zones: Lessons from the State Government Experience." In *Source of Metropolitan Growth*, edited by Edwin S. Mills and John F. McDonald. New Brunswick, NJ: Center for Urban Policy Research, pp. 161–182.

Feller, Irwin. 2004. "Virtuous and Vicious Cycles in the Contributions of Public Research Universities to State Economic Development Objectives." *Economic Development Quarterly* 18, no. 2: 138–150.

Fitzgerald, Joan, and Nancey Green Leigh. 2002. *Economic Revitalization: Cases and Strategies for City and Suburb*. Thousand Oaks, CA: Sage.

Florida, Richard. 2002. *The Rise of the Creative Class*. New York: Basic Books.

Florida, Richard, and Donald F. Smith, Jr. 1992. "Venture Capital's Role in Economic Development: An Empirical Analysis." In Edwin Mills and John F. McDonald, eds., *Sources of Metropolitan Growth*, New Brunswick, N.J. Center for Urban Policy Research, pp. 183–209.

Furdell, Phylis A. 1994. *Poverty and Economic Development: Views of City Hall*. Washington, DC: National League of Cities.

Greenhut, M., and M. Goldberg. 1962. *Factors in the Location of Florida Industry*. Tallahassee: Florida State University Press.

Howlett, Michael, and M. Ramesh. 2003. *Studying Public Policy*. New York: Oxford University Press.

Holtz-Eakin, Douglas. 1993. "Correspondence: Public Investment in Infrastructure." *Journal of Economic Perspectives* 7, no. 4 (Fall): 231–234.

Jacobs, S., and M. Wasylenko. 1981. "Government Policy to Stimulate Economic Development: Enterprise Zones." In *Financing State and Local Governments in the 1980s: Issues and Trends*, edited by N. Walzer and D. L. Chicoine. Cambridge, MA: Oelgeschlager, Gunn, and Hain, 175–201.

Jones, Brian, and Lynn W. Bachelor. 1993. *The Sustaining Hand*, 2nd ed. Lawrence: University of Kansas Press.

Krumholz, Norman. 1984. "Recovery of Cities: An Alternate View." In *Rebuilding America's Cities: Roads to Recovery*, edited by Paul R. Porter and David C. Sweet. New Brunswick, NJ: Center for Urban Policy Research, pp. 173–190.

Leonard, Herman P., and Jay H. Walder. 2000. *The Federal Budget and the States*, 24th ed. Cambridge, MA: Taubman Center for State and Local Government, John F. Kennedy School of Government.

Luce, Thomas. F. 1994. "Local Taxes, Public Services, and the Intrametropolitan Location of Firms and Households." *Public Finance Quarterly* 22, no. 2 (April): 139–167.

Lynch, Robert G. 2004. *Rethinking Growth Strategies: How State and Local Taxes and Services Affect Economic Development*. Washington, DC: Economic Policy Institute.

Maguire, Steven, and Joseph S. Hughes. 2018. "Private Activity Bonds: An Introduction." July 13. Washington, DC: Congressional Research Service.

MassDevelopment. 2003. *Annual Report 2003*. Boston: MassDevelopment.

MassDevelopment. 2018. *Annual Report 2018*. Boston: MassDevelopment

Meir, Robert. 1984. "Job Generation as a Road to Recovery." In *Rebuilding America's Cities: Roads to Recovery*, edited by Paul R. Porter and David C. Sweet. New Brunswick, NJ: Center for Urban Policy Research, pp. 160–172.

Mueller, Eva, Arnold Wilken, and Margaret Woods. 1961. *Location Decisions and Industrial Mobility in Michigan*. Ann Arbor, MI: Institute for Social Research.

Munnell, Alicia. 1990. "Why Has Productivity Declined? Productivity and Public Investment." *New England Economic Review* (January/February): 3–22.

Munnell, Alicia. 1992. "Policy Watch: Infrastructure Investment and Economic Growth." *Journal of Economic Perspectives* 6, no. 4 (Fall): 189–198.

Noll, Roger G., and Andrew Zimbalist. 1997. *Sports, Jobs, and Taxes: The Economic Impact of Sports Teams and Stadiums*. Washington, DC: Brookings Institution.

Pack, Howard, and Kamal Saggi. 2006. "Is There a Case for Industrial Policy? A Critical Survey." *The World Bank Research Observer* 21, no. 2 (July): 267–297.

Pagano, Michael A., and Ann Bowman. 1995. *Cityscapes and Capital*. Baltimore: Johns Hopkins University Press.

Parilla, Joseph, and Sifan Liu. 2018. "Examining the Local Value of Economic Development Incentives." March. Washington, DC: Brookings Institution, Metropolitan Policy Program.

Pelissero, John P., ed. 2003. *Cities, Politics, and Policy: A Comparative Analysis*. Washington, DC: CQ Press.

Pew Center on the States. 2012. "Avoiding Blank Checks: Creating Fiscally Sound State Tax Incentives." December. Washington, DC: Pew Research Center.

Pianin, Eric. 2017. "Some States Spend Billions on Economic Tax Incentives for Little or No Return." *The Fiscal Times*, May 7.

Pollin, Richard, and Dean Baker. 2009. "Public Investment, Industrial Policy and U.S. Economic Renewal." *Working Paper Series Number 211*, December. Washington, DC: Center for Economic and Policy Research.

Reich, Robert. 1982. "Why the U.S. Needs an Industrial Policy." *Harvard Business Review* 60:1 (January). https://hbr.org/1982/01/why-the-us-needs-an-industrial-policy

Rubin, Marilyn. 1991. "Urban Enterprise Zones in New Jersey: Have They Made a Difference?" In *Enterprise Zones*, edited by Roy Green. Newbury Park, CA: Sage.

Sagalyn, Lynne B. 1997. "Negotiating for Public Benefits: The Bargaining Calculus of Public-Private Development." *Urban Studies* 34, no. 12 (December): 1955–1971.

Sanders, Heywood T. 2002. "Convention Myths and Markets: A Critical Review of Convention Center Feasibility Studies." *Economic Development Quarterly* 16, no. 3 (August): 195–210.

Sanders, Heywood T. 2014. *Convention Center Follies: Politics, Power, and Public Investment in American Cities. Philadelphia, PA*. University of Pennsylvania Press.

Selingo, Jeffrey J. 2018. "States Decision to Reduce Support for Higher Education Comes at a Cost." *Washington Post*, September 8.

Simon, Herbert A. 1997. *Administrative Behavior*, 4th ed. New York: Free Press.

Solow, Robert M. 1956. "A Contribution to the Theory of Economic Growth". *Quarterly Journal of Economics*. 70 (1) (February): 65–94

Soule, David, Joan Fitzgerald, and Barry Bluestone. 2004. "The Rebirth of Older Industrial Cities: Exciting Opportunities for Private Sector Investment." Boston: Center for Urban and Regional Policy.

State of California. 2003. *California State Abstract*. Table C-3. December. Sacramento: California Department of Finance.

Stensrud, Christian. 2016. "Industrial Policy in the United States." October. London: Civitas: Institute for the Study of Civil Society.

Stephenson, Max O. 1987. "The Policy and Premises of Urban Development Action Grant Program Implementation: A Comprehensive Analysis of the Carter and Reagan Presidencies." *Journal of Urban Affairs* 9, no. 1 (Winter): 19–35.

Strom, Elizabeth. 2002. "Converting Pork into Porcelain: Cultural Institutions and Downtown Development." *Urban Affairs Quarterly* 38, no. 1 (September): 3–22.

Tripp, Simon. 2020. "New Empirical Evidence: How One Innovation District is Advancing the Regional Economy." March 12. *The Global Institute on Innovation Districts*. https://www.giid.org

US Bureau of the Census. 2007. "State and Local Government Finances by Level of Government and by State: 2004–05." Table 1. May. https://www.census.gov/programs-surveys/gov-finances/data/datasets.All.html

US Department of Housing and Urban Development. 1999. *Now Is the Time: Places Left Behind in the New Economy*. Washington, DC: Government Printing Office.

US Department of Labor, Office of Inspector General. 1993. *Targeted Jobs Tax Credit Program*. Washington, DC: Government Printing Office.

US General Accounting Office. 1991. *Targeted Jobs Tax Credit*. Washington, DC: Government Printing Office.

Wagner, Julie, Bruce Katz, and Thomas Osha. 2020. "The Evolution of Innovation Districts: The New Geography of Global Innovation." *The Global Institute on Innovation Districts*. https://www.giid.org/the-evolution-of-innovation-districts/

Walker, Robert and David Greenstreet, 1991. "The Effect of Government Incentives and Assistance on Location and Job Growth in Manufacturing." *Regional Studies* 25(1) (February): pp. 13–30.

Wasylenko, Michael. 1986. *The Effect of Business Employment on Employment Growth*, Vol. 2. Minneapolis: Minnesota Tax Study Commission Staff Papers.

Questions and Exercises

1. Manufacturing industries often provide good jobs at reasonably good wages for workers who have not completed college. Using the following website from the US Bureau of Labor Statistics, select ten metro areas of your choice and calculate manufacturing's percentage of total employment in each: https://www.bls.gov/opub/ee/2019/sae/tabled3_201901.htm.

   • Which of these metro areas has the highest manufacturing percentage?

   • Which of these metro areas has the lowest manufacturing percentage?

   • For the most recent period, has manufacturing employment been on the increase or decrease in each of these metro areas?

2. StatsAmerica has a powerful tool that identifies what individual cities and towns are doing to promote economic development. This can be found at http://www.statsamerica.org/innovation/sitemap.html.

   • Using this data source, first study how the innovation index is calculated noting what factors are used to derive it.

   • Using the data in this website, select ten counties across the country of your choice and see how the innovation index varies among them.

   • Which three of the counties you chose has the highest innovation indices? Which three have the lowest?

   • Using your browser, see what you can learn about the specific economic development policies used in the three counties you selected.

Urban Well-Being and Civic Engagement in the Twenty-First Century

17

LEARNING OBJECTIVES

- Describe the advantages and disadvantages of common interest developments such as business improvement districts or homeowners' associations

- Explain Hirschman's concepts of exit, voice, and loyalty and apply them to a current issue that affects metropolitan areas

- Define social capital and show how it may be used to assess the situation of individuals within a community

- Explain Newman's concept of defensible space and apply it to the physical design of neighborhoods

- Discuss the complex ways in which the COVID-19 pandemic might have affected the location decisions of households and businesses

- Describe the Rawlsian concept of the veil of ignorance and explain the influence it might have on the ways people might describe their ideal city

Chicago suffered a brutal heat wave in July 1995 during which there were more than 700 heat-related deaths. Those likeliest to die were elderly poor people who lived alone. Yet as Eric Klinenberg (2002) discovered in *Heat Wave,* his "social autopsy" of the event, two equally poor neighborhoods experienced strikingly different death rates for their most vulnerable residents. He found that a person's chance of surviving depended not only on individual characteristics such as age and income, but on the characteristics of the neighborhood in which that person lived.

The same was true when the COVID-19 pandemic struck. The Commonwealth of Massachusetts published infection rates and death rates for each of its 351 municipalities during the outbreak. In the Greater Boston metropolitan area, the highest rates per 100,000 residents were found in the lowest incomes communities.

In Chelsea, just north of Boston, the infection rate was 8,830; in Brockton just south of Boston, the rate was 4,426. By contrast, Boston itself had an infection rate of 2,429 while the richer suburbs of Brookline, Newton, and Dover were all under 1,000 per 100,000 residents (Huddle and Bailey-Wells, 2020).

Why are some communities and neighborhoods better able to protect their most vulnerable residents? What constitutes a good neighborhood? As a society, what can we do to promote healthy communities? As we have done throughout this book, we use the criteria of social equity and economic efficiency to examine these questions and look closely at issues of consumer sovereignty and positive and negative externalities.

What Do We Want from Our Neighborhoods and How Do We Get It?

If we asked a thousand individuals to describe their ideal neighborhood, we would likely receive a thousand different and conflicting answers. One person might say the ideal neighborhood must contain a skateboard park, while another thinks that skateboarding should be prohibited; one might say that it should be an area where pets can roam freely, while another might want pets to be closely confined. Nevertheless, there are some fundamental characteristics of a good neighborhood on which we would expect wide agreement.

- A good neighborhood is a place where people feel safe and secure inside their own homes or out and about. It is a place where the most vulnerable residents—children, the elderly, the infirm—are protected.

- A good neighborhood facilitates good health for its residents and is free of environmental hazards that pollute the earth, air, and water.

- A good neighborhood minimizes intrusions such as noise, garbage, and other assaults on the senses. It is a place where people are respectful both of common areas and of other peoples' property.

- A good neighborhood is a place where schoolchildren can flourish and all people—not just children—can continue to grow and to learn.

- A good neighborhood provides access to transportation beyond its boundaries for employment, shopping, and other purposes.

- A good neighborhood is responsive to the needs and desires of its residents. It is a place where people feel a civic responsibility to the community and to each other.

- A good neighborhood is a place where people care about each other and the broader community.

Since some elements of a good neighborhood are widely shared beliefs while others may vary from one individual to another, the ability of households to sort themselves according to their preferences—to "vote with their feet" and move to an area populated with like-minded individuals who share their preferences with regard to local taxing and spending patterns—would seem to maximize satisfaction and epitomize efficiency in the use of resources. This is the Tiebout hypothesis we examined in Chapter 7. Tiebout (1956) used this approach to argue that the division of a metropolitan area into many small and varied jurisdictions was desirable precisely because it allowed each household to choose the public-sector package that maximized its satisfaction.

The Tiebout Hypothesis and the Privatization of Public Space

Tiebout was theorizing about how to maximize satisfaction from the collective consumption of goods provided by local government. In recent decades, private organizations have been formed with the same purpose in mind. These **common interest developments** refer to ways in which individual households or businesses form associations to pursue common goals through shared consumption. In some respects, these associations have taken on some of the traditional roles of local government. A **business improvement district (BID)**, for example, is comprised of businesses within a neighborhood that form an association and assess fees from their members to provide such services as additional street cleaning or private security patrols beyond the level of service provided by the municipality. The association might provide sidewalk amenities such as the planting of trees and flowering bushes. It might engage in marketing and promotional activities. Some BIDs have even more ambitious capital improvement and social service programs.

Several questions have been raised about the way BIDs operate. For example, since BIDs give large property owners disproportionate weight in decision-making, are they democratic? Since BIDs operate with a high degree of autonomy, are they accountable to the citizens of the jurisdiction? Since BIDs provide extra security within their boundaries, do they actually reduce crime or do they simply displace it to neighboring areas, thereby causing negative spillovers (Briffault 1999; Hoyt and Gopal-Agge 2007)?

Homeowners have also formed associations to provide themselves with services over and above those provided by the municipality. Like the business improvement districts, fees assessed by the homeowners' association might cover private security patrols, street cleaning, and snow removal. If the homeowners' association precedes the development's construction, which is usually the case, streets inside the development might be wholly owned and maintained by the association.

When households buy property that is part of a homeowners' association, they must agree to join the association and abide by its rules. These might include a lengthy list of restrictions: no outside clothes lines, exterior paint choice limited to a handful of acceptable shades, no garbage cans visible from the street, no multicolored Christmas lighting, and a host of other restrictions. A household that moves into such a development gives up its right to place an unregistered car on cinder blocks in its driveway in return for the assurance that none of its neighbors will be able to do so either. Essentially, the household surrenders some of its consumer sovereignty in order to reduce the possibility of suffering a negative externality.

While a municipality is limited in its ability to place restrictions on household behavior through zoning laws, a homeowners' association, condominium organization, or housing cooperative can accomplish a far greater degree of control through its contractual bylaws. Whatever amenities such community associations agree to provide—a swimming pool, a golf course, tennis courts—will be paid for by association members and their use will be limited to members only. In this sense, it is, though usually on a smaller scale, a private-sector analog to the local public-sector theory developed by Tiebout.

The number of US households belonging to community associations has increased dramatically since 1970. Back then there were about 10,000 such associations nationwide, with just 2.1 million households living in 700,000 housing units. By 2018, such housing had become so popular that there were 347,000 such organizations with 73.5 million resident members living in nearly 27 million housing units. Over this period, the proportion of the US population living in housing governed by a private community association has risen from less than 1 percent to more than 22 percent (Community Associations Institute 2019). In some instances, homeowners' associations beyond the boundaries of growing cities provide services in the absence of local government and continue to provide these services even after annexation has occurred.

Robert Nelson (2005) argues that while municipal zoning represents one response to dealing with externalities, private associations represent another response through the establishment of private property rights. This is analogous to the Coasean solutions we discussed in Chapter 13. Arguing within this framework of maximizing the role of the market and minimizing the role of government, Nelson posits that it would be desirable to allow neighborhood-size private communities to replace local government even to the extent of replacing the "one-person one-vote" process of decision-making in the public sector with the "one-share one-vote" process of decision-making among stockholders in private corporations.

Such a proposal flies directly in the face of long-standing democratic principles. The principle that each citizen is entitled to equal representation was reaffirmed in the landmark 1967 US Supreme Court decision *Avery v. Midland County*—referred to at the time as the principle of "one man, one vote." Moreover, as eminent economist Arthur Okun warns in his examination of the balance between political rights and economic rights, although there is a place for the market, we must know when to "keep the market in its place" and not impinge on basic human rights in a free society (Okun 1975).

Gated Communities and the Avoidance of Dis-Amenities

In some instances, homeowners' associations have gone beyond the step of creating developments in which everything, including the streets, is privately owned and maintained. They have erected walls, fences, and gates to exclude those who do not own property within. These gated communities have been growing in popularity over the last few decades. According to a study by City Lab, some 6 to 9 million Americans lived in gated communities in 2013, with the highest proportion in western and southern states (Goodyear 2013).

The United States is not alone when it comes to gated communities. In Brazil, particularly in Sao Paulo and Rio de Janeiro, the most widespread gated community is called a *condomínio fechado* (closed housing estate) where the upper classes desire to live. These closed housing estates are really small private towns with their own infrastructure, including a reserve power supply, sanitation, and security guards (Low 2001). Likewise, there are many gated communities in Argentina, especially in Greater Buenos Aires, some of which date back to the 1930s and 1940s. Gated communities can be found in cities around the world including Shanghai, Cairo, New Delhi and Mumbai; outside of Beirut; in Monterrey, Mexico City, and Guadalajara; in Lima; and even in Moscow.

Blakely and Snyder (1997) identify three different types of gated communities: (1) the recreation and retirement communities organized around leisure lifestyle activities such as golf and tennis, (2) the elite communities of the rich and famous, including celebrities who wish to maintain their privacy and noncelebrities who wish to enjoy the prestige of living in such an expensive and exclusive area, and (3) the embattled zone areas in which barriers are retrofitted onto vulnerable communities in an effort to reduce high crime rates. Many of the communities in this last category have little in common with the previous two, in which boundaries are intended to be impermeable and space is privately owned. They include neighborhoods in which road barriers prevent the passage of automobiles, but where pedestrians can move freely. They include public housing projects in which gates were installed despite residents' objections. Notwithstanding this last category, most gated communities attract households that have a great deal of choice about where to live and intentionally choose to withdraw into a private realm.

While the Tiebout hypothesis emphasizes maximization of household choice about a community's spending and taxing patterns, the flip side of associating with those whose preferences most closely match one's own is the aversion to associating with those who are different. In *Behind the Gates,* sociologist Setha Low (2003) interviewed residents of several gated communities. Some of these communities were in the West and Southwest, others in the Northeast; some were middle income, others were upper-middle income or high income. Some fell into the "lifestyle" category described by Blakely and Snyder, while others were in their "elite" category. The common theme that emerged in all these communities was a concern for safety and security and, in some instances, fear of others who were of different race, ethnicity, or income class. Low argues that the focus on safety and security may be unwarranted given that the nongated alternatives generally available to this group are comprised of other neighborhoods in which crime rates are already quite low.

In a few instances, gated communities in California and Florida have incorporated as municipalities, taking privatization of public space to its logical conclusion. While Nelson might see this as a triumph of private property rights, Blakely and Snyder view it as secession from civic responsibility. In the context of a rapid growth in the number of gated communities, Blakely and Snyder ask, "Can this nation fulfill its social contract in the absence of social contact?"

Dissatisfied Citizens and Their Choices: Exit Versus Voice

As we can imply, the Tiebout hypothesis can be considered the public-sector analog to the theory of competition in the private sector. Households vote with their feet to choose the jurisdiction that best satisfies their local public-sector taxing and spending preferences, just as they maximize satisfaction in the private sector by choosing from an array of alternatives for restaurant meals, shoes, or deodorants.

In *Exit, Voice, and Loyalty,* the noted economist Albert O. Hirschman (1970) referred to these choices as "exit." If one is dissatisfied with a good or service, and if alternatives are readily available, it is easy enough to choose an alternative and that is what we would expect people to do. Through competition, the restaurants that do not please their customers will close; those that do will flourish. The market outcome will be efficient. This assumes, of course, that there are no economies of scale and no externalities to cloud the sunny outcome predicted by the workings of the competitive marketplace.

But exit is not the only choice, nor is it always available or desirable. Say you have accumulated a substantial number of frequent flyer miles with one airline. The airline adopts a new policy stating that the frequent flyer miles can only be used to book travel during times in which there is a full moon. You are very unhappy with the new policy, but exit is not a real option here since your frequent flyer miles have no value on another airline. Instead, you are likely to complain in an effort to change the airline's new policy. As an individual, you might send angry notes to the customer service department. You might call your Congressional representative. You might band together with other individuals to picket the company's offices or otherwise embarrass them. The group might consult an attorney to see if legal action is warranted. In Hirschman's terminology, you would be exercising "voice," rather than "exit." You would try to remedy or improve the existing situation instead of withdrawing from it.

To the extent that individuals perceive that voice has been successful, their sense of loyalty to the organization will grow. Those individuals who would otherwise exit might similarly be induced to remain if they perceive that the concerns they have expressed have been addressed. Thus, voice, if acknowledged, can be a powerful way to build loyalty.

Under what circumstances would individuals choose voice rather than exit? Consider the case of the nearby employer paying higher wages. If you have not been working for your current employer for very long, the cost of exit is low and you are likely to leave in response to higher wages elsewhere. However, if you have been with your current employer for many years, you may have accumulated some valuable seniority rights—more weeks of vacation, priority in being able to select the vacation time of your choice, or protection against being laid off if the company downsizes. In this case, the cost of exit is high. You might decide to exercise voice instead by requesting a raise or promotion to a better paid job category, joining with other coworkers to form a union or lobby management, or writing letters to the corporate board of directors asking them to review their personnel policies. Similarly, as Fischel (2001) pointed out in his home voter hypothesis, many homeowners might choose voice rather than exit because their single most important asset, the value of their homes, is tied to a specific place.

In other circumstances, there is no choice because exit is impossible. What happens when exit is an option for some, but not for all? Going back to our frequent flyer example, what if rival airlines decide to honor your airline's frequent flyer miles but only for those who have accumulated more than 500,000 miles (these individuals might be particularly desirable as a source of future business given how much they travel). In this instance, the individuals with the greatest motivation to exercise voice, those who perceive themselves to have the most at stake, will be siphoned off. The remaining individuals will lose their most powerful and well-connected spokespeople and advocates and thus their chances of improving their situation by using voice will have been greatly reduced. The airline might experience its comeuppance sometime in the future when it fails to attract new customers to its frequent flyer program, but that will not remedy the situation for the existing group of frequent flyers who cannot exit.

What if we were discussing public education rather than frequent flyer miles? What if, in response to a decline in the quality of an area's public schools, exit could be chosen only by households wealthy enough to pay private school tuition or move to a jurisdiction with better public schools? With such restricted exit, voice becomes a less effective strategy for those who remain. Initial inequality breeds even greater inequality and the disparity in education resources across the income spectrum grows wider.

In this case, competition does not improve the outcome for all. Those who can exit may benefit but those who cannot fare even worse than before. In this context, it is easy to understand why parents in poor-performing school districts often support voucher programs that would provide them with the exit option they currently lack. Political scientist Terry Moe (2001) found that while 60 percent of the general population expresses support for vouchers, 77 percent of inner-city public-school parents do. While 63 percent of White parents support vouchers, 75 percent of Black parents and 71 percent of Latinx parents do.

Former secretary of labor Robert Reich (1991) has written about the "secession of the successful" and why it is potentially so problematic. He argues that growing income disparities are one result of structural changes underway in the economy. With the increase in globalization, those US workers whose skills command a high value in the international marketplace find their incomes growing while other US workers, typically those with less education, find that they cannot compete against lower-paid workers in other parts of the world. As manufacturing jobs continue to be lost, the supply of workers to the remaining low-paid service jobs grows. This additional supply puts pressure on wages, keeping them from rising as fast as they otherwise would. The resulting growth in income disparities has exacerbated an already high degree of residential segregation by income levels. Sharing public services within communities now means sharing resources within a relatively homogeneous group, firmly bounded by the town's borders.

Reich argued that as the income gap between the most prosperous 20 percent of the population and the other 80 percent grows ever wider, those at the top are less inclined to share resources with those below. Their exit takes many forms such as moving to expensive suburbs or into city enclaves where privately provided schools, clubs, and other recreational activities supplant those provided through the public sector. Even the charitable offerings of this group are more likely to support institutions whose services they themselves consume (e.g., private educational or cultural institutions) rather than those that help to ameliorate the situation of those who are less fortunate.

The devolution of many federal government responsibilities—the shift of responsibility from the federal level to lower levels of government—has amplified the fiscal disparities between local jurisdictions. Even as poor jurisdictions face a greater need to provide more services to their residents, they have fewer resources from higher levels of government to support them. In Reich's view, this is yet another form of exit and one that raises fundamental questions about the responsibility of one citizen to another.

Reich's "secession of the successful" can be seen as the triumph of exit over voice. If exit can be employed only by the more privileged, its use will widen income disparities and worsen conditions for those who must remain.

How Do We Create Better Communities?

More than 600 years ago, Ambrogio Lorenzetti, a painter in Siena, Italy, created murals for its town hall. These murals were titled "Allegories of Good and Bad Government and Their Effects in the City and in the Countryside." In the case of good government, guided by wisdom and justice, the outcome was peace, prosperity, happiness, a vibrant life in the city, and abundance and well-tended crops in the countryside. In the case of bad government, the forces of tyranny, betrayal, and fraud resulted in a city destroyed by war, famine, hatred, and idleness, and a countryside that was barren. In these murals, created from 1338 to 1340, Lorenzetti believed that the fate of the city and the countryside were intertwined. Do we still believe that today? What are the elements of good government that will lead to peace and prosperity for communities, city and countryside alike?

The Role of Social Capital and Civic Engagement

As the poet John Donne famously said, "No man is an island, entire of itself." We are all connected to other individuals through networks of family and friends, concentric rings of those who are closest to us, as well as those to whom we are connected in increasingly more marginal ways. We might rely on the people in our networks for advice, information, support, leads on promising jobs or apartments, or even introductions to potential mates. New high school graduates might rely on their networks to find entry-level jobs; new college graduates might do the same. But networks can work for or against you. It all depends on who is in your network. New college graduates whose friends' parent or parents' friends are successful and well-connected might have access to better opportunities than they could come up with on their own; new high school graduates living in low-income communities among poorly educated adults are likely to find only dead-end jobs through their networks. They would be better off searching on their own.

Social capital refers to the ability of individuals to harness the resources they need through their network of friends and relatives. It may be as trivial as knowing which friend to call to obtain the name of a quick, reliable, and relatively inexpensive moving company. Or it may be a matter of life and death. As we learned in the aftermath of Hurricane Katrina, most of those who perished during the flooding of New Orleans were very poor, elderly, or infirm members of the Black community who could not easily flee the city because they did not own cars and could not ask for help from anyone who did. The circumstances of extreme racial and income segregation under which they lived meant that many residents of severely flooded neighborhoods knew only other people whose situation was as bad as their own.

In his pathbreaking book *Bowling Alone*, Robert Putnam (2000) explains the importance of social capital, both for the individual and for the larger society. In a neighborhood where friends watch your house while you are away and you do the same for them, both homes are safer. By making this a safer area, even those families who are not part of this reciprocal arrangement will benefit. In this way, social capital yields positive externalities. In a larger sense, building social capital means building trust. This may take time and effort, but once trust has been established, many benefits flow. It is much easier to do business with others if you are confident that they deserve your trust. People who live in areas where trust is warranted have greater life expectancies because their day-to-day encounters are less stressful.

Putnam distinguishes between **specific reciprocity** in which the donor of a good deed is paid in kind by the recipient ("I'll buy the first round of drinks, you'll buy the next") and **general reciprocity** in which the donor might expect to be rewarded in some cosmic sense, but not necessarily by the recipient. There are many catchphrases that embody this notion of general reciprocity: "one good turn deserves another," "what goes around comes around," "practice random kindness and senseless acts of beauty," or the notion of "creating good karma." There are many instances in which fortunate people from humble beginnings describe their charitable acts as "giving back" to the community. It is this general reciprocity that is crucial in establishing trust and that benefits all.

Putnam distinguishes between **bonding social capital** (making firmer connections with people who share some fundamental identities—for example, immigrants who live in the same ethnic enclave) and **bridging social capital** (making firmer connections with those who may come from different backgrounds but seek a common purpose—for example, an environmentalist group). Bonding social capital is based on homogeneity and exclusion; bridging social capital is based on heterogeneity and inclusion.

While it is more difficult to build bridging social capital, it may be more useful both to the individual and to society. Sociologist Mark Granovetter (1973) describes the "strength of weak ties," in which an individual's best opportunities come not from the people closest to them whose networks already overlap with their own but from acquaintances outside their inner circle whose networks are more likely to provide new contacts ("Need some help with this? I know a guy"). Moreover, bridging social capital expands horizons and fosters tolerance and empathy. Without it, bonding social capital alone can produce gangs and ethnic hatreds, where trust and reciprocity are limited only to those within the group while those outside are treated with contempt or, in the extreme, might be subject to annihilation. Bridging social capital can be a powerful force for helping overcome the damage caused by racism, sexism, and other forms of discrimination.

Social capital is an important component of vibrant communities. In communities where people know each other, not only are they more likely to live in greater safety, but they are apt to live longer and healthier lives. In addition, they are better able to advocate effectively for the changes they seek—whether it be the installation of a traffic light at a busy intersection or the establishment of an on-site after-school day-care program in the area's elementary schools. Social capital is therefore crucial for voice to be a viable alternative to exit. But without bridging social capital, it can lead to segregated communities and the negative effects of NIMBYism ("Not In My Backyard").

Just as in Lorenzetti's murals in Siena, good government begets happiness and prosperity, and bad government begets famine and strife. It is therefore a matter of great concern, according to Putnam, that levels of social capital and civic engagement have been falling in the United States since the late 1960s. A study by McPherson et al., "Social Isolation in America" (2006), provides additional confirmation of this decline. In the last 20 years, the average number of people whom Americans say they turn to when they want to discuss serious matters in their lives has fallen from three to two, and the likelihood they will discuss these matters only with family members has risen. In addition, in the 2004 General Social Survey (GSS), about one-quarter said that they have no one in whom to confide, an increase from 10 percent who responded this way in the 1985 GSS.

Why has social capital declined? The reasons are complex and include such disparate factors as generational change (the dying off of the generation whose high degree of public spiritedness was shaped by the Depression and World War II), increases in television viewing (which promotes passivity rather than engagement), and the increase in work hours among women as well as men (which reduces the amount of time and energy available for other activities). With the dramatic increase in digital technology use around the world, researchers have studied whether smart phones and the internet have increased social isolation or perhaps reduced it. While this technological advance now provides individuals with an unprecedented level of convenience, dependence on smartphones and other digital devices makes it less necessary for people to acquire new knowledge through face-to-face conversations. These shifts are reducing opportunities for people to build connections with others through work and social activities. A major study of loneliness based on a survey of over 10,000 Americans carried out by the Cigna Corporation in 2019 found that three out of five adults (61%) report that they sometimes or always feel lonely. Among young workers 18–22 years old, the rate is even higher (73%) and has been growing over time. The survey suggests that loneliness is higher among those who use social media more frequently. Seven out of ten (71%) heavy social media users reported feelings of loneliness compared to only 51 percent of light social media users (Coombs 2020).

In this case, correlation may not infer causation. Those who use social media more often may be those who are seeking to reduce their sense of social isolation, using Facebook and other apps to interact more often with friends and colleagues. This was particularly true during the COVID-19 pandemic, when the critical need for social distancing encouraged a much higher use of digital technologies such as Zoom to connect with family and friends.

Social Capital, Suburbanization, and Sprawl

As we saw in Chapter 4, newer suburbs were built around the automobile in contrast to the transit-oriented suburbs of the pre–World War II era. As residences and workplaces have shifted farther out and as the extreme segregation of land use between residential, commercial, and industrial structures has grown, the amount of time Americans spend in their cars has risen and in the majority of car trips, the driver is alone.

Other aspects of suburban development have had adverse effects on the development of social capital. Income segregation and the consequent growth of homogeneous communities have reduced opportunities for creating bridging social capital. Segregation of land use through zoning and the prohibition against building neighborhood stores, restaurants, or bars in residential suburban neighborhoods reduces the serendipitous encounters that help neighbors get to know each other.

Earlier in this chapter, we discussed the privatization of public spaces but along with this privatization there has been a withdrawal from public spaces and public life. As newly constructed homes grow ever larger, suburbanites spend more time within their own houses and yards in a completely private sphere with a small, inner circle of intimates. The grandest of the new houses, which encompass thousands of square feet and are equipped with specialized rooms for exercising or viewing media make it easier for families to turn inward, to be more self-sufficient, and to require fewer outside contacts. As the proportion of the population living in the newer suburbs continues to grow, it is not surprising that according to the McPherson et al. study (2006) mentioned earlier, the percentage of those who confide only in family members rose from 57 percent in 1985 to 80 percent in 2004.

Social Capital and Neighborhood Form

A clear implication of the previous section on social capital, suburbanization, and sprawl is that a person's physical environment influences their behavior. The spatial configuration of newly built suburbs makes it more difficult to foster the interactions through which social capital is created. The housing reform pioneers of the previous century believed in this cause-and-effect relationship between physical environment and social environment. Reformers such as Catherine Bauer, who was instrumental in drafting the Housing Act of 1937—the law that created the public housing program—believed that the way to eliminate the antisocial behavior found in poor slums was to eliminate the slums themselves (Oberlander and Newbrun 1999).

Slum clearance and the replacement of poor-quality housing with newly built public housing of better quality presumably would create the necessary changes in the physical environment. It was expected that when the physical environment changed, the social environment would change as well. People living in better housing, it was believed, would change their behavior and stop engaging in violent and unlawful acts. This did not happen. Many public housing projects became as dangerous as the slums they replaced; many became more dangerous. The reformers were ridiculed for their naiveté in thinking that merely changing peoples' surroundings would change their behavior.

Yet nowadays, we are once again exploring the relationship between physical environment and social environment. The housing reformers of the early twentieth century may well have had the right idea in thinking that one's physical environment mattered. Where they went wrong was in the way they executed their insight.

In her seminal 1961 book *The Death and Life of Great American Cities*, Jane Jacobs offered a scathing critique of the then-current conventional wisdom on how to rebuild cities. She argued that the typical urban renewal project of the time—where small city blocks were consolidated into megablocks and where mixed-use neighborhoods were replaced with single-use, large-scale developments—sucked the energy out of cities, killing off vibrant street life. For Jacobs, the public housing projects of the 1950s epitomized everything that was wrong with contemporary urban development. Their isolation from the surrounding urban fabric and their pattern of high-rise buildings separated by large swaths of poorly maintained and often useless grounds were antithetical to her ideal of building "on a human scale."

For Jacobs, what mattered was a physical environment that fostered human contact: small blocks, mixed uses, clear distinctions between public space and private space, and serendipitous meetings of neighbors. What Jacobs described was a neighborhood conducive to building social capital. She argued that the best way to control crime was to have lively streets, and that "eyes on the street" would provide fewer opportunities for criminal activity. The best way to promote eyes on the street, she argued, was to have many reasons for people to be out and about throughout the day and evening. Although hers was a voice in the wilderness for many years, her ideas have now taken hold and are reflected in many of the precepts of the new urbanism. This approach to architecture and design, as noted in Chapter 13, emphasizes walkable neighborhoods that contain a mixture of commercial and residential properties, a mixture of residential types (single-family homes, apartments, and town houses), a connected network of narrow streets (no cul-de-sacs), and the placement of buildings (often with porches) close to the sidewalk.

Areas in which people have a reason to walk around, where there are well-designed public spaces, and areas characterized by mixed use tend to promote the formation of social capital. Conversely, areas where people are more dependent on automobiles, those that are devoid of public spaces and occupied by low-density residential development, are not as conducive to the development of social capital.

Every major city has its low-income areas, but it is a mistake to think that because of poverty they are alike. During her research, Jacobs found evidence of her theory about the importance of physical space as conducive to social capital in several neighborhoods including the North End of Boston. In this neighborhood during the 1950s and 1960s incomes were low and banks, viewing the area as a slum, would not grant mortgages or home-improvement loans. Yet the area was safe. In addition to its low crime rate, social indicators that measured health status and school attendance and completion rates showed that this was a healthy community despite its very modest physical surroundings. This was an area that had all the characteristics she valued: short blocks, mixed residential and commercial land use, high residential density, a vibrant street life, and surroundings attuned to a human scale.

Research in urban public health (e.g., Kawachi and Berkman 2003) demonstrates that an individual's health depends in part on that individual's own characteristics, including age and income, as well as the characteristics of the neighborhood where the individual resides. In other words, individuals who are 75 years old and living below the poverty line will fare better if they live in a neighborhood with a low crime rate compared to similar seniors who live in a more crime-ridden area, even if they are not crime victims themselves.

This is what Klinenberg found in his study of the 1995 Chicago heat wave, which we mentioned at the very beginning of this chapter. Two neighborhoods in the same part of Chicago, Little Village and North Lawndale, had similar proportions of their elderly populations who were poor and who lived alone—demographic factors that put people at higher risk of dying during a heat wave. Yet the death rate in North Lawndale was ten times higher than the death rate in Little Village. The contrast, Klinenberg argues, was not due to the differences between individuals but the differences between the two neighborhoods where they lived. Little Village is a low-income neighborhood that exemplifies the healthy urban environment described by Jane Jacobs. It has a busy street life, lots of commercial establishments mixed in with high-density residential development, and a low crime rate. It is currently a Latinx area with a growing population. Many of the elderly residents are remnants of a previous generation of White ethnics who once lived there. Even though they did not share the culture or language of the current residents, the fact that they routinely left their homes to walk on the safe streets or to buy items from the local merchants meant that they were less isolated and that they had easy and regular access to places that were air-conditioned.

By contrast, North Lawndale was a high crime rate area that had lost population and where there were many abandoned lots and few stores. Older people in this neighborhood were not as likely to venture outside their homes, for it was too dangerous and there was no place to go. Poor elderly people living alone in Little Village had the "suitable living environment" promised in the 1949 Housing Act. Elders in North Lawndale did not, and for some, it was the difference between life and death.

While Little Village was a very low-income neighborhood and well below middle class, the economic conditions in North Lawndale were far more severe. While the elderly there had incomes similar to the elderly in Little Village, the latter was an area of concentrated poverty—defined as a neighborhood in which more than 40 percent of the residents live below the poverty line. In concentrated poverty areas, poor people are likely to interact only with others who are poor. The extreme segregation and isolation from the world of the nonpoor has toxic effects on residents of these areas. These are high-crime areas in which everyday life is full of stress affecting mental and physical health. Poor health affects children's performance in school and adults' prospects on the job market. These self-reinforcing effects make it difficult for people in such circumstances to improve their situations.

According to Jargowsky (2003), 10.3 percent of those who lived below the poverty line in the United States in 2000 resided in neighborhoods with concentrated poverty. In New Orleans, 37.7 percent of the poor lived in these circumstances— the second-highest rate of concentrated poverty among large cities. Only Fresno, California had a higher rate, at 43.5 percent. In New Orleans, while 10.9 percent of poor Whites and 18 percent of poor Latinx lived in neighborhoods with concentrated poverty, 42.6 percent of the city's Black population lived in these dire circumstances.

This high degree of concentrated poverty was, in part, a result of government decisions about where to relocate tenants of condemned public housing projects. According to historian Douglas Brinkley (2006), the condemned projects were close to downtown and accessible by public transportation. The new locations in the Seventh Ward and New Orleans East were more isolated. As Brinkley says, "Many of those new to the neighborhood had worked in what Blacks called the 'servant industry,' toiling as hotel maids, parking attendants, or domestic help for well-to-do Whites. It was an honest living. Suddenly, with their relocation, they had no easy way to get to work downtown." The geographical and social isolation of these communities left their residents, too poor to own cars, without access to any of the resources that might have allowed them to escape to safer places.

Being poor in America is no picnic, but it does not have to be a death sentence. Misguided government policies contributed to the growth in concentrated poverty in the late twentieth century especially during the 1970s and 1980s. The economic prosperity of the 1990s with its low unemployment rates spurred some reduction in the extent of concentrated poverty. That improvement, however, did not last. Data from the American Community Survey comparing rates of concentrated poverty in 2000 to the five years from 2005 to 2009 and the subsequent five years from 2010 to 2014 show growth in the number of concentrated poverty census tracts and the proportion of poor people who live in them. By the 2010–2014 period, 13.5 percent of all poor people lived in concentrated poverty census tracts, but the incidence was much higher for minorities: 5.5 percent of Whites, 17.6 percent of Latinx, and 25.1 percent of Blacks lived in such areas (Kneebone and Holmes 2016). While there has been some improvement in the lives of the most impoverished in America, by 2020 more than one in eight US residents still lived below the official poverty line. Keep in mind that a household of four was only counted as poor by 2020 if its annual income was below $26,200 or a total of about $500 per week. In many cities in the United States, poverty rates using this low-income standard approached 30 percent (Sauter 2020).

Neighborhood Form and Crime Reduction

Where people desire to live, if they have a choice, is often related to their perception of neighborhood safety. The fear of crime is a potent force, and it has self-reinforcing effects. If people perceive an area to be unsafe, they will avoid it and the now-abandoned area will, in fact, be a more dangerous place. While many factors affect an area's crime rate, our focus here is to expand a bit farther beyond our discussion in Chapter 12 on the link between physical design and social capital and the impact of that link on crime prevention.

In the early 1970s, criminologist C. Ray Jeffery (1971) developed the approach known as Crime Prevention Through Environmental Design (CPTED). Architect Oscar Newman's approach, termed **defensible space**, fits within this framework (Newman 1972). Building on the ideas of observers including Jane Jacobs, this framework examines how the physical design of an area can be used to deter crime by changing the behavior of both the potential criminal and the area's residents. The idea is to discourage the potential perpetrator from committing the crime in the first place by raising the likelihood that any such crime will be seen and reported. This is achieved through maximizing visibility in an area (e.g., replacing high fences or bushes that can serve as hiding places with lower ones; making sure that outdoor areas are well-lit) and through creating public spaces that foster a sense of ownership and responsibility among residents (e.g., small areas used by relatively few households rather than broad swaths of ground that become, literally, "no man's land"). These steps foster social capital, which keeps the area safer and encourages residents to watch for and report suspicious behavior.

Poorly maintained areas reduce social capital formation while well-maintained areas encourage it. Therefore, the CPTED approach has expanded from its original formulation in the 1970s to include the broken windows theory expounded by Kelling and Wilson in 1982 and explored in Chapter 12. If small problems in a neighborhood are not resolved including broken windows, graffiti, and litter, it sends a message that no one cares, no one will act, and, therefore, that more serious offenses will be tolerated.

New York City implemented the broken windows theory in its zero-tolerance approach to subway fare jumpers, squeegee men, and graffiti artists. Although its crime rate dropped, there is controversy over the extent to which broken windows policies should be credited. Other factors, such as demographic change (e.g., fewer young men), economic change (e.g., an improved economy and lower unemployment in the late 1990s), and additional resources for law enforcement agencies and improvements in the criminal justice system and in other social service agencies played extremely important roles. Unlike in a physical science laboratory, it is difficult to run controlled experiments in the messy real world, so it is extraordinarily challenging to isolate the actual contribution, if any, of broken windows policies.

The Effect of Social Capital on the Lives of the Most Vulnerable

Most individuals in low-income communities do not possess large stocks of physical capital such as valuable homes or human capital in the form of a postsecondary education. Therefore, the presence or absence of social capital is particularly important to the quality of their lives. In this respect, the overall decline of social capital may have its worst impact in these communities. Vulnerable individuals in low-income communities are like the proverbial canaries in the coal mine. If, as a society, we cannot protect our most vulnerable citizens, it does not bode well for the rest of us either. As Franklin Delano Roosevelt said in his second inaugural address in 1937, "The test of our progress is not whether we add more to the abundance of those who have much; it is whether we provide enough for those who have too little."

The preamble to the Housing Act of 1949 states as a national goal the provision of "a decent home and a suitable living environment for every American family." Even though this has been an explicit national goal for more than seven decades, governments at all levels—federal, state, and local—have failed to achieve it, at least in the United States. In too many instances those who are poor have neither, especially if they are elderly, infirm, or part of a racial or ethnic minority group. During times of crisis such as the COVID-19 pandemic these vulnerable groups are at greater risk of dying and are less likely to receive the protection that governments are expected to provide for their citizens during public emergencies.

More than 1,800 people died as a result of Hurricane Katrina in 2005; more than 700 people died in a severe Chicago heat wave in 1995; by Summer 2021, with cases still rising, more than 600,000 US residents had already died during the COVID-19 pandemic. In these instances, those who were at greatest risk of dying were poor, elderly, and infirm. Being Black compounded the risk. In each of these instances, there were scandalous failures on the part of government agencies. Existing disaster plans were seriously deficient and in the case of the coronavirus, the federal government downplayed the severity of the pandemic to the point that millions were infected and deaths mounted month after month. In each of these cases, government agencies failed to follow even these deficient plans.

The Future of Metropolitan Areas

No one can predict future events with absolute certainty. That's what makes a horserace—the odds are with the favorite, but every so often the longshot entry is the winner. Whether they are referred to by financial experts as "black swan" events or by medical diagnosticians as "zebras" rather than horses, sometimes outcomes are unexpected, even unanticipated. So rather than trying to predict the future of metropolitan areas, we will examine the interplay of forces that can produce what cities might be like in the future.

In the United States during the spring and summer of 2020, several dramatic forces that might influence the nature of metropolitan areas converged: a novel coronavirus created a public health crisis and a subsequent economic crisis; instances of fatal police brutality served as a catalyst for outrage against an accumulation of racial injustices going back months, years, decades, and even centuries; and an impending election in which gerrymandering, voter suppression, and stymied efforts to expand the ability to vote by mail led to greater get-out-the-vote efforts. For months after he was soundly defeated at the polls, President Trump tried to challenge the result. These forces occurred against a backdrop of other continuing issues affecting metropolitan prospects, particularly the challenges of climate change and of the extreme growth in income and wealth inequality. These issues are interconnected: climate change drives some species from their natural habitats and makes pandemics more likely; extreme inequality leaves lower income minorities at greater risk from pandemics and with fewer resources to protect themselves; efforts to reopen the economy and get people back to work were intertwined with progress in controlling the virus.

There is a parable, originally from the Indian subcontinent, about a group of blind men encountering an elephant for the first time. Each man touches a different portion of the elephant's body, each has a different description, and they argue about who is right. The implication is that with limited information and experience, it is easy to jump to the wrong conclusion. Similarly, contemporary punditry with regard to the impact of COVID-19 on the future of metropolitan areas ranges from those who expect the permanent decline of large cities, those who expect a temporary decline and then a rebound, and those who do not expect much significant change over time. Choose your own adventure.

The adage "never let a good crisis go to waste" has most recently been attributed to Rahm Emanuel, advisor to former President Barack Obama after serving as the mayor of Chicago. Before that the phrase was attributed to community organizer Saul Alinsky, and before that, to British Prime Minister Winston Churchill. Crisis can indeed create opportunities to achieve goals that would be difficult to achieve otherwise, but the goals themselves will depend on who is taking advantage of the opportunities. Members of President Donald Trump's administration used the COVID-19 crisis to promote private schooling at the expense of public education and to further erode environmental regulations. Neither of these initiatives were favored by the general public. Previous crises, such as the Great Depression of the 1930s, have led to major reforms including the creation of the Social Security System, which has been an important part of the nation's social safety net, especially for older citizens, ever since.

Pandemics and the Future of Metropolitan Areas

As the saying goes, "timing is everything." In the summer of 2020, much of the developed world had the virus under control and many nations were engaged in cautiously reopening their economies with their citizens resuming much of their normal lives, albeit safeguarded with masks and social distancing as necessary and with some trepidation about the dangers that colder weather would bring in the fall. The United States was the outlier, with the virus still raging and no end in sight. By the summer of 2021, the availability of new vaccines in the US allowed cases to fall, while they rose in many other parts of the world where availability was limited. Even in the US, however, the ability of the virus to create more communicable variants, combined with substantial vaccine hesitancy and outright resistance, caused cases to rise, with the most severe effects (hospitalizations and deaths) concentrated within the unvaccinated portion of the population.

With our inability to truly conquer the virus, the question of how life might change takes on greater relevance. Some trends, such as an enhanced ability for many white-collar workers and professionals to work remotely, have accelerated. One implication is that the demand for office space will fall. When this happened in Manhattan in the wake of the terrorist attacks of September 11, 2001, jeremiads predicted the end of the city. Instead, many downtown office buildings were converted to residential use and the area became vibrant 24 hours a day rather than just during business hours.

Similarly, some observers see vacant office space as an opportunity for cities, especially those with high housing costs, to expand their supply of housing and make those areas more affordable. In the recent past, when families with children moved from city to suburb, they were replaced by an influx of new residents—young workers, students, empty nesters, and immigrants. The future of cities (Grabar 2020) may partly depend on whether that influx continues.

Large cities have shown resilience in the past because as Eduardo Porter, the economics columnist for the *New York Times* has observed, they are valuable. In the period leading up to the crisis that unfolded in 2020, an increasing share of the nation's output could be attributed to the dynamic economies of the metropolitan areas that relied on highly skilled workers. "Altogether, ten cities, home to under a quarter of the country's population, account for almost half of its patents and a third of its economic production" (Porter 2020). Can remote work generate the same benefits of agglomeration that required proximity before the virus struck? Instead of congregating in close proximity, can researchers, engineers, and scientists collaborate at a distance using Zoom and other digital technologies? Given the limits of telemedicine, there are times when people will want to see their doctors in person, but will they need to meet their lawyers or accountants face-to-face? Whether cities in the United States and around the world will continue to be population magnets or their growth will slow depends on the answer.

Crosscurrents in the Impact of COVID-19 on US Metropolitan Areas

By the fall of 2020, some aspects of the impact of the pandemic on US cities became clearer while others were still unknown. The United States, with 4 percent of the world's population, had sustained nearly 20 percent of worldwide COVID-19 deaths. A virus that first affected the large coastal metropolitan areas had expanded into the nation's midlands where it also affected those living in smaller cities and rural areas. White-collar and professional workers continued to be employed from home while essential workers worked in person in hospitals, nursing homes, public transportation, grocery stores, and pharmacies, often being exposed to higher risks of infection. Workers in retail trade, where e-commerce trends had accelerated, and in the hospitality industry, had high rates of unemployment as many stores, hotels, and restaurants closed down and a substantial number went out of business.

Those predicting the demise of large metropolitan downtown areas could point to high vacancy rates in commercial real estate and nearby rental housing. Anecdotal evidence described wealthy urbanites retreating to second homes in more bucolic areas and deciding to stay there, perhaps permanently. Home sales in rural areas rose dramatically. One story told of an influx to a tiny Vermont town that was glad to stem its previous loss of population, while another told of a rural town in upstate New York dealing with the problems of gentrification and the loss of affordable rentals for its prepandemic population (Barry 2020; Heller 2020). Companies including Facebook offered its workforce the option to leave San Francisco and work from home permanently in any area with a lower cost of living in exchange for lower wages (Sen 2020).

And yet one illustration of the crosscurrents affecting the future of large metropolitan areas is that Facebook, having made the work-permanently-from-home offer, also made a large commitment to rent the entire former main post office across from Penn Station—730,000 square feet—bringing its total office space in that area of Manhattan to more than 2.2 million square feet, all leased within the last year (Haag 2020). Similarly, Amazon purchased a large former department store in midtown Manhattan and has plans to expand its presence in other cities including Dallas, Denver, Detroit, Phoenix, and San Diego (Weise and Haag 2020).

While the *New York Daily News* and the *Charlotte Observer* in North Carolina have closed their physical newsrooms permanently, Fred Hiatt, the editorial page editor of the *Washington Post*, has argued that the ability of newspapers and many other organizations to operate remotely, yet still effectively, is not something that can be maintained indefinitely. He argues that the effectiveness of remote work in the months following the start of the pandemic is a product of the social capital that has been built up by colleagues who have worked together for years. That social capital will become depleted without a workplace culture, and the loss will be compounded as some workers leave and new ones are hired. He discusses the loss of serendipitous interactions that lead to useful new ideas, the within-organization analog to the bump rate of Chapter 8 in which we explain why the agglomeration economies of large metropolitan areas lead to higher rates of innovation (Hiatt 2020). Twitter started experimenting with work-from-home policies in 2018 before the pandemic hit. Its goal is to have half of its workforce working from home worldwide. Yet it is retaining all its office real estate. Its biggest concerns are the ability to form and maintain social capital, especially for its new employees (Dwoskin 2020).

Regeneration for Whom? Rebuilding Central City Neighborhoods

As we saw in Chapter 2, in recent years a good number of central cities have undergone a renaissance. Crime rates have fallen, population has risen, and many central city locations are now attractive to young professionals, empty nesters, and new waves of immigrants. This was not necessarily what one might have expected as late as the 1970s, when cities including New York were almost considered relics. With so many families fleeing to the suburbs and with the city government virtually bankrupt as properties were abandoned and property tax revenue plummeted, many thought that New York, along with other older cities, would continue to lose population and the people who were left in the city would be increasingly poor. Such speculation has reappeared as a result of the pandemic, but a replay of the 1970s seems unlikely.

In some cities, low-income residents who have worked hard to make their neighborhoods safer now find that they have been priced out of once-affordable housing. What are the challenges of building desirable communities within central cities? In *When Work Disappears*, William Julius Wilson (1996) described the hopelessness in many Black Chicago neighborhoods where crime and drug trafficking ran rampant, many adults were locked into low-wage jobs, and others were disconnected from the world of work altogether. In this urban dystopia, communities were depopulated, local stores could not survive, and vacant lots and abandoned buildings were common. School dropout rates were high, academic achievement scores were low, and the next generation was doomed to continue the pattern.

Between 1970 and 1990, most large US cities had similar areas of despair and concentrated poverty, particularly affecting Black households because they often faced greater racial segregation than other low-income minorities. Then, during the 1990s, many inner cities, once designated as areas of concentrated poverty, began to experience a comeback. While severe problems persist in many areas, some neighborhoods were able to improve the circumstances under which their residents lived.

What accounts for the turnaround that some places were able to achieve? One answer lies in the creation of new urban organizations. Starting in the late 1960s in some cities, local residents and merchants, often joined by local religious organizations and other stakeholders, formed nonprofit groups—community development corporations (CDCs)—to improve conditions in their low- and moderate-income neighborhoods, primarily through housing construction and job creation. The Ford Foundation created the Local Initiatives Support Corporation (LISC) in 1980 to provide technical and financial support to many of these organizations. According to the National Congress for Community Economic Development, CDCs across the United States had created 550,000 units of affordable housing and 247,000 private-sector jobs by 1998.

Despite this early success, CDCs nevertheless have been the subject of controversy. In a widely disseminated *New York Times Sunday Magazine* article, the journalist Nicholas Lemann (1994) questioned the entire strategy of ghetto job development including the role played by CDCs. He argued that offering economic inducements to get major firms that operate in national or international markets to locate in inner-city neighborhoods that they would otherwise avoid simply does not work. He pointed out that the emphasis on job development inside the ghetto through these inducements was misplaced as long as jobs can be found elsewhere. After all, most people do not live and work in the same neighborhood.

He concluded that for political reasons, it was more acceptable for CDCs to emphasize their role in job creation even though their major contributions have been in the creation of housing. While criticizing what was, in his view, a futile effort focused on economic development, Lemann nevertheless lauded the social service role that CDCs play in delivering affordable housing, health services, childcare, and education and training programs.

In *Comeback Cities*, Paul Grogan (a former president of LISC) and Tony Proscio (2000) describe the four ingredients they view as necessary to transform inner-city neighborhoods. CDCs are one of them as they are the agencies through which housing, small business, and social capital can be rebuilt in places where it has been destroyed. Through CDCs, residents and other local stakeholders can develop their own leadership to respond to the needs of the existing community.

Private investment is a second. As social capital is accumulated, as depopulation is halted, and as new housing is built, the area becomes more inviting to privately owned and operated local businesses. When merchants are willing to invest in a formerly run-down neighborhood, a virtuous cycle begins—more jobs and housing are created, abandoned buildings are recycled, and vacant lots are filled in. Exit gives way to voice, and some residents who have the option of leaving choose to stay and work toward further improvement.

Retail trade is one of the areas for private investment where inner cities actually have an advantage. While the average household income in central city neighborhoods, particularly those with large numbers of low-income families, is well below the average household income of suburban residents, the much greater density of housing in the inner city means that the average retail demand per square mile in central city neighborhoods is usually much higher than in the suburbs. According to a 1998 study by the Boston Consulting Group (BCS), retail demand per square mile for food and apparel was an estimated $116 million in Harlem, New York, compared with $53 million across the rest of the New York metropolitan area. In other cities, similar disparities in retail demand per square mile were found. In Chicago, the BCS estimated that households' combined retail demand per square mile was $57 million, compared with $27 million across the entire metro area. In Boston, the inner city to metro region ratio was $71 million to $12 million per square mile (Boston Consulting Group 1998).

Based on such studies and the proselytizing by the Initiative for a Competitive Inner City, an organization formed by Harvard University's Michael Porter, several inner-city retail malls have been established in cities including New York and Boston. Those similar to the South Cove Mall in the Dorchester neighborhood of Boston have attracted national chain stores that include Home Depot, Stop & Shop Supermarkets, and Staples. They generally report higher sales volume per square foot of retail space than their suburban outlets because of the density of the demand per square mile and the general absence of competition in the inner-city communities where they have built stores. By diversifying their product lines to appeal to inner-city multiracial and multiethnic communities, many of these stores are prospering. In 2007, Wal-Mart decided to build 50 stores in low-income urban neighborhoods to take advantage of the retail opportunities there (Miara 2007).

In addition to the role of CDCs and the role of private markets, Grogan and Proscio argue that the two other necessary ingredients for the renaissance of low-income, inner-city neighborhoods are the reduction of crime rates—part of which automatically occurs as the virtuous circle begins to increase the liveliness of the area's streets and provides jobs for local residents—and a reduction in the monolithic force of the welfare, public housing, and public school bureaucracies. Local, state, and federal governments have important roles to play in facilitating these reforms: a shift to community policing, an income maintenance system that promotes independence and supports work effort, a redesign of public housing that avoids large-scale high-rise buildings, and a school system that offers more choice and is more accountable for its outcomes.

Citing the failure of the 1960s War on Poverty to eliminate poverty altogether and the recognition that the elimination of poverty is not a goal likely to be reached in the foreseeable future, the real task, say Grogan and Proscio, is to create decent neighborhoods for low- and moderate-income households today. With these four ingredients in place, they argue that it is possible for low-income households to live in decent circumstances despite their poverty.

Demographic Change and Low-Income Communities

One important demographic change in central cities cited by Grogan and Proscio (2000) is the recent large wave of immigration. They argue that although changes in the legislation that affect immigration—whether the restrictions put in place in the 1920s or their removal in 1965—never had the explicit purpose of affecting the well-being of urban areas, they have nevertheless had an important unintended consequence for central cities. The roughly 40-year period in the mid-twentieth century in which immigration was severely reduced coincided with the decline in central city fortunes. As residents of central city neighborhoods departed for the suburbs, there was no one to replace them, and thus the depopulation trend commenced. With the flow of new immigrants restored after 1965, depopulation in the gateway cities was finally halted. Those cities that are not destinations for immigrants continue to suffer.

Across the globe, immigration has played a role in revitalizing cities. According to recent census figures, of the largest cities in the world, Miami boasts the largest foreign-born population. In 2016, more than 58 percent of the city's population was foreign born, with large numbers coming to the city from Latin America and Eastern Europe. Toronto was in second place with 47 percent of its residents foreign born. Both Sydney and Melbourne have immigrant populations of 40 percent or more. Other world cities with large immigrant populations include Los Angeles (37.7%), New York City (37.5%), London (36.4%), and Amsterdam (32.1%). These cities have vibrant economies that attract foreign workers, but those who come, including highly educated scientists, engineers, and physicians, help to enhance the vibrancy of the cities they now call home.

College students and young professionals are another source of new residents. Urban-based institutions of higher learning, once viewed primarily in an adversarial role by their host cities, have stabilized neighborhood economies in many low-income areas. Though tensions persist, universities and the communities in which they are located have tried to find common ground in pursuing mutually beneficial outcomes.

Along with immigrants, students, and young professionals, artists have long been attracted to areas with cheap housing and available loft space. New York and Boston are not the only places that have benefited from artists helping to stabilize an area. Even smaller cities, such as the very old industrial mill town of Pawtucket, Rhode Island, have tried to attract artists to converted mill space as a strategy for regeneration.

The Perils of Success

What happens when a neighborhood is successful in regenerating itself? What are the rewards for the hard efforts of those who survived the bad times to share in the newfound safety and stability? In some instances, the area becomes so attractive that real estate values soar and residents are victims of their own success. Property owners might reap the windfall of higher values, but residential renters and small business owners who lease retail or commercial space may find that they are priced out of the area.

Neighborhoods that are initially attractive to higher-income households because of their economic and racial diversity become less diverse over time as property values soar. Similarly, small business owners in successful retail districts are succeeded by franchises of national companies who can afford to outbid them for retail space. This can be a double-edged sword. On the one hand, cities benefit from higher tax receipts and all neighborhood residents stand to benefit from the economic and political power of higher-income residents who have committed themselves to city living and who demand, and often receive, better public services. To the extent that an influx of more privileged families means cleaner and safer streets, better public schools, and more frequent bus service for everyone in the neighborhood, the longer-term residents who preceded the gentrification wave may be better off.

On the other hand, without some protection against soaring rent increases, there is a "killing the goose that laid the golden egg" aspect to this process. The initially attractive features of the area as someplace unique begin to disappear as the one-of-a-kind funky stores and restaurants are displaced by the more standardized fare available in any generic shopping mall. The longer-term residents who gave the place its character and stability and who endured when the area suffered through hard times are replaced by new arrivals who are generally younger and better educated. The area becomes less diverse—more segregated—not only by race and income, but by age.

As a society, we have been effective in fulfilling the desires of those who seek segregation. Through market forces reinforced by public policy decisions, we have created communities segregated by race and income. We have been far less effective in fulfilling the desires of those who seek diversity. Our record in creating and sustaining communities integrated both by race and by income has been disappointing.

Over the next few decades, the influx of new immigrants and their children will continue to change the racial and ethnic mix of our society. As the baby-boom generation ages and as life expectancies grow, the age composition of our nation will change. Long-term economic changes in our industrial structure—the impact of globalization and new technologies—will affect how and where we work and the nature of work itself. If present trends continue, the earnings gap between those who are highly educated and those who are not will continue to grow and economic inequality will be even more pronounced. In a society that is demographically more diverse but more unequal with respect to income and wealth, will we be able to move any closer toward achieving the goal of providing a decent home and a suitable living environment for every American family, which was set more than 70 years ago?

An Urban Thought Experiment

In *A Theory of Justice*, published in 1971, the influential political philosopher John Rawls argues that in an ideal world when people make decisions about how their society should function, and especially when they consider the moral principles upon which that society is based, they should do so behind a **veil of ignorance**. That is, in thinking about how best to organize society, they should begin without knowing about their own place in the society they are designing. Since, as we have seen, our society treats individuals differently depending on a range of factors including race, gender, ethnicity, social class, educational attainment, age, and disability, the moral principles of the society should be decided without knowing what one's own individual circumstances would be. In order to be sure that once you came out from behind the veil you yourself do not end up disadvantaged in this ideal society, Rawls argued people would design a society which has a great deal of equality of opportunity and equality of outcomes.

In response to discussions of how the multiple crises in 2020—including the COVID-19 pandemic and the Black Lives Matter movement—new initiatives were undertaken in several cities that affected urban form. For example, in New York City and many other cities across the world more pedestrian streets were closed to automobiles, more bike lanes and paths were developed, and more neighborhood parks were created. *Gothamist,* a news website owned by New York's public radio station WNYC, asked, "Given that this is an opportunity for real change, what is your utopian idea of how NYC could look in the future?" (Carlson 2020). The question was quickly reframed along Rawlsian lines: "Another way to think of it is to imagine that you did not know who you would be in a new New York—what race or color, what age, what religion, what gender or orientation, whether you would be with or without a disability, healthy or unhealthy, what national origin, your political views, and what zip code you would live in. If you had no idea what or who you might be, what talents you might have or lack, then what sort of New York would you devise?" This really is the ultimate question for human society, no matter where you live.

- How diverse would you like your neighborhood to be in terms of income, race, ethnicity, and talent?

- How might you reform urban institutions including schools, police departments, and virtually all the other services offered by the city to assure more equal opportunity and a fair way of dealing with all of the residents who live in your city?

- What changes might you make in your city's transportation system to make it more efficient?

- What would you do to help make it possible for more of your city's residents to find good jobs at decent pay?

- What would you do to make your city an exciting place to live for everyone from young children to great grandparents?

Gothamist's focus is New York City, but these questions can be asked of any community. We have come full circle from the beginning of this chapter where we asked what makes a good neighborhood. Now everyone should give some thought to this question.

References

Barry, Ellen. 2020. "The Virus Sent Droves to a Small Town. Suddenly, It's Not So Small." *New York Times*, September 26.

Blakely, Edward J., and Mary Gail Snyder. 1997. *Fortress America: Gated Communities in the United States*. Washington, DC: Brookings Institution.

Boston Consulting Group. 1998. "The Business Case for Pursuing Retail Opportunities in the Inner City." June. http://imaps.indygov.org/ed_portal/studies/bcg_inner_city_retail.pdf.

Briffault, Richard. 1999. "A Government for Our Time? Business Improvement Districts and Urban Governance." *Columbia Law Review* 99, no. 2: 365–477.

Brinkley, Douglas. 2006. *The Great Deluge: Hurricane Katrina, New Orleans, and the Mississippi Gulf Coast*. New York: HarperCollins.

Carlson, Jen. 2020. "What Do You Want NYC to Look Like? We Asked New Yorkers." *Gothamist*, July 20. https://gothamist.com/arts-entertainment/the-future-of-new-york-city

Community Associations Institute. 2019. "Community Associations in the United States." https://foundation.caionline.org/wp-content/uploads/2020/08/2020StatsReview_Web.pdf

Coombs, Bertha. 2020. "Loneliness Is on the Rise and Younger Workers and Social Media Users Feel It the Most." *Cigna Survey*, January 23. https://www.cnbc.com/2020/01/23/loneliness-is-rising-younger-workers-and-social-media-users-feel-it-most.html

Dwoskin, Elizabeth. 2020. "Americans Might Never Come Back to the Office, and Twitter Is Leading the Charge." *Washington Post*, October 1.

Fischel, William. 2001. *The Homevoter Hypothesis: How Home Values Influence Local Government Taxation, School Finance, and Land-Use Policy*. Cambridge, MA: Harvard University Press.

Goodyear, Sarah. 2013. "The Threat of Gated Communities," *Bloomberg Citylab*, July 13. https://www.bloomberg.com/news/articles/2013-07-15/the-threat-of-gated-communities

Grabar, Henry. 2020. "What's a City Without the Office?." What's Next TBD Podcast Series on The Future of Cities, *Slate Magazine*, July–August. https://slate.com/podcasts/what-next-tbd/2020/07/cities-offices

Granovetter, Mark. 1973. "The Strength of Weak Ties." *American Journal of Sociology* 78, no. 6 (May): 1360–1380.

Grogan, Paul S., and Tony Proscio. 2000. *Comeback Cities: A Blueprint for Urban Neighborhood Revival*. Boulder, CO: Westview Press.

Haag, Matthew. 2020. "Facebook Bets Big on Future of N.Y.C., and Offices, With New Lease." *New York Times*, August 3.

Heller, Karen. 2020. "Welcome to Woodstock 2020: Peace, Love . . . and Urban Exiles Fighting Over Real Estate." *Washington Post*, September 22.

Hiatt, Fred. 2020. "We're Doing Our Best with Zoom. But We'll Still Need Offices—and Each Other." *Washington Post*, August 23.

Hirschman, Albert O. 1970. *Exit, Voice, and Loyalty: Responses to Decline in Firms, Organizations, and States*. Cambridge, MA: Harvard University Press.

Hoyt, Lorlene, and Devika Gopal-Agge. 2007. "The Business Improvement District Model: A Balanced Review of Contemporary Debates." *Geography Compass* 1, no. 4: 946–958.

Huddle, Ryan, and Peter Bailey-Wells. 2020. "Town-by-Town COVID-19 Data in Massachusetts." *Boston Globe*, August 5.

Jacobs, Jane. 1961. *The Death and Life of Great American Cities*. New York: Random House.

Jargowsky, Paul A. 2003. "Stunning Progress, Hidden Problems: The Dramatic Decline of Concentrated Poverty in the 1990s." *Living Cities Census Series.* Washington, DC: Brookings Institution, May. https://www.brookings.edu/research/stunning-progress-hidden-problems-the-dramatic-decline-of-concentrated-poverty-in-the-1990s/

Jeffery, C. Ray. 1971. *Crime Prevention through Environmental Design.* Beverly Hills, CA: Sage Publications.

Kawachi, Ichiro, and Lisa F. Berkman. 2003. *Neighborhoods and Health.* New York: Oxford University Press.

Kelling, George L., and James Q. Wilson. 1982. "Broken Windows." *Atlantic Monthly* 249, no. 3 (March): 29–38.

Klinenberg, Eric. 2002. *Heat Wave: A Social Autopsy of Disaster in Chicago.* Chicago: University of Chicago Press.

Kneebone, Elizabeth, and Natalie Holmes. 2016. "U.S. Concentrated Poverty in the Wake of the Great Recession." March 31. Washington, DC: Brookings Institution.

Lemann, Nicholas. 1994. "The Myth of Community Development." *New York Times Sunday Magazine*, January 9, pp. 27–31, 50, 54, 60.

Low, Setha. 2001. "The Edge and the Center: Gated Communities and the Discourse of Urban Fear," *American Anthropologist* (March): 45–58.

Low, Setha. 2003. *Behind the Gates: Life, Security, and the Pursuit of Happiness in Fortress America.* New York: Routledge.

McPherson, Miller, Lynn Smith-Lovin, and Matthew E. Brashears. 2006. "Social Isolation in America: Changes in Core Discussion Networks over Two Decades." *American Sociological Review* 71, no. 3 (June): 353–375.

Miara, James. 2007. "Retail in Inner Cities." *Urban Land* (January): 98–105.

Moe, Terry M. 2001. *Schools, Vouchers, and the American Public.* Washington, DC: Brookings Institution Press.

Nambiar, Melanie. 2019. "2019 Global Consumer Trend 'Social Isolation': How'd We Do?" https://www.mintel.com/blog/new-market-trends/2019-global-consumer-trend-social-isolation-howd-we-do

Nelson, Robert H. 2005. *Private Neighborhoods and the Transformation of Local Government.* Washington, DC: Urban Institute Press.

Newman, Oscar. 1972. *Defensible Space: Crime Prevention through Urban Design.* New York. Macmillan.

Oberlander, N. Peter, and Eva Newbrun. 1999. *Houser: The Life and Work of Catherine Bauer.* Vancouver: University of British Columbia Press.

Okun, Arthur M. 1975. *Equality and Efficiency: The Big Tradeoff.* Washington, DC: Brookings Institution Press.

Porter, Eduardo. 2020. "Coronavirus Threatens the Luster of Superstar Cities." *New York Times*, July 21.

Putnam, Robert D. 2000. *Bowling Alone: The Collapse and Revival of American Community*. New York: Simon & Schuster.

Rawls, John. 1971. *A Theory of Justice*. Cambridge, MA: The Belknap Press of Harvard University Press.

Reich, Robert B. 1991. *The Work of Nations: Preparing Ourselves for 21st-Century Capitalism*. New York: Knopf.

Sauter, Michael. 2020. "Cities with the Highest Poverty Rates." *24/7 Wall Street*, March 19. https://247wallst.com/special-report/2018/11/19/cities-with-the-highest-poverty-rates-4/

Sen, Conor. 2020. "Why Is Facebook for Remote Work? It Wants Pay Cuts." *Bloomberg*, May 29. https://www.bloomberg.com/opinion/articles/2020-05-29/facebook-s-remote-work-plan-driven-by-desire-to-cut-tech-pay

Tiebout, Charles. 1956. "A Pure Theory of Local Expenditures." *Journal of Political Economy* 64, no. 5 (October): 416–424.

Weise, Karen, and Matthew Haag. 2020. "Amazon Sticks with Office Expansion Plans in New York and Elsewhere." *New York Times*, August 18.

Wilson, William J. 1996. *When Work Disappears: The World of the New Urban Poor*. New York: Knopf.

Questions and Exercises

1. The population of individual regions, states, and metro areas in the United States is constantly shifting as households make choices as to where to live and earn a living. The US Census Bureau keeps track of the change in population for regions and states at its website:

   https://www.census.gov/data/tables/time-series/demo/popest/2010s-state-total.html#par_textimage. Within this website go to Population, Population Change, and Estimated Components of Population Change: April 1, 2010 to July 1, 2019 (NST-EST2019-alldata) and use the spreadsheet data columns for the state populations in 2010 and 2019. Calculate the 2010–2019 percentage change in population for each state and then sort the data by the percentage.

   • Which five states have had the largest increases in population?
   • Which five states have had the smaller increases or largest decrease?
   • Given what you have studied while using this textbook, what do believe are the key factors explaining these population changes?

2. Now repeat this exercise for US metro areas using the following US Census Bureau website:

https://www.census.gov/data/tables/time-series/demo/popest/2010s-total-metro-and-micro-statistical-areas.html

- Which five metro areas have had the largest increases in population?
- Which five metro areas have had the smaller increases or largest decrease?
- Given what you have studied while using this textbook, what do believe are the key factors explaining these population changes?

3. Now repeating this exercise for US cities using the following US Census Bureau website:

https://www.census.gov/data/tables/time-series/demo/popest/2010s-total-cities-and-towns.html.

- Which five cities have had the largest increases in population?
- Which five cities have had the smaller increases or largest decrease?
- Given what you have studied while using this textbook, what do believe are the key factors explaining these population changes?

Glossary

ABILITY-TO-PAY PRINCIPLE—A principle of taxation that says wealthier households should pay for a larger share of publicly provided goods and services because they have greater means to do so.

ABSOLUTE ADVANTAGE—The ability of one firm, region, or country to produce a commodity using fewer resources per unit of output than any other firm, region, or country.

ACCELERATED DEPRECIATION—Under this provision of the federal income tax, firms (or landlords) can deduct a large proportion of the cost of maintenance in the early years of such an investment rather than spreading out the deduction in equal shares over the full expected life of the property improvement. This reduces the amount of income tax paid by the firm or landlord.

ADAPTATION (CLIMATE CHANGE)—Adjustment in natural or human systems to a new or changing environment that exploits beneficial opportunities or moderates negative effects.

ADAPTIVE CAPACITY (CLIMATE CHANGE)—The ability of a system to adjust to climate change to moderate potential damage or to cope with the consequences.

AFFORDABLE HOUSING—According to the US Department of Housing and Urban Development, housing for which the household pays no more than 30 percent of its own income in rent or in mortgage payments including taxes and utilities.

AGGLOMERATION ECONOMIES—Reduced costs in an economic activity that result from enterprises or activities locating near one another. There are two types of agglomeration economies: localization economies and urbanization economies.

ALLOCATION ROLE OF GOVERNMENT—The role that governments play when they change the amount of goods and services that would otherwise be produced in a market economy.

ALLOCATIVE EFFICIENCY—The use of resources to produce the particular combination of goods and services that maximizes consumer satisfaction.

AMORTIZE—To pay off a debt (e.g., a mortgage) through periodic agreed-upon installments, gradually reducing the balance owed.

ANNEXATION—The extension of the geographic boundaries of a city or town by adding a neighboring area or municipality to its jurisdiction.

ASYMMETRIC INFORMATION—Unequal information held by the buyer and seller in a market exchange. For example, a used car dealer may know more than the prospective buyer about the quality of a car being sold.

ATTRIBUTES THEORY OF CONSUMER BEHAVIOR—An approach to understanding consumer behavior emphasizing that a good is actually a combination of attributes (characteristics), and that these attributes hold value for a consumer. From this perspective, the source of consumer demand for a specific good (e.g., a house or a car) is the demand for a specific combination of attributes exhibited by that good.

BASIC/NONBASIC APPROACH—An approach to understanding urban economic growth in which production is divided into two sectors. "Basic production" and related "basic jobs" pertain to firms that produce goods or services for export to other regions in return for payments from consumers from those other regions. Export can refer to sales to other municipalities, states, or nations. "Nonbasic production" and "nonbasic jobs" pertain to firms whose goods or services are not exported, but instead are only sold locally.

BENEFIT PRINCIPLE—A principle of taxation that says households that gain from a publicly provided good or service should be the ones who pay for it.

BID RENT—The amount renters or buyers are willing to offer in order to gain access to and use of a specific parcel of land.

BID RENT CURVE—A graph that shows the maximum amounts (represented on the vertical axis) that a type of land user (e.g., commercial businesses) would be willing to pay for land, as the distance from the city center increases (represented on the horizontal axis).

BOARDS OF HEALTH—Individuals appointed by state or local governments to oversee the quality of public health in an area, to pursue initiatives designed to increase health-related services, promote healthy behavior, and prevent disease and injury.

BONDING SOCIAL CAPITAL—Making firmer connections with people who share some fundamental identities.

BRIDGING SOCIAL CAPITAL—Making firmer connections with those who may come from different backgrounds but seek some common purpose.

BROKEN WINDOWS/ZERO TOLERANCE—An approach to crime prevention that emphasizes police response to vandalism and minor disorder. The underlying reasoning is that if potential criminals notice such response, they are likely to believe that residents and city government care about what happens in those locations, that criminal activity is more likely to be observed and reported in that area, and that arrest is more likely.

BUDGET CONSTRAINT—The limit on a household's purchasing power due to the limited money the household has available to spend. In graphs, the budget constraint is a line that represents the various combinations of goods and services a household can buy with a given income.

BUILDING CODES—Standards and specifications contained in government regulations, designed to establish minimum safeguards for the construction of buildings, and to protect the people who live and work in them from fire, threats to health, and other hazards.

BUILDING CONSTRUCTION GUIDELINES—Regulations covering the type and quality of materials used, design, size, height, or other aspects of building construction.

BUMP RATE—The frequency with which two or more parties come into contact with each other and share ideas.

BUSINESS CYCLE—A fluctuation in the level of economic activity where output expands and then contracts or vice versa.

BUSINESS IMPROVEMENT DISTRICT (BID)—An association formed by businesses within an area to provide services (such as street cleaning or security patrols) beyond the level of services provided by the municipal government.

CAP AND TRADE—See "emissions trading."

CAPITAL—Buildings (e.g., factories, offices) and equipment (e.g., tools, machinery) used in the production of goods and services.

CARBON TAX—A price placed on carbon dioxide emissions to reduce the amount produced.

CENSUS TRACT—An official small statistical subdivision of a county or city that usually contains between 1,200 and 8,000 persons.

CENTRAL BUSINESS DISTRICT (CBD)—A densely developed center of a city, used primarily for business activities.

CENTRAL CITY—The largest municipality, containing more than 50,000 population, in a metropolitan area. Under certain conditions regarding size and commuting patterns, there can be more than one central city in a given metropolitan area. Also known as a "principal city."

CENTRAL PLACE THEORY—A theory asserting that there is a hierarchy of size and function among cities and towns within any given region, based upon the market areas of different types of firms located in each city or town. At the top of the hierarchy are cities that contain industries producing goods and services for export widely throughout a region, nation, or the globe. Lower in the hierarchy are municipalities that produce goods and services for local consumption or for consumption in those cities at the top of the central place hierarchy.

CENTRIFUGAL FORCE—Factors that encourage dispersal of activities away from a center toward the outskirts.

CENTRIPETAL FORCE—Factors that encourage locational choice toward the center of a city.

CETERIS PARIBUS—a Latin phrase used in economics to mean "holding everything else constant"; a theoretical condition used frequently in economic explanations. To focus attention upon a limited number of factors, other things that could change are assumed to be held constant.

CHARTER SCHOOLS—Schools established by private groups that provide publicly funded education under contracts (charters) with designated government educational authorities.

CIRCULAR CAUSATION WITH CUMULATIVE EFFECT—The theory that a small change in one direction leads to a large effect in that direction, while a small change in another direction leads to a large effect in that direction. As an example, small differences in initial schooling can lead to large changes in life opportunities.

COASE THEOREM—The theory that externalities do not necessarily require government intervention and that private bargaining between those producing externalities and those that they potentially affect will lead to optimal outcomes if three conditions hold. These conditions are that property rights are clearly specified, the number of parties involved is small, and the costs of bargaining are negligible.

COGNITIVE MAPS—Mental "maps" of a community created by employers and other decision-makers that reflect their beliefs about the strengths and weaknesses of each location as a place to live, establish a business, or from where to hire new employees. Cognitive maps can be based on impressions and beliefs rather than objective reality and can lead to certain forms of discrimination.

COMBINED STATISTICAL AREA (CSA)—As defined by the US Bureau of the Census, a large, urbanized area that links together metropolitan statistical areas (MSAs) where there is a substantial amount of commuting between individual metropolitan areas. These combined statistical areas can cover hundreds of square miles.

COMMON INTEREST DEVELOPMENTS—Private organizations formed by individual households or businesses to pursue common goals through shared consumption of goods and services.

COMMUNICABLE DISEASES—Diseases that can be transmitted through contact with other humans or contact with other living organisms. Communicable diseases can be contrasted with noncommunicable diseases, such as scurvy, which arise because of nutritional or other deficiencies, and are not transmittable.

COMMUNITY-BASED ORGANIZATIONS (CBOS)—Any of a broad range of nonprofit organizations based in urban neighborhoods and dedicated to improving the quality of life for their residents.

COMMUNITY DEVELOPMENT CORPORATIONS (CDCS)—Nonprofit groups formed to improve conditions in low- and moderate-income neighborhoods, primarily through housing construction and job creation.

COMMUNITY-ORIENTED POLICING—An approach toward crime that emphasizes the creation of a close relationship between police and neighborhood residents, with the objective of building neighborhood residents' capacity to prevent crime, solving neighborhood problems that may be related to crime levels, and linking crime prevention by police and residents with other municipal services.

COMPARATIVE ADVANTAGE—A country or region has a comparative advantage in producing a good or service, relative to another region or country, if the relative cost of producing the good or service—its opportunity cost in terms of other goods forgone—is lower than it is in the other region. Even if one region has an absolute advantage in the production of two goods, the region without absolute advantage has comparative advantage in the production of the good whose opportunity cost is less than the opportunity cost of the region with absolute advantage. Under comparative advantage, maximum output and maximum utility is achieved when each region concentrates its resources in the production of the good or service for which its opportunity cost of production is lowest and then trades some of this good or service for some of the good or service produced in the other region.

COMPETITIVE ADVANTAGE—The success of a firm (or region, or nation) in a particular industry against rival firms (or regions or nations) producing the same, or a similar, product. Competitive advantage can be gained either through low-cost production or product differentiation—producing a unique product or one that is considered to be of higher quality or more innovative.

COMPLEX GOOD—A good that embodies several different characteristics of importance to a consumer. Because the characteristics of a complex good typically involve several types of value, consumers' choices about such goods involve trade-offs between the different types of value. For example, housing may be valued for its size, layout, amenities, proximity to work, and the quality of the school district where the house is located. The choice of a particular house depends upon how much the home buyer values each of these different aspects relative to each other and the trade-offs that he or she is willing to make in terms of these varied attributes.

COMPREHENSIVE COMMUNITY HEALTH CENTERS—Centers funded by the US Congress to provide a wide array of medical services and health outreach in urban and rural low-income areas.

CONGESTION PRICING—Varying the tolls on a roadway, bridge, or tunnel so that motorists are charged the most during periods of heaviest traffic (congestion).

CONSOLIDATED METROPOLITAN STATISTICAL AREA (CMSA)—As defined by the US Bureau of the Census and used until 2003 for what is now termed a combined statistical area (CSA).

CONSTRAINED MAXIMIZATION—Maximizing a particular goal given a set of limits on resources. For example, a consumer seeks to maximize the utility he or she gets from the consumption of a set of goods and services subject to a budget constraint on the amount he or she can spend.

CONSUMER MARKETS—The sale of goods and services from firms to households, or the locations in which such sale takes place.

CONSUMER SOVEREIGNTY—The idea that the desires of individual consumers either (1) are paramount in an economy, or (2) that they should be paramount. The first way of using the term asserts that what consumers want actually determines what is produced in a society. The second way of using the term is an assertion about how things should be: that consumers should decide for themselves what to buy, rather than having their purchases affected by government regulations that influence production or choice.

CONTAGIOUS DISEASES—Diseases that can be passed from one person to another. Contagious diseases are one category of communicable diseases (diseases that can be either passed from human to human or contracted through contact with other living organisms).

CORE-BASED STATISTICAL AREA (CBSA)—As defined by the US Bureau of the Census, a term in use since 2003, to refer either to a metropolitan or micropolitan statistical area.

CORPORATE WELFARE—A term used by some journalists to describe the public provision of direct and indirect subsidies for capital and other costs as incentives to businesses.

COST-BENEFIT ANALYSIS—A study to determine whether a proposed project is worthwhile, by assessing current and future costs and benefits from the project. The general mathematical framework in which cost-benefit analysis occurs expresses the present value of the difference between the stream of current and future benefits and the stream of current and future costs: $\Sigma \ (\text{benefits}_t - \text{costs}_t) \ / \ (1 + r)_t$.

COST-BURDENED HOUSING—Housing costs that exceed 30 percent of a household's pretax annual income (see "affordable housing").

COST-EFFECTIVENESS ANALYSIS—A technique closely related to cost-benefit analysis that attempts to find the least cost method for obtaining a particular objective even when the value of the objective cannot be judged against the cost of obtaining it.

COST-OF-LIVING INDEX—An index of the cost of maintaining a given standard of living. This is found by measuring the total cost of a specified set of goods and services commonly bought by consumers and measuring the change in the cost of purchasing this market basket of goods and services over time.

CREATIVE CLASS—As defined by Richard Florida, the group of workers in science and engineering, architecture and design, education, arts, and music and entertainment whose economic function is to create new ideas, new technology, and new creative content.

CREATIVE DESTRUCTION—The replacement of older industries and economic activity in a region with new industries and economic activities.

CROSS-SUBSIDIES—Paying for services that operate at a loss using the revenue derived from other services that operate at a profit.

CULTURAL, TOURISM, AND RECREATION CENTERS—Cities (or metropolitan areas) where activities tied to recreation, culturally significant venues, and historically important sites constitute a large part of the economic base, or where such activities are the dominant source of economic growth.

DECISION ANALYSIS—A tool that is similar to cost-benefit analysis but focuses on a decision made by a specific interested party such as a homeowner, an industrial firm, or a particular government department or division rather than society as a whole.

DE FACTO—A Latin term meaning "from reality." De facto is often used to indicate that a phenomenon is occurring without formal legal authorization (in other words, not "de jure"). For example, de facto segregation is segregation that exists due to economic factors or social behavior, not imposed by law.

DEFENSIBLE SPACE—An architectural term referring to design elements that deter crime. This can be accomplished through the physical design of an area by raising the likelihood that a crime will be seen and reported, reducing the number of places in which a perpetrator could hide, and creating public spaces that foster a sense of ownership and responsibility among residents.

DEINDUSTRIALIZATION—The rapid loss of factories and factory-related jobs to other parts of the country or to other nations or to the cessation or sharp reduction of production activities in key industries for any reason.

DE JURE—A Latin term meaning "from law." For example, de jure segregation is segregation that is written into law and maintained through the enforcement of such law.

DEMAND—The quantity of a good or service that an individual, group, or nation is willing and able to buy at a specified price.

DEMOGRAPHIC SHIFTS—Changes in the population characteristics of a city, suburb, or other geographic area. These would include changes in the racial and ethnic composition of the population, as well as changes in its age structure, its nativity, or number of people per household.

DESIGN ZONING—Regulating the use of land to promote efficient use of a city's infrastructure or to conserve open spaces.

DISCOUNT RATE—A computational tool that adjusts for the present value of costs or benefits that will occur in the future.

DISECONOMIES OF SCALE—Factors that cause long-run average cost to increase as a firm attempts to increase its output. For example, diseconomies of scale may arise from problems in communication or coordination as a large organization continues to grow.

DISEMBODIED KNOWLEDGE—Knowledge that has been written down by people with skills and insight, so that it can be learned by others rather than only learned through experience.

DISSIMILARITY INDEX—A measure of the difference in the patterns in which two population groups are spread across a geographic area. Used in studies of housing markets and social dynamics, the dissimilarity index shows the extent to which each census tract or neighborhood within the geographic area replicates the racial composition of the area as a whole.

DISTRIBUTIONAL ROLE OF GOVERNMENT—The role that governments play when they change the access to income or to goods and services from what market forces would otherwise have produced.

DIVISION OF LABOR—A system of production in which different people are assigned different types of work.

DOWNWARD FILTERING—A succession of ownership (or rental residency) that moves down income levels from higher-income families to middle-income families to lower-income families.

DROIDS—In package delivery, autonomous robots that deliver packages to households and businesses.

DUAL LABOR MARKET—A labor market in which there is a primary sector, containing jobs that pay relatively high wages, provide good working conditions and reasonable employment stability, and offer chances of advancement; and a secondary sector, containing jobs that tend to be low paying with poor working conditions and considerable instability, little chance for advancement, and high turnover.

ECONOMIC BASE—Economic activities that produce goods and services that can be sold outside the metropolitan area, generating income for those in the metro area from those residing in other regions. Economic base theory states that such firms are the primary determining factor in the economic growth of a town or region.

ECONOMIC PROFIT—The return that a business owner receives over and above what is necessary to keep him or her willingly in business. This is typically thought of as the amount above the return the owner would receive in the owner's next-best business alternative.

ECONOMIES OF SCALE—Factors that cause a firm's long-run average cost to decrease as the firm's output increases. For example, large-scale production permits specialization in the use of labor, buying in bulk, and other ways of acquiring and using resources, all of which may help to lower costs.

ECOSYSTEM—A community or group of living organisms that live in and interact with each other in a specific environment.

EDGE CITIES—A term used to describe a pattern of urban growth where there are concentrations of economic activity and residences in the outer rings of metropolitan areas. Edge cities are typically built around large retail malls or the intersection of two major highways. According to Joel Garreau, who introduced the term in the early 1990s, an edge city must include at least 5 million square feet of leasable office space and 600,000 square feet of retail space.

EDUCATION PRODUCTION FUNCTION—A mathematical representation of the relationship between inputs in the educational process, such as the teacher/student ratio in a school or the number of library books, and educational outcomes, such as graduation rates or scores on standardized tests.

EDUCATION VOUCHERS—Educational systems in which households are entitled to a certain amount of public funding for a child's education, regardless of whether the child attends public, private, or parochial (religiously oriented) schools. Parents of school-age children typically receive a document (called a voucher) that can be used toward the payment of tuition at any school within the voucher system.

EFFICIENCY—Using resources in the most optimal way. This entails either maximizing output (being as productive as possible) with a given set of inputs, or minimizing the amount of inputs needed to produce a given amount of output.

ELITISM—The belief that public-sector decision-making reflects the interests and values of powerful individuals or groups, rather than the interests of the public at large.

EMERGENCY MEDICAL SERVICES (EMS)—The provision of emergency services, such as cardiopulmonary resuscitation, control of bleeding, administration of lifesaving drugs, and other potentially lifesaving techniques, by trained personnel from the public or private sectors, who specialize in on-the-scene medical interventions for injured or ill people prior to and during transportation to hospitals.

EMERGENCY MEDICAL TECHNICIANS (EMTS)—Trained personnel who travel to a scene in ambulances to provide emergency medical services.

EMINENT DOMAIN—The power of local government to take private land for public use.

EMISSIONS TRADING—A market-based solution to reducing carbon dioxide (or other) emissions by setting an overall limit and allowing firms to trade pollution permits within that established limit.

EMPOWERMENT ZONE—An economically distressed area eligible for tax and regulatory relief under the Federal Empowerment Zone program, initiated in 1993.

ENTERPRISE ZONE (EZ)—An economically distressed area eligible for tax and regulatory relief (e.g., sales tax exemptions, tax waivers, building permit fee waivers, subsidies) under state enterprise zone laws.

ENTITLEMENT—A benefit available by law automatically to all qualifying individuals or households.

ENVIRONMENTAL JUSTICE—Fairness to all racial, ethnic, or socioeconomic groups, with respect to the environmental impacts of industrial, municipal, and commercial activities and with respect to the environmental impacts of government policies and programs.

EPIDEMICS—Diseases that affect many more people than usual, and rapidly spread to others.

EQUITY—Fairness in the distribution of resources or income.

EXCLUDABLE—Capable of being provided to one person and not to others. Excludable goods/services can be purchased and consumed by one person, without others having access to the good/service that has been purchased. This contrasts with nonexcludable goods, which, once they are provided, are accessible to everyone. For example, most privately purchased goods (e.g., an ice cream cone) are excludable. A good like national defense is nonexcludable since, if it is provided, all presumably benefit from it.

EXCLUSIONARY ZONING—Regulating the use of land to bar one or more demographic groups (e.g., racial groups, ethnic groups, or income groups) from areas of a city or town.

EXPORT BASE THEORY—A theory that posits the demand from other regions for an area's exports is the key driving force in that area's economic prosperity.

EXPULSIVE ZONING—The use of local zoning ordinances to bar use of land for activities that produce negative externalities in areas populated by a particular race/ethnicity group, while allowing those activities in areas populated by other race/ethnicities. The unwanted externalities are essentially expelled from the former areas into the nonprotected areas.

EXTERNAL DISECONOMIES—A cost that arises from an economic activity that does not fall on the person or firm producing or consuming the goods or services produced by that activity.

EXTERNAL ECONOMIES—A benefit that arises from an economic activity that does not accrue to the person or firm producing or consuming the goods or services produced by that activity.

EXTERNALITIES—A cost or benefit in production or consumption that does not accrue solely to the producer or consumer of the commodity, but to others.

EXTERNALITY ZONING—Regulating the use of land to separate activities that create negative externalities from other activities that may be adversely affected by those externalities.

EXURBAN REGIONS—Areas or towns that are located in the rural areas beyond those considered to be the suburbs of a city.

FEE—A fixed amount of money charged for a service or privilege.

FEE SIMPLE—A legal tradition in which, at the most fundamental level, land is owned by government, and the ownership of private property by individuals and other private entities is a right conferred by government. The implication of fee simple is that governments can revoke the right of ownership. This is the legal underpinning for eminent domain.

FINANCIAL CENTERS—Cities (or metropolitan areas) where access and expertise that link firms and individuals to financial services (such as potential investors, sources of loans, accounting, wealth management, and insurance) constitute a large part of the economic base, or where such activities are the dominant source of growth.

FIRST-MOVER ADVANTAGE—The benefit from being first into a market with a new product.

FISCAL ZONING—Regulating the use of land to bar changes that would adversely affect tax revenue or the municipal budget.

FIXED COSTS—Costs that do not vary with the level of output.

FREE RIDER PROBLEM—The ability of individuals or firms to legally enjoy consumer goods or services without having to pay for them. This phenomenon exists in the case of nonexcludable goods where no provision for payment through taxes or special user fees is established.

GATED COMMUNITIES—Privately owned residential areas created by homeowners' associations where fences, gates, and walls exclude those who do not own property within.

GENERAL RECIPROCITY—The expectation that someone who does a good deed will be rewarded, though not necessarily by the beneficiaries of that good deed.

GENERAL TAX INCENTIVES—Inducements given to all firms meeting qualifications specified in the applicable tax law.

GENTRIFICATION—The displacement of low- and moderate-income residents from an area due to rising housing values, and their replacement with higher-income families.

GLOBALIZATION—The increased integration of economic activity (including trade, investment, production, technological change, and other activities) across national boundaries.

GREENHOUSE GASES—gases such as carbon dioxide, methane, nitrous oxide, and fluorinated gases that contribute to global warming.

GROWTH MACHINE—A concept that emphasizes the role of real estate investors, bankers, and other local business interests acting out of self-interest to promote intensification of land use as their primary objective.

HARD COSTS—The costs of capital, labor, and taxes incurred by developers as contrasted with the soft costs of regulation such as legal costs and time delays.

HAZMAT TRUCKS—Trucks that carry industrial waste, nuclear waste, chemicals, or other materials that are potentially hazardous to humans.

HEDONIC PRICE INDEX—A statistical technique that seeks to quantify the value of each of the various attributes of a complex good.

HERD IMMUNITY—A situation in which high levels of immunization protect both those who have received the vaccine and those who have not.

HIGHEST AND BEST USE—The use of market competition to determine the most productive use for land or other goods.

HOUSING TRUST FUNDS—Low-cost loans made available to housing developers if they agree to set aside a minimum number to be rented or sold at prices affordable to low- and moderate-income households.

HUMAN CAPITAL—Skills, knowledge, or other attributes that render a worker more productive.

IMPORT SUBSTITUTION—A strategy for increasing output and employment in a region by producing goods or services for local consumption that were once imported into the region from other locations. The strategy of import substitution can be contrasted with that of export promotion, where industrial effort is focused on the production and goods and services that can be sold to other regions to generate local income.

INCLUSIONARY ZONING LAWS—Municipal laws that provide housing developers with waivers of previously existing limits on the number of units per acre in return for the developer building a number of affordable housing units in the development or contributing to an affordable housing trust fund used for building low-income housing.

INCOME ELASTICITY—A measure of how much a specified variable changes in response to changes in income (both expressed in percentage terms). For example, the income elasticity of demand for food is the percentage increase in demand for food divided by the percentage increase in income. An income elasticity of 0.2 would mean that if income rises by 1 percent, the demand for food rises by 0.2 percent.

INDIFFERENCE CURVES—A line or curve that shows all combinations of consumption goods that yield the same level of total satisfaction (utility) for an individual. Because they each yield the same level of satisfaction, the individual would be indifferent as to which combination was received.

INDUSTRIAL POLICY—The strategic effort by a federal, state, or local government to encourage the development and growth of a particular sector of the economy, a particular industry, or business.

INDUSTRIAL REVENUE BONDS—Bonds issued by municipal governments to raise funds to provide land, buildings, and equipment that will be leased by a private industrial company for a set number of years. Such bonds are often used to attract companies to an area, or to provide funding for expansion of companies that already exist in the area.

INDUSTRIAL TRANSFORMATION—The prosperity and growth of some industries, while others become obsolete (see also "creative destruction").

INDUSTRY CLUSTERS—Groups of firms located near each other, that are in the same industry or in related industries (through their roles as suppliers or purchasers of each other's products, or through their reliance upon the same set of inputs).

INELASTIC DEMAND—Demand for a good or service for which consumers are not highly sensitive to changes in price. Often these are commodities without good substitutes, so many consumers will continue to purchase them despite higher prices.

INFANT MORTALITY RATE—The proportion of deaths among children during their first year of life. The infant mortality rate is calculated by taking the number of deaths of children before their first birthday during a year and dividing it by the number of live births during that same year.

INFORMAL ECONOMY—See "underground economy."

INNOVATION CENTERS—Cities (or metropolitan areas) where activities (such as research and development, universities, and medical facilities) related to the discovery of new ideas and new products constitute a large part of the economic base, or where such activities are the dominant source of growth.

INNOVATION DISTRICTS—An approach to economic development that bring together in close proximity within a city all of the ingredients needed to spawn new industry.

INPUT-OUTPUT ANALYSIS—A technique for studying the interdependence in production among the entire array of industrial sectors of an economy. An input-output table calculates all flows of goods and services between sectors of origin (and factor services) and sectors of destination. As an example, an input-output analysis will show how much steel is consumed in the production functions of each industry (including the steel industry itself).

INTERDISTRICT CHOICE—An educational system in which families are allowed to select and send their children to public schools in school districts other than the ones in which they reside.

INTEREST-GROUP THEORY—The belief that public-sector decision-making can best be understood through the realization that decision-makers face competing pressures and demands from formal and informal groups of individuals, with each group trying to persuade the decision-makers to make decisions favorable to that group.

INTERGENERATIONAL EQUITY—Fairness with regard to how the costs of providing a service are divided across generations. Intergenerational equity is an issue in financing major projects for which services and payments will continue across generations.

INTERNAL ECONOMIES OF SCALE—Economies of scale that result from factors within the firm. Internal economies of scale contrast with external economies of scale (such as agglomeration economies), which result from factors outside the firm.

INTRADISTRICT CHOICE—An educational system in which families are allowed to select and send their children to any public school within the boundaries of the school district in which they reside.

JOB MULTIPLIER—The relationship between employment in economic base (basic) industries and employment in the economy as a whole. The job multiplier is calculated as total employment divided by export employment in the economic base industries. Economic base theory states that the job multiplier is a measure of the number of jobs in the overall economy of an area that will be created as the result of each additional job in basic industries.

KNOWLEDGE SPILLOVERS—The spread of new skills, insights, and information from one application to another or from one firm to another. Knowledge spillovers can occur through formal arrangements, such as industry symposia designed to spread new knowledge, or through informal channels, such as when workers from different firms within a field socialize with each other.

LABOR MARKET SEGMENTATION—A labor market containing two or more segments that provide very different wages and working conditions (see "dual labor market").

LINKAGE PROGRAMS—Municipal laws that require developers of commercial and industrial property to make payments to a housing fund for the construction of affordable housing to offset pressure on the housing market that presumably will be caused by the hiring of new employees in the businesses occupying those properties.

LOCALIZATION ECONOMIES—Agglomeration economies that result from firms in the same industry locating near one another (see "agglomeration economies").

LOCALLY UNWANTED LAND USES (LULUS)—Land uses that residents do not want to have nearby (such as industrial plants and hazardous waste sites).

LOCATION-EFFICIENT MORTGAGES—Mortgages that offer better terms for home purchases in areas where there is less need to commute by private automobile. Such mortgages are currently available in only a few cities.

LOCATION QUOTIENT—A statistical measure of the extent to which a particular economic activity is over- or underrepresented in the economy of a region, compared to its representation in the economy as a whole.

LONG RUN AVERAGE COST CURVE—The total cost per unit of output during a time period sufficiently long that increases in plant and equipment can occur. Thus, the long-run average cost curve depicts production costs when all inputs can be increased.

LOW BIRTH WEIGHT—The weight of a newborn who is less than 2,500 grams (about five and a half pounds). Babies with low birth weights are more likely to be at risk for life-threatening complications.

MACROECONOMICS—The study of the behavior of a national economy as a whole, including the study of gross domestic product, inflation, unemployment, and economic growth.

MAGNET SCHOOLS—Public schools with a specialized curriculum or a distinctive approach to learning that are open to students throughout a school district, regardless of the school to which they would normally be assigned.

MANUFACTURING CITIES (CENTERS)—Cities (or metropolitan areas) where the production of finished consumer goods or components for use as inputs in further manufacture constitute a large part of the economic base, or where such activities are the dominant source of growth.

MARGINAL PRODUCT—The additional quantity of output that is generated by one more unit of a single input. For example, the marginal product of labor is the increase in the amount of output that comes from one more worker.

MARKET-ORIENTED FIRMS—Firms for which transportation costs are the primary determinant of location, and in which those costs are minimized by locating production close to the market where the final consumer is located.

MARKET POWER—The ability to influence the terms on which a market exchange is made. As most commonly used, the term market power describes the ability of a monopoly or oligopoly to raise prices. A firm with no market power has to sell at the same price that other sellers of the same good are charging.

MARKET VALUE—The price that a good would receive if sold on the open market.

MATERIALS-ORIENTED FIRMS—Firms for which transportation costs are the primary determinant of location, and in which those costs are minimized by locating production close to the source of raw materials.

MEDIAN FAMILY INCOME—After arraying all families according to income from lowest to highest, the income that divides the distribution in half. Fifty percent of all families have an income lower than the median; 50 percent have an income above it.

MEDICAID—A joint state/federal health insurance program to fund healthcare for individuals with low income and few resources. Created in 1965, in the same legislation that created Medicare, Medicaid is managed by the states, and is available only to individuals who fall under specified income and resource criteria.

MERIT GOOD—Also called "merit wants." A good whose consumption is deemed to be intrinsically beneficial, but which, due to imperfect knowledge or unaccounted- for externalities, is purchased by consumers in insufficient quantities. The consumption of merit goods (such as basic education or housing) is often encouraged by government through public provision or subsidy because of the beneficial results that presumably ensue to society.

MERIT WANTS—See "merit good."

METROPOLITAN AREA (MA)—A geographic area containing a large population nucleus, together with adjacent communities that have a high degree of economic and social integration with that nucleus (some metropolitan areas are defined around two or more nuclei). Metropolitan areas are designated by the federal Office of Management and Budget in terms of one or more counties or, in New England, county subdivisions (primarily cities and towns).

METROPOLITANISM—Cooperation between central cities and their surrounding suburbs to work toward common goals.

METROPOLITAN STATISTICAL AREAS (MSAS)—Defined by the US Office of Management and Budget as an area that includes a city of at least 50,000 population or an urbanized area of at least 50,000 with a total metropolitan area population of at least 100,000. Generally, an MSA consists of one or more counties, except in New England, where MSAs are defined in terms of county subdivisions (primarily cities and towns).

MICROECONOMICS—The study of the behavior of individual consumers and firms, including the study of how prices are determined in markets for specific goods or services, how goods are distributed among the population, and how income from market exchange is distributed.

MICROPOLITAN STATISTICAL AREA—As defined by the US Office of Management and Budget, urban areas too small to be classified as metropolitan areas, but having at least one urban cluster of between 10,000 and 50,000 inhabitants.

MINIMUM WAGE—A minimum level of pay established by law for workers in general. The federal minimum wage law covers the vast majority of US workers; many states have minimum wage laws that supersede federal law.

MONETARY WEIGHT—The monetary cost of transporting a product times the weight of that product. Monetary weights are used in the determination of the most cost-effective location for a transportation-cost-oriented firm.

MONOCENTRISM—The characteristic of having one center of activity

MONONUCLEARITY—Having one, and only one, center of key activity, with other parts of the urban area dependent upon this one central area.

MONOPOLIST—A business that is the only seller of a particular good or service for which there is no close substitute.

MONOPOLY—The existence of only one seller for a given product for which there is no close substitute.

MULTIPLE IDENTITIES—A situation in which an individual may have one persona within a specific group at one time and a completely different persona with another group at another time.

MUNICIPAL HEALTH CENTERS—Centers established and funded by municipal governments to provide medical services, health education, health-related outreach, and other services. The extent of services provided is determined by individual city governments.

MUNICIPALITIES—Legally established cities or towns, usually pursuant to state legislation.

MUNICIPAL PUBLIC WELFARE DEPARTMENTS—Municipal offices established to help coordinate and deliver publicly and privately financed social services to poor people.

NATURAL MONOPOLY—The existence of a monopoly in which economies of scale are so large that no entry by competitors is possible once an incumbent firm is established.

NEW GROWTH THEORY—A theory of economic growth that emphasizes the role of education and technology in the growth process. Within new growth theory, education not only has direct effects on productivity, but also has spill-over effects that enhance a region's competitive advantage.

NEW TRADE THEORY—An approach to understanding trade between countries or regions that emphasizes the effect of economies of scale in production and the barriers that existing large-scale production pose for the entry of new firms to an industry.

NEW URBANISM—An approach to urban planning that seeks to recreate more vibrant civic life through architectural and design elements, such as higher-density housing, front porches, and other elements that encourage interaction along lively streets.

NOMINAL WAGES—The dollar amount of the pay received; the amount shown on a paycheck (contrast with "real wages").

NONAMORTIZING MORTGAGES—Mortgages in which only the interest is paid during the term of the mortgage, and a large payment, consisting of the entire principal, is due at the end of the mortgage. This contrasts with amortized mortgages, where the amount of the principal is gradually reduced through payments during the mortgage term.

OCCUPATIONAL SAFETY AND HEALTH ACT—A federal law, passed in 1970 that requires employers to provide workers with safe and sanitary workplaces.

OFFSHORING—The relocation of a production center, or some other part of a firm, to another country, using a central office in the original country simply to coordinate production and distribution. Offshoring is particularly notable in recent decades, as some firms have moved part of their operations to areas with cheaper labor or better access to other inputs.

OLIGOPOLIST—A firm that is one of only a few producers in its industry.

OLIGOPOLY—The existence of only a few producers in an industry.

OPPORTUNITY COST—The value of the best alternative given up (forgone) when income or time is used to consume something else.

OPPORTUNITY STRUCTURES—The access to resources and institutions that individuals possess. Access is affected by where individuals live, as well as by race, ethnicity, income, wealth, and other factors, and is continuously shaped by government policies, private-sector decisions, and the choices of individuals.

OPTION VALUE—The value that consumers who do not usually use a good or service place on the standby availability of that good/service (that is, its availability), should they want or need to use it in the future. An example would be a city park that may be seldom used by a particular resident but is still available to that resident if he or she chooses to visit it. Also refers to the value of completing a given education degree in terms of the completion permitting one to go on to a higher level of schooling.

OUTSOURCING—Moving functions originally performed within a company to another firm that performs the function and sells the resulting parts or services to the original firm. It is called outsourcing because after the functions have been moved, the source of the parts or services is outside the original firm.

OVERCROWDING—A situation in which a housing unit contains more than one person per room.

OVERZONING—A restriction on land development in the absence of negative externalities that arise from incompatible land uses.

PARETO OPTIMALITY—The condition of an allocation of goods such that no shift of resources is possible without reducing the satisfaction of at least one consumer.

PATERNALISM—Governmental action where the judgment of government decision-makers is substituted for the judgment of individual citizens or consumers.

PATH DEPENDENCY—The situation that occurs when elements of the past or present affect future conditions; historical circumstances or choices made by individuals open up some possibilities for the future, while closing off other possibilities.

PHILLIPS CURVE—Statistical observation by A. W. Phillips of an inverse relationship between the rate of inflation and the unemployment rate.

PHYSICAL INFRASTRUCTURE—The basic underlying capital equipment (such as pipes, roads, cables, etc.) used to provide services to the general public (such as transport, telecommunications, water, and sanitation).

PLURALISM—Another name for interest-group theory; the belief that public-sector decision-making can best be understood through the realization that decision-makers face competing pressures and demands from formal and informal groups of individuals, with each group trying to persuade the decision-makers to make decisions favorable to that group.

POLICE POWER—The right of local government to protect the health, safety, and general well-being of its citizens by imposing appropriate regulations. This is the legal basis for building codes, zoning, health regulations, and other measures that restrict the activities that occur within a government's jurisdiction.

POPULATION DENSITY—A statistical measure of the number of people who live within a certain land area (total population divided by area). Also, a descriptive attribute meaning large numbers of people living in close proximity to each other.

PORK BARREL POLITICS—Government spending that is intended to benefit constituents of a politician, such as private urban developers or defense contractors in return for their political support, either in the form of campaign contributions or votes.

POVERTY RATE—The proportion of the population in a given area with income below the poverty thresholds (which differ according to family size) established by the US government.

PRESENT DISCOUNTED VALUE—The value now of a stream of future income payments, taking into account that payments made in the future are worth less than payments made today because a current payment can accumulate interest.

PRICE ELASTICITY OF DEMAND—The percentage change in quantity demanded resulting from a 1 percent change in price.

PRICE ELASTICITY OF SUPPLY—The percentage change in quantity supplied resulting from a 1 percent change in price.

PRIMARY METROPOLITAN STATISTICAL AREA (PMSA)—Now obsolete, this term was defined by the US Bureau of the Census to refer to a metropolitan statistical area (MSA) that was part of a larger consolidated metropolitan statistical area (CMSA).

PRIMARY SECTOR INDUSTRIES—Agriculture, timber, mining, and fishing industries (see also "secondary sector industries" and "tertiary sector industries").

PRINCIPAL-AGENT PROBLEM—The problem that exists when the interests of an agent acting on behalf of a client (the principal) diverge from the interests of the client. For example, the interests of the manager of a corporation may differ from the interests of the stockholders who hired the manager.

PRINCIPAL CITY—The largest city in a metropolitan area, along with any cities in a metro area with a population of at least 250,000 or in which 100,000 or more persons work, and other cities in the metro area that meet specified official standards of population size and employment. This term is often a synonym for "central city."

PRISONER'S DILEMMA—A situation where the pursuit of self-interest by separate individuals without regard for the well-being of others keeps all individuals from reaching goals that actually maximize their self-interest.

PRIVATE SECURITY GUARDS—Individuals hired by private groups to provide screening, monitoring, and control of behavior, and other activities related to the security of the people or firms who have hired them.

PROBLEM-ORIENTED POLICING—An approach to crime prevention that relies on the police attempting to systematically understand the causes of recurring crime and react with a concerted effort of problem solving, planning, mediating, and organizing the community to fight it.

PRODUCTION COSTS—The costs incurred in the manufacture of a good, including the cost of labor, raw material, machinery, rental property, energy, and taxes and fees.

PRODUCTIVE EFFICIENCY—Producing goods at the lowest possible cost per unit.

PRODUCT LIFE CYCLE THEORY—An approach to understanding firm location and urban prosperity that emphasizes how the location of production for a particular good may change over time due to changes in production and marketing needs and competitive forces as the product moves from initial introduction into the market to widespread market circulation.

PUBLIC CHOICE THEORY—A branch of economics concerned with the application of economics to the analysis of nonmarket public decision-making. One assumption of public choice theory is that public employees will seek to maximize personal utility, and in the absence of adequate monitoring by government, decisions may be made that benefit the employees' interests rather than the interests of the overall public.

PULL FACTORS—Positive characteristics of an area that attract migration of residents or firms from other regions or nations.

PURE PUBLIC GOODS—Goods that are nonexcludable (once they are provided, they are available to everybody), and nonrival (consumption or use by one person does not diminish the amount of that good or service available for other individuals).

PUSH FACTORS—Negative characteristics of an area that encourage migration of residents or firms to other regions or nations.

REAL ADJUSTED WAGES—The dollar amount of the pay received adjusted for changes in prices over time; the purchasing power of wages compared to the purchasing power of the same nominal wage in the past.

REDLINING—A practice where banks (or other lenders) refuse to make mortgage or home repair loans for specific areas in a city. Historically associated with racial discrimination, the practice is known as redlining because some lenders drew red lines on maps to indicate the areas that were not to be given loans.

REFUSE—Also known as "solid waste," refuse is leftover material that has been thrown away by households, businesses, and other parties (see "solid waste").

REGIME THEORY—An approach to understanding the relationships between government and private sectors as decisions are made that affect urban areas. Regimes are informal coalitions that represent business, government, and others who are working toward a goal that requires the participation of both private and public sectors. Parties within the coalition may not have the same exact interests but are willing to participate in movement toward a goal because of the benefits that are expected from achieving the goal, or because of promises that have been made from other members of the coalition to acquire their cooperation.

REGRESSION ANALYSIS—A statistical technique that seeks to explain changes in an outcome (a dependent variable) in terms of changes in other variables (independent variables) that are, based on theory, believed to be causes of the outcome.

REGULATORY COSTS—Costs incurred by businesses in the course of complying with local, state, and federal laws.

RENT—In discussion of housing (or commercial property), rent is the price paid to the owner of a property for use of the home (or commercial space). In microeconomics, rent is sometimes used to refer to the amount paid for an input (e.g., to a worker with unique talents) above the amount of that input's opportunity cost (its next-best-paying alternative use).

RESIDENTIAL PARADOX—The situation in which lower-income families tend to live closer to the central parts of cities on more expensive land and where higher-income families live in the suburbs on less expensive land. The paradox is explained by the high-density living conditions of lower-income families so that the price per square foot per person is lower in the higher-priced central city than in less expensive suburbs.

RESIDENTIAL SEGREGATION—A residential pattern where households of different races or members of particular ethnic groups live in separate neighborhoods within a city or metro area.

RESILIENCE (CLIMATE CHANGE)—A capability to anticipate, prepare for, respond to, and recover from significant multihazard threats with minimum damage to social well-being, the economy, and the environment.

RETIREMENT CENTERS—Cities (or metropolitan areas) that attract large numbers of individuals retiring from their former jobs, and where income from retirement earnings and activities related to retirement constitutes a large part of the economic base, or where such activities are the dominant source of growth.

RISK—The situation that exists when future outcomes are not known but probabilities of various outcomes can be calculated from data.

RISK (CLIMATE CHANGE)—A combination of the magnitude of the potential consequences of climate change impacts and the likelihood that the consequences will occur.

RISK MANAGEMENT—An analytic tool which is used to consider cases where there is a need for information about the relative likelihood of a variety of possible events or variation in the intensity of an event.

RIVAL—The characteristic of a good or service where consumption or use by one person diminishes the amount of that good or service available for other individuals.

SCALE ECONOMIES—See "economies of scale."

SCHOOL CHOICE—An educational system in which parents can decide which school their children attend, rather than having schools assigned by residential address or other criteria.

SECONDARY MORTGAGE MARKET—The market in which banks or other financial institutions sell their existing mortgage contracts with households to other parties (such as other financial institutions and pension funds). The secondary mortgage market provides cash (or other short-term assets) to the bank that originally sold the loan, while providing a longer-term flow of funds (from the household) to the new mortgage holder.

SECONDARY SECTOR INDUSTRIES—Construction and manufacturing industries (see also "primary sector industries" and "tertiary sector industries").

SELECTIVE MIGRATION—Migration in which those who leave an area come disproportionately from specific demographic groups. For example, the migration away from depressed areas tends to be composed disproportionately of younger, better educated individuals.

SETTLEMENT HOUSES—Organizations (and the buildings out of which they operated) that were established to provide social, educational, and health services to immigrants and to low-income residents of cities in the late 1800s and early 1900s. The most widely known settlement house was Hull House, founded in Chicago by Jane Addams.

SEVERELY COST-BURDENED HOUSING—Housing costs that exceed 50 percent of a household's pretax annual income.

SHADOW ECONOMY—See "underground economy."

SHORT RUN AVERAGE COST CURVE—The total cost per unit of output during a short enough time period that no changes in plant and equipment can take place. Any increase in output is due only to increased use of labor and raw materials.

SITE ASSEMBLY PROBLEM—The problem confronted by developers when a certain amount of land is needed for a development project but parts of the needed land are owned by a variety of individuals, some of whom are willing to sell to the developer and others who are not.

SITE COSTS—Costs incurred to procure—and make any necessary adjustments to—the land and buildings that a business occupies.

SMART GROWTH—Planned development to limit suburban sprawl through measures that increase density. Among current smart growth initiatives are transit-oriented development, urban growth boundaries, location-efficient mortgages, transferable development rights, and new urbanism. Proponents of smart growth development believe that it can improve central cities, promote environmental quality, save public resources, lower energy consumption, and preserve rural land and open space.

SOCIAL BENEFIT—The sum of the gains or benefits to society as a whole from an activity or project. This includes benefits accrued both by the particular consumers of the activity or project and by others who are not directly party to the consumption. A common example is the social benefit that derives from the education of other people's children.

SOCIAL CAPITAL—The ability of individuals to harness the resources they need through a network of friends and relatives. Social capital depends upon intangible things with economic value that either are contained within or are transmitted through social relationships. Examples of social capital include trust, information, and obligations.

SOCIAL COST—The full opportunity cost to society of using resources to produce a particular good or service rather than using the resources for some other purpose.

SOCIAL INFRASTRUCTURE—An area's ability to produce human capital as measured by the quality of its education and training institutions as well as its health care facilities.

SOCIAL NETWORK—A social structure made of nodes (which are generally individuals or organizations) that are tied together by one or more specific types of relations, including kinship, employment, or business links. Social networks play a critical role in determining the way problems are solved, organizations are run, and the degree to which individuals succeed in achieving their goals.

SOCIAL SECURITY—A federal program to provide retirement income, disability income, and income for surviving spouses and children of deceased workers.

SOFT COSTS—The legal costs and time delays developers experience due to regulation as contrasted with the hard costs of capital, labor, and taxes.

SPATIAL MISMATCH—A situation where lack of access to suburban housing (due to housing discrimination or to high prices for houses) and lack of access to transportation prevent jobseekers in cities from reaching jobs that are located in the suburbs.

SPATIAL RELOCATION—The movement of households, businesses, and other activities from one geographic area to another. Spatial relocation includes movement from one country to another, from one metro area to another, or from city to suburb (and vice versa).

SPECIAL TAX BREAK—Inducements given to a specific firm or group of firms, keyed to considerations such as the number of new workers hired or to specified neighborhoods within a municipality.

SPECIALIZATION—Dividing up production tasks so that people (or places) concentrate on tasks in which they have an advantage—that is, that they can perform more efficiently than other people (or places). Specialization normally results in higher levels of output, or improved quality of output.

SPECIFIC RECIPROCITY—The expectation that someone who does a good deed will be rewarded by the beneficiaries of that good deed.

SPILLOVER EFFECTS—The positive or negative impact of an exchange on third parties who are neither the buyers nor the sellers involved in the transaction.

STANDARD METROPOLITAN STATISTICAL AREAS (SMSAS)— As defined by the US Office of Management and Budget, a term used between 1959 and 1983 to refer to large metro areas. In 1983 the term "standard" was dropped, and large metro areas were subsequently referred to simply as "metropolitan statistical areas" (MSAs).

STATISTICAL DECISION THEORY—See "decision analysis."

STATISTICAL DISCRIMINATION—Judging an individual not on his or her own credentials, but on beliefs about the characteristics of the average or typical member of a demographic group to which the individual belongs.

STEERING—The practice by real estate agents of limiting housing options by showing to prospective home buyers only the housing in neighborhoods with population characteristics similar to their own (e.g., showing White households properties only in White areas and showing minority households properties only in minority areas).

SUPPLEMENTARY SECURITY INCOME (SSI)—A federal program to provide income support for low-income elderly and disabled individuals.

SUPPLY—The amount of a good or service offered for sale at any given price.

SUPPLY CHAINS—The systems of firms, processes, and transportation that are involved in producing a good and making it available for purchase. Supply chains can extend from extraction of the basic raw materials from which the good is made, through all steps in manufacturing, and end with final sale of the finished product.

SUSTAINED COMPETITIVE ADVANTAGE—The ability of firms and regions to innovate in order to successfully maintain a competitive advantage over an extended period of time.

SYSTEMIC SOCIAL DISORGANIZATION APPROACH—An approach to crime that emphasizes the ability of neighborhood residents to build social capital (such as trust and shared norms) that will increase their influence on the behavior of individual residents. Adherents of this approach try to change patterns of social interaction among families in ways that will build social capital.

TAX—Financial obligation imposed by a government upon individuals, businesses, and other entities to provide funds used to support government activities.

TAX EFFORT—The tax rate per dollar of assessed property value; the total property tax collected by local governments divided by the total value of assessed property in their jurisdictions.

TAX EXPENDITURES—Preferential tax treatment that reduces revenue flowing to government, and increases the income retained by a particular group of households or firms. Essentially, it is the cost to government of tax exclusions, exemptions, deductions and deferrals provided to particular groups of households or firms. An example of a tax expenditure is the provision in federal tax laws that allows homeowners to reduce their taxable income by the amount of their home mortgage interest.

TAX INCREMENT FINANCING (TIF)—The financing of local development projects through the issuance of municipal bonds backed by the expected increase (increments) in tax revenue from future increases in property values within the designated TIF area. The proceeds from the bond sales can be used for site clearance, utility installation, street construction and repair, and other purposes that reduce costs for private businesses willing to locate in depressed areas where TIF districts are permitted.

TAX REVOLT—Initiatives by voters to limit the tax rates that governments can charge on property and other taxable items.

TECHNOLOGICAL PROGRESS—The use of new or recent scientific knowledge in ways that lead to new innovations, inventions, and insights.

TELECOMMUTING—Performing a job from home, rather than coming into a central workplace, and communicating with the employer and other workers in the office or elsewhere through use of the internet or telephone.

TELECONFERENCING—Using telecommunications equipment (such as conferencing telephones or the internet) to conduct live meetings among three or more people in different locations.

TEMPORARY ASSISTANCE FOR NEEDY FAMILIES (TANF)—A federal program to provide income support mainly for single-parent families with dependent children. In place since 1995, it replaced the older Aid to Families with Dependent Children (AFCD).

TERTIARY SECTOR INDUSTRIES—Wholesale and retail trade and business and personal service industries (see also "primary sector industries" and "secondary sector industries").

TIPPING POINT—The small action in the course of a series of actions that leads to a major change in a trend or behavior. For example, when a new racial group begins to reside in what was once a segregated neighborhood, there may be little change in racial composition until the proportion of the new racial group reaches a critical point and then the racial composition of the neighborhood changes dramatically.

TOTAL COST (TC)—The sum of a firm's fixed costs and variable costs.

TOTAL REVENUE (TR)—The total receipts that a firm takes in from selling its goods and services.

TRADE—The exchange of goods and services for money, or for other goods and services.

TRADITIONAL APPROACH TO URBAN CRIME—A police department approach to crime that emphasizes rapid response and raising the probability of arrest through the use of crime laboratories and investigatory techniques. This was the dominant police department approach to crime throughout most of the twentieth century.

TRANSFERABLE DEVELOPMENT RIGHTS (TDRS)—Government programs that use market forces to promote conservation in agricultural land and open space areas while encouraging smart growth in developed or rapidly developing sections of a community. In a TDR program, a community identifies a local area it would like to see protected from development (the "sending zone") and another area where it desires more concentrated development (the "receiving zone"). Landowners in the sending zone are allocated a number of development credits that can be sold to developers, speculators, or the community itself to help compensate for the loss of market value that preservation entails. Meanwhile, the purchaser of the development credits can apply them to develop at a higher density than otherwise allowed on property within the receiving zone.

TRANSIT-ORIENTED DEVELOPMENT—An approach to urban planning that emphasizes locating higher-density housing and mixed-use development near transit routes, to reduce an area's reliance upon automobiles.

TRANSPORTATION-COST-ORIENTED FIRMS—Firms for which transportation costs are the key factor determining where the firm should be located. The two basic types of transportation-cost-oriented firms are market-oriented firms and materials-oriented firms (sometimes called "resource-oriented firms").

TRANSPORTATION COSTS—Costs incurred in moving inputs to producers (procurement) and shipping the output to points of sale (distribution).

TRANSPORTATION HUBS—Cities where activities related to transportation lines (such as switching goods or people from one mode of transportation to another, redirecting goods or people in new directions, or breaking large shipments of goods into smaller shipments) constitute a large part of the economic base, or where such transportation-related activities are the dominant source of growth.

UNCERTAINTY—The situation that exists when future outcomes are not known and probabilities of various outcomes cannot be calculated because the process leading to the outcome is random or arbitrary. This contrasts with "risk," a term used when it is possible to calculate the probabilities of various outcomes.

UNDERGROUND ECONOMY—This unregulated and poorly measured part of the economy consists of both legal activities (with the exception that taxes are usually not paid on their proceeds) and a range of illegal activities, from unsanctioned gambling and prostitution to the sale of drugs.

UNDERZONING—A failure to prevent negative externalities that arise from incompatible land use.

UNEMPLOYMENT COMPENSATION—A federal/state program to provide temporary partial wage replacement for workers who lose their jobs.

UNEMPLOYMENT RATE—The number of people who are without a job but actively seeking work divided by the number of people in the labor force—those who are either working or actively seeking work.

UNINTENDED CONSEQUENCES—Unforeseen impacts of actions consciously taken by an individual, business, or government. Unintended consequences can be either positive or negative.

UNION DENSITY—The rate of unionization (the ratio of union members to all workers) within a geographic area, industry, or occupation.

UNION SHOP—Places of employment where, under the contract with the employees' union, new employees are required to join the union within a specified period after being hired. In contrast to a closed shop, new hires in a union shop do not need to be union members before being hired.

UPWARD FILTERING—A succession of ownership (or rental residency) that moves up income levels from lower-income families to middle-income families to higher-income families.

URBAN AREA—All territory located within an urban cluster or urbanized area (see "urban cluster" and "urbanized area").

URBAN CLUSTER—A smaller version of an urban area. As defined by the US Bureau of the Census, an urban cluster has a census population of 2,500 to 49,999, at least one core of blocks with a population density of at least 1,000 people per square mile, and adjacent block groups and blocks with at least 500 people per square mile.

URBAN GHETTO—A term used by social scientists to refer to sections of the city that contain high proportions of very poor households. It often refers to neighborhoods that contain poor minority households.

URBAN GROWTH BOUNDARY—A geographic area within which future growth will occur, as established by legislation that limits future development to within a certain radius of the core city.

URBANIZATION ECONOMIES—Agglomeration economies that result from economic activities being concentrated in urban areas. As an example, having a concentration of accounting, advertising, and marketing services available in a central business district reduces the cost to businesses that require all these services.

URBANIZED AREA—As defined by the US Bureau of the Census, a densely settled area that has an overall population of at least 50,000, at least one core of blocks with a population density of at least 1,000 people per square mile, and adjacent block groups and blocks with at least 500 people per square mile.

URBAN POPULATION—As defined by the US Bureau of the Census, all people living in official urbanized areas plus people outside of urbanized areas who live in urban clusters (i.e., towns with more than 2,500 inhabitants).

URBAN PUBLIC AMENITIES—Municipal services intended for voluntary leisure use by the public.

URBAN SLUM—Sections of a city where a concentration of poor people leads to a concentration of poverty-related social problems.

URBAN SPRAWL—Land-use patterns characterized by low density, clusters of activity with only one use (such as housing subdivisions, malls, and industrial parks), and automobile dependency, with resulting negative effects upon a variety of issues that may be of concern to environmentalists, urban planners, and others.

USER FEES—Fees charged to the actual users of government-provided goods or services, in contrast to paying for these items out of general tax revenue. Examples of user fees include charging tolls to cross a bridge, metering households for the amount of water they use, and adopting admission prices for city zoos.

USER TAX—A tax that is charged only to individuals who use a good or service, but which may not, as in the case of a user fee, be prorated on the amount of good or service consumed.

USE VALUE—The subjective value that an individual places upon using or owning a good.

VACANCY RATE—The percentage of housing stock in a neighborhood, city, or metro area that is available for purchase or rental.

VARIANCES—Decisions by city government to approve a specific application for land use that would otherwise be barred by zoning laws. Variances do not change the zoning laws but give permission for the single nonconforming application.

VEIL OF IGNORANCE—The assumption that citizens making choices about their society will do so without knowing what position they will have in that society.

VICIOUS CYCLE—A course of events where predictable factors perpetuate and reinforce an undesirable outcome.

VIRTUOUS CYCLE—A course of events where predictable factors perpetuate and reinforce a desirable outcome.

VOCATIONAL EDUCATION—Educational training that provides practical experience in a particular occupational field.

VOUCHERS (HOUSING)—A document issued by government to low-income families that can be used to pay a portion of the costs of housing, schooling, or other needs.

VULNERABILITY (CLIMATE CHANGE)—The degree to which a system is susceptible to, or unable to cope with, adverse effects of climate change and is a function of the character, magnitude, and rate of climate variation to which a system is exposed.

ZERO-SUM GAME—A game where the sum of the gains to winners equals the sum of the losses to losers. Zero-sum games are contrasted with positive-sum games, where gains for all participants are possible and negative-sum games, where all parties may be worse off as a result of some joint activity.

Index